Joe "Flash" Gordon

Joe "Flash" Gordon

A Biography of the Hall of Fame Second Baseman

Judy Gordon *and* Erik Simpson

McFarland & Company, Inc., Publishers
Jefferson, North Carolina

ISBN (print) 978-1-4766-9797-0
ISBN (ebook) 978-1-4766-5638-0

Library of Congress cataloging data are available

Library of Congress Control Number 2026000463

© 2026 Judy Gordon and Erik Simpson. All rights reserved

No part of this book may be reproduced or transmitted in any form or by any means, electronic or mechanical, including photocopying or recording, or by any information storage and retrieval system, without permission in writing from the publisher.

Front cover image: New York Yankees second baseman Joe "Flash" Gordon (National Baseball Hall of Fame Library, Cooperstown, New York)

Printed in the United States of America

*McFarland & Company, Inc., Publishers
Box 611, Jefferson, North Carolina 28640
www.mcfarlandpub.com*

Table of Contents

Acknowledgments	vii
Introduction	1
1. Spring Training with the Yankees, 1937	3
2. Mining Towns (1915–1921)	7
3. The Sandlots of Portland (1921–1928)	11
4. The Original "Flash" Gordon (1928–1932)	16
5. Semipro and College Ball (1932–1936)	22
6. Joe the Pro! (1936–1937)	28
7. A Rookie Year to Remember (1938)	39
8. "Greatest Team of All Time" (1939)	54
9. A Horse Race of a Pennant (1940)	64
10. World Series "Hero" (1941)	72
11. An MVP Year (1942)	86
12. World Series Records (1943)	97
13. "G.I. Joe" (1944–1945)	107
14. Goodbye, New York (1946)	121
15. The "Flash" Is Back! (1947)	136
16. A Storybook Season (1948)	145
17. High Hopes Dashed (1949)	160
18. The Old Pro Calls It a Career (1950)	166
19. California, Here We Come! (1951–1957)	170
20. "For a Baseball Man, This Is the Ultimate" (1958–1961)	182
21. A Remarkable Career (1962–1971)	199

Table of Contents

22. Farewell, "Flash" (1972–1978)	205
23. Cooperstown at Last (2008–2009)	210
Epilogue	225
Chapter Notes	227
Bibliography	267
Index	273

Acknowledgments

We are greatly indebted to the following persons and organizations, whose help and encouragement inspired us to write this book about Judy's father and Erik's grandfather, Joe "Flash" Gordon.

Louise (Evans) Gordon (1893–1984)—Joe Gordon's mother and most ardent fan, whose detailed scrapbooks and collection of letters and photos chronicling her son's life and baseball career led us to this endeavor. Dorthy "Dottie" (Crum) Gordon (1914–1992)—Joe Gordon's beloved wife and mother of their two children, Judy and Joey. Dottie compiled scrapbooks and photo albums of Joe's years playing professional ball, his time in the military, and some of his years managing. Joseph Michael "Joey" Gordon—Judy's brother, who recalled memories of their lives as "baseball brats" from the 1940s through 1960s, in addition to proofreading our chapters.

Those especially instrumental throughout our many years of research and writing include award-winning author Daniel R. Levitt; Senior Museum Curator Brian Richards of the New York Yankees Museum; the National Baseball Hall of Fame and Museum; the New York Yankees; the Cleveland Indians and Cleveland Guardians; the Society for American Baseball Research; Baseball-Reference.com; Baseballinwartime.com; the University of Oregon; Matt Rothenberg; Bill Francis; Jim Gates; John Horne; Scot Mondore; Cary Smith; Gary Bedingfield; Michael Haupert; P.J. Dragseth; Larry Doby, Jr.; Mary Lou Holoboff; Dennis Hollenbeck; Joe Humasti; Savannah Webb; Idaho Falls Family Search Center; Gary Mitchem; Sophia Lyons; Susan Kilby; Bill Madden; Jerry Izenberg; Idaho Falls Public Library; Dean Hoffman—whose absolutely invaluable help in tracking down people and information continues to this day; "Dave O"—for his fantastic website and audio interviews; and Matt Dahlgren—grandson of major league first baseman Babe Dahlgren—for his encouragement and faith that we could complete our book. And we did!

We are blessed in having corresponded with some of Joe Gordon's former teammates and other ballplayers before they passed on, including Bobby Doerr, Charlie Silvera, Albie Pearson, Dr. Bobby Brown, Bob Feller, Eddie Robinson, Harry Dunlop, Yogi Berra, and Joe Morgan. And a heartfelt thank you to friends, old and new, family, and many ballplayers, fans, and others who contributed in a myriad of ways, including much-needed moral support throughout our multi-year journey. We could not have written our book without your help. We hope you enjoy it!

Introduction

Joe "Flash" Gordon was the baseball player that time almost forgot. This would change, however, on December 8, 2008, when Jane Forbes Clark, chairman of the Board of Directors of the National Baseball Hall of Fame and Museum, announced that the former New York Yankees and Cleveland Indians second baseman was the only player selected by the Veterans Committee for induction into the Hall of Fame in 2009.

In just 11 seasons, Joe Gordon accumulated impressive statistics. As a 23-year-old rookie in 1938, he became the first American League second baseman to hit 20 or more home runs in a season. Playing in just 127 games that year, he wrapped up the season with 25 homers (24 as a second baseman and one as a pinch-hitter) to set a first-year record that would stand for 68 years. Had a Rookie of the Year Award existed back then, he most certainly would have been in the running.

In his first year in the majors, Gordon gave rise to something baseball had rarely seen before—a power-hitting second baseman, nipping at the heels of, and sometimes surpassing, the American League's top home run producers. He led all American League second basemen in home runs for nine of his 11 seasons, and he was the first among them to hit 25, 30, and 32 homers in a season.

Gordon played for six pennant winners and five World Series champions. He unquestionably would have been named the Most Valuable Player of the 1941 World Series had that honor existed back then. Yankees manager Joe McCarthy was so elated with Gordon's performance he afterward declared, "[T]he greatest all-around ball player I ever saw—and I don't bar any of them—is Joe Gordon."[1]

Joe Gordon won the American League Most Valuable Player Award in 1942, beating out Boston Red Sox slugger Ted Williams despite Williams attaining baseball's coveted Triple Crown that year. Gordon also recorded a career-high 29-game hitting streak in 1942, which has not been equaled or surpassed by a Yankee since.

He finished in the top 10 in MVP balloting five times during his career and was selected for nine All-Star Games, missing that honor only twice—his rookie and final seasons. His total of 246 home runs while playing as a second baseman (out of a career total of 253) set an American League record that would stand for a remarkable 66 years.

Gordon was one of the most acrobatic second basemen the American League has ever seen. He was exciting to watch as he completed seemingly impossible defensive plays that no other second baseman could accomplish. Offensively, he was widely recognized for "coming through in the clutch" when it counted the most.

But this is only part of his legacy. After wrapping up his playing days in the majors, Gordon became a minor league and major league manager, coach, batting instructor, and scout.

So why did it take 30 years after his death for Joe Gordon to receive the Hall of Fame recognition that teammates and opponents alike said he deserved? His own family believes that perhaps some of the explanation can be attributed to Gordon himself. He seldom spoke about his own baseball career, either publicly or privately. Until his family showed up for the 2009 Hall of Fame Induction Ceremony, even *they* didn't know that he *still* held the American League home run record for second basemen!

Family members cannot recall a single instance of Gordon sharing stories of his playing days with family or close friends. Joe's daughter, Judy, told reporters at a press conference before the 2009 Hall of Fame Induction Ceremony that baseball simply was not a topic of discussion in the Gordon home. She described how her father would change the subject, usually to hunting, fishing, or golf, whenever anyone wanted to talk baseball. On the other hand, he almost always obliged every request for his autograph from his young admirers and many fans.

The story would have ended here, if not for a large stack of scrapbooks and personal letters that Joe's mother, Louise Gordon, kept, chronicling her son's baseball career from his sandlot days in Portland, Oregon, in the 1920s until he retired from playing in the majors in 1950. Joe's wife, Dottie, also compiled scrapbooks containing countless newspaper and magazine articles, photographs, and documents related to his career.

Family members would eventually discover a treasure trove of information in the old scrapbooks and personal letters. They also found that a few long-held beliefs about Joe Gordon, which continue to be discussed by sports columnists and bloggers alike, were undeniably wrong. The oft-reported accounts that his father died when Joe was just a young boy were proven untrue. Even the story behind his legendary nickname "Flash" was found to be incorrect.

This book is about Joe "Flash" Gordon's life and distinguished career in baseball. It also relates stories about many of the players, managers, and club owners who, with Gordon, contributed to the "golden age" of the game. It is written for those who love the game of baseball, especially as it was played from the mid–1930s through the late 1960s.

This is also an American success story—about a boy named Joe, who spent his first six years in the gold- and copper-mining camps of Arizona, even living for a time in a canvas wall tent. Moving to Portland, Oregon, in 1921, with his mother and brother Jack, young Joe learned to play ball on the sandlots of Portland to become a highly acclaimed, multi-sport athlete in high school and college. After spending only two years in the high minors, he went on to a distinguished career in major league baseball, eventually earning a plaque in the National Baseball Hall of Fame and Museum.

Joe Gordon's contributions to the game may have been forgotten over time, but it is the authors' hope that his story reinforces the belief that anyone—no matter their family circumstances or upbringing—can excel and reach the pinnacle of a sport through dedication, talent, and hard work. Sportswriters and historians alike have called Gordon "the second baseman of his era."[2] How he became that was largely unknown—until now.

Chapter 1

Spring Training with the Yankees, 1937

During 1936, attendance at major league baseball games finally had begun to recover, after having dipped to lows three years earlier because of the Great Depression. The New York Yankees were reaping great rewards from their fledgling rookie outfielder, Joe DiMaggio. After not having missed a game since June 1, 1925, Yankees first baseman Lou Gehrig would complete his 12th full season with the Bronx Bombers. And, Joseph Vincent "Marse Joe"[1] McCarthy, who'd managed the Yankees since 1931, piloted them to another world championship in 1936.

Following his outstanding first season of professional ball as shortstop for the 1936 Pacific Coast League Oakland Oaks, Joe Gordon hurried back to Eugene to enroll in the fall term at the University of Oregon.[2] He was a senior, majoring in Physical Education.

Early that fall, a letter had arrived at the Gordons' home in Portland, Oregon. Yankees veteran scout Bill Essick, who had signed Joe to his first professional baseball contract in June 1935, arranged for him to report to the 1937 Yankees spring training at St. Petersburg, Florida.[3] Manager McCarthy wanted a look at him.

In late February 1937, 22-year-old Joe Gordon traveled the 3,500 miles by train from Portland to St. Petersburg. Being invited to try out with the world champion New York Yankees had to have been one of the most cherished dreams of every red-blooded American man and boy of that era.

He arrived in St. Petersburg the first of March. A banner hung across one of its main streets, proclaiming the town the "Permanent Training Ground of the World Champion Yankees."[4] The club had trained there since 1925.[5] How Joe Gordon would measure up against baseball's greatest athletes, many at the pinnacles of their careers, was one of the questions that he and sportswriters who followed the Yankees asked.

Carrying a small, tightly-packed valise, Gordon stepped up to the front desk of the Suwannee Hotel—"The St. Petersburg Home of the New York Yankees."[6] He was a clean-cut young man, with neatly trimmed dark hair and bright hazel eyes, standing 5 feet, 10½ inches tall and weighing a fit 170 pounds.

A year later, writer Stanley Frank asked Joe Gordon to narrate a 10-page article for *Street & Smith's Sport Story Magazine*. In the article, Joe talked about his arrival and his two weeks at St. Petersburg: "There was no reservation for me at the team's hotel. Nobody apparently knew I was expected. I didn't know a single soul, and I was thirty-five-hundred miles from home! I didn't even have a contract [for the 1937 baseball season]!"[7]

Gordon checked his bag and headed out to the ballpark at Miller Huggins Field, figuring he'd get acquainted with some of the other rookies trying out with the Yankees. He later told Stanley Frank, "Joe McCarthy was extremely cordial and helpful when he learned I was in camp and assured me it was all right [sic] for me to get into uniform for the second day of practice."

The following day, Gordon reported at the ballpark and introduced himself to the Yankees' longtime clubhouse manager, Fred "Pop" Logan. He asked for a uniform—but Logan flatly refused to give him one. Years later, Bobby Brown, who'd signed with the Yankees as a rookie in early 1946, told author Judy Gordon, "Logan, the clubhouse man, treated me [in 1946] exactly like he treated your dad."[8]

"You're not down on my list," Logan told Gordon. Per strict orders from manager McCarthy, absolutely *no one* was allowed to suit up or go out onto the field unless their name was on the Yankees' official roster.

"But Mr. McCarthy just told me to come out," Gordon protested.

Later Gordon would say, "Logan insisted that I leave the clubhouse, and I stormed out, discouraged and almost ready to catch the next train home."

When McCarthy came onto the scene, he asked why the young rookie wasn't in uniform. It was then that Gordon told him what had happened.

"It's my fault for not telling Logan about you," McCarthy chuckled. "He has to be suspicious of every new player because so many hitch-hikers barge in on him, asking for uniforms."

"Everything was all right after that," Gordon recalled. He suited up in the Yankees' pinstripes, grabbed his glove, and went out onto the field. Later he told about the thrill of that first day: "Not until I had got into a Yankee uniform and gone out on the field did I believe it…. I got a warm welcome from the world champions. I was introduced around and at once treated like one of the boys. That was a big boost, a kick for my morale."[9]

After the team finished batting practice, Yankees coach Art Fletcher grabbed a fungo stick and began hitting grounders toward Gordon, who was covering second base. At first, Fletcher hit a few easy ones. Then he tried hitting past Joe and into the outfield.

Jack Smith wrote for the *Daily News*, "Gordon came up with one [fungo] after the other. Old timers around the camp, Dickey, Rolfe, Crosetti, Lazzeri, forgot whatever they were doing. They just stood there in amazement watching this kid they didn't even know make plays nobody then in the big leagues could make."[10] Rud Rennie reported for the *New York Herald Tribune* that, after just a few looks at Gordon, "McCarthy was delighted."[11]

Gordon trained with the Yankees for two weeks. During that time, manager McCarthy, second baseman Tony Lazzeri, and the team's coaches taught him some of the finer points of batting and playing second base.[12] The Yankees were switching him from his previous position as a shortstop to second base.

Joe McCarthy himself had played 15 years in the minor leagues, much of it at second base. Future Hall of Famer "Poosh 'Em Up Tony" Lazzeri had been with the Yankees since 1926, almost the entire time playing the keystone corner. But Lazzeri was 33 years old, and the Yankees were looking for his eventual replacement.

A year later, Gordon would tell more about his two weeks training with the 1937 Yankees: "The Yankees were a swell gang and gave me every consideration. Still, it wasn't a social trip; my immediate job was learning how to play second base, and learning it well enough to replace Lazzeri when he decided to quit."[13]

Chapter 1. Spring Training with the Yankees, 1937

Earlier that spring, Yankees scout Bill Essick had arranged for instructors at Jess Orndorff's National Baseball School in Los Angeles to tutor Gordon on the basics of playing second base.[14] A year later, Joe was quoted saying that he liked playing second base better than shortstop.[15]

By the 10th day of training, manager McCarthy figured that the team had drilled enough to play a nine-inning intrasquad practice game. The players were divided into two teams, the Regulars and the Yannigans (a nickname for a rookie or "scrub" baseball team), with Gordon playing second base for the Yannigans. More than 2,000 local fans and tourists showed up to watch. Not surprisingly, the Regulars shut out the Yannigans, 8–0.[16]

Wasting no time, McCarthy wanted to see for himself what this Gordon kid could do during a "real" game. The young rookie was slated to play the National League Boston Bees in the Grapefruit League's[17] opening game of 1937 on Saturday, March 13, at St. Petersburg's Waterfront Park. The game was reported as drawing the largest Opening Day crowd in local spring training history. More than 4,600 fans filled every seat of the stands and bleachers, even overflowing onto the ball field.[18]

In his first major league spring training game, playing in a borrowed uniform and batting eighth in the order, Joe Gordon was described by writer Red McDonald as "the day's sensation."[19] In four plate appearances, he pounded out three singles, scored twice,

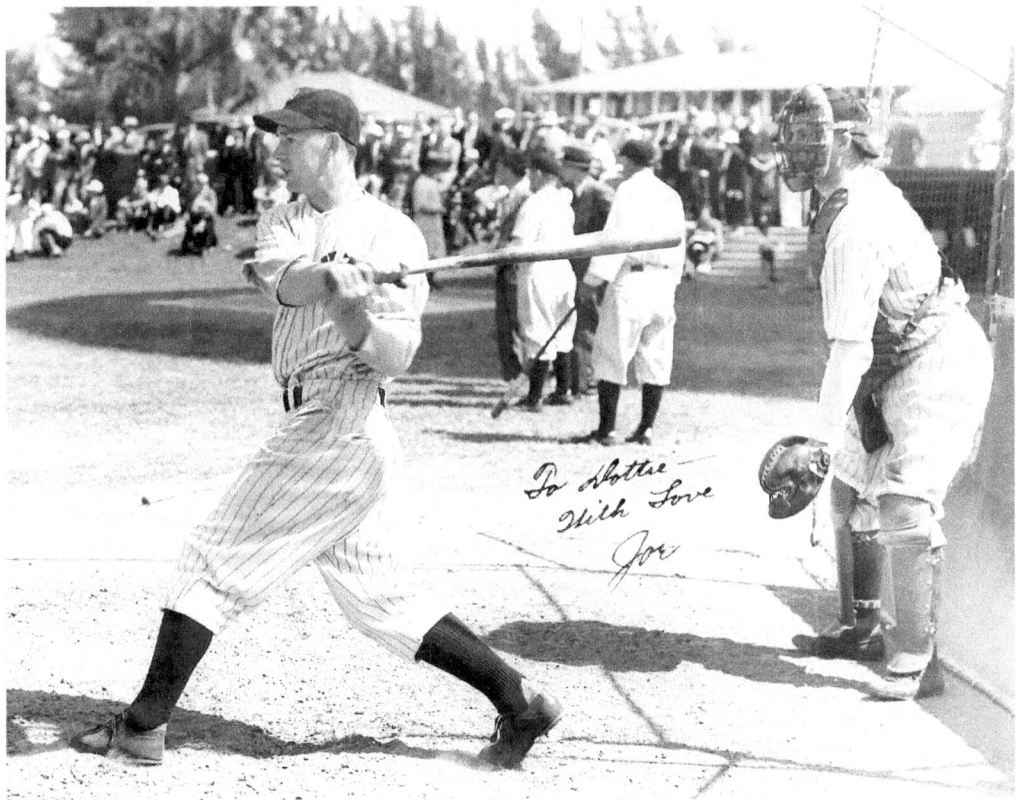

Joe Gordon swings away during New York Yankees spring training batting practice at St. Petersburg, Florida, in early March 1937. Joe signed this photograph and mailed it to his girlfriend, Dottie Crum, who lived in Los Angeles (Gordon family collections).

and walked once. His fielding was exemplary; he executed four putouts and five assists without an error as the Bombers stomped the Bees, 13–4. Without a doubt, Yankees management was well pleased with their young prospect, Joe Gordon.

A few days later, for an article headlined "View Gordon, Coast Lad, as Lazzeri's Successor," acclaimed sportswriter Max Kase wrote, "Even with so star-studded a gang as the Yankees, Gordon is the talk of the place. The hardboiled Yankee strategy board enthuses over his prospects. He's a little away as yet, but the master minds are looking past the horizon and see Gordon as the possible successor to Tony Lazzeri when the gallant old warhorse retires to pasture."[20] It was about this time that sportswriters began calling the young rookie "Flash Gordon," after the comic-strip character of the same name. The nickname would stick with him his entire career.

On March 15, Yankees owner Colonel Jacob Ruppert was sitting in the stands on a hot, muggy day, scrutinizing his players during their two-hour workout. It was reported that the Colonel was "keenly interested" in young Joe Gordon.[21] After watching Gordon work out, Ruppert signed him to a contract with the Yankees' top farm club, the 1937 Newark Bears of the Class AA International League.[22] At the time, Class AA was the highest level of play in the minor leagues. It also was well known that "Newark was where the Yankees sent their very brightest and most advanced rookies for post-graduate schooling."[23]

Meanwhile, the Yankees kept Gordon around to play one more exhibition game before sending him off to the Bears' spring training. He traveled with the team by bus to Daytona Beach, Florida, to play the St. Louis Cardinals, where the Yankees won again. Gordon didn't get any hits that day, though his fielding was flawless—again without error.[24]

Two days later, Rud Rennie reported how manager Joe McCarthy described Joe Gordon as "the best-looking kid I've seen come into camp in a long time.... I'll go overboard on this kid. He's gonna be a good ball player."[25]

Chapter 2

MINING TOWNS (1915–1921)

Two months after riding the train to Los Angeles, California, with just her luggage and 14-month-old son Jack, 22-year-old Lulu Pearl (Evans) Gordon gave birth to her second son, Joseph Lowell Gordon, on February 18, 1915.[1]

Baby Joe was born in the "Golden State" at the home of Lulu's sister and brother-in-law, Bertha and Joe Rusche. Three months later, Lulu, baby Joe, and young Jack rode the train back to Needles, California, then motored on to their home in the soon-to-be-booming gold-mining town of Oatman, Arizona. There, Joe would meet his father, Benjamin Lowell Gordon, for the very first time.

Family photos depict Lulu as a pretty young woman, standing barely five feet tall, with dark hair and bright hazel eyes. She was born in Houghton, Michigan, in 1893, and raised in the large, close-knit family of James and Matilda (Grose) Evans.

Not long after graduating from high school, Lulu departed Michigan and joined her brother, George Evans, in the busy mining town of Globe, in the East-Central foothills of what was then the Territory of Arizona.[2] It was there that she met Ben Gordon, perhaps at some celebration of Arizona becoming the 48th State of the United States in February 1912.

Benjamin Lowell Gordon was born in Bainbridge, Indiana, in 1875, the first of three children of John Riley Gordon and Martha Ann (Darnall) Gordon. Orphaned at the age of 15, Ben wouldn't remain long in any one place. By 1900, he had departed Indiana and was shearing sheep in Central Montana.[3] In 1910, "bitten" by the proverbial "gold and silver bugs," he was working for wages as a miner near the remote mining town of Cerbat, Territory of Arizona.[4] By 1912, Ben had moved again—this time clear across the State of Arizona to work as a mining engineer in Miami's busy copper-mining industry.

Lulu and Ben married in Globe, Arizona, on December 3, 1912, and resided in the nearby town of Miami.[5] Ten months later, the Gordons' first child, John Robley "Jack" Gordon, was born at the home of Lulu's sister in Los Angeles. By the time Lulu returned to Arizona by train with new baby Jack, Ben had moved the family's few belongings to Oatman, Arizona, which would be their home for the next six and a half years.

When times were prosperous, Ben purchased or built a very small, wood-framed home for his family at Ryan Addition, located about a half-mile from the newly established township of Old Trails and a half-mile south of Oatman.[6]

The United States entered World War I on April 6, 1917. Soon, work ceased at almost all the gold mines near Oatman. Nationally, there was a more vital need for copper in support of the war effort. Ben and many gold miners found themselves out of work. To

This Gordon family photograph taken about 1915–1916 shows the desolate area surrounding the Gordons' home at Ryan Addition, located about half a mile from the newly established township of Old Trails and a half-mile south of Oatman, Arizona (Gordon family collections).

support his family, 43-year-old Ben found employment back across the state near Globe, where he worked as a copper miner for the Old Dominion Co.[7] Housing was in very short supply, so Lulu and their two boys remained at their home near Oatman.

Joe (left) and Jack Gordon, along with their father, Benjamin Lowell Gordon, pose for a photograph on the beach near Los Angeles, when the Gordon family visited Lulu Gordon's sister and brother-in-law about 1918 (Gordon family collections).

Chapter 2. Mining Towns (1915–1921)

The war ended on November 11, 1918, and exploration and mining for gold began ramping up again. Ben moved back home with his family and went to work for wages at a nearby mine.[8]

But gold mining was an unpredictable occupation. Soon the Gordon family was on the move. When Joe was just five years old, they lived at or near at least four Arizona mining towns. From the Oatman area, they moved for a time to the barren southern Arizona desert near Gila Bend, where it's assumed that Ben prospected for gold.[9]

During part of the winter of 1920–1921, the Gordon family lived in a windowless tent house near the town of Jerome, Arizona. Lulu Gordon wrote on the back of this photograph: "This was my house at the Jerome Copper. Jack is standing in the door but you can hardly see him" (Gordon family collections).

The family moved again—this time living part of the winter of 1920–1921 in a primitive, windowless tent house on a steep, snow-covered hillside near Jerome Copper in Central Arizona.[10] Close by was the infamous mining town of Jerome, sometimes referred to as "The Wickedest City in Arizona."

Having moved from mining camp to mining camp, Lulu Gordon finally reached the limits of her endurance in late 1920 or early 1921. She and her two boys went back to Miami, Arizona, probably to be close to her brother, George Evans, who still lived in nearby Globe.[11] It's not known if Ben went with them.

By late January 1921, Lulu left Ben, and Arizona, for good. She and their boys, Joe (almost six) and Jack (age seven) moved to Portland, Oregon, to be near her sister and brother-in-law, Bertha and Joe Rusche, who'd relocated there two years earlier.[12]

As far as the present-day Gordon family has been able to determine, Ben never again had contact with his two sons, Joe and Jack. Apparently, the boys were told that their father had died. Throughout Joe's baseball career, whenever sportswriters asked about his early life, he would tell them that his father had died when he was a young boy.[13] Likewise, after moving to Portland, Lulu represented herself as a widow.

Although it's believed that Ben Gordon had no contact with his boys after January 1921, many years later, he was well aware that his son, Joe Gordon, was a famous major league ballplayer. Ben once told an acquaintance how proud he was of his son.[14]

Late in life, Ben was described as being "down on his luck ... living literally day by day and taking any kind of work he could get."[15] When questioned by a friend why he didn't ask his family for help, Ben said that he'd left them when they needed him, and he didn't think it right that he should expect them to assist him.

During World War II, when Joe was serving in the U.S. Army at Hamilton Field, California, Ben Gordon lived in Sonora, only 140 miles away. However, sadly, it appeared that neither Joe nor Jack Gordon ever knew that their father was still alive.

Benjamin Lowell Gordon died of a stroke at the age of 70 on May 12, 1946, in Sonora, California. He was buried in the paupers' section of the town's Mountain Shadow Cemetery.[16] A quote from the *Oatman News* perhaps best sums up the plight of Ben Gordon's peripatetic life, which eventually led to the loss of all contact with his sons, Joe and Jack: "When gold began to talk, the first word it learned to say was 'Good-bye.'"[17]

Chapter 3

THE SANDLOTS OF PORTLAND (1921–1928)

Departing Arizona in January 1921 with just their mother Lulu, young Joe and Jack Gordon soon discovered a sense of kinship and community in the big city of Portland, Oregon. They stayed for a short time with Lulu's sister and brother-in-law, Bertha and Joe Rusche. Lulu soon obtained employment as a stenographer with Zellerbach Paper Co. where she worked for the next 37 years.[1]

She registered both boys at Holladay Grammar School, a large school with an enrollment of about 700 students spanning the 1st through 8th grades.[2] Joe excelled academically, and in the following years he skipped Grades 2A and 3B. Jack did well in the lower grades but struggled a bit later on and repeated Grade 7B. This resulted in both boys graduating from grammar school together in January 1928.[3]

Soon after moving to Portland in early 1921, Lulu Gordon and her two boys, Joe (left) and Jack, have their picture taken together (Gordon family collections).

Interviewed by writer Dan Daniel in 1938 for a large article in *The Sporting News*, Joe Gordon recalled about his youth, "I must have been six when I started playing ball—softball, in the playground. I gradually went into all sports. We kids in the Albina section [of Portland] had no dough, but we had a good time, just the same."[4] Joe also was interviewed for an article in the *Oregon Journal*, saying, "When I started playing baseball—and that's from just about when I first started remembering things—I wanted to be and was a catcher. My brother Jack was pitcher, and I was catcher."[5]

Years later, Lulu told how her son Joe, at the age of eight, had "sparked a sandlot team to a neighborhood pennant."[6] He already was formulating the first of his three simple rules for learning to play baseball—rules that he would teach other young players many years later: (1) Play all the baseball you can, (2) See all the good players you can in action, and (3) Copy the style of the best players.[7]

But it wasn't always just a life of clean living and playing ball for the Gordon boys, as Joe later revealed about his not-always-law-abiding youth:

> As long as I can remember, I always have had a baseball and a bat in my hands. When I was a kid, things were not so easy financially. A nickel was a lot of money. As for $2, the price of a ball and bat, that was an unheard of sum. The obvious way was to "borrow" from the more fortunate.
>
> On a Saturday afternoon, after our morning double-header, the gang would attend the nearest independent game. As we slapped our heroes on the back, I am very much afraid we sidled up to the bench. I also am afraid that as somebody in authority hollered "scram" we dashed off with bats in our pants-legs, and baseballs in our arm-pits.[8]

Joe and Jack Gordon weren't bad kids, by any means, but what they did lack was a father-figure in their lives. During an interview many years later, sadly, Joe would say that he didn't even remember his father.[9]

In early 1923, Lulu Gordon married for the second time. She and her boys and new husband moved to a large apartment building just a few doors from where her sister, Bertha Rusche, and family lived. But according to later court testimony, Lulu's husband deserted her after only two months of marriage. She and her boys were on their own again.

Going by the name of "Louise" instead of Lulu, she moved with her boys for a fourth time, to a place just around the corner from where her sister and brother-in-law lived. Money was tight.[10] Yet at least she had a steady job throughout all the years of the Great Depression.

About a year after her hapless second marriage ended, Louise and her sons were befriended by a man she met through work. Andrew J. "Andy" Lampert became an influential, lifelong friend and mentor to Joe and Jack Gordon. Andy taught them how to golf and play handball and other sports, and to hunt and fish. Happily, many years later, Louise Gordon and Andy Lampert would marry, with the blessings of their delighted family.[11]

When Joe was 12 and Jack just a year older, they were proud members of the "hot-shot" Crosby Juniors baseball team, named after Crosby Street near where they lived. Nine neighbor boys made up their team (no subs—"[a] guy could go the route, or else").[12] Louise Gordon sewed the letters "CJ" on their team sweatshirts. Joe later said that one of his greatest treasures as a kid was his Crosby Juniors sweatshirt.

They played their games on the rough, pitted sandlots of Portland, and the boys sold newspapers to earn money to buy their baseball equipment. After their games, they

Chapter 3. The Sandlots of Portland (1921–1928)

Jack (left) and Joe Gordon are all dressed up in their Sunday best for an outing with their friend and mentor, Andy Lampert, in Portland on May 25, 1924 (Gordon family collections).

Here are the 1927 Crosby Juniors baseball players, posing for a team photograph on one of their sandlot diamonds in Portland. Front row, from left: Jack Gordon, Bruno Humasti, Martin Berg, and Joe Gordon. Back row, from left: Virgil Morse, Walter Anderson, Jack Eatch, probably John Seaten, and probably Emil Berg (courtesy of Bruno Joseph Humasti).

hung out at Ellen's Café, where teammate Bruno Humasti's mother, Ellen, watched over and fed them.[13]

In 1927, Louise and her boys moved for a fifth time, to a house close to Jefferson High School. There they would remain until Joe and Jack graduated from high school in 1932.

Louise enrolled her sons in several Young Men's Christian Association (YMCA) sports programs in Portland, hoping to keep them occupied with respectable pursuits. Joe and Jack played YMCA hockey and "Y" basketball clear into their high school years.[14] Joe also played soccer for Portland's Rosebud Juniors.[15]

As a 14-year-old in 1929, Joe won first-, second-, and third-place ribbons in the broad jump, 75-yard dash, and 8-pound shot put in the Second Annual Portland Area YMCA Track and Field Meet.[16] He also participated in gymnastics and tumbling at Portland's YMCA. This inspired Louise to begin compiling scrapbooks to record both of her boys' athletic achievements, which she continued doing throughout their lives.

Some of Joe's and Jack's most-treasured memories were of their summers spent at YMCA's Spirit Lake Camp, located at the base of Mount St. Helens in Washington State. They hiked, backpacked, climbed mountains, fished, golfed, swam, and competed in track meets—activities fostering their love of the outdoors. Joe once told S.T. Wright of the *Sunday Oregonian* that he might have turned into one of those "juvenile problems" if

Chapter 3. The Sandlots of Portland (1921–1928)

it wasn't for the YMCA.[17] Sadly, many years later, Spirit Lake Camp was destroyed by the colossal volcanic eruption of Mount St. Helens on May 18, 1980.

But it wasn't just the YMCA and sports that kept Joe and Jack Gordon on the right side of the law. Louise was a very loving mother, but she also was quite strict. Years later, granddaughter Judy asked her how she'd kept Joe and Jack from becoming juvenile delinquents, especially since she had to be at work all week. Louise's answer was simple, yet pragmatic: "They [Joe and Jack] *always* had to be home before dark!"

As a way of keeping young Joe out of mischief and at the same time introducing him to a little culture, Louise signed him up for violin lessons. She insisted that he practice at least an hour every day after school and on Saturdays. As he became more proficient, Joe played in the 110-piece Ted Bacon String Orchestra and took lessons from his concertmaster for over five years.[18] He even fostered ambitions of someday becoming a professional musician—that is, until sports became his passion![19]

Chapter 4

The Original "Flash" Gordon (1928–1932)

Over the years, sportswriters reported that Joe Gordon's iconic nickname "Flash" was originally based on Alex Raymond's comic strip character *Flash Gordon*, but this was not true. The authors discovered that Joe's nickname "Flash" had already appeared in print in his high school yearbook, *The Spectrum: Class of June '32*, at least a year and a half before Alex Raymond's comic strip was first published in January 1934.[1]

Joe Gordon played on many sports teams, from his early years in Oregon through 11 seasons as a major league ballplayer. His teams often dominated their opponents—sometimes to the point that they're remembered, even today, as some of the greatest of local, state, and national sports powerhouses. Soon it became evident that Joe was one of the key players who served as a spark or catalyst for his teammates, helping to spur them on.

When the Gordon boys enrolled as freshmen at Portland's Jefferson High School in January 1928, Louise Gordon phoned the school's principal, Hopkin Jenkins, telling him that she was a widow and asking him to watch her boys closely. Years later, Jenkins recalled about Joe, "I'll never forget him when he came here. He was a little fellow and very serious. He was an excellent student."[2]

Jefferson's high school baseball coach, Lindsey C. Campbell, also talked about when young Joe Gordon turned out for baseball in 1930: "[H]e was so small he didn't look like he'd ever be an athlete. He was a junior before he started to grow. But what he lacked in size, he made up in fire. He had lots of 'pepper' and was a smart fielder."[3]

Not surprisingly, Joe's grades in gym class almost always were Es for excellent—but with *one* exception. In the spring of 1930, he received a grade of U for unsatisfactory in gym, when he "sassed" his baseball coach and was "fired" from the team.[4] Yet from the next term on, Joe earned all Es in gym, most likely "motivated" by a stern reprimand from his mother. The authors found not a single instance of Gordon ever "talking back" to any of his coaches or managers from that time forward.

Joe was amazingly multi-talented. He joined Jefferson High School's soccer team in 1930, lettering for three years, and was elected captain of his team in 1932. They won the Portland Interscholastic Soccer League Championship three years in a row. During the 1932 championship game, Joe led the scoring attack with four goals. At season's end, he was selected for Portland's First Team All-Stars.[5]

He also played as an amateur in the Oregon State Soccer Football Association, an adult men's league. His Vikings team won the 1931–1932 Portland Soccer Association Championship.[6]

Chapter 4. The Original "Flash" Gordon (1928–1932)

Weighing just 140 pounds, Joe tried out for high school football in 1930, but as he later said, "[I] got little encouragement in that game, and gave it up."[7] A year later and five pounds heavier, he returned to the gridiron: "In the fall of 1931, weighing exactly 145 pounds, I was induced to go back to football. I became the right halfback on the Jefferson High eleven which won the city and state titles, and *never was scored on* [italics added]. Next to me in the backfield was Bobby Grayson, the marvelous back who did such great things at Stanford."[8] The undefeated 1931 Jefferson High School football team is still regarded as one of Oregon's three most outstanding high school teams of the twentieth century. Joe lettered in football, but as he later explained to Dan Daniel of *The Sporting News*, "I got the baseball bug bad and quit the gridiron."[9]

On New Year's Day 1932, the *Morning Oregonian* published the photos of 10 star athletes of 1931—mostly adults who had some connection to Oregon. Sixteen-year-old Joe Gordon was one of the athletes, along with his Jefferson High School football teammate, Bobby Grayson.[10]

Joe also competed on Jefferson's track team and broad-jumped 21 feet. He lettered in track his senior year.[11]

Both Gordon boys played on Jefferson's baseball team the spring of their junior year, Jack as a pitcher and Joe a center fielder, then catcher.[12] Years later, Joe talked about his days as a center fielder, saying that he played with a first baseman's mitt.[13] He also talked about switching positions to catcher: "After two years of trying out, I finally managed to make the team. As a catcher. Up to this time I had tried playing every position, including pitching, and had started the season as a center fielder. Then came an injury to our regular catcher, and as we had no other, I decided it was the spot for me. There was no chance of being beaten out of that job."[14]

While baseball became Joe's passion, his mother's insistence that he continue practicing the violin interfered with what he *really* wanted to do: "I couldn't play all the ball I wanted to, because I had to practice on the violin more than an hour a day, and every Saturday afternoon, when the other boys were out playing their pick-up games, I was confined indoors rehearsing with a symphony orchestra. In 1931, when I was just past fifteen [years old], I put the violin aside long enough to make the varsity baseball team at Jefferson."[15]

The Jefferson High School "Democrats," coached by Lindsey C. Campbell, finished second in a field of eight high school teams in the 1931 Portland Interscholastic Baseball League. Both Joe and Jack Gordon lettered in baseball that year.[16] End-of-season records show Joe (a catcher) batting .327, and Jack (a pitcher) right on his brother's heels at .312. Joe was awarded a tiny gold charm engraved with ".327 JHS JG."[17]

The summer of 1931, Joe and three of his former Crosby Juniors teammates, in addition to at least two from his Jefferson High School baseball team, joined Portland's American Legion Post No. 1 East Side Commercial Club team, coached by Bill Garbarino and managed by Harry Dorman. During the previous two summers, Garbarino had coached American Legion Junior Baseball teams to back-to-back Division titles, in addition to 1929 Oregon State and Northwest Regional Championships.[18]

After Joe had played a few games for the East Siders, Bill Garbarino switched him from catcher, to third base, and finally shortstop. Years later, Al Stump wrote an article for *Argosy for Men* magazine, revealing what Garbarino recalled about switching Joe Gordon to shortstop: "The first ground ball he fielded almost took off his head. It was a screamer that hopped once. But Joe got in front, blocked it with his chin. Then he picked up the ball and threw his man out. I knew then for sure where he belonged."[19]

Five of Portland's American Legion Post No. 1 East Side Commercial Club teammates pose for a photograph before heading to their game during the summer of 1931. We could positively identify only two team members: Bruno Humasti, left, and Joe Gordon, second from left (Gordon family collections).

In 1937, in an article Dan Daniel asked Gordon to write for the *New York World-Telegram*, Joe told about switching positions at 16 years of age: "I decided I wanted to play third base. Under the watchful eye of Billy Garbarino, I made the switch to shortstop. Through his steady coaching that summer I finally found what I believed to be my best position."[20] Throughout his life, Joe remained especially grateful for everything that coach Garbarino had done for him: "Bill Garbarino made an infielder out of me. He was an infielder himself and knew all the tricks. I'm terribly indebted to him."[21]

Joe's "fire in the belly" for baseball took off that summer. He later recalled how the first semi-serious notions of a professional career had crept into his mind:

> That summer of 1931 ... the germ of the idea was planted in me. I played shortstop for [c]oach Billy Garbarino's East Side Commercial team in the American Legion League in Portland, and I had a faint notion that there might be something in this baseball business for me, after all.
>
> In high school, we played games once a week; but the American Legion teams had three or four games a week, and the constant practice brought out talents I never realized I possessed.[22]

In 1931, the City of Portland claimed two American Legion Junior Baseball teams: East Side Commercial Club and Post Office Pharmacy. The city championship came down to the final game of a three-game playoff, with East Side stomping Post Office Pharmacy, 12–5, and capturing the title.[23]

The East Siders traveled to The Dalles, where they were victorious; then on to Ontario, where they wrapped up the Oregon State Eastern Division title. This qualified

Chapter 4. The Original "Flash" Gordon (1928–1932)

them for the three-game playoff held at Oregon State College in Corvallis, to determine the American Legion Junior Baseball Champions of Oregon.[24]

Photos of the players and coaches from Oregon's two finalist teams, Portland's East Side Commercial Club and Salem, appeared in the *Sunday Oregonian*.[25] The playoff was a highly celebrated event, held in conjunction with Oregon's American Legion Annual Convention.

Salem won the first game, 12–8, and East Side evened up the series by taking game two, 11–8.[26] The Oregon State American Legion Championship came down to a close, fast-moving final game in which Portland's East Side Commercial Club nosed out Salem, 5–4, in just one hour and 36 minutes.[27] Each player from the winning team received a gold medal engraved with "1931 American Legion Championship."

Sixteen-year-old Joe Gordon was voted Outstanding Player of the three-game championship series, as reported in the *Sunday Oregonian*: "The balloting was

In this photograph from the September 1931 issue of *The Oregon Legionnaire*, shortstop Joe Gordon of Portland's East Side Commercial Club American Legion Team is holding the Harry Dorman Individual Trophy after being named Outstanding Player of the Junior Baseball Series on August 8, 1931, at Corvallis, Oregon. Also pictured are Roy "Spec" Keene of Salem (left) and Dan Sowers of New York, "Papa" of the American Legion Junior Baseball Program (courtesy Jared R. Dyer and *The Oregon Legionnaire*).

Portland's Jefferson High School varsity baseball team proudly lines up for a team photograph in the spring of 1932. Joe Gordon is ninth from the right, with the big smile on his face. This was Joe's final year playing high school baseball (Gordon family collections).

unanimous, all three umpires voting in favor of Gordon.... When Dan Sowers read off Joe's name as being the lucky winner, the young chap just stood and gasped for breath. He was so surprised that he could hardly speak as he walked up to receive the bronze statuette presented by Harry Dorman."[28]

The victorious East Side Commercial Club traveled by train to Butte, Montana, to compete in the American Legion Northwest Regional Tournament against the State Champions of Idaho, Montana, and Washington. In their first game, the Oregonians thrashed Idaho, 21–1. The account in the *Morning Oregonian* is electrifying: "The flashy bunch of youngsters making up Portland's entry in the American Legion [J]unior [R]egional [B]aseball [T]ournament here descended upon New Plymouth, Idaho, like a tornado here today, all but sweeping them off the field with the power of their attack.... Joe Gordon, Portland shortstop, poled two homers."[29] But in the final game of the tournament, the Seattle, Washington team "vanquished" Oregon, 11–8, to capture the Northwest Regional Championship.[30]

Sometime that summer of 1931, two East Side Commercial Club teammates, shortstop Joe Gordon and catcher Vern Richards, aspired to show off their newfound athletic prowess. They brazenly walked, totally uninvited, right into the clubhouse of the Class AA Pacific Coast League Portland Beavers and out onto the field to barge in on the team's batting practice. Richards caught the entire practice, while Gordon "bounced around the infield" and took a few turns at bat. Needless to say, Beavers manager Spencer Abbott was *not* impressed with the two 16-year-old upstarts. Billy Step later wrote for *The Oregonian* that the two intruders "weren't even given as much as, 'Nice work, boys,' by Abbott.... [T]hey departed after the shower and never came back." Step also wrote, "It proves beyond doubt that you never can tell what is in the offering until given a fair trial." Years later, manager Abbott would lament, "I'll give any kid a chance even if he looks like a Joe Bush. No more [Joe] Gordons are gonna slip out of the reach of the Portland club."[31]

Chapter 4. The Original "Flash" Gordon (1928–1932)

During the spring of 1932, Joe's senior year, he played for Jefferson High School's varsity baseball team, starting as a catcher and finishing the season as shortstop. He was elected captain of his team and lettered in baseball for the second year in a row. Jefferson finished third in Portland's Interscholastic Baseball League, and Joe Gordon was selected as shortstop for the league's First-Team All-Stars. Howard Hobson, coach at rival Benson High School, was quoted in the *Sunday Oregonian*, saying, "Joe Gordon, the slender Jefferson player, is the best shortstop and there were several outstanding.... He is fast and has a fine throwing arm. He also hits."[32]

In June 1932, Joe (age 17) and Jack (18) graduated from Jefferson High School, both having completed the school's college preparatory course of study. It is noted in *The Spectrum: Class of June '32* that both boys planned on attending the University of Arizona at Tucson, Joe to study Mining Engineering and Jack as yet undecided.[33] But due to financial limitations during the Great Depression, their plans soon changed. In the meantime, both young men were *more* than eager to make their marks playing semipro ball that summer!

Chapter 5

SEMIPRO AND COLLEGE BALL (1932–1936)

During the summer of 1932, Joe Gordon's future in baseball slowly began to take shape. Both Joe and Jack Gordon signed contracts to play for Portland's West Side Babes, a semipro team in the newly organized, six-club Oregon State Baseball League.[1] The West Side Babes were a young team, with most of their players coming onboard right after graduating from high school.

However, back in 1931 there had been a controversy (referred to as the "Joe Lillard Affair") within the Pacific Coast Conference (PCC), concerning whether athletes who participated in semipro sports were eligible to play college ball.[2] The authors believe this may have prompted Joe Gordon to sign with the West Side Babes as an amateur in order to ensure his eligibility for playing college ball.

The Oregon State League was well underway by late June 1932, when a photo of Joe appeared in the *Morning Oregonian*, captioned, "State League Shortstop Star: Joe Gordon, member of the West Side Babes of the Oregon [S]tate circuit, is causing quite a sensation throughout the state. Joe, among the younger stars developed in American Legion [J]unior [B]aseball, is leading hitter of the State [L]eague, with an average of .667."[3]

In addition to their State League games, West Side's manager, Ray Brooks, booked his club to play at least three barnstorming teams during the summer of 1932. One was advertised as an "all-girls' team,"[4] and two were men's teams.

Brooks scheduled his "cocky" West Side Babes to play the barnstorming Gilkerson's Union Colored Giants of Chicago. The visitors overpowered West Side but scheduled a return to Portland two weeks later for a three-game rematch, with the Babes winning two of the three.[5,6]

Next, the popular House of David team of Benton Harbor, Michigan, arrived in town. The "Bearded Beauties" were considered one of the greatest barnstorming teams in the nation.[7] They lived up to their reputation, too, sweeping the four-game series against West Side, including two night games and a Sunday afternoon doubleheader.[8]

Joe Gordon wrapped up his first season of State League semipro ball with a .420 batting average.[9] Joe and Jack Gordon then headed to Eugene, where Joe enrolled at the University of Oregon (UO) and Jack began working for the Zellerbach Paper Co.[10] The West Side Babes, minus the two Gordon brothers, finished the season winning the Oregon State League championship.[11]

Joe enrolled as a freshman Physical Education major. Several years later, he explained why he ended up attending school there: "[Bill] Reinhardt [*sic*], then baseball coach at the University of Oregon, almost bowled me over when he told me I might

Chapter 5. Semipro and College Ball (1932–1936)

have a chance to make a good living from baseball, if I applied myself to it. For the first time, I began to bear down and wonder if he was overoptimistic or kidding me. But I knew Reinhardt [sic] was a good coach and had some connections with the Yankees, so I matriculated at Oregon after graduating from high school."[12]

Joe went out for freshman football that fall and was described in one newspaper article as "[an] outstanding ball-carrying candidate," and in another article as "fast and shifty, but light [weight]. He is a triple-threater [sic]."[13] He earned his "numeral" playing halfback that fall, which qualified him to report for football practice the spring of 1933, although he opted not to play then.

That spring, Joe played shortstop for the University of Oregon freshman baseball team, coached by Johnny Londahl. He was heralded as "one of the best infield prospects to enroll at Oregon for some time. He is in a class by himself as far as classy fielding is concerned. He is a sure regular for the 1934 Webfoot [Ducks] varsity."[14]

After completing an outstanding season with the UO frosh baseball team, 18-year-old Joe Gordon signed to play semipro ball that summer for Wolfer's Federals of the Oregon State League. This was a new club based in Portland, comprising many players from the West Side Babes and piloted by their previous year's manager, Ray Brooks.[15] They played a *lot* of baseball that summer, even taking on a team of sailors from the U.S.S. *Greer*, one of four Navy destroyers docked at Portland for the city's annual Rose Festival.[16] Joe finished his second season of semipro ball with a league-leading .400 batting average. And for the second year in a row, Ray Brooks's club won the Oregon State League championship.[17]

When Joe enrolled as a sophomore at the University of Oregon in the fall of 1933, head football coach Prince G. "Prink" Callison tried to convince him go out for varsity football, but Joe already had made up his mind—he wanted to be a baseball player and didn't want to risk getting injured.[18] He did, however, play a little fraternity football and captained his Sigma Chi Fraternity team.[19]

While attending college, Joe worked part-time for the R.A. Babb Hardware Co. in downtown Eugene, and his brother Jack continued working for the Zellerbach Paper Co. to help with Joe's college expenses. After Joe signed with the New York Yankees organization in June 1935, Jack enrolled at the University of Oregon and played varsity baseball for the 1936–1938 Ducks, with UO winning the PCC Northern Division championship in 1937.

In the spring of 1934, Joe joined the UO varsity baseball team, coached by Bill Reinhart. They played a 16-game schedule in the five-team Northern Division of the Pacific Coast Conference. Their opponents included the Oregon State College Beavers, University of Idaho Vandals, University of Washington Huskies, and Washington State College Cougars. Coach Reinhart bragged about his new shortstop (Joe Gordon) and second baseman (Ray Koch): "I have one of the sweetest second-base combinations ever in varsity baseball."[20]

One writer described Gordon's play during a game in mid–May, revealing the fun, cocky side of the Ducks' 19-year-old shortstop: "On one short fly ball[,] Little Joe took three steps for a warm-up and took off into the ozone and speared the ball. That was only part of it. He did a double flip and came down to a hand-stand. Now to most of the public that was quite a feat.... 'That's nothin,' said Joe, 'you oughta see me on the hard ones.'"[21]

Winning their final doubleheader of the season against Oregon State College, the Ducks clinched the 1934 PCC Northern Division championship.[22] It was a *prodigious* victory for the University of Oregon—the first time they'd won a PCC baseball championship outright since 1918. One sportswriter raved about their keystone combination: "Ray Koch, second baseman, and Joe Gordon, shortstop, are as immovable as the Rock of Gibraltar. Koch and Gordon are as fine a double-play combination as ever wore the Webfoot colors."[23] Joe was named All-Conference shortstop. He and Koch also were two of the 10 UO varsity baseball players awarded the University's coveted "O" letters that spring.[24]

In addition to Joe playing baseball, *Oregon Journal* sports editor George Pasero later revealed, "He also headed the Letterman's Club boxing smoker, and that was a talent that [people] … perhaps didn't know Joe possessed. He was a superb boxer, and ring guys of the time thought he had the potential to be a champion [boxer]."[25]

As soon as the 1934 UO varsity baseball season wrapped up, Joe signed to play semi-pro ball that summer for the Eugene Townies of the Oregon State League.[26] Jack Gordon also played outfield for the club. The Townies finished the State League season tied for second place with the Bend Elks.[27]

Also that summer, Bill Garbarino, who had coached Portland's East Side Commercial Club American Legion team in 1931, recruited a select team of Portland-area all-stars—including the Gordon brothers and Ray Koch—to play the barnstorming Van Dyke Colored House of David team of Sioux City, Iowa. The Portland All-Stars stomped the House of David, 13–7.[28]

By the fall of 1934, Joe Gordon had put on some weight and learned that the University of Oregon varsity football team needed backfield players, so he decided to go out for football again. He later explained why: "When I enrolled for my junior year, the coach was a little short of backfield material and said he would fix me up with a scholarship if I would play. I reported for practice the first day."[29] But after the *Morning Oregonian* published an article about Gordon joining the football team,[30] a life-changing letter arrived from New York Yankees scout Bill Essick. In Joe's own words:

> It [the letter] was from Bill Essick, the famous Yankee scout. He advised me against playing football if I entertained any ideas of continuing with baseball after college.
> Like all baseball men, Essick's only objection to football was the ever-present danger of a wrenched arm or leg which might make a fellow useless for baseball.
> For the first time, I had been given some indication that a major-league ball club knew I even existed. Also for the first time, that letter was a very small step, but nevertheless a step, toward playing baseball as a means of livelihood….
> The next day, I turned in my football suit. I had been convinced there might be something in baseball for me if the Yankees, rich in talent and resources, thought enough of me to watch my activities and advise me accordingly.[31]

Later that fall, Joe met someone very special—a beautiful, statuesque, blue-eyed, honey-blonde young lady with a dazzling smile. Dorthy Irene "Dottie" Crum was a former Oregon State College coed from Los Angeles. She just happened to be in Eugene, visiting her brother Newton at the University of Oregon. As the story goes, she attended a Sigma Chi Fraternity party one night with some of her Pi Beta Phi Sorority sisters. There she met the handsome, fun-loving, UO Ducks varsity baseball star, Joe Gordon. Joe always was the "life of the party," wherever he went. And this night was no exception. The two talked and danced the night away—it was "love at first sight." Although Dottie had to return home to Los Angeles, the story would not end here.

The mid-winter break before UO varsity baseball started up in the spring of 1935 didn't stop Joe from participating in sports. He competed in intramural football and for

Chapter 5. Semipro and College Ball (1932–1936)

the UO gymnastic team.[32] He was featured in tumbling and horizontal-bar exhibitions during halftimes at UO basketball games, in addition to representing his Sigma Chi Fraternity in handball tournaments.[33]

After 12 seasons as head baseball and basketball coach, the eminently regarded Bill Reinhart announced that 1935 would be his final year at the University of Oregon. He had accepted a job at George Washington University in Washington, D.C.[34] With nearly the entire 1934 UO varsity baseball team returning for 1935, Reinhart was very enthusiastic about the Ducks' prospects for his final season. Due to Eugene's cold, rainy weather, the players practiced indoors in early March, and Joe Gordon was voted captain of their team.

Meanwhile, William "Vinegar Bill" Essick had been scouting the University of Oregon's outstanding Gordon-Koch keystone duo for quite some time now. Having worked as a West Coast scout for the New York Yankees since 1925, Essick was well known for signing such outstanding Yankees as Lefty Gomez, Joe DiMaggio, and Frank Crosetti. He'd also gained a reputation of fair dealing with college athletes, usually advising them to finish at least their junior year of school before signing a professional baseball contract.[35]

In March 1935, Essick invited Joe Gordon and Ray Koch to spend their spring break in Los Angeles, California, as guests of the New York Yankees. But first, Joe had to get approval from his mother. Before Louise Gordon would even *consider* letting her son go to Los Angeles for two weeks, he had to *promise* her that he would finish college, even if it meant that he might have to enroll for only one term each year until he graduated.[36]

Years later, Essick would say about Joe Gordon, "I sent him expense money to come down to Los Angeles during [s]pring vacation, stuck him on a semi-pro team and got him a tryout…. Joe might not have come except that his girl, Dorothy [sic] Crum … lived in L.A."[37]

While in Los Angeles, Joe got to spend some time

While visiting Southern California as a guest of the New York Yankees in late March 1935, Joe Gordon got to spend a little time on the beach with his girlfriend, Dottie Crum, who lived in Los Angeles (Gordon family collections).

with his girlfriend, Dottie Crum, meeting her family and friends, and frolicking on California's beautiful beaches. Even though Joe had to return to school in Oregon, Dottie and her mother would see him again soon. Later that spring, they traveled to Eugene to visit Dottie's brother, Newton; his new wife, Janis; and, of course, Joe.

Ever since early April, rumors had been circulating within Oregon sports circles about Yankees scout Bill Essick's keen interest in signing both Joe Gordon and Ray Koch to contracts.[38] However, recruiting the two would have to wait until after the college baseball season was finished.

In anticipation of the Ducks' first varsity game of 1935, April 26 was proclaimed "Baseball Day" in Eugene.[39] A record crowd of 2,700 fans cheered the Ducks on, as their star pitcher, Don McFadden, hurled a two-hitter to shut out the Oregon State Beavers, 17–0.[40] It was reported that Joe Gordon led the defense with three put-outs and five assists, in addition to a pair of hits and two intentional walks. Batting leader Ray Koch belted a home run, two doubles, and a single. The Ducks were off and running!

But baseball can be a fickle game. The following day, the Beavers stomped the Ducks, 12–7.[41] Gordon went hitless, and Koch logged just a single.

On May 10, three major league scouts (Bill Essick, the Detroit Tigers' Marty Krug, and the St. Louis Browns' Willis Butler) were sitting on the sidelines, watching the University of Oregon Ducks play the University of Washington Huskies.[42] The Ducks got by the Huskies by just one run that day. But knowing that three big-league scouts were watching may have been too much for Gordon and Koch. Although Joe managed to belt a two-run homer in the first inning, he committed *three errors*, and Ray Koch went hitless.

After observing the Ducks playing that spring, Boston Red Sox scout Earl Sheely told L.H. Gregory of *The Oregonian*: "Been looking over some of the collegians up here. I like Joe Gordon of Oregon. Fast, great pair of hands, he gets the ball away beautifully, hits well and has the instinct. Joe is the best varsity prospect on the Pacific [C]oast, better right now than some of the professional shortstops you see. It's easy to vision what he'll be in two or three years."[43]

The race to the 1935 PCC Northern Division championship went down to the wire. Four of the five conference teams were in contention. With just two games left, both against second-place Oregon State College, the University of Oregon was in first place by one game. The Ducks would have to take both games to win the championship outright.[44]

They sailed through their first game at Corvallis. Then, playing their final game at home, they beat Oregon State to capture their second consecutive PCC Northern Division championship.[45] The Ducks ended the 1935 season with 11 victories and five defeats, a full game ahead of the University of Washington Huskies.

Joe Gordon finished his final season of college ball, leading the PCC Northern Division with a .415 batting average and, once again, was named All-Conference Shortstop.[46] Coaches from the five conference schools selected a dozen players for the PCC Northern Division All-Star Team, with Gordon and Koch both on that list.

Bill Essick didn't lose any time in recruiting 20-year-old Joe Gordon. There already were too many other clubs looking to sign the Ducks' star shortstop.[47] On May 31, Joe accepted the terms of the contract offered him by the Yankees organization, and, after his final college game, he signed on June 7, 1935, with their Class AA International League Newark Bears farm club.[48] However, by the time Joe signed, minor league

Chapter 5. Semipro and College Ball (1932–1936)

baseball already had been underway for almost two months, which explains why his contract specified that he begin his professional playing career in 1936. Joe also received a $500 signing bonus from the Yankees.[49]

Louise Gordon also had to sign Joe's contract, because her son was not of legal age, which was 21 years old then. Several years later, Essick talked about the day that he signed Joe Gordon: "I'll never forget that first afternoon I had lunch with Joe's mother. 'You and I,' I told her, 'will be traveling to New York some day to see that son of yours playing in a World Series.' That wasn't all bunk. I really felt it.... An hour and a half later the Red Sox scout got around to the Gordons' house. I opened the door. 'Too late,' I [Essick] told him."[50]

Yet shortly after signing with the Yankees, Joe had second thoughts, as he told writer Stanley Frank a few years later:

> The very next day after I had signed with Essick two more offers were made. One was from Earl Sheeley [sic], a scout for the Red Sox, and the other from the Los Angeles club, a [Chicago] Cub farm. And both offered much more money than the Yankee proposition.
>
> I wondered whether I had made a serious mistake in accepting the Yankee offer so quickly. The way I figured things, the Red Sox and Los Angeles must have had a much higher opinion of me than did the Yankees if they bothered to make their bids so much more attractive....
>
> Then Bill Reinhardt [sic], my college coach, told me the facts of baseball life....
>
> "The Yankees pay the best salaries and they're always up there in the pennant race. That means bonuses and World Series shares. Five years from now, you'll realize you got the best break a young ball player could possibly get."[51]

The summer of 1935, Joe Gordon and Ray Koch played for the Hop Golds of Vancouver, Washington, another new semipro club managed by Ray Brooks in the Oregon State League. The Hop Golds were a traveling team, playing all their games on the road, and were considered one of the strongest clubs Brooks had ever put together.[52] By mid-July, it was reported that Joe Gordon was leading the State League with a .470 batting average.[53] After a spring and summer full of baseball, he played his final game for the Hop Golds and departed for college in Southern California.[54]

He enrolled at the University of Southern California the fall semester of 1935, carrying a full load of 16 units.[55] L.H. Gregory wrote in the *Sunday Oregonian*, "Joe Gordon, Oregon's shortstop, is playing Saturday and Sunday winter league baseball in Los Angeles under the sponsorship of Bill Essick, who signed Joe last summer [June 1935] to a Newark [Bears] contract.... Joe is having a fine time playing winter baseball and his hitting is much better."[56]

While Gordon was in Los Angeles, Yankees scout Bill Essick also enrolled him in Jess Orndorff's National Baseball School. Daniel R. Levitt's biography, titled "Bill Essick," on the Society for American Baseball Research website at www.sabr.org, states, "The Yankees scout who signed a player played a key role in determining at which minor-league team and level the player would debut. In Gordon's case, Essick anticipated starting him in a low minor league in Joplin, Missouri." Several years later, Orndorff wrote to *The Sporting News*, saying that it was he who persuaded Essick and the New York Yankees to option Joe Gordon to the Class AA Pacific Coast League Oakland Oaks for 1936, instead of to the Class C Western Association Joplin Miners at Joplin, Missouri, where Essick had originally determined that Joe begin his professional career.[57] This would turn out to be a career-changing move for 21-year-old Joe Gordon.

Chapter 6

JOE THE PRO! (1936–1937)

1936 Oakland Oaks

Joe Gordon completed his fall semester at the University of Southern California on February 6, 1936,[1] and headed home to Portland. He stopped off at Eugene, where he was greeted with nicknames of "Joe-Joe" and "Hollywood" by friends delighted to hear about his upcoming first year in professional baseball.[2]

Joe and his former University of Oregon teammate, Ray Koch, soon were on their way south to Modesto, California, hitchhiking to the spring training camp of the Class AA Pacific Coast League (PCL) Oakland Oaks, who were affiliated with the New York Yankees from 1935 to 1937.[3] During the first half of the twentieth century, the PCL was considered one of the "premier" baseball leagues in the nation. In 1936, the league comprised eight teams, ranging from Seattle to San Diego.[4]

Billy Meyer, the Oaks' new manager, had seen Joe Gordon play ball in Los Angeles that winter and wanted a better look.[5] Gordon and Koch arrived at Modesto several days early, reportedly upsetting Oaks management—until Gordon explained that they were early because of being so eager to start playing pro ball.[6]

The two Oregonians and a host of other rookies trained under the watch of manager Meyer and Yankees scouts Bill Essick, Joe Devine, and Bobby Coltrin.[7] How well they performed during spring tryouts would determine whether they'd be optioned to the Oaks or sent on to one of the Yankees' other farm clubs.

After working out for several days, Gordon was described as "A great ground coverer, with a strong arm, and to date a pretty fair-looking hitter."[8] He recorded a base hit and a bases-loaded triple in one of his first practice games. During an intrasquad game, playing shortstop for Billy Meyer's Billies, he belted two doubles and executed five putouts and four assists without an error.[9] It was a good start.

But by mid–March, both Gordon and Koch were still slated to begin their professional careers with the Yankees' Joplin Miners farm club in the Class C Western Association.[10] Despite predicting "great things in baseball" for Gordon, manager Meyer didn't think Joe was quite ready for Class AA ball.[11]

Then a series of "lucky breaks" came Gordon's way.[12] During an intrasquad game just a few days before the PCL season opened, and with Joe already booked to board the train later that day for Joplin, he belted a line-drive home run and a long single, which likely changed Meyer's mind about keeping him.[13]

Yankees farm system director George Weiss wired Oakland Oaks president Vic Devincenzi that rookie Joe Gordon was being optioned to Oakland.[14] Joe signed his contract with the Oaks on the opening day of the PCL season. His salary was later reported

Twenty-one-year-old Joe Gordon poses for a photograph in his 1936 Oakland Oaks uniform. We think this snapshot was taken right about the time that the Yankees optioned Joe to the Oaks in late March 1936. From the dirt on his uniform, it looks like he's been practicing his sliding (Gordon family collections).

as a very generous one for the time, $350 per month—however, he had to prove within 15 days that he potentially was a Class AA player.[15]

Gordon's University of Oregon teammate, second baseman Ray Koch, was not so fortunate. Ray was assigned to the Yankees' farm club at Joplin, Missouri, where he played second base until a knee injury ended his very promising career.[16]

The PCL season began on March 28. On April 5, during the nightcap of a doubleheader, the Oaks' 35-year-old shortstop, Bernie DeViveiros, injured his back, forcing him to sit out several games.[17] Three days later, manager Meyer sent Joe Gordon in to play the last half of a game against the visiting Portland Beavers. In Joe's first game as a pro, a 10-minute-long riot broke out in the 12th inning over an umpire's ruling, resulting in fans pelting the official with bottles and cushions until three policemen rushed onto the scene. The game eventually went 15 innings before Portland finally edged out the Oaks, 7–5.[18]

The following day, Gordon played the entire game as shortstop and leadoff batter against the Beavers, recording two hits, scoring a run, and taking part in a double play in the Oaks' victory.[19] Eddie Murphy wrote for the *Oakland Tribune*, "He's [Gordon's] the kind of newcomer who makes old timers recall the best shortstops they've ever seen, and he hits sharply."[20]

Gordon held onto the shortstop position until DeViveiros was back playing again, after which time he substituted regularly. He took over the position permanently in early May, when DeViveiros got hurt again.[21]

Following a "disastrous series" at the end of May when they lost seven out of eight games at Seattle, the Oaks' next stop was Portland.[22] This was Joe Gordon's first time playing pro ball in his hometown. In the first game of the seven-game series and with his mother, brother, and family friend Andy Lampert watching from the grandstands, Joe went 4-for-4, with a home run, double, two singles, and a walk. He drove in four runs and scored three in the Oaks' 13–3 victory over the Beavers.[23] However, the following night, Joe went 0-for-5 and committed an error while playing third base, as the Beavers toppled the Oaks, 13–4.[24]

These autographs are of five players from the 1936 Pacific Coast League Oakland Oaks and Mission Reds clubs: Dario Lodigiani (Oaks), Joe Gordon (Oaks), Harry Rosenberg (Reds), Max West (Reds), and Frenchy Uhalt (Oaks). This is the earliest autograph that the Gordon family has from Joe Gordon's time playing professional baseball (Gordon family collections).

After an exciting series against the Mission Reds in late June, Eddie Murphy wrote for the *Oakland Tribune*, "The youthful keystone combination of Joe Gordon at short and Dario Lodigiani at second won hundreds of transbay supporters by their work around the second bag and also with the willow [bat]. Gordon collected a total of 16 hits in 31 times charged at bat for an average of .516."[25] A large photo of him appeared in the *Oakland Tribune*, titled "Keeping Oaks in Race for 1936 P.C.L. Championship." The caption read, in part, "[S]cribes and fans tout him [Gordon] as the best major league prospect in the [Pacific] Coast League today."[26]

Joe's defense was outstanding, too, as noted following a game in mid–July: "The young shortstop had only four fielding chances, but one of them was of the most spectacular ever witnessed here."[27] Later that month, an article in the *Seattle Post-Intelligencer* forecast, "Gordon is coming fast and the boy has the physique and the cold-blooded nerve to be a major league star."[28]

In late July, *The Sporting News* published a column headlined "Minors Worth Watching," saying, in part, "Hustlin' Joe [Gordon] has raised himself into the .300 class of hitters and is generally regarded as the most improved rookie in the Pacific Coast League."[29]

Perhaps no greater praise can be paid to a ballplayer than from a rival team's manager. In Gordon's case, the accolades came in mid–August from player-manager Bill Sweeney of the league-leading Portland Beavers: "Never have I seen a greater prospect than this kid, and I've been playing ball for more years than I care to remember. He's not only the outstanding rookie of this league, but of every other league. I saw him make plays in our series at Portland that were absolutely impossible. How he ever came up with them I don't know, but he did. And he can hit too."[30]

Also that summer, baseball legend Lefty O'Doul, manager of the PCL San Francisco Seals, revealed his personal all-star dream team, picked from among current players of the eight 1936 PCL ballclubs.[31] Lefty named Oakland rookie Joe Gordon as his all-star shortstop, one of only two players selected from the Oaks.

The race to the finish of the 1936 season was one of the closest in PCL history. On the final day, Oakland toppled the Sacramento Solons in both games of a doubleheader. They ended up tied with the San Diego Padres for second place, just 1½ games behind the first-place Portland Beavers.[32]

Gordon wrapped up his first season of professional baseball, batting an even .300 in 143 games, with 56 RBI and six home runs. Beavers manager Bill Sweeney again praised him: "Greatest young infielder in this league ... was Joe Gordon ... playing shortstop for Oakland, and I don't see how he can possibly miss as a big leaguer.... He has the size, the speed, big hands, is a great judge of either a ground or a fly ball, and at bat, has lots of power.... The New York Yanks got one of the prizes of baseball when they signed Gordon."[33]

In the postseason best-of-seven-game Shaughnessy semifinals, the first-place Portland Beavers went up against the fourth-place Seattle Indians,[34] while the tied-for-second-place San Diego Padres and Oakland Oaks took on each other. The Padres' roster comprised a powerhouse of future major leaguers, including Ted Williams, Bobby Doerr, and Vince DiMaggio. Moreover, the club was reported as possessing "an unwarranted feeling of confidence ... because they had won the season series from the Oaks 17–11."[35]

Playing the first two games of the semifinals in Oakland, the Oaks beat the Padres in both games. But due to reported "bad blood" between the clubs because of a couple of questionable calls in the second game, PCL president William C. Tuttle ordered that the two teams travel to San Diego in separate railroad cars and not intermingle en route. After arriving at San Diego, it was reported that Padres owner Bill Lane refused to allow the Oaks to work out at Lane Field on the two days off before resuming the semifinals.[36]

Oakland won Game Three, and San Diego took Game Four. In a very close Game Five, in which the two clubs used four pitchers each, the Oaks wrapped up their semifinals, four games to one.[37]

Meanwhile up north, the Portland Beavers had won four straight from the Seattle Indians and enjoyed several days of rest while the Oaks were playing their fifth game and traveling two days from San Diego to Portland for the finals. Playing to overflow crowds, the Beavers took all three of the games. The two teams traveled to Oakland, where the Oaks won Game Four, but lost the championship in Game Five.[38]

Of the $10,000 total prize money, the Beavers were awarded $2,500 for their first-place finish in the regular season, plus $3,000 for winning the championship. The Oaks received $2,000 for coming in second, which amounted to about $80 per player. The San Diego Padres and Seattle Indians were awarded $1,250 each.[39]

Immediately following the playoffs, Joe Gordon hurried back to Eugene, in time to enroll for the fall semester at the University of Oregon.[40]

1937 Newark Bears

In late January 1937, a small paragraph in *The Sporting News* noted, "Joe Gordon, a young infielder who displayed considerable ability with the Oakland [Pacific] Coast [L]eague club last season … will play Saturday ball in Los Angeles for Bob Little's Yanks, a semi-pro outfit guided by [s]cout Bill Essick. Essick wants to look over Gordon, who is a shortstop, before sending him on to Newark [Bears] of the International League."[41]

While at Los Angeles, Gordon also attended Jess Orndorff's National Baseball School to learn some of the fundamentals of playing second base.[42] The New York Yankees were planning on converting Joe into a second baseman, as future replacement for their longtime keystone sack star, 33-year-old Tony Lazzeri.

The 1937 Newark Bears were one of eight clubs in the International League, ranging from Quebec to Baltimore. Like the Pacific Coast League, the International League was Class AA, the highest level of play in the minors.

The Bears were widely regarded as the Yankees' top farm club[43] and played their home games at Ruppert Stadium in Newark, New Jersey. The 1937 team had undergone major rebuilding from the ground up. Well over half of their players were new to the club, and their roster was replete with former and future major leaguers.

Newark's manager, Oscar "Ossie" Vitt, had piloted the Bears to a third-place finish in 1936. After Gordon spent two weeks at the 1937 Yankees' spring training, manager Joe McCarthy told Vitt, "Take Gordon with you and make a second baseman out of him. He looks like the man to take Lazzeri's place when Tony's pins [legs] give out on him."[44] Although Vitt was regarded as a veritable taskmaster by many players, Gordon got along well with his manager, saying, "When I was sent to Newark, I got all the encouragement in the world from Oscar Vitt."[45]

The Bears conducted their spring training at Sebring, Florida, and played exhibition

Chapter 6. Joe the Pro! (1936–1937)

games against five major league clubs, including the Yankees, in addition to the Toronto Maple Leafs and Baltimore Orioles of their own league.[46] By the time the team departed Florida on their barnstorming trip north to Newark, it was reported that spring training had "uncovered" three promising players for the Bruins (a nickname for the Bears): infielders Joe Gordon and Frank Kelleher, and outfielder Charlie Keller. Gordon was reported in *The Sporting News* as "the find of the year."[47]

The Bears opened the season at home on a wet, sunless April 22. Although only about 5,000 brave souls showed up to watch amidst intermittent showers, notables in attendance included International League president Frank J. Shaughnessy, Yankees owner Colonel Jacob Ruppert, Newark's Deputy Mayor William S. Fox, and a Yankees contingent composed of general manager Ed Barrow, farm system director George Weiss, Ruppert's personal secretary George Perry, and scout Paul Krichell. Joe Gordon was nursing a wrenched ankle that had to be taped, yet he played the entire game, recording a hit and scoring a run, plus five putouts and three assists for Newark's Opening Day triumph over the Montreal Royals, 8–5.[48]

Many years later, iconic New Jersey sportswriter Jerry Izenberg (nicknamed the "Walking Encyclopedia of Baseball") told author Judy Gordon, "When you played for the Bears, you were family."[49] The ballplayers lived at the Hotel Riviera in Newark's Springfield/Belmont neighborhood. Izenberg wrote about how "kids ... stood outside Chris [sic] Chop House, where the Bears ate, and felt as though they walked with gods when the players permitted them to walk back to the team hotel alongside them."[50]

Earl Harper broadcast the Bears home games live from Ruppert Stadium on radio station WNEW. He even broadcast play-by-play coverage of their road trip games, with the help of Ed Weinstein, who traveled with the team and telegraphed the live action back to Harper in Newark.[51]

Joe "Flash" Gordon takes time for a photograph before a Newark Bears game at Ruppert Stadium in Newark. Sitting in the grandstand behind Joe are his steady girlfriend, Dottie Crum, and his teammate Frank Kelleher's bride Frances. Dottie rode the train 3,500 miles from Los Angeles, California, to visit Joe during the Bears' long homestay in mid-June 1937 (Gordon family collections).

Joe Gordon gained a large fan following at Newark with loyal admirers who tracked his every game. Some ardent enthusiasts even presented him with a Bulova watch inscribed "J. Gordon, Radio Fans, 1937." Although Joe's teammates nicknamed him "Mercury" or "Merk," probably for his speed around the keystone bag, his fans and the media called him "Flash."[52]

By early July, an article in Gordon's hometown newspaper proclaimed, "Joe Gordon Best of Stellar Yankee Farm Players," describing him as "perhaps the deadliest clutch hitter in the league." He also was portrayed as "greased lightning around second [base]."[53]

Midway through the 1937 season, Newark already was leading the second-place Montreal Royals by 18 games.[54] In his regular spot as leadoff batter, during a night game at Baltimore on July 8, Gordon went 4–for–5, belting *three* home runs and driving in five runs, in addition to handling four chances defensively without an error. The "Bruins" stomped the Orioles, 17–3, in front of a reported 10,000 fans.[55] A photo of Joe appeared in the next day's *New York Herald Tribune*, captioned, "Joe Gordon, second baseman, called the best infielder in the league."[56]

Later that season, sports columnist Hy Goldberg wrote, "Players who have shuttled between the Yankees and Bears this year report that [Joe] Gordon fields ground balls [Tony] Lazzeri couldn't reach with a 10-foot pole.... [A]nd as for pop flies that ordinarily drop for hits behind second base, Newark fans never have seen any one [*sic*] run so far to catch them." Goldberg also noted how International League president Frank Shaughnessy remarked that the Bears have a "fourth outfielder" with Joe Gordon on second base.[57]

Gordon was blessed with an outstanding mentor—the 34-year-old shortstop and captain of the Bears, Nolen Richardson. Years later, Joe told writer Ed Fitzgerald of *Sport* magazine, "Until I played with Richardson, I always wondered what they meant when they said a fellow was a playmaker. He showed me by the way he fitted his play to mine and the way he made every maneuver a team operation. He taught me how to shift for hitters with the pitch, how to shorten my position in double-play situations, and a million other things."[58]

The Bears clinched the International League pennant on August 23, reported as the earliest such date in league history.[59] They wrapped up the 1937 season at Ruppert Stadium on September 12, defeating the Baltimore Orioles in both games of a doubleheader.[60] With a record of 109–43 (.717), the Bears finished a whopping, league record 25½ games ahead of second-place Montreal. Newark's top four pitchers, Joe Beggs (21-4 record and 2.61 ERA), Atley Donald (19-2), Vito Tamulis (18–6), and Steve Sundra (15–4), posted an astounding 73-16 (.820) combined record that year![61]

Joe Gordon played in 151 of the Bears' 152 games, batting .280 with 89 RBI, notable in that he almost always was the leadoff batter. He recorded 178 hits and 109 runs (both second in the league to teammate Charlie Keller's 189 and 120), in addition to 26 home runs (first on his team and second in the league to the Orioles' Ab Wright's 37). Gordon's batting average belied the fact that he was widely feared as a clutch hitter, coming through when it counted the most. It also was reported that he led International League second basemen in putouts, assists, double plays, and errors. Although his .948 fielding average was not the highest in the league, it was reported that he covered more territory and handled about 50 more chances than any other second baseman.[62]

The International League playoffs began with a best-of-seven-game Shaughnessy semifinals, with the first-place Newark Bears facing the third-place Syracuse Chiefs,

Chapter 6. Joe the Pro! (1936–1937)

and the second-place Montreal Royals playing the fourth-place Baltimore Orioles. The Bears' first game against the Chiefs ended in a storybook finish. In the bottom of the ninth inning, with two outs and Syracuse leading, 1–0, Joe Gordon and Jimmy Gleeson belted back-to-back home runs on just *three* pitches, to win the game, 2–1.[63] Newark players and fans went wild! In reporting for the *Newark Star Eagle*, sports editor Murray Robinson *twice* described the game as "the most dramatic game of baseball we have ever seen."[64]

Newark, "the wonder team," swept all four games against the Chiefs. Gordon wrapped up the semifinals batting .474, including three home runs, his last one an inside-the-park round-tripper to clinch Game Four. An exciting media account reads, in part, "[O]nly an exhibition of superb base running enabled Gordon to score seconds ahead of the relay. He tripped head over [c]atcher Dee Moore, who was blocking the plate, and touched the dish [home plate] with his hands, just as the ball bounced over Moore's shoulder."[65]

Next, the best-of-seven-game International League finals saw the Newark Bears going up against the heavy-hitting Baltimore Orioles, who had just won their last four of five games against Montreal in the semifinals. In Game One, Newark's Joe Beggs pitched a "brilliant" one-hitter to shut out the Orioles, 2–0, at Newark's Ruppert Stadium.[66]

Game Two may be remembered more for the wild scuffle between Orioles shortstop Chester "Wimpy" Wilburn and home-plate umpire William "Bick" Campbell than for the Bears' second victory of the International League finals, 6–5.[67] As the last player up in the top of the ninth inning, his *fourth* time called out on strikes, Wilburn vigorously protested the call, tearing at the umpire's chest protector and swinging in a rage.[68] Both benches emptied, and several fans took to the field to join in the fray. Umpire Campbell was escorted off the field for his own safety.

After the teams traveled to Baltimore, the outcome of Game Three shifted back and forth until the Bears triumphed, 7–5. Along with their victory, 10–7, in Game Four, the Bears accomplished a *first* in International League playoff history—sweeping both the semifinals and finals without losing a game! During the eight games, Charlie Keller batted .455, followed by Joe Gordon at .385, Jimmy Gleeson .344, and George McQuinn .324.[69] The Bears won the 1937 International League Governors' Cup[70] and $4,000 in prize money, in addition to qualifying to play the American Association Columbus Red Birds in the "Junior World Series" (also known as the "Little World Series").[71]

The best-of-seven-game Junior World Series kicked off on September 29, with the first three games scheduled to be played at Newark.[72] Yankees dignitaries were out in force for Game One: Colonel Jacob Ruppert, Ed Barrow, George Weiss, Joe McCarthy, George Perry, and three scouts, including Bill Essick, who'd signed Joe Gordon to his first professional contract in 1935.[73] Game One oscillated back and forth until Columbus prevailed, 5–4, despite Joe Gordon's home run in the bottom of the ninth.[74]

Game Two was played at night, drawing more than 17,000 fans, eager to see their hometown Bears even the score. But the Red Birds slipped by, 5–4, this time in 11 innings.[75]

Game Three drew another near-capacity crowd of 17,000. But Newark fans ended up greatly disheartened when Columbus toppled their beloved Bears, 6–3.[76] Departing immediately after the game, the Bruins' special train to Columbus was replete with almost palpable gloom. Everyone *knew* that they had to accomplish the all-but-impossible—win the next four games in a row—and in their opponents' home stadium to boot!

Yet Lady Luck was smiling down on the Bears in Game Four the following night, as they easily bested the Red Birds, 8–1, in their first win of the Series.[77]

After a day off due to rain, Game Five saw one of the Bears' star hurlers, Atley Donald, pitch a "masterpiece" of a three-hitter to shut out Columbus, 1–0, assisted by Joe Gordon driving in the winning run.[78] The mood in the Bears' camp changed—it was the spark they needed!

Spud Chandler, who earlier that year had pitched in 12 games for the Yankees before sent down to Newark due to a sore arm, held Columbus to just one run in the Bears' hitting-spree of a Game Six, 10–1, to even the Series at three games apiece.[79] It was reported in *The Sporting News* that "Joe Gordon ... played sensationally in the sixth game, handling ten chances at second [base] in flawless style, several being of a spectacular nature."[80]

Game Seven was the clincher. In his book, *The 1937 Newark Bears: A Baseball Legend*, author Ronald A. Mayer wrote, "Although the crowd was slim, slightly under 4,000 (it rained hard an hour before game time), the tension throughout the park was evident. This was it. The string had run out. There would be no next game."[81]

With Newark leading, 3–2, in the bottom of the fourth inning, manager Vitt sent in veteran southpaw Phil Page to relieve Joe Beggs. With the bases loaded and two outs, Red Birds first baseman Dick Siebert hit a slow grounder toward second base. Mayer described Joe Gordon's play as he charged, scooped, and flipped the ball to first base for the third out, delivering "the fielding gem of the game."[82] The Bears stormed ahead, triumphing over the Red Birds, 10–4, to win the 1937 Junior World Series, four games to three. Newark outfielder Jimmy Gleeson later told how manager Oscar Vitt had motivated their team to victory: "After we had lost the first three games [at Newark], everybody on the club was down, but Vitt was still certain we could win. He literally drove us to the championship."[83]

The players' pool for winning the Junior World Series amounted to $22,328. The Bears' portion was 60 percent, which they divided into 19½ shares, with each player receiving $687.[84] It was reported that Joe Gordon used his winnings to help his mother put a down payment on buying her first home in Portland.[85] During Joe's first two and a half years in professional baseball, he turned all of his paychecks over to his mother, except for a small amount that he kept for incidentals. The authors believe that Joe may have done this to help with his brother Jack's college expenses.

Immediately after the final game of the Series, Joe flew home from Columbus to enroll in the fall semester at the University of Oregon.[86] He would miss the huge welcoming celebration when the Bears arrived back at Pennsylvania Railroad Station, the ticker-tape motorcade through downtown Newark, and Colonel Jacob Ruppert's victory dinner at the Commodore Hotel in New York City.[87]

The International League team managers selected their all-star team for 1937. A remarkable 10 of the 14 players were from the Newark Bears: George McQuinn (first base), Joe Gordon (second base), Babe Dahlgren (third base), Nolen Richardson (shortstop), Charlie Keller (right field), Bob Seeds (center field), Willard Hershberger and Buddy Rosar (catchers), and Steve Sundra and Joe Beggs (pitchers).[88] Likewise, when 22 sportswriters who'd followed the International League throughout the 1937 season picked their all-star team, it, too, was composed of nearly all Newark Bears.[89]

It was reported that International League president Frank Shaughnessy favored Newark's Oscar Vitt as the league's top manager of 1937 and rated Joe Gordon as the

Chapter 6. Joe the Pro! (1936–1937) 37

This outstanding 1937 Newark Bears autographed baseball is signed by manager Oscar Vitt and 19 of the team's players, including Joe Gordon (Gordon family collections).

league's standout player.[90] *The Sporting News* later named the Bears' 21-year-old outfielder, Charlie Keller, as their 1937 Minor League Player of the Year.[91]

The 1937 Newark Bears were one of the youngest teams in the history of the International League.[92] They still are regarded by countless baseball fans and historians as the "greatest team in minor league baseball history." In 2001, as part of the 100th anniversary of Minor League Baseball, veteran baseball historians Bill Weiss and Marshall Wright ranked their favorite "100 Best Minor League Teams of the 20th Century." They placed the 1937 Newark Bears third, following the 1934 Los Angeles Angels and 1921 Baltimore Orioles—although Bears fans may passionately beg to differ.[93]

Right after the Junior World Series, manager Oscar Vitt praised his young second baseman, Joe Gordon: "[H]e could step right into the Yankee lineup right now and give 'em a lot of help. He'll be with the Yankees next season. He is an exceptionally good hitter and he's going to town. He certainly did a big lot to put the Bears up where they are."[94]

In mid–October 1937, the Yankees released their longtime second baseman, Tony Lazzeri. Soon thereafter, Oscar Vitt told writer Harry Grayson, "He'll [Gordon will] make the Yanks forget Lazzeri. I've never seen a better young second sacker."⁹⁵ Vitt also told writer Emmons Byrne of *The Sporting News*, "I've seen most of the great ones in action, and that Gordon kid made plays last summer [1937] that Eddie Collins or [Nap] Lajoie couldn't have touched. That's how good I think he is."⁹⁶

The authors are especially drawn to a quote from Oscar Vitt in February 1938, summing up his assessment of Joe Gordon: "He's a wonderful fielder, a dangerous hitter in the pinch and, best of all, he has marvelous team spirit and the will to learn."⁹⁷

Chapter 7

A Rookie Year to Remember (1938)

Expectations were widespread throughout the baseball world for the New York Yankees' 23-year-old rookie second baseman Joe Gordon to perform brilliantly in his first season in the major leagues.[1] The Flash, however, would not only redefine how second base was played, he also would own it!

Gordon had a lot going on the winter of 1937–1938, as he got ready to join the Yankees at spring training in St. Petersburg. He completed his fall term early at the University of Oregon, then headed to Southern California to play winter ball under the "watchful eyes" of Yankees scout Bill Essick.[2] While Joe was in Los Angeles, the Yankees once again enrolled him in Jess Orndorff's National Baseball School—this time to work on his batting.[3]

Joe was happy to be back in California, where his girlfriend, Dottie Crum, lived. He played semipro ball on Sundays for the Montebello Merchants, in addition to joining in on "pick-up [sic] nines" with local college teams during the week.[4] A photo of him wearing a Montebello Merchants uniform along with his 1937 Newark Bears baseball cap appeared in several newspapers, including the *Los Angeles Times* and *The Oregonian*.[5]

In late January, the Yankees purchased Joe Gordon's contract from their Newark Bears farm club, making him a "full-fledged Yank." He signed his 1938 contract for a salary of $6,500 per season—$1,500 more than the amount originally listed on the contract and personally okayed by Yankees owner Colonel Jacob Ruppert.[6] This was an excellent starting salary for a rookie, especially when the average family income in the United States at the time was just a little more than $2,000 per year.

In the 1930s, major league players' contracts almost always were for just one year. Lou Gehrig's wife, Eleanor, pointed out in her book, *My Luke and I*, "[T]here were no baseball pensions in those days. You played, if you were lucky, and you left when they found somebody else younger and stronger. It's a business, we accepted that."[7]

In mid–February 1938, *The Sporting News* published a photo of Joe Gordon and several other rookies. In the accompanying article, Gordon was referred to as "perhaps the brightest prospect of them all."[8] *The Sporting News* was a highly regarded, St. Louis-based sports weekly, established back in 1886 and often referred to as "The Bible of Baseball."

Right before Joe departed for Yankees' spring training, Dottie Crum held a farewell party for him at her parents' home in Los Angeles. During the evening's festivities, the young couple surprised the partygoers by announcing their engagement.

Joe arrived at St. Petersburg a week early for spring training, along with the Yankees' advance squad of pitchers and catchers.[9] Unlike the "rocky" reception he'd received at 1937 spring training, this time he had a room waiting for him at St. Petersburg's

The New York Yankees' rookie second baseman, Joe Gordon (seated, front-center), is welcomed by his teammates in the clubhouse during spring training at St. Petersburg, on March 1, 1938. From left: Bill Dickey, Steve Sundra, George Selkirk, Monte Pearson, Kemp Wicker, and Ivy Andrews (The SABR-Rucker Archive).

Suwannee Hotel. Moreover, he "started off under noble auspices" by being assigned Babe Ruth's former locker in the clubhouse at Miller Huggins Field, in addition to being entrusted with Tony Lazzeri's old Number 6 for his uniform.[10]

At first, Gordon may have been somewhat apprehensive about joining the much-revered New York Yankees. His concerns would be short-lived, however, as he later told Stanley Frank in *Street & Smith's Sport Story Magazine*: "I knew Tony Lazzeri had been a great favorite with the team and I couldn't help but feel that some of the veterans might resent my appearance, regard me as an interloper. I felt as if I had just hit a homer with the bases loaded and two out in the ninth [inning] … when the Yankees gave me a swell reception at St. Petersburg … in March 1938. Everybody gave me a glad hand; everybody remembered my name. This time I really felt that I 'belonged.'"[11]

Lou Gehrig, Joe DiMaggio, and a few others still hadn't signed their contracts by the time spring training began. It was said that Colonel Ruppert reminded the "holdouts" that their earnings would be boosted by their World Series winnings.[12] This had been true the previous two years (1936 and 1937); but no matter how good the club's prospects seemed, there were no guarantees. Joe DiMaggio would hold out for so long in 1938 that he missed spring training altogether, as well as the Yankees' barnstorming trip from Florida to New York and their first dozen games of the season.[13]

Manager McCarthy experimented with Gordon's batting, getting him to move closer to the plate and try to hit more to right field.[14] During the 1938 season, McCarthy delegated Joe Gordon to hit seventh or eighth in the batting order, spots usually reserved for a team's less-consistent hitters.

As spring training progressed, Gordon's defensive skills were reported as improving from "great to greater." Joe McCarthy said that the Yankees were executing plays at second base that he'd not seen since becoming manager of the team in 1931.[15]

They played their first exhibition game on March 12 against the National League St. Louis Cardinals, drawing a record spring training crowd of 6,948 enthusiastic fans. Gordon's bases-loaded ground-rule triple into the center field crowd contributed three runs to the Yankees' six-run sixth inning to clinch the game, 6–4.[16]

Lou Gehrig, the Yankees' longtime first baseman and captain, signed his 1938 contract for a reported $39,000 (a $3,000 raise over his previous year's salary) and arrived at St. Petersburg about a week late. He had spent most of the winter in Hollywood, California, filming the movie *Rawhide*, which premiered at St. Petersburg during spring training.[17]

Gordon, though, was just being cautiously optimistic about the likelihood of remaining permanently with the Yankees. On the very day that McCarthy made up his mind to keep his rookie second baseman, Gordon still was unaware of his manager's decision and admitted to a writer, "If McCarthy wants me to go back to Newark[,] I won't be disappointed. I know that making the grade in this league is tough business."[18]

Yet by the third week of training, McCarthy officially endorsed his new rookie: "We could not make double plays last year [1937]—finished last in our league with 130 [actually 134]. Gordon will remedy that. He can do everything in the field."[19] By the time the Yankees headed out from St. Petersburg, Joe McCarthy was telling the sportswriters, "Gordon is going to fit well into our infield. He'll cover more ground than did Tony [Lazzeri], and I wouldn't be surprised if he hits better in our league than he did in the International [League]."[20]

The Yankees traveled in two or three Pullman cars in which the players ate and slept as they barnstormed, usually with another major league club, throughout the Southeast by train, then northward to New York.[21] The Gordon children still recall a funny story about how their father had always been blessed with an uncanny ability to fall sound asleep at a moment's notice, especially when riding the train. During one of the Yankees' excursions between cities, Joe's teammates took advantage of their new rookie's catching forty winks. Reminiscent of a fraternity prank, they painted Joe's toenails with bright-red nail polish while their subject slept unaware, only to awaken and discover his haphazard pedicure.

Arriving in New York, the Yankees and Brooklyn Dodgers played their traditional three exhibition games at Ebbets Field. They now were ready to begin the 1938 season.

Wearing new traveling uniforms with 1939 World's Fair patches on their left sleeves,[22] they opened the 1938 season at Boston on April 18. Gordon, batting eighth, went 0-for-4 in his first major league game, striking out his first two times at bat, flying out to right field, and finally grounding into a double play. The Red Sox won, 8–4.

In the opener of the following day's doubleheader at Boston, the Flash recorded his first major league hit and drove in two runs in the Yankees' 5–3 victory. He also hit a double in the nightcap, although Boston shut out the Bombers, 6–0. Remarkably, that was the first of only *two* shutouts of the Yankees the entire 1938 season. Boston took the final game of the series, and the Yankees headed home for their series against the Washington Senators. (The American League baseball club in Washington, D.C., was officially named the Washington Senators from 1901 to 1904, Washington Nationals from 1905 to 1955, and Washington Senators again from 1956 to 1960. For simplicity, the authors have chosen to refer to them as the Senators.)

It may seem incredible to readers today, but reliable sources reported that Joe Gordon had never even *seen* the inside of Yankee Stadium until his first game there on April 22.[23] Yankee Stadium had a well-known reputation for penalizing right-handed power hitters such as Gordon. Left-handers had a marked advantage, due to right field's considerably shorter distance from home plate (straightaway 344 feet) versus left field's (straightaway 402 feet).[24] Only three Yankees regulars of 1938 (Frank Crosetti, DiMaggio, and Gordon) were right-handed batters. The other five (Bill Dickey, Lou Gehrig, Tommy Henrich, Red Rolfe, and George Selkirk) batted left-handed, although Dickey, Rolfe, and Selkirk threw right-handed.

Joe DiMaggio finally came to terms for his 1938 contract and was on his way from California to New York. However, he would miss the first 12 games of the season, for which, reportedly, Yankees owner Jacob Ruppert docked his pay.[25]

In *Ed Barrow: The Bulldog Who Built the Yankees' First Dynasty*, author Daniel R. Levitt described opening ceremonies at Yankee Stadium as "chaotic."[26] New York City's Acting Mayor, Newbold Morris, was scheduled to toss out the first pitch, but was conspicuously absent. While waiting for Morris, Captain Sutherland's 7th Regiment Band paraded the Yankees and Senators ballplayers to the center field flagpole. Yankees general manager Ed Barrow stood at attention as he and the two managers, Joe McCarthy and Bucky Harris, waited for the raising of Old Glory and the Yankees' "World Champions of 1937" flag.[27] The assemblage remained by the flagpole a full 15-20 minutes before Morris finally made his entrance, after having refused to cross a picket line.[28]

It was the top of the fifth inning when Joe Gordon's fielding drew the accolades of the day: "[Rick] Ferrell grounded to Gordon and 'Flash' flicked the ball to Frankie Crosetti, giving the 25,000 customers their first glimpse of the new keystone combination at high-speed operation…. There were no hits in Gordon's bat … but he won his way into the hearts of the Bronx fans with his arm."[29] The Yankees shut out the Senators, 7–0.

At Philadelphia on April 26, in addition to taking part in completing three double plays, Gordon hit his first major league home run, with one man on base. The Yankees triumphed over the Athletics, 5–3, on Gordon's "upper-tier" left field round-tripper.[30]

On Friday, April 29, the Bronx Bombers held their first Ladies Day in the 15-year history of Yankee Stadium. A reported 4,903 ladies attended for free except for tax. Thirty-four-year-old first baseman Lou Gehrig, who'd been experiencing an uncharacteristically slow start this year, was cheered on by all his lady fans and recorded his first two-hit game of the season, raising his batting average from .088 to .132, as the Yanks topped the Red Sox, 6–4.[31]

April 30 saw the Yankees on the road again, this time playing at Washington, D.C. Gordon had played all the games, with this being his 13th start. This also was Joe DiMaggio's first game of the 1938 season.

In the bottom of the sixth inning, second baseman Joe Gordon, center fielder Joe DiMaggio, and left fielder Myril Hoag all took off after a high fly ball hit to short-center field. While trying to make the catch, DiMaggio and Gordon collided head-on, with both players knocked unconscious.[32] Somehow, Hoag caught the ball for the out, and the Yankees went on to win the game. Both DiMaggio and Gordon were rushed to the hospital and kept overnight for x-rays and observation.[33]

Chapter 7. A Rookie Year to Remember (1938)

DiMaggio returned to play the following day, while Gordon watched from the grandstands.[34] Years later, in *The DiMaggio Albums, Vol. 1: 1932–1941*, Joe DiMaggio wrote:

> The year 1938 was a troublesome one. It began with a contract dispute. We did not have long-term contracts in those days.... I ended up holding out, in fact did not come to terms with the Yankees until the end of April. Then, when I was finally back on the field [April 30], I collided with Joe Gordon, the second baseman we had acquired to replace Tony Lazzeri.... Gordon, however, left the field via a stretcher, and I was booed for the first time that I can remember in my baseball career.[35]

Within four days, Gordon was ready to play again—but manager McCarthy had other ideas. "Marse Joe" had decided to bench his young rookie for a while, which turned out to be 30 games. McCarthy talked about that a month later: "I knew Joe had it all the time. But he lacked something. Strange to say, it was complete confidence. Externally he looked cocky, invincible in spirit. But he came up with the feeling that he was taking the place of a superman [Tony Lazzeri], and that the league was full of men whose class it would take him years to match.... And I knew he would not lose that feeling unless he could get the proper perspective—from the bench."[36]

Years later, McCarthy gave more insight into his practice of occasionally benching a rookie: "My benching ... doesn't mean I have decided he hasn't the skill. I benched Crosetti when he broke in, I did it with Joe Gordon, I have done it with so many of our players. The idea is to take off the strain, at times, and let a man wear into a job."[37]

Right before spring training, the Yankees had acquired 26-year-old utility infielder Bill Knickerbocker from the St. Louis Browns, as backup for Frank Crosetti at shortstop or Joe Gordon at second base.[38] With Gordon relegated to the bench for what turned out to be five and a half weeks, Knickerbocker took over the keystone sack.

During that time, Gordon sat next to Joe McCarthy in the dugout, observing every play of every game—all the while picking up valuable pointers from his manager. Years later, Ed Barrow wrote about McCarthy: "[T]he asset that placed him above all other managers was his ability to handle young ballplayers.... He had a great patience with young players, and was unmatched in giving a young fellow confidence."[39]

During Gordon's time on the bench, the 23-year-old rookie got to know, respect, and admire his 51-year-old manager. The present-day Gordon family believes that McCarthy may have even become somewhat of a father figure to the young rookie, although strictly in a baseball sense. The two men's backgrounds were remarkably similar: both had lost their fathers at a young age, both learned to play baseball on the sandlots and played in college, and both were amateur magicians.[40]

While watching from the bench, Gordon had the opportunity to observe his teammate, center fielder Joe DiMaggio, who was playing his third season with the Yankees. Years later, author Maury Allen quoted Gordon about his teammate: "He [DiMaggio] was the best hitter I ever saw.... He was an easy guy to get along with. He didn't make any fuss. Didn't ask for any privileges. Just got into his uniform and did his work."[41]

In Gordon's 11 years in the majors, he *rarely* talked with writers about teammates or other ballplayers. His remarks about Joe DiMaggio are some of the few that the authors came across during their many years of research.

With DiMaggio joined up with the Yankees, and Knickerbocker soon batting better than Gordon's .156 average, the club started moving up in the American League standings. By the end of May, they had a record of 20–14–1 (.588) and had advanced from fourth to second place behind the league-leading Cleveland Indians.

The Flash, however, did get to play in one game during his hiatus—an exhibition game on May 16 at Butler, Pennsylvania, against the Butler Yankees of the Class D Pennsylvania State Association.[42] In the second inning, Gordon was hit on the head by a pitched ball from Butler's 19-year-old right-hander, John Kernoski. Joe dropped to the ground. Yet recovering quickly, he insisted on playing the remainder of the game. And play he did—belting *three* home runs over the left field fence that day! The Yankees stomped their farm club, 18–2, with the game finally called after the top of the seventh inning when more than 2,000 young autograph seekers swarmed onto the field.[43] The *Chicago Daily Tribune* reported, "Because Butler failed to play in the seventh [inning], the score reverted to the sixth, with New York ahead, 16 to 2."[44]

Two historic events took place on the last two days of May 1938. In addition to the Yankees' three victories over the visiting Boston Red Sox, a paid attendance of 81,891, reported as "the largest crowd in the history of baseball," packed Yankee Stadium for a doubleheader on Decoration Day (now known as Memorial Day) on May 30.[45] On May 31, Lou Gehrig played in his 2,000th consecutive game.[46] The Bronx Bombers' rookie second baseman, Joe Gordon, was there for both occasions—but still watching from the bench.

As the first of June rolled around, Joe may have wondered if he *ever* would get back in the Yankees' lineup. It was pointed out in a newspaper article that, "although the youngster [Gordon] has recivered [recovered], [s]econd [b]aseman Knickerbocker has been filling his shoes too effectively to warrant a change in the New York infield."[47]

Meanwhile, Joe and his fiancée, Dottie Crum, decided that they didn't want to wait any longer to be married. They had been limited to a mostly long-distance relationship for the previous three and a half years. But first, Gordon had to ask Joe McCarthy and Ed Barrow for "official permission" to marry.[48] He later revealed what happened when he talked with his manager: "I was scared to death because I knew McCarthy didn't like his players to get married during the [baseball] season. But when I asked his permission, he said, 'Sure. Can she cook?' 'Yes, sir,' I told him—and left as fast as possible."[49] But it must have taken more than just a little bit of courage to ask the Yankees' stern general manager; yet Barrow gave his approval, too.

With permission granted so easily, Gordon may have figured that Bill Knickerbocker would be holding down the Yankees' second base job for the remainder of the season. Nevertheless, on June 4, 1938, a day when the Yankees' game was postponed because of rain, Joe and Dottie eloped to Elkton, Maryland—also known as the "Gretna Green of the East Coast."[50] Dottie later wrote, "We were married, and returned to New York to find that Walter Winchell, the gossip columnist and radio commentator, had already spread the news. The next morning when we went down to breakfast in our hotel, almost the entire New York Yankee team was there to greet us!"[51]

Four days later, on June 8, in the bottom of the ninth inning of the nightcap of a doubleheader at home against the Chicago White Sox, manager McCarthy sent Joe Gordon into the game to pinch-hit. With his new bride, Dottie, watching from the grandstand, the Flash came through, belting a home run to deep left field with one man on base. Although the Yankees lost the game, McCarthy liked what he saw of his young rookie, and Joe Gordon had his job back at second base—for the rest of the season. The following day, the Flash justified his manager's confidence in him by smashing a triple to drive in the winning run. The Yankees won six games in a row, and Joe Gordon played every day the rest of the season.

Chapter 7. A Rookie Year to Remember (1938)

The newlyweds settled into a small apartment at the Concourse Plaza Hotel in the Bronx, where they would reside each baseball season from 1938 to 1943. The 12-story luxury hotel had opened in 1923 and was conveniently located about two blocks from Yankee Stadium.

Dottie was the ideal baseball wife, and the Gordons became close friends with the six to eight other Yankees couples living at the hotel. She attended all the home games, as well as a few on the road. She also became an avid scorekeeper, keeping score of nearly every baseball game that she attended from that time forward. Years later, she would teach their two children to keep score, too.

Theirs was a "marriage made in Heaven." In all their years together, Joe and Dottie's children never once heard their parents argue or even exchange a cross word. Dottie was sweet-natured and friendly with everyone.

Game by game, Gordon's batting got better and better. Multiple times, he was credited with game-winning hits or runs. Playing at St. Louis on June 20, Lou Gehrig, Joe Gordon, and Spud Chandler each hit home runs in the sixth inning, reported as tying a record and clinching the win against the Browns.[52] Gordon's round-tripper was an inside-the-park home run to deep center field.

Beginning on June 25 at Detroit, the Yankees launched a nine-game winning streak. Batting 3–for–4 with two RBI that day was great for Joe Gordon, but not so good for his head. After the Flash singled in the seventh inning, Tigers catcher Rudy York tried to pick him off first base. As Joe dove headfirst back to the bag, York's throw hit him in the back of the head—so hard that the ball rebounded clear back to home plate.[53] Joe was taken to the hospital for x-rays, where it was determined that he was not seriously hurt.

In less than two months, Gordon had suffered three severe blows to his head. This prompted his teammates to begin calling him "Rockhead," in addition to their usual nickname for him, which was "Trigger," in reference to his passion for guns and hunting. A few days later, writer Jack Smith characterized Joe Gordon as "strong of heart, fleet of foot and stout of skull."[54]

The Flash was on a roll. Some attributed it to him getting married, which probably was somewhat true. Sid Mercer wrote about Gordon's play during a June 29 doubleheader at home against the Philadelphia Athletics: "No American League freshman ever had a better day than Gordon."[55] He went 4–for–4 in the first game, including a home run, double, and two singles. In the nightcap, he singled, walked, and homered. Joe's batting average climbed from .288 to .322 in just one afternoon! Five days later, during 13 innings of the nightcap on July 4, Gordon handled 18 fielding chances without an error.[56] The authors don't know if his 18 chances during a 13-inning game set a record, although it certainly would have been close. Soon, Joe Gordon was being mentioned for the "American League rookie laurels of 1938."[57]

The 6th Annual Major League Baseball All-Star Game was scheduled for July 6 at Cincinnati's Crosley Field. The Detroit Tigers' future Hall of Famer, Charlie Gehringer, was chosen to play second base for the American League. The National League beat the American League, 4–1.

As the 1938 season progressed, Joe Gordon's fielding became more and more outstanding. On July 26, during the first game of a doubleheader at St. Louis, besides belting his 13th home run of the season, he tied a major league record for second basemen when he participated in five double plays.[58] Dan Daniel wrote in *The Sporting News*,

"[W]e find that the chief story in the Yankee camp is Joe Gordon. I think this boy is making the greatest second base plays we have seen in the history of the Yankees—the greatest in the major leagues today."[59]

First baseman Lou Gehrig talked with sportswriters several times about his young teammate, Joe Gordon. Two photos of Joe, headlined "Lou Gehrig Calls Him the Best Ever," appeared in the *Chicago Daily News* along with the caption, "'He'll be the best second baseman in the big leagues,' says Lou Gehrig when he speaks of Joe 'Flash' Gordon.... Gehrig predicts Gordon will outshine Detroit's great Charlie Gehringer within two years."[60]

Gehrig also was quoted in Gordon's hometown newspaper, *The Oregonian*: "It would be unfair to him [Gordon] to make comparisons this early. But I believe he'll be another Charlie Gehringer. I never have to catch pop flies anymore; he takes 'em all. He's all over that second base patch and works like a charm. And he'll drive that ball as far as anybody. Maybe not as often, but in the pinch, when it counts."[61]

Although Gordon never had a reputation for being combative either on or off the field, there was one instance, during a game on July 30, when he got pushed to his limit. Milton Gross wrote in *Collier's* magazine about a scrap Joe got into with White Sox pinch-hitter Gee Walker in the bottom of the ninth inning: "Walker came into second [base] with legs flying, banged into Gordon making the play at the bag and bowled him over.... Gordon went at Gee and it was hot and heavy before they were separated."[62]

August 1938 was a highly successful yet exhausting month for the Yankees. Besides their regularly scheduled games, they had to make up several that had been postponed because of rain. They traveled six times by train (with no air conditioning) and played 36 games in 26 days, including 10 doubleheaders. During the seven days from August 21–27, they played *six* doubleheaders in a row, with just *one* day off (for travel)! Their 28 wins in August set a one-month American League record that still stands.

Years later, Gordon told author Maury Allen about road trips:

> I roomed with Red Rolfe, and when we got into a town we put our bags in the room and got right back down to the lobby. You had to.... They didn't have any air conditioning in those days, and if you opened the window in July and August ... you got nothing in there but some more hot air. Rolfe and I used to figure the lobby was the coolest place, out of the sun and with a little breeze from the people going in and out. A lot of those places had revolving doors, and that would keep the air moving.[63]

During the "dog days" of August, it wasn't surprising that rookie Joe Gordon's batting average dropped from .289 to .263. Yet he still was drawing rave reviews, including one from Washington Senators manager Bucky Harris: "The Yankees again have landed the prize rookie of the year in our league. In Joe Gordon they have the greatest young second baseman I have seen come up in my 19 years in the circuit.... You cannot overestimate the value of Gordon in the rise of the New York club. Until he got going, they [the Yankees] ran second, didn't they?"[64]

During August, first baseman Lou Gehrig may unknowingly have been experiencing early symptoms of amyotrophic lateral sclerosis (ALS),[65] the disease that eventually took his life. Yet that month, Lou's batting average actually climbed—from .278 to .293.

From August 23 through September 5, the Yankees were scheduled to play 20 games at home, including six doubleheaders. Looking forward to the club's long homestay, Joe's mother, Louise Gordon, rode the train from Portland to New York City to visit Joe and Dottie. During her two-week stay, the Yankees' record was an outstanding 14–6 (.700).

Chapter 7. A Rookie Year to Remember (1938)   47

In the nightcap of the doubleheader on August 27, Louise and Dottie were privileged to see Yankees pitcher Monte "Hoot" Pearson hurl Yankee Stadium's first no-hitter, over the Cleveland Indians, 13–0.[66] Joe Gordon and Tommy Henrich belted two home runs each in the game, with Gordon driving in six runs and Henrich four.

On September 4, with his mother and wife watching from the stands, the Flash hit his 20th and 21st round-trippers, in addition to two doubles. This was Joe's third time hitting two homers in a game that year. Two records were set that day. First, when Joe hit his 21st home run, he would forever be memorialized in the record books as the first American League second baseman to hit 20 home runs in a season. (He had hit one home run as a pinch-hitter back on June 8.) Going 4-for-4 was a great day, not to mention his seven assists and no errors. Writer Rud Rennie's account in the *New York Herald Tribune* resonated with, "Gordon, the league's prize rookie, really had a day for himself."[67] The Flash would total 25 home runs in 1938.

The race to the single-season home run record for American League second basemen was close—very close. Charlie Gehringer was hot on Gordon's heels late in 1938. Gehringer hit his 20th (a career high) home run on September 27, just 23 days after Joe Gordon's 20th home run.

Yet this was not the only record set that day. Gordon's 21st home run on September 4 also brought the New York Yankees a record of five teammates each hitting *more than* 20 home runs in the same season: Joe DiMaggio, Lou Gehrig, Bill Dickey, Tommy Henrich, and Joe Gordon.[68] And the season was not yet over! DiMaggio, Gehrig, Dickey, and Gordon each added several more round-trippers that year. The Yankees' record would stand for 27 years until topped by six players on the National League Milwaukee Braves in 1965.

On September 9 in Washington, Lou Gehrig played in his 2,100th consecutive game, an unbroken string that had begun back in June 1925.[69] He celebrated the occasion by going 4-for-4, as Yankees pitcher Bump Hadley hurled a one-hour and 38-minute,

(From left) Lou Gehrig, Joe Gordon, Tommy Henrich, Joe DiMaggio, and Bill Dickey take aim with their bats from the dugout steps while on the road. We believe that this photograph was taken at Chicago about September 20–22, 1938, commemorating Joe Gordon hitting his 21st home run on September 4, to bring the New York Yankees a new record of five players each hitting *more than* 20 home runs in the same season (Jeff Kelch/The Digital Archive Group).

2–0 shutout. After the game, Gehrig had high praise for his teammate Joe Gordon: "Gordon is the best defensive second baseman in our league, and he has been for months. Better than Charley Gehringer? Yes, I'd say so…. Gordon is a marvel in the field…. He is an exceptionally good fielder now, but he is going to get better with more experience. He is on the way to developing into one of the greatest defensive second basemen the American [L]eague ever had."[70]

Others raved about the Yankees' young second baseman, too: "Gordon is a big league ball player now—and good as he is, he is getting better constantly…. The last time the Red Sox were at the [Yankee] Stadium, Joe Cronin [manager of the Boston Red Sox and future Hall of Famer] said, 'Gordon is the best second baseman I ever saw. I don't mean that he is going to be. I mean he is.'"[71]

Yet in baseball, like other sports, almost nothing lasts forever. The Bombers won only three of their 10 western road trip games in mid–September and suffered a six-game losing streak from September 17–21. On September 21, it was reported that Gordon's two errors, plus one by shortstop Crosetti, "handed the [White] Sox five unearned runs on a platter and ruined an otherwise well-pitched ball game for Lefty Gomez."[72] Gordon's second error occurred when his double play throw hit a Chicago baserunner in the head, causing the ball to ricochet into the stands.

The Yankees clinched the American League pennant at St. Louis on September 18, under what one sportswriter called "embarrassing circumstances," when the next-to-last-place St. Louis Browns took both games of the doubleheader.[73] Even so, Joe McCarthy threw a celebration party to end all parties that evening. Rud Rennie wrote that "McCarthy was hoisted onto the top of the piano and serenaded with 'For He's a Jolly Good Fellow.'"[74] Sid Mercer later wrote, "Gordon was thrilled about his first big league season. He danced, he vaulted over tables, he jitterbugged with marvelous rhythm and he was just about the happiest yearling the Yanks ever raised."[75] But the Yankees may have celebrated a little too much, as the next day they lost their third game in a row to the seventh-place Browns.

A week before the World Series was scheduled to begin, *Associated Press* writer Dillon Graham pointed out that "certainly, if Gordon had failed, the Yanks would not be the American [L]eague entry [in the World Series]…. His speed has enabled Lou Gehrig to stick closer to first base and has pepped up Frank Crosetti at shortstop. Crosetti and Gordon are working like twins on double killings."[76]

The Yankees wrapped up their 1938 season at Boston on October 2, finishing 9½ games ahead of the second-place Red Sox. Their record of 99–53 (.651, with five ties) was just one win short of manager McCarthy's goal of 100. They turned 177 double plays that year—particularly pleasing to their manager, especially since they'd recorded only 134 the year before.

Joe Gordon completed his rookie season batting .255, although as author Donald Honig wrote, "it was a lethal .255."[77] The Flash hit 25 home runs and drove in 97 runs, quite commendable in that he almost always batted eighth in the order. His 24 home runs while playing as a first-year second baseman set a record that would stand for 68 years—even more remarkable in that he'd played in only 127 of the Yankees' 157 games. Gordon's home runs and RBI ranked fourth for his team—right on the heels of such star-studded teammates as Joe DiMaggio (32 and 140), Lou Gehrig (29 and 114), and Bill Dickey (27 and 115). One can only wonder what he might have done while playing a full season. Had a Rookie of the Year Award been in existence in 1938, unquestionably,

Chapter 7. A Rookie Year to Remember (1938)

Gordon would have been in the running. (The first Major League Rookie of the Year Award would be presented in 1947 to Brooklyn Dodgers infielder Jackie Robinson, the first African American player in National and American League history.)

The "[S]eries-wise" and "battle hardened" Bronx Bombers rode the *New York "Yankees" Special* train to Chicago to play the first two games of the 1938 World Series against the Chicago Cubs.[78] Joe Gordon, Spud Chandler, and Tommy Henrich were the only Yankees regulars who had never played in a World Series.[79] Most of the Yankees already were veterans of multiple Fall Classics: Gehrig (6), Ruffing (3), Crosetti (3), Dickey (3), and Gomez (3); DiMaggio, Rolfe, Selkirk, Pearson, Murphy, Powell, Hoag, and Hadley were veterans of two; and pitcher Ivy Andrews of one.[80]

Joe Gordon was thrilled about his first World Series. He told staff writer David W. Hazen of *The Oregonian*, "You can't beat it, getting to play in a [W]orld [S]eries my first season in major league ball."[81]

For the second time that year, Joe's mother took leave from her stenographer's job, this time riding the *Union Pacific Streamliner* from Portland to Chicago, where the World Series would begin. Joe's wife, Dottie, wearing a fur coat to ward off the unseasonably cold weather, met her mother-in-law at the Chicago train station.

Tickets for the Series were hard to come by. An estimated 12,000 eager fans waited in line, some of them all night, to buy one of the 8,000 bleacher tickets available for Game One. Just before the game began, 22 stowaways were discovered hiding inside Wrigley Field.[82] Three were found, unshaven and hungry, after three days of hiding out; four others were discovered concealed in the huge roller used to store the stadium's canvas infield cover.

This was the Yankees' tenth World Series since Colonel Jacob Ruppert purchased the club back in 1915. But this year the Colonel would not get to watch his team play. Suffering from phlebitis, he'd been restricted to home by his doctor. Fortunately, the games were broadcast across much of the nation by radio.[83] The *Portland News-Telegram* published a photo of Joe Gordon's Jefferson High School principal, Hopkin Jenkins, and baseball coach Lindsey C. Campbell listening to a radio broadcast of their former student in his first World Series.[84]

Game One was played on an exceptionally chilly October 5 day, with gale-like winds sweeping across Wrigley Field.[85] Lou Gehrig was quoted saying, "You'd have to have a propeller on the ball to get it into the stands against this wind."[86]

In Joe Gordon's first time at bat, with runners on first and third and the Yankees leading, 1–0, the Flash smashed a hard single past Cubs third baseman Stan Hack in the second inning. This scored Bill Dickey and turned out to be the game-winning run for Yankees pitcher Red Ruffing's 3–1 triumph. Writing for the *Chicago American*, Jim Gallagher praised the defense work of the Yankees' keystoners: "Crosetti and Flash Gordon were true rally-busters around that second sack…. Gordon's backhand stop to get [Ripper] Collins in the fifth [inning] was amazing."[87]

In the second inning of Game Two the following day, with two men on base and two outs, Gordon hit an easy roller to the left of Cubs pitcher Dizzy Dean. But third baseman Stan Hack and shortstop Billy Jurges collided going after the ball. As the two lay on the ground, the ball trickled slowly into short left field, giving Gordon a double and scoring DiMaggio and Gehrig to put the Yankees ahead, 2–1.[88] Homers by Crosetti in the eighth inning and DiMaggio in the ninth gave Yankees southpaw Lefty Gomez his 6–3 victory, his record *sixth* World Series win going back to 1932.

The nine New York Yankees starters line up for a photograph before Game One of the 1938 World Series at Chicago's Wrigley Field on October 5: (from left) Frank Crosetti, Red Rolfe, Tommy Henrich, Joe DiMaggio, Bill Dickey, Lou Gehrig, George Selkirk, Joe Gordon, and Red Ruffing (Jeff Kelch/The Digital Archive Group).

The two teams traveled on separate trains to continue the World Series at Yankee Stadium. On October 8, two and a half hours before Game Three was scheduled to begin, tickets for bleacher and unreserved grandstand seats went on sale for $1.10 and $3.30, respectively.[89] Writer Rud Rennie previewed the upcoming game in the *New York Herald Tribune*: "It is an old axiom that a great club must be strong through the middle. So where is there anything stronger than Dickey, Crosetti, Gordon and DiMaggio? Crosetti and Gordon were the talk of their league as a second-base combination. In this [S]eries[,] oldtimers in the stands are saying they never saw anything like them."[90] In the top of the fourth inning, Gordon made a sensational leaping catch of Billy Jurges' line drive, what one writer called "probably the finest fielding play of the [S]eries to date."[91] But in the top of the fifth, he fumbled Phil Cavarretta's "bounder," with the ball bouncing off his shins for an error and setting the stage for an unearned run for the Cubs.

On the next play in the same inning, Gordon's throw to first base for the double play hit umpire Charley Moran square in the face from about four feet away.[92] Blood gushed from the umpire's nose and mouth, and play was halted for several minutes while Yankees trainer Doc Painter patched up Moran. Signaling that he was all right, Moran shook hands with Gordon and continued umpiring. The Flash was "considerably upset," saying afterward, "I didn't stop to look before wheeling and throwing—I hadn't time. Then I heard the crack as the ball hit Moran in the face and saw blood dripping from his mouth where he had been cut…. I'm awfully sorry it happened, but Moran sure can take it. He never even went down."[93]

In the bottom of the fifth inning, with two out and two strikes, Joe Gordon belted a "soaring" home run deep into the lower left field box seats, "atoning" for his previous error and tying the score at 1–1. The Flash's round-tripper also put a screeching halt

Chapter 7. A Rookie Year to Remember (1938)

to Cubs pitcher Clay Bryant's 4⅔-inning no-hitter. Garry Schumacher wrote, "Bryant's confidence deserted him right there, and he faded fast thereafter."[94]

With the Yankees leading, 2–1, in the bottom of the sixth inning, Gordon smashed a bases-loaded single into left-center to score DiMaggio and Gehrig, which eventually clinched the game.

In the top of the ninth, Cubs second baseman Tony Lazzeri, former fan favorite of the New York Yankees, received "the loudest cheer of the day" when he came to the plate to pinch-hit. Lazzeri grounded out, Gordon to Gehrig. One more out, and pitcher Monte Pearson had Game Three, 5–2. David Hazen wrote in *The Oregonian*, "When shadows fell on Yankee field Saturday, Joe Gordon, the Cub killer, was the hero. Joe batted in enough runs to win the game."[95] Monte Pearson and Joe Gordon were heralded the "co-stars" of Game Three.

After umpiring the game, Charley Moran went to the hospital and received three stitches. He was quoted in the *New York Times*, saying, "It was just one of those things. I had to be on top of that play at second [base] and was there. Gordon hadn't time to look before throwing, and I hadn't time to skip out of the line of fire."[96] Tough guy that he was, Moran umpired the following day's game, too.

Almost 60,000 fans turned out for Game Four, the majority of them there to cheer the Yankees on to their fourth straight victory against the Cubs, 8–3, and set a record of winning three world championships in a row (1936, 1937, and 1938). Frank Crosetti, Joe Gordon, Bill Dickey, Monte Pearson, and Red Ruffing were named "standouts" of the 1938 Fall Classic. Frederick G. Lieb reported in *The Sporting News*, "Joe Gordon was a constant source of annoyance to the Cubs, whether in the field or at bat. In the eighth position in the batting order, he was as dangerous as a clean-up hitter."[97]

Bill Dickey and Joe Gordon led the Yankees, both batting .400 for the four-game Series. Gordon and Frank Crosetti shared top RBI honors with six apiece. Lou Gehrig and Joe Gordon were the only two Yankees to hit safely in all four games.

After the final game, Cubs first baseman Ripper Collins quipped this well-remembered one-liner from the losers' clubhouse: "We came, we saw and now we are going home."[98] Writer Harry Ferguson summed up the 1938 World Series with, "A good ball club was beaten by a great one, and the scores tell the story."[99]

After the Series, Harry Grayson wrote an article in the *Seattle Star*, headlined "Joe Gordon Stands Out as Sensational AL [American League] Rookie of 1938." The article said, "Gordon contributed more to the success of Col. Jacob Ruppert's club this season than any other member of the party…. The all-powerful Yankees would not have won their third consecutive world championship had not Gordon stood up 100 per cent [sic] in the most important position in the lineup."[100]

Shortly after the World Series, *The Sporting News* announced their "All-Freshman Team" of first-year major leaguers of 1938. Joe Gordon was selected as the outstanding freshman second baseman, and his teammate, Spud Chandler, as one of two outstanding right-handed pitchers. Dick Farrington wrote, "At second base, Gordon of the Yankees, who carried his starry freshman year right through the World's [sic] Series, had little or no competition…. [N]one came near Joe's 25 homers, 84 runs scored [actually 83] and 97 driven in."[101]

Later that year, Yankees catcher Bill Dickey talked with legendary sportswriter Grantland Rice about teammate Joe Gordon: "I got another laugh when they talked about one or two great plays Joe made in the last [W]orld [S]eries. I've seen him make 30 or more plays through the season that were far more brilliant than anything he showed against the Cubs. I'm telling you[,] this Gordon is a great ball player. Not a good one—a great one…. He hasn't even started yet."[102]

In his freshman year in the majors and playing in just 127 games, second baseman Joe Gordon placed 12th in the voting for the 1938 American League Most Valuable Player (MVP) Award. First baseman Jimmie Foxx of the Boston Red Sox won his third MVP Award that year, batting .349 with 50 home runs and 175 RBI.

From the World Series emblems awarded to each Yankee for winning the world championship, Joe Gordon selected the 1938 men's ring. Of the Flash's five world championships during his 11-year playing career, this was the only time that he selected the men's ring.

Each player's share of the winner's pool was a reported $5,729.[103] With part of his winnings, Joe and Dottie purchased a new Buick Special in Detroit and headed for California to visit her parents. On the way, they drove through Oatman, Arizona, so Joe could show Dottie where he and his family had lived when he was a young boy.

Dottie picked up her belongings and her cocker spaniel, Rusty, from her parents, and the young newlyweds headed for home in Eugene, Oregon. Joe planned on enrolling in the winter term at the University of Oregon to complete his degree in Physical Education, yet first he had several hunting trips before classes began in January.

Later that winter, Joe and Dottie purchased a small acreage in the Braes Addition of southwest Eugene. The property was nestled in a beautiful rural setting in the

Joe "Flash" Gordon's 1938 New York Yankees world champions ring is engraved inside, "Presented by Baseball Commissioner to Joseph Gordon" (Gordon family collections).

Chapter 7. A Rookie Year to Remember (1938)

foothills, with many mature fir trees and few, widely scattered neighbors. It came with a small, fenced pasture and a gentle sorrel gelding named Gold. Joe and Dottie planned on building their first home there the following fall.

Nineteen-thirty-eight was an amazing year. Joe "Flash" Gordon's storybook rookie season won over Yankees management, his teammates, and baseball fans and media alike. And the Flash was just getting started!

Chapter 8

"Greatest Team of All Time" (1939)

In a poll that winter of sports editors throughout the nation, who had considered athletes from all sports including baseball, Joe Gordon was forecast as "The star that will blaze brightest across the world of sports in 1939."[1]

However, in sports as in life, along with the high points, sometimes adversity follows. The New York Yankees' 71-year-old owner, Colonel Jacob Ruppert, passed away at home on January 13, 1939. He was eminently respected throughout the baseball world by club owners, team managers, and players alike. Upon hearing of Ruppert's passing, manager Joe McCarthy spoke of his boss, "Col. Ruppert was a real gentleman. He was loved by all the players. He was a real asset to the baseball world and a man who cannot possibly be replaced."[2]

The Colonel had bequeathed ownership of the New York Yankees, in trust, to two of his nieces and a longtime friend, Helen Weyant.[3] At a meeting of the club's Board of Directors four days after Ruppert's death, Yankees general manager Ed Barrow was elected president of the club,[4] and he served with distinction in that capacity for the next six seasons (through 1944).

Fulfilling the promise that he had made to his mother in the spring of 1935, Joe Gordon completed work for his Bachelor of Science Degree in Physical Education at the University of Oregon in February 1939. Because graduation ceremonies were held only in June, his diploma, dated June 4, 1939, would be mailed to him.

Departing for spring training with his 1939 Yankees contract unsigned, Gordon insisted that he was not holding out for more money: "I'm no holdout; I'm just going down and talk it over with the boss."[5] This would be Joe's *modus operandi* for most of his career—preferring to talk with his bosses in person, rather than by phone. John Drebinger wrote in the *New York Times*, "[I]t is generally felt that among those to receive a substantial boost [in salary for 1939] is the youthful Joe Gordon, who as a rookie product of the Newark farm [club] concluded the year [1938] as one of the most brilliant second basemen in the game."[6]

Being a major league ballplayer domiciled in Oregon entailed extensive cross-country travel for the Gordon family. Each year that Joe played for the Yankees (except 1943), the family embarked on an 8,000-mile, circuitous journey by car, from their home in Oregon, to Florida for spring training, to New York for the baseball season, and then back home to Oregon in the fall.

Arriving at St. Petersburg in early March, Joe immediately headed out to the ballpark, even though not scheduled to report for several days.[7] The following day, he accepted the terms of his 1939 contract for $10,000 per season, an outstanding $3,500 raise over his rookie-year salary.

Chapter 8. "Greatest Team of All Time" (1939)

While at spring training, Yankees first baseman Lou Gehrig again praised his young teammate, Joe Gordon: "I want to see that kid in two years. He can't miss developing into the head man at his job. I think we have the highest mentally-geared infield in the history of baseball, and I am not talking about the first sacker."[8]

The Yankees again appeared to be well on track to repeat their previous years' success.[9] Following their third consecutive world championship in 1938, the cry "Break Up the Yankees" was heard coming from the media, other ballclubs, and the fans themselves—so much so, as to be called a "movement" by some.[10] When questioned by *Oregon Journal* reporter Richard H. Syring, Gordon responded, "Why! I don't see why they would want to break us up. Every club has the same chances to get ball players."[11]

The National Baseball Centennial Commission designated 1939 as the "Centennial Year of Baseball," and all major and minor league players would wear the Baseball Centennial Patch on their uniforms that year.[12] After being rained out for two days, the Yankees opened their season at home on April 20, which also was Boston Red Sox rookie Ted Williams's first game. In his book, *My Turn at Bat: The Story of My Life,* Williams told about opening the season at Yankee Stadium: "I hit one to right center just a foot from going into the bleachers. I'd gotten under it a little bit or it would have gone out. When I got to second base, there was [Joe] Gordon. We had played against each other on the coast [in the Pacific Coast League] in 1937 [actually 1936], and he came over, smiling. 'You nervous [Joe asked]?' I [Williams] said, 'Boy, am I. Nervous as hell.'"[13] Red Ruffing shut out the Red Sox, 2–0, the first time since back in 1933 that the Yankees won their season opener.

May 2, 1939, with the club on the road in Detroit, would be a very sad day for the New York Yankees and for all of baseball. Due to 35-year-old Lou Gehrig's undiagnosed health problems, he requested that manager Joe McCarthy bench him, thus ending "The Iron Horse's" remarkable record of playing in 2,130 consecutive games dating back to June 1, 1925.[14]

Ellsworth "Babe" Dahlgren took over for Gehrig at first base, hammering a double and home run in the Yankees' 17-hit win over the Tigers, 22–2. Grantland Rice portrayed the 26-year-old Dahlgren as "the forgotten man of the Yankees…. His value lies in his defensive work—and he is giving full value…. They [Gordon and Dahlgren] had clicked together in Newark a couple of years ago [1937] and they are clicking again."[15]

The Yankees forged ahead, posting a record-setting 24–4 (.857) mark for May, including a 12-game winning streak from May 9 through 23. Joe Gordon's bat had come alive, and he was batting .277, with five home runs to his credit. During the 1939 season, manager McCarthy would move Gordon from seventh or eighth in the batting order to sixth or even fifth.

On June 12, 1939, the quaint village of Cooperstown, New York, celebrated the Centennial of Baseball, along with official dedication of the National Baseball Hall of Fame and Museum.[16] While George Selkirk, Arndt Jorgens, and manager Joe McCarthy were away at Cooperstown, the Yankees traveled by overnight train from St. Louis to Kansas City to play an exhibition game against their Kansas City Blues farm club. A near-record exhibition game crowd of 23,864 fans turned out as the Yankees defeated the Blues, 4–1, in Lou Gehrig's last appearance as a player.[17]

After the game, Gehrig flew to Rochester, Minnesota, for a week-long medical assessment at the Mayo Clinic. On June 19, his final day there, on his 36th birthday, Dr.

Harold Habein presented him with a letter explaining the results of his examination, which read, in part, "[I]t was found that he [Gehrig] is suffering from amyotrophic lateral sclerosis [ALS]. This type of illness involves the motor pathways and cells of the central nervous system and, in lay terms, is known as a form of chronic poliomyelitis—infantile paralysis."[18]

Gehrig returned to New York a few days later and revealed the results of his medical exam to Yankees management and his teammates.[19] Yankees president Ed Barrow provided the media with a copy of Dr. Habein's letter. Tragically, "The Iron Horse" would never play baseball again.

The Yankees kept Gehrig on their active roster and payroll, and as captain of their team, a position he'd held since 1935 and would continue to hold until his death. In his 17 years playing for the Yankees, he had accrued an impressive string of records, and he remains one of the most widely revered sports figures of all time.[20]

In a special tribute in December 1939, the members of the Baseball Writers' Association of America (BBWAA) voted unanimously, by acclamation, to "suspend the rules and present [Lou] Gehrig to the Hall of Fame [C]ommittee as the association's nominee without an election."[21] But because of Gehrig's poor health during 1940 and untimely death in 1941, in addition to our nation's entrance into World War II in December 1941, Gehrig would not be formally inducted into the Hall of Fame until July 28, 2013, along with Rogers Hornsby (Hall of Fame Class of 1942) and 10 members of the Class of 1945.[22]

During Major League Baseball Winter Meetings in December 1938, the American League had approved a limited number of night games for 1939, virtually the same thing that the National League had done three years earlier.[23] Yankees president Ed Barrow—not a fan of nighttime baseball himself—later consented to his team playing one night game at each of the American League's lighted stadiums at Philadelphia, Cleveland, and Chicago.[24]

Traveling to Philadelphia for a three-game series at Shibe Park, the Yankees made their night-game debut on June 26, with the Athletics winning, 3–2. Up until then, the Bombers had not lost to the Athletics in eight previous games. Some players remarked that the ball appeared to travel faster at night, especially grounders. Night ball also was said to favor the pitcher. All told, Philadelphia's night game against the Yankees was considered a great success. Louis Effrat reported in the *New York Times*, "Perhaps the most impressive thing of all was the huge turnout at Shibe Park. If the game had been played in the afternoon[,] 3,000 persons would have been considered a fine attendance. But the biggest crowd of the season here, 33,074, was on hand [for the night game] and such figures cannot be brushed aside."[25]

Two days later, the Bronx Bombers retaliated for their previous night-game loss to the Athletics, putting on a record-setting display "that saw home runs booming from Yankee bats every few minutes."[26] Six Yankees "broke the all-time record for the most home runs in one game by clouting eight [homers] off three Philadelphia Athletic pitchers in the first game" of the doubleheader: Dickey, DiMaggio (two), Selkirk, Dahlgren (two), Gordon, and Henrich.[27] The Bombers stomped the Athletics, 23–2. As of this writing, the record of 10 home runs in one game was set by the Toronto Blue Jays on September 14, 1987, while beating the Baltimore Orioles, 18–3.

However, the Yankees were not yet done! In the nightcap, they belted five more round-trippers (Crosetti, Gordon [two], DiMaggio, and Dahlgren) behind Lefty Gomez's three-hit shutout, 10–0. Their record of 13 home runs during a doubleheader still stands. Tommy Henrich wrote in his book, *Five O'Clock Lightning: Ruth, Gehrig, DiMaggio,*

Chapter 8. "Greatest Team of All Time" (1939)

Mantle and the Glory Years of the NY Yankees, "Babe Dahlgren, Joe D. and Joe Gordon each hit three homers, if you can believe that: three players on the same team hitting three home runs each in the same day."[28] By the end of June, Joe Gordon was batting .328, third-highest on his team after Joe DiMaggio's .413 and Bill Dickey's .338.

The Yankees designated July 4, 1939, as "Lou Gehrig Appreciation Day," drawing the largest crowd of the season, a reported 61,808 loyal fans. The Stadium was bedecked with ceremonial flags and bunting, and Gehrig's teammates from the 1927 "Murderers' Row" Yankees were invited to attend.[29] During the between-games ceremony at home plate, New York City Mayor Fiorello LaGuardia, U.S. Postmaster General James A. Farley, Yankees president Ed Barrow, manager Joe McCarthy, and Babe Ruth each spoke briefly. Gehrig's 1939 teammates presented him with a silver trophy engraved with their signatures and a poem written by John Kieran of the *New York Times*.[30] The emotional "Iron Horse," Lou Gehrig, had to be coaxed to speak and delivered his "Luckiest Man" speech, one of the most poignant and memorable addresses of all time. At the end of the 1939 season, the Yankees retired Lou Gehrig's uniform Number 4, the first time in baseball history that a player's number was retired.[31]

In early July, Joe Gordon received a letter from American League president William Harridge, notifying him that he'd been selected as one of the players for the 7th Annual Major League Baseball All-Star Game on July 11. Harridge wrote, in part, "[W]e are assuming that you will be prepared with your home uniform, baseball shoes, gloves, bats and whatever other paraphernalia you will need for participation in the All-Star Game. Please see that your uniform is in perfect condition."[32]

For the first time in the seven-year history of MLB All-Star Games, this year's "Midsummer Classic" was scheduled for Yankee Stadium. At the Winter Meetings in December 1938, the American League had chosen the immortal, 76-year-old manager of the Philadelphia Athletics, Connie "The Tall Tactician" Mack, to pilot their All-Star Team in this, the Centennial of Baseball. Later, however, due to a stomach ailment, Mack asked to be relieved of his duties, and Joe McCarthy, manager of the 1938 title-winning New York Yankees, took his place.[33] Lou Gehrig was designated honorary captain of the American League team, which included six Yankees as starters: Bill Dickey (catcher), Joe DiMaggio (center field), Joe Gordon (second base), Red Rolfe (third base), Red Ruffing (pitcher), and George Selkirk (left field). Rounding out the American League starting team were Hank Greenberg (Detroit Tigers, first base), Joe Cronin (Boston Red Sox, shortstop), and Doc Cramer (Red Sox, right field). Years later, an editorial appeared in *The Sporting News* about the 1939 All-Star Game, saying, "Some critics rapped McCarthy for employing so many of his own players, but they couldn't fault him on results. The American League won, 3–1."[34]

Joe Gordon didn't record any hits in his first All-Star Game, yet it was reported that he didn't need to. Published in several newspapers, *United Press* staff correspondent Henry McLemore wrote, "Gordon *was* [italics added] the [A]ll-[S]tar [G]ame. DiMaggio was great with his home run; Feller was superb with his fireball pitching; Lombardi was deadly with his hitting. But it was Joe Gordon who stole the show, and it was Joe Gordon who spelled the difference between victory and defeat for the American [L]eaguers."[35]

After the game, Boston Red Sox manager Joe Cronin said about Gordon's defensive play: "There never was a second baseman like him. Eddie Collins was great and so was Nap Lajoie and so is Charlie Gehringer. But they never saw the day they could make plays around second [base] such as Gordon makes."[36]

In late July, Teachers College, Columbia University, in upper Manhattan held its 3rd Annual Summer Baseball School for teachers and coaches from across the nation, presided over by former major league outfielder Ethan Allen.[37] Fourteen classes were offered, nine of which were jointly taught by Allen and other major leaguers, including five Yankees: Lefty Gomez, Joe Gordon, George Selkirk, Red Rolfe, and Monte Pearson. Reportedly, Joe Gordon was the first "guest professor" requested by the attendees. Looking back, it seems amazing that a 24-year-old, with just 215 regular-season games under his belt, was chosen for this honor, let alone considered a "professor" at how second base should be played.

Also during that busy summer of 1939, Joe Gordon and Frank Crosetti joined forces to film an infield tutorial in which they were heralded as "outstanding guardians of the keystone sack, the crack double play combination of the World Championship New York Yankees, speaking in their own voices and in slow motion fundamentals of play cover important points at shortstop and second base." Their tutorial would become part of a movie titled *Touching All Bases,* promoted as "The Official American League Motion Picture of 1940."[38]

Sometime in the spring or summer of 1939, Joe Gordon found time to write a six-page tutorial pamphlet, titled *How to Play Second Base*, which was first published in August 1939. Copies were included with Joe Gordon Personal Model 4205 baseball gloves sold by Montgomery Ward.[39]

Yankees second baseman Joe Gordon demonstrates his batting techniques to a class of teachers and coaches at the 3rd Annual Summer Baseball School at Teachers College, Columbia University, in Manhattan, New York, on July 26, 1939 (Society for American Baseball Research).

Chapter 8. "Greatest Team of All Time" (1939)

On their final western road trip of the 1939 season, the Yankees stopped off at Cooperstown, New York, to play an exhibition game on August 21 at Doubleday Field, against their Newark Bears farm club. Drawing an overflow crowd of 10,000 fans, the junior club slipped by the Yankees, 5–4, in 11 innings.[40] While at Cooperstown, the players also visited the National Baseball Hall of Fame and Museum, where, unbeknownst to them at the time, six of the 1939 teammates would eventually be enshrined: Lou Gehrig (Class of 1939), Bill Dickey (1954), Joe DiMaggio (1955), Red Ruffing (1967), Lefty Gomez (1972), and Joe Gordon (2009).

On August 22, the Yankees played a night game at Chicago before a crowd of some 50,000 fans under Comiskey Park's brand-new stadium lights. The luminosities didn't seem to bother the Bronx Bombers this time. Crosetti, Dahlgren, Gordon, Rolfe, and DiMaggio all belted home runs as the Yankees stomped the White Sox, 14–5. The following day, the Bombers took both games of the doubleheader, giving them *three* victories within just 21 hours and 50 minutes, thought to be an American League record.[41] In the nightcap, Joe DiMaggio homered and Joe Gordon hit a grand slam in the Yankees' 16–4 victory.

The Flash continued batting close to .300 throughout August, prompting *The Sporting News* to report:

> Joe Gordon's improvement in hitting this season hasn't just happened.... He did everything possible in the way of study to improve his hitting.... [H]e studied all of the other outstanding hitters in the league, Foxx, Greenberg, his own teammate, DiMaggio, young Williams and others. He questioned Gehrig about all he had learned about hitting, and then proceeded to make a study of the various pitchers, both when they pitched to him and to other

ALL-STAR SECOND BASEMAN, OF WORLD'S CHAMPION NEW YORK YANKEES

Joe Gordon wrote this six-page tutorial pamphlet, titled *How to Play Second Base*, which was published in August 1939 and included with Joe Gordon Personal Model 4205 baseball gloves sold by Montgomery Ward (Gordon family collections).

Yankees. The result is he has tacked on 40 points to his average this year, when most of the other hitters are off from their 1938 figures.[42]

In the meantime, hostilities on the world scene were escalating throughout Europe. Early in the morning of September 1, 1939, Germany invaded Poland, bombing multiple cities and annexing Danzig.[43] This marked the beginning of the devastating, global

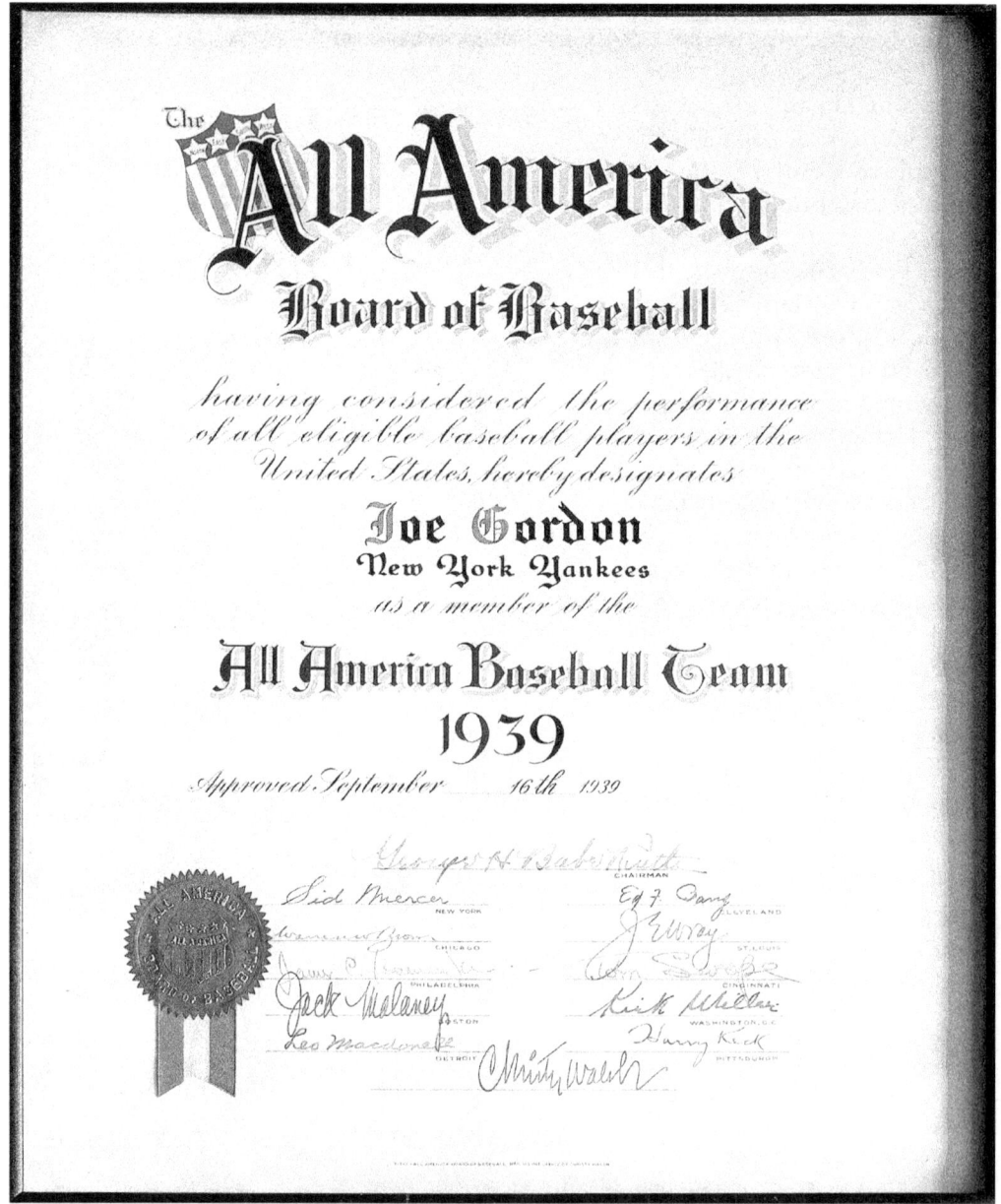

On September 16, 1939, Joe Gordon is designated an honorary member of the All America Baseball Team of 1939 and presented with this framed plaque signed by Babe Ruth, Christy Walsh, and one sportswriter from each of the 10 cities hosting major league clubs (Gordon family collections).

Chapter 8. "Greatest Team of All Time" (1939)

World War II. Although not fully realized at the time, the war would fundamentally affect major and minor league baseball, as more and more players joined American and Allied Armed Forces to fight multiple adversaries around the world.

In mid–September 1939, the All America Board of Baseball designated the following 10 major leaguers as honorary members of the All America Baseball Team of 1939: Joe Cronin, Bill Dickey, Joe DiMaggio, Jimmy [sic] Foxx, Joe Gordon, Joe Medwick, Red Rolfe, Red Ruffing, Bucky Walters, and Ted Williams.[44] An All America Baseball Team had been selected each year since 1922 by a committee comprising Chairman Babe Ruth, writer/sports agent Christy Walsh, and one sportswriter from each of the 10 American cities or boroughs hosting one or more major league clubs.

During a game on September 15, Joe Gordon tied the major league record for second basemen with his 11 assists in one game.[45] The following day, September 16, the Yankees clinched their record fourth consecutive American League pennant—two days earlier than their previous year's pennant.[46]

The Bronx Bombers wrapped up the 1939 season on September 30 with a 106–45–1 (.702) record, 17 games ahead of the second-place Boston Red Sox. Four Yankees finished with more than 20 home runs: Joe DiMaggio (30), Joe Gordon (28), Bill Dickey (24), and George Selkirk (21). Because of a torn leg muscle in late April, DiMaggio played in only 120 games, but still won the first of his three AL Most Valuable Player (MVP) Awards (1939, 1941, and 1947).

In just his second year of major league ball, Joe Gordon placed ninth in the voting for the MVP of the American League Award of 1939. He ended his outstanding season with a .284 batting average, 28 home runs, and 111 RBI (second to DiMaggio's 126).

The Yankees' run differential (runs scored minus runs allowed) of +411 that year was the best in American and National League history.[47] Including pitchers, eight Yankees batted better than .300: Spud Chandler (.400), Joe DiMaggio (.381), Charlie Keller (.334), Red Rolfe (.329), Monte Pearson (.321), Red Ruffing (.307), George Selkirk (.306), and Bill Dickey (.302).

Defensively, the Yankees finished atop their league with a fielding percentage of .978 and second with 159 double plays, and committed the fewest errors (126) of any team *by far*. In *The Sporting News*, Dan Daniel portrayed the 1939 Yankees as having "the greatest infield it has been your correspondent's privilege to watch."[48] Joe Gordon led American League second basemen in defensive games played (151), chances (859), putouts (370), assists (461), and double plays (116).

Their pitching was outstanding, with a .702 winning percentage and 3.31 ERA. Thirty-four-year-old Red Ruffing led Yankees hurlers with his 21–7 record in this, his fourth consecutive season of 20 or more wins and 22 or more complete games. *Six* more Yankees pitchers posted double-digit wins: Atley Donald (13–3), Monte Pearson (12–5), Bump Hadley (12–6 and 2.98 ERA), Lefty Gomez (12–8), Steve Sundra (11–1 and 2.76), and Oral Hildebrand (10–4). The Bombers were shut out only *once* the entire 1939 season, yet they dealt out 15 shutouts to their opponents. Relief pitcher Johnny Murphy topped both leagues with 19 saves. In general, the concept of recording a pitcher's "saves" or games saved was not official until first adopted for the 1969 major league season. Baseball researchers, however, have gone back, retroactively, through game records before 1969 and amended pitchers' statistics to include their saves.

Tragically, on October 3, just one day before the start of the 1939 World Series, Joe Gordon's beloved father-in-law, Frank Crum, passed away in Los Angeles. He had been in poor health for several years, due to a train accident. Joe Gordon missed his team's batting and fielding practice that day, in addition to the Yankees' team photoshoot, as he rushed to the airport to meet his mother-in-law, who was arriving from Los Angeles, unaware that her husband had died while she was en route.[49] Dottie and her mother left immediately for California. The Yankees had their official team photo retaken later, with Joe Gordon in it, although earlier photos, with Gordon missing, still are floating around on the Internet. Joe's mother and several of the Gordons' friends traveled from Oregon to watch Joe play in his second World Series.[50]

This was the Cincinnati Reds' first Fall Classic since 1919. Yankees pitcher Red Ruffing held the Reds to just four hits and retired the last 14 batters in a row for the Yankees' 2–1 victory in Game One. In the clubhouse after the game, Yankees third base coach Art Fletcher was called the "unsung hero of the game." Fletcher told about Joe Gordon's mad dash home from first base on Babe Dahlgren's double in the fifth inning to score the tying run: "I waited till I saw where Berger [Cincinnati's left fielder] would throw. When he tossed to second [base] I knew there wouldn't be a cutoff because Myers [Cincinnati's shortstop] wasn't in position. Then, knowing that Gordon is one of the best baserunners in the game, I waved him home. Boy, that Gordon is fast!"[51]

In Game Two on October 5, Monte Pearson staged "one of the finest pitching exhibitions in [World] [S]eries history," giving up only two singles and shutting out the Reds, 4–0.[52] For seven and one-third innings, he was pitching his way to the first no-hit game ever hurled in a Fall Classic. Breaking the spell, the Reds singled once in the eighth and again in the ninth, but couldn't put together any runs.

Game Three on October 7, at Cincinnati's Crosley Field, saw the Reds outhit the Yankees, 10-to-5, yet the Bombers came through with the runs for the 7–3 victory. Yankees rookie outfielder Charlie Keller belted two home runs and drove in four runs, in addition to home runs by Joe DiMaggio and Bill Dickey.

In Game Four, Cincinnati outhit the Yankees once again but couldn't outscore them. The Bombers took the game in 10 innings, 7–4. Winning the World Series a record fourth time in a row, the Yankees let loose with what was reported as "the noisiest clubhouse victory celebration they have ever have [sic] staged."[53] Each player's share of the winner's pool was reported as $5,542.[54] As his emblem for the Yankees winning the 1939 world championship, Joe Gordon selected the pocket watch on a long chain with an attached pocketknife.

After the 1939 World Series, there was, and continues to be, considerable debate regarding which team was the greatest in the history of Major League Baseball, the 1927 or the 1939 New York Yankees. Veteran New York sportswriter Dan Daniel compared the two teams for his "Over the Fence" column in *The Sporting News*, ultimately selecting the 1939 Yankees as the better team. Daniel wrote that the 1939 team had the better infield in terms of defense, speed, conditioning, and balance. Despite giving the nod to 1927 players like Babe Ruth and Lou Gehrig over their 1939 counterparts, he said the younger team did something the 1927 Murderers' Row squad couldn't do, which was win four consecutive world championships! Daniel wrapped up his comparison with, "You know, a great ball club must win two straight pennants. It takes a super-team to win three, a miracle club to take four."[55]

The Sporting News also published an article by Frederick G. Lieb, headlined "Precedent-Smashing Yanks Hailed as Team of Century," part of which reads, "One can write of these powerful, amazing [1939] Yankees only in superlatives…. [T]hey have come closer to perfection than any other club in the first 100 years of baseball.... Like other clubs before them, the [Cincinnati] Reds went down before a club which many believe to be the greatest in all baseball history."[56]

Joe Gordon drove home to Oregon with his friends Joe and Mary Brown, who had come east to watch the World Series and take in the World's Fair.[57] Dottie Gordon was still in Los Angeles, helping her widowed mother. Once Joe and Dottie were both back in Eugene, they contracted to have a home built on their property in The Braes. It was a comfortable, two-bedroom, one-bath Colonial, paneled in knotty pine with a large brick fireplace in the living room.

In mid–November, some of Joe Gordon's Oregon friends and fans honored him at a 100-plate dinner at the Multnomah Athletic Club in Portland, Oregon.[58] It was reported that, as great as the Flash was on the ball field, he never did lose track of his roots and those who'd helped him along the way. Harry Leeding, a writer covering the event, praised Gordon's poise and humility in paying tribute to his schoolmates and sandlot teammates, in addition to his early mentors and coaches.[59]

During his first two years in major league baseball, Joe "Flash" Gordon was fortunate to play in and win two World Series championships. Yet championships are somewhat akin to beautiful fall days—enjoy them while you can—because the harsh reality of winter, where sometimes only the strongest survive, may soon follow.

Chapter 9

A Horse Race of a Pennant (1940)

In January 1940, Babe Ruth was quoted in *The Sporting News*, talking about Joe "Flash" Gordon: "That kid can think, he makes plays that no one else thought of trying and, most important, comes through in the clutch at the plate."[1] Ruth was also quoted in another newspaper article, headlined "Babe Ruth Credits Joe Gordon for Yankee Dominance": "Do you know who made this team? Joe Gordon. He came along just at the right time. The club needed a spark and he gave it."[2]

Also in January, *The Sporting News* announced their results of polling 259 Baseball Writers' Association of America members to name the newspaper's prestigious Major League All-Star Team of 1939.[3] *The Sporting News'* team was an end-of-season annual selection of the top player at each position (eight position players and three pitchers) from among all major leaguers. Although the team names are similar, *The Sporting News'* annual Major League All-Star Team was not connected in any way to the annual Major League Baseball All-Star Game, usually played in July.

The Sporting News' 1939 Major League All-Star Team comprised nine players from the American League and two from the National League. This was second baseman Joe Gordon's first year selected, and he was accompanied by three other first-timers: Bucky Walters, Bob Feller, and Ted Williams. Four of Gordon's teammates (Joe DiMaggio, Bill Dickey, Red Ruffing, and Red Rolfe) also were selected for the team.

Joe and Dottie Gordon headed for spring training in mid–February by way of Los Angeles to visit Dottie's recently widowed mother. While in the City of Angels, a reporter asked Gordon how he thought the Yankees would fare in 1940. Joe predicted that the Boston Red Sox would be the team giving them the most trouble: "If any team's going to beat us I'd rather it would be the Red Sox, but confidentially I don't think any club is going to keep the Yankees from winning their fifth straight pennant."[4]

The Gordons arrived at Yankees spring training several days before Joe was scheduled to report. After brief discussions with manager McCarthy, he accepted the terms of his 1940 contract for a salary of $14,000, a $4,000 raise over his 1939 salary.[5]

The Flash was in uniform the following day, thrilling the onlookers. Rud Rennie reported in the *New York Herald Tribune*, "Gordon made the camp followers quit looking at anyone else.... You looked at Gordon, not because he did anything spectacular, but because of the way he moved for the ball and got rid of it—with such ease, sureness and grace. He has a great pair of hands. He has the knack of sliding to get in front of the ball. And he is always down low, like a frog."[6]

With the escalation of World War II in Europe, it was inevitable that professional

Chapter 9. A Horse Race of a Pennant (1940)

Onlookers watch from the sidelines as eight New York Yankees wearing mock military helmets take aim with their bats during 1940 spring training at St. Petersburg. Joe Gordon, Bill Dickey, and George Selkirk are somewhere in this group, but we can't tell who's who (Gordon family collections).

ballplayers had the conflict on their minds. During spring training, Dottie Gordon captured some unique photos of the Yankees wearing mock military helmets and taking aim with their bats during simulated drills at St. Petersburg.

Boston Red Sox slugger Jimmie Foxx was watching the Yankees work out one day, when someone asked him what he thought of the team. Foxx's droll comment was, "If they are any better this year than they were last year [1939] we had all better go on home."[7]

After wrapping up spring training in Florida, the Yankees barnstormed their way to New York. John Drebinger reported in the *New York Times*, "It seems as if the champions ... are more determined than ever to smash another American League pennant race to smithereens."[8] While in Kentucky, the Yankees and their Brooklyn Dodgers traveling companions toured Hillerich & Bradsby Co., manufacturers of Louisville Slugger baseball bats. Gordon was photographed inspecting one of his new "Joe Gordon" model bats as it was crafted by Fritz Bickel.[9]

Arriving in New York City, the Yankees and Dodgers were greeted by rain and snow. The two teams were scheduled to play their traditional three exhibition games at Ebbets Field right before the season opened. But due to the inclement weather, they managed to get in just one game.[10] In the ninth inning, Joe DiMaggio badly wrenched his right knee sliding into second base,[11] causing him to miss the first 15 games of the 1940 season. Several other players were also beset with injuries or medical problems: Joe Gordon (persistent "charley horse" in his left thigh), pitcher Atley Donald (with sciatica), and catcher Bill Dickey (a bruised shinbone).[12] Gordon later revealed that his road trip roomie Red Rolfe's infected tonsils bothered the third baseman's eyes most of the 1940 season.[13]

The Yankees opened the season at Philadelphia on April 16. It was a close game, with the Athletics winning, 2–1, in 10 innings. James P. Dawson wrote, "Even the defeat could not becloud a spectacular day for the spectacular Joe Gordon, back in action after shaking off a charley horse. The Rock [Gordon] handled a dozen [fielding] chances and was all over the place."[14] The Athletics' 77-year-old manager, Connie Mack, then in his 43rd season as a major league manager, marveled at Gordon's defensive work and conceded, "Some of those plays just aren't a part of baseball, as we know it."[15]

Yankee Stadium's home opener fell on a "cold, damp and dark" April 19, drawing a small crowd of a reported 15,299 loyal fans.[16] In the first inning, Joe Gordon belted Yankee Stadium's first home run of 1940, deep into the upper left field balcony, with one man on base.[17] The Yankees beat the Washington Senators, 5–3.

However, by the end of April, the Bombers were in fifth place, with an uncharacteristic record of 4–6. From May 4 through May 11, they lost eight games in a row at home, dropping them to last place with a 6–14 record; by then, Joe Gordon had raised his batting average to .237. It was a long, uphill battle, and on May 28 the Yankees moved into the first division in fourth place.

On Memorial Day, May 30, 1940, Yankee Stadium hosted one of the largest crowds in baseball history, with a reported paid attendance of 82,437 fans packed into the grandstands and bleachers.[18] Dottie Gordon was so awestruck by the crowd that she took a snapshot of it that day, as the Yankees and the league-leading Boston Red Sox split the doubleheader. The Yankees finally arrived at a .500 record on June 1, and by June 3, they'd won 10 of their last 11 games.

The 8th Annual Major League Baseball All-Star Game was scheduled for July 9 at Sportsman's Park in St. Louis. As was the custom, approximately 25 players had been chosen for each team by the eight managers in each respective league. John Drebinger

Dottie Gordon's snapshot taken at Yankee Stadium on Memorial Day, May 30, 1940, shows part of the tremendous crowd of a reported 82,437 fans watching the doubleheader against the league-leading Boston Red Sox (Gordon family collections).

wrote, "Because Joe McCarthy, manager of the four straight pennant-winning Yankees, wearied of the responsibility and asked to be excused, the American League team [would] be directed by Joe Cronin, manager of the [1939 second-place] Red Sox."[19] Seven Yankees were selected for the American League All-Star team: Bill Dickey, Joe DiMaggio, Joe Gordon, Charlie Keller, Monte Pearson, Red Rolfe, and Red Ruffing.

Five National League pitchers held the American League to just three hits and no runs, as the "sweltering crowd of 32,373" baked in the St. Louis sun, while watching the first shutout, 4–0, in the eight-year history of the All-Star Game.[20]

During the All-Star Game break, Dottie Gordon had flown home to Los Angeles to visit her family and friends. The Gordons were expecting their first child in August.

Following the Midsummer Classic, it appeared as though the Yankees were stuck in fourth place. Dan Daniel wrote an article conjecturing how at least 11 of their players were "fighting for their jobs." He also noted that "the relief pitching of the Yankees looks to be in a state of collapse." As Daniel pointed out, in the club's seven extra-inning games through July 6 (the 11-inning game on June 20 was later ruled a "no decision" game), they had lost every one of them.[21]

The Flash's hitting came alive in July. He belted 13 home runs during the month's 29 games, his career-best month for round-trippers *by far*. But injuries, advancing age, and at times exhaustion plagued the Yankees. Joe Gordon and first baseman Babe Dahlgren were the only two team members to play in all 155 games that year. Hot weather was also a factor. During a game in the oppressive heat of St. Louis on July 25, the temperature was estimated to be between 110 and 120 F on the playing field.[22] Gordon, who always maintained that he performed better in the heat, belted two home runs with three RBI in Red Ruffing's 13–8 victory over the Browns.

However, early August brought a downturn to the Bombers, dropping them back to the second division after losing a string of games at Cleveland and Boston. Perhaps partly out of desperation, for a doubleheader at Boston on August 7, manager McCarthy tried switching Joe Gordon to the top of the batting order. This was not unfamiliar territory to the Flash, as he'd batted leadoff the entire season for the 1937 International League Newark Bears. Reportedly, McCarthy told Gordon before the game, "What this club needs is somebody who can hit singles…. You just get on base, Joe, let the other boys move you around."[23]

McCarthy's experiment worked! Gordon's switch to leadoff gave the Yankees the spark they needed. He recorded six hits in seven at-bats that day, in addition to three walks. A week later, a sportswriter noted, "McCarthy's trial has proven successful, for in the nine games since then the Oregon Flash has hit safely in each contest, reached base 29 times in 45 at bats, poled out three homers and batted at a .553 clip."[24] During 1940, Gordon would bat leadoff in 56 games, batting .318, versus games in the fourth, fifth, sixth, or seventh positions, batting just .258. Columnist Sid Mercer mused about the switch: "Marse Joe McCarthy[,] watching his left at the post Yankees making a remarkable back stretch spurt[,] must wonder what the story might have been if Joe Gordon had been elected to head the batting order at the beginning of the season."[25]

In mid–August, the Yankees played the Boston Red Sox in a doubleheader at Yankee Stadium. Joe Gordon went 2-for-5 and belted his 22nd home run of the season in the opener and 2-for-4 with two RBI in the nightcap. The Bombers stomped Boston, 9–1 and 19–8. Their 19 runs in the nightcap were the most they scored in a game all season. Yankees home run hitters included Joe Gordon, Red Rolfe, Joe DiMaggio (two, one a grand slam), and Babe Dahlgren. Red Sox round-trippers were hit by Jim Tabor, Jimmie Foxx, and Ted Williams.

Joe and Dottie Gordon's first child was born at 7:52 P.M. that evening at Manhattan's Flower and Fifth Avenue Hospital. Given the two rain delays in the opening game, the 20-minute break between games, and the abundance of scoring in the nightcap, the games went well more than five hours, and the nightcap was called after the top of the seventh inning in the Yankees' favor because of approaching darkness.[26] Needless to say, new Papa Gordon didn't quite make it to the hospital in time for his baby daughter's arrival.

Dottie didn't have a girl's name picked out, so she chose the name "Judith Anne" out of the New York City phonebook. Dottie's mother, Irene Crum, came from California to help care for Dottie and baby "Judy."

Except for two games at Philadelphia, the Yankees were scheduled to play almost three weeks at home, allowing Joe plenty of time to get acquainted with his new baby daughter. He was a doting father, later entertaining his little girl with his magic tricks and remarkably realistic ventriloquist sidekick named "Amen."

With no warning, on Sunday morning, August 18, with the Yankees in fifth place, 10 games behind the league-leading Cleveland Indians, the *Sunday Daily News* published two highly controversial articles written by their sports editor, Jimmy Powers—himself said to be no stranger to controversy.[27] One article was headlined in large, bold type, "Has 'Polio' Hit the Yankees?" and the other, in smaller type, reading "Slumping Yanks."[28] The articles were accompanied by a distasteful cartoon of a "Yanks" player recoiling on the ground beneath storm clouds and blowing debris.

In trying to determine why the 1940 Yankees were so far behind in league standings compared with previous years, Powers conjectured in his first article, "Has the mysterious 'polio' germ, which felled Lou Gehrig, also struck his former teammates, turning a once-great team into a floundering non-contender?"[29] Gehrig, though, had been diagnosed as suffering not from polio, but from amyotrophic lateral sclerosis (ALS), which was then, and still is, considered non-contagious. However, the letter that Mayo Clinic's Dr. Harold Habein had written in 1939 explaining Gehrig's diagnosis said, in part, that Gehrig's illness "in lay terms, is known as a form of chronic poliomyelitis—infantile paralysis."[30] Powers's publisher and lawyers would later claim that when Powers wrote his articles, he had misinterpreted Dr. Habein's words as the greatly-feared communicable disease "polio."[31]

In his second article, headlined "Slumping Yanks," Powers specifically mentioned 10 Yankees by name: Red Ruffing, Lefty Gomez, Monte Pearson, Johnny Murphy, Bill Dickey, Joe Gordon, Red Rolfe, Steve Sundra, Atley Donald, and Oral Hildebrand. He ended this article with the following questions (in all caps): "CAN COINCIDENCE EXPLAIN THESE SIMULTANEOUS AILMENTS? COULDN'T THE 'POLIO' GERM BE THE COMMON CAUSE?"[32]

Lou Gehrig and his Yankees teammates were outraged by the articles. Gehrig filed a $1 million libel suit against Powers and the owners of the *Daily News*, and later added Tribune Publishing, owners of the *Chicago Tribune*. As Jonathan Eig wrote in his biography, titled *Luckiest Man: The Life and Death of Lou Gehrig*, "The case never went to trial. The newspaper publishers paid Gehrig $17,500 to settle the suit."[33]

The 10 players named by Powers in his article filed a separate $2.5 million civil libel suit,[34] the outcome of which was never made public. Many years later, for his book, *Pride*

Chapter 9. A Horse Race of a Pennant (1940)

of October: What It Was to Be Young and a Yankee, author Bill Madden talked with retired pitcher Marius Russo about the players' lawsuit. Russo told Madden, "We all had to go to the courthouse. The whole team was subpoenaed, although none of us was asked to testify. Needless to say, Powers didn't have much of a case. He was wrong all the way."[35]

Powers's articles hit the newsstands the morning of August 18. Later that day, the Yankees were scheduled to play a doubleheader at Philadelphia. In the nightcap, they would face the Athletics' 27-year-old right-hander Johnny Babich, a relatively unknown pitcher who'd bounced around the minors since 1931 and spent 1934–1936 in the National League before being sent back to the minors. Acquired by the Yankees in late 1938, Babich had pitched for their 1939 Kansas City Blues farm club and posted a very respectable 17–6 record. Yet for some reason, the Yankees didn't bring him up to the majors and allowed him to be drafted by the Philadelphia Athletics that October, apparently something Babich never forgave them for.[36]

Babich already had beaten the Yankees two of the three times he'd faced them in 1940, both complete games, so the fervor leading up to the August 18 nightcap against him must have been intense. In the opener, Joe Gordon went 4-for-5 in the Bombers' 9–1 victory. But in the nightcap, Babich beat the Yankees again, this time 7–3, and went the distance in just one hour and 45 minutes. The only solace was Joe Gordon's 23rd home run of the season.

Back on their own home turf, the Yankees won their next 14 out of 15 games. On August 29, they may have set a record in the first game of the doubleheader against the St. Louis Browns, amassing all 10 runs in the fifth inning, which "saw the bases filled nine times as 16 men went to bat."[37] Each Yankee scored at least once, and Gordon scored twice in their 10–3 victory.

On September 2, the Yankees again lost the nightcap of a doubleheader to Philadelphia's Johnny Babich, this time at Yankee Stadium and this time a shutout, 3–0. It was the Bombers' fourth loss to Babich in five games.

In the meantime, one sportswriter said of the tight 1940 pennant race that "the whole first division in the American [L]eague could be covered by a handkerchief."[38] On September 8, the Yankees were still "in the thick of the fight" and only one game behind the tied-for-first-place Tigers and Indians. Playing at Boston, Joe Gordon hit for the cycle. As the first batter up, he belted his 25th home run of the season. He followed up with a single, triple, and double, all in the first five innings. He topped off his perfect day with two walks. At the time, his hitting for the cycle was just the 10th occasion in Yankees history: Bert Daniels (1912, New York Highlanders), Bob Meusel (1921, 1922, and 1928), Tony Lazzeri (1932), Lou Gehrig (1934 and 1937), Joe DiMaggio (1937), Buddy Rosar (1940), and Joe Gordon (1940). It was later reported that it was the Flash's "berserk behavior with the stick that enabled the Yanks to drub the Boston Red Sox, 9–4" that day.[39] Another writer noted, "[T]he only thing Joe Gordon didn't do was steal first [base]."[40]

September went down to the wire in the Bombers' valiant pursuit of a fifth consecutive American League pennant. Gordon hit his 26th and 27th home runs on September 14, as his team demolished six Detroit pitchers to beat the first-place Tigers, 16–7. He hit his 28th home run a week later at Yankee Stadium. Three days after that, the Yankees won a doubleheader at home against the Senators, bringing them to within 2½ games of league-leading Detroit. In the first game, Gordon went 5-for-6, including three doubles.

In the nightcap, he went 1-for-3, with his 29th home run. Jack Mahon wrote, "The fire of champions—a flame that just will not die—blazed as brightly as even [ever] in the Stadium at dusk yesterday as your Yankees swept desperately onward in quest of their 5th straight AL [American League] pennant, taking a double-header from the Senators to climb on the backs of the second-place Indians."[41]

Ballparks were packed for every game. The battle cry "The Yanks are coming!" resonated on sports pages across the country.[42] With six games left to play—all on the road—they would need to win every game, or they would be eliminated from the pennant race.[43]

Right before the Yankees' final road trip, Grantland Rice talked with Joe Gordon for the writer's "Sportlight" column, titled "Still Shooting." Forever the optimist, Joe told Rice, "We are still shooting, and don't think we have quit. We'll be shooting to the last out.... We knew a week ago we had to win something like twelve straight—and we've already clipped off half this number.... At this stage we can't afford to lose a ball game.... It can be done if we can only get away with this Philadelphia series."[44]

On the morning of September 26, just a few hours before the Yankees were scheduled to begin a do-or-die three-game series at Philadelphia, the *Daily News* published another multi-column article by sports editor Jimmy Powers, this time boldly headlined "Our Apologies to Lou Gehrig and the Yankees."[45] The article was a follow-up to Powers's inflammatory articles of August 18, serving as a lengthy, detailed explanation and apology, perhaps partially a reaction to Lou Gehrig's $1 million libel lawsuit. Yet the timing of Powers's article, and why he waited well more than a month to apologize, still seems somewhat curious.

The Yanks won their September 26 doubleheader against the Athletics, with Gordon belting his 30th and final home run of the season in the opener. This left four must-win games remaining—one more against the last-place Athletics and three against the seventh-place Washington Senators. But the following day, September 27, the Yankees were slated to face their nemesis: "slider-ball specialist" Johnny Babich. Up until then, the Yankees had lost four of their five games against him.

Moreover, back on September 19, *The Sporting News* had published an inconspicuous, one-paragraph article titled "Babich Guns for Champs." It was reported that Johnny Babich had asked Athletics manager Connie Mack to let him pitch against the Yankees on September 27. Evidently, Johnny *still* resented that the Bombers had let him be drafted by the Athletics after his 17-6 season for the Yankees' 1939 Kansas City Blues farm club. Babich was quoted, saying, "I'm not through with the Yankees yet, and nothing would please me more than to beat them at Shibe Park, September 27, and if I can, put them out of the running [for the pennant]."[46]

Ultimately, a fifth consecutive pennant was not in the cards for the 1940 Bronx Bombers. John Drebinger wrote, "The American League's spectacular pennant race came to a dramatic and abrupt end today [September 27] on two fronts when Detroit's fighting Tigers conquered Bob Feller and the Indians, 2-0, an hour or so after the tidings had been flashed in from Philadelphia that the Athletics had brought to a close the four-year reign of the world champion Yankees."[47] Johnny Babich, "their worst tormenter through the campaign," had held the Yankees to just five hits in the Athletics' 6-2 victory.[48]

The Yankees ended their 1940 season in third place with an 88-66 (.571) record, two games behind the pennant-winning Detroit Tigers and one game behind the second-place Cleveland Indians. They placed third in the American League in runs scored, third in RBI, and first in home runs, yet *last* in hits and team batting average. There were no 20-game winners for the Yankees this year. Only two pitchers won in double digits: Red Ruffing (15–12) and Marius Russo (14–8).

However, the 1940 season rivaled, if not surpassed, Joe Gordon's best year thus far. He started all 155 games, batted .281 with 30 home runs and 173 hits, both second on his team on the heels of Joe DiMaggio's 31 and 179. He recorded 103 RBI (also second to DiMaggio's 133), as well as 18 stolen bases (first). Columnist H.G. Salsinger pointed out that, even though Gordon was handicapped by being switched to leadoff batter after midseason, remarkably, he still drove in 103 runs while playing for the weakest-hitting team in the league.[49] Gordon finished in the top 10 in almost all categories of batting in the American League (games, at-bats, runs, total bases, triples, home runs, RBI, and stolen bases). Defensively, he led the American League with 505 assists, while fielding .975.

Interviewed months later by *United Press* correspondent Henry McLemore, Joe Gordon gave some insight as to what he thought had happened to the 1940 Yankees: "We had a terrible spring in Florida … and even if it sounds like an alibi, that is what cost us our fifth straight pennant. Every man on the club had charleyhorses [*sic*] for the first month of the season. We got off bad and never could make it up."[50]

Gordon also talked with sports editor Dick Strite of his hometown *Eugene Register-Guard*. He said he thought his club's downfall could be directly attributed to the cold, rainy weather at spring training, which didn't allow the players to get in condition. He also noted that their late-season relief pitching had handicapped the team.[51]

Joe, Dottie, and seven-week-old baby Judy headed for Oregon by way of Los Angeles to visit Dottie's mother. Once back home in Eugene, Joe spent part of the off-season completing the upstairs of their new home. Then he joined his brother Jack and friend Ford Danner to hunt deer, pheasant, and ducks in central and southern Oregon.

In late December, Joe embarked on an entirely new adventure—flying. He received instruction in a variety of 65- and 75-horsepower, two- and three-seat "taildragger" airplanes (Taylorcraft, Piper Cub, and Piper Cub Cruiser). He was an excellent student, soloing after just eight hours of instruction.[52]

Joe Gordon would spend little, if any, time reliving the 1940 baseball season. Exciting things awaited the Yankees' second baseman in 1941, including a new but highly unusual assignment.

Chapter 10

WORLD SERIES HERO (1941)

During early January 1941, rumors of a Yankees "purge" or "winter housecleaning" were circulating in the media.[1] It was reported that only three Yankees regulars were sure of their jobs: center fielder Joe DiMaggio, second baseman Joe Gordon, and catcher Buddy Rosar. Although rating the Yankees as the team to beat, George Kirksey reported in the *Oregon Journal*, "Fifteen of the 35 players on the Yankee roster are newcomers."[2] Most notable was that the talented keystone combination of second baseman Jerry Priddy and shortstop Phil "Scooter" Rizzuto was scheduled to come on board from the Yankees' Kansas City Blues farm club.[3]

Also in January, *The Sporting News* announced the 11 players selected for the newspaper's prestigious Major League All-Star Team of 1940. This time, Joe Gordon and Joe DiMaggio were the only two Yankees voted onto the team by 308 members of the Baseball Writers' Association of America.[4]

In mid–February, Joe, Dottie, and six-month-old Judy set out by car on their annual 3,400-mile drive to Yankees spring training at St. Petersburg, Florida.[5] As Joe typically did each year, he brought along his Yankees contract unsigned, so he could "talk things over" with Joe McCarthy and Ed Barrow.[6]

The Gordons were still en route when a headline appeared in the *New York Times*, announcing, "Yankees Sell First-Baseman [sic] Dahlgren to Bees in Straight Cash Transaction."[7] The sale of Babe Dahlgren was a surprise to everyone, it seems—everyone but Joe McCarthy and Ed Barrow.[8]

Rud Rennie wrote in the *New York Herald Tribune*, "This automatically makes Johnny Sturm, a rookie from Kansas City, the Yankees first baseman. He is the only recognized first sacker on the roster now that Dahlgren has gone. But Joe McCarthy, the manager, says, rather significantly: 'For the present, Sturm is our first baseman.' Which leads every one [sic] to suspect that the Yankees have something else on the fire."[9] Writer Dan Daniel later revealed how the narrative unfolded: "When the Yankees sold Dahlgren, Joe McCarthy announced [Johnny] Sturm was the new first baseman…. But Joe [Gordon] had not yet signed his contract and McCarthy had to keep mum about his plans until he had lured Gordon into the fold."[10]

The Gordons arrived at St. Petersburg several days before the reporting date.[11] As standard practice with the Yankees, no players were allowed to work out with the team until they had a signed contract.[12] Gordon still was discussing contract terms with manager McCarthy when he admitted to a reporter that he probably would be in uniform on Monday, his scheduled reporting date, but he "had no idea whether his first workout would be at first, second or third base."[13]

Joe agreed to the terms of his contract on March 3 and signed the following day for

Chapter 10. World Series Hero (1941)

$15,000, a raise of $1,000 over his previous year's salary.[14] The Yankees' third-place finish in 1940 affected all of their players' salaries for 1941. Gordon was one of just a handful of players to receive a raise—while several received reductions in salary.

Daniel later told what happened after Gordon signed his contract: "Then the scheme was sprung on the writers."[15] McCarthy ended all speculation about what he planned on doing with two second basemen (Gordon and Priddy) and two shortstops (Crosetti and Rizzuto). He announced that Gordon would be the Yankees' first baseman, Priddy and Rizzuto the new keystone combo, and Crosetti the utility infielder.[16] McCarthy told Daniel, "Turning Gordon into a first baseman is not the result of an overnight decision. I had this thing in mind last summer [1940]."[17] Daniel later noted, "Gordon did not relish the shift. But the club said, 'Play first [base],' so Joe went out and got a drugstore mitt and pre-empted the terrain on which had trod the great Iron Horse [Lou Gehrig]."[18]

McCarthy told the reporters, "Gordon will be my first baseman until he shows me he cannot hold the job. I'm sure, however, that Joe will be able to make the shift."[19] He further explained, "What I'm trying to do, is add speed and punch to my infield. Any one [sic] who handles the ball as beautifully as Gordon should be able to play first base. I think he can do it. He thinks he can do it. We'll see."[20]

Shifting Gordon to first base did seem like an odd move, especially considering how brilliantly he'd played the keystone sack the previous three years. Dan Daniel wrote, "But Marse Joe was willing to take the gamble and rely on his judgment of players—particularly his judgment of Gordon."[21] No doubt the switch was tough on the Flash—but he ***didn't*** complain.

The Yankees' 21-year-old rookie second baseman, Jerry Priddy, was portrayed in the media as a somewhat cocky, brash young man; although his keystone partner, 23-year-old shortstop Phil Rizzuto, was just the opposite, very quiet and shy. Bill Madden wrote in *Pride of October: What It Was to Be Young and a Yankee,* that during 1941 spring training, Priddy walked up to Joe Gordon in the clubhouse and told him, "I'm the better second baseman. I can make the double play better than you … do everything better than you."[22] Rich Marazzi and Len Fiorito also noted the same incident in their book, *Baseball Players of the 1950s: A Biographical Dictionary of All 1,560 Major Leaguers,* and added that Joe Gordon had just laughed in Priddy's face at the rookie's comments.[23] This sounds typical of Joe's confident, light-hearted nature. Gordon's daughter Judy agrees: "I can just *see* my father laughing in Jerry's face, as Dad was a great kidder!"

On the other hand, multiple Gordon family photos indicate that Priddy's boastful comments to Joe Gordon very well may have been made in jest. The two players and their wives certainly appeared to be good friends, and they even vacationed together in the Pocono Mountains of Pennsylvania on a day off in September 1941.

Meanwhile, baseball pundits expressed considerable reservations about McCarthy's decision to move Joe Gordon to first base. St. Louis Browns first baseman George McQuinn, who had been Gordon's teammate on the 1937 Newark Bears, said, "Gordon is the greatest second baseman I ever saw, and I can't see the percentage in converting him into a first baseman. I don't care who they play at second, they can't fill Gordon's shoes."[24]

Babe Dahlgren, who had taken over first base when Lou Gehrig retired early in 1939, had played alongside Joe Gordon in 144 games in 1939 and 155 games in 1940. Shortly after being sold to the Boston Bees in 1941, Dahlgren said, "When the Yanks informed me I had been sold to the Bees, I told a San Francisco sports writer that Joe

Dottie Gordon's photograph of Joe (right) with Jerry and Evelyn Priddy was one of several taken while the two couples vacationed together in the Pocono Mountains of Pennsylvania, on a day off in September 1941 (Gordon family collections).

Gordon would play first [base] for the club. Gordon is the kind of ball player who can play any place…. I wouldn't be surprised if Joe is playing first base in mid-season like he had been there all his life."[25] "The Iron Horse," Lou Gehrig, told John Kieran of the *New York Times*, "He [Gordon] can't miss! He's really a great ballplayer. Just give him a little time to practice and he'll be a whiz at first base."[26]

Most important, though, was what Gordon himself thought about the switch. On the first day at his new position, he said, "Throw me that mitt and watch the fireworks. This is not altogether new to me. I played the bag as a semi-pro. However, it's new stuff for me since I broke in with Oakland in 1936. There are tricks of playing first [base], as there are tricks around second, and it will take some time to get the hang of the job—and the new glove [mitt]."[27]

Gordon, however, was confident he'd have his new position mastered by the time the season opened in mid–April. The thing that seemed to bother him the most was getting used to the not-so-subtle differences between a second baseman's glove and the first baseman's mitt. He practiced by the hour, catching the ball in the webbing of his mitt, instead of in the palm of a glove, like he was used to doing.[28]

During a spring training exhibition game in mid–March, it was reported that "Gordon took a dozen chances in stride at first [base].... [I]n 10 days, Joe has conquered the difficult task of playing first [base] and has come along so rapidly [that] press box critics are saying he may be one of the best first-sackers in the American [L]eague before the 1941 season is over."[29]

Manager McCarthy took occasion to poke fun at the skeptics: "Gordon came to me as a shortstop. I first changed him into a second baseman. Now he is playing first [base]. Joe could do a great job at third if he had to. Don't be surprised if some day I let Gordon open at first [base] and work him all the way around the infield."[30]

Meanwhile, and most likely unbeknownst to Yankees management, Joe Gordon took up where he had left off with his most recent passion—flying. He took two lessons with a flight instructor and made two solo flights in a small Taylorcraft training plane at St. Petersburg. He would fly seven more times that summer—in New York and Cleveland—in a variety of aircraft, including seaplanes.[31]

The Yankees began their 1941 season on April 14 at Washington, with President Franklin D. Roosevelt throwing out the first ball in front of 32,000 sweltering fans.[32] The Bombers shut out the Senators, 3–0, on Marius Russo's three-hitter. Rookie second baseman Jerry Priddy had sprained his ankle during one of the Yankees' final exhibition games, so he missed the first three games of the regular season. Gordon was moved back to second base, playing between two rookies, Phil Rizzuto at shortstop and Johnny Sturm at first base. Clark Griffith, owner of the Washington Senators, talked with reporter Francis E. Stan about Opening Day: "Gordon beat us, you know, in the opening game.... Russo was all right. So were Di Maggio [sic] and a few others. But that catch Gordon made in right field off Chapman saved the game for the Yanks.... Only great ball players [sic] do that sort of thing at the right time.... That was the ball game, that catch, and as far as Gordon playing first base, I'd say he could play anywhere."[33]

After three games at the keystone sack, Joe Gordon was back playing first base, with Priddy at second and Rizzuto as shortstop, where they played until mid–May. Dan Daniel wrote, "Whether this arrangement will continue is by far the most absorbing question in the bailiwick of the Bombers."[34]

Baseball pundits speculated about whether Gordon's new position would "eat into his hitting."[35] On April 20, the Flash silenced the naysayers by going 3–for–5 including two home runs in the Bombers' 19–5 pummeling of the Philadelphia Athletics. At first glance, moving Gordon to first base seemed to be working. By the end of April, the Flash was batting a robust .313 and had made only one error.

On May 15, and barely noticed at the time, Joe DiMaggio hit a run-scoring single during a game at Yankee Stadium, although the White Sox crushed the Bombers, 13–1. This was DiMaggio's first game of an amazing 56-game hitting streak that has yet to be surpassed or even approached in major league baseball.

The Yankees had just lost five games in a row and were in fourth place behind Cleveland, Chicago, and Boston. Suddenly on May 16 and seemingly with *no* advanced warning, Joe McCarthy benched Jerry Priddy and Phil Rizzuto, moved Joe Gordon back to second base, and brought in Frank Crosetti to play shortstop and Johnny Sturm at first base.

It wouldn't be until June 1, during the nightcap of a doubleheader at Cleveland, with Joe DiMaggio's streak at 18 games, that sportswriters began to pay attention to what was evolving.[36]

Sadly, on June 2, 1941, Lou Gehrig, one of the most respected and beloved players in the history of baseball, passed away at his home from amyotrophic lateral sclerosis (also known today as "Lou Gehrig's disease"). The following day, ballpark flags were lowered to half-staff as players and fans stood with bowed heads to honor the memory of "The Iron Horse."[37]

Two weeks later, the Yankees were in second place, playing the league-leading Cleveland Indians at Yankee Stadium. During the top of the second inning, Joe Gordon dove "flat on his stomach" going after a grounder and "rolled the ball to [shortstop] Crosetti while [still] on [the] ground for [the] putout."[38] During the play, 30-year-old Crosetti was badly spiked on his hand by Cleveland's Hal Trosky sliding into second base.[39] McCarthy sent in rookie Phil Rizzuto to play shortstop. Twenty-three-year-old "Scooter" would start all the remaining games that season except for four.

Dan Daniel later wrote, "That Gordon was the pivot of this Yankee machine quickly was demonstrated. With Joe back at second base, the Yankees began to move.... Phil [Rizzuto] thought he had played short [shortstop] for Kansas City. He confessed that in a month he had learned more from Gordon and [third baseman] Rolfe than he had been able to master in [four years in] the minors."[40] Many years later, Rizzuto talked with a writer about his former keystone partner Joe Gordon: "When I broke in [in 1941], Joe could have made me look bad. I was taking Frank Crosetti's place and he [Joe] was Cro's buddy, but he [Joe] helped me in every way."[41] The Yankees posted an outstanding month of June, winning 19 of their 26 games for a one-month percentage of .731.

On June 24 at Yankee Stadium, Joe DiMaggio's hitting streak was at 35 games and generating more and more interest each day. St. Louis Browns rookie pitcher Bob Muncrief had held "The Yankee Clipper" hitless through three previous appearances at bat. Then, in the bottom of the eighth, after Rolfe walked and Henrich homered, the score was at 6–0 with no one on base. DiMaggio singled to left field and would score on Dickey's single. Gordon blasted his 11th home run of the season to score Dickey. Muncrief was pulled from the game for a new pitcher, who retired the rest of the side. After the game, reportedly, St. Louis manager Luke Sewell wondered why Muncrief hadn't walked DiMaggio. The pitcher answered, "Because, that wouldn't have been fair—to him or to me. Hell, he's the greatest ballplayer I ever saw."[42]

June 28 would be the first time the Yankees faced "Yankee-Killer" Johnny Babich since the Athletics' pitcher had crushed the Bombers' pennant chances back on September 27, 1940.[43] Kostya Kennedy wrote in **_56_**: *Joe DiMaggio and the Last Magic Number in Sports*, "Now, facing the Yankees for the first time since that game, Babich had let it be known to his teammates—and in turn word had come to the Yankees and to DiMaggio—that he [Babich] intended to stop Joe's hitting streak right where it was at 39 straight games. He had a simple plan to do it too. If he could get DiMaggio out once,

Chapter 10. World Series Hero (1941)

then he would walk him the rest of the game. In this way the Yankee-slayer would make his most dramatic kill."[44]

The first inning went according to Babich's scheme, when DiMaggio popped out to short. But as the leadoff batter in the third inning, DiMaggio let Babich's three intentional far-outside pitches go by, leaving the count 3–0.[45] Realizing that Babich intended to intentionally walk DiMaggio as threatened, manager McCarthy signaled for DiMaggio to swing away at the next pitch. DiMaggio reached for Babich's high-outside pitch and blasted a line drive through the pitcher's box for a double to center field—and his 40th consecutive game with a hit. It was reported that Babich fell to the ground, barely in time to avoid being hit by the ball.[46] Kennedy wrote that DiMaggio later called it "the most satisfying hit of the streak." Giving up 10 hits and five runs, Babich was replaced with a pinch-hitter in the bottom of the sixth and would be charged with the loss. Beating their nemesis, Johnny Babich, on his home turf, the Bombers claimed the league lead for the remainder of the season.

From the nightcap of the doubleheader on June 1 through the nightcap of June 29, the Yankees set a record by hitting at least one home run in 25 consecutive games, amassing a total of 40 round-trippers in the process.[47] In the nightcap on June 29, Joe DiMaggio hit safely in his 42nd consecutive game, breaking George Sisler's single-season major league record of 41 games, set back in 1922.[48] However, "The Yankee Clipper" was not done yet. On July 2, connecting in his 45th consecutive game, DiMaggio broke "Wee Willie" Keeler's "slightly questionable" 44-game streak back in 1897, when foul balls were not counted as strikes.[49] In 1978, Pete Rose would come closest to DiMaggio's 56-game record by hitting in 44 consecutive games for the Cincinnati Reds.

In early July, Joe Gordon received a letter from American League president William Harridge, notifying him that he'd been selected for the 1941 Major League Baseball All-Star Game on July 8, at Detroit's Briggs Stadium. In addition to the standard admonition, "Kindly see that your uniform is in perfect condition," Harridge wrote, "You will be furnished with railroad and [P]ullman transportation from New York to Detroit and from Detroit to St. Louis. You will also be reimbursed for your incidental expenses, including taxicab hire, meals, etc."[50] Net proceeds from the All-Star Game were designated for the United Service Organizations (USO) nonprofit, founded in February 1941 to provide entertainment and other programs for members of the U.S. Armed Forces and their families.

Cleveland Indians pitcher Bob Feller started the game for the American League, and the Dodgers' Whit Wyatt for the National League. After eight and a half innings and eight pitchers (four from each team), with one out in the bottom of the ninth inning, the National League was leading, 5–3. American League pinch-hitter Ken Keltner singled, and Joe Gordon followed suit. Cecil Travis walked to load the bases. Joe DiMaggio forced Travis at second base, but Keltner scored, narrowing the National League's lead to 5–4. Then the *hero* of the 1941 Midsummer Classic, 22-year-old Ted Williams, with two runners on base, smashed one of his "trade-marked line-drive homers" deep into the upper right field stands for the American League's 7–5 victory.[51] Jack Smith wrote, "No movie plot could have been more thrilling than the one which bared itself in explosive blasts before the 54,674 tickled fans who jammed Briggs Stadium."[52]

The Yankees won 14 consecutive games from June 28 through July 13. They'd already racked up 100 double plays by July 11. It was reported that "the way the Bombers are making those double killings, they look sure to set a new record."[53] Meanwhile, Joe

DiMaggio hit in his 50th consecutive game, surpassing the previous modern record by nine games.[54]

But playing at Cleveland on July 17, Indians pitchers Al Smith and Jim Bagby, shortstop Lou Boudreau, and third baseman Kenny Keltner, with "two sensational backhanded stops" of hot grounders down the line, finally put a halt to Joe DiMaggio's record-setting hitting streak at 56 games.[55] It was said to be the largest crowd ever to see a night game up to that time, a reported attendance of "67,468 roaring fans."[56]

Throughout Joe DiMaggio's electrifying 56-game hitting streak, the Yankees won 41 games, lost 13, and tied two, for a .759 winning percentage. As fate would have it, beginning with the following day's game on July 18, DiMaggio took up where he'd left off and hit in the next 16 consecutive games. Unfortunately, "The Yankee Clipper" sprained his ankle on August 19 and would not get back in the lineup again until September 9.[57]

Shortly after DiMaggio's 56-game hitting streak ended, Joe Gordon wrote to his friend Dick Strite, sports editor of the *Eugene Register-Guard*, giving a one-of-a-kind, first-hand account of teammate Joe DiMaggio's hitting streak and the Yankees' mid-season charge to the 1941 pennant. The authors are especially grateful to Christopher Pietsch of the *Eugene Register-Guard* for allowing us to quote from Gordon's letter:

> Dear Dick—
>
> We have just finished seeing probably the most outstanding feat in the history of baseball—DiMag's consecutive games hitting streak. It is hard for anyone not in the game to realize the practical impossibility of it, but you can take my word for it. It means consistent hitting of all types of pitching, of which there are plenty in the league (I can testify to that also). That is, hitting two, three and sometimes four balls hard per game to get that one hit.
>
> We believe DiMag is the only player in the game with the ability to do that. As great a hitter as he is, he needed that little thing called a break now and then, such as a handle hit, or a bad hop over someone's head to keep it going. However, you could count the times that he actually benefited from that on one hand. In fact it was the opposite kind of break that stopped him in Cleveland or he would be going yet.
>
> Two hard smashes down the third base line that [Ken] Keltner fielded somehow backhanded to throw him out by a step.
>
> I don't think we will live long enough to see his [DiMaggio's] record approached....[58]

The Yankees won 25 games and lost only four during July—a winning percentage of .862.[59] In the *Cleveland Plain Dealer*, Gordon Cobbledick titled one of his columns, "Gordon's Return to Keystone Sack Supplies Spark for Yankees' Sensational Spurt to the Top." Cobbledick contended that "the more one sees of Joe Gordon[,] the more outrageous seems the early-season experiment by which he was converted into a first baseman. Gordon is the greatest second baseman in the major leagues. No one is close to him now and few in all the game's history have approached him.... Not only is he playing superb ball himself, but he has helped Rizzuto to become a better shortstop than he has ever been before."[60]

In 1941, Joe "Flash" Gordon was one of three celebrities featured on the backs of Wheaties "Breakfast of Champions" cereal boxes, in a series of "Champ Stamps" called "Champs of the U.S.A."[61] Included along with Gordon were former U.S. Postal Service aviator George I. Myers and Chicago Cubs third baseman Stan Hack. Athletes first appeared on the backs of Wheaties boxes beginning in 1934.[62]

On July 28, a well-deserved day off, the Gordons, Priddys, Rolfes, Chandlers, and several other Yankees and guests attended a party at renowned bandleader Tommy

Chapter 10. World Series Hero (1941)

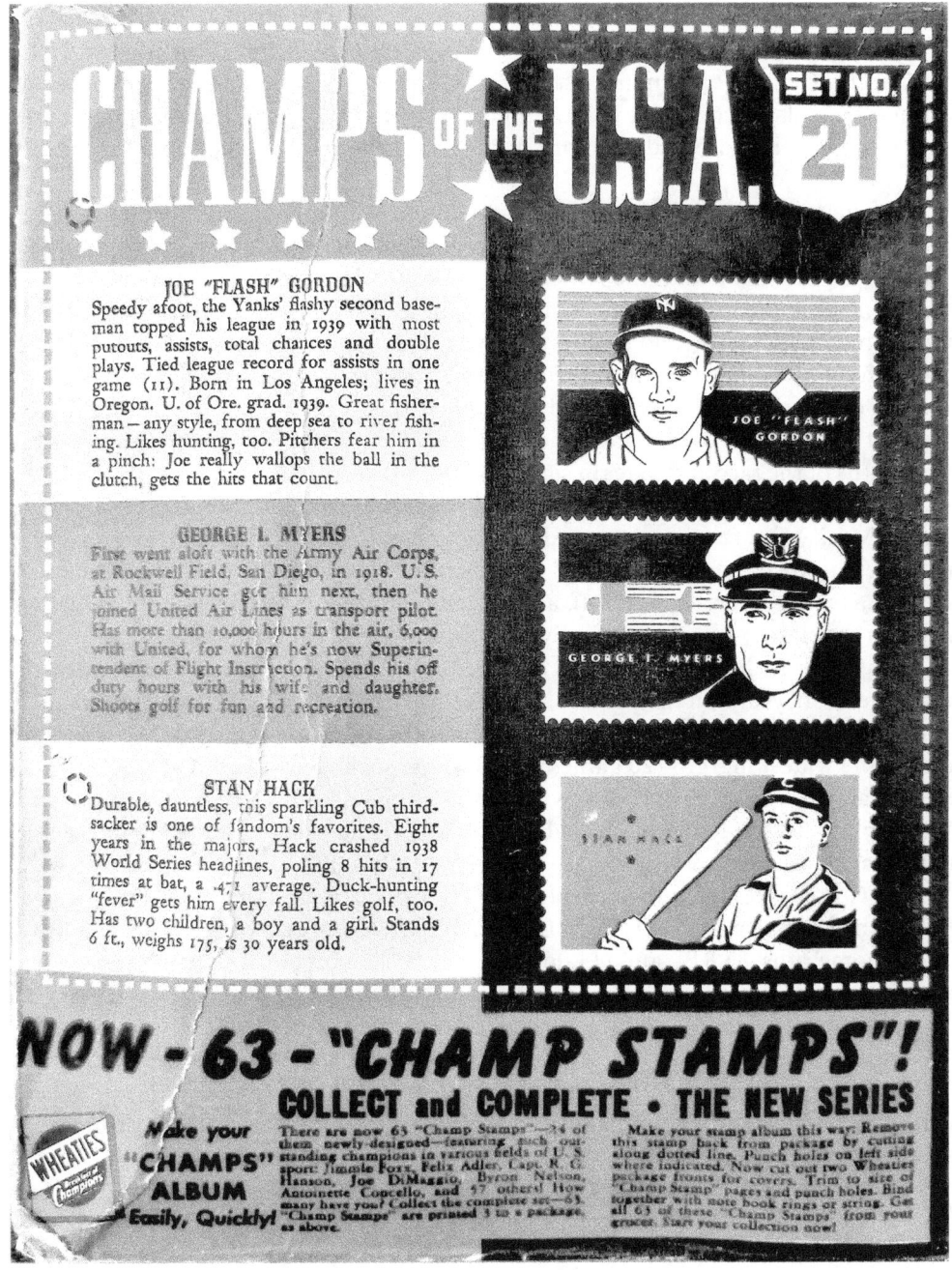

In 1941, Joe "Flash" Gordon was one of three celebrities featured on the backs of Wheaties cereal boxes in a series of "Champ Stamps" called "Champs of the U.S.A." (Gordon family collections).

Dorsey's home in New Jersey, for a day of swimming, badminton, tennis, clay-pigeon shooting, lunch, and dinner.[63]

In mid–August, Washington Senators manager Bucky Harris, a former second baseman himself and future Hall of Famer, talked with sports editor Harry Grayson, referring to Joe Gordon as "the best defensive second baseman he [Harris] ever saw." Harris also told Grayson, "[Nap] Lajoie, [Eddie] Collins, Rogers Hornsby, Frank Frisch and Charley Gehringer, to name five, outhit Gordon with plenty to spare, but not even Collins could play second base like the young man from Oregon." Harris also unhesitatingly rated Phil Rizzuto and Joe Gordon as among the greatest keystone combinations of all time.[64]

In a newspaper article headlined "Yankee Infield Combination Rated Best in Short Series," Gayle Talbot wrote, "It would be difficult to exaggerate Gordon's fielding wizardry or his importance to the American [L]eague champions. Old-timers, who have seen them all in the so-called modern era, say he makes stops and throws that they only faintly imagined before, and that he has never had an equal as a pivot man on double plays." In the same article, Talbot praised Gordon's keystone partner: "[Phil] Rizzuto has fulfilled every expectation of the Yankees, both afield and at bat. After being benched early in the season, he came back to powder the ball at better than a .300 clip in the closing months of the race and to team sensationally with Gordon."[65]

Before a game at Yankee Stadium, the venerable Philadelphia Athletics manager Connie Mack, one of the most revered men in baseball, said, "Gordon is the greatest second baseman we have seen in the last ten years. I wish we had him. We'd give them all a battle…. He is in a class by himself, a whole club in himself, a marvelous play-maker, a driver in the clutch, a marvelous individual and a wonderful team player."[66]

Playing at Boston, the Yankees clinched the American League pennant for their fifth time in six years. In the process, they set two new American League records. They clinched the pennant on the earliest date (September 4) in the history of the league, and also by the widest margin (20 games ahead of the second-place Chicago White Sox).[67] They wrapped up the 1941 season with a 101–53 (.656) record, 17 games ahead of the second-place Boston Red Sox. They also turned 196 double plays, breaking the previous major league record of 194 set by the Cincinnati Reds in 1928.

Joe Gordon was the only major leaguer to play 156 games that year. He placed seventh in the voting for the 1941 AL Most Valuable Player Award, with a .276 batting average, 24 home runs, 87 RBI, and 144 double plays (35 as a first baseman and 109 at second base).

Due to injuries, teammate Joe DiMaggio played in just 139 games, batting .357 with 30 home runs and a major league-leading 125 RBI. "The Yankee Clipper's" 56-consecutive game hitting streak, coupled with his outstanding play as a center fielder, earned Joe DiMaggio his second MVP Award. Runner-up was Boston Red Sox left fielder Ted Williams with his career-high .406 batting average—the last player to bat .400 or more in a single season.

Joe Gordon's mother, Louise, flew to New York City via commercial airline to watch her son play in his third World Series. Joe and Jack Gordon's boyhood mentor and lifelong friend, Andy Lampert, also came from Oregon to watch the Series. Andy received his World Series tickets along with a handwritten note from manager Joe McCarthy, reading "Compliments of the New York Yankees from Joe McCarthy."[68] Dottie's mother, Dr. Irene Crum, also came from California to watch the Series and help care for one-year-old granddaughter Judy.

It was reported that the Yankees' wives were rooting for the Brooklyn Dodgers to win the National League pennant so there would be a "Subway Series." Although the date of the first use of the term "Subway Series" is uncertain, starting in 1941 it was

Chapter 10. World Series Hero (1941)

a nickname for a World Series played between two of the three New York City baseball clubs (the American League New York Yankees, and the National League New York Giants or Brooklyn Dodgers). Fans only had to board the subway in order to travel to either of the ballparks and attend the Series.

When Dottie Gordon found out that Brooklyn had won the National League pennant, a sportswriter quoted her saying, "It'll be a short [S]eries. Our boys will win four straight. No road trips! Good, old Brooklyn."[69] The Yankees already had played in five Subway Series (1921–1923, 1936, and 1937) against the Giants,[70] but 1941 would be the first for the Brooklyn Dodgers.

The day before the first game of the World Series, Alex Raymond, renowned cartoonist and creator of the epic *Flash Gordon* comic strip, visited Yankee Stadium and talked with Joe Gordon. Raymond confessed that Gordon was his baseball idol. Joe likewise told Raymond, "'Flash Gordon' has been an inspiration to me and I've always wanted to meet its creator."[71]

Even before the Series got underway, it was reported that Dodgers manager Leo Durocher was saying, "We're not afraid of DiMaggio or Keller. The man we fear is [Joe] Gordon."[72]

Game One on October 1 at Yankee Stadium drew a record World Series crowd of 68,540 to watch Red Ruffing hurl a "brilliant" six-hitter against Dodgers starter Curt Davis and two relief pitchers. In the second inning, Joe Gordon belted the first home run of the 1941 Fall Classic, reported as a "Ruthian Sock" into the 12th row of the left field seats.[73] Bill Dickey's tremendous 400-foot double in the fourth inning scored Charlie Keller. In the sixth inning, Gordon singled to score Keller for the winning run of the Yankees' 3–2 victory.

The Dodgers fired back to take Game Two, 3–2, ending the Yankees' string of 10 consecutive World Series victories dating back to 1937. Attendance was reported as "another tremendous turnout of 66,248." The Bombers outhit the Dodgers, 9–6, but couldn't put together enough runs, as Brooklyn's pitcher, Whitlow Wyatt, got better, and "his fast ball appeared to grow faster," until "toward the last the Yanks were lucky to touch him."[74] Gordon walked three times (one an intentional pass) and singled once. But in the top of the sixth inning, he bobbled a "screaming" grounder that took a "nasty hop," and his hurried throw to first base pulled Johnny Sturm off the bag.[75] This cost Gordon a critical error, which led to the Dodgers winning the game. Yet as Harry Ferguson wrote, "[P]robably no other second baseman in the game could have put his hands on [that ball]."[76]

Gordon's error did not diminish any of the praise he received in the media. Cartoonist Burris Jenkins, Jr., noted in a newspaper cartoon, "Except for his one error, Joe Gordon has done about everything for the Yanks except pick up the bats—a dervish on defense and still batting 1.000."[77] Harry Ferguson later pointed out "in the first two games he [Gordon] reached first base every time he went to bat. He was the only Yankee regular who did not strike out at least once [and, actually, in the entire Series]."[78] Jimmy Powers wrote, "If you are one of the 80,000,000 newsreel fans who will see the [S]eries footage at your neighborhood theatre, notice the electric aura Joe Gordon gives off on that frame. Joe is like a high tension wire. He anticipates every play."[79]

After Brooklyn's victory in Game Two, Dodgers president Larry MacPhail[80] joined his players in the clubhouse to celebrate their triumph over the Yankees. Charles Dunkley wrote in *The Oregonian*, "[Dodgers manager] Durocher had particular praise for the aggressiveness and hitting ability of Joe Gordon…. He declared emphatically that Gordon was the man to stop in the Yankee attack. 'I still think he's the toughest in the outfit,' Leo said. 'If you make one mistake, you can go out in the seats to get it. He's really a tough hitter—and I mean tough.'"[81]

Tensions were high as the Series moved across the Brooklyn Bridge to Ebbets Field for Game Three on October 4. A reported 33,100 fans jammed into the stadium to see its first World Series game since 1920, back when the Dodgers were known as the Brooklyn Robins. Tragically, in the top of the seventh inning, a line drive off Yankees pitcher Marius Russo's bat hit Dodgers pitcher, 40-year-old Freddie Fitzsimmons, on the left kneecap, sending him to the hospital.[82]

With the game still scoreless going into the top of the eighth inning, four consecutive singles (by Rolfe, Henrich, DiMaggio, and Keller) scored two runs for the Yankees. The Dodgers followed with one run in the bottom of the eighth. No one scored in the ninth, and the Yankees won Game Three, 2–1, on young Russo's brilliant four-hitter. Joe Gordon went 1-for-3 with a triple and base on balls, and was batting .667 after three games.

Edward Zeltner summed up Game Four in the *New York Daily Mirror* with, "A World Series game was WON—and LOST—on one pitch … and Lady Luck once more frowned on the ill-fated Dodgers who bowed, with victory seemingly in their grasp, 7 to 4, in the weirdest climax to a championship game in baseball history."[83] The Yankees scored one run in the first inning and two in the fourth; the Dodgers scored twice in the bottom of the fourth and two "rejuvenating runs" in the fifth to pull ahead, 4–3.

The game saw no more runs until the top of the ninth. With two out, no one on base, and the count 3–2, Tommy Henrich swung at Hugh Casey's next pitch, a sharp-breaking curve, and missed. But the ball deflected off Dodgers catcher Mickey Owen's mitt, and the astonished Henrich wasted no time dashing to first base, while Owen chased after the ball. Up next, Joe DiMaggio singled, sending Henrich to second. Charlie Keller doubled high against the right field fence, driving Henrich home, with DiMaggio close behind, sliding in ahead of the throw. With the Yankees leading, 5–4, Bill Dickey walked, and Joe Gordon sent a tremendous double to deep left field, scoring Keller and Dickey and bringing the tally to 7–4. In the bottom of the ninth, Yankees relief pitcher Johnny Murphy set down the Dodgers, one, two, three, for the Yankees' third win of the Series. Charlie Keller was the game's hero with four hits, including his game-winning double. Gordon went 2-for-5 with a single, double, and two RBI.

In Game Five the following day, 6-foot 2-inch, 215-pound right-hander Ernest "Tiny" Bonham held the Dodgers to just four hits and one run, as the Yankees captured their fifth world championship in six years. The largest crowd of the three games at Ebbets Field, approximately 34,072 fans, turned out to watch "the most turbulent tussle" of the Series. It was reported that "the two teams fought the umpires and each other at every turn in one long continual wrangle."[84] In the second inning, Keller walked, Dickey singled, and, with Gordon at bat, Keller scored from third on a wild pitch over the catcher's head. Gordon belted a "scorching single" to right field, sending Dickey home, and the score was 2–0, which was enough for the win. The Dodgers scored a run in the third inning. Henrich homered in the fifth inning for the spare one-run edge, 3–1. Jack Smith reported in the *Daily News*: "For the Dodgers it was the third failure in three shots (1916, 1920, and 1941) at the highest goal in baseball."[85]

Joe Gordon topped all players in the five-game Series, batting .500 in 14 at-bats, with seven hits (including a home run, triple, and double), five RBI, seven walks, and no strikeouts. He was the only regular not to strike out, recording an on-base percentage of .667 and a slugging percentage of .929. Defensively he handled 26 chances and committed one error, for a .962 fielding percentage. Columnist Bill Corum portrayed Gordon as "an infielder out of another world."[86]

Each Yankee's share of the 1941 World Series winner's pool was $5,943.[87] This was Joe Gordon's third time being awarded a World Series championship emblem. He chose the 1941 lady's ring for his wife, Dottie. Anxious to get home to his hunting, it was reported that Joe's first comment after the Series was, "Now bring on the ducks!"[88]

Brooklyn Dodgers president Larry MacPhail was quoted in a newspaper article headlined "MacPhail Picks Best Players," saying, "The hero was Joe Gordon.... If you ask me, the difference between the Yankees and the Dodgers in this [S]eries was at second base.... And they had Joe Gordon.... And Gordon did everything right."[89]

Henry McLemore's article, "From First to Last It Was Joe Gordon," began, "The [W]orld [S]eries between the Yanks and the Brooklyns can be boiled down to one word—Gordon." McLemore quoted Larry MacPhail talking about Gordon: "The standout guy, the guy who licked us. He must have cut off 10 runs with plays that no other infielder between here and heaven could make. Give me that guy next year and we'll win the National [League] by 20 games."[90]

In the Yankees' clubhouse after the final game, McLemore said to Gordon, "You're the hero of the [S]eries." But Joe replied, "Yeah. What about Ruffing and Russo and Bonham and Keller and the other guys? ... [I]t was fun to lick the Dodgers. Tough ball club. They gave us a whale of a battle.... Of all the [W]orld [S]eries this club has won since I've been with them, this is the one they [our guys] really got a kick out of winning."[91] Years later, in his book, *Five O'Clock Lightning: Ruth, Gehrig, DiMaggio, Mantle and the Glory Years of the NY Yankees*, the Bombers' former outfielder, Tommy Henrich, echoed Gordon's words: "Of all the World Series championships that I was part of with the Yankees, 1941 was by far the sweetest. Every one of us felt that way."[92] In a newspaper column, titled "Joe Gordon—The Real Story of World Series," Joe Williams wrote, "Don't miss Gordon the next time you come to a ball game, because when you take a look at him you are taking a look at something you only see once."[93]

Yankees president Ed Barrow said, "Gordon is the absolute feature of this Series. He's a champion all the way, head and shoulders above every other second baseman or any other player as a competitor. There are none like him. I haven't seen one in 52 years in the game."[94]

In a newspaper article titled "Pilot Votes Gordon Best All-Around," manager Joe McCarthy was quoted saying:

> "You talking about great ball players?" Joe McCarthy demanded with some heat the other night at the Yankee victory party.
> "Well, I'll say right now the greatest all-around ball player I ever saw—and I don't bar any of them—is Joe Gordon."
> ... Somebody suggested McCarthy look at Gordon's .277 [actually .276] batting average for 1941.
> "I don't know what he hit, and neither does Gordon. I don't care if he hit a hundred, and neither does Gordon.
> "He don't give a dang, so long as we win."[95]

Gordon's proud mother, Louise, got to attend the Yankees' victory dinner and meet manager McCarthy and all the players. Once back home in Oregon, she told a reporter,

Joe Gordon, one-year-old daughter Judy, and wife Dottie say goodbye at City Hall, right before heading home to Oregon on October 7, the day after the Yankees won the 1941 world championship. Baseball writers from nine New York newspapers unanimously voted Joe Gordon the outstanding player of the 1941 World Series (Society for American Baseball Research).

"This was the most thrilling of all the [W]orld [S]eries Joe's played in…. The games this year were all so close, and Joe played the best ever."[96]

Baseball writers from nine New York newspapers voted unanimously in selecting Joe Gordon as the outstanding player of the 1941 World Series.[97] On the steps of City Hall the next morning, Acting Mayor Newbold Morris presented Gordon with a $150 ermine-beaver hat from Young's Hat Stores of New York City. Standing nearby, holding 14-month-old daughter Judy, was Joe's wife, Dottie. Immediately after the presentation, the Gordons headed for home in Oregon. The Flash had some duck hunting to do!

Years later, Don Doerr, son of Boston Red Sox second baseman and Hall of Famer Bobby Doerr, commented about the year 1941: "Your dad had a fabulous [S]eries. I think this had to be an incredible period in baseball. [It] was an amazing year with [Joe] DiMaggio's 56-game streak, [Ted] Williams [batting] .406, the [S]ubway [S]eries, and, to think, just two months before Pearl Harbor."[98]

Tragically, just before 8 A.M. on Sunday, December 7, 1941, our nation and the entire world became abruptly transformed by Japan's devastating air attack on the U.S. Naval Base at Pearl Harbor, Oahu, Territory of Hawaii. More than 3,500 Americans were killed or wounded in the attack. In addition, eight battleships and more than 300 airplanes were destroyed or seriously damaged. The following day, United States President Franklin D. Roosevelt addressed a joint session of the U.S. Congress and the nation, delivering his "A Date Which Will Live in Infamy" speech, resulting in Congress declaring war against the Empire of Japan. On December 11, 1941, just hours after Germany declared war on the United States, the Congress of the United States also declared war on Germany.

The future of Major League Baseball, the United States of America, and the embattled world would change dramatically over the next several years. In the meantime, Joe Gordon was formulating his own plans in support of the war effort—and his plans did not involve baseball!

Chapter 11

AN MVP YEAR (1942)

With the United States declaring war against the Empire of Japan on December 8, 1941, the nation's war machine began ramping up and transporting thousands of ships, aircraft, and troops to the islands of the Pacific Ocean. At first, just a few major leaguers were drawn into the war effort. But eventually hundreds of major league and thousands of minor league players would trade in their bats, balls, and mitts for guns and bullets. Meanwhile, baseball continued to be played at home during the war years.

Twenty-six-year-old Joe Gordon became more focused on joining the nation's war effort—hoping to become a pilot for the U.S. Navy or U.S. Army Air Forces. At home in Oregon, he continued to fly several times a week, obtaining instruction in stalls and spins, building up solo hours, and completing his solo cross-country flights.[1] He received his Private Pilot Airman Certificate—Airplane, Single Engine, Land; 0–80 horsepower on January 5, 1942.[2]

Also in early January 1942, *The Sporting News* published the results of their end-of-season polling of 356 Baseball Writers' Association of America (BBWAA) members to select the newspaper's Major League All-Star Team of 1941.[3] Yankees on the team included center fielder Joe DiMaggio, second baseman Joe Gordon, and catcher Bill Dickey.

On January 15, 1942, *The Sporting News* published a large, front-page cartoon by Jim Berryman, portraying 10 highly acclaimed second basemen, ranging from the legendary Napoleon "Nap" Lajoie (whose major league career had begun back in 1896), to relative newcomers Joe Gordon and Bobby Doerr.[4] Accompanying the cartoon likeness of Gordon were the words, "*but ... the currently reigning king of the keystone players is ... Joe Gordon* an important cog in 1941's best piece of diamond machinery, the Yankees." Along with Berryman's cartoon was an article by Dan Daniel comparing past and present second basemen, headlined "Joe Gordon Succeeds Gehringer as High Man at Position Whose Guardian Makes or Breaks Team."[5]

Also on January 15, United States President Franklin D. Roosevelt wrote a historically significant letter (referred to as baseball's "Green Light Letter"), in response to Baseball Commissioner Kenesaw M. Landis's previous letter and agreeing that baseball should continue to be played during 1942.[6]

Joe and Dottie Gordon and 18-month-old daughter Judy headed to Yankees spring training early in 1942.[7] Because his contract had not arrived in the mail by the time the family departed Oregon, Joe didn't know what the Yankees were offering in the way of salary. In the meantime, he figured his contract would catch up with them either at Los Angeles or when they got to Florida.

On their way, the Gordons stopped for a week in Los Angeles to visit Dottie's

Chapter 11. An MVP Year (1942) 87

Upon arriving at New York Yankees spring training in St. Petersburg in early March 1942, Dottie Gordon is warmly greeted by infielder Jerry Priddy (Gordon family collections).

mother. On February 18, Joe's 27th birthday, he headed out to Wrigley Field, home of the Pacific Coast League Los Angeles Angels, where *The Pride of the Yankees* motion picture was being filmed. While there, Joe spoke with Yankees catcher Bill Dickey, actor Vernon Rickard, and Yankees icon Babe Ruth, who were taking part in filming the movie starring Gary Cooper as Lou Gehrig.[8]

Arriving at spring training about March 2, Joe Gordon accepted the terms of his contract on March 9 for $17,000, a raise of $2,000 over his previous season's salary.

The following day, he made his debut in an exhibition game against the Boston Red Sox at Sarasota, Florida. This marked the first year that the Yankees played exhibition games against teams in their own league during spring training.[9] It was reported that "Gordon really was a revelation. He established his old authority in the field right at the start."[10]

But the Flash had more on his mind than just baseball that spring. Three months after the Japanese attack on Pearl Harbor, he already was thinking (albeit secretively) about going to war—firmly planted in the pilot's seat of a military fighter, bomber, or transport aircraft. Joe's *Pilot's Flight Log* indicates that, during the month of March 1942, he rented airplanes and flew for an hour or so a total of 19 times.[11] This continued until the Yankees headed out from St. Petersburg, barnstorming their way to New York. Joe even managed to get in one flight along the way at Nashville, Tennessee.

Joe continued to fly during the 1942 baseball season—at Cleveland; St. Louis; Chicago; Washington, D.C.; Long Island; Yonkers; and Detroit. He received his Seaplane Rating in mid–June.[12] He also flew at night and received instruction in several large aircraft, working toward adding additional ratings to his pilot's license. In all, during spring training and the 1942 baseball season, Joe flew four dozen times and added 43 hours to his logbook. S.T. Wright later wrote, "The hobby [flying] was a secret one

DATE	AIRCRAFT FLOWN			CROSS-COUNTRY		No. PASS.	REMARKS OR INSTRUCTOR'S SIGNATURE CERT. NO. & RATING
	MAKE AND MODEL	CERTIFICATE NUMBER	ENGINE	FROM	TO		
3/3/42	T Cr.	24060	Cont 65	St. Pete Fla.			
3/4/42	T Cr	"	"		"		
3/6/42	T Cr	"	"		"		
3/7/42	Cub	30607	"		"		
3/10/42	T Cr.	24060	"		"		
3/11/42	Cub.	37970	"		"		
3/13/42	Stins.	11,156	Lyc. R680		"		
3/14/42	J. Cr.	24060	Cont 65		"		
3/15/42	J Cr.	"	"		"		
3/17/42	T Cr.	"	"		"		
3/19/42	Cub	30607	"		"		
3/20/42	J. Cr.	24060	"		"		

Joe Gordon's *Pilot's Flight Log* shows where he recorded his 19 flights made while at Yankees spring training in St. Petersburg during March 1942 (Gordon family collections).

because 'Uncle Ed' Barrow, president of the Yankees, would have been uneasy about his ace player risking his neck flitting around the skies in rickety old training planes."[13]

For the second year in a row, the Yankees opened the season at Washington. Red Ruffing hurled a three-hitter to shut out the Senators, 7–0, in front of approximately 31,000 fans.[14]

It was reported that the Bronx Bombers had "suffered little so far from the [military] draft," and their overall strength appeared "as great as ever, both offensively and defensively." Bob McShane wrote, "With Dickey behind the plate, Gordon on second base and Joe DiMaggio in the center field spot, the Yankees have the strongest 'pennant line' in baseball."[15]

After 10 games, the Yankees were in first place by one game. Joe Gordon, typically a slow starter in the spring, was leading both leagues, batting .487. Harry Leeding reported in the *Oregon Journal*, "[A]lways before in the big leagues[,] 'Flash' couldn't buy a base hit for love or money early in the season."[16]

However, while trying to complete a double play on April 29, Gordon badly wrenched his back, causing him to miss the next three games.[17] This was his first time out of the Yankees' lineup since April 25, 1939, reportedly ending a string of 471 consecutive games played.[18] While Gordon was recuperating, third baseman Jerry Priddy switched to second base, Frank Crosetti came in to play third, and Phil Rizzuto continued as shortstop. Losing four games in late April and early May, the Yankees dropped back to third place. Yet on May 6, during a game lasting only one hour and 24 minutes, the Bombers again captured the lead—this time to stay!

Playing at Cleveland on May 13, and probably not even noticed at the time, Joe

Chapter 11. An MVP Year (1942)   89

Gordon went 1-for-4 with an uneventful single in the top of the ninth inning. This marked the beginning of a career-best hitting streak for the Flash, continuing from May 13 to June 14. During that time, he hit in 29 consecutive games, recording 48 hits (including six home runs and 26 RBI) in 112 at-bats and raising his batting average from .350 to .396 to top all players in both leagues.[19]

It was reported that "Gordon has been having the greatest spring of his baseball career." Meanwhile, he was said to be under the watchful surveillance of the "diamond diagnosticians," who reached a few conclusions of their own: "First, Gordon is not going after so many bad balls.... Second, Gordon has changed his batting style and is levelling [sic] instead of hitting upward on so many balls."[20]

By late May, Joe Gordon and a fellow Oregonian, Boston Red Sox second baseman Bobby Doerr, were neck-and-neck, leading both leagues in batting.[21] Bob Considine wrote in the *New York Daily Mirror*, "Physically, we think he [Gordon] is capable of leading the league.... [H]e has the coordination and the guts of a great hitter. But such a goal has always seemed rather trite to him. He is the perfect team player. His interest in personal glory is always secondary."[22]

Gordon's 29-game hitting streak finally was halted on June 14 by St. Louis knuckleballer Johnny Niggeling, during the nightcap of a doubleheader at Yankee Stadium. The Flash went down swinging—but not in vain. Baserunners Joe DiMaggio and Charlie Keller pulled a double steal on Gordon's third strike, with DiMaggio scoring when Browns catcher Rick Ferrell's throw went wild into left field.[23] The Yankees won both

Ten of the New York Yankees' wives celebrate Bill Dickey's 35th birthday in June 1942. Dottie Gordon is second from the right, sitting on the couch, and Violet "Vi" Dickey is in the back, wearing a white blouse with a dark collar (Gordon family collections).

games that day, putting them 9½ games ahead of second-place Boston. Gordon's hitting streak tied two earlier 29-game hitting streaks by Yankees, the first by shortstop Roger Peckinpaugh in 1919, and the second by outfielder Earle Combs in 1931. As of this writing, Gordon's hitting streak has not been surpassed or even equaled by a Yankee since then.[24]

This year's All-Star Game would be the first of three wartime Midsummer Classics (1942, 1943, and 1944). Because World War II was still ongoing in 1945, the All-Star Game was not played that year. July 6, 1942, fell on a rainy twilight evening at the Polo Grounds, home of the New York Giants.[25] Joe McCarthy piloted the American League team, starting four of his nine Yankees who were on the roster: Tommy Henrich, Joe DiMaggio, Joe Gordon, and Spud Chandler.

Associated Press writer Judson Bailey summed up the game with, "The American [L]eague made a travesty of the tenth [M]ajor-[L]eague [A]ll-[S]tar spectacle in one inning Monday night, knocking the National [L]eaguers groggy with three runs on two homers in the first frame and coasting to a 3-to-1 triumph."[26] Spud Chandler pitched a flawless two-hitter for the first four innings and was credited with the win.

Joe Gordon handled five fielding chances flawlessly, although he struck out three times and grounded out once. Meanwhile, and perhaps with a bit of prophetic foresight, Gordon Cobbledick of the *Cleveland Plain Dealer* expressed high praise for the All-Star Game's keystone combination of Yankees second baseman Joe Gordon and Indians shortstop Lou Boudreau: "[T]he American League's second base combination can be written down as the greatest ever put together on a ball field…. If Lou Boudreau and Joe Gordon could play together for a full season they would overshadow every pair from Tinker and Evers down to the present…. Their double play in the first inning tonight was faster than the lightning that had been playing around the Polo Grounds a few minutes before."[27]

After defeating the National Leaguers, the victorious American League All-Stars traveled to Cleveland to play the All-Service All-Stars, managed by U.S. Navy Lieutenant Gordon "Mickey" Cochrane, a former player/manager of the Detroit Tigers. Following opening ceremonies at Cleveland's Municipal Stadium including "marching men, rumbling tanks, and flowing banners,"[28] a lineup of American League All-Stars hammered the All-Service All-Stars, 5–0, sending "Cleveland's idol," U.S. Navy Chief Boatswains Mate Bob Feller, to the showers in the second inning.[29] Red Sox second baseman Bobby Doerr played the entire game for the American League, though, like Joe Gordon the night before, he went hitless.

From the nightcap of a doubleheader on July 12 through the game on July 28, the Yankees won a phenomenal 15 of 16 games, both at home and on the road. During the club's long western road trip, the Gordons' second child, Joseph Michael "Joey" Gordon, was born at the Fitch Sanitarium in the Bronx, weighing in at a hefty 8 pounds and 6 ounces.

Papa Joe wouldn't get to meet his baby son until two weeks later, although he did get to see Joey's photo in the newspapers. In those days, there was no time off for a player to go home for the birth of a baby. Dottie's mother, Irene, flew from California to help care for Dottie and Joey. Meanwhile, the Gordons sent for their Oregon babysitter, 21-year-old college student Helen Deedon, to help care for almost-two-year-old Judy.

After five games at home, the Yankees were on the road again. Joe Gordon was still one of the top three American League leaders in batting, along with Boston's Ted

Chapter 11. An MVP Year (1942)

Williams and Chicago's Taft Wright.[30] By then, Boston's Bobby Doerr had dropped back of "Baseball's Big Six," which was an *Associated Press* daily tabulation of the top three batters of each league, published in newspapers throughout the country.

Gordon had occasion to talk with a reporter about his batting: "I used to think maybe I was hitting over my head, but I don't know now. No, I don't guess I can call it an accident any more.... I never worried about averages. If you hit a single every inning but don't drive in a run or score, what good is that high batting average? I'd rather get fewer hits and have 'em count."[31]

But what set the Flash apart from other second basemen was his defensive play. On August 14, "[u]nder lights and amid the applause of a hostile gathering of 17,955 fans" at Philadelphia's Shibe Park, the Yankees set a record by turning *seven* double plays in one nine-inning game![32] As one reporter witnessed, "[N]ot one play was close at any base! ... [N]o line drives for automatic double plays were included in the record-shattering performance. They all had to be made the hard way.... Nor were there any liners hit to infielders."[33]

The Yankees "got a tremendous kick" out of their accomplishment. After beating the Athletics, Joe Gordon talked with a reporter about the record they had just set:

> This was the biggest jolt I ever got out of a defense job. Not that we were so wonderful, but everything had to break just right for us and we were able to come up with every one of those plays. When you realize that no other team ever did it before and we made the last five [double plays] on ground plays it gives you a kick. I count it one of the greatest and most unusual records the Yankees ever made. It may never be equalled [*sic*]. The odds against everything meshing properly for a duplicate performance must be about a million to one.[34]

Shortstop Phil Rizzuto told writer Dan Daniel, "That guy Gordon hounds me all the time.... He keeps hollering 'faster' all through the game, and I am starting and pivoting in double plays we would not have made last year."[35] The Yankees' record stood unmatched for almost 27 years until tied on May 4, 1969, by the Houston Astros. It would be tied again on August 17, 2018, by the Chicago Cubs.[36] As of this writing, the record has not been broken.

Playing a doubleheader at home against the Washington Senators on Sunday, August 23, the New York Yankees donated an estimated $80,000 of their gate receipts to U.S. Army and Navy Relief Funds.[37] The huge triple-decked Yankee Stadium was bedecked with flags and bunting. Two iconic Hall of Famers were featured as the between-games attraction: 47-year-old Babe "The Bambino" Ruth and 54-year-old Walter "The Big Train" Johnson. Johnson pitched nearly a score of times to Ruth, who belted several long balls into the right field grandstands, to the delight of the more than 69,000 fans. The Senators took the first game. Then Yankees pitcher Ernie "Tiny" Bonham won the six-inning nightcap with his 3–0 shutout and 16th victory of the season.[38]

On August 30, Yankees right fielder Tommy Henrich played his final two games before heading out for three years of military service with the U.S. Coast Guard.[39] George Selkirk, who'd previously been sidelined with a leg injury, took over in right field until Roy Cullenbine was acquired from the Washington Senators. Cullenbine played 21 games for the 1942 Yankees and hit .364, in addition to playing all five games of the 1942 World Series.

At Cleveland on September 14, Tiny Bonham hurled an 8–3 victory over the Indians to clinch the 1942 pennant for the Yankees, their sixth pennant in seven years. Bonham also was the first American League pitcher to win 20 games that year,[40] on his way to his career-best, league-leading 21–5 (.808) record and 22 complete games. Three days later, the Yankees recorded their 100th win for the eighth time since 1903, six of those years under manager Joe McCarthy.

Right before the Yankees' final game of the season, Joe Gordon wrote a letter to his mother from Boston's Copley-Plaza Hotel. This would be one of scores of letters that Joe wrote to her during his many years in baseball: "We are waiting to go out to play our last game of the season & then the big event [World Series]. It looks like the Cards [St. Louis Cardinals] are in [the Series].... They will be tough for us to beat, as they have 4 or 5 real tough pitchers, but we will sure be bearing down on them."[41]

The Yankees wrapped up their 1942 season with a 103–51 (.669) record, nine games ahead of the second-place Boston Red Sox. They finished first in their league in runs scored (801), home runs (108), RBI (744), fielding percentage (.976), and double plays (190), all the while committing the fewest errors (142) *by far*. Five Yankees hurlers (Bonham, Chandler, Ruffing, Borowy, and Donald) finished with double-digit wins.

Joe Gordon finished the season with 18 home runs and 103 RBI, in addition to his career-best .322 batting average and .409 on-base percentage. His batting average topped teammate Joe DiMaggio's .305 with plenty to spare. Gordon's fielding was exemplary, participating in 121 of the Yankees' league-leading 190 double plays. He finished fourth in the American League in batting average and RBI, fifth in on-base percentage, and sixth in home runs. On the other hand, he held the dubious distinction of leading both the American and National Leagues with his 95 strikeouts, although DiMaggio was third with 87.

The 1942 World Series began on September 30 at Sportsman's Park, home of the St. Louis Cardinals. In front of a crowd of 34,769 in Game One, Yankees pitcher Red Ruffing hurled a "masterpiece" of a one-hitter through eight innings.[42] But giving up four hits and charged with four runs in the bottom of the ninth, he was relieved by Spud Chandler, although he would be credited with the win to become the first major league pitcher to win seven World Series games. Somewhat ominously, though, in the Yankees' 7–4 triumph over the Cardinals, only three of their seven runs were earned. Moreover, the noticeably "flashless" Joe "Flash" Gordon had batted a much-out-of-character 0-for-5 and struck out three times.

Gordon did a little better in Game Two by hitting a double, yet he struck out two more times. The Yankees outhit the Cardinals, but the young, aggressive St. Louis club took the game, 4–3, to tie the Series at one game apiece.

Game Three was played at Yankee Stadium on October 3 and attended by "69,123 rabid fans." It was reported as the "greatest crowd" for a World Series game. Yet it also turned out to be the first shutout inflicted upon the Yankees in a Fall Classic since 1926, which, ironically, also had been against the St. Louis Cardinals in Game Three. With the Cardinals leading, 1–0, in the top of the ninth inning, two hotly contested calls, one at second base and another at third, caused pandemonium among the Yankees. The first occurred when Yankees reliever Marv Breuer's "fiery toss" pulled shortstop Phil Rizzuto's foot off second base, causing umpire George Magerkurth to call Cardinals runner Jimmy Brown "safe." It was reported that "instantly the husky Magerkurth was the dark-suited center of a ring of raging Yanks. [But] [t]hey didn't change his mind."[43]

The second altercation broke out in the same inning: "[A] violent argument ensued when [u]mpire Bill Summers called [Cardinals runner] Terry Moore safe at third base as he slid into the bag as Frank Crosetti took Joe DiMaggio's throw from center field."[44]

Chapter 11. An MVP Year (1942)

The scene escalated further when, "Trying to walk away from the hysterical Frank Crosetti, … Summers was jerked around roughly by the enraged player. The burly custodian of the baseball law wheeled around and just as roughly pushed Crosetti away. The Yankee players again screamed for a good ten minutes, and the old trouble between Rizzuto and Magerkurth broke out spontaneously in another section of the field."[45]

A month after the 1942 World Series, Commissioner Landis fined Joe Gordon $250 "for having tossed indecorous language at [u]mpire George Magerkurth" over the call at second base. But more significantly, Frank Crosetti was fined $250, *plus* suspended for the first 30 days of the 1943 season, for shoving umpire Bill Summers after the decision at third base. An editorial in *The Sporting News* later revealed that the umpires had been instructed to *not* eject players from the games and, instead, let Commissioner Landis handle any infractions after the World Series was over.[46]

Joe Gordon batted 0–for–4 and struck out once in Game Three's loss to the Cardinals, 2–0. He was joined by teammates Cullenbine, DiMaggio, Chandler, Crosetti, and Ruffing, all of whom were fanned by Cardinals southpaw Ernie White.

Game Four on October 4 saw St. Louis advance to within one game of the championship as they beat the Yankees, 9–6. Gordon again went hitless, although he did score a run. Topping the previous day's attendance and revenues, the "thrill-soaked mob of 69,902 paid $269,408 to watch the turbulent contest."[47]

Writer Bob Considine summed up Game Five with, "A great American sports era ended here Monday, while a vast crowd of 69,052 God-sped it into history. The St. Louis Cardinals, a superbly dauntless young team, ended the reign of the seemingly unshatterable [sic] New York Yankees by winning the 1942 [W]orld [S]eries, taking the fifth and final game of the [C]lassic, 4 to 2."[48]

Wrapping up an extremely disappointing World Series, the final inning of the final game may well be termed as "disastrous" for Joe Gordon. With the Yankees down by two runs, he opened the bottom of the ninth inning with a single. An error on Bill Dickey's grounder advanced Gordon to second base. He led off the bag about 10 feet, as Johnny Beazley pitched a "high fast one" to Jerry Priddy.[49] In the blink of an eye, Cardinals catcher Walker Cooper rifled a throw to shortstop Marty "Slats" Marion, to pick off the "horrified" Joe Gordon diving headfirst back to the bag for the out. Priddy popped out and pinch-hitter George Selkirk grounded out to end Game Five, 4–2. The Cardinals took home the world championship, four games to one.

Perhaps Gordon's only consolation was that he committed no errors in the five-game Series. He batted 2–for–21 (.095) and struck out seven times, the most of any player in that year's Fall Classic. Several years later, Grantland Rice quoted Joe McCarthy in an article published in *The Oregonian*: "But he was the same Gordon. He just figured that was the best he could do at that particular time. Things happen that way. You are not always on top when you want to be."[50]

Each Yankee's share of the loser's pool was reported as $3,352.[51] With proceeds from the World Series, Major League Baseball presented the United Service Organizations with a check for $362,926 to be used for "service for American soldiers, sailors, marines and coast guardsmen."[52]

An article in the September 29, 1957, issue of *This Week* magazine identified several "Toppled Idols" who had been upended in Fall Classics of past years. The list included Ty Cobb (in 1909), Babe Ruth (1922), Rogers Hornsby (1929), Bill Dickey (1936), and Joe Gordon (1942).[53] Aside from a bruised ego, Gordon was in rather "noble" company.

Sometime in the fall of 1942, Gordon found out that, due to his age (soon turning 28) and three dependents, he wasn't eligible for a U.S. Navy or U.S. Army flying job. Although very disappointed, Joe decided to return to the Yankees for the 1943 baseball season and waited to be drafted.[54]

On November 3, the Baseball Writers' Association of America announced its selection of Joe Gordon as the Most Valuable Player (MVP) of the American League for 1942.[55] The selection committee comprised 24 members of the BBWAA (three sportswriters from each of the eight cities hosting an American League club). As standard procedure, the balloting had taken place before the World Series, so as to be impartial to candidates not playing in the 1942 Fall Classic.

The voting was close. With first-place votes counting 14 points, second-place 9 points, third-place 8 points, … , down to 10th-place votes counting 1 point, Joe Gordon received 270 points to Boston Red Sox left fielder Ted Williams's 249. Twelve of the 24 members of the 1942 selection committee placed Gordon first versus nine for Williams. Two of the remaining three first-place votes went to Boston Red Sox shortstop Johnny Pesky, and one to St. Louis Browns shortstop Vern Stephens. When notified of his selection, Gordon said, "I'm floored…. It's always been my ambition to be

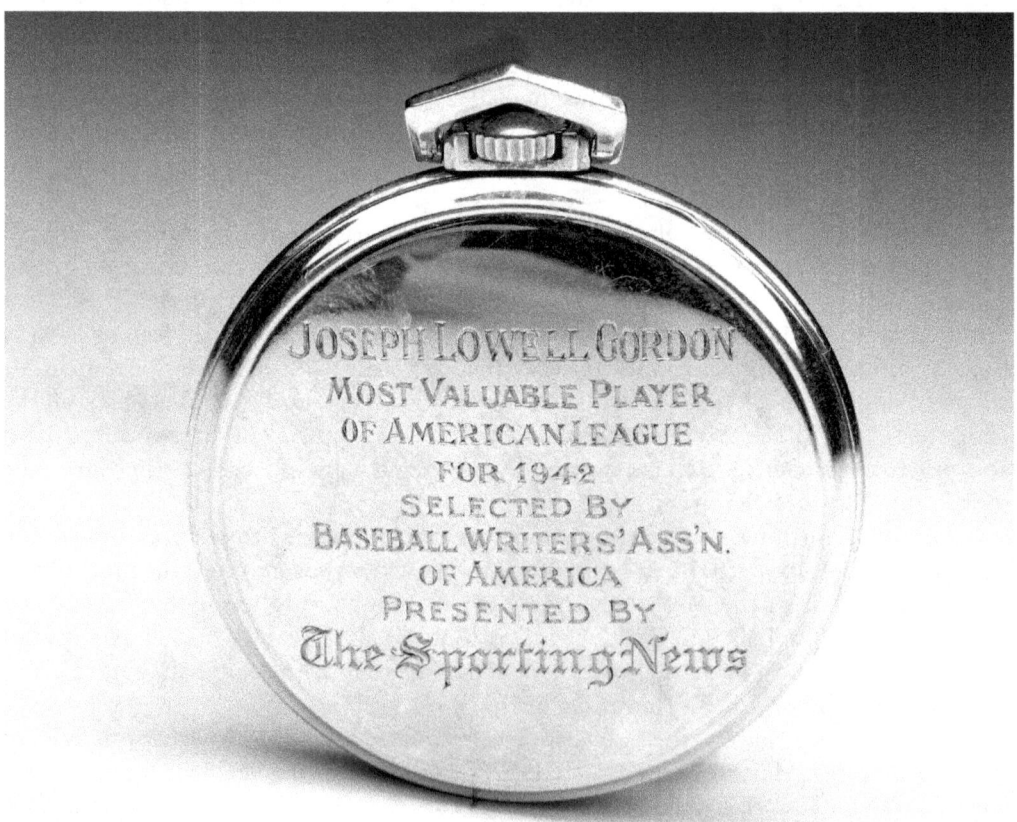

The engraving on Joseph Lowell Gordon's 1942 Most Valuable Player of the American League Award pocket watch reads, "Joseph Lowell Gordon Most Valuable Player of American League for 1942 Selected by Baseball Writers' Ass'n. of America Presented by *The Sporting News*" (courtesy Milo Stewart, Jr./National Baseball Hall of Fame and Museum).

selected for *The Sporting News* award, in fact it's the ambition of all ball players, but I never expected it."[56]

In December 1942, *The Sporting News* awarded Ted Williams its coveted 1942 Player of the Year Award for the second year in a row.[57] At an awards dinner in early 1943, the New York Chapter of the BBWAA presented Williams with its 1942 Player of the Year plaque, in recognition of his Triple Crown.[58]

Years later, in his book, *My Turn at Bat: The Story of My Life*, Ted Williams wrote about the 1942 Most Valuable Player Award:

> I felt I should have been given a little more consideration because I won the [T]riple [C]rown—.356 average, 137 RBI's [sic], 36 home runs—but Joe Gordon got it. Gordon had his greatest year and the Yankees won the pennant again. And we [the Boston Red Sox] were second again. The voting tends to go to the team that wins [the pennant], which is right.[59]

Williams also wrote that, if he had to pick an all-star team of players that he had ever played with or against in the American League, second base would be his toughest position to choose: "I saw Bobby Doerr and Joe Gordon, how good they were. Gordon would have the edge for power at bat and range afield, but I would still consider Doerr his equal, with Nellie Fox a close third."[60]

There was in 1942, and remains to this day, considerable debate over Joe Gordon receiving the MVP Award over Ted Williams.[61] On the other hand, as has been said many times, batting is not everything in evaluating a player's value to his team or to the game of baseball.

An article in *The Sporting News* noted multiple Boston sportswriters, whose "practically unanimous" opinions concurred with the BBWAA's selection of Joe Gordon as MVP over Red Sox left fielder Ted Williams. It was reported that Jack Conway of the *Boston American* commented, "Selection of Gordon over Williams as the [M]ost [V]aluable [P]layer was a good one. Gordon was consistent through the season, one of the chief factors why the Yankees won [the pennant]. Williams flashed brilliantly, but lacked Gordon's steadiness." Arthur Siegel of the *Boston Traveler* was quoted as saying, "But as between Gordon and Williams, there was no question as to which rated the award. Ability to hit a baseball does not make the most valuable player. Sportsmanship and team play are two stipulations, I believe, in the matter of the award." *Boston Herald* writer Bill Cunningham concurred: "The vote is for team value. Gordon qualifies." From Howard G. Reynolds of the *Boston Post* came, "[B]ut Gordon was certainly the sparkplug of the Yankees and I believe led them to the pennant more than any other single player." Harold Kaese of the *Boston Globe* also said, "No man can measure intangibles, but he can form opinions. That's what this decision is—an opinion that Gordon was more valuable to the Yankees than Williams was to the Red Sox."[62]

Due to the ongoing war, presentation of the 1942 MVP Award to Joe Gordon was delayed until September 26, 1943, just a day after the Yankees clinched the 1943 American League pennant.[63] Between games of the Sunday doubleheader at Yankee Stadium, former U.S. Postmaster General James A. Farley presented Gordon with a gold Longines pocket watch engraved with the following: "Joseph Lowell Gordon Most Valuable Player of American League for 1942 Selected by Baseball Writers' Ass'n. of America [and] Presented by *The Sporting News*."[64] For 1942, *The Sporting News* presented the MVP Award to the player selected by the vote of the BBWAA. This ended after 1943, when each entity voted and presented separate awards.[65] *The Sporting News* discontinued their MVP Awards in 1946.

In mid–January 1943, *The Sporting News* announced that Joe Gordon had topped *all* players in both the American and National Leagues in number of votes received for the newspaper's prestigious Major League All-Star Team of 1942.[66] This was Gordon's fourth consecutive year voted onto the team as second baseman, receiving 255 of the 260 total votes cast by members of the BBWAA. After Gordon, the next highest vote-getters were St. Louis Cardinals pitcher Mort Cooper (250 votes), Ted Williams (247 total votes for left field and right field combined), and Joe DiMaggio (215 total votes for center, left, and right field combined). Also voted onto *The Sporting News'* team was Yankees pitcher Tiny Bonham (197 votes).

Chapter 12

WORLD SERIES RECORDS (1943)

With the war raging throughout Europe, Southeast Asia, and the Pacific area, many changes were in store for all of baseball in 1943. Because of wartime demands on the nation's railroads, the Director of the U.S. Office of Defense Transportation requested that Major League Baseball "explore the possibilities for curtailing travel during spring training and the regular season."[1]

In early January, representatives from the American and National League ballclubs met in joint session with Commissioner Landis to plan for spring training and the 1943 baseball season. In order to cut back on travel, the spring training sites were restricted to those located north of the Potomac and Ohio Rivers, and east of the Mississippi, except the two St. Louis ballclubs (the Browns and the Cardinals) were given the option of training in Missouri. Due to colder weather further north, spring training was scheduled to begin several weeks later than usual. Likewise, Opening Day of the 1943 baseball season was delayed about a week, with the season running from April 21 to October 3.[2]

In mid–January, the Yankees announced that they would conduct their spring training at the seaside resort town of Asbury Park, New Jersey.[3] The facilities included a 7,200-seat high school stadium, locker rooms and showers, and an adjoining gymnasium. The batterymen were scheduled to begin training on March 15, with the remainder of the players reporting a week later.

Once again, Yankees president Ed Barrow predicted that his club would win the American League pennant, even though they already had several key players join the military (Ruffing, Henrich, Hassett, Selkirk, and Rizzuto) and one voluntarily retire (Rolfe).[4] Catcher Buddy Rosar and outfielder Roy Cullenbine had been traded to the Cleveland Indians for outfielder Roy Weatherly and infielder Oscar Grimes.[5] At the end of January, Yankees utility infielder Jerry Priddy and Newark Bears pitcher Milo Candini were traded to the Washington Senators for pitcher Bill Zuber and cash.[6] It was reported that all of the players on the Yankees roster were military draft status III-A, except for pitcher Atley Donald, who was IV-B because of medical issues.[7]

The Yankees mailed their 1943 contracts to 30 players the end of January.[8] Two and a half weeks later, word was received that their star center fielder, Joe DiMaggio, was joining the U.S. Army.[9] "The Yankee Clipper" would serve with the U.S. Army Air Forces for the next two and a half years, both Stateside and on the Hawaiian Islands.

Throughout the off-season, Joe Gordon kept in excellent physical condition at home in Oregon. He managed and played on the Man's Shop Guards basketball team twice a week, with their team winning the last 16 consecutive games to capture Eugene's City Basketball League championship.[10] He also played handball, trained with the University of Oregon baseball team, and worked at a livestock feed company.[11] By the time

Joe reported to Yankees spring training, he said he was in the best early-season physical condition of his career.

Prior to spring training, however, Gordon experienced a near-tragedy in mid–March. While still home in Oregon, he was flying as a passenger in a small training airplane that he co-owned with pilot John Shaeffer. On approach to landing at the Klamath Falls Airport, the plane hit a power line, came down on the east-west runway, skidded a considerable distance, and came to a stop with a damaged propeller and landing gear but did not overturn.[12] Luckily, no one was hurt.

Several media outlets caught word of the accident. An article in *The Sporting News* also noted that, soon after the accident, Gordon sold his airplane to the government. And, at the insistence of his wife, Dottie, and Yankees president Ed Barrow, Joe quit flying—at least for the time being.[13]

The Yankees' batterymen began training at Asbury Park in mid–March. They were joined a week later by the remainder of the team—minus their last two holdouts—second baseman Joe Gordon, "the rock of the Yankee infield," and Charlie Keller, "slugging guardian of left field."[14] This was the second year that Gordon had held out on signing his contract—both times coming to terms about a week late. Negotiating with Ed Barrow via long-distance phone, Joe agreed to the terms of his contract on March 29, for a salary of $20,000, a $3,000 raise over his 1942 MVP-season salary.[15] He immediately headed for New Jersey via commercial airline.[16] Dottie and the Gordon children followed later by train.

There were only *two* infielders remaining from the 1942 Yankees: second baseman Joe Gordon and shortstop/third baseman Frank Crosetti. But Commissioner Landis had suspended Crosetti for the first 30 days of the 1943 season for shoving umpire Bill Summers during the 1942 World Series, so he would not be available to play until May 21.[17]

Quick to effect changes, Ed Barrow and Joe McCarthy assembled an infield that included: Nick Etten (a first baseman obtained from the Philadelphia Phillies); Joe Gordon (second base); and rookies Billy Johnson (third base) and George "Snuffy" Stirnweiss (shortstop), both brought up from the Newark Bears. On the bright side, though, the Yankees were reported as having the best pitching in the American League, with Tiny Bonham, Hank Borowy, Spud Chandler, Atley Donald, Marius Russo, and reliever Johnny Murphy on the roster, as well as several promising newcomers.[18]

The players did not look forward to training in the cold, wet climes of New Jersey in March. Joe Gordon recalled, all too well, how training in Florida during the unseasonably cold spring of 1940 had led to severe charley horses for him and his teammates, which, he said, had contributed to the Yankees not winning the pennant that year.[19]

To cut back on travel, pre-season exhibition games were sharply reduced from approximately 35 in previous years to 12 in 1943.[20] In early April, the Yankees played their Newark Bears farm club in nearby Newark. Then on to Yankee Stadium and Ebbets Field for a scheduled series of nine exhibition games against the National League Brooklyn Dodgers, Boston Braves, and New York Giants.[21] The Bombers lost all the games they were able to get in, with three of the nine cancelled due to rain, snow, or cold weather. In the meantime, manager McCarthy said, "We're not as bad as we look…. We need work, and some warm weather."[22]

Dottie and the Gordon children, as well as their 13-year-old babysitter, Phyllis Morgan, traveled by train from Oregon to New York. During their five-day, cross-country trip, nine-month-old Joey learned how to crawl, practicing his newly-discovered talents up and down the aisles of the Pullman cars. Years later, Phyllis wrote about living with the Gordons during the summer of 1943:

> We stayed in the Concourse Plaza Hotel in the Bronx, New York.... Joe and Dorothy [sic] were wonderful to me and kept me from being lonesome or homesick! Sometimes I was able to go to the baseball games and sit in the "wives" box while Dorothy [sic] stayed home with the children. Joe often invited other players who lived in our hotel to come and have a cocktail with him. He would open the window and blow on his duck call to "send the message" to come for a drink.[23]

The Yankees were scheduled to play Opening Day at home on April 21 against the Washington Senators, but due to rain, the game had to be rescheduled.[24] A day later, they opened to "wretched weather" and a disappointingly small turnout of "[o]nly 7,057, of whom 5,860 paid." It was reported that there were 832 civilian and 365 military guests of Yankees president Ed Barrow in attendance. Throughout the war years, military personnel in uniform were admitted for free.[25] Batting fourth in the order, Joe Gordon belted the Yankees' first home run of the season in the eighth inning, and the Bronx Bombers "stumbled home" with a 5–4 win over the Senators.[26]

By the end of April, only *two* American League players had hit home runs: Joe Gordon on April 22 and St. Louis Browns first baseman George McQuinn on April 25. Baseball was seeing the effects of the new balata ball used during 1943. Due to critical shortages in the United States, rubber had been banned for use in all items not essential to the war effort. Instead, a considerably less-elastic, rubber-like material called balata was used in the manufacture of official Spalding baseballs.[27] Fortunately, however, with the expansion of synthetic rubber production in the United States, baseballs would be back to normal in 1944. The Yankees played well, winning five of their seven games, to end April tied for first place with the Cleveland Indians. Joe Gordon had a fairly good start and was batting .276.

But by the latter part of May, the Yankees' hitting, particularly that of Joe Gordon, had taken a marked downturn. Before the game on May 22, Joe was batting just .205 and was reported as being "in the first serious slump of his career." He told writer John Cashman, "The only way I can account for my poor showing is to blame it on the weather. We have played four games since May 9. You hang around the hotel and get soggy and lose your swing. At least that's how it has hit me." In all of May, *nine* games had to be rescheduled due to inclement weather. Manager McCarthy didn't seem too concerned, telling Cashman, "Joe [Gordon] is doing some funny things at the plate. But such slumps will affect the greatest hitters; Ruth had them; Gehrig and DiMaggio suffered through them. Besides, Joe has not fallen down in the field; he still plays the best second base in the game."[28]

Losing four games in a row in late May, the Yankees relinquished the American League lead and dropped briefly back to third place. But they didn't remain there long. Regaining first place on May 30, they never looked back.

In early June, manager McCarthy decided to shake up the Yankees' batting order, bumping Gordon from fourth down to either fifth or sixth in the lineup and moving outfielder Johnny Lindell to the cleanup spot. Although Gordon's batting still wasn't up to par, he and shortstop Snuffy Stirnweiss "collaborated in a fancy fielding display around second base on June 10, handling a total of 22 chances without a flaw" at Philadelphia.[29]

Nineteen-forty-three would be the first year that the Major League Baseball All-Star Game was billed as a night game,[30] even though a year earlier, the twilight

All-Star Game had been delayed by weather and was played under the lights. This year the American League was the "home club," with the Philadelphia Athletics' octogenarian manager, Connie Mack, the host at Shibe Park. The American League All-Star team was piloted by Yankees manager Joe McCarthy, and the National League team by Cardinals manager Billy Southworth. Net proceeds from the game, in addition to contributions, were allocated for baseball's Ball and Bat Fund, to provide athletic equipment for America's servicemen.

Six Yankees had been selected for the American League team: Tiny Bonham, Spud Chandler, Bill Dickey, Joe Gordon, Charlie Keller, and Johnny Lindell. But manager McCarthy played *none* of his Yankees! Years later, Frederick G. Lieb wrote, "Six Bombers rode the bench." Lieb pointed out that "if McCarthy offended many persons by the way he stuck to [playing] his Yankees in earlier [All-Star] [G]ames, he literally thumbed his nose at his critics in the 1943 night contest in Philadelphia, when he got away with one of the most audacious gambles ever taken in baseball. Joe [McCarthy] proved he could win an All-Star Game without calling on a single Yankee."[31] Fortunately, McCarthy had Boston Red Sox second baseman Bobby Doerr, who belted a three-run homer in the second inning.

In previous Midsummer Classics, and in particular in 1937 and 1939, McCarthy had been criticized for playing too many of his Yankees.[32] Lieb called to mind a "one-liner" circulating at the time: "The National League could beat a team of American League All-Stars, but they can't beat the Yankees."[33] In 1943, McCarthy decided to show the critics that he could win by playing none of his Yankees! The American League won, 5–3, in what was described as "a rather unexciting All-Star contest."[34]

The Yankee players got a "big kick" out of being spectators.[35] When asked why he didn't use any of his Yankees—and known as a man of very few words—McCarthy answered, "I didn't need 'em." The game was broadcast by radio across the country, as well as to American and British servicemen and servicewomen around the world.[36]

Right before the Yankees headed out on their third and final western road trip of the season, Grantland Rice wrote a column titled "Yankee Manager Praises Joe Gordon as Ideal Type of Team Player." Rice had asked manager McCarthy what he thought made a winning ballclub, with "Marse Joe" answering, "First, good ball players. Second, team players. And I'd rather take a chance on the second group. I want players working for the club, not their own individual averages.... I haven't any interest in a .400 hitter, who hasn't some interest in the rest of the team and how the game comes out." Rice also asked McCarthy if he thought Joe Gordon's current batting average of .225 worried or upset the Flash. McCarthy assured the writer, "Not a bit. Gordon is strictly a team player—one of the best team players I ever saw.... His idea is to win ball games.... I know he would rather hit .200 if we won the pennant than to bat .400 and have us lose."[37]

By August 10, Joe Gordon hadn't missed a game all season. But during a force out at second base in the first inning of that day's game, a St. Louis runner slid hard into him and bowled him over. Joe had to retire from the game in the fifth inning with a strained back and sat out the next three games.[38]

On August 26, the *New York Journal-American* and the U.S. Treasury Department sponsored an "admission-by-war-bonds-only" exhibition game at the Polo Grounds, home of the New York Giants. The game featured an all-star team of players selected from among the three New York City clubs (the Yankees, Giants, and Dodgers). Before the game, showman Billy Rose staged an entertainment extravaganza packed with a "gala array of screen and radio stars."[39] Among the reported 40,000 spectators were approximately 300 wounded servicemen, home from the war. As part of the pregame show, Walter "The Big Train" Johnson pitched to fellow Hall of Famer Babe Ruth, until the slugger "parked one" high into the upper right field grandstands.[40] Also featured was a Hall of Fame "dream team" comprising "idols of yesteryear," suited up on the field: Duffy Lewis, Eddie Collins, Roger Bresnahan, Connie Mack, Red Murray, George Sisler, Honus Wagner, Frankie Frisch, Babe Ruth, Walter Johnson, Tris Speaker, and umpire Bill Klem.

The New York City All-Stars faced off against the U.S. Army's Camp Cumberland baseball team, "augmented by a flock of former major leaguers ... in [the] service," including Hank Greenberg, Birdie Tebbetts, Johnny Beazley, Billy Hitchcock, Sid Hudson, Enos Slaughter, and Tommy Hughes.[41] Playing for the New York City All-Stars, Joe Gordon belted a double off the left field wall and scored the first run of the game. The All-Stars won, 5–2. Arthur Daley wrote for his "Sports of the Times" column, "This was a great show ... [for] a great cause. Baseball can be proud."[42]

The Yankees put together an excellent August, September, and October, winning 43 of their 64 games, including a string of nine straight wins in September. A *New York Journal-American* article headlined "Gordon in Old Form at Plate," said, "As the Yankees continue their torrid pace toward their third straight pennant, they are greatly encouraged by the recent good stick work of Joe Gordon, their flashy second baseman."[43] By mid–September, the Yankees were leading the American League by almost a dozen games, with no signs of letting up. Winning a 14-inning game against the Detroit Tigers on September 25, they clinched their seventh American League pennant in eight years.[44] Joe Gordon's bat had finally come alive—evidenced by his .336 batting average and five home runs during September and October.

The Yankees wrapped up their 1943 season with a record of 98–56 (.636), finishing 13½ games ahead of the second-place Washington Senators. They had played 36 double-headers in 1943, partially because of fewer road trips due to restricted train travel during World War II and partially because of having to reschedule games cancelled because of weather. They were swept in seven of those double-headers. The Yankees played only three (scheduled) doubleheaders in 2024 and one in 2025!

Thanks to right fielder Bud Metheny's homer in the opener on October 2 and Joe Gordon's 17th and final round-tripper of the season in the nightcap, the Bombers achieved their goal of hitting 100 home runs for a record 19th consecutive year. Winning both games of the twin bill also set a new American League record of sweeping both games of 14 doubleheaders that season.[45] In addition to their home runs, the Yankees topped the American League in runs (669), triples (59), RBI (635), and bases on balls (624). Another *great* year!

The Yankees' pitching was definitely a strong suit. Five hurlers each won 12 or more games: 36-year-old Spud Chandler (career-best, league-leading 20–4 [.833] record and major league-leading 1.64 ERA), Tiny Bonham (15–8 and 2.27), Hank Borowy (14–9 and 2.82), rookie Charles "Butch" Wensloff (13–11 and 2.54), and reliever Johnny Murphy (12–4 and 2.51). Spud Chandler won the 1943 Most Valuable Player Award. As of this writing, he is the only Yankees pitcher who ever attained that honor.

Joe Gordon played in 152 games in 1943, recording his lowest batting statistics thus far in his six years in the majors: batting average (.249), home runs (17), runs (82), and RBI (69). However, he also recorded a career-high 98 walks. Although the authors found no record of him ever talking about the balata baseball used during 1943, it's conceivable that his batting suffered because of it. More likely, though, was what writer S.T. Wright alluded to in the *Morning Oregonian*: "Gordon has been restless because he is at home and in baseball [not in the military]."[46]

Due to wartime travel restrictions, the first three games of the 1943 World Series were played at Yankee Stadium, with all remaining games played in St. Louis. Notables in attendance for Game One on October 5 included: New York Governor Thomas E. Dewey; former U.S. Postmaster General James A. Farley; World War I fighter ace Captain Eddie Rickenbacker; former Brooklyn Dodgers president Lieutenant Colonel Larry MacPhail; Baseball Commissioner Kenesaw M. Landis; and former Yankees Babe Ruth, Lefty Gomez, U.S. Navy Lieutenant Buddy Hassett, Red Rolfe, and Bump Hadley.[47]

As Dottie Gordon had done during the 1938, 1939, and 1941 World Series, she brought along her movie camera to try to film her husband playing in the 1943 Series. (Apparently, Dottie had not filmed Joe during his disastrous 1942 World Series—or, if she did, she hadn't saved the film.) In 1943, Dottie had the chance to film Babe Ruth, sitting next to his wife, Claire, and signing autographs for a lucky serviceman during Game One.

Just like they'd done back in 1942, the Yankees toppled the Cardinals in Game One of the Series. Judson Bailey wrote in *The Oregonian*:

In this single-frame photograph obtained from Dottie Gordon's home movies filmed at Yankee Stadium during Game One of the 1943 World Series on October 5, Babe Ruth is sitting next to his wife, Claire, and signing autographs for some lucky serviceman (Gordon family collections).

Chapter 12. World Series Records (1943)

> In one of the oddest, most obstreperous games in the history of the [W]orld [S]eries the New York Yankees conquered the St. Louis Cardinals, 4 to 2, Tuesday before 68,676 fans who packed the [S]tadium for the opening contest of the 1943 [D]iamond [C]lassic. It was a triumph for the pitching prowess of Spurgeon (Spud) Chandler ... and a spectacular comeback for [s]econd [b]aseman Joe Gordon.... Gordon hit a ringing [reported as a 450-foot] home run in the fourth inning and gave a miraculous defensive performance during which he made eight assists to tie a [W]orld [S]eries record for second basemen and handled 12 fielding chances, just one short of the record.[48]

Jack Cuddy wrote, "Gordon performed so magnificently that [m]anager Billy Southworth of the Cards said after the game, '[W]ithout Gordon, we would have made at least four more base hits. That guy was like a net out there.'"[49]

Louis Effrat compared Gordon's play with that of the 1942 Series: "The Rock cast himself in a different role yesterday at the Stadium. For the classy Yankee second baseman was the undisputed hero of the opening game of the [W]orld [S]eries."[50]

Gordon's towering home run was unique. First, he was able to showcase his talents in front of his childhood idol, Babe Ruth. Second, in a statistic that no one knew at the time, Gordon would be the first "reigning" Most Valuable Player (of the previous year) to hit a home run in Game One of the following year's World Series. Gordon started one of the most exclusive "clubs" in baseball history, joined only by Reggie Jackson (1974), Joe Morgan (1976), Barry Bonds (2002), Albert Pujols (2006), and Cody Bellinger (2020).[51]

Duplicating the score of Game Two of the 1942 World Series, the Cardinals won, 4–3, on October 6, in a "stirring drama, the full story of which was unknown to most of the 68,578 fans."[52] Cardinals pitcher Mort Cooper and his teammate and brother, catcher Walker Cooper, had learned only a few hours before the game about the sudden death of their father, yet both chose to play.

Game Three on October 7 set a new World Series attendance record of 69,990, as the Yankees turned back the Cardinals, 6–2, sparked by their rookie third baseman, Billy Johnson's bases-loaded triple in the eighth inning.[53] Joe Gordon went 1-for-4, drove in a run, and handled five chances defensively.

The teams traveled by train to St. Louis's Sportsman's Park for Game Four on October 10. Yankees southpaw Marius Russo pitched the entire game and reportedly "carved out a great chunk of personal glory for himself ... before 36,196 sweltering fans by pitching and batting the New York Yankees to a 2-to-1 victory that gave New York a commanding three-games-to-one lead over the St. Louis Cardinals."[54] Joe Gordon's double in the fourth inning, followed by Dickey's single to score the Flash, yielded the Yankees' first run. The Cards tied the game in the seventh inning, which led to a noisy demonstration as the energized St. Louis fans "littered the outfield with hundreds of bottles and other debris." This halted play for several minutes while "park attendants carrying bushel baskets cleaned up the playing field." Hitting a long double in the eighth, Russo himself scored the Yankees' winning run after Tuck Stainback's sacrifice bunt and Frank Crosetti's sacrifice fly. Gordon handled 10 chances defensively in the game.

The Cardinals outhit the Yankees in Game Five, but Spud Chandler held his opponents at bay on runs to win, 2–0, on Charlie Keller's single followed by Bill Dickey's home run in the sixth inning. Chandler was "backed all the way by sparkling infield defense, particularly on the part of the crack second-base combination of Frank Crosetti and Joe Gordon."[55] Gordon handled 12 chances in Game Five, wrapping up the

1943 World Series with a new record of 43 total chances and no errors. Each full share of the 1943 World Series winner's pool was $6,139 per player.[56]

The elated Joe McCarthy's remarks after the Series perhaps said it all: "Like all my players, the big kick we get out of this [S]eries is that we beat the club which licked us last year. Beating any other National League team would never have given us the same amount of satisfaction. They [the Cardinals] made us look bad last year. This time I think we repaid the compliment. I think it was a very fine [S]eries."[57] Unknown at the time, this would be McCarthy's seventh and final world championship in nine World Series. (In 1929, McCarthy's Chicago Cubs lost the Series to the Philadelphia Athletics, and in 1942, the Yankees lost to the St. Louis Cardinals.)

It was reported that 12 new records were added to the books, and seven others tied during the 1943 Fall Classic. Of those, Joe Gordon topped the field by setting three new individual records and tying another with his "spectacular defensive play," as he "broke fielding performances of long standing."[58] The Flash's three new records included: (a) 43 fielding chances without an error, breaking the previous five-game World Series record for second basemen of 35 chances in 1910 by Eddie Collins of the Philadelphia Athletics[59]; (b) 20 putouts by a second baseman in a five-game Series, topping the record of 19 set by George Cutshaw of the Brooklyn Robins in 1916[60]; and (c) 23 assists, surpassing the 21 by Herman "Germany" Schaefer of the Detroit Tigers in 1907 and Johnny Evers of the Chicago Cubs in 1908.[61] Gordon also tied the previous record for most assists by a second baseman in a single World Series game, with his eight assists in Game One.[62]

After the Series, *United Press* staff correspondent Oscar Fraley wrote, "The hero's wreath could go to several of the Yankee players, but Joe Gordon certainly rates a chance to try it on for size. The second baseman played superbly throughout the [S]eries and more than made up for his miserable showing last year [1942]."[63]

Dan Parker wrote in *The Sporting News*, "THE HERO—Joe Gordon, whose brilliant fielding saved the Yankees countless times."[64] Marlowe Branagan penned in the *Oregon Journal*, "Joe Gordon draws our vote as the outstanding player in the past [1943] [S]eries. True enough, he didn't hit like his rookie third base mate, Billy Johnson, but recall, if you will, the marvelous plays he made on seemingly impossible stops and recall he hit an all-important home run in the first game which was the knockout punch to the Cards."[65]

After the final game, Joe Gordon talked with Grantland Rice about playing in a World Series:

> The trouble with a short [S]eries, is that you begin to run out of games too quickly, so you feel you have to get away to a flying start. If you do, you feel more relaxed. But if you don't, the strain begins to get worse each day and suddenly things begin to happen to you. If you make a mistake, it is always at a critical point, which makes it look worse. You'd be surprised how many people forget what has happened all through the season. They only remember what has happened in the [W]orld [S]eries. Last fall [1942], for example, I got away badly, striking out three times [in the first game]. I never recovered my balance. This season I got away well enough and had little to worry about. You can afford to make mistakes here and there through 154 games [of the regular season]. You can't in just a few games [of the World Series].[66]

In late December, Joe McCarthy was named *The Sporting News*' Major League Manager of the Year for 1943.[67] This was "Marse Joe's" third time honored (1936, 1938, and 1943). This year he was recognized for "his skill in overcoming war losses [of players going into the military] and putting together a team that won the American League pennant by a wide margin [13½ games] and defeated the Cardinals for the manager's seventh world championship [1932, 1936–1939, 1941, and 1943]."[68] In addition to winning the 1943 AL Most Valuable Player Award, Yankees pitcher Spud Chandler also was named *The Sporting News*' Major League Player of 1943.[69]

The Gordon family and their babysitter, Phyllis Morgan, headed for home from St. Louis.[70] Once back home, Joe took off for Central and Eastern Oregon with his brother, Jack, and friends for their annual deer, waterfowl, and pheasant hunts.[71]

While Joe was gone hunting, newspaper headlines across the country unexpectedly blared with, "Gordon Again to 'Quit' Ball" and "Joe Gordon Quits Baseball 'for Good.'" Earlier, when questioned about 1944 spring training, reportedly Joe had said, "Well, there won't be any spring training [in 1944]. And if there is, I won't be there. I'm tired of baseball."[72] The *New York Herald Tribune* also quoted him saying, "I'm just tired of baseball, that's all. And I'm tired of living conditions that go with baseball in the East. I don't like to be separated from my family, and I miss this Oregon climate in the summer time [sic]."[73] Gordon, however, had excelled during the 1943 World Series, which made media accounts of him quitting baseball even more puzzling. Yet nothing could be verified until he returned home from hunting.

It was reported that the Yankees' front office "expressed amazement at Gordon's abrupt declaration," with one club official saying, "[T]his is the first we've heard about it."[74] At the time, the club's 75-year-old president, Ed Barrow, was in the hospital, recovering from a heart attack suffered after the first game of the 1943 World Series.[75] Barrow issued this statement: "The club knows nothing whatever concerning Joe Gordon's retirement."[76]

Joe's wife, Dottie, also appeared to be totally in the dark about the rumors of her husband quitting, saying, "I'm sure Joe expects to play baseball if baseball is played next spring. He hasn't said anything to me that would indicate anything else."[77] Dan Daniel, however, wrote in *The Sporting News*, "Yes, Joe Gordon definitely has been thinking of the war for some two years and he may have something in mind."[78]

Back home from hunting, Joe disavowed all the media reports: "They got me wrong, that statement I made was misinterpreted."[79] He explained what he had meant was that he doubted that major league baseball could continue if the military kept drafting fathers. He also indicated that, if baseball was played in 1944, he hoped to do his spring training in Eugene, where weather conditions were decidedly better than the cold, winter climes of New Jersey: "I can get in better condition here at home and be ready to go when the season opens."[80]

Meanwhile, Commissioner Landis decreed, "Major league clubs will train in the North next year [1944] as they did in 1943."[81] Yankees manager Joe McCarthy also squelched the idea of his players training anywhere other than with the team: "The place for a ball player when the training season starts is with his ball club. I certainly won't favor letting any of our players do their own work at home."[82] Yet regarding Gordon training in Oregon, McCarthy said, "What difference would it make. Gordon is the sort of ball player who never gets out of shape. He could walk through that door tomorrow and play ball in a couple of days."[83]

Trying to explain how the media had misquoted him, Gordon telegraphed Dan Daniel: "Somebody asked me about the future of wartime baseball and I said that the father draft left us all wondering. This was garbled as it passed from mouth to mouth and I was made to say something I never uttered. If I am available and McCarthy still wants me, I will be back at second [base] for the Yankees next season [1944]."[84]

Then, suddenly, in mid–November, a photo of Gordon appeared in the *New York Herald Tribune,* titled "Joe Gordon a Walking Ad for 'Ducks Unlimited.'"[85] It showed him returning from hunting with a large string of ducks draped over his shoulder. The photo allegedly spawned a "flood of complaints to the War Department" from people insisting that "Gordon should have gone into some war work immediately after the [baseball] season's conclusion."[86] Yet what most people didn't know was that Gordon already was working in an essential war job at Ben Weber's livestock feed company in Eugene.[87]

The Yankees mailed a form letter to each of their players, wanting to know what their draft status and plans were for 1944. Upon receiving Gordon's response, Ed Barrow told writer Joe Williams, "Here's a letter from Joe Gordon. Says he's still 3-A [draft classification] and can't wait until the season starts…. You'd have to shoot him to keep him out of the game."[88]

In the meantime, wartime requirements changed, allowing more fathers of young children to be drafted. Quite unexpectedly, in mid–December, the soon-to-be 29-year-old Joe Gordon announced that he intended to enlist in the military. He said, "I plan to return to the Yankees after the war, if I'm still young enough."[89]

Gordon wired Ed Barrow the following message: "Will be unavailable for 1944 season, as expect to enter some branch of [A]rmed [S]ervice before start of spring training. Regards, Joe Gordon."[90] Barrow wanted more details about the "Gordon situation" and sent the Yankees' West Coast scout, Bill Essick, to Eugene to talk with Joe.[91] Gordon told Essick that his decision to enter the military was subject to passing the physical exam.[92] Passing the physical was considered somewhat questionable, as Gordon had a "trick hip" that sometimes had to be strapped when he played ball, an ankle that had been taped most of the 1943 season, and a chronic bad back.[93]

Some of Joe's close friends revealed that he had "recently expressed keen disappointment … that his age and family circumstances [three dependents] prevented him from joining the Naval Air Forces."[94] A commentary in *The Oregonian* indicated that he had visited the U.S. Navy Recruiting Office in Portland.[95] Clearly, ever since early 1942, Gordon had been focused on joining the military as a pilot, as evidenced by his accumulating flight hours and building time in different types of aircraft.

Joe's friends in Oregon, in addition to media accounts, indicated that he still retained some hope of becoming a pilot for the U.S. Navy or U.S. Army Air Forces. Dick Strite wrote in the *Eugene Register-Guard,* "But between you, me and the lamp post, the thing 'Trigger Joe' would like best of all, right now, would be one of Uncle Sam's 'buzz boys.'"[96]

Chapter 13

"G.I. Joe" (1944–1945)

Joseph Lowell Gordon was reclassified I-A for the military draft and passed his pre-induction physical exam on March 17, 1944, at the U.S. Armed Forces Induction Center in Portland, Oregon.[1] It was reported that he requested assignment with the U.S. Army Air Transport Command—but there were no guarantees.

After hearing about catcher Bill Dickey being accepted by the U.S. Navy and two days later Joe Gordon by the Army, manager Joe McCarthy reflected about the loss to the Yankees: "I guess that we have to take these things as they come. Dickey and Gordon—that's a ball club, isn't it?"[2] James P. Dawson, in the *New York Times*, quoted McCarthy saying, "I can say with emphasis we'll miss Gordon. He's the best second baseman I ever handled and a great player's player. I hope he'll come back safe and sound so that he can resume when this thing [the war] is over."[3]

While waiting for his call from Uncle Sam, Joe played basketball for the Man's Shop Guards, defending champions of Eugene's City Basketball League.[4] He also joined up with the town's semipro all-star baseball team for a four-inning practice game attracting more than 1,000 spectators.[5] The Flash belted a bases-loaded home run and drove in nine runs in the all-stars' victory over the Oregon Army Air Corps Fliers, 16–0.

Joseph L. Gordon was inducted into the U.S. Army on May 8, 1944.[6] He spent a week as a new recruit at the Monterey (California) Presidio Reception Center, receiving his immunizations, undergoing processing and classification, and putting in time at kitchen duty.[7] Yet the Flash was a celebrity, even in the Army, which meant that his days didn't end like other recruits'. At night, he was summoned to attend personal appearances and bond-selling campaigns at nearby military camps and civilian communities.

Gordon was assigned to the U.S. Army Air Transport Command, likely due to the efforts of Detroit Tigers catcher George "Birdie" Tebbetts. At the time, Lieutenant Tebbetts was helping to recruit major league and minor league ballplayers into the U.S. Army Air Corps (the permanent statutory organization).[8]

More than two dozen Yankees would serve their country during World War II,[9] including such well-known players as: Spud Chandler, Bill Dickey, Joe DiMaggio, Joe Gordon, Tommy Henrich, Charlie Keller, Johnny Murphy, Phil Rizzuto, and Red Ruffing. Most baseball players who served in the military or in national defense occupations during the war missed two or three full seasons, although some missed even more.

Joe Gordon arrived at the U.S. Army Air Transport Command Training Center at Camp Luna, New Mexico, on May 17, 1944, to begin his basic training.[10] Commissioner Landis notified Joe by mail that he'd been placed on the National Defense Service List (NDSL) of the New York Yankees.[11] An editorial in *The Sporting News* referred to the NDSL as "representing men [ballplayers] now in the service whose contracts are held by those organizations [ballclubs] and who, on returning from the war, are expected to report to them for assignment."[12]

Like many professional ballplayers serving in the armed forces, Joe Gordon's Military Occupational Classification (MOS) was Athletic Instructor.[13] Within a week of arriving, Joe was busy organizing and playing shortstop for Camp Luna's Airtrancos baseball team, in addition to fulfilling his basic training requirements.[14] In his first game, Gordon belted two singles and a double in five times at bat, in addition to fielding flawlessly in the Airtrancos' 10–4 victory over the Las Vegas (New Mexico) All-Stars.

During Joe's time at Camp Luna, the Airtrancos traveled to military bases in New Mexico, Texas, and Colorado, playing exhibition games against other U.S. Army Air Forces teams.[15] *The Sporting News* reported about Gordon playing ball at Camp Luna, "Since joining the Airtrancos, the Flash has been playing shortstop, fielding spectacularly and hitting like a demon. In a two-game series against the Santa Fe [New Mexico] M.P.'s on a recent week-end [sic], Gordon, batting in the cleanup spot, collected eight hits in 11 trips. The ex–Bomber had three-for-six in the first game, won by the Airtrancos, 22 to 16, and boasted a perfect five-for-five in the second tiff, also won by Camp Luna, 16 to 6."[16] It was reported that the Airtrancos won the Southwestern Semi-Pro

The Camp Luna Airtrancos baseball team poses for a photo at their ball diamond at the U.S. Army Air Transport Training Center at Camp Luna, New Mexico, in June or July 1944. Thanks to Sal Guerriero, son of pitcher Raffaele "Lefty" Guerriero, for providing us with this photo. Sal could positively identify only two players, both in the back row: Raffaele "Lefty" Guerriero (far left) and Joe Gordon (fourth from left).

Baseball Tournament at El Paso, Texas, beating the Hobbs (New Mexico) Army Airfield team, 6–0, in the championship game.[17]

Dottie and the Gordon children, Judy (almost four) and Joey (almost two), joined Joe at Camp Luna in late May. The family lived for a time in temporary housing on-base, then moved to the nearby town of Las Vegas, New Mexico, staying in furloughed servicemen's homes and apartments, as they became available.[18]

Shortly after Joe arrived at basic training, U.S. Army Chief of Staff General George C. Marshall issued orders for "breaking up the powerhouse sports teams at Army posts [Stateside] and sending the soldier-sports [sic] luminaries out to buck up morale in combat outfits."[19] This order would significantly affect Joe Gordon's future assignments in the military.

After just eight weeks at Camp Luna, Gordon's basic training was cut short, and he was transferred to the Army's Air Transport Command at Hamilton Field, California.[20] Dottie and the children returned home to Oregon.

But Gordon's stay at Hamilton was less than a week. Orders direct from Washington, D.C., stated that he be transferred, by air, to Hickam Field, Oahu, Territory of Hawaii, on loan to the U.S. Army's Seventh Air Force (also known as the 7th Army Air Force or 7th AAF).[21] The outfit must have wanted Joe in a big hurry, as other ballplayers destined for the 7th AAF baseball team had traveled from Seattle to Hawaii by ship, arriving in June.[22]

Joe arrived at Hickam Field on July 14, and, two days later, he was playing ball for the 7th AAF Fliers, one of the top service teams in Hawaii.[23] The team's roster comprised a veritable powerhouse of mostly major league and high minor league ballplayers: Rugger Ardizoia, Johnny Beazley, Bob Dillinger, Joe DiMaggio, Ferris Fain, Joe Gordon, Hal Hairston, Walt Judnich, Don Lang, Will Leonard, Al Lien, Dario Lodigiani, Mike McCormick, Jerry Priddy, Red Ruffing, Bill Schmidt, Charlie Silvera, and manager Tom Winsett.[24] The 7th AAF Fliers traveled throughout the Hawaiian Islands, drawing tremendous crowds to their games.[25]

In early 1937, Yankees manager Joe McCarthy had switched Joe Gordon from shortstop to second base, and from all appearances the Flash had never looked back. It's interesting, however, that Gordon played shortstop almost exclusively during his time in the military.[26] Although normally a right-handed batter, Joe also switched to batting left-handed during at least five games during the summer of 1944 in Hawaii. Batting lefty in one game, he logged two triples, a double, and a single, and drove in seven runs in five times at bat.[27] He later told writer Gene Karst in *The Sporting News*, "I went into a slump, so I decided to take advantage of the right field fence. It was a short one, and the wind usually blew in that direction.... I did pretty well for a while, but then they [the pitchers] caught up with my weakness as a lefthanded hitter, and I went back to the other side of the plate."[28]

At times, the caliber of baseball played in the military during World War II was beyond imagination. During one game in Hawaii against the Schofield Redlanders, it was reported that Gordon's 7th AAF Fliers teammate, St. Louis Browns center fielder Walt Judnich, hit *five* consecutive home runs, in addition to two singles and a double, going 8-for-8 for the Fliers' 30–2 victory.[29]

But being in the military was not all just fun and games. The ballplayers still had their regular Army jobs, in addition to playing ball. Gordon's duties included working at the motor pool, "latrine orderly," and "everything from salvaging cigarette butts to standing guard duty."[30]

In the summer of 1944, Joe also played ball for the 7th AAF Fighters (possibly a softball team), along with Captain Donal J. Broesamle, a pilot with the 7th AAF Fighter Command and a fellow graduate of the University of Oregon.[31] From early August through October 1944, Joe Gordon flew 15 times with Captain Broesamle, in both single- and multi-engine military aircraft (C-47-A, RA-24-B, and UC-78). The flight logs show that they flew to airfields throughout the Hawaiian Islands (Hickam, Kaneohe, Hilo, Maui, Kauai, and Molokai), with Private Joe Gordon logging 31.5 hours of dual time and 25 landings.[32]

Gordon and Broesamle also were so-called "charter members" of a small, informal group of eight enlisted men and officers, calling themselves the "Nimrod Association of the World," probably after Nimrod in Genesis 10:9: "He was a mighty hunter before the Lord." On their rare days off, the members hunted pheasants on Hawaii's Big Island and several other islands.[33]

In mid–September, the 7th AAF Fliers baseball team was said to be "going so strong that it has swept about everything."[34] An article in the *New York Herald Tribune* reported that they had won 60 games and lost only 13 in capturing the pennants of both the Central Pacific Area Service League and the Hawaii League.[35] Gordon finished the season with a "tremendous hitting burst" and was named one of the Central Pacific League All-Stars.[36]

Gene Karst quoted from an article appearing in the *Honolulu Star-Bulletin* extoling Joe Gordon's play as shortstop: "After watching The Flash work out here ... it just isn't possible to believe that anybody can come close to carrying Gordon's shoes.... Joe has pulled plays here that people would swear are impossible unless they had seen them with their own eyes." Gordon told Karst, "We had Don Lang, Bob Dillinger, Walter Judnich, Dario Lodigiani, Mike McCormick and Red Ruffing on our club. At one point we had a streak of about 31 straight wins. I think we finished with about an .800 average."[37]

That fall, Joe Gordon and a score of his 7th AAF Fliers teammates were selected to play the U.S. Navy in the 1944 Central Pacific Area Service World Series (also known as the "Army-Navy World Series" or the "Service World Series"). Meanwhile, the phenomenal success of the 7th AAF Fliers that summer and early fall had prompted Navy to bring in player reinforcements from all parts of the Pacific (including major leaguers Phil Rizzuto and Dom DiMaggio from Australia), in order to shore up Navy's all-stars, "supposedly on direct order from Adm. Nimitz himself."[38] Once the Army discovered what Navy was up to, they sent for last-minute reinforcements from the States. But Army's players would be thwarted in their attempt to get to Hawaii, when a football team commandeered their flight. Army's reinforcements had to travel by ship and arrived in Hawaii after the Army-Navy World Series was over.

The much-anticipated Army-Navy World Series was scheduled to begin on September 22, 1944, at Furlong Field, Pearl Harbor Naval Base, Oahu, Territory of Hawaii.[39] It was reported that "both service teams are as good as, if not better than, the majority of clubs in the major leagues in the States."[40]

The Series was originally scheduled as a best-of-seven-game competition, with all seven games to be played, regardless of outcome. Yet the games were so popular that, eventually, the Series was expanded, so more servicemen had the opportunity of watching three dozen major leaguers in action.[41]

The two teams weren't even close to being evenly matched—but that didn't matter—the goal was to entertain service members. Navy had gone to great lengths in mustering up a team of 36 players, of whom 27 were major leaguers. Army, on the other hand, was able to assemble only 28 players, including just nine major leaguers.[42] Yankees catcher Lieutenant Bill Dickey managed Navy's All-Stars, and Dodgers former outfielder Lieutenant "Long Tom" Winsett piloted Army's. Four brothers were on the rosters: Joe DiMaggio (Army) and Dominic DiMaggio (Navy), and Bill and George Dickey (both Navy). Although included on Army's roster, Staff Sergeant Joe DiMaggio was unable to play in the Series, because of recently released from the hospital after suffering from ulcers. He did get to watch most of the Army-Navy World Series, however.[43]

Army's All-Stars also included African American pitcher Harold "Hal" Hairston, who, after the war, would play for the Homestead Grays of the Negro National League. In the States, even in the military, African American ballplayers were rarely allowed to play on white teams, due to the deplorable laws and attitudes in the United States at the time. When stationed abroad, however, sometimes ways of thinking were more relaxed, and, occasionally, African American servicemen played on white teams, as in the case of Hairston in Hawaii.[44] Hal pitched in several games of the 1944 Army-Navy World Series, two and a half years before Jackie Robinson and Larry Doby broke the "color barrier" in the National and American Leagues in 1947.

The games were played exclusively for military personnel, but there was such a demand for seats that not everyone who wanted to attend could obtain tickets. Yet it was reported how some enterprising Seabees solved their dearth of tickets for the games at Furlong Field: "[A]fter a conference, they brought in a bulldozer, piled up dirt and built their own stands. Then they put a guard on the stands throughout the night, and the next afternoon had the best seats in the park."[45]

During pregame ceremonies at the opener of the Army-Navy World Series on September 22, the Commander in Chief of the Pacific Fleet, Admiral Chester W. Nimitz, led the salute to the colors during the National Anthem and gave a speech to the approximately 20,000 spectators, before tossing out the first ball. Armed Forces Radio broadcast the games to servicemen both at sea and stationed on forward-island bases in the Pacific.

Navy shut out Army, 5–0, in the first game, "spearheaded by the brilliant, airtight [four-hit] pitching of Virgil Trucks." Army's Joe Gordon "turned the fielding gem of the day, starting a triple play in the eighth inning, when, playing shortstop, he pulled down a line drive, stepped on second and threw to first base for a triple killing [scored as 6–6–3]."[46] Joe DiMaggio would later talk about Gordon playing shortstop in Hawaii: "If you think he was good at second [base], wait until you see him at short."[47]

Navy also won the next three games, 8–2, 4–3, and 10–5, to clinch the "mythical championship."[48] But they were not done yet. Navy also took Games Five and Six, 12–2 and 6–4, before Army finally salvaged the seventh game of the Series, 5–3. Attendance was reported as ranging from approximately 10,000 to 20,000 servicemen at each of the seven games played on the Island of Oahu.

Traveling to Kahului, Maui, for Games Eight and Nine, Navy shut out Army, 11–0, before Army squeaked by with their second victory of the series, 6–5, on a game-winning run scored by Joe Gordon in the ninth inning.[49] At Hilo on the Island of Hawaii, the tenth game went to a 6-to-6 tie in 14 innings, before being called because of approaching darkness. The last game was played at Kalaheo, Kauai, drawing an estimated 20,000 spectators, with Navy winning, 6–5, in 10 innings. The final tally was Navy eight games, Army two, and one game tied.

Private Joe Gordon was flown back to the States at the end of October 1944, to resume his assignment with the U.S. Army Air Transport Command at Hamilton Field, California. After six months of active duty, he was granted a 15-day furlough to visit his family in Oregon.[50]

However, Dottie wasn't sure when to expect him home on leave. Daughter Judy, then just four years old, still vividly remembers the night when she and her mother and two-year-old brother Joey were heading home from town in their car. Gas was very scarce during the war, so they hadn't ventured far. Customary of the times, Dottie stopped to give a ride to a hitchhiking serviceman in uniform, who appeared in the car's headlights, trudging up their dark country lane lugging a big duffle bag. It was a *huge* surprise for the kids when they finally realized it was their Dad—home for a visit!

After his furlough, Gordon served as Athletic Instructor in the Physical Training and Special Services Program of Hamilton's Air Transport Command.[51] In a letter to his mother, Joe wrote, "Right now I am manager, coach, general flunky & what not of the ball team, and besides my classes, am trying to get some more ball players from the big shots, get what players we have off work, & in shape, & build a ball field, all at once."[52]

Sergeant Ed Dooley wrote in the *Sunday Oregonian*, "The former New York star [Joe Gordon] is considered by his GI constituents at Hamilton [F]ield as a 'regular guy,' one of the most popular men in his outfit. You'll find him pulling his regular kitchen police detail with the rest of the GIs, and he has won 'expert' many times on the latrine firing line with his accurate mop and scrub-brush work—a weekly assignment for him."[53]

Dottie and the children joined Joe in California in early January. The family couldn't find a place to rent, so they ended up buying a 988-square-foot, two-bedroom, one-bath home in the Sun Valley neighborhood of San Rafael.[54]

The Hamilton Field Flyers (also written as Fliers in the media) were a young team, with only two major leaguers, Private First Class Joe Gordon and his good friend, Philadelphia Phillies outfielder Sergeant Joe Marty.[55] The Flyers played the Oakland Oaks, San Francisco Seals, and Sacramento Solons during Pacific Coast League spring training, even winning a few games.[56]

Private Gordon kept busy, both on and off base. He was placed in charge of Hamilton Field's "March of Dimes" program.[57] He attended the 16th Annual Hot Stove League[58] gathering of the Alameda (California) Elks, along with Ty Cobb, Tony Lazzeri, and scores of other ballplayers.[59] Joe also appeared in an auditorium program and visited bedridden patients at the U.S. Naval Hospital at Mare Island, California, along with Ty Cobb, Oscar Vitt, Tony Lazzeri, Lefty O'Doul, Dolph Camilli, Joe Marty, and other "world famous baseball players of the past and present baseball world."[60] He also played shortstop and managed an Army Air Forces All-Stars team for a benefit game at Seals Stadium in San Francisco, against the Sherry Liquors All-Stars (also known as the "Yankees of the West"), with all receipts going toward purchasing athletic equipment for service teams.[61]

But soon, Gordon's comparatively tranquil life serving in the States would change. On April 25, 1945, the AFATC (Air Forces Air Transport Command) Enlisted Personnel Branch of the U.S. War Department in Washington, D.C., sent a "Restricted" message to the Commanding General, Pacific Division Air Transport Command at Hamilton Field, directing that Private Joe Gordon be transferred to Hickam Field, Oahu, Territory of Hawaii.[62]

Gordon's commanding officer at Hamilton, Colonel Curtis A. Keen, replied to the directive with a strongly worded objection, saying, in part:

Chapter 13. "G.I. Joe" (1944–1945)

> There is every possible military objection to transferring Private Joe Gordon.... Subject Enlisted Man cannot be spared from the Physical Training Section of this Command without a suitable replacement and even with a suitable replacement as far as his MOS is concerned, this Command would suffer considerable loss from a morale standpoint if it were generally known that he had been taken from his present assignment[,] where he is doing a good job[,] for assignment to some other organization primarily because he is an outstanding ball player.... We request that subject Enlisted Man be permitted to remain at this Station until made available by this Command on regular rotation on the basis of his MOS and performance as a soldier, rather than for his publicity value.[63]

But rank won out, and Gordon, who by then had been promoted to Corporal, departed Hamilton Field on May 14 on his way back to Hawaii.[64] He played ball for Army's Wheeler Field Wingmen the short time he was there.[65] On June 16, 1945, Joe Gordon and 11 other members of their team played their final game for the Wingmen.[66]

Almost a month later, Joe wrote home from Tinian, one of the two largest islands in the Northern Mariana Islands:

> This is about the first chance I've had to mail a letter for over two weeks now, as we have been riding the bounding main on a troop ship. We saw land once before we got here—Eniwetok [Enewetak Atoll], on July 4, but didn't get off. That ride was some experience.... Hot, dirty, sweaty, crowded—below two decks, bunks five high—alerts, drills, guard duty....
>
> Well, we got in Saipan a couple of days ago, and then they flew some of us over here to Tinian where we are now attached to the 58th Bomb Wing which was the old 20th AAF in China & India. The bunch I am with were supposed to go to Guam, but something came up, and we may go in a few weeks or not at all....
>
> We live in a big tent with coral & dirt floor or I should say ground & sleep on canvas cots.... Yesterday it rained hard & we had a river right thru the middle of the tent, so we had to go dig a trench around us.
>
> Yesterday we watched the B29s take off for Japan—less than 1500 mi. away, & then later sweated them back in. It was a sight I will never forget.[67]

Saipan, Tinian, and the nearby island of Guam had been captured (or, in the case of Guam, recaptured) by Allied forces during critical battles of World War II the summer of 1944. Tinian became the busiest airbase of the entire war, with its long runways enabling U.S. Army Air Forces B–29 *Superfortress* bombers within strategic reach of the Philippines, Ryukyu Islands (including Okinawa), and mainland Japan itself.

The 20th AAF assembled three baseball teams, two on Tinian and one on close by Saipan: the 58th Bombardment Wing Wingmen based at West Field, Tinian, and managed by Captain "Birdie" Tebbetts; the 313th Bombardment Wing Flyers at North Field, Tinian, managed by Corporal Lew Riggs; and the 73rd Bombardment Wing Bombers at Isley Field, Saipan, managed by Lieutenant "Buster" Mills.

Playing ball in the Northern Mariana Islands was not like playing in Hawaii or the States. The ballplayers had to help build their own ball diamonds, "leveling out the cane fields, and digging out coral rocks."[68] Gordon wrote home about their ballpark:

> First we fixed up our own barracks & clubhouse with bomb crates for lockers; then we went to work on a ball field. It was some job, but it finally is beginning to look like something. The main trouble is the coral—it just seems to keep coming up, so we had to have loads of dirt & spread it. The ground work [*sic*] is about done now & starting today [July 23] we are putting up bleachers and fences, so it will be a pretty nice park soon. We open up on it next Sunday [July 29] against the other club stationed here [the 313th Bombardment Wing Flyers].[69]

The 58th Bombardment Wing Wingmen ballplayers based at West Field, Tinian, lined up for a team photograph in the summer of 1945. Some of the unidentified players may also be from the 313th Bombardment Wing Flyers based at North Field, Tinian. Although the late Charlie Silvera is not in the photograph himself, many thanks go to him, as he played for the 73rd Bombardment Wing Bombers based on nearby Saipan, and thus could identify some of the players for us. Front: unknown. Middle row, from left: Birdie Tebbetts, Enos Slaughter, Stan Rojek (73rd Bombardment Wing Bombers), unknown, Roy Pitter, Art Lilly, Don Lang, Chuck Stevens, unknown, unknown. Back row, from left: unknown, unknown, unknown, Joe Gordon, unknown, unknown, George Gill, Joe Marty, Howie Pollet, and Billy Hitchcock (Gordon family collections).

When on their "home" islands of Tinian or Saipan, the ballplayers still had their regular Army jobs to fulfill in addition to playing ball. Gordon also learned how to drive large, earth-moving equipment, while trying to keep their ball field in decent playing condition.

By late July, the three teams were ready to play exhibition ball for Uncle Sam's forward-area troops. Even on such rough, makeshift ball fields, the games drew thousands of wildly appreciative G.I.s, eager to see well-known major and minor leaguers in action. The three teams kicked off a multi-game round-robin series on July 27 on Saipan.[70] Playing shortstop for the 58th Bombardment Wing Wingmen, Joe Gordon belted a home run in the opening game, although his team lost to the 73rd Bombardment Wing Bombers, 4–3.[71]

A few days later, Corporal Gordon, under the guise of being a newspaper correspondent, was flown, secretively, to the island of Guam, to play in a softball game between the News Correspondents and the Press Censors of Admiral Nimitz's Advanced Pacific Fleet Headquarters.[72] Introduced as "Joe Hollister" of the *Philadelphia Bulletin*, he was sent in to pinch-hit for the Correspondents. Before being "exposed" as an impostor, he fouled off the first pitch, high upon a hill way beyond the ball field. The Press Censors immediately became suspicious and recognized that they had a celebrity in their midst. They stopped the game, and Gordon was ejected. The Censors went on to beat the Correspondents, 22–13.[73]

When his 58th Wing Wingmen team wasn't playing, sometimes Joe Gordon umpired the 73rd Wing Bombers vs. 313th Wing Flyers games during the summer and fall of 1945 in the Northern Mariana Islands. We are unable to identify the officer standing next to Joe (Gordon family collections).

The three 20th AAF baseball teams flew from island to island, playing exhibition ball for the troops. As weather permitted, they managed to get in about 27 games on the islands of Saipan, Tinian, Iwo Jima, and Guam. It was estimated that about 180,000 servicemen had the rare opportunity of watching approximately four dozen major and minor league ballplayers playing ball. Some of the accounts on Gary Bedingfield's www.baseballinwartime.com website and in his book, *Baseball in Hawaii During World War II*, give graphic descriptions of the conditions under which some of their games were played.[74]

On August 6, and most likely unbeknownst to most of the ballplayers stationed on Saipan and Tinian, the *Enola Gay B-29 Superfortress*, piloted by Colonel Paul W. Tibbets, Jr., took off from North Field, Tinian, loaded with the *Little Boy* atomic bomb, which was dropped over Hiroshima, Japan. On August 9, the *Bockscar B-29 Superfortress*, piloted by Major Charles W. Sweeney, took off, also from North Field, Tinian, to drop the *Fat Man* plutonium bomb over Nagasaki, Japan. Two days later, Joe Gordon wrote home:

> We heard all the big peace news last nite—and most of the guys went wild, and surely you can't blame them.... [I]t was the best news ever heard, if it goes thru the big shots O.K. But some of us have our doubts if it will be accepted. There are too many people who don't want it to end. Boy, if they left it up to the GIs, it would be over now. All we can do now is hope & hope that it works out the right way, and that way is peace. It will surely save lives.[75]

At 7:00 P.M. on August 14, 1945, President Harry S. Truman summoned reporters to the White House to announce the unconditional surrender of Japan.[76] Soon after Joe Gordon heard the news, he again wrote home: "Well, the big news finally came after hours and days of waiting and hoping with ears glued to the radio. As far as all the guys

This Army Air Forces flyer advertises the 20th AAF All Stars POA (Pacific Ocean Areas) games played on Tinian and Iwo Jima in late August and early September 1945 (Gordon family collections).

out here are concerned, it was the best news ever heard. Now we have something to look forward to—going home. Don't know when or how, but we'll get there."[77]

The three 20th AAF baseball teams remained in the Central Pacific another two months, playing exhibition games for our returning troops and liberated prisoners

Chapter 13. "G.I. Joe" (1944–1945)

of war.[78] In August, two teams of 20th AAF All Stars were selected, one composed of mostly American League players and the other mostly National Leaguers, to play in the "AAF All Stars POA (Pacific Ocean Areas) Series."[79] The first game was played on Tinian on August 26.[80]

Joe Gordon wrote home the following day: "We finally finished our season here on Tinian yesterday with an American-National League all-star game. We [American League] won 3–2 in a real good ball game. There was some crowd, too; everyone from Privates to three-star Generals was there. We are to leave for Iwo Jima today for our week's series there. Then we are to go to Guam to end the season around Sept. 20th. From then on it is anybody's guess what will happen to us."[81]

The second AAF All Stars POA game was played on September 2 on the island of Iwo Jima, with the National Leaguers beating the American Leaguers, 5–1.[82] Iwo Jima is one of the Volcano Islands, located about halfway between the Northern Mariana Islands and Japan. After a horrific five-week battle, the island had been captured by the Americans in late March 1945. The battle was immortalized by a legendary photo of six U.S. Marines raising the Stars and Stripes atop Mount Suribachi. However, it was estimated that approximately 3,000 enemy fighters remained hidden in caves and tunnels on the island.

Boston Braves outfielder/first baseman Max West's vivid memories of playing ball on Iwo Jima are described in Todd W. Anton's book, *No Greater Love: Life Stories from the Men Who Saved Baseball*.[83] Departing Tinian early one morning in the dark, the teams were flown to Iwo Jima. Enemy snipers still hiding on the island necessitated the ballplayers being housed in dirt-covered Quonset huts, set in deep pits at the end of the runway. The U.S. Navy Seabees worked all night, bulldozing a ball field out of the island's rock and sand. In his book, *Birdie: Confessions of a Baseball Nomad*, Tebbetts described their playing field: "The boundary of left field was the Pacific Ocean. The boundary of center field was the Pacific Ocean. The boundary of right field was the Pacific Ocean."[84] The Seabees chalked the batter's box and baselines and set out the bases and home plate. Empty bomb crates and packing cases were used for seating. There was no backstop.

U.S. Marine Corps marksmen were posted in the outfield to protect the ballplayers in case of enemy snipers. As West noted, "We had our helmets with us on the bench. Some guys wanted to wear them in the outfield."[85] The players' names and their former teams were announced as they lined up on the first base line, to the cheers of what Birdie Tebbetts described as "12,000 grimy, cheering, gun-toting, battle-torn soldiers and marines."[86] Max West didn't remember who won the game, but he did recall, "It was called the greatest game ever played or something like that."[87] Sergeant Stan Rojek, one of the players with the 73rd Wing Bombers, later told writer Cy Kritzer that, everywhere they played, the soldiers' enthusiasm made it like "playing before 80,000 in Yankee Stadium. We gave everything we had. There was no loafing or protecting yourself. Not before those crowds."[88]

Joe Gordon wrote home about the games they played on Iwo Jima: "We got back from Iwo [Jima] yesterday [September 4]—played four games and they [the troops] really turned out in masse. There's not much for the guys to do up there—it's just a small place, and hot and dusty—no trees or grass. Saw a lot of guys I knew from Holladay [Grammar School] thru [University of] Oregon—CB's, Army & Navy…. Today we move out of here for Guam for the last two weeks of the season. From then on, we don't know what the score is."[89]

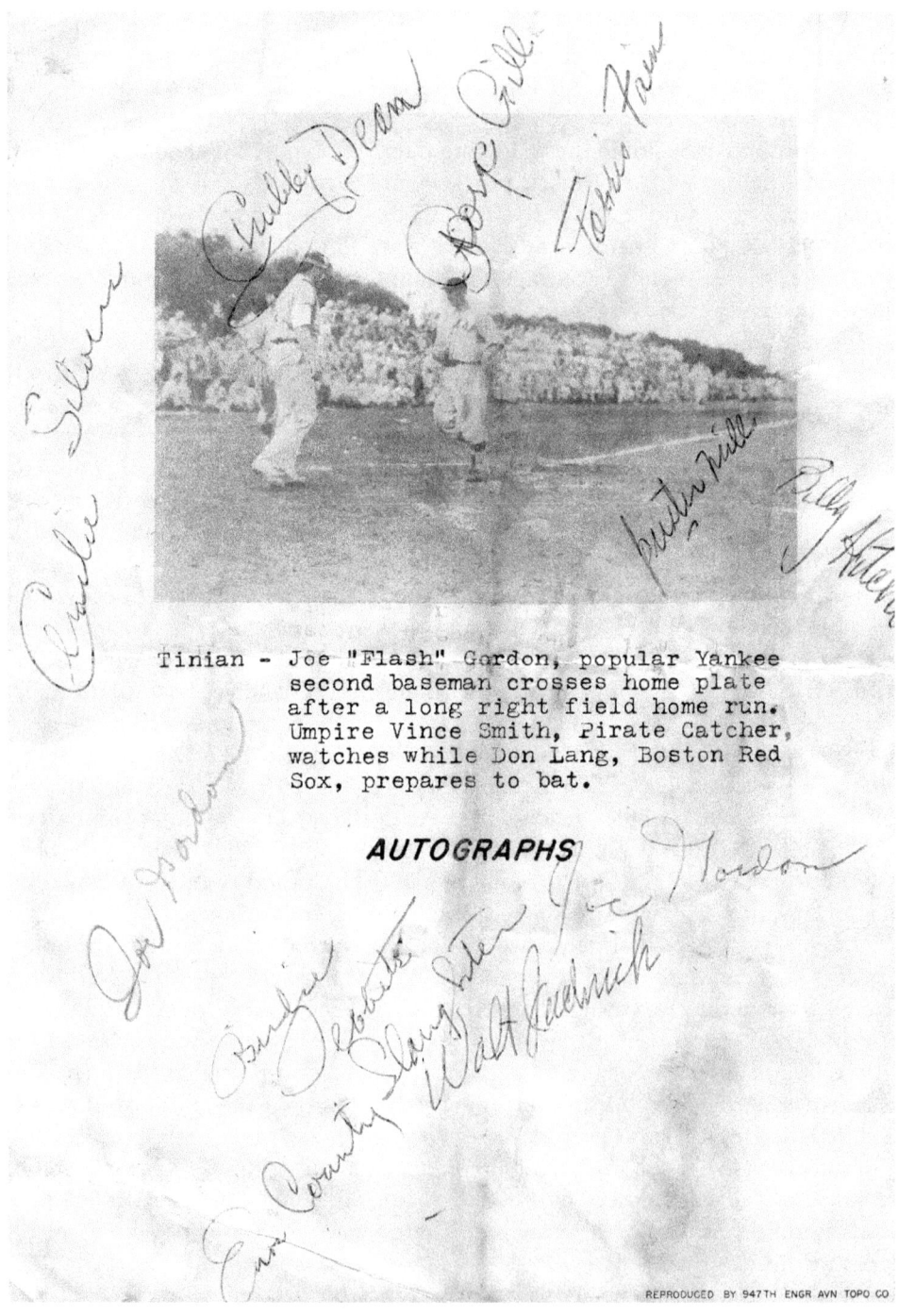

Some of the ballplayers autographed the back of this USASTAF Special Services Major League Baseball Stars flyer advertising their final game on Guam in late September 1945. Flyers autographs include Joe Gordon, Billy Hitchcock, Birdie Tebbetts, Enos Slaughter, and Walt Judnich. Wingmen autographs include Charlie Silvera, Chubby Dean, George Gill, Ferris Fain, and Buster Mills. The photograph on the flyer is of Joe Gordon crossing home plate after hitting a home run in a previous game on the Northern Mariana Islands (Gordon family collections).

Chapter 13. "G.I. Joe" (1944–1945)

The ballplayers were flown to the nearby island of Guam and divided onto two teams of 22 players each, called the Flyers and the Wingmen.[90] By then, they were under the auspices of the U.S. Army Strategic Air Forces (USASTAF) Special Services, headquartered on Guam. They were scheduled to play eight games, although the rain and mud permitted only three.[91] Gordon wrote, "It's hard to keep busy and not go nutty around here."[92]

Their playing season concluded with an American Leaguers versus National Leaguers all-star game, after which Joe wrote, "We finished up our last game finally, losing to the Nat'l [L]eague 7–2. I managed to hit a homer to wind up the season. Boy we are all sure glad it's over."[93]

The players headed home for the States on the U.S. Navy attack transport ship U.S.S. *Cecil*,[94] departing Guam on October 17 and arriving at Los Angeles on November 2, 1945.[95] Corporal Joseph L. Gordon reported to the Separation Center at Camp Beale, California, and received his Honorable Discharge from the U.S. Army on November 14, 1945.[96]

Dottie and the Gordon children had been living in San Rafael, California, since early 1945. Once Joe got home, the family drove to Oregon to visit friends in Eugene and Joe's mother in Portland. Then Joe took off on a much-anticipated hunting trip with his buddies.[97]

After the war, Joe didn't talk much about his time spent in the Army, except for the many friends he made there. His children, however, do remember him telling stories

Some of the 20th AAF ballplayers pose for a photograph on the ship returning home to the United States in October/November 1945. Front row, from left: Chuck Stevens and Stan Rojek. Back row, from left: Lew Riggs, Dario Lodigiani, Joe Gordon, and unknown. Thanks to the late Charlie Silvera for identifying the players for us (Gordon family collections).

about learning to drive heavy, earth-moving equipment while maintaining their ball fields, a job he loved and would put to good use years later.

After Gordon was discharged from the Army, the rumors and second guessing about him began popping up again in the media. There was much speculation about what Yankees manager Joe McCarthy was going to do with two second basemen: Snuffy Stirnweiss and Joe Gordon.[98] Stirnweiss had played the entire 1944 and 1945 seasons, leading the American League and the majors in several categories both years, in addition to being voted fourth and third place, respectively, in Most Valuable Player Award balloting.

Even so, one thing was hoped to be true—that the Selective Training and Service Act of 1940, and its subsequent additions and alterations, would ensure that ballplayers returning from the military were reinstated to their pre-war positions and salaries, or equivalents, at least for the 1946 baseball season.[99]

Despite the challenges of being away from his family and juggling war responsibilities for the previous year and a half, new challenges awaited Joe Gordon upon his return to the New York Yankees in 1946. How he responded to those challenges would either make or break his legacy in baseball.

Chapter 14

GOODBYE, NEW YORK (1946)

Few athletes could have bounced back after the year Joe Gordon experienced in 1946. Although rarely one to complain, Joe wrote to his mother in mid-August, telling her, "I will sure be glad when this year is over, as it has been the worst I have ever spent in baseball."[1]

This also would be the first year that Dottie Gordon did not compile a scrapbook chronicling her husband's baseball career. Moreover, she would not return to keeping scrapbooks until 1951–1952, when Joe was managing the Pacific Coast League Sacramento Solons. Fortunately, though, from her home in Portland, Oregon, Joe's mother, Louise, faithfully continued her "mission" of compiling scrapbooks throughout her son's entire playing career.

Looking back, it doesn't seem possible that Joe "Flash" Gordon could have experienced such a bad year. However, newspaper and magazine articles, personal letters from Joe to his mother, later accounts by Joe himself, and the recollections of his two children remain to tell the story of what took place that fateful year.

In January 1945, the New York Yankees had been sold by the administrators of Colonel Jacob Ruppert's estate, along with Yankee Stadium, the club's minor league franchises, and title to several hundred ballplayers. It was reported that the new owners, Larry MacPhail, Del Webb, and Dan Topping, purchased the club for the wartime bargain price of $2.8 million.

Ever since late 1920, Ed Barrow had served in the dual capacity as the Yankees' business manager and general manager, and then as club president in the six years since owner Jacob Ruppert had passed away in January 1939.[2] Barrow was quoted several times saying, "Only over my dead body will (Larry) MacPhail buy the Yankees."[3] Yet he had little control over the matter, since he was just a minority (10 percent) stockholder.

With the sale of the Yankees came many changes in the organization's front office and Yankee Stadium itself. The outspoken, flamboyant, and at times hot-tempered Larry MacPhail (also known as the "Roaring Redhead") became a very engaged president of the Yankees. He took full charge of the club from the reserved, conservative, 76-year-old Ed Barrow.[4]

The new owners relegated Barrow to a mostly symbolic advisory position as Chairman of the Board of Directors, which he would resign from effective December 31, 1946.[5] In his book, *My Fifty Years in Baseball*, Barrow reflected on the sale of the club: "I would have preferred someone else [had bought it]. After all, the best years of my life had been put into the Yankees. I had pride in what they stood for."[6]

Despite rumors to the contrary, Larry MacPhail vowed repeatedly that Joe McCarthy would be kept on as the Yankees' field manager.[7] On the other hand, as Arthur Daley forewarned in the *New York Times*, "McCarthy and MacPhail are as different as night and day. They may even be as insoluble as oil and water."[8]

Minus many of their pre-war stars still in the military, the Yankees finished fourth in 1945. Soon after season's end, it was reported that Larry MacPhail was in Havana, Cuba, checking out hotel accommodations and negotiating with Cuban sports officials regarding the Yankees playing spring training exhibition games there in early 1946.[9] MacPhail had done this before as president and general manager of the 1941 Brooklyn Dodgers.[10] But this time the negotiations fell through, likely due to financial considerations.[11]

Two weeks later, MacPhail announced that the Yankees would conduct dual spring training camps in 1946, one based at St. Petersburg, Florida, and the other across Tampa Bay at Bradenton. Two locations were necessary because of the large number of players (approximately 70) expected to report to spring training, in addition to the tight post-war housing situation.[12] The two camps would train independently and even barnstorm north separately. Joe McCarthy would be in charge of the headquarters camp at St. Petersburg, which consisted mostly of players returning from military service. He also would oversee the Bradenton camp, with coach Johnny Neun directing the activities there.[13]

MacPhail planned on installing stadium lights and kicking off night games in 1946, in addition to making major improvements to Yankee Stadium itself. Plans for adding some 10,000 box seats and double-decking the bleachers were expected to raise the seating capacity to about 80,000.[14]

Joe Gordon was honorably discharged from the U.S. Army in mid–November 1945. Once back home in Oregon, he planned on spending the next three months reconnecting with his family and friends, having been gone the past year and a half.

At least twice during the Flash's major league career (right before the 1942 World Series and again late fall of 1943), rumors had run the gamut regarding him quitting baseball.[15] After being discharged from the Army, however, it was reported that Joe was eager to play ball again.[16]

It was also reported that Gordon had looked as good as ever while playing ball for the Army during 1944 and 1945. He soon began his own physical fitness program at home in Oregon, playing handball and refereeing basketball games, figuring he had plenty of time to get in shape before reporting to Yankees spring training, which normally began around the first of March.[17]

During the winter of 1945–1946, Joe and two of his close friends, Walter Hummel and Bob Shisler, purchased the R.A. Babb Hardware Co. located in downtown Eugene, later renaming it Joe Gordon Hardware. Besides being a hardware store, it also became a favorite hangout for local sportsmen, hunters, and fishermen.[18]

In January 1946, the Yankees announced that for the first time in two decades, the players' wives would not be invited to stay with the team during spring training. The shortage of hotel beds in Florida affected not only the Yankees, but other major league clubs as well. Most of Florida's hotels had been taken over by the U.S. Government in 1942 and converted into military barracks and training facilities.[19]

Also to the dismay of a few players, Larry MacPhail announced that the Yankees would be traveling by air instead of rail to the more distant cities (Chicago, Cleveland, Detroit, and St. Louis) during the 1946 season.

As the days counted down, MacPhail began exploring options on how to offset some of the club's spring training expenses. A small paragraph appeared in *The Sporting*

News in late December, noting, "Larry is said to be on his way to Panama, to talk terms for a series [of games] with the Yankees down there in February."[20]

Preliminary details of the Panama venture hit the newsstands in early January 1946.[21] The schedule would eventually include the Yankees spending a full three weeks in Panama, with training to begin there on February 10, almost three weeks earlier than usual.[22] Joe McCarthy was in charge of the Panama contingent, which was composed of almost all of the Yankees returning from military service.

The New York sportswriters had plenty to say about MacPhail's plans. In a column titled "Join MacPhail and See the World," widely-read *New York Herald Tribune* writer Red Smith penned, "This isn't a training trip. It's a circus tour. It is the sort of hippodrome stunt which has been anticipated ever since MacPhail threw in with the once staid Yankees."[23] John Drebinger of the *New York Times* described MacPhail's plans as "one of the most pretentious spring training campaigns ever undertaken by a major league ball club."[24]

Joe Gordon was reinstated from the National Defense Service List to the New York Yankees' active players list on January 21, 1946. Thanks to the Selective Training and Service Act of 1940 (also known as the G.I. Bill), Gordon signed his contract with the Yankees for $20,000, the same salary that he'd received in 1943 before joining the military.[25]

Meanwhile, in anticipation of the upcoming baseball season, manager McCarthy faced a dilemma—who would play second base, Joe Gordon or Snuffy Stirnweiss? While Gordon was in the Army during 1944 and 1945, Stirnweiss had been the Yankees' second baseman and led the American League in runs, hits, triples, and stolen bases, as well as in batting average in 1945. On the other hand, before drafted by Uncle Sam, Gordon had played six seasons as the Yankees' keystoner, been selected for five All-Star Games, and won the 1942 Most Valuable Player Award.

Once assembled at Miami, Florida, the Yankees' contingent heading to Panama included: manager Joe McCarthy, road secretary Arthur Patterson, coach John Schulte, clubhouse/equipment manager Pete Sheehy, trainer Ed Froelich, 33 ballplayers, and eight sportswriters. They departed on two Pan-American DC–4 airplanes in the early-morning hours of February 9.[26] Landing in the Canal Zone among the war planes parked at Albrook Army Airfield, the Yankees received a warm welcome from U.S. military and Panamanian dignitaries.[27] Joe McCarthy wasted no time—training would begin the following morning.

The Yankees paid the U.S. Army $8.50 per day for room and board for each member of the team housed at Albrook, in addition to paying to use the base's vehicles for transportation. The players were housed in the modern three-story officers' living quarters, greeted by a huge "Home of the Yankees" banner posted out front. Another sign announced "Yankee Headquarters" at a barracks converted into the players' dressing room. A sign over the mess-hall door proclaimed, "Through these portals pass the greatest ball players in the world." The food was excellent, with plenty of butter, sugar, and steaks—luxuries either in very short supply or nonexistent during the war years.[28]

In 2014, author Judy Gordon had the privilege of talking on the phone with former Yankees catcher Charlie Silvera on his 90th birthday. Charlie gave a colorful account of the team's three weeks in Panama: "We liked it down there. It was like getting out of jail [the Army or Navy]. We were mostly ex-service guys and lived at the Officers' Club. McCarthy didn't put any restrictions on us. It was relaxed with no pressure. It was just like a vacation—[that is] until we got back to Florida. Your dad was very instrumental in helping me get to the major leagues. I owe him an awful lot."29

Training began the following day at nearby Balboa Stadium in the Canal Zone. The weather was hot and humid under a "broiling sun." About 700 onlookers showed up to watch the Yankees work out. After a little more than an hour of mostly drills, the players' wool uniforms were drenched with sweat. McCarthy scheduled only one workout per day from then on.30

On the second day of practice, the players drilled a full two hours, putting on an impressive show of long-ball hitting for 900 enthusiastic spectators.31 Due to the scarcity of official major league baseballs after the war, ball retrievers were stationed at various positions to retrieve balls hit out of the park. Out of necessity, 25 dozen balls had to be set aside for the upcoming 11 exhibition games.32

Once word got out that admission was free, the team's daily practices saw a large upturn in spectators. Rud Rennie reported in the *New York Herald Tribune,* "Joe Gordon and Phil Rizzuto performed brilliantly around second base."33 The temperatures were in the 80s F, accompanied by 12-mph trade winds—picture-perfect weather for watching world-class baseball. Joe McCarthy announced that the first intrasquad game would take place the upcoming weekend.

Gordon enjoyed his time in Panama and went fishing whenever he had free time. It was reported that "Joe Gordon, Yankee second baseman, is not having any trouble finding his way around Panama. He speaks Spanish like a native."34

Joe Gordon enjoys some time off for fishing during the Yankees' spring training at Panama in February 1946. Note how Joe's suntan ends where his baseball glove had covered up his left hand when he was playing ball. This is the only photograph the family has of him in Panama (Gordon family collections).

On February 15, the Yankees went through a two-hour drill to get ready for the following day's six-inning intrasquad game. Joe McCarthy again voiced his dilemma of who would play second base during the season, Joe Gordon or Snuffy Stirnweiss. It was generally believed that Gordon would hold down the keystone position, with Stirnweiss playing third base. Yet it also was noted that Stirnweiss still had not signed his contract or reported to spring training.[35]

The Yankees' first intrasquad game saw the "La Guardias" taking on the "Amadors," named after the Panamanian promoters Ernesto de La Guardia and Juan de Dios Amador, who had advanced $30,000 for the Yankees to come to Panama. Joe Gordon belted a home run and a single as the La Guardias shut out the Amadors.[36]

Larry MacPhail and his wife, along with American League umpire Charlie Berry (who would officiate the exhibition games), arrived in Panama on February 18, Joe Gordon's 31st birthday. MacPhail finally got to meet his ballplayers, many for the first time. While in Panama, MacPhail also watched the Yankees play another intrasquad game, where Gordon executed "a brilliant backhand stop and pounded two singles."[37]

Years later in his book, *The Scooter: The Phil Rizzuto Story*, Gene Schoor wrote about the Yankees training in Panama: "Joe DiMaggio, Charlie Keller, Bill Dickey, and Joe Gordon would take turns swatting the ball out of the park. Joe Gordon and Phil Rizzuto put on almost unbelievable exhibitions of dexterity in the infield. It was all choreographed by MacPhail—that is, the order of performances was arranged by MacPhail—and the play of Gordon and the Scooter [Rizzuto] around second base came as the climax of each training session."[38]

The final day of conditioning and practice saw the players sweating it out during a two-hour drill in "torrid" weather, cheered on by another large, enthusiastic crowd.[39]

The Yankees were scheduled to play a series of 11 exhibition games in Panama. Railroad schedules on both sides of the Canal Zone were changed to accommodate the large numbers of spectators expected at the games.[40]

The series opened on February 21 at Olympic Stadium, with the Yankees playing the Panama Professional Baseball League All-Stars.[41] Reserved seats were sold out, and the near-capacity crowd was estimated at 15,000. The Yankees' lineup consisted entirely of war veterans: Phil Rizzuto, Johnny Sturm, Tommy Henrich, Joe DiMaggio, Charlie Keller, Joe Gordon, Hank Majeski, Ken Silvestri, and pitchers Spud Chandler and rookie Bill Wight. Provisional President of the Republic of Panama Enrique Adolfo Jiménez threw out the ceremonial first pitch. Early in their training, the Yankees were considered the underdogs, although they managed to edge out the Panama All-Stars, 5–4.[42]

Victorious over the Canal Zone League All-Stars the following day and then defeating the Panama Professional League All-Stars twice more, the Yankees extended their winning streak to four in a row. Next, they traveled by motor convoy to Cristóbal on the Caribbean side of the Canal Zone, where they recorded 17 hits in defeating the U.S. Army All-Stars, 12–4, at Mount Hope Stadium.[43]

After visiting Panama for a week, the MacPhails flew back to the States. Writer Red Smith quoted the Yankees' president talking about his ballplayers: "D'Maggio [sic], Gordon, Keller and Rizzuto look as though every one of 'em might have the best year of his life. DiMaggio hit a homer in every game I saw. Keller hit the longest ball ever seen down there. Gordon may be a step slow, I don't know. I asked McCarthy, and he said it was too early to tell. But you ought to see him around that bag [second base]."[44]

The authors believe that MacPhail's remarks in the media about Joe Gordon being a "step slow" in Panama may have been one of the first indications of tensions beginning to arise between the two men. Contrary to MacPhail's statement, after the players returned to Florida in early March, it was reported that "clockers watching the Yankees exhibition games reveal that Henrich has been caught [timed at] under four seconds three times in going down [running] to first base, with [c]atcher Ken Silvestri the second fastest and Joe Gordon third."[45]

Meanwhile, back in the States, Snuffy Stirnweiss agreed to the terms of his contract and headed to St. Petersburg, although too late to join the Yankees in Panama.[46]

It was reported that the exhibition games in Panama were "voted a success by the Yankee players, [m]anager McCarthy, the coaches, and the local promoters."[47] The Yankees won eight of the 11 games, and Joe DiMaggio recorded 14 hits in 40 at-bats to lead the Yankees in batting average at .350. Joe Gordon logged the most hits, with 16 in 48 at-bats, for a .333 average. Charlie Keller hit safely in all 11 games and led the club with five home runs. Gordon and Keller played every inning of every game. More than 50,000 fans attended the games, resulting in the promoters clearing almost $50,000 in gate receipts.[48]

The Yankees flew back to Miami, then on to Bradenton for a few days until Joe McCarthy could get the St. Petersburg training camp sorted out.[49] Even though the players were reported as being a bit "dog-eared" after three weeks in Panama, they also were said to be in remarkably good condition. Gordon wrote home on March 8, saying, "Here we are back in our own stomping grounds finally, and it's sure a good feeling to know … that Dorthy and the kids will be here about Monday. I found a nice apt. [apartment] down near the [b]each, so we are all set, and will have till [sic] the 29th [of March] here with them…. I guess I have done pretty good so far, as Mc [McCarthy] has moved Stirnweiss to 3rd [base], and I feel real spry in spite of my 31 years."[50]

The Yankees were scheduled to play 17 exhibition games against other major league clubs. Toughened up from their three weeks in the tropics, they began like a "house afire," winning their first seven in a row against the St. Louis Cardinals, Detroit Tigers, and Boston Red Sox.

But on March 19, during a game at St. Petersburg against the Cardinals, things changed dramatically. While heading off St. Louis rookie Bob Rhawn trying to steal second base, Joe Gordon was spiked clear through his glove, suffering a completely severed extensor tendon of the middle finger of his left hand. The Yankees' winning streak ended that day.[51]

Gordon was taken to St. Petersburg's Mound Park Hospital, where Dr. Robert C. Lonergan reconnected the severed tendon, stitched the wound, and splinted Joe's finger.[52] Daughter Judy still remembers her father's description of the surgery after he got home that night. Living up to his nickname, "The Rock," he'd remained awake so he could watch the doctor reconnect his tendon. He was lucky—the injury could have ended his baseball career right then. X-rays the next day revealed that he also had a chipped bone in his finger.[53]

The doctor ordered his patient to do absolutely nothing for the first week.[54] After that, Joe was eager to try his luck at fishing. However, he'd been warned not to get his cast wet, so Dottie rigged several of the children's balloons to keep his cast dry while he fished.

Chapter 14. Goodbye, New York (1946)

Joe Gordon and his children, Joey and Judy, enjoying a day on the beach in early April 1946 at St. Petersburg, while Joe is recuperating from surgery on his left hand (Gordon family collections).

Judy also remembers flying with her dad as he piloted a small, two-seat seaplane, while recovering from surgery. One time they flew alongside the St. Pete-Bradenton Ferry transporting the Yankees across Tampa Bay on their way to Sarasota for a game against the Red Sox.[55] The Flash rocked the wings of the plane in greeting as he buzzed very close by the ferry.

New rookie infielder Bobby Brown had just signed with the Yankees that February and was on the ferry boat. Years later, during a recorded interview with nationally syndicated radio host "Dave O," Bobby corroborated Judy's account: "[W]e were going from St. Petersburg over to Bradenton, and in those days they didn't have a bridge. You had to take a ferry or a ship…. He [Gordon] was in an airplane, and he buzzed the ship [ferry boat]. And everybody says, 'That's Joe Gordon.'"[56] Frank Gibbons also wrote how, when Joe McCarthy was told who was flying the plane, the Yankees' skipper yelled, "Get him down, get him down[!]"[57]

It was estimated that Gordon would be out of action for at least four weeks.[58] Utility infielder Oscar Grimes filled in at second base, while Snuffy Stirnweiss continued learning his new position playing third base. The Yankees wrapped up their 17-game exhibition schedule against the Cardinals, Tigers, Red Sox, Indians, and Dodgers with a record of 9–7–1, winning only two games after Gordon got spiked.[59]

The Gordons remained at St. Petersburg as the Yankees headed out barnstorming through Louisiana, Texas, Georgia, and then northward.[60] Just 19 days after surgery, Joe joined the team and had recovered enough to begin light workouts the following day.[61] By April 13, it was reported that he was able to practice his bunting.[62]

The day before the 1946 season opened, Gayle Talbot wrote, "Of 119 sports writers polled by the *Associated Press*, 78 picked the Yanks to finish first."[63] Playing to an Opening Day crowd of 37,472 at Philadelphia on April 16, the Yankees' 38-year-old pitcher, Spud Chandler, hurled a five-hit shutout to beat the Athletics, 5–0. Major league baseball was back in full swing, with post-war attendance over the top!

Gordon didn't play on Opening Day, but the following day, just four weeks and a day after surgery, he was back in the lineup at the keystone sack, where he would play every game through May 6. A year later, he told Dan Daniel: "Eventually, I got back into action, but far ahead of time. I should have been out another fortnight, but Joe [McCarthy] was in a tough spot. I had to play. That did me no good."[64] The Yankees were stacking up injuries. Shortstop Phil Rizzuto missed the first eight games of the season due to a pulled leg muscle, and left fielder Charlie Keller had to sit out the first five games because of a persistent charley horse.[65]

The Yankees' home opener on April 19 drew a reported paid attendance of 54,826, at the time said to be the largest turnout for an opening game in major league history other than Yankee Stadium's inaugural game in 1923.[66] The Stadium had undergone major additions, renovations, and remodeling during the off-season. Rud Rennie wrote, "The people wanted to see a ball game with Joe DiMaggio, Joe Gordon, Tommy Henrich, Johnny Lindell, Bill Dickey and all the old stars in it."[67] The Yanks edged the Washington Senators, 7–6, behind Joe DiMaggio's "superlative" hitting.

On April 30, Cleveland Indians right-hander Bob Feller hurled a no-hitter to defeat the Bronx Bombers, 1–0. It was the first no-hitter ever pitched *against* the Yankees at their own Yankee Stadium.[68]

By May 2, Joe Gordon had played 15 games, recording an early-season batting average of .339, second only to teammate Charlie Keller's .378. The Flash looked as great as ever, and the Yankees were only two games behind the league-leading Boston Red Sox. But just two days later, Gordon pulled a muscle in his leg while playing on a wet day. Although he toughed it out for three games, the injury finally forced him to sit out five games.[69]

Things were changing fast for the Yankees. On May 13, the team flew from New York's La Guardia Field to St. Louis on a chartered four-engine United Air Lines DC-4 (also reported as a C-54–type transport), aptly christened the *Yankees Mainliner*.[70] Although the Yankees had flown to and from Panama, in addition to a few cities during 1946 spring training, this was their first regular-season road trip by air. The Bronx Bombers became the first major league club to fly on a regular basis. One of the advantages of flying, besides the much shorter travel time, was that the players got to spend their nights in hotels, instead of having to sleep in Pullman car berths en route. The players were almost unanimously in favor of flying, except for a few who elected to continue traveling by rail.

In the starting lineup on May 14 at St. Louis, "Gordon looked like his old self back at second [base] after a week's enforced idleness, handling six chances flawlessly."[71] He also belted one of the Yankees' three home runs that day.

During a doubleheader at Cleveland on May 19, a rare, unexpected side of the jovial, easy-going Joe Gordon was observed by James P. Dawson of the *New York Times*: "Gordon's slugging in the opener was done with his fists upon Allie Reynolds, who had a smooth one-hit pitching performance up to the ninth [inning]. Allie made the mistake of trying a rough tackle in an attempt to take Gordon out of a double play in the Tribe [Cleveland Indians] eighth, and was massacred by a couple of Gordon right hooks while lying on the ground near second [base] after the twin killing had been completed."[72]

The Yankees won both games that day. Gordon Cobbledick later wrote about the slugfest in *Sport* magazine, saying, "The Flash would be an excellent guy *not* to have sore at you. Among his varied hobbies is boxing.... On the baseball field, however, he is no brawler."[73]

Playing at Detroit on May 22, five Yankees took part in a wildly executed triple play, scored as 3-2-5-4-6-4-3-6. At the time, it was just the 411th triple play recorded in American and National League baseball history going back to 1876.[74] Moreover, it was an unusual execution, in that it involved the entire Yankees infield except for pitcher Jake Wade. The Tigers had runners on first and third with no outs. Dick Wakefield grounded to Yankees first baseman Nick Etten, whose throw to catcher Bill Dickey trapped Detroit runner Eddy Mayo between third base and home. Dickey threw to third baseman Snuffy Stirnweiss, who ran down Mayo and tagged him out. Stirnweiss propelled the ball to second baseman Joe Gordon, who relayed to shortstop Phil Rizzuto, who threw to Gordon to tag Jimmy Outlaw out at second. Meanwhile, the batter, Wakefield, had dashed toward second base and was run down and tagged out after relays from Gordon to Etten to Rizzuto. Even Yankees right fielder Tommy Henrich got in the action while backing up the play, but ended up with a spiked ankle, requiring a trip to the hospital and several stitches.[75] Yankees manager Joe McCarthy was out sick, so he missed seeing his team's triple play and 5–3 victory over the Tigers.

The next day, Joe Gordon belted two home runs and a double in the Bombers' 17-hit routing of five Detroit pitchers. McCarthy also missed that game and his team's record-tying three consecutive home runs in the fifth inning (DiMaggio, Etten, and Gordon).[76] It was reported that "Marse Joe" was suffering from gallbladder trouble and had flown home to Buffalo.

Then, suddenly and seemingly with no warning, on May 24, just 35 games into the 1946 season, manager Joe McCarthy submitted his resignation to Yankees president Larry MacPhail, citing health reasons.[77] At the time, the club was in second place with a record of 22–13 (.629), five games behind the Boston Red Sox. McCarthy leaving was a *huge* loss to the Yankees. In his 15 full seasons (1931–1945) of managing the team, the venerable "Marse Joe" had piloted the club to a remarkable eight pennants and seven world championships.

In a column titled "Exit for Marse Joe," Arthur Daley wrote, "It had to happen sooner or later.... Both men [McCarthy and MacPhail] like fiercely to win. But there their similarity ends. Marse Joe is an ultra-conservative man who hates change, emotionalism, gloss or glitter. Larry [MacPhail] is a radical who relishes change, flash, color, excitement and argument.... That they'd some day [sic] come to a parting of the ways was absolutely inevitable."[78]

Nevertheless, "Marse Joe" would not be away from baseball for long. By mid–September, and with his health restored, reportedly he told Frank Yetter of the *Philadelphia Evening Bulletin*, "There's no use denying I'd like to be back.... When I quit managing the Yanks all I wanted was to get my health back.... For three years I had been under a nervous strain that just about broke me up."[79] McCarthy would finish out his distinguished 24-year major league managerial career piloting the Boston Red Sox to second-place finishes in 1948 and 1949, each year just one game back. After 59 games in 1950, he retired due to poor health.

Years later, in *Five O'Clock Lightning: Ruth, Gehrig, DiMaggio, Mantle and the Glory Years of the NY Yankees*, former outfielder Tommy "Old Reliable" Henrich wrote about that ill-fated year 1946:

> We weren't able to maintain our Opening Day success over the course of the season, and 1946 became the kind of year you don't associate with the New York Yankees.... To make matters even more un–Yankee, we had dissension both on the field and in the front office.
>
> Larry MacPhail had joined the Yankees after serving as a major in the [A]rmy. He eased Ed Barrow out of his job, and the friction hurt us. MacPhail and McCarthy simply never got along. Joe [McCarthy] was gone as our manager after only thirty-five games. MacPhail said he fired him. Joe said he quit.
>
> Regardless, Joe was gone, and I [Henrich] was crushed. All of us were in a state of shock. McCarthy was the only manager many of us had ever played for in the big leagues.[80]

Joe Gordon also had never played major league ball under any other manager. For more than six seasons, McCarthy had been one of the Flash's most influential teachers and mentors. Five days after stepping down, "Marse Joe" visited the Yankees' clubhouse before a game, to thank all the players for their years of faithful service. After the game, he bid goodbye to the New York sportswriters, declaring, "I'm still a Yankee."[81]

The Yankees replaced McCarthy with one of their own—11-time All-Star catcher Bill Dickey as their player-manager. After serving with the U.S. Navy and almost 39 years old, Dickey had returned for his 17th season with the Bronx Bombers.

Losing two out of three games at Boston, the Bombers headed home for Yankee Stadium's first-ever night game on May 28. They were in second place, six games behind the Red Sox. Battling cold, windy weather and under "baseball's most brilliant floodlights," the game drew a tremendous mid-week crowd of 49,917.[82] Twenty-one-year-old rookie Clarence "Cuddles" Marshall, making his first career start, stayed in for seven innings, although the Senators eventually triumphed, 2–1.

When the Philadelphia Athletics arrived to town, "[a]mid the roars of 60,851 eyewitnesses" in addition to "a couple of dazzling fielding plays by Joe Gordon ... and Phil Rizzuto," the Yankees swept their first home doubleheader of the season on May 30.[83] Back under the lights on the last day of May and playing to a reported 60,895 fans, the Bombers won their fourth game in a row. They were finally on a roll, and attendance skyrocketed. Yet the Red Sox kept up their first-place pace, and the Bombers remained multiple games back.

Yankees president Larry MacPhail was fixated on winning the pennant. However, by the last day of May, only one regular (Charlie Keller) was batting over .300, whereas the league-leading Boston Red Sox had three players batting over that mark (Ted Williams, Dom DiMaggio, and Johnny Pesky). Moreover, the average age of Red Sox players (seven regulars, a catcher, and five first-string pitchers) was a youthful 28 years old, compared with an equivalent group of Yankees who averaged 31½ years of age.[84]

Chapter 14. Goodbye, New York (1946)

The month of June was just around the corner, but with it would come more troubles for Joe Gordon. Trying to pin down when they began, the authors believe that one of the precipitating events may have occurred during the first game of a doubleheader at Boston back on May 26. In the bottom of the seventh inning, Boston's Johnny Pesky hit a "difficult grounder" toward Gordon, whose throw to catch Red Sox baserunner George Metkovich at second base pulled Phil Rizzuto off the bag. Gordon was charged with an error on the play, eventually leading to an unearned run and Boston's 1–0 victory.[85]

In a game at home on June 1 against the St. Louis Browns, during an attempted double play in the second inning, Gordon's throw to first base went wild into the grandstands, eventually resulting in an unearned run and a 4–3 victory for the Browns.[86] Gordon adamantly claimed interference on Browns baserunner Johnny Berardino, but the umpire charged Joe with responsibility. Photos published in several newspapers the following day clearly substantiated Joe's claim—showing Berardino, who'd already been called out at second base, sliding *way* past the bag, trying to take out Gordon.[87]

Two years later, Gordon talked with sportswriter Gordon Cobbledick about what happened next. He said he was ordered to report to Yankees president Larry MacPhail's office. As soon as Gordon stepped through the door, MacPhail unleashed his anger and accused Joe of not trying. Joe fired back at MacPhail and walked out. Manager Bill Dickey, who also was at the meeting, asked Joe to come back and explain to MacPhail that he'd been nursing leg injuries. But when Joe returned, the two went at it again. When MacPhail told Dickey that he was not to play Gordon again, Dickey turned to the president, hotly telling MacPhail that no one from the front office was going to tell him how to manage the team. Joe told Cobbledick that, at that moment, he knew he was finished with the Yankees, and so was Dickey.[88]

The June 15 trading deadline was fast approaching, but Gordon was still recovering from leg injuries, which made a trade highly unlikely. MacPhail also may have had second thoughts about getting rid of Gordon midseason, because the Flash was so popular with Yankees fans.

The authors believe that Larry MacPhail's growing animosity toward Joe Gordon during 1946 perhaps had its roots in MacPhail's memories of the Flash's out-of-this-world play in the Yankees' five-game defeat of the Brooklyn Dodgers in the 1941 World Series.[89] MacPhail had been president of the 1941 Dodgers and had seen, firsthand, Gordon's outstanding play in the Series. So he was well aware of what Joe had been capable of, both offensively and defensively. The authors also believe that much of MacPhail's animosity toward Joe Gordon during 1946 had to do with the Yankees president's frustration with the club as a whole, especially when they couldn't seem to catch the league-leading Boston Red Sox.

Ed Fitzgerald later wrote in *Sport* magazine, "Unfortunately, from the time that he [Gordon] first reported back to the New York ball club in the [s]pring of 1946, after his discharge from the service[,] Joe had trouble with the new president, Larry MacPhail. The [New York] writers who traveled with the team watched the friction increase until they reluctantly concluded that the only logical resolution of the problem would be the dispatching of Gordon to greener pastures."[90]

For the remainder of the 1946 season, Gordon remained resolutely closed-mouthed about his contentious run-in(s) with MacPhail. The authors didn't come across a single instance of Joe talking or writing about what had happened. Being the team player that he was, it was evident he didn't want to disrupt his teammates. Also, since he figured he'd be traded anyway, he didn't want to jeopardize his chances of ending up with a good ballclub.

A doubleheader against the visiting Cleveland Indians on June 9 boosted the Yankees' total paid attendance to 1,010,977, the earliest that any club had ever topped the million mark.[91] However, shortstop Phil Rizzuto twisted his knee in the top of the first inning of the opener, benching him for the next three games. In the same game, Joe Gordon severely strained his right leg, causing him to sit out 10 games except for pinch-hitting twice.

On June 21, Joe wrote to his mother from Detroit: "I finally broke back into the lineup today—didn't get any hits, but it sure felt good to play again. My leg seems to be about cured, & sure hope it stays that way for keeps this time. I sure hate to sit on the bench. We have gained three games on Boston this trip and if they keep going as lousy as they have been, we have a good chance to come close to them by the time we get home. If we can stay around five games from them, we always have a chance."[92]

The 13th Annual Major League Baseball All-Star Game was scheduled for the afternoon of July 9 at Boston's Fenway Park. Net proceeds from the game were designated for the Baseball Welfare Fund, aiding aged and disabled ballplayers and their families, in addition to the families of nine Spokane, Washington, minor league players who had died in a tragic bus accident in late June 1946.[93]

Six Yankees (Spud Chandler, Bill Dickey, Joe DiMaggio, Joe Gordon, Charlie Keller, and Snuffy Stirnweiss) were chosen for the 1946 American League All-Star team, with Keller starting and playing the whole game, hitting a two-run homer.[94] Just two days before the All-Star Game, Joe DiMaggio had severely injured his left knee and ankle while sliding into second base, causing him to miss the next 22 games of the season—a huge loss for the Bombers.[95] Gordon and Stirnweiss each played the final five innings of the All-Star Game, both contributing to the total run count. Although some mumbling was heard that several players chosen for the All-Star Game didn't merit selection based on their 1946 performances, there still existed an unspoken edict that the fans deserved to see their favorite pre-war stars in this, the first post-war Midsummer Classic.

The American League shut out the National League, 12–0, with Rud Rennie describing the contest as "the most lopsided game in All-Star history."[96] Going 4-for-4 with two home runs, two singles, a walk, and five RBI, Ted Williams set *six* new All-Star Game records and tied two others.[97] An All-Star Game scoring record was set that day, a record not broken until 1983, when the American League beat the National League, 13–3, at Chicago's Comiskey Park.

Meanwhile, about four days after the All-Star Game, the *New York News* published a very small article with a headline reading, "Gordon Swap Due Next Year." In the article, Joe was described as "the New York Yankees' 'flop of the year,'" in addition to saying that he would be offered to the Cleveland Indians in exchange for manager/shortstop Lou Boudreau that winter.[98]

The following day, the *New York Herald Tribune* published an article by Rud Rennie, saying, "Larry MacPhail is planning for next year. He told Bill Veeck, new president of the [Cleveland] Indians, that there will be the greatest turnover of Yankee players this winter that baseball ever has seen. One of the players slated to be 'turned over' is Joe Gordon, and the Indians are interested."[99]

But things would get even worse! *International News Service* sportswriter Davis J. Walsh let loose with a scathing article, headlined "Yank Vets—Headed by Gordon—at

Chapter 14. Goodbye, New York (1946)

Odds with Dickey." Walsh didn't identify his so-called "source," except to say that this person's "contact with both players and management is intimate and reliable."[100]

With the Yankees trailing the league-leading Red Sox by 11 games, Larry MacPhail called a special press conference before the July 15 night game and handed out a full-page communique, saying emphatically, "I have never talked with Veeck or anyone else on any club about a trade involving Gordon. I have never talked with Veeck or anyone else on the Cleveland club about a deal involving Boudreau." Indians president Bill Veeck also denied that he had ever talked with MacPhail or anyone else about any deal for Joe Gordon or Lou Boudreau.[101]

But the rumors ran rampant. In spite of this, Gordon remained silent and continued to play every day. Adding to the chaos, the third-place Tigers were hot on the Bombers' heels.

On July 17, at the urging of several of his teammates, Gordon summoned an unprecedented press conference in the Yankees' clubhouse before the opener of a doubleheader against the St. Louis Browns. He "emphatically denied" all of the published reports about him being "ringleader of a revolt" against manager Bill Dickey: "Such a report is an out and out lie. I want it understood that Dickey and I are the best of friends, and that there is no dissension in the club whatsoever."[102] After Gordon spoke, Bill Dickey invited the reporters to talk with the players. To a man, each player backed up their manager and strongly denied that there was any dissension among them.[103] This seemed to extinguish the rumors and clear the air—at least for a while.

The Yankees won both games of the doubleheader, in addition to setting a major league home-attendance record of 1,510,934, even topping the Chicago Cubs' full-season record set back in 1929. But during the nightcap, Yankees shortstop Phil Rizzuto was hit on the temple by a pitched ball, rushed to the hospital with a concussion, and would miss the next 10 games.[104] Forty-one-year-old pitcher Red Ruffing, who'd been hit on the knee by a line drive on June 29, was finally diagnosed with a split kneecap and placed on the club's disabled list, ending the season with a 5–1 record and 1.77 ERA.[105] Coupled with Joe DiMaggio's still-ongoing recovery, injuries posed a substantial setback for the Yankees their entire season.

Adding to their plight, Gordon fractured his left thumb on July 30 at Detroit, while trying to break up a double play.[106] He would be out of commission the next 16 games except for pinch-hitting twice.

In mid–August, Joe wrote to his mother: "It sure has been a long time since I've written, but it seems as if there never is any good news to write this year. I will sure be glad when this year is over, as it has been the worst I have ever spent in baseball. As soon as I get over one thing, something else happens. My thumb is nearly well now—another two or three days—and I'm just wondering what will be next."[107]

The last half of August, the Yankees stalled out in second place, 12 to 14 games behind the Red Sox. Although Joe Gordon's batting suffered because of his thumb, he did manage to hit his 10th and 11th home runs on August 23 and 29.

The club headed out on September 9 for a 10-game western road trip. About that time, Larry MacPhail hired longtime player and manager Bucky Harris as his "administrative assistant."[108] Losing two games at Cleveland slipped the Bombers to third place behind Boston and Detroit. In the meantime, Yankees manager Bill Dickey, suspecting that he might not be rehired for 1947, notified MacPhail that he didn't want to be considered as manager for the following year.[109] Suddenly, on September 13, during the middle of a "do-or-die" three-game series at Detroit in the close battle for second place, MacPhail handed the Yankees' managerial reins over to coach Johnny Neun.[110] Neun managed the team their final 14 games of the season, going 8–6.

Bill Dickey wrapped up his only major league managerial season, a position he'd never wanted anyway, with a 57–48 record.[111] Later, Joe Gordon said that Dickey did a great job of managing the 1946 Yankees—"in an impossible situation."[112]

Even before the 1946 season was over, widely circulating rumors predicted that Joe Gordon would be sold or traded to either the Detroit Tigers or Cleveland Indians.[113] In late September, and likely not known by Gordon himself, the Yankees requested American League waivers on him.[114] However, he was claimed by Detroit, Chicago, Cleveland, Washington, and Boston, and the Yankees withdrew him from waivers on September 25.

Gordon finished the 1946 season having played in a career-low 112 games. He had to sit out 42 games due to multiple injuries (severed tendon in his left hand, pulled leg muscle, severely strained right leg, and broken thumb). He batted a career-low .210, with career lows of 11 home runs and 47 RBI. It was a *very* disappointing year.

Gordon had played seven seasons for the New York Yankees, recording exactly 1,000 hits in 1,000 games, hitting 153 home runs with 617 RBI. He'd also received the Most Valuable Player Award in 1942; been selected for six All-Star Games; and played in five World Series, winning four world championships.

The Yankees wrapped up the 1946 season in third place, trailing the pennant-winning Boston Red Sox by 17 games and the runner-up Detroit Tigers by five games. Their record of 87–67 (.565) was the lowest in Joe Gordon's seven years with the club. Several players (Etten, Gordon, and Henrich) had posted career-low batting averages. Joe DiMaggio's .290 average was a career low for him until his final year of play in 1951, when he batted .263.

On a brighter note, 39-year-old Spud Chandler topped all Yankees pitchers with his 20–8 record and 2.10 ERA. Other double-digit winners, however, were few and far between: Bill Bevens (16–13 and 2.23) and Randy Gumpert (11–3 and 2.31). The Yankees set a new major league attendance record of 2,265,512.

While attending the 1946 World Series at Fenway Park, Yankees president Larry MacPhail and the Cleveland Indians owner/president of less than four months, Bill Veeck, put together a trade that would define the remainder of Joe Gordon's playing career. On October 11, Veeck announced that the Indians' 29-year-old pitcher, Allie Reynolds, was being traded to the New York Yankees for 31-year-old second baseman Joe Gordon.[115] Gordon was released outright to Cleveland on October 19.

One of the Flash's first public comments after hearing about being traded was, "That automatically means ten points more on my 1947 batting average. I won't have to hit against Bob Feller now."[116] Joe also said that he was "tickled to death" to be going to Cleveland, and he already had begun a conditioning program to get ready for 1947.[117]

Joe's fellow Oregonian, Boston Red Sox second baseman Bobby Doerr, told *Cleveland Plain Dealer* sports editor Gordon Cobbledick, "I'll tell you what I'm waiting to see. I want to see Gordon and Boudreau working together around that bag. They'll do tricks that'll make your eyes pop right out of your head."[118] Doerr also said in early 1947, "I saw a lot of Gordon out on the coast [in Oregon] this winter.... He's ready.... [H]e started to get himself into condition the day he heard about the trade."[119]

Bill Veeck was unable to restrain his delight in obtaining Joe Gordon. It was later revealed that Veeck gleefully told Cleveland sportswriters during supposedly "off-the-record" conversations, "We just won the pennant!"[120] Author Gerald Eskenazi

Chapter 14. Goodbye, New York (1946)

later wrote about the trade in *Bill Veeck: A Baseball Legend*: "So Gordon became an Indian and Reynolds became a Yankee, where he also was to become the best clutch pitcher in baseball. Gordon, though, was brilliant with Cleveland."[121]

In his book, *Player-Manager*, Lou Boudreau described Indians president Bill Veeck as "the grinning, plain-talking, tie-hating ex–Marine."[122] Boudreau also wrote about Joe Gordon: "[K]nown to every baseball follower in America as the Flash, was a second baseman of impressive proportions.... Getting him on our side proved to be nothing less than a stroke of genius.... Even though Joe had had a miserable season with the Yankees in 1946, his acquisition was greeted by shouts of joy in Cleveland."[123]

Boudreau wrote more in his later book, *Lou Boudreau: Covering All the Bases*: "But Gordon also gave us exactly what we needed. He complemented me as I did him, and we became an even better shortstop-second base combination.... Joe was happy to come to Cleveland because he'd been under such great pressure with the Yankees. He ... looked forward to playing for the Indians."[124]

Many years later, Bill Veeck talked with Harry Jones of the *Cleveland Plain Dealer* about what had taken place at Fenway Park on October 11 during the fifth game of the 1946 World Series. Veeck was sitting in a box seat when Larry MacPhail walked by. Veeck stopped MacPhail, telling him that the Indians had an extra pitcher and the Yankees had an extra second baseman. Veeck offered either Allie Reynolds or Red Embree to the Yankees for Joe Gordon. With that verbal offer, MacPhail went over and asked Joe DiMaggio whom he would choose. Without hesitation, DiMaggio told MacPhail to pick Reynolds. Veeck said he and MacPhail then wrote up the trade agreement on a paper napkin. Veeck said it was the quickest and best deal he'd ever made, because the Indians would never have won the pennant in 1948 without Joe Gordon.[125]

After the trade was announced, Ed McAuley quoted Bill Veeck in *The Sporting News*: "I want the best team I can get every year. That's why I traded for Joe Gordon.... I hardly can wait until spring to watch Lou Boudreau and Gordon work together."[126]

Years later in his book, *Where Have You Gone, Joe DiMaggio?*, author Maury Allen quoted Gordon saying, "They [the Yankees] were going to trade me anyway; it was just a question of which pitcher they wanted. The '46 season was a bad year."[127]

Once Gordon was back home in Oregon, Joe Gordon Hardware sponsored a weekly radio program called "Sportman's Clubhouse" on Eugene's station KUGN, with Joe providing the duck-calling audio.[128] To this day, the two Gordon children still remember that their father was the best duck- and goose-caller they ever heard!

At first, Gordon rarely talked with anyone in the media about being traded. In late 1946, however, he did open up to a few of his Oregon sportswriter friends, telling them, "The best thing MacPhail ever did for me was trade me."[129]

Larry MacPhail remained just one more year as co-owner and president of the New York Yankees. Immediately after the Bronx Bombers won the 1947 World Series, several heated confrontations initiated by MacPhail led to him resigning and his partners Dan Topping and Del Webb buying him out of the Yankees.[130]

However, to Larry MacPhail's credit, the authors did not come across a single instance in the media of MacPhail ever bad-mouthing his former second baseman, Joe Gordon, after trading him to the Cleveland Indians. As Don Warfield later wrote in his book, *The Roaring Redhead: Larry MacPhail—Baseball's Great Innovator*, "MacPhail was not one to hold grudges."[131]

Chapter 15

THE "FLASH" IS BACK! (1947)

Joe Gordon signed his 1947 contract with the Cleveland Indians on December 26, 1946. He was paid the same $20,000 salary he'd received from the New York Yankees the year before, in addition to incremental attendance bonuses potentially totaling an additional $2,000.[1]

In early February, Commissioner Albert Benjamin "Happy" Chandler announced that the American and National Leagues, in joint session, agreed to implement a pension plan (including an annuity and life insurance), effective April 1, 1947, for participating players, coaches, and trainers on the rosters of the 16 American and National League clubs on the last day of the 1946 regular season or on Opening Day of 1947.[2] Upon participants reaching the age of 50, the plan paid $50 per month for life to those who were vested with five seasons of service in the majors and up to $100 per month for those vested with 10 or more seasons. Funding of the plan would come from players' dues, contributions by the ballclubs, annual Major League Baseball All-Star Game receipts, and World Series radio broadcast rights.

Once Joe Gordon had a signed contract with the Cleveland Indians, he opened up to a few of his sportswriter friends about his 1946 season. L.H. Gregory wrote in *The Oregonian*, "Gordon feels he got a break in being traded to Cleveland.... He had a runin [sic] or two with the Yankee's [sic] red-headed [president/]general manager last season and MacPhail said point-blank he would get him off the club.... Joe cares not a whit who knows he doesn't like MacPhail, but says he was hurt clear through by stories last summer [July 1946] of his alleged feud with [m]anager Bill Dickey."[3]

During extensive research of Joe Gordon's many years in baseball, the authors discovered that there was only *one* person Joe ever spoke disparagingly about (at least, "on the record")—and that was Yankees president Larry MacPhail. Moreover, during numerous interviews, Gordon insisted that there never was one iota of truth to persistent rumors that he and Bill Dickey had ever had a run-in. Dickey, too, backed up Joe's claims, saying that stories of any altercation between the two were false and "spread by idle gossips."[4]

Dickey also talked about Joe Gordon as a player, calling him "the greatest defensive infielder of his [Dickey's] long experience in the American League." He told Dan Daniel, "In his prime, Gordon not only got Boudreau's jump on the ball but added his amazing acrobatics and the speed of a great pair of legs.... I used to watch balls travel into Gordon's locality and say to myself, '[N]ot even Joe can get that one,' only to see the incredible move and the throw to the base.... Gordon was the grandest playmaker and covered more ground than any other infielder I have ever seen."[5] High praise indeed, by one of the greatest catchers in the history of baseball.

Chapter 15. The "Flash" Is Back! (1947)

After engaging in some "serious training" by playing handball and officiating basketball during the winter months, Joe Gordon was in excellent physical condition and several pounds lighter by early February, when he headed to 1947 spring training.[6] This was the first year that the Cleveland Indians conducted their spring training in Tucson, Arizona—establishing the "Cactus League" along with the New York Giants, who trained in Phoenix.[7]

Indians president Bill Veeck invited Joe Gordon to come to Arizona early, to hunt on the Veecks' Lazy Vee Ranch located at the foot of the Rincon Mountains, east of Tucson.[8] The two men got along great. Veeck later wrote in *Veeck—As in Wreck: The Autobiography of Bill Veeck*, "If I had to put in time on a desert island I can think of no one I'd rather have along than Joe [Gordon], because even on a desert island he would always find a few ways to keep the hours dancing along."[9]

Gordon checked in at spring training a week early so he could attend Rogers Hornsby's batting school. He donned his Cleveland Indians uniform Number 4 for the first time on February 18, his 32nd birthday. *The Sporting News* published a photo of Indians manager Lou Boudreau and coach Bill McKechnie presenting Joe with a birthday cake, decorated with replicas of Arizona's saguaro cactus.[10]

Writer Abe Chanin quoted Gordon talking about his previous season with the Yankees and subsequent trade to the Indians: "'The change will do me good,' he [Gordon] said of his trade to Cleveland. 'Last year was a nightmare for me and the whole Yankee club. Before the season started, I could have sworn we would win the pennant. But it turned out to be one of those years when nothing went right.'"[11]

Soon after spring training began, Ed McAuley wrote an article, headlined "Indian Infield Shaping Up as League's Best," saying, "On the opening day of the 1947 training season, big Ed Robinson took up his station at Randolph Field's first base. Joe Gordon was at second, Lou Boudreau at shortstop and Ken Keltner at third. The ensuing workout was so electrifying that even the pitchers, who had been excused for the day, sat along the sidelines to watch the show."[12]

A week later, McAuley followed up with more observations: "Boudreau and Gordon make our eyes pop out.... [Rogers] Hornsby has been widely quoted as calling Boudreau and Gordon the best second base combination in the history of the game.... [T]he Redskins [a former nickname for the Cleveland Indians] put on a show which has the Arizona tourists goggle-eyed.... You'll have to pinch your sunburned arm to make sure that you're awake."[13]

Gordon's close friend, Boston Red Sox second baseman Bobby Doerr, kidded about Joe joining the Indians: "[Commissioner] Chandler ought not to allow two guys like Boudreau and Gordon on one team."[14]

The first in a series of spring training exhibition games was played against the New York Giants at Tucson on March 8. The Indians triumphed "before a capacity crowd of 4,934, which was generously sprinkled with ten-gallon hats, both the genuine article from the ranges and the fancy variety from the dude ranches."[15]

In 2018, former Indians first baseman Eddie Robinson, then 97 years old, wrote to Judy Gordon about when her father first joined the club in 1947:

> Joe joined the team in 1947 and it didn't take him long before he had an impact on the team. In spring training we were playing the Chicago Cubs and one of their hitters hit a hard ground ball back over the pitcher's mound, over second base, and I thought into center field. But no, Joe was playing the hitter behind second base and he fielded the ball. I [Robinson]

didn't cover 1st base. All the players were yelling at me to cover 1st! I looked and realized Joe had the ball. I ran for 1st base, and Joe led me with the throw, and we just got the runner out. After that I always looked to see where Joe was positioned on the infield. That play let every player on the team know that Joe was a different type [of] player.[16]

Everything was going well in mid–March 1947 when Gordon told special correspondent Johnny McCallum of *The Oregonian*: "Tell Greg [L.H. Gregory, sporting editor of *The Oregonian*] he can quote me very truthfully as saying I am happier here [with] Cleveland than I have ever been in baseball. I like the bosses, I like the club and I especially like [m]anager Lou Boudreau and the way he handles his club, as well as his shortstopping. He and I work together beautifully and I'm looking forward to a great season."[17]

Years later, Boudreau wrote about the 1947 season in *Lou Boudreau: Covering All the Bases*: "The changes were coming fast and furious."[18] Due to its larger seating capacity, owner Bill Veeck had scheduled all of the Indians' home games at Cleveland's massive Municipal Stadium, no longer alternating between there and the old League Park like the year before. Just two weeks into the season, Veeck, the master entrepreneur, unveiled one of his most controversial brainstorms—a moveable outfield fence, constructed of five-foot-high sections of woven wire and designed, allegedly, to "reduce the vastness of the Cleveland Stadium outfield."[19]

The fence was installed for the first time during a pregame ceremony on April 28, complete with a marching band playing "Don't Fence Me In."[20] Depending on the longball power of each visiting team, Veeck could have the fence moved either in or out a maximum of 60 to 70 feet. Lou Boudreau described Veeck's invention as "Anything to get even the slightest advantage."[21] American League president William Harridge later ruled that the fence could not be either moved or removed, once the season had begun.

But the fence wasn't the only "obliging and adaptable" item in the repertoire of the Indians' zany president. He noted in *Veeck—As in Wreck: The Autobiography of Bill Veeck*:

> There was also the matter of our infield. We had, in Cleveland, the Michelangelo of the grounds keepers [*sic*], Emil Bossard.... Our mound at Cleveland always changed according to the pitcher of the day.... At second base, our needs were entirely different. Joe Gordon was an acrobat, swift of foot and sure of hand. Joe could make plays on hard-hit balls that no other second baseman in the league could touch. The grass toward second, then, was clipped to the nubbin and the base paths between first and second were kept as hard as a rock.[22]

The Indians got off to a mediocre 5–5 start in April. Joe Gordon was batting just .229 with one homer to his credit. Yet things would soon change. Playing at home on May 2, he belted his second home run of the season—a game-winner for Bob Feller's 10th one-hitter of his ongoing 18-year pitching career.[23] The following day, the Flash blasted two more home runs (the second one a grand slam) good for five RBI in Charles "Red" Embree's 9–3 victory over the Red Sox. It was reported that "three of the Tribe's four homers landed beyond the fence in the area known as the 'happy hunting grounds.'"[24]

On a day off in early May, Joe wrote home to his mother from Cleveland's Tudor Arms Hotel, where he was living until his family arrived from Oregon. Telling her how he was playing, he wrote, "The way I feel, no one can get me out."[25]

On May 11, the Flash again belted two home runs in one game, as well as a single, driving in four runs in the Indians' 16–1 stomping of the St. Louis Browns. This temporarily boosted Joe's batting average to .317. He was leading the American League with six home runs and was tied with Boston's Bobby Doerr for the lead in RBI with 16.[26] It was reported that the overjoyed Bill Veeck "went into an ecstacy [sic] over Joe Gordon, who had poled a couple of important homers over the new barrier [fence]."[27] Veeck said, "The deal which gave us Gordon was the greatest the Cleveland club has made in more than a decade and will look better as we go along."

Word of Gordon's play spread across the country. A headline in the *San Francisco Examiner* declared, "Gordon, the Old Flash Again, Causes Flag Talk in Cleveland." In the article, the writer claimed, "What a difference a player makes…. The guy who is causing hope to spring eternal in the hearts of Cleveland followers is the former Yankee star second baseman, Joe (Flash) Gordon."[28]

May 18 was Joe Gordon's first time back at Yankee Stadium, in addition to his first time playing against his former Yankees teammates since being traded to the Indians. Al Stump wrote an article for *Argosy for Men* magazine titled "Mr. Second Sack is Back," describing Gordon's first appearance at the Stadium: "The crowd drew a long breath as a lean, goose-necked figure in a Cleveland Indians uniform trotted from the visitors' dugout onto the field. Then an uproar hit the place. With a full-lunged shout, the stands exploded—'Joe Go-o-ordon. Yaaaaa, Flash!'"[29]

The Flash enjoyed a perfect day—going 3-for-3, including two singles and two walks (off starter Allie Reynolds) and a home run (off of reliever Joe Page) in the Indians' 5–3 victory over the Bombers. Ironically, the player that Gordon had been traded to the Indians for—Allie Reynolds—was charged with the Yankees' loss.

The Indians made a clean sweep of their three-game series against the Yankees. Gordon went 4-for-9 (.444), with a home run, double, and two singles. Defensively, he handled 11 putouts and six assists.

While the Indians were in New York City, veteran sportswriter Dan Daniel had the opportunity to talk with Joe Gordon. The two men first met 10 years earlier, when 22-year-old Gordon had been summoned to 1937 Yankees spring training. Daniel quoted Gordon comparing the Indians' organization with that of the Yankees: "I always believed the Yankee organization to be the greatest in baseball, but take it from me, this man Veeck, this [m]anager Boudreau, the atmosphere in Cleveland, the general picture—well, MacPhail never did a ball player the kind of favor he did me, when he shipped me to the Indians for Allie Reynolds."[30]

As soon as Oregon's schools let out for the summer, Dottie and the two Gordon children headed for Cleveland to join Joe. Typically, the Gordons traveled three times a year (to spring training, then to New York City or Cleveland for the baseball season, then back home to Oregon), but sometimes more.

The Gordon children remember loving their family's cross-country adventures. Over the years, they got to do and see things that most kids never dreamed of, such as riding the train or driving clear across the country twice or more each year; swimming in the ocean at St Petersburg, Florida; visiting the Empire State Building, Statue of Liberty, Bronx Zoo, and Madison Square Garden in New York City; seeing Mount Rushmore soon after it was completed; and watching the bison, elk, and lots of bears at Yellowstone National Park. Perhaps most memorable, however, was when they also got to attend baseball games at Yankee Stadium and Cleveland's Municipal Stadium, and experienced the excitement of sometimes 50,000 or more fans cheering and throwing hats in the air whenever *their* dad hit a home run or completed an especially thrilling double play!

The Gordons were fortunate in finding a three-bedroom home to rent in Rocky River, Ohio, a quiet western suburb of Cleveland. Their landlord, Oscar Grimes, had been a utility infielder for the Indians, Yankees, and Athletics, although in 1947 he was playing for the Toronto Maple Leafs of the International League.[31] Grimes had been the player who substituted for Gordon at second base when Joe got spiked so badly during 1946 Yankees spring training.

Out on the ball field, the keystone combination of Joe Gordon at second base and Lou Boudreau at shortstop was performing like clockwork. During the first 23 games of the season, it was reported that they "cleanly fielded" 246 out of 249 chances, for a .988 fielding average.[32]

With Bill Veeck's "ingenious promotional schemes," the Cleveland Indians were drawing record numbers of fans to their games. Adding live music, Veeck stationed a band beyond the new outfield fence and roaming troubadours playing musical requests before and during the games.[33] Lou Boudreau wrote, "You couldn't be around the Indians in those days without being caught up in the sweep of events. It was more than mere showmanship, much more than the simple giving away of nylon stockings, the fireworks displays after night games, the vaudeville acts, the hiring of specialists in baseball clowning like Jackie Price and Max Patkin. It was a new spirit, a new outlook on life. You felt that you belonged to an organization that was going places come hell or high water."[34]

Joe Gordon was hitting well enough that he ended the month of May batting .279. But by early June, he would get mired in a downward-spiraling slump, eventually bottoming out at .229 on July 1. Meanwhile, the club was bouncing in and out of the American League's first division.

On the morning of July 3, Bill Veeck released a historically significant and far-reaching announcement that the Cleveland Indians were purchasing second baseman Larry Doby from the Newark Eagles of the Negro National League.[35] Doby joined up with the Indians on July 5, while the team was on the road at Chicago. On that day, just 11 and a half weeks after Brooklyn Dodgers infielder Jackie Robinson had become the first African American ballplayer to play in the National League, 23-year-old Larry Doby debuted with the Cleveland Indians as the first African American ballplayer in the American League. It was a momentous occasion for baseball and the future of our nation.

It was reported that Doby signed his contract "at high noon" and "before a battery of cameras" in an office at Chicago's Comiskey Park on July 5. He was escorted to the visitors' clubhouse and introduced to manager Lou Boudreau. After dressing in his Indians uniform, he talked briefly with his manager about "signs, club rules and related matters." As to when Doby was introduced to his teammates, accounts vary widely about what happened and are included in multiple sources.[36]

As Doby was escorted out onto the field, reported *Cleveland Plain Dealer* sports editor Gordon Cobbledick, he received applause, swelling to "the proportions of an ovation." It also was reported that "Lou [Boudreau] himself warmed up with the newcomer on the sidelines before infield practice began. Then as they took [to] the diamond for their pregame drill he [Boudreau] introduced him [Doby] to Joe Gordon, with whom he [Doby] shared the second base duties in practice."[37]

Almost all accounts agree that second baseman Joe Gordon was the first player to ask Doby to "have a catch" during infield practice.[38] Many years later, *Newark Star-Ledger* writer Jerry Izenberg reported what Doby had told him at Cooperstown just

Chapter 15. The "Flash" Is Back! (1947)

hours before Doby was inducted into the National Baseball Hall of Fame on July 26, 1998: "It was my first day with the Indians. I stood at the edge of the field, as alone as I had ever been. I wore the same [Cleveland Indians] uniform but nobody would throw me the ball. Gordon saw it and he walked over and he said: 'Hey, rookie, you gonna pose or do you wanna warm up?' I will never forget that."[39]

Boudreau later wrote, "Joe [Gordon] was great with Larry, not just that first day, but every day."[40] Gordon's grandson and coauthor of this book, Erik Simpson, who knew his grandfather well, says, "He [Grandpa Joe] was truly color blind." During her acceptance speech for the induction of her father into the National Baseball Hall of Fame on July 26, 2009, Joe's daughter Judy said, "This was not just an isolated occurrence—this was how my father lived his whole life."[41]

Hall of Fame second baseman Joe Morgan also told about Larry Doby's high regard for Joe Gordon: "[H]e [Doby] did tell me about Joe Gordon and always spoke highly of him. Doby told me that the first day he went on the field to warm up with the [Cleveland] Indians, no one would throw with him. But Gordon stepped up and said, 'I'll play catch with you.' Doby spoke in glowing terms about how much that meant to him. Because Gordon was an All-Star, many of Doby's teammates fell in line after that."[42]

On July 26, 2009, literally minutes before Judy Gordon took to the stage at Cooperstown, Joe Morgan made a special point of talking with Judy about how much Larry Doby admired her father.[43] Joe Morgan's comments still mean the world to Judy and to her family!

Trailblazing sports journalist Claire Smith also told how Dottie Gordon was one of the Indians players' wives who befriended Doby's wife, Helyn: "So, while Joe Gordon forever won Larry Doby's friendship by becoming the first Cleveland player to offer to have a catch, Helyn Doby found a soul mate [sic] in Gordon's wife. And in [Bill] Veeck's, Jim Hegan's, Bob Lemon's, [and] Steve Gromek's."[44]

Larry Doby was not in the Indians' starting lineup on July 5. But with one out in the top of the seventh inning, Chicago leading, 5–1, and Cleveland runners Hank Edwards on first base and Joe Gordon on third, manager Boudreau sent Doby in the game to pinch-hit. Doby "got a rousing hand from a Comiskey Park crowd of more than 18,000 as he stepped up to bat for [p]itcher Bryan Stephens."[45] Although Doby, a left-handed batter, struck out on a 2–2 pitch in his only time at bat that historic day, he was given a stirring round of applause on his way back to the bench.

Over the years, differing accounts emerged of Doby striking out in his first and only time at bat. One account, in particular, portrayed Joe Gordon batting immediately after Doby and striking out on purpose, then returning to the bench to sit beside Larry, dejectedly holding his head in his hands. This version may have originated 14 years later, when Bill Veeck, who sometimes was known to embellish a bit, was interviewed on a New York radio show.[46] Veeck's version, however, was not what actually took place. Joe Gordon was the runner on third base when Doby struck out in his one and only time at bat that day. Furthermore, anyone who ever saw Gordon play ball would *know* that he never struck out on purpose—unless, for some bizarre reason, he was ordered to do so by his manager.

Still at Chicago on July 6, manager Boudreau penciled Doby's name on the Indians' lineup card to play first base, a position he had not played since high school.[47] Borrowing a first baseman's mitt, Larry played the whole game and recorded his first hit and RBI, in addition to eight putouts without an error.[48]

During the 1947 season, Doby appeared in just 29 games, with only 33 plate appearances and one complete game. Besides getting to play so infrequently, it was an extremely tough three months for the new American Leaguer.[49] Years later, upon his well-deserved election to the National Baseball Hall of Fame, a tribute to Doby was published in the *U.S. Congressional Record: Proceedings and Debates of the 105th Congress, Second Session*, titled "Congratulations to Larry Doby on His Introduction [*sic*] to the Baseball Hall of Fame." The tribute reads in part:

> Doby suffered the same kind of appalling treatment as the far more famous [Jackie] Robinson—beanball pitches at the plate and brutal tags on the basepaths [*sic*] from opponents, the silent treatment or worse from teammates, boos and insults from fans, segregated accommodations on the road—and he endured it with the same kind of quiet dignity and outstanding on-field performance that distinguished [Jackie] Robinson's career. These unbelievably courageous and self-disciplined men did much to change American attitudes and pave the way for the civil rights revolution of the 1960s.[50]

Russell Schneider, author of *The Boys of the Summer of '48*, years later quoted Doby saying that his three months during the 1947 season were "the toughest time I went through in my entire baseball career."[51]

The 14th Annual MLB All-Star Game was scheduled for the afternoon of July 8 at Wrigley Field, home of the Chicago Cubs. Boston Red Sox manager Joe Cronin piloted the American League All-Stars, and St. Louis Cardinals manager Eddie Dyer led the National League's. Net proceeds from the game were designated for the players' pension fund.[52]

Baseball fans throughout the country got to vote for the eight starting players (other than pitchers) for each team, with the starters playing at least the first three innings.[53] A reported 1,973,493 fans took part in the polling, which was sponsored by 193 newspapers, radio stations, and magazines, with the results tabulated by the *Chicago Tribune*.[54] Two Cleveland Indians players started for the American League: shortstop Lou Boudreau and second baseman Joe Gordon. Indians catcher Jim Hegan was selected for the American League's 18-player reserves, in addition to the American League's winningest pitcher of 1947, Bob Feller.[55]

Gordon played the first 5½ innings of the game, hitting a double and striking out once in two at-bats. In the bottom of the sixth inning, Boston's Bobby Doerr replaced Gordon at second base, and Doerr scored the game-winning run in the top of the seventh. Lou Boudreau played the entire game, executing a tremendous, game-saving fielding play in the eighth inning.[56] The American League edged out the National League, 2–1.

Playing at home on July 10, Indians right-hander Don Black hurled a no-hitter in the first game of the twi-night doubleheader, a 3–0 victory against his former Philadelphia Athletics. It was the first no-hit game ever pitched at Cleveland's Municipal Stadium. After the game, Black expressed high praise for Joe Gordon's brilliant catch in the third inning, dashing at full speed into right field with his back to the plate: "That catch of Gordon's really saved me, though, didn't it?" Bill Veeck celebrated the momentous occasion with a big, between-games fireworks display.[57] Three days later, playing against Boston, Gordon belted his 15th home run of the season to tie Ted Williams for the American League lead.[58]

Gordon's hitting improved in August. The Indians were drawing huge crowds at home, and, by August 10, they'd already surpassed their previous whole season's 1,057,289 attendance.[59] In a late–August article in *The Sporting News*, Ed McAuley wrote

Chapter 15. The "Flash" Is Back! (1947)

about Joe Gordon's batting and defense: "Since Gordon found his stride, his pace has been well over the .300 mark. But his real value is not reflected in his batting average. He is the club's leader in homers with 22, in runs-batted-in with 62, in bases on balls with 48, and in runs scored with 69. Add to this impressive record his flawless work in the field, and you have a day-after-day star."[60]

But while at bat in late August, the Indians' 26-year-old first baseman, Eddie Robinson, fouled an Allie Reynolds fastball off his right leg, breaking his ankle and putting him out of action for the remainder of the season.[61] Thirty-two-year-old Les Fleming took over at first base and played the rest of the games.

The Indians swept the St. Louis Browns in a twin bill at Cleveland on September 1 to climb back into the first division—in fourth place. Ten days later, Joe Gordon set a record for Cleveland Indians right-handed batters with his 27th home run in the first game of a doubleheader at Boston.[62] He belted his 28th and 29th round-trippers in the first game of a doubleheader at Philadelphia on September 16, again tying Ted Williams for the American League lead.[63] Gordon also hit a 30th home run at Detroit on September 21, but "[w]inds and rain of near hurricane violence" washed out the game after three innings, with the score tied at 2–2, which also washed the Flash's home run out of the record books.[64]

On September 27, 1947, Gordon became vested as a "ten-year man" in the major leagues. By then, he had played eight full seasons in the American League, and, like other ballplayers who'd served their country during World War II, he was given credit for his service in the U.S. Army during 1944 and 1945. This was significant, in that upon reaching the retirement age of 50, he would be eligible to receive an annuity paying him $100 per month for life.[65]

Joe Gordon wrapped up his "comeback season" with 29 home runs, second in the American League to 1947's Triple Crown winner Ted Williams's 32 four-baggers, and nine more than his former Yankees teammate Joe DiMaggio's 20 round-trippers. The BBWAA voted Joe DiMaggio his third Most Valuable Player Award (1939, 1941, and 1947), this time by just *one* point over second-place Ted Williams.[66] Lou Boudreau placed third in the MVP voting by one point over Yankees southpaw Joe Page. Joe Gordon placed seventh by one point over Indians pitcher Bob Feller.

The Cleveland Indians finished in fourth place with an 80–74 record, 17 games behind the pennant-winning New York Yankees, five games back of second-place Detroit, and three games behind third-place Boston. They topped their previous year's home attendance by almost 500,000 and set a new Indians attendance record of 1,521,978, guaranteeing Joe Gordon his full $2,000 bonus. Bob Feller was the only American League pitcher to win 20 or more games, finishing with a 20–11 record, 2.68 ERA, and major league-leading 196 strikeouts and 299 innings pitched. Former infielder-outfielder-turned-pitcher Bob Lemon posted an impressive 11–5 record, while pitching just the second half of the season. Ed Klieman tied the American League for the most saves with 17. It also was reported that the Indians set a new major league fielding percentage record of .983.[67]

Joe Gordon's eighth season in major league baseball, at 32 years of age, 1947 was a great year for the Flash. He led his team in games played (155), runs (89), home runs (29), RBI (93), slugging percentage (.496), and stolen bases (7). His fielding average of .978 set a new record for Indians second basemen.[68] In *The Sporting News*, Doc Goldstein quoted Gordon's teammate, Larry Doby saying, "I used to watch Joe [Gordon] and [Lou]

Boudreau in practice and just shake my head." Doby also described Gordon as "simply out of this hemisphere," noting how, in his opinion, "Gordon was chiefly responsible for the Indians winding up in a first division slot."[69]

Joe Gordon was named *The Oregonian's* Professional Athlete of the Year for 1947. Bill Hulen reported, "Gordon made one of the year's great comebacks with the Indians. He batted .272, belted 29 homers, was selected by the nation's fans as the American [L]eague second baseman for the [A]ll-[S]tar [G]ame, and was named to the same position … in an *Associated Press* poll of 233 baseball writers."[70] The "Flash" was back! And 1948 promised to be an even greater year!

Chapter 16

A Storybook Season (1948)

In October 1947, Cleveland Indians president Bill Veeck declared, "To me, [n]othing on this earth is more important than winning the pennant."[1] The Indians had not won a pennant since 1920, when they also won the World Series, five games to two, over the Brooklyn Robins (later the Dodgers).

In late January 1948, *The Sporting News* announced their Major League All-Star Team of 1947.[2] The Cleveland Indians topped all 16 clubs with three players voted onto the team: Lou Boudreau (shortstop), Joe Gordon (second base), and Bob Feller (pitcher).

By mid–January, Joe Gordon had received his 1948 Cleveland Indians contract in the mail, offering him a raise of $5,000 to $25,000.[3] Bill Veeck also assured Joe that he, again, would be eligible for an attendance-based bonus at the end of the season.[4]

Daughter Judy was in second grade, so the Gordon children remained at home in Eugene with their grandmother, while Joe and Dottie drove to Tucson, Arizona, for the 1948 Indians' spring training. The Gordons arrived a week early and vacationed at the Veecks' Lazy Vee Ranch, where they enjoyed horseback riding and exploring in the nearby mountains. Cleveland sportswriter Gordon Cobbledick wrote in *Sport* magazine about how Joe lightheartedly practiced his calf roping skills on his "obedient," good-humored wife Dottie, while at the Lazy Vee.[5] Indians rookie infielder Ray Boone later talked about attending a rodeo in Tucson, where Gordon rode one of the bucking horses and stayed on for the full eight seconds.[6]

Although the Flash was 33 years old, he was down to a trim 175 pounds after having played basketball and handball, and hunted and fished throughout the winter months.[7] As the players arrived at training, Bill Veeck assigned some of them new road trip roommates.[8] Years later, Joe Gordon's 1948 roomie, first baseman Eddie Robinson, told Judy Gordon, "Oftentimes people ask me who was my favorite teammate, and I say, 'Joe Gordon.' I think of Joe often. He was just one hell of a guy."[9]

Lou Boudreau wrote in *Player-Manager* that he was committed to going "all out" to try to win the 1948 pennant. He scheduled two workouts per day, focusing on instilling "a spirit of confidence and determination" in his players.[10] Boudreau also was blessed with an outstanding coaching staff: veteran infielder and 24-year major league manager Bill McKechnie, longtime catcher and coach Muddy Ruel, and the Indians' 20-year pitching great, Mel Harder.[11] Hall of Fame second baseman Rogers Hornsby again coached the Indians in batting during spring training.[12] Bill Veeck also brought the Detroit Tigers' former home run king, "Hammerin' Hank" Greenberg, onboard as his right-hand man and confidante, and subsequent vice president of the club.[13]

The mutual respect between manager Boudreau and second baseman Gordon remained strong in 1948, as it had been the previous year. Joe was quoted in *Sport* magazine, saying, "I forget to play second base because it's such a pleasure to watch that guy [Boudreau] play shortstop." Likewise, Boudreau voiced high regard for Gordon's defense: "If I seem to be in a daze out there, it's probably because I'm wondering if Joe really did what he did or if I dreamed it."[14] Gordon was one of Boudreau's closest confidants on the team, as well as extremely well-liked by his teammates, who looked up to him as a team leader.[15]

The 1948 Cleveland Indians again were armed with a rock-solid infield: Eddie Robinson at first base; veterans Joe Gordon at second, Lou Boudreau at shortstop, and Kenny Keltner at third; and one of the best catchers in baseball, Jim Hegan.[16] Their pitching staff included future Hall of Famers Bob Feller, Bob Lemon, and later Satchel Paige; in addition to Steve Gromek, Don Black, Eddie Klieman, and rookie southpaw Gene Bearden. In early April, Bill Veeck purchased "iron-armed relief hurler" Russ Christopher from the Philadelphia Athletics.[17] Christopher would finish the 1948 season as one of the major leagues' top relievers. Just hours before the midnight June 15 trade deadline, Veeck acquired southpaw Sam Zoldak from the St. Louis Browns.[18]

At the suggestion of Biz Mackey (Larry Doby's former manager with the Negro National League Newark Eagles), coach Bill McKechnie and manager Lou Boudreau decided in late 1947 to convert Doby from a second baseman to an outfielder, under the tutelage of Hall of Fame outfielder and former Indians player-manager Tris "The

The Cleveland Indians infield is ready to go on April 8, 1948, at spring training, probably in Tucson, Arizona: (from left) third baseman Kenny Keltner, team manager and shortstop Lou Boudreau, second baseman Joe Gordon, and first baseman Eddie Robinson (*Cleveland Press Collection, Michael Schwartz Library, Cleveland State University*).

Grey Eagle" Speaker.[19] Speaker later praised his talented pupil, saying, "I've never seen a young player with such a high potential…. I used to dream of that kind of a rookie when I was managing the Indians."[20]

Wrapping up their training in Arizona, the Indians barnstormed toward home along with the New York Giants.[21] On the train, Joe Gordon and his trusty "accomplice," utility infielder Johnny Berardino, wrote, produced, and starred in a "suspenseful mystery drama" titled "The Case of the Missing Meal Money."[22] Berardino, years later simplifying his name to John Beradino, became a well-known film and TV actor, probably best-known for his role as Dr. Steve Hardy in the TV soap opera *General Hospital*.

The Indians opened their 1948 season on April 20, playing at home against the St. Louis Browns, to a colossal attendance of 73,163, at the time the largest Opening Day crowd in major league history.[23] Indians fans reveled in Bob Feller's two-hit shutout, 4–0. Winning their first six games in a row, they ended April in first place—a great start!

In 2016, writer Christian Red interviewed former Indians first baseman Eddie Robinson, who was then 95 years old. Robinson recalled what Joe Gordon had told him after the club's fourth win in 1948: "We're going to win the pennant."[24]

Playing at Boston on May 10, the Indians executed a triple play in the bottom of the eighth inning, scored as 6–4–3 (Boudreau to Gordon to Robinson). Gordon and Doby both homered in their 12–7 victory over the Red Sox.

Playing the visiting Boston Red Sox on May 20, the Indians recorded a whopping 18 bases on balls during their 13–4 victory. They were in first place, with a 16–6 (.727) record.

On May 23, with the Yankees playing at Cleveland for the first time that year, the attendance of 78,431 set a new record for Municipal Stadium, including the overflow crowd of 2,000 standing-room-only fans on the grass behind Veeck's portable outfield fence.[25] In the opener of the twin bill, Yankees center fielder Joe DiMaggio belted three home runs to drive in all six runs for the Yankees' 6–5 victory. The Indians bounced back to take the nightcap, 5–1. But following the doubleheader, Joe Gordon was beset with painful back troubles, which benched him for the next eight games and part of a ninth.[26] Johnny Berardino, the Indians' jack-of-all-trades utility infielder, took over at second base.

The Indians dropped back to second place, although not lingering long. They recaptured first place in early June. At the time, it was reported that they were leading all major league clubs in holding their opponents to an average of just 3.41 runs per game.[27]

Playing a four-game series at Yankee Stadium in mid–June, Cleveland won three out of four. Gordon's play in the June 12 doubleheader was portrayed in the media as, "Ex-Yankee Joe Gordon had a field day on the eve of the celebration of the opener of Yankee [S]tadium, pacing the American [L]eague leading Cleveland Indians to a double victory over the world champion New Yorkers today 7–5 and 9–4 before a capacity throng of 68,586."[28] The Flash belted three home runs that day, one in the first game off Allie Reynolds and two in the nightcap off Spec Shea, in addition to recording six RBI and executing four double plays. Lou Boudreau later wrote, "Joe has always been a prime favorite in Yankee Stadium but the 68,586 people who jammed the place that day must have been happy to see him disappear through the dugout door after we got the Yankees out in the ninth inning of the second game."[29]

On April 18, 1923, the New York Yankees had dedicated their brand-new $2.5 million Yankee Stadium.[30] Twenty-five years later, the Bombers planned to commemorate their Stadium's Silver Anniversary, in addition to retiring Babe Ruth's uniform Number 3. However, the Yankees were on the road Opening Day of 1948. That, coupled with Babe Ruth's recent declining health and multiple hospitalizations, resulted in the 25th Anniversary celebration being scheduled for June 13, 1948, when warmer weather would be more amenable to "The Babe's" well-being.

Members of the 1923 world champion New York Yankees suited up for a two-inning exhibition game against a team of Yankees stars of subsequent years. The players were introduced as they came out onto the field. Joe Gordon, wearing his old Yankees uniform for the exhibition game, was given a "tremendous ovation" by his many, still-loyal fans.[31]

Babe Ruth, donning his Yankees uniform for the last time, stepped out from the dugout, waving his cap to a "thunderous roar" from the fans. His uniform Number 3 was permanently retired that day and later displayed in the National Baseball Hall of Fame and Museum. Speaking barely above a whisper, the great "Bambino" said, "Ladies and gentlemen, I just want to say one thing. I am proud I hit the first home run here against Boston in 1923. It is marvelous to see these 13 or 14 players who were my teammates going back 25 years. I'm telling you it makes me proud and happy to be here. Thank you."[32]

Babe Ruth makes his final appearance at Yankee Stadium on June 13, 1948. We believe that Joe Gordon is standing fourth from the right in the line of uniformed players along the first base line. Gordon is wearing his old Yankees uniform for the two-inning exhibition game against the 1923 Yankees Stars of Yesteryear (photograph "The Babe Bows Out" by Nat Fein).

This would be "The Babe's" final appearance at Yankee Stadium. Sadly, he passed away from throat cancer two months later on August 16, 1948, at the age of just 53.

Back in his Cleveland Indians uniform for the scheduled game against the Yankees, Joe Gordon went 2–for–3 and scored a run. But as Rud Rennie wrote in the *New York Herald Tribune*, "It was a pleasantly memorable day for all the Yankee family except Gordon, who donned a Yankee uniform to be introduced along with other former Yankee stars before the game. Back in his own uniform, Gordon doubled and scored the Indians' run in the fourth. Then he was fated to make the error which lost the game."[33]

On Father's Day, June 20, two future Hall of Famers, Bob Feller and Bob Lemon, pitched a doubleheader, as Cleveland's Municipal Stadium welcomed a "major-league record crowd of 82,781." The Indians swept both games from the second-place Philadelphia Athletics.[34] Their elated president, Bill Veeck, proclaimed the record crowd as "the biggest thrill of his career." It also was reported that 70,000 hot dogs and 120,000 bottles of soft drinks and beer were sold that day.[35]

Playing a night game at Detroit on June 30, Bob Lemon hurled a no-hitter, striking out four and giving up just three walks, to blank the Tigers, 2–0. After the game, Lemon was asked if he knew that he had a no-hitter going and answered, "The fellows on the bench wouldn't talk to me from the sixth inning on. I thought at the time it was funny, but didn't quite know what was happening. Boy, oh boy, what a thrill it was when that last out was made."[36]

A week before the 1948 MLB All-Star Game, Joe wrote home about his performance so far during the 1948 season: "I guess I made the All-Star Game again. It seems like I never get any older. Everyone says I am as fast as I ever was, which makes me feel good, as I'm pretty old [age 33] for an infielder."[37]

Almost a year to the day that the Cleveland Indians signed Larry Doby in 1947, Bill Veeck signed iconic right-handed pitcher LeRoy "Satchel" Paige, formerly of the Kansas City Monarchs of the Negro American League. "Satch" later recalled in his book, *Maybe I'll Pitch Forever*, "I got to Cleveland on July 7, 1948. That was my forty-second birthday and I was about to get me the best birthday present I'd ever had.... I wasn't as fast as I used to be, but I was a better pitcher. If I couldn't overpower them, I'd outcute [sic] them."[38]

During a night game at home on July 9, Paige was the first of three relievers of starter Bob Lemon against the visiting St. Louis Browns. "Satch" recalled about walking out to the mound: "There were about thirty-five thousand in those stands and lots of them were there just hoping they'd get to see me.... It seemed like a mighty long walk from the bullpen to the pitcher's mound. I didn't go fast. No reason for wearing myself out just walking. I just shuffled along and every time I shuffled[,] the stands busted loose like they never was so happy to see anyone in their life."[39]

Everyone *loved* when Satchel Paige pitched, and especially the Gordon kids! "Satch" appeared in 21 games for the 1948 Cleveland Indians, mostly as a reliever. He also started seven games to finish the second half of the season with an excellent 6–1 record and 2.48 ERA.

The 15th Annual MLB All-Star Game was played on July 13 at Sportsman's Park, home of the American League St. Louis Browns and National League St. Louis Cardinals. Three members of the Indians started for the American League: shortstop Lou Boudreau, second baseman Joe Gordon, and third baseman Ken Keltner.[40] Bucky Harris, manager of the American League All-Stars, also picked two Cleveland Indians for

Joe Gordon's membership plaque is in recognition of him being just the 25th player in the history of the major leagues to join the 200 Home Run Club, which he achieved on July 19, 1948, at Griffith Stadium in Washington, D.C. (Gordon family collections).

his pitching staff, Bob Feller and Bob Lemon, although neither pitched in the game.[41] The American League beat the National League, 5–2, with net proceeds from the game going to the ballplayers' pension fund.[42]

During a night game on July 19 at Griffith Stadium in Washington, D.C., Joe Gordon hit the 200th home run of his career.[43] Although home run records have soared since then, Joe Gordon was just the 25th player in the history of the American and National Leagues to achieve this record.[44]

Losing a doubleheader at Boston on July 24, the Indians' almost seven-week sojourn either in or tied for first place came to an abrupt end, and they dropped back to third. On August 3, the "largest night crowd in Cleveland baseball history," a reported 72,434 lucky fans, got to watch LeRoy "Satchel" Paige start his first American League game and hurl "seven strong innings" in the Indians' 5–3 victory over the Washington Senators.[45] His win boosted the club into a four-way tie for first place with the Yankees, Red Sox, and Athletics.

Three days later, it was Joe Gordon's turn for a big night, going 3-for-3 and hitting his 21st home run of the season, with three RBI to help beat the Yankees, 9–7. Ed McAuley wrote an article in the *Cleveland News*, titled "The Flash," a condensed version of which was printed in the August 1948 issue of *Sportfolio* magazine, saying, in part, "At 33, the oldest man on the Cleveland roster [except for Satchel Paige], Gordon still handles his second base assignment with the agility of a rookie and with infinitely more success."[46]

The Indians oscillated between first and second place in early August and were in second place, trailing first-place Philadelphia by one-half game after a twilight-night doubleheader at St. Louis on August 12. They lost the opener but bounced back in the nightcap, belting 29 hits to beat the Browns, 26–3. Including that game, they posted a string of eight consecutive wins, five of them shutouts (including two by Satchel Paige), which had them back in first place by three games on August 20.

But back in the nightcap of a doubleheader at Chicago on August 15, Joe Gordon had badly sprained his ankle, forcing him to sit out the next four games.[47] A few days later, Dottie Gordon wrote a note to Joe's fishing buddy, *Eugene Register-Guard* sports editor Dick Strite, telling him, "Cleveland has pennant fever and they all have their fingers crossed."[48]

Coming up on 28 years since Cleveland had won their only pennant in 1920, they continued to break their own home attendance records. On August 20, Satchel Paige hurled a one-hour and 50-minute, three-hit shutout, with Larry Doby driving in the lone run to beat the Chicago White Sox, 1–0.[49] The game set another new attendance record for major league night games, with its monumental crowd of 78,382. The next day, the Indians' string of holding their opponents scoreless for 47 consecutive innings topped the old American League record of 41 innings set by the Indians back in 1903.[50]

But the outlook did not remain all rose-colored forever. They lost three in a row to Chicago plus one more at Boston on August 24, dropping them to second place.[51] A few days later, they succumbed to the Yankees in the stifling 98-degree heat of New York City and dropped back to third.[52] By then it looked as though there might be three contenders for the American League pennant: Boston, New York, and Cleveland.

September held the keys to the pennant—or almost! The Indians went into the month in third place, 1½ games behind Boston and a half-game back of New York. Splitting a doubleheader at Chicago on Labor Day, September 6, they dropped back to 4½ games behind the Red Sox.[53] Years later, Gordon Cobbledick, sports editor of the *Cleveland Plain Dealer,* recalled how Joe Gordon had exhorted his dispirited teammates to action during the between-games break: "What in hell is wrong with you guys? Here you're breezing along to a pennant and you act like a lot of dead men."[54] The pep talk worked. They bucked up and took the nightcap, 1–0, on Bob Feller's three-hit pitching. What's more, they forged ahead to win their next six games in a row, too.

In the meantime, center fielder Larry Doby was in the midst of a 20-game hitting streak from August 22 through September 9, before injuring his thumb and having to sit out six games. Back in the lineup on September 16, his first-inning grand slam clinched the game for the Indians and his 21st consecutive game with a hit.[55]

It was now or never. With the prospects of the pennant riveted in their sights, the team pulled together an impressive sprint, chalking up a September/October record of 22 wins, eight losses, and one tie, for a .733 winning percentage.

Likewise, Joe Gordon upped his home run production with an epic run of his own. During September/October he belted nine home runs and drove in 24 runs in 31 games (including the tied game) for a .304 average. Third baseman Kenny Keltner kept right on Gordon's heels, with six homers and 29 RBI for a .351 average, including a *very* crucial three-run round-tripper on October 4 at Boston.

However, tragedy struck the Indians on September 13. While at bat during a game at home against the St. Louis Browns, the Indians' 32-year-old pitcher, Don Black, suffered a cerebral hemorrhage and was rushed to the hospital in extremely critical condition.[56] Don would remain hospitalized for six weeks while recovering from his tragic, career-ending ordeal. Bill Veeck declared September 22 as "Don Black Night" at Municipal Stadium and donated the Indians' gate receipts of more than $40,000 to the pitcher and his family.[57] That night, Bob Feller hurled a "magnificent" three-hitter, striking out six and walking just two, to beat the Red Sox, 5–2. The Indians were now tied with the Red Sox for first place, just .002 points ahead of the Yankees.

The following day, Commissioner Chandler authorized the Indians to print tickets in anticipation of playing in the World Series. Prices were $8 for box seats, $6.25 for reserved, and $1 for bleachers.[58]

The Gordon children still remember how, earlier that summer, some enterprising Cleveland merchants had decided to sweeten the race to the pennant by awarding the Indians' two top home run leaders, Joe Gordon and Ken Keltner, a case of Wheaties and a case of bubble gum for every round-tripper they hit. The Gordon family ate Wheaties every day for breakfast and sometimes for lunch, and even fed some to their dog, Rex. They gave away bubble gum to all the kids in their neighborhood. Eventually, Gordon and Keltner donated their Wheaties and bubble gum to various children's group homes in the Cleveland area.[59]

With Cleveland schools about to begin that fall, and the International League baseball season already wrapped up, the Gordons' landlord, Oscar Grimes, and his family were returning to their home in Rocky River.[60] The Gordons had to find another place to live. At first, they tried staying at the Westlake Hotel in Rocky River. But the two kids were wild, riding the elevator up and down until the hotel manager had to ask the very embarrassed Dottie to please rein them in a bit. Finally, Joe found a small, furnished home to rent, close to a grammar school in Willoughby, Ohio, a suburb of Northeast Cleveland.[61] Judy was in the third grade, and Joey was just starting first grade.

After seven consecutive wins, the Indians lost a close game at Detroit on September 24, to find themselves in a three-way tie for first place with the Red Sox and Yankees. Needing to plan ahead in case the pennant race ended in a tie, American League president William Harridge held a coin-toss ceremony in his Chicago office to determine where any playoff game (or games) would take place.[62] The Indians were not lucky in either case. If they tied the Red Sox, they'd have to travel to Boston for the playoff game; if they tied the Yankees, they'd have to go to New York.

A newspaper article about the September 29 game reads, "As has been the case in recent days, the big bats of Joe Gordon and Ken Keltner furnished most of the fireworks. Between them they drove in all Cleveland's runs to give the [T]ribe their 18th victory in their last 21 games."[63] The Indians ended September in first place, 1½ games ahead of the Red Sox and Yankees.

The week before the 1948 World Series was scheduled to begin, the *Oregon Journal* published an article about their hometown hero, Joe Gordon. In the article, Indians president Bill Veeck said: "The deal I made with the Yankees for Joe Gordon is the best I ever made in baseball."[64]

The Indians lost at home on October 1, when Detroit's Jimmy Outlaw came into the game late and "played the villain's role" by driving in two runs for the Tigers in the ninth inning.⁶⁵ The next day, the Indians bounced back, as southpaw Gene Bearden "blanked the Tigers on eight scattered hits[,] ensuring at least a tie in the final standings."⁶⁶

October 3 was the final game of the regular season. It was played under what was reported as "extremely adverse conditions, with a howling wind whipping through [Municipal] Stadium from Lake Erie and the temperature more like an Oregon steelhead fishing day than one for a game designed to be played under a broiling sun."⁶⁷ But the pennant would not be won that day—not yet. Bob Feller plus a "parade of five Cleveland flingers" (Zoldak, Klieman, and Gromek; in addition to two rookies up from the minors, Mike Garcia and Ernest Groth) took a "7–1 beating" from future Hall of Famer Hal Newhouser and his Tigers teammates.⁶⁸ This locked the Indians in a dead-heat tie with the Boston Red Sox, both teams with 96–58 (.623) records. The Yankees were out of the race, two games back. Bill Veeck's pronouncement after the Indians' loss spoke for itself: "We'll beat the Red Sox in the play-off [sic] tomorrow [October 4]. There's no use talking about today's game."⁶⁹

Even before the game had ended, manager Boudreau asked Joe Gordon who his choice would be to pitch the playoff game at Fenway Park the following day against the Boston Red Sox. The two men agreed—it should be southpaw knuckleballer Gene Bearden.⁷⁰

Immediately after losing to the Tigers, the Indians gathered in their clubhouse to discuss the next day's pitcher. Boudreau ordered the door barred and had a policeman stand outside.⁷¹ No members of the press or anyone else were allowed in. After Boudreau announced Gene Bearden as his choice to pitch the playoff game, only one player voiced concern.⁷² Bearden was a rookie and would be pitching the Indians' most important game of the 1948 season—after only one day of rest. But the Red Sox had four left-handed batters (Ted Williams, Billy Goodman, Johnny Pesky, and Stan Spence) in their regular lineup, and Bearden was the Indians' only southpaw who had started and finished a complete game at Boston's Fenway Park during the 1948 season (a 2–0 shutout on June 8).⁷³

In support of his manager's decision, Joe Gordon spoke up, saying, "Lou, we went along with your choice for 154 games and finished in a tie. There's not a man in this room who, two weeks ago, wouldn't have settled for a tie. I'm sure we can go along with you for another game."⁷⁴ Boudreau later wrote in *Player-Manager*, "That, coming from the most respected individual on our club, cut off any further debate…. The meeting was over. We were agreed on our purpose and we were agreed on our tactics."⁷⁵ Boudreau asked his players to keep Bearden's name a secret until game time, which they did.

The year 1948 was the first time in the 48-year history of the American League that two teams had finished the regular season tied. In 1946, the National League season also had ended in a tie, although their pennant winner was determined by a best-of-three-game playoff, won by the St. Louis Cardinals over the Brooklyn Dodgers in two games.

The winner-take-all, one-game playoff between the Cleveland Indians and Boston Red Sox would be played at Boston the next day, October 4. There would be *no* day off for travel! However, departing Cleveland on the overnight train, the players even managed to do a little partying along the way.⁷⁶

The players' wives would travel from Cleveland to Boston after the playoff game— *if* the Indians won the tiebreaker. The Boston Braves had clinched the National League pennant a full week earlier, and the World Series was scheduled to begin at Braves Field on October 6.

Arriving at Boston mid-morning October 4, contrary to what one might expect, the Indians were reported as "loose as a goose" in the visitors' clubhouse right before the "sudden death" playoff game.[77] Years later, Gene Bearden told how: "Gordon was the glue that held all of us together. He'd been through the pressure of pennant races before, with the Yankees, and helped keep all of us loose."[78]

Right before the playoff game, Joe Gordon was photographed talking with two distinguished visitors: Elmer Smith and Bill Wambsganss. Both men had played for the Cleveland Indians in the 1920 World Series.[79] Smith, a right fielder, was renowned for hitting the first grand slam in a World Series; and Wambsganss, a second baseman, for the only unassisted triple play ever recorded in World Series history.

After just one day off from pitching, 28-year-old Gene Bearden hurled a six-strikeout, complete-game five-hitter to win the most important game of his career, 8–3, and, along with his teammates, capture the 1948 American League pennant. Remarkably, this was Bearden's sixth start and sixth win (five of them complete games) in the final drive to the pennant.

Lou Boudreau led the charge in the playoff game—going 4-for-4, homering twice, singling twice, walking once, and scoring three times. When he came to bat in the ninth inning, he was given a well-deserved standing ovation—from Red Sox fans in their own home stadium![80] Ken Keltner smashed three hits, including his 31st home run of the season, which drove in three runs. Joe Gordon singled, leading to him scoring on Keltner's homer, in addition to turning two double plays. When the game ended, pitcher Gene Bearden was carried off the field on the shoulders of his jubilant teammates.[81] Amidst pandemonium in the clubhouse, Bearden managed to utter the words, "Am I happy? What a game to win, what a way to win it; what a spot to come through; what a gang of fellows to have behind you with their bats."[82]

Manager Joe McCarthy, who had just finished his first year of piloting the Boston Red Sox, said, "I've been licked before and I can be licked again. I'm sorry for the boys, that's all."[83]

Manager Boudreau wrote about the "riotous victory party" held at Boston's Kenmore Hotel.[84] During the celebration, Joe Gordon grabbed a microphone and gave a short speech: "As the player representative, I've been asked to propose a toast, and here it is. Let's all drink to the greatest major leaguer in the business, Lou Boudreau."[85]

The 1948 Cleveland Indians' regular season finally was over. Multiple players enjoyed career-best years. Playing in 144 games, 33-year-old Joe Gordon recorded career-bests in RBI (124) and home runs (32), leading the club in both categories while batting .280. One sportswriter wrote, "The Indians had no better clutch player. It was Joe's best season since 1942 at least and, perhaps, his best ever, all things considered."[86]

Sports Album magazine published an article, titled "Still the Flash," avowing, "The record books will never do justice to the play of the Oregonian [Joe Gordon]. You had to see him to believe he was as good as advertised."[87]

Just days shy of 32 years old, third baseman Kenny Keltner wrapped up his 1948 season with career bests of 119 RBI and 31 home runs in 153 games, including a game-winning three-run homer in the playoff game.

Between them, the Indians' four regular infielders amassed 432 RBI on their way to capturing the pennant: Gordon (124), Keltner (119), Boudreau (106), and Robinson (83).[88] David Kaiser, in *Epic Season: The 1948 American League Pennant Race*, wrote, "The heart of the 1948 Indians was their three veteran right-handed infielders, Joe Gordon,

Chapter 16. A Storybook Season (1948)

LouBoudreau, and Ken Keltner, who for that one season—together with Eddie Robinson—probably made up the greatest infield of all time."[89]

Indians regulars batting over or almost .300 included Lou Boudreau (.355) and Ken Keltner (.297); and outfielders Dale Mitchell (.336), Allie Clark (.310), Larry Doby (.301), and Bob Kennedy (.301). Joe Gordon's 32 home runs ranked second in the American League to Joe DiMaggio's 39 circuit clouts. It also was noted that Gordon placed third behind Joe DiMaggio and Ted Williams in RBI average (runs batted in per at-bat).[90] Ford Sawyer tagged Joe Gordon as the "home run king in nocturnal games, with ten round-trippers," noting that the Flash "belted the ball at a .309 clip after dark."[91] The Indians' dominance in night games proved to be one of the deciding factors in them winning the American League pennant.[92]

Pitching definitely was a strong suit. Three Cleveland pitchers finished with double-digit wins: Bob Lemon (20–14, 2.82 ERA, league-leading 293⅔ innings pitched and 20 complete games, and major league-leading 10 shutouts, in addition to his .286 batting average); rookie southpaw Gene Bearden (20–7, league-leading 2.43 ERA, with 15 complete games and six shutouts); and Bob Feller (19–15, league-leading 38 games started, and major league-leading 164 strikeouts). Indians reliever Russ Christopher tied with a major league-leading 17 saves. Lemon and Feller combined for 38 complete games.

The 1948 Indians also led defensively, missing by just .001 of tying their fielding percentage record of .983 set in 1947. Twice during 1948, Joe Gordon participated in five double plays in a single game, tying that record for second basemen.[93]

To Bill Veeck's delight, the Indians also set a new major league home attendance record of 2,620,627, topping their 1947 attendance by more than a million. Their record would stand for 14 years until broken by the Los Angeles Dodgers in 1962.[94]

Indians player-manager Lou Boudreau won the 1948 Most Valuable Player Award, "virtually by acclamation."[95] Bob Lemon finished fifth in the voting for MVP, Joe Gordon tied for sixth with Tommy Henrich of the Yankees, and Gene Bearden placed eighth. Bearden also placed second in the voting for the 1948 Major League Rookie of the Year (ROY) Award and later was named the Cleveland Indians' Man of the Year for 1948.[96] Beginning in 1949, there would be two ROY Awards, one for the American League and one for the National League.

Indians pitcher Bob Lemon received *The Sporting News'* prestigious American League Pitcher of the Year Award for 1948. *The Sporting News* also named Indians president Bill Veeck as baseball's Major League Executive of the Year.

The Indians enjoyed a much-needed day off on October 5, holding just an early-afternoon workout at Braves Field, home of the National League's pennant-winning Boston Braves. The World Series was scheduled to begin there the following day. Bill Veeck, in what some called "a stroke of genius," proposed that the games be scheduled on seven consecutive days, with no days off for travel. Somehow he convinced Braves owner Lou Perini to agree to it.[97] But this also meant that the two teams had to travel by overnight trains from Boston to Cleveland after Game Two on October 7, and from Cleveland back to Boston after Game Five on October 10—*if* more games were needed. Each team, though, probably figured they wouldn't need more than five games to wrap up the Series.

Game One on October 6 was a pitchers' duel from start to finish. Years later, Bob Feller wrote in *Now Pitching, Bob Feller*, "When the game started, I was as ready as I've ever been in my life. This was what all of us wanted, that we had worked for, and what I had been dreaming about since I was a boy."[98] Feller gave up only two hits and one run, yet Boston's Johnny Sain hurled a four-hit shutout for the Braves' 1–0 victory over the Indians.

The game turned out to be one of the most controversial in World Series history, when National League umpire Bill Stewart's hotly disputed call of "safe" during Feller's attempted pickoff of Braves pinch-runner Phil Masi at second base in the bottom of the eighth inning, eventually led to Masi scoring the winning run. A widely published four-photo sequence of the play *clearly* showed that shortstop Boudreau had tagged Masi out by a foot or more.[99] Years later, Stewart admitted to Feller that he "blew it" (the call).[100] And many years later, Masi himself was said to have acknowledged in his personal will that he should have been called out.[101]

International News Service staff correspondent Bob Considine wrote about Game Two on October 7: "The Cleveland Indians regained consciousness Thursday and yanked the Boston Braves out of their rose-colored paradise by whipping them solidly, 4 to 1, in the second game of the 1948 [W]orld [S]eries. The victory, astonishingly colorless, enabled the again strongly favored Cleveland club to draw abreast of the Braves at one game apiece."[102] The Braves' only run scored off Bob Lemon was reported as "bred and reared" on Joe Gordon's fumble in the first inning, followed by two Braves singles. Gordon, however, redeemed himself in the fourth inning, knocking in the Indians' first run to tie the game and scoring another on Doby's single.

Riding overnight sleeper trains from Boston to Cleveland, the Indians and Braves resumed play in Game Three on October 8. Indians southpaw Gene Bearden, coming off a well-deserved three days of rest, hurled a five-hit shutout, 2–0, in just one hour and 36 minutes, to put the Indians one game ahead in the Series.

Game Four on Saturday, October 9, played at Cleveland's mammoth Municipal Stadium, drew a record World Series crowd of 81,897 to what was reported as "the fourth and most spirited game of the championship." The portrayal of the game in the *Morning Oregonian* evokes excitement, even today: "The greatest mob in the history of that bizarre American ritual known as the [W]orld [S]eries bellowed madly Saturday as their treasured Cleveland Indians beat Johnny Sain and the Boston Braves, 2–1."[103] Steve Gromek, coming off his season's 9–3 record and 2.84 ERA, went up against the top major league hurler of 1948, Johnny Sain (24–15 and 2.60). But it took Gromek only one hour and 31 minutes to wrap up his complete-game victory. Larry Doby's decisive 425-foot home run over the right-center field fence in the third inning clinched the Indians' victory, after Lou Boudreau doubled in a run in the first inning.[104] Doby's homer was the first of the 1948 Fall Classic, in addition to the first ever hit by an African American ballplayer in a World Series. The historic photo of Steve Gromek and Larry Doby joyfully embracing after the game appeared in newspapers throughout the country.[105] Moreover, in 2023, that photo would be the incentive for a very special commemorative gold coin—the *Congressional Gold Medal*—minted in honor of Larry Doby and presented to Larry Doby, Jr., and his family by The Congress of the United States.[106]

Joe Gordon's mother, Louise; brother Jack; and their lumberman friend, Ben Cheney, traveled from Oregon to watch Joe play in what would be his sixth and final World Series (1938, 1939, 1941–1943, and 1948).[107]

There was tremendous anticipation that this would be "Rapid Robert" Feller's time to attain what he had longed for his entire life—a World Series victory. After the fifth

Chapter 16. A Storybook Season (1948)

inning, Cleveland led, 5–4. But Bob Feller and four relievers (Ed Klieman, Russ Christopher, Satchel Paige, and Bob Muncrief) could not thwart the resolute Braves, who came away with the victory, 11–5, on Warren Spahn's magnificent one-hit, seven-strikeout relief work in the final five and two-thirds innings.

The only bright spot for Cleveland fans that day was getting to see Satchel Paige come in to relieve in the top of the seventh inning—the first African American player to pitch in a World Series. "Satch" later told what he experienced: "They [the fans] kept chanting, 'We want Satchel.' ... [A]nd they yelled louder than they had any other time in the World Series up to then."[108] He pitched two-thirds of an inning, which included a sacrifice and a balk called on him because of his "hesitation pitch."

Rookie Al Rosen pinch-hit for Paige in the bottom of the seventh, adding to Game Five being a landmark in World Series history. Although not the first time that African American players were in a Fall Classic, 1948 was the first time they played for the winning team. Al Rosen's participation also marked one of the few times that a Jewish American had played in a World Series. At the time, the Cleveland Indians were the most racially and ethnically diverse team to win a world championship.

The sendoff crowd at Cleveland's Terminal Station after Game Five was estimated at between 10,000 and 15,000 well-wishing Indians fans.[109] The team's 13-car special pulled out of the train station at 5:30 P.M., scheduled to arrive in Boston the following morning at 8:00 A.M. Two more trains carried members of the press, and another 13-car special transported fans.

Played at Braves Field on October 11, Game Six would be remembered as "the best game of the championship."[110] Bill Voiselle started for the Braves, and Bob Lemon for the Indians. Cleveland scored in the third inning, and Boston tied it up in the fourth. Joe Gordon opened the sixth with a "booming home run [that] cleared the advertisement sign in left field and put the Indians in the lead for the second time."[111] Another run that inning boosted their lead to 3–1. Braves ace Warren Spahn came in to relieve in the top of the eighth on *no* days of rest, and Eddie Robinson singled in a run, bringing the score to 4–1.

In the bottom of the eighth, with the bases loaded and only one out, Gene Bearden came in to relieve Bob Lemon. The Braves scored two runs (charged against Lemon). Ed McAuley later revealed in his book, *Bob Lemon: The Work Horse*, that Lemon had been pitching at "[t]wenty pounds below his normal weight."[112]

In the bottom of the ninth inning, Gene Bearden wrapped up Game Six and the 1948 world championship, saving Bob Lemon's second win of the 1948 Fall Classic, 4–3. For the second time that week, the lanky knuckleballer was hoisted onto the shoulders of his "deliriously happy teammates."[113] Not to be forgotten, the Indians' great catcher, Jim Hegan, caught every inning of the six-game World Series.

Manager Lou Boudreau expressed tremendous praise for his rookie southpaw, Gene Bearden: "It was Bearden's [S]eries all the way, all his. Gene was the key to our success."[114]

Charles Heaton wrote in the *Cleveland Plain Dealer*, "A veteran [W]orld [S]eries campaigner while with the New York Yankees, Joe [Gordon] admitted that this probably topped them all. 'I've been in on a lot of baseball excitement,' the grinning veteran explained, 'but nothing like that pennant drive. It's sure great to be with a winner again.'"[115]

(From left) Indians second baseman Joe Gordon, starting pitcher Bob Lemon, manager and shortstop Lou Boudreau, and game-saving pitcher Gene Bearden celebrate in the clubhouse after winning the sixth and final game of the 1948 World Series, 4-3, against the Boston Braves on October 11, 1948 (The SABR-Rucker Archive).

Larry Doby played all six games of the Series, leading the Indians by batting .318. He was followed by Eddie Robinson, who played all six games and batted .300. With two runners on base in the top of the eighth inning of Game Six, Robinson singled in Kenny Keltner for the winning run—and the world championship. The payout to the winners set a new World Series record of $6,772 per share.[116]

It had been 10 years, almost to the day, since Joe Gordon won his first World Series championship ring while playing for the 1938 New York Yankees. Winning his fifth and final world championship emblem, the Flash chose the beautiful 1948 Cleveland Indians lady's ring for his wife, Dottie.

The celebration on the overnight train back to Cleveland was wildly spirited and boisterous. Gordon again toasted Lou Boudreau: "To the greatest leatherman I ever saw, to the damnedest clutch hitter that ever lived, to a doggone good manager, Lou."[117] It was reported that the overjoyed teammates basically trashed the railroad car they were celebrating in, which ended up costing Bill Veeck a reported $6,000 to $6,500 in damages.[118]

Amidst "[t]ooting horns, screaming sirens, and raining confetti," the baseball-happy Clevelanders welcomed their returning world champions by staging what was reported as the "biggest and loudest demonstration in the city's history." Estimates of the crowd size ranged from 200,000 to 500,000 worshipping fans. The players rode in open convertibles along the parade route strewn with roses and confetti.[119]

Fifty years later, author Russell Schneider summed up the 1948 season with, "And so ended the Indians' greatest—*most thrilling, exciting, wondrous, glorious,* take your choice—season in the history of the franchise."[120] In a letter to Judy Gordon in 2016, former first baseman Eddie Robinson, then 96 years old, wrote, "Joe was a tremendous factor in our winning. We could not have won without him."[121]

Chapter 16. A Storybook Season (1948)

Results of *The Sporting News'* polling of 296 members of the Baseball Writers' Association of America to select the players for the newspaper's Major League All-Star Team of 1948 were published immediately after the World Series.[122] Three Cleveland Indians were chosen: shortstop Lou Boudreau, second baseman Joe Gordon, and pitcher Bob Lemon. This was Gordon's sixth and final year voted onto the newspaper's prestigious team.[123]

The official movie of the 1948 World Series premiered on November 30 at Toots Shor's Restaurant in New York City. An instructional film, titled *The Double Play Kings of Baseball*, accompanied the World Series movie, featuring the keystone combinations of the Cleveland Indians (Lou Boudreau and Joe Gordon), St. Louis Cardinals (Marty Marion and Red Schoendienst), Boston Red Sox (Vern Stephens and Bobby Doerr), and New York Giants (Buddy Kerr and Bill Rigney).[124]

That year, the Gordon family took their time driving home to Oregon, stopping along the way in South Dakota for Joe to hunt pheasants, at Mount Rushmore for the kids to see, and Yellowstone National Park for Dottie. Seventy-five years later, the Gordon children still cherish the memories of that special trip. Their always zany father kept them in stitches whenever they ate in restaurants along the way, making hilarious faces and pretending to drink from a straw in his nose. Sometimes he had the kids laughing so hard, they could hardly eat. Dottie, who was considerably more reserved than her husband, sometimes got so embarrassed that she'd go wait for them in the car.

As of this writing, six Cleveland Indians players from that storybook 1948 season have been inducted into the National Baseball Hall of Fame: Bob Feller (in 1962), Lou Boudreau (1970), Satchel Paige (1971), Bob Lemon (1976), Larry Doby (1998), and Joe Gordon (2009). Bill Veeck was inducted into the Hall of Fame as an executive in 1991. Nineteen-forty-eight was a magical year!

Chapter 17

High Hopes Dashed (1949)

Thirty-four-year-old Joe Gordon checked in a week early at 1949 Cleveland Indians spring training and worked out every day. Abe Chanin quoted him saying, "I feel good. Maybe I've got two more good years to go.... Yes, I'm in pretty good shape." Joe also talked with Chanin about the Indians' chances of winning the pennant again: "It will probably be a lot like last year. Three of four clubs could finish in front. New York, Boston, and, of course, Cleveland are all dangerous. Detroit is an outside possibility. I don't look for the Athletics to be as strong as last year."[1]

Gordon signed his contract on March 8 for a salary of $35,000, an outstanding $10,000 raise over his 1948 salary.[2] Bill Veeck again included a clause in Joe's contract awarding him a bonus of $2,500 if the club's home attendance amounted to 1,750,000 paid admissions, plus an additional $2,500 if attendance reached 2,250,000 or more.

After watching the Indians play exhibition games in California, Frank Gibbons wrote an article, headlined "Gordon Hits Homer, Sparkles Afield to Prove He's Ready."[3] However, during an exhibition game at Los Angeles, Joe strained his throwing arm, bad enough that he had to have it x-rayed. Manager Boudreau had Joe rest it for several days, yet even by mid–April, his arm still wasn't quite right.[4] Also during spring training, the Indians' star southpaw of 1948, Gene Bearden, hurt his leg. Years later, he told author Russell Schneider, "I pulled a hamstring in my right leg real bad and got all messed up.... I didn't pitch for a couple of weeks, and when I tried to come back I couldn't stride right."[5]

As the 1949 season approached, "optimism was rampant" regarding the club's prospects for another fantastic year.[6] But opening the season at St. Louis on April 19, Indians starter Bob Feller was able to pitch only two innings, and the Browns won, 5–1. Afterward, Feller said he felt something "stretch" in his arm every time he pitched,[7] causing him to not start another game until May 5.

The Indians won their 10-inning home opener against the Tigers on April 22. Bob Yonkers described the Flash's sensational launch of a "lightning-fast double killing," drawing high praise from manager Boudreau: "That was a July play. Joe didn't even have time to think what to do. It was all instinct."[8]

By the time April ended, things were looking pretty good. The Indians had six wins in nine starts and were just 2½ games behind the red-hot, first-place Yankees. On May 5, Bob Feller was back in the rotation and pitched a complete-game victory over the Red Sox. Gordon was batting .333 with four home runs, including two round-trippers the previous day against the Athletics.

But several things came up early in the 1949 season, any one of which could have been enough to squelch the Indians' chances of repeating 1948's phenomenal season.

Chapter 17. High Hopes Dashed (1949)

President Bill Veeck was going through a divorce and quietly looking to sell the club. By his own admission, in *Veeck—As in Wreck: The Autobiography of Bill Veeck*, "I suspect now that mixed in there, unconsciously, was the feeling that I had done everything that could be done in Cleveland and that the time had come to pick myself up and wander on. It may have been, too, that some instinct for self-preservation warned me that the time had come to stop running and take a little rest."[9]

As often happens in sports, circumstances arise that are totally unplanned for. It seemed as though the Indians had more than their share of injuries early in the season, starting with their pitchers: Bob Feller (injured shoulder), Bob Lemon (torn rib cartilage), Early Wynn (severe case of hives), and Gene Bearden (pulled hamstring); in addition to second baseman Joe Gordon (strained arm), shortstop Lou Boudreau (broken finger), and third baseman Kenny Keltner (badly-spiked leg).[10]

Perhaps even more unsettling, Bill Veeck had contracted with Republic Pictures to film a movie, titled *The Kid from Cleveland*, starring George Brent and Lynn Bari, and introducing young Rusty Tamblyn. It was billed as "The story of a kid, a city ... and 30 Godfathers!" The filming involved all of the Indians players, in addition to Bill Veeck, vice president Hank Greenberg, and trainer Lefty Weisman.[11] Many years later, Lou Boudreau wrote about how he regretted that his players had participated in the movie:

> The filming began early in the season at [old] League Park, and usually about nine o'clock in the morning. We'd break for lunch, then shower and dress in street clothes and a couple of hours later report to the stadium [Municipal Stadium] for our game that night. It was like being on the road every day and went on like that until about the first of June [actually a little longer].
>
> It was more than tiring; it also was a great distraction. I know it hurt me and there's no doubt it had a negative effect on the whole team. Though Veeck never admitted it, I've got to believe he was sorry he let us go ahead with it, but by then it was too late to back out.[12]

May began with the club in second place and winning their first three of four games. But things went downhill from there. In *Distant Drums: The 1949 Cleveland Indians Revisited*, author Bruce Dudley aptly titled one of his chapters "A Miserable May."[13] On May 22, after a disappointing 11 losses in their previous 13 games, the Indians were in next-to-last place, and Joe Gordon was batting just .247.

They wrapped up May with a record of 11–15 (.423), their worst month that year, although they had bounced back to win five of their last six games. It's significant that during May and early June, the players were preoccupied with rehearsing and filming *The Kid from Cleveland*.[14] One can only wonder how 1949 might have turned out, had the Indians not been involved in filming a movie.

On May 31, a local businessman, Charley Lupica, distraught that his beloved Indians were "mired" near the bottom of the American League's second division, on a dare, climbed a 40-foot-high flagpole above his store and attached a four-foot by six-foot enclosed platform to the pole. There he vowed to remain until the Indians either took over first place or were eliminated from the pennant race. Lupica's "living quarters" eventually were outfitted with lights and a portable radio, TV, telephone, and bucket to haul things up and down. He drew huge crowds of curious onlookers. And loyal fan that he was, Lupica even remained on his perch when his wife gave birth to their fourth child, a son, in early August.[15]

After losing both games of a doubleheader at home to the Philadelphia Athletics on June 5, Bill Veeck called an "emergency conference" with player-manager Boudreau and the team's coaching "brain trust," to discuss their "serious slump." The lineup was altered, with Boudreau moving to third base and rookie Ray Boone coming in to play shortstop. Boudreau ordered the players to report to practice two hours earlier than usual for their June 6 game. The shakeup must have worked, as the Indians beat the Athletics, 11–5. Joe Gordon hit his seventh home run of the season and drove in three runs.[16] Two nights later, he belted his eighth round-tripper, and his batting average climbed to .283.

On the road on June 14, the Indians beat the Red Sox and finally were back in the first division. Gordon belted a grand slam, his 11th home run of the season, three more than he'd hit by the same date in 1948. By June 16, he was batting .285.

The 16th Annual MLB All-Star Game was scheduled for July 12 at Brooklyn's Ebbets Field, with the starting lineups announced in early July. Eight starters for each team (other than pitchers and utility players) were selected by polling baseball fans throughout the nation. Strangely, the polling results did not include *any* starters from either the 1948 world champion Cleveland Indians or the National League's pennant-winning Boston Braves, although manager Billy Southworth did pick Braves southpaw hurler Warren Spahn to start for the National League. The fans' choice to start at second base for the American League was White Sox 23-year-old second baseman Cass Michaels, who'd received 1,306,808 votes to Joe Gordon's 1,247,153 in the polling.[17] However, five Cleveland Indians were on the American League All-Star team's 25-player roster: Larry Doby, Joe Gordon, Jim Hegan, Bob Lemon, and Dale Mitchell.[18]

This was the first year that African American ballplayers were chosen to play in the Midsummer Classic. Brooklyn Dodgers second baseman Jackie Robinson played the entire game for the National League. Indians outfielder Larry Doby pinch-ran for Joe DiMaggio in the top of the sixth inning and played the remainder of the game. Dodgers pitcher Don Newcombe (later voted the 1949 National League Rookie of the Year) and catcher Roy Campanella each played part of the game.

This was Joe Gordon's ninth and final All-Star Game of his 11-year career. He replaced Cass Michaels in the bottom of the fifth inning and doubled in the top of the seventh, scoring a run in the American League's 11–7 triumph. In the nine years that Gordon was an All-Star (1939–1943 and 1946–1949), the American League won eight Midsummer Classics.

Leading up to the All-Star Game break, the Indians had won nine of their first 11 games in July and regained second place. Things were looking pretty good. But they still were 5½ games behind the league-leading Yankees. However, beginning with the game on July 15, Joe Gordon got into a prolonged batting slump and recorded only *one* hit and *no* RBI in his next 21 at-bats in seven games. Daughter Judy still remembers her parents spending hours and hours searching through photos and home movies, trying to analyze her father's batting stance and swing to figure out what he was doing wrong. Even though baseball never was discussed in front of the Gordon children, at almost nine years old, Judy still knew what was going on.

Batting just .258, Joe finally broke out of his slump on July 21, going 2-for-4 and belting his 14th home run of the season, although the Indians lost to the Yankees that day. They held onto second place until August 12, when, surrendering to the Chicago White Sox, they dropped back to third.

Sometime that spring and early summer, Joe Gordon found time to write an article, titled "Double Play!" published in the August 1949 issue of *Boys' Life* magazine.

Chapter 17. High Hopes Dashed (1949)

Although he was struggling with his batting, his tutorial reveals how much he still loved the game of baseball, in this, his 10th year in the majors: "The double play is one of the most thrilling defensive plays in baseball. There are many possible ways for a double play to be made, and any one of them generally adds up to a load off the pitcher's mind. It not only kills off the batter, but it takes care of one of the opponents who has gotten on base. Instead of having a potential run on first [base], the batting team finds itself with two outs and the runner erased."[19]

On September 1, the Indians set a remarkable major league record by posting their 17th consecutive win in extra-inning games. Beating the Philadelphia Athletics, 2–1, in 11 innings, Bob Lemon also went the distance with his 17th win of the season. The Indians would wrap up their 1949 season with an 18–1 (.947) record in extra-inning games, an achievement still one of the best of all time.[20]

On September 2, a day off for the club, Republic Pictures held the world premiere of its movie, *The Kid from Cleveland*, at Loew's Stillman Theater in Cleveland, complete with a reception including movie stars and ballplayers. The event drew packed crowds to both the daytime and nighttime showings. Ed McAuley wrote about one of Joe Gordon's and Larry Doby's scenes in the film: "There's a terrific—if entirely fictitious—bit in which Joe Gordon and Larry Doby collaborate in a pantomime which couldn't have been done better if the highest-salaried Hollywood actors had played it." But, as McAuley had perceptively picked up on, "the [w]orld [c]hampion Indians spent as much time [on the film] early this summer as they spent trying to defend their title."[21]

Because the team was scheduled to be on the road much of September, Dottie Gordon decided to drive home to Oregon early, so the children could start school on time. Before they left Ohio, it was reported that she told their landlord's wife, "We're not coming back [next year]. Joe is quitting."[22]

From September 18 through 24, the Indians lost six games in a row, two each to the Yankees, Red Sox, and Tigers. The loss at Boston on September 20 mathematically eliminated them from winning the pennant.[23] On September 23, during a pregame ceremony at home against Detroit, Bill Veeck, ever the showman, drove a horse-drawn hearse, leading a faux funeral procession to a mock burial of the club's 1948 pennant flag behind the fence in center field, complete with cardboard tombstone inscribed with "1948 Champs." Continuing the somber tone of the evening, Detroit shut out the Indians, 5–0. Yet still resolute and only 2½ games behind the third-place Tigers, the Indians were not ready to give up on capturing third place.[24]

After being eliminated from the pennant race, Bill Veeck had "1949 Cleveland Indians Flagpole Sitter" Charley Lupica transported, "pole and all," to Municipal Stadium via a specially fitted truck.[25] On September 25, the Indians' last home game of the season, Lupica finally gave up his 117-day vigil and came down from his flagpole. "Nervous, speechless and nearly in tears," and with a band playing *Charlie, My Boy*, he kissed home plate and his wife and four children, including his infant son, Charles Junior, who'd been born during Lupica's vigil.[26] Veeck awarded the stalwart fan and his family a truckload of gifts, including a new automobile. Many years later, one of Lupica's grandsons said about his grandfather, "He talked about it all the time. He would never have traded the experience for anything."[27]

Perhaps it was Charley Lupica's example of devotion and perseverance that spurred the Indians on, as they made a final, valiant push and won their last seven games to nudge the Tigers out of third place. Playing at Detroit on October 1, Joe Gordon hit into a triple play in the first inning. Yet he redeemed himself by going 2-for-4 with two RBI for Mike Garcia's 4–0 shutout and 14th win of the season. This guaranteed the Indians at least a tie for third.[28] The last day of the season, they clinched solo third by defeating the Tigers, 8–4.[29]

They wrapped up their 1949 season with an 89–65 (.578) record, eight games behind first-place New York and seven back of Boston, who for the second year in a row finished just one game out of first place.

Although the Indians' batting left much to be desired, their .983 fielding percentage and 3.36 earned run average led the majors. Four Cleveland pitchers won in double digits: Bob Lemon (22–10, 2.99 ERA, and 22 complete games); Bob Feller (15–14); rookie Mike "The Big Bear" Garcia (14–5 and a major league-leading 2.36 ERA); and Early Wynn (11–7). Thirty-eight-year-old reliever Al Benton finished with a 9–6 record and 10 saves.

Thirty-four-year-old Joe Gordon played in 148 of the Indians' 154 games, batting .251 with 20 home runs and 84 RBI. Outfielder Larry Doby led the team with 24 home runs and 85 RBI. Dale Mitchell led in batting average at .317, the only regular over .300. The club's total home attendance of 2,233,771 guaranteed that Joe Gordon would collect half of his bonus.

The Indians' not winning the 1949 pennant would become the subject of considerable conjecture and second-guessing. Ed McAuley wrote an "extensive post-mortem analysis" for *The Sporting News*, headlined "Indians a Vanished Tribe, Without '48 Zip."[30] Years later, Bruce Dudley wrote a month-by-month account of the 1949 season in *Distant Drums: The 1949 Cleveland Indians Revisited*.[31] To this day, it remains true that winning back-to-back pennants is extremely difficult to accomplish.

Although not a surprise, the Cleveland Indians were sold on November 21, 1949, for a reported $2.2 million, to a syndicate of Cleveland businessmen headed by new president Ellis W. Ryan. Hank Greenberg was signed to a three-year contract as the club's new general manager, and Lou Boudreau, with a year to go on his contract, was kept on as field manager.[32]

Just a week later, Al Gould wrote a long article for the *Oregon Journal*, headlined "Gordon Seeks Tribe Release; Wants Pacific Coast Berth."[33] Joe said he didn't have any differences or complaints with the Indians, but was seeking his unconditional release, hoping to play in the Pacific Coast League so he could remain closer to his home in Oregon.[34] He had hinted at quitting major league baseball a couple of times before, while playing for the Yankees. In late June 1949, Frank Gibbons also had noted, "Joe Gordon is 34 years old and every once in a while he sort of gets to hankering for the calm life of a hardware merchant, or a minor league baseball owner. He was saying the other day that this might be his last year…. He said it before, but this time he sounded as though he meant it."[35]

Soon after the news that Gordon was seeking his release from the Indians, it was reported that two Pacific Coast League clubs, the Portland Beavers and the Sacramento Solons, expressed interest in him. There also was speculation in the *Idaho Evening Statesman* that Gordon possibly was looking at buying into the Boise Pilots of the Pioneer League.[36]

But it appeared as though the Cleveland Indians had no intentions of releasing Joe Gordon—at least not in 1950. In a December newspaper article headlined "'Out of the Question,' Says Tribe to Gordon," general manager Hank Greenberg said, "I'm

Chapter 17. High Hopes Dashed (1949)

convinced Gordon will be back [for 1950].... We consider him the best second baseman in baseball, and we couldn't possibly turn him loose. We'll send Joe a contract the same time we send out all the others, and I'm sure he'll sign it and send it back. We can use him."[37]

Yet just four days after Greenberg's statement to the press, the Indians asked for American League waivers on Gordon. He was claimed by the Boston Red Sox, but the following day Cleveland withdrew him from waivers. The authors discovered that the Indians had also asked for American League waivers on Gordon back on June 11, 1949, right before the trading deadline. He'd been claimed by both the Athletics and the Yankees, but the Indians had withdrawn him that same day, too.

In *Ed Barrow: The Bulldog Who Built the Yankees' First Dynasty*, Daniel R. Levitt wrote about waivers: "Teams often requested waivers on players for the purpose of sending them to the [m]inor [l]eagues or trading them to the other [m]ajor [l]eague. Teams strove to keep the names of the waived players secret from the public and the players themselves. Because most waivers were revocable, teams commonly withdrew waivers if another team claimed the player. Therefore, they did not want a player distracted by knowing he might be designated for the [m]inors or a trade."[38]

It was reported in the Gordons' hometown *Eugene Register-Guard* that Joe "received hundreds and hundreds of letters from Cleveland fans asking that he return for another season with the Indians."[39] Manager Boudreau said, "I hope Joe (Gordon) changes his mind. I want him bad and we can certainly use him. Where would we find a better second baseman?"[40] Meanwhile, Indians general manager Hank Greenberg and new president Ellis Ryan expressed confidence that Gordon was just a victim of "winter fever" and would show up for spring training in 1950.[41]

Chapter 18

THE OLD PRO CALLS IT A CAREER (1950)

On January 13, 1950, and probably unbeknownst to Joe Gordon himself, the Cleveland Indians again asked for American League waivers on him, perhaps exploring the prospects of trading him to a National League club. However, Gordon was claimed by the Boston Red Sox, and the following day, the Indians withdrew him from waivers.

In early February, *The Sporting News* published an article about the 48 "ten-year men" of the approximately 600 ballplayers on the rosters of the 16 American and National League ballclubs.[1] Having attained that status in September 1947, Joe Gordon was one of 31 "ten-year" players in the American League, including eight Indians: Al Benton, Johnny Berardino, Lou Boudreau, Bob Feller, Joe Gordon, Ken Keltner, Bob Kennedy, and Mike Tresh. Attaining 10-year status had advantages in the ballplayers' pension plan, in addition to having more say as to when a player could obtain an unconditional release.[2]

Meanwhile, the *Oregon Journal* announced that Joe Gordon had been chosen by a readers' poll as the outstanding baseball player produced in the Northwest during the first half of the twentieth century. It was reported that he received more votes than the other 19 nominees combined.[3]

Also that month, Joe said that he had come to terms with the Cleveland Indians on his 1950 contract, for a reported salary of $35,000.[4] He noted that he was "very much satisfied" with the terms, but disappointed in not being promised his unconditional release at the end of the season. He did admit, however, "I can see that it would be asking quite a bit to be given a release."[5] Hank Greenberg explained that Gordon was too valuable to be released.

Arriving at spring training in Tucson, Arizona, 35-year-old Joe Gordon again was in excellent physical condition after playing handball several hours a day during the off-season. By early April, he was reported as playing "with the zeal of a rookie trying to make the team."[6] Another writer noted, "Joe Gordon looks as good as he ever did at second base ... and the 'Flash' has also been getting a fair number of home run raps this spring."[7]

In mid–April, the Indians granted their 11-year third baseman Ken "Butch" Keltner his unconditional release.[8] Thirty-three-year-old Keltner was still experiencing leg troubles after being badly spiked in early 1949 and appearing in only 80 games that year. Twenty-six-year-old rookie Al "Flip" Rosen took over Keltner's spot at the "hot corner" and would experience a fantastic season, batting .287 in 155 games, with 116 RBI and a league-leading 37 home runs.

Chapter 18. The Old Pro Calls It a Career (1950)

The club got off to a fair start in 1950, despite getting in only seven games in April. As May began, Joe Gordon was struggling with an .087 batting average. Hitting his first two home runs on May 2 and 3, plus a couple more several weeks later, he finally raised his batting average up to .220. The Indians slipped into the second division for several weeks, but climbed back out later that month, although never managing to get in the lead.

Having requested American League waivers on Joe Gordon in mid–January, the Indians asked for waivers on him again on February 20, May 23, and September 13, although he wasn't claimed. Right before the trading deadline on June 15, rumors circulated that the National League Pittsburgh Pirates were trying to acquire Gordon. Reportedly, they offered $35,000 for him, perhaps thinking of eventually naming him their manager.[9]

On Sunday, June 18, the Indians toppled the visiting Philadelphia Athletics in both games of a doubleheader. In the bottom of the first inning of the nightcap, their 14 runs set a modern major league record for runs scored in the first inning by one team, and their 14 runs also tied the modern major league record for runs scored by one team in any inning.[10] Every player batted twice except pitcher Mike Garcia. The final score was 21–2.

Although Gordon experienced a rather hapless first half of the season, batting just .211 with eight home runs, he rallied in the second half, batting .266 with 11 homers and 30 RBI. Twenty-six-year-old rookie Bobby Ávila, a second baseman from Mexico who had appeared in just 31 games the previous year, played in 80 games in 1950, batting a solid .299.

Gordon's Oregon friend and sports editor Dick Strite noted in his "Highclimber" column that Cleveland writer Ed McAuley observed the Flash taking on new life in July: "In Fenway Park, July 16, he [Gordon] staged a demonstration of ground-covering which would have been most creditable for the Gordon of ten years ago."[11] During the first game of a July 17 doubleheader at Boston, "Gordon rapped four singles and a home run for a perfect game."[12] Lou Boudreau commented on Gordon's play, "I knew Joey still had a lot of baseball left in him."[13] Although the 35-year-old Flash posted a .307 average in July, his rally was short-lived, and he slipped back to .217 in August and .238 in September/October.

In a game at home on August 2 against the Senators, the Indians' 26-year-old center fielder, Larry Doby, belted home runs in his first *three* times at bat. Also that night, Joe Gordon recorded his 13th round-tripper of the season, and pitcher Bob Lemon hit his fifth homer and had three RBI in addition to hurling a three-hit shutout, 11–0.

During the fifth inning on August 15, the Indians turned a triple play (9–6–3) against the visiting Tigers. Just two days later, the visiting St. Louis Browns launched a "triple killing" against Cleveland (5–5–4). The Indians battled throughout the summer, climbing to within just 1½ games of the lead in late August. But by the end of the month, six close losses in a row, partly due to a rash of injuries to Ray Boone, Larry Doby, Bobby Ávila, and Luke Easter, dropped the club back to fourth place.[14] There wasn't any risk of ending the season in the second division, though, as the fifth-place Senators were 23 games behind Cleveland and would drop back even further by season's end.

The Indians' optimistic manager, Lou Boudreau, insisted that they were going to win the pennant: "In all my years as manager we've never had such a fine group [of players].... Our pitching is excellent and I see signs of our hitting returning."[15] But his predictions were not to be. Yet after a lackluster first half of September, the Indians put together a heroic finale, winning nine of their last 10 games to end the season in fourth place.

The Flash hit his 19th and final home run of 1950 and of his career, on September 22. As leadoff batter in the bottom of the ninth inning and the score tied, 3–3, Gordon's round-tripper was a "walk off" against Tigers future Hall of Fame pitcher Hal Newhouser to clinch Bob Feller's 4–3 victory. This brought Joe's total home runs in his four years with the Cleveland Indians to an even 100—and his total in his 11-year major league career to 253.

Cleveland wrapped up the 1950 season in fourth place with a 92–62 (.597) record, six games behind the pennant-winning Yankees, three games behind Detroit, and two games back of Boston. The Indians topped the American League in home runs with 164, thanks to the club's newfound cadre of long-ball hitters: rookie Al Rosen (37 home runs and 116 RBI), 6-foot 4-inch American League rookie Luke Easter (28 and 107), and Larry Doby (25 and 102). Joe Gordon played in 119 games in his final year of major league baseball, batting .236 with 19 home runs and 57 RBI.

Cleveland's pitching was outstanding. They led the American League, *by far*, with their 3.74 ERA. Five pitchers finished the 1950 season with double-digit wins. Living up to his nickname, "The Work Horse,"[16] Bob Lemon led both leagues in wins (23) and topped the American League in games started (37), strikeouts (170), innings pitched (288), and complete games (22). Other double-digit winners included Early Wynn (18–8, and a league-leading 3.20 ERA), Bob Feller (16–11), Mike Garcia (11–11); and Steve Gromek (10–7).

Right after the 1950 season ended, Ed McAuley wrote an article in *The Sporting News*, headlined "'Old Pro' Gordon Calls It Career."[17] Ever since mid–September, rumors had been circulating that Joe Gordon might be in line to manage the Pacific Coast League Portland Beavers or Seattle Rainiers.[18] It was reported that the Indians had given Gordon permission to "make a deal" for himself as a player-manager with a Pacific Coast League club.[19]

Things moved quickly once Joe knew that the Indians would not hold him to his contract's reserve clause,[20] and that he had "Cleveland's blessings" to look for another job. It appeared that he favored the Pacific Coast League Sacramento Solons—if a job opened up there—as Dottie preferred living in California rather than the rainy climes of Portland or Seattle. Joe also had spent some time in Sacramento while playing for the 1936 Oakland Oaks, as well as during World War II, so he was familiar with the area.[21] When Solons manager Joe Marty resigned in mid–October 1950 and signed with the club to play outfield, the Solons were in the market for a new pilot.[22] On October 18, Solons general manager Joyner "Jo-Jo" White announced that, once Gordon cleared waivers, he would be hired as player-manager of the Sacramento Solons for 1951 and 1952.[23] Gordon said, "I am happy to get into the [C]oast [L]eague in a manager's slot. I want two years here in Sacramento and perhaps I can go back up there [the majors].... I like this city. I like the people and I like the climate."[24]

However, formal signing of Gordon's contract would have to wait until he cleared American League and National League waivers, in accordance with Major League Rule 8—Unconditional Release.[25] The Indians requested unconditional-release waivers on him, but again he was claimed by the Boston Red Sox, who would not give him waivers to leave the majors. As a "ten-year man" in the majors, though, Gordon had another option, that is, getting himself declared a free agent by the Cleveland Indians. Afterwards, Gordon said that he was very grateful to Indians general manager Hank Greenberg, "who made it possible."[26]

On October 27, Gordon signed a two-year contract as player-manager of the 1951–1952 Sacramento Solons. It was later reported that he received a salary of $22,500, in addition to attendance bonuses.[27]

Thus Joe "Flash" Gordon's 11-year major league playing career was brought to a close. During seven years with the New York Yankees and four with the Cleveland Indians, he played for *six* pennant winners and won *five* world championships (1938, 1939, 1941, 1943, and 1948). The Baseball Writers' Association of America (BBWAA) had voted Joe Gordon recipient of the MVP Award in 1942. He'd been included in the MVP voting during eight of his 11 seasons in the American League, finishing five times in the top 10. He was chosen for *nine* MLB All-Star Games (1939–1943 and 1946–1949) and played in eight of those.[28] The BBWAA voted Joe Gordon onto *The Sporting News*' prestigious Major League All-Star Team an impressive six times (1939–1942, 1947, and 1948), tying the record for second basemen with the great Charlie Gehringer and in the same company as outfielders Babe Ruth and Al Simmons, third baseman George Kell, and catcher Bill Dickey.[29]

Throughout his career, Joe Gordon set multiple batting records for second basemen, some standing for many decades. He was the first American League second baseman to hit 20 or more home runs in a single season, and the first to hit 25, 30, and 32. He hit 20 or more home runs seven times (1938–1941 and 1947–1949), in addition to 30 or more homers twice (1940 and 1948).

Playing in just 127 of the Yankees' 157 games in 1938, rookie Joe Gordon also set records for first-year second basemen with 24 of his 25 home runs (one home run was hit while pinch-hitting). His record would stand for 68 years. His 32 round-trippers in 1948 also set a record for American League second basemen that would stand for 53 years. He drove in more than 100 runs four times (1939, 1940, 1942, and 1948), a rarity for second basemen of that era. Upon completion of his final major league season in 1950, Gordon's 246 home runs while playing as a second baseman set an American League record that would stand for 66 years. Even his family didn't know about his still-standing home run record until watching the big-screen video at Cooperstown, New York, during Joe Gordon's induction into the Hall of Fame in 2009!

Defensively, Gordon often ranked in the top 10 among major league second basemen in various stats.[30] In four seasons (1939, 1940, 1943, and 1947), he led the American League in assists, and during three years (1939, 1941, and 1942) in double plays by a second baseman. As of this writing, Joe Gordon still ranks 19th in career double plays by a second baseman with 1,160, which he accomplished in just 11 years.[31] His average of 105.5 double plays per season as a second baseman ranks second in major league history, right on the heels of his good friend Bobby Doerr's 107.6. During the 1943 World Series, Gordon also set records for chances, putouts, and assists by a second baseman in a five-game Series.

In 2001, in celebration of the Cleveland Indians' 100th anniversary, the club announced their "Top 100 Greatest Cleveland Indians."[32] A panel of veteran baseball writers, historians, and executives named Joe Gordon as one of the Indians' nine greatest second basemen.

Chapter 19

CALIFORNIA, HERE WE COME! (1951–1957)

1951 Sacramento Solons

Within a week of Joe Gordon signing his contract to manage the 1951–1952 Sacramento Solons of the Pacific Coast League (PCL), the Gordons put their home in Eugene up for sale and headed for California. Arriving in Sacramento, they rented a small, two-bedroom home and enrolled the children in school.

The Pacific Coast League was Class AAA in 1951 and comprised eight teams, with a star-studded host of managers: Rogers Hornsby (Seattle Rainiers), Fred Haney (Hollywood Stars), Stan Hack (Los Angeles Angels), Bill Sweeney (Portland Beavers), Mel Ott (Oakland Oaks), Del Baker (San Diego Padres), Joe Gordon (Sacramento Solons), and Lefty O'Doul (San Francisco Seals). Gordon was the only player-manager in the PCL this year.[1]

During 1950 and 1951, the Solons had a "two-year working agreement" with the Chicago White Sox, primarily for what was reported as "player-feeding purposes." The White Sox could option players to the Solons, in addition to having first chance at buying players at the season's end.[2] Unfortunately, Sacramento had seen six different field managers during the five years before Joe Gordon was hired, and the club finished in the cellar, 37 games behind the first-place Oakland Oaks in 1950.[3]

As manager, Gordon was instrumental in recruiting several major leaguers for his team: heavy-hitting third baseman Ken Keltner and right-handed reliever Ed Klieman, both teammates of his on the 1948 world champion Cleveland Indians; and pitcher Al Benton of the 1949 and 1950 Indians.

He also was successful in acquiring first baseman Bob Boyd, formerly of the Memphis Red Sox of the Negro American League, the "one man he [Gordon] wanted most."[4] In addition to Boyd, the Solons obtained Negro American League catcher Sam Hairston on option from the Chicago White Sox organization.[5]

Unseasonably wet weather seriously hampered the Solons' workouts and practice games throughout much of the club's spring training at Stockton, California.[6] It was reported that manager Gordon and coach Merv Shea "scampered all over Stockton in an effort to find a large building in which the athletes could limber up. Included on the list of sites inspected were a winery, a sheep pen, airplane hangars, gymnasiums and an [A]rmy ordnance depot."[7]

As for Gordon's managing style, one sportswriter described him as a "gentler and kinder" type of manager, who led more by example than by dictating strict training rules and restrictions. Joe said, "These fellows are grown men who know what's right and what's wrong for them. Why have a lot of rules?"[8]

The Solons opened the 1951 season at Sacramento's Edmonds Field on March 27, to an overflow crowd of more than 12,400 fans. Joe's brother, Jack, and their mutual friend, Ben Cheney, flew in from Tacoma, Washington, to be there for Joe's first game as manager. Former Chicago White Sox pitcher, 31-year-old Orval Grove, won the game, 5–4, over the Hollywood Stars, thanks to Bob Boyd's eighth-inning home run with a man on base.[9]

Losing their next six games in a row dropped the Solons to next-to-last place, just a notch above the San Francisco Seals.[10] They lingered in the second division until April 21, when six straight wins miraculously boosted them into second place for a day.[11]

Gordon later told writer John B. Old that he credited his former manager, Joe McCarthy, with much of his success: "Managing just seems to come natural. That's because when I played under McCarthy for the Yankees, he practically made managers of all of us. He kept pounding into us every phase of the game."[12]

During one of the Solons' road trips south to play the Hollywood Stars, manager Gordon and four of his teammates were invited to visit Republic Pictures Studios and meet cowboy film star Roy Rogers.[13] Joe was a huge fan of Roy Rogers' movies and comic books. Likewise, Roy was a big admirer of the Flash. While there, Joe got to ride Roy's beautiful palomino stallion, Trigger. Gordon's teammates later told how their manager had been "walking around in a dream world" for a week after riding Roy's horse.[14]

Meanwhile, 36-year-old Gordon, who'd sometimes been portrayed as a "slow starter" during early spring in the majors, was belting home runs and driving in runs like mad. Bill Conlin, sports editor of the *Sacramento Union*, observed, "Every baseball man who has watched Gordon this spring invariably comes up with a variation of the same comment: '[T]he Flash still belongs in the American League.'"[15]

Solons president Eddie Mulligan was delighted: "I've never seen such team spirit. Joe Gordon's got our gang putting out like a college club instead of a bunch of old pros. It's remarkable.... A dozen San Francisco people came up and told me that they'd never seen a [Pacific] Coast League team put so much determination and spirit into their play."[16]

The Flash kept up his barrage of hitting. By early June, he'd hit 19 home runs with 65 RBI.[17] Reporters had "a field day" writing about the Solons' new player-manager. One Los Angeles columnist wrote, "Pacific Coast League's rookie of the year is probably Joe Gordon."[18] A San Francisco writer observed, "Joe Gordon has introduced a new method of managing a ball club—he simply waits until a couple of his hirelings get on base, then he whacks a home run." New Hall of Famer Mel Ott, manager of the Oakland Oaks, quipped, "Gordon doesn't belong down here [in the PCL] playing with us kids."[19] Ott also said, "Joe could be playing regularly for any club in the majors right now. If he's slowed down any, it doesn't show."[20]

Once again, the baseball rumor mill started up. Bill Veeck, former owner of the Cleveland Indians, was negotiating for controlling interest of the St. Louis Browns.[21] Veeck wrote in *Veeck—As in Wreck: The Autobiography of Bill Veeck*, "My first choice to replace Zack Taylor [field manager of the Browns] was Joe Gordon, then in his first year of managing at Sacramento. Joe would have come gladly if I could have talked his wife, Dorothy [sic], into it. But Dorothy [sic] felt he had more security in Sacramento."[22]

Solons president Eddie Mulligan announced that he would not release Gordon from his contract during the current season.[23] Actually, though, it was Gordon himself who had no intentions of cutting short his tenure with the Solons.[24]

On June 20, with the Solons in second place, their slugging right fielder, Joe Marty, was hospitalized with a compound dislocation of his right thumb.[25] Marty was batting .322 when he had to sit out for a month.[26] Solons catcher Al Lakeman also was out with a pulled back muscle.

In mid–July, Gordon was leading the PCL in home runs (33) and RBI (105), and Solons first baseman Bob Boyd was leading in batting average (.349).[27] But just as Joe Marty returned to play after being out for a month,[28] Gordon was experiencing painful muscle spasms in his back and neck and had to sit out 10 games except for pinch-hitting.[29] Soon the Solons had dropped back to the second division.[30]

On July 28, coming off the bench in the seventh inning to pinch-hit, a player that Lenny Anderson described as "[a]n invalid named Joe Gordon," limped to the plate to smash his 34th round-tripper of the season, a grand slam, to singlehandedly beat the Seattle Rainiers, 4–3.[31] Back in the swing again, the following week the Flash belted four more home runs.[32]

Playing at Portland in August with the Solons in fifth place, manager Gordon decided to shake up his lineup, putting Sam Kanelos in at second base.[33] Joe would play about a dozen games at shortstop that year.

That summer, Joe and Dottie Gordon purchased a modest three-bedroom home in the Sierra Oaks Vista subdivision of Sacramento.[34] Eleven-year-old Judy enrolled at Arden Elementary School in September and wouldn't have to change schools again until she entered high school.

The Solons lost three players to voluntary retirement at various times throughout the summer of 1951: pitcher Mike Palm, catcher Al Lakeman, and third baseman Ken Keltner.[35] During a game in early September, a Hollywood Stars baserunner crashed into Gordon, injuring Joe's right shoulder and putting him on the bench for the final few games of the season except for pinch-hitting.[36] With just a week remaining of the PCL season, the Chicago White Sox called up Solons first baseman Bob Boyd to the majors.[37] This was a huge loss for the Solons. At the time, Boyd ranked second in the PCL with his .342 batting average and was leading the league with 41 stolen bases.[38]

On the last day of the season, the Solons won both games of the twin bill against the last-place San Francisco Seals to boost themselves out of the cellar and clinch seventh place.[39] They finished with a 75–92 (.449) record, 24 games behind the first-place Seattle Rainiers.

Joe Gordon had played in 148 of the Solons' 167 games, running away with the PCL's top honors in home runs (43) and RBI (136), while batting .299. He also set the Solons' "all-time records" in home runs and RBI.[40]

Soon after the PCL season ended, the Gordons and their hardware store partner, Walter Hummel, learned that their controlling interests in Joe Gordon Hardware in Eugene had been sold.[41] This freed the Gordons of any business ties remaining in Oregon.

Late that fall, L.H. Gregory wrote in *The Oregonian*, "It has leaked out that Joe Gordon could have gone to either of two major league clubs, the Boston Red Sox or Cleveland Indians, when the Coast [League] season ended last fall—but personally turned down both opportunities. The Red Sox, with Bobby Doerr hurt, had to have a second baseman and tried hard to buy Joe from the Sacs [Sacramento Solons]; while Cleveland, with infield and batting problems, also wanted him back."[42]

Chapter 19. California, Here We Come! (1951–1957)

1952 Sacramento Solons

Gaining approval from both the minor and major leagues during winter meetings in late 1951, George M. Trautman, president of the National Association of Professional Baseball Leagues (the umbrella organization for the minor leagues), announced the formation of the Pacific Coast League's (PCL's) new Open Classification. PCL president Clarence Rowland said, "This is another step toward what the Pacific Coast League hopes will be eventual major league status."[43]

The step above Class AAA to Open Classification would, among other things, make it more difficult for major league clubs to draft PCL players. Moreover, the PCL could begin working toward trying to meet the requirements (e.g., surrounding population, park capacity, attendance, salaries, etc.) for becoming the third major league, although they never did attain that status. The New York Giants and Brooklyn Dodgers relocated to the West Coast in time for the 1958 season, and, eventually, the National and American Leagues would almost double the number of clubs spread across the country. The PCL remained Open Classification from 1952 to 1957, after which time it returned to Class AAA.[44]

In early February 1952, because of the PCL's recent change in classification, Joe Gordon signed a new contract with the Sacramento Solons, even though he still had a year remaining on his previous managerial contract. Joe, like most Pacific Coast League players that year, voluntarily waived their rights to be drafted by a major league club.[45]

The Solons held their 1952 spring training at Modesto, California, hoping for warmer, drier weather than they'd faced the previous year. With only 11 regulars carried over from 1951, the club hoped for an improved showing in 1952 and signed several young players.[46]

They opened the 1952 season at home on April Fools' Day to an enthusiastic, record-breaking crowd of 13,621 fans. In the bottom of the fifth inning, with the Los Angeles Angels leading, 1–0, Joe Gordon singled, then advanced to third on a ground-rule double. Trying to score on a wild pitch, Joe was thrown out at home plate. But his angry protest of umpire Bill Doran's call earned him an early trip to the showers. The home team ended up losing their April 1 opener, 1–0.[47]

The Solons won their first game on April 4, but by then they were tied for last place.[48] Eventually they would get as high as fourth place for a few days, but even before April was done, they were back in the cellar for the remainder of the season except for a few forays into seventh place.

To make up a rained-out twin bill against the Portland Beavers, a doubleheader was scheduled for Monday night, July 21, at Sacramento. During the first game, while chasing an off-the-wall line drive, Solons center fielder Len Attyd crashed into the wall and was knocked unconscious. He was rushed to the hospital and kept for several days. In the nightcap, Gordon was hit on the head by a pitched ball. He didn't lose consciousness but reported that he "saw plenty of stars" and was taken to the hospital. The Solons and Beavers split the 24-inning twin bill.[49]

Manager Gordon, sporting a bruised and cut head, flew south with his team the following day, but had to sit out their first game against the Hollywood Stars. Because Solons utility infielders Eddie Bockman and Bob Dillinger also were out with injuries, pitcher Frank Nelson played second base and catcher Jim McKeegan played third. Substituting for Gordon, Nelson belted a home run against the Stars![50]

The year 1952 marked the New York Yankees' 50th season in the American League. Joe Gordon was invited to play in their Sixth-Annual Old-Timers Day game in place of Tony Lazzeri, who had passed away in 1946. With the blessings of Solons management, Joe flew to New York to play against a team of Yankees All-Stars in the two-inning exhibition game on August 30.[51]

In the meantime, the Sacramento Solons' strings of losses in August and September doomed them to a last-place finish in the PCL. They ended the 1952 season with a 66–114 (.367) record, 43 games behind the first-place Hollywood Stars. Manager Joe Gordon played in 122 games, batting .246 with 16 home runs and 46 RBI. It was a *very* disappointing season for the Solons' owners, players, coaches, fans, and, especially, manager Gordon.

Joe resigned as manager of the Solons on the last day of September, reported as parting "on the friendliest of terms."[52] L.H. Gregory later reported how much Gordon was admired by his Solons teammates: "[W]e haven't run into a Sacto [Sacramento] player yet who was with Gordon but swears by him as the finest fellow that ever led a ball club."[53]

The baseball rumor mill came to life again that fall, trying to predict what the Flash would do in 1953. It was speculated that he might take a position with the Boston Red Sox, because former Indians manager Lou Boudreau was piloting the club.[54] But this was not in Joe's future.

1953–1956 Detroit Tigers

In early October 1952, the Detroit Tigers offered Joe Gordon a position as director and supervisory scout of their revamped Pacific Coast scouting system for 1953.[55] Besides scouting, Joe's job included organizing and conducting baseball clinics and schools on the West Coast; attending Tigers spring training at Lakeland, Florida; and instructing young players at the club's Tigertown minor league training camp. It was reported that Joe had signed for a "whopping salary" of $22,500 to $25,000; however, as L.H. Gregory later noted, "Even head scouts don't get that kind of money."[56] Gordon's salary actually was $7,500, as documented in his contract information archived at the National Baseball Hall of Fame and Museum.

Joe enjoyed scouting on the West Coast. In mid–February 1953, he conducted a two-day tryout camp at Lodi, California, assisted by Ray Perry, Larry Williams, and Tony Zupo.[57] Dick Strite also reported that a reader wrote in to say, "Saw Joe Gordon at Glendale [California] last week and he seems happy and enthusiastic with his scouting work with the Detroit Tigers."[58] In April, Joe spent a week in Oregon, scouting college teams. By mid–June, he'd signed three players from Oregon State College, in addition to Santa Clara University player Dick Camilli, son of Dolph Camilli, winner of the 1941 NL Most Valuable Player Award.[59]

Following their distant sixth-place finish in 1953, the Tigers released two of their coaches, prompting a "very strong rumor" that Gordon might be hired as a Tigers coach. However, Joe said that he preferred remaining on the West Coast.[60]

In early 1954, besides attending Tigers spring training in Florida, Gordon was assisted by his former Oakland Oaks teammate, Bernie DeViveiros, and minor league player-manager Bob Mavis in conducting another training camp at Lodi, for a group of minor leaguers.[61]

Despite his baseball responsibilities, Joe and his friends still found time to hunt ducks and geese. After a successful day's hunt, they'd take their harvest to their favorite eating place, Frank Fat's Chinese Restaurant, in downtown Sacramento.[62] The cooks prepared Chinese pressed duck, and the hunters and their wives, children, and friends would gather for an evening of fine Chinese cuisine. It was a fun time.

After the 1954 baseball season ended, Detroit Tigers manager Fred Hutchinson resigned and was replaced by longtime major league manager Bucky Harris. Joe Gordon had been mentioned as a possible successor to Hutchinson, but he quashed any rumors of returning east again, saying that he preferred remaining as a scout.[63]

A year later, though, he changed his mind. In late 1955, he was offered a job as the 1956 Tigers' first base coach under manager Harris, at an annual salary of $10,000.[64] Gordon said, "I have always liked to work with the young players in baseball, and this appointment presents a fine opportunity for me. Although I never have played for Bucky Harris[,] I have known him for a long time and have always admired him." Harris, too, spoke highly of his new coach: "I've always had a lot of respect for Joe. He'll do a good job for us."[65]

In mid–February 1956, the Tigers held a two-week "instructional school" at Lakeland, Florida, for 50 young ballplayers. Tigers management brought in a full cadre of instructors from their scouting and coaching staffs, including Joe Gordon.[66] A month later at Tigers spring training, the club was reported as experiencing "big gaps" at second base. Forty-one-year-old Gordon had been working out regularly with the team and was said to be "sensational in hitting drills" and even mentioned as a possible fill-in player.[67] Although most likely amused by the reports, Joe said he intended to remain as a coach.

After school let out for the summer, Dottie and the Gordon children left Sacramento and headed for Detroit to join Joe. Shortly after the family got settled into a rental house, the fifth-place Tigers got mired in a string of 10 losses and one tie at home, dropping them to sixth place. Tigers co-owner/president Walter O. "Spike" Briggs, Jr., publicly criticized manager Bucky Harris and the players, in addition to challenging the competence of general manager Herold "Muddy" Ruel and the club's three coaches: Joe Gordon, Billy Hitchcock, and Jack Tighe.[68]

In late June, the *New York Herald Tribune* published a small article, headlined "Gordon May Quit as Tiger Coach." Joe told reporters, "I can't say anything definitely at this time. Naturally I'm disturbed. When a team is in a slump like this one … and the president starts criticizing the manager, the coaches and everyone else, it would be hard to be any other way."[69]

Suddenly, right before the Tigers headed out on a road trip, Gordon informed manager Bucky Harris and general manager Muddy Ruel that he was resigning. At the time, Briggs was in Florida on a business-pleasure trip. Reportedly, the Tigers' president apologized and shouldered "all the blame for this entire mess," but Gordon had made up his mind.[70]

The only thing Judy and Joey Gordon recall about leaving Detroit was being told to pack their bags because they were moving back home to California. Until doing the research for this biography of their father, neither Judy nor Joey ever knew why they had left Detroit so suddenly, in the middle of the 1956 season. In all the years that Joe was in baseball, he and Dottie *never* talked baseball in front of their children. It simply was not a subject ever discussed at home. In hindsight, the two children now realize that their parents were just doing the best they could to give them as normal a childhood as possible—in a *very* public arena.

A short time later, the Detroit Tigers were sold by the administrators of the Briggs family's estate, with the new owners keeping Walter O. Briggs, Jr., on as executive vice president and, later, general manager. In the spring of 1957, it was reported that Briggs either resigned or was asked to resign.[71]

1956 San Francisco Seals

Joe Gordon spent only a few days without a job. On July 9, he was hired to replace Eddie Joost as manager of the Pacific Coast League (PCL) San Francisco Seals.[72] During 1956 and 1957, the Seals were affiliated with the American League's Boston Red Sox. It was reported that Gordon was hired to manage the club because of his proven ability in tutoring young players. Wilbur Adams wrote in his "Between the Sport Lines" column, "Sometimes the job is made for the man and the man is made for the job."[73] This would prove especially true in Gordon's case.

When Gordon took over the Seals, they were struggling with a 44–59 (.427) record and in seventh place. Going 33–29 the remainder of the season, the club finished sixth, with an overall 77–88 (.467) record and was fourth in the league in batting, pitching, and fielding. Seals management was well pleased with Gordon's work with their young team during 1956, prompting club president Jerry Donovan to announce on September 11 that Joe was being hired to manage the club in 1957.[74]

1957 San Francisco Seals

In early January 1957, Joe Gordon and his contractor friend, Tom Sertich, took advantage of California's great steelhead fishing. It was reported that Joe caught a 26-inch, 7¾-pound "beauty" on the American River, which runs through the middle of Sacramento.[75]

Spring training for the Seals' batterymen began in early March at Fullerton, California, with the balance of the players reporting a week later. Planning on boosting the club's ranks with a number of former major leaguers, manager Gordon forecast that the club would be a "definite pennant contender" and finish in the first division in 1957.[76]

By the time everyone arrived at training camp, the Seals had a squad of 35 players, including "a mixture of teenaged youngsters as well as oldsters."[77] Gordon, however, did face a predicament—he had to pare the team down to the PCL's 21-player limit by the May 11 deadline.[78] Lefty O'Doul, manager of the PCL Seattle Rainiers, later remarked, "They [the Seals] have one of the best-balanced clubs of recent Coast [L]eague history."[79]

The 1957 Pacific Coast League season began in mid–April, with reporter Tom Kane predicting, "San Francisco is the No. 1 choice to win the pennant after the Boston Red Sox staffed it with top rated players. Manager Joe Gordon's team had an excellent spring record and if the pitching goes as expected it has an excellent chance to take it all."[80]

During 1957, any talk about the future of the Pacific Coast League would be sure to promote fascinating conversation if one paid attention to all the speculation about the relocation of two major league ballclubs to the West Coast. For some time, the prospects

Chapter 19. California, Here We Come! (1951–1957)

of the New York Giants moving to San Francisco and the Brooklyn Dodgers to Los Angeles kept the PCL club owners, ballplayers, and fans in suspenseful anticipation.

In late May, the National League club owners voted unanimously to allow the Giants to move to San Francisco and the Dodgers to Los Angeles, if both decided to do so.[81] This placed the future of the San Francisco Seals in a state of uncertainty for much of the summer, as it was a given that San Francisco could not adequately support a PCL team if a popular major league club moved there, too.

The New York Giants Board of Directors announced in mid–August that they intended to relocate to San Francisco in time for the 1958 season.[82] The Brooklyn Dodgers followed suit in early October, announcing that they were moving to Los Angeles.[83]

San Francisco Seals manager Joe Gordon poses for a fan to take his photograph out on the field at Seals Stadium, before a home game against the Seattle Rainiers in April 1957. The fan wrote on the back of this photograph: "Here is a little memento, Joe, 4/20/57" (Gordon family collections).

In early July, Alan Ward, sports editor of the *Oakland Tribune*, wrote a column, headlined "Gordon Predicts Flag for Seals." Ward noted, "It is axiomatic in professional baseball that the team leading the loop [on] July 4 is the team which, all being even, will win the pennant…. One of the optimists is Joe Gordon."[84]

In *The 1957 San Francisco Seals: End of an Era in the Pacific Coast League*, P.J. Dragseth wrote a game-by-game chronicle of the Seals' 1957 season. She characterized the first game of their July 14 hometown doubleheader as "a true, unabridged slugfest."[85] During the free-for-all, manager Gordon called on eight pitchers and every one of his 21 players except for the nightcap's pitcher and catcher. But the Hollywood Stars triumphed, 18–17.[86] The 35-run slugfest set a scoring record for a single game at Seals Stadium. Yet the good news was—the Seals *still* were in first place by three games.[87]

On their way north to play the Portland Beavers, the Seals stopped off at Eugene on July 15 to play an exhibition game earmarked as "Joe Gordon Night," against the Class B Northwest League's Eugene Emeralds. At the time, the Seals were leading the Pacific Coast League, and the Emeralds were the first-half champions (and eventual champions) of the Northwest League. Special guests at the game included Gordon's wife, Dottie, and their son, Joey; former Red Sox second baseman Bobby Doerr and his son, Don; and a host of Gordon's former teammates from the 1935 University of Oregon Pacific Coast

Conference Northern Division champions. The Seals beat the Emeralds, 5–3, thanks to a pair of homers by Albie Pearson and one by Sal Taormina, in addition to runs scored by Ken Aspromonte and Nini Tornay.[88]

At Portland for a series against the seventh-place Beavers at Multnomah Stadium, the Seals took six of the seven games and departed Portland in first place by five games.[89]

During August, the Seals were scheduled to play every team in the Pacific Coast League, with only one day off all month.[90] Mid-month, the rumor mill ramped up to high gear, speculating about what would happen if the San Francisco Seals won the pennant. A headline in the *Eugene Register-Guard* posed the question: "If SF [San Francisco] Wins and Giants Move, What Happens to Joe Gordon?"[91]

But with just two weeks remaining in the PCL season, Boston called up Seals second baseman Ken "Chip" Aspromonte to replace keystoner Ted Lepcio, who'd broken his wrist.[92] When Aspromonte headed east, he was leading the PCL with a .334 batting average. The Seals signed 40-year-old veteran infielder Lou Stringer.[93] Yet with the outcome of the PCL pennant still up in the air, the loss of Aspromonte presented a substantial dilemma, leaving manager Gordon to juggle infielders as best he could for the balance of the season.

Early September saw the Seals on the road, playing the Hollywood Stars, San Diego Padres, and Los Angeles Angels, posting an 8–6 record. But they ended their road trip with three consecutive losses to the Angels, which left the outcome of the pennant still up in the air. Moreover, several players, in addition to manager Gordon, had come down with the Asian flu while on the road.[94] Fortunately, their final four games of the season were at home against the Sacramento Solons, who themselves were in a battle with the Portland Beavers for last place.

On lucky Friday the 13th of September, southpaw Bob "Riverboat" Smith pitched a four-hitter as the Seals shut out the visiting Sacramento Solons, 3–0, to clinch the PCL pennant just two days before season's end.[95] There were no playoffs in 1957, so the Seals also won the Pacific Coast League championship. It was the club's first championship since 1946, in their storied 55-year history as charter members of the PCL.

Writer Tom Kane, who'd known Joe Gordon ever since his days as player-manager of the 1951 and 1952 Sacramento Solons, wrote, "Joe is credited with doing a magnificent job in leading the Seals to the title. His pitching staff was made up mostly of relief hurlers and some of his athletes had a lot of miles behind them." Kane also praised Gordon for overcoming the many predicaments he faced in having to constantly juggle his lineup, rest some players while buoying up others, and maneuver his "non too deep pitching staff."[96]

With the pennant clinched and just three home games left, Bert Thiel pitched one more for good luck on September 14, an 11-inning, complete-game 3–2 victory over the Solons.[97]

The Seals played their final two games on Sunday, September 15, against the Solons, who were still in a battle with the Portland Beavers for seventh place. Originally designated as "Seals Appreciation Day," the celebration was renamed "Glenn 'Cap' Wright Day" in honor of the team's coach, who had recently undergone surgery to remove a malignant tumor from his jaw and throat.[98] The surgery was successful, and Wright lived 27 more years.

The largest crowd of the season, 15,484 loyal fans, turned out to watch their beloved San Francisco Seals play, probably for the very last time. The first game of the doubleheader saw the Solons beat the Seals to clinch seventh place in the PCL.[99]

Chapter 19. California, Here We Come! (1951–1957)

Receiving a "tremendous ovation" when introduced at the microphone, manager Joe Gordon described his team as the greatest he'd ever worked with. He told the fans, "They [the players] did their best for you all year. It has been a wonderful experience playing here this summer. You fans have been wonderful and your loyalty unforgettable." Seals president Jerry Donovan presented the 18-foot-long by 9-foot-high "Champions 1957" pennant to Gordon and his teammates at home plate.[100]

The seven-inning nightcap turned out to be "probably the most hilarious game ever played in the [Pacific] Coast League" in its 55-year history and appeared as though "every rule in the baseball book was violated."[101] Seals outfielder Albie Pearson started the game as the pitcher, giving up four runs in the first inning and going into the record books with a record of 0–1 and 36.00 ERA.[102] Pearson then took turns playing the entire infield circuit.

Bent on everyone having a great time, Joe Gordon came out of retirement and played second base and shortstop, pitched, and took a stint at umpiring while PCL umpire Chris Pelekoudas took Joe's place on the pitcher's mound, in full umpire attire minus his chest protector.[103] At 42 years old, yet still plenty adept with a bat, Gordon went 2-for-3, included in the official record books, as is his pitching record, 0–0. It was reported that "Sacramento won with fourteen runs. No one was sure of the Seals' total."[104] The score went into the record books with the Solons winning, 14–7.

The final out of the final game of the San Francisco Seals' final season was a force play by Solons third baseman Harry Bright. Fighting off the mob of souvenir hunters pouring onto the field, Bright handed the ball to Joe Gordon, who lost his cap and had his uniform torn in the tussle. Gordon and Seals president Jerry Donovan later signed the ball and donated it to the National Baseball Hall of Fame and Museum.[105]

Gordon gave all the credit to his players: "This is the hustlingest [sic] bunch of players I've ever been associated with in all my years in baseball." In paying high praise to his players and field manager, Seals president Jerry Donovan said, "I'll be very surprised if Joe [Gordon] isn't drafted by a major league club."[106]

The San Francisco Seals wrapped up their 1957 championship season with a 101–67 (.601), 3½ games ahead of the second-place Vancouver Mounties. Second baseman Ken Aspromonte won the Pacific Coast League batting crown with his career-best .334 average.[107] Right on Aspromonte's heels were teammates Grady Hatton (.317), Frank Kellert (.308), and Albie Pearson (.297). Bill Renna hit 29 home runs and had 105 RBI, and Kellert hit 22 home runs and drove in 107 runs. The only PCL pitcher to win 20 or more games was Seals southpaw Leo Kiely, with his 21–6 record and 2.22 ERA. Amazingly, Kiely posted 20 of his wins as a reliever![108] He was followed by teammates Bill Abernathie, who topped PCL hurlers in winning percentage with his 13–2 (.867) record; Bob "Riverboat" Smith (13–10 and a league-leading six shutouts); and Jack Spring (11–9). Each Seals player received a $400 bonus for winning the Pacific Coast League championship.[109]

United States Vice President Richard Nixon sent a telefax to San Francisco Mayor George Christopher, saying, in part, "Please extend my warm congratulations to all of the players and particularly to Joe Gordon who managed this championship team. Dick Nixon."[110]

Years later, Ken Aspromonte wrote the Foreword to P.J. Dragseth's book, *The 1957 San Francisco Seals: End of an Era in the Pacific Coast League*, saying, "That season was memorable for all of us…. We had a good ballclub and that's always a big help to individual players.... And we played under a good man, Joe Gordon, who was my favorite manager."[111] After a seven-year major league playing career, Ken Aspromonte managed the Cleveland Indians from 1972 to 1974. In an audio interview recorded by radio host "Dave O" in 2016, Aspromonte talked about playing for the San Francisco Seals under manager Joe Gordon: "He was a players' manager.... It was just terrific.... He just said, 'Go play your game the way it should be played.'"[112]

In mid–October 1957, Horace Stoneham, owner/president of the New York/San Francisco Giants, announced the swap of their Class AAA American Association Minneapolis Millers franchise for the Open Class PCL San Francisco Seals franchise of the Boston Red Sox.[113] Rumors speculating that Joe Gordon would be offered the manager's job at Minneapolis soon proved true. Red Sox general manager Joe Cronin said, "[The] job is Gordon's if he wants it."[114] But Joe indicated that he preferred a West Coast scouting job if he didn't come up with a job managing in the majors.

Several Seals players went on to the majors (Ken Aspromonte, Marty Keough, Leo Kiely, Albie Pearson, Bill Renna, and Bob "Riverboat" Smith); some to the Minneapolis Millers of the American Association; and others to various minor league clubs.[115]

Outfielder Albie Pearson played his first major league season for the 1958 Washington Senators and was voted the American League Rookie of the Year by both *The Sporting News* and the Baseball Writers' Association of America. In March 2014, Judy Gordon was privileged to have a phone interview with 79-year-old Albie:

> Joe Gordon was the best manager I ever had. What made him so good was that he always encouraged us to go and play as hard as we could. "Just go and play," he'd say. He had a short memory if we made mistakes, too. He was a players' manager.
>
> When Joe was with the Yankees, he was a great low-ball hitter. When I was in a hitting slump with the San Francisco [Seals], Joe'd tell me to chop at the ball, right toward the pitcher's feet, but it would always go good, up in the air.
>
> He always backed me 100 percent. His reports about me were always positive.
>
> After Gene Autry bought the Los Angeles Angels and they became an American League team, Joe Gordon was [their] hitting coach in 1962. He was famous for teaching batters to "chop" at the ball. I can't tell you how many players he helped. One of them was Billy Moran. Joe got ahold of him, and Billy got to be one of our best hitters. I [Pearson] led the American League in runs scored [115] that year. Joe was the key; he was always willing to help. I loved your dad. He was a special guy.[116]

In 1958, Bucky Walter, a veteran sportswriter for the *San Francisco News*, wrote an article, headlined "Gordon Called Smart, Daring Pilot," saying, "Joseph Lowell Gordon earned his managerial credentials last year [1957] when he picked up the San Francisco Seals by the scruff of the neck and captured the Pacific Coast League pennant. Gordon passed another critical test. He won the respect and comradeship of the cynics of the press box.... Gordon not only led the Seals to the pennant but also helped develop Bosox [Boston Red Sox] farmlings. With patience and tutelage, he brought along such fledglings as Ken Aspromonte, Albie Pearson, Marty Keough and Heywood [*sic*] Sullivan."[117]

In the fall of 1957, Joe Gordon joined the Robert D. Metcalf Insurance Agency in Sacramento as a special sales representative for The Equitable Life Assurance Society of the United States, the company that underwrote Major League Baseball's pension plan.[118]

In late November, Joe and Dottie, along with their good friends, Jack and Helen Renwick, flew to Mexico in their Piper Tri-Pacer airplane for a two-week vacation. One day, while fishing with light tackle from a small boat, Joe and Jack chanced onto an exciting adventure off the coast of Mazatlan. Joe hooked onto a 20-foot-wide giant manta ray, which towed them out to sea for five miles before they finally had to cut it loose.[119]

While the Gordons were vacationing in Mexico, Joe's name was mentioned as a frontrunner in the Sacramento Solons' search for a new manager. Upon hearing the news, Joe said, "I would have to give a lot of thought to it before making a decision on taking any manager's job."[120] Eventually he decided to drop out of consideration, saying, "After several exploratory talks with Solon officials, I've decided to devote full time to my insurance business. I want to give this insurance business a good try."[121] Meanwhile, it was reliably reported that he'd also turned down a coaching job with the Detroit Tigers.[122]

Chapter 20

"For a Baseball Man, This Is the Ultimate" (1958–1961)

1958 Cleveland Indians

The Gordon family spent a quiet winter and spring of 1957–1958 at home in Sacramento. Joe sold life insurance and annuities, and he enjoyed his contacts with old friends and new acquaintances. Yet when a reporter asked him if he missed baseball, he responded with an enthusiastic, "You betcha."[1]

In late June 1958, in what the media described as "a startling move," Cleveland Indians general manager Frank Lane hired 43-year-old Joe Gordon to replace Bobby Bragan as the team's field manager for the remainder of 1958 and all of 1959.[2] Lane, himself just seven months into his job as general manager, gave a somewhat generic explanation of why they were changing pilots: "We are making this change with the hope that there will be a general improvement in the club."[3] At the time, the Indians were tied for sixth place, with a 31–36 record and 12 games behind the league-leading New York Yankees.

Other than in 1954, when Cleveland won the American League pennant but lost the World Series to the New York Giants, the Indians had experienced steadily declining attendance since their 1948 world championship season. *The Sporting News* published an editorial, saying, "We're especially interested in the [managerial] switch at Cleveland.... If Gordon can help reverse this situation [declining attendance], he will bring financial benefits not only to the Indians' stockholders, but to every club in the American League."[4]

When former Indians owner Bill Veeck heard about Joe Gordon being hired as the club's new manager, he told writer Harry Jones, "This is one of my two or three all-time favorite athletes. He's just a wonderful guy, a lot of fun. And a real good manager, too. He'll do a first-class job."[5]

Before heading east, Joe said, "It's a real homecoming for me.... I'm delighted to be coming back.... For a baseball man, this is the ultimate."[6]

Columnist Ed McAuley expressed high praise for the Indians' new manager: "Joe starts with a shining asset. He's a major leaguer, through and through. He'll have the respect of his players, the press and the public.... Everyone who knows him likes him."[7]

Joe was eager to get started. He caught an overnight flight to Cleveland, arriving mid-morning on June 27. Greeted at the airport by his boss, Frank Lane, and about 100 fans, he said, "I'm tickled to death he [Lane] offered me the job and I have enough confidence in myself to feel I can improve the club. Otherwise I wouldn't be here today."[8]

Amazingly, Gordon and Lane *still* had not discussed contract terms or salary.[9] Joe later talked about what happened: "When Frank offered me the job, I didn't even ask him [about the contract]. I accepted right away. He [Lane] said, 'Hey, don't you want to know the terms?' He told me my contract would run through '59, but it wouldn't have made any difference if he had said it was only until the end of this year. And as for money, what the heck is money when you've got a big league manager's job?"[10] Gordon's contract records indicate that his salaries for both 1958 and 1959 were $30,000 per season.

Having traveled all night, Joe checked in for a catnap at the Cleveland hotel where he'd be living until his family arrived. Next, he attended meetings, first with Lane, then his coaches, and finally his players.[11] That night, a reported 9,607 fans were there to welcome back Joe "Flash" Gordon, one of their heroes of the legendary 1948 world champion Indians. Joe received "a heartening ovation the first time he walked toward home plate with his lineup cards."[12] Rocky Colavito and Bobby Ávila hit home runs for their manager's inaugural game, and the Indians posted a come-from-behind 6–5 victory over the Baltimore Orioles. The next day, they toppled the Orioles—again by 6–5.

Gordon planned on keeping the club's present staff of coaches: Mel Harder, Red Kress, and Eddie Stanky.[13] He also brought his good friend, former Tigers outfielder and Indians scout Joyner "Jo-Jo" White onboard as third base coach.[14]

It had been eight years since Gordon played for the Indians. Several of his former teammates were with the 1958 club: first baseman Mickey Vernon; second baseman Bobby Ávila; left fielder Minnie Miñoso; center fielder Larry Doby; and pitcher Bob Lemon, although 37-year-old Lemon would be released in early July.[15]

Gordon said that his first order of business was to establish a set lineup: "That's my first objective, a regular starting team.... It will take a while because I want to get a good look at all the players. I hope to make up my mind before the All Star [G]ame."[16] By July 6, Joe was well pleased with his team's six wins in his first 10 games.[17]

Following a seven-game winning streak, they were in second place on August 2, although trailing the Yankees by a whopping 17 games. But they ran mostly cold in August, ending the month in sixth place.

Rallying again in September, they ended the season in fourth place, 14½ games behind the Yankees, but only 1½ games out of third place. Their record after Gordon took over in late June was a solid 46–40 (.535).

Outfielders Rocky Colavito and Minnie Miñoso produced outstanding seasons under Gordon's management.[18] Colavito ended the 1958 season with 41 home runs and 113 RBI, and topped both leagues with his career-high .620 slugging percentage. He placed third in the voting for the 1958 Most Valuable Player Award. Thirty-four-year-old Miñoso, nicknamed the "Cuban Comet," drove in 80 runs in addition to a career-high 24 home runs.

Finishing in the first division guaranteed the Indians a share of the 1958 World Series players' pool, with manager Gordon and his players taking home an extra $518.61 each.[19] Disappointingly, though, their reported attendance of 663,805 was their lowest since 1945.

After the season ended, Frank "Trader" Lane got busy doing what he loved best—putting together multiple player transactions in anticipation of 1959. One trade, in particular, triggered a front-page article in the *Cleveland Plain Dealer*, stating, "Frank Lane's 12-month search for a second baseman ended last night when he obtained the one he so relentlessly pursued—Billy Martin [from the Detroit Tigers]."[20] But in obtaining Martin, two of the Indians' good young pitchers, Ray Narleski and Don Mossi, were traded to Detroit, where, ironically, southpaw Mossi would post a 17–9 record for the 1959 Tigers.

Not realized at the time, two of Lane's transactions that fall would cause manager Joe Gordon and the Indians considerable concern during 1959 and 1960—the acquisitions of second baseman Billy Martin from the Detroit Tigers and, shortly thereafter, center fielder Jimmy Piersall from the Boston Red Sox.[21] Yet on the up side, both Martin and Piersall were widely recognized as hustlers and certain to bring color and excitement to the Indians.

1959 Cleveland Indians

Joe Gordon was his usual optimistic self in January 1959, when he spoke at the annual Ribs and Roasts Dinner of the Cleveland Chapter of the Baseball Writers' Association of America. Arriving late, because his flight from California had been delayed by bad weather, Joe told the capacity crowd of more than 600 attendees, "Why pussyfoot around? I think we're gonna have a helluva fine ball club. I'm really excited about it. We're more than dangerous. We can win. I really believe it."[22] It was announced at the gathering that popular right fielder Rocky Colavito had been voted the Cleveland Indians Man of the Year for 1958.[23]

As the Indians assembled for spring training at Tucson, Frank Lane was busy touring spring training camps in Florida, "checking rival clubs and pursuing all trade possibilities."[24] Indians vice president George Medinger talked about how Lane's rebuilding of the team, along with adding Joe Gordon as manager, already was triggering an "uplift of enthusiasm" in Cleveland. Medinger also noted, "Gordon has gone on record as saying that the Indians will be good enough, with a few breaks, to go all the way [to the pennant].... We could be a big surprise."[25]

Similar to his managing style in the Pacific Coast League, Joe Gordon continued his more relaxed practices while managing the Cleveland Indians. He also was recognized for his hands-on approach in helping young players with their batting and fielding. His children still remember their dad teaching his "chop-chop" or "tomahawking" method of leveling out a player's swing to avoid uppercutting.[26]

The Indians opened their 1959 season winning their first six games in a row, losing one game, then winning four more in a row. Manager Gordon talked about his team: "They may not be the best team in the world, but they think they are and I'm not going to tell them otherwise. We have the cockiest team in baseball."[27] The Indians wrapped up April in first place, with a 10–4 record. In early May, an article in *Sports Illustrated* described Joe Gordon as the "most secure manager of the week."[28]

The Indians posted identical 15–13 records in May and June, their worst two months of the 1959 season. During a night game on June 10 at Baltimore's Memorial Stadium, 24-year-old right fielder Rocky Colavito became just the eighth ballplayer in American and National League history to hit *four* home runs in one game! What's even more impressive, Colavito was just the third player to hit his round-trippers in four successive trips to the plate, joining Bobby Lowe of the Boston Beaneaters (in 1894) and Lou Gehrig of the New York Yankees (1932).[29]

Dottie Gordon and 18-year-old daughter Judy headed to Cleveland in late June to join

Chapter 20. "For a Baseball Man, This Is the Ultimate" (1958–1961)

Indians manager Joe Gordon intently observes his players during a game in 1959 (*Cleveland Press* Collection, Michael Schwartz Library, Cleveland State University).

Joe. Son Joey remained at home in Sacramento to work for the summer. The Gordons lived at the Westlake Hotel in Rocky River, which was convenient for Judy, as Cleveland's city bus schedule had a stop right near the hotel, so she was able to attend all of the Indians' home games while she was back east that summer.

In what was called a "break from tradition," Major League Baseball scheduled two All-Star Games for 1959. Four Indians (Rocky Colavito, Minnie Miñoso, Vic Power, and Cal McLish) played in one or both of the games. The first game was played on July 7 at Forbes Field, home of the Pittsburgh Pirates, and saw the National League winning, 5–4. The American League won the second game, 5–3, on August 3, at the Memorial Coliseum, home of the Los Angeles Dodgers. The playing of two Midsummer Classics would continue each year through 1962, reportedly for the purpose of boosting the players' pension fund.[30]

In first place much of the season thus far, the Indians were just .002 percentage points ahead of the Chicago White Sox on July 15. Manager Gordon expressed caution about the American League pennant: "Anyone who says flatly that this team or that team will win the pennant just doesn't know what he's talking about. There isn't a team [in the league] strong enough to pull away from the rest."[31]

Meanwhile, attendance at Indians home games was making a big comeback. On August 2, the reported paid attendance of 34,682 at their doubleheader put them over the one-million mark for the first time since 1955.[32]

On August 5, the Indians were playing at Washington, two games behind league-leading Chicago. The first player up to bat in the nightcap of the doubleheader was Cleveland's second baseman, Billy Martin. The Gordons' daughter, Judy, was traveling with the team, watching the game from about halfway up the third base stands. Tragically, on the third pitch, Martin was hit square in the face by a fastball from Senators pitcher Tex Clevenger.[33] Judy still vividly remembers when Martin was hit. Viewed from where she was sitting, it looked as though the ball caught him in the mouth and sounded like a rifle shot. At first, it was feared that Martin was dead. But miraculously, he revived slightly and was carried, semiconscious, from the field on a stretcher and rushed to the hospital. X-rays revealed a severely fractured left jaw and cheekbone. His doctors predicted that he would be out of action at least four to six weeks.[34]

Following reconstructive surgery, Billy Martin was released from the hospital after 17 days, but remained on the Indians' disabled list a full month.[35] Unfortunately, his injury had ended his ongoing eight-game hitting streak, and he would not play another game that season.

During mid– to late–August, the Indians pulled together an eight-game string of wins at home against Washington, Baltimore, Boston, and New York, to move within just one game of the league-leading White Sox on August 26. By then, the other clubs were far back. But at the very end of August, their high hopes would be almost totally crushed when they were swept in a disastrous four-game series at home by the frontrunning White Sox, putting them 5½ games back.

In the meantime, in early September, reports about general manager Frank Lane's second-guessing of Joe Gordon's managing appeared more and more frequently in the media. When asked if Gordon would be offered a contract for 1960, Lane was noncommittal. He admitted, though, that he'd been guilty of second-guessing many of Gordon's decisions on the field that year.[36]

Still in the race in early September, the Indians won two of three games at Chicago, kicking off a six-game winning streak and showing they still had a chance to win the pennant.[37] Yet they were 4½ games behind the league-leading White Sox, with just 16 games left to play.

In mid–September, sports editor Gordon Cobbledick wrote, "[E]ach day that passes without a definite announcement that [t]he Flash will pilot the team in 1960 would seem to lessen the likelihood that his contract will be renewed."[38] Lane told the press he would make his decision regarding Gordon before the World Series.[39]

With just eight games left, Frank Lane's weeks-long outspoken second-guessing and criticism of Joe Gordon's managing finally drew a priceless retort from the Flash: "If he [Lane] wants to run the team on the field, he should sit close enough so he can signal."[40] An editorial in the *Cleveland Plain Dealer* hinted that "it would have been far better, in our opinion, if Lane had kept his mouth shut until the season ended. No manager likes to be second-guessed by his boss in the sports columns."[41]

In a startling move on September 18, Joe Gordon removed himself from consideration as manager of the Indians for the following year. He informed Lane, "Please do not consider me a candidate." Gordon's announcement came amidst rumors (later substantiated) that Lane was trying to recruit longtime National League manager Leo Durocher to pilot the Indians for 1960.[42]

The blowback from Indians fans was overwhelmingly supportive of Gordon. The *Cleveland News* conducted a survey of its readers and reported that "94 out of 100 persons questioned" favored retaining the exceptionally popular Joe Gordon as manager.[43] As the team returned home from their road trip to Kansas City, and with just five games remaining, they still were in the pennant race. They were greeted at the airport by about 400 fans carrying a large sign reading, "WE WANT JOE."[44]

Even so, the club's slim pennant chances would be crushed during a game at home on September 22, when the league-leading White Sox defeated the Indians, 4–2, in front of 54,293 heartbroken fans. At the start of the game, Gordon's loyal supporters gave him a five-minute standing ovation when he brought his lineup cards to home plate. Ironically, the Indians were knocked out of the pennant race that night by 1959 Cy Young Award winner and future Hall of Famer, 39-year-old Early Wynn, whom Frank Lane had traded to the White Sox two years earlier.[45]

Chapter 20. "For a Baseball Man, This Is the Ultimate" (1958–1961)

Shortly after the defeat, Joe Gordon announced that he'd been relieved of his managerial duties, which Lane had forewarned would happen if/when the Indians lost the pennant. Although some newspapers reported that Gordon was "fired," he actually was just relieved of his managerial duties for the final four games of the 1959 season. Veteran pitching coach Mel Harder took over managing the team. After telling Harder, "You're it," Gordon was asked where he'd be during the season-ending four games against Kansas City. In true Gordon fashion, Joe quipped, "Upstairs with Lane second guessing the new manager."[46]

Then, in what the media called a "bizarre and startling development," less than 24 hours after Gordon had been relieved of his managerial duties, Frank Lane called a press conference to announce that Joe Gordon was being hired to pilot the Cleveland Indians in 1960 and 1961, along with a raise to $35,000 per season.[47] Gordon's new contract also contained an additional clause, stating, "[I]n the event the [m]anager should obtain employment with another baseball organization during the period covered by this contract [1960 and 1961], then any compensation therefor [sic] is deductible from this contract." Lane told the press, "As evidence of my confidence in Joe Gordon, we've offered him a two-year contract. The best man to succeed Joe Gordon, I thought, was Joe Gordon."

Gordon stated that he and Lane had straightened out their differences and blamed their disagreements on "two hotheads in the pennant race." He also said, "[T]here has never been any serious disagreement between Frank Lane and I [sic]." After Lane's announcement, Gordon wisecracked: "The fact that Frank Lane gave me a two-year contract must mean that he really doesn't think I'm as bad a manager as he sometimes says I am." Meanwhile, a prophetic quote from Gordon would prove especially true during 1960: "You never know what's going to happen in Cleveland."[48] As far as the present-day Gordon family has been able to determine, Joe Gordon and Frank Lane remained friends throughout their many future associations in baseball.[49]

September was the 1959 Indians' "do or die" month in trying to overtake the Chicago White Sox. Even with all the distractions due to the Lane-Gordon squabbles, the team put forth a valiant effort, winning 14 games and losing 10 that month. They finished the season leading their league in home runs, RBI, and runs scored, and tying Kansas City in team batting average.

During the Indians' 89–65 season in 1959, they posted an even 11–11 mark against the New York Yankees, who finished a distant third at 15 games behind Chicago. But it was their dismal 7–15 record against the White Sox that cost them the pennant by five games.[50] The record-setting players' pool from the 1959 World Series between the Los Angeles Dodgers and Chicago White Sox resulted in shares to the Indians players of a reported $1,799.94 each.[51]

On a positive note, the 1959 Indians finished second to the New York Yankees at the gate, with a reported attendance of 1,497,976, a remarkable 834,171 increase over their previous year's gate.[52]

Indians third base coach Jo-Jo White said, "The future is bright for the Cleveland Indians to win the American League pennant in the next year or two.... If ever a ball club fought to the last ditch for Gordon it was the Indians.... [T]he spirit on the club was tremendous. Joe kept the team loose and we won games just through spirit."[53]

Years later, Gordon would tell writer Dennis Lustig that his biggest disappointment in baseball was piloting the Cleveland Indians to a second-place finish in 1959 instead of the pennant.[54]

1960 Cleveland Indians

In mid–December 1959, the Cleveland Indians traded second baseman Billy Martin, rookie first baseman Gordy Coleman, and pitcher Cal McLish to the National League Cincinnati Reds for All-Star second baseman Johnny Temple.

Then, suddenly, several weeks before the start of 1960 spring training, *The Sporting News* published an article, headlined "Piersall Standing on TNT, Told Not to Light Matches: Lane Reminds Jim He Was Obtained as Player—Not Clown."[55] Piersall's antics on the field the previous season, coupled with his .246 batting average in just 100 games, had posed a considerable distraction to the Indians, as well as to management.

Manager Gordon agreed with Lane: "I want the fans to cheer for him [Jimmy] for his bat and his glove and not for his antics. I'm for it 100 per cent [*sic*]. I'm sure Jimmy has more ability than he displayed last year [1959]."[56]

As in the previous two years, Frank Lane again was involved in back-and-forth contract negotiations with outfielder Rocky Colavito in early 1960. It was reported that the contract had "made the rounds three times already." The two men finally came to terms in early March, and Colavito headed to spring training.[57]

The Indians were reported as having the youngest team in the American League, with their eight "likely" regulars averaging just 27 years of age.[58] Gordon's opening pep talk with his players included words of encouragement: "Each of you can improve yourself just as I can improve as a manager. All it requires is three or four hours of hard work and concentration out here every day.... We'll have a helluva club this year."[59] Even center fielder Jimmy Piersall seemed to be exhibiting a "surprising transformation" in attitude, arriving at camp a week early and working hard at reining in what Lane referred to as Piersall's "yakking all the time."[60]

Despite optimistic reports of the Indians' hitting and fielding prospects, several sportswriters expressed pessimism about their pitching. Harry Jones wrote, "The state of Cleveland pitching is so precarious that only a supreme optimist could pick the Indians to win the pennant this season."[61]

Then just two days before Opening Day and apparently with *no* heads-up, Frank Lane announced a player transaction that would rattle Indians fans to the core.[62] On April 17, Lane traded right fielder Rocky Colavito to the Detroit Tigers for All-Star outfielder Harvey Kuenn. During 1959, Harvey had topped the American League with his .353 batting average, 198 hits, and 42 doubles. Despite Colavito's outstanding .620 slugging percentage in 1958 and league-leading 42 home runs in 1959, his batting average had dropped to just .257, which is thought to have contributed to Lane's decision to trade him.

Just a day later, Lane traded southpaw pitcher Herb Score to the Chicago White Sox for right-handed pitcher Barry Latman.[63] Score had not posted a winning season for the Indians since, tragically, he was hit in the eye by a line drive on May 7, 1957. He had returned to pitch for the Indians in 1958 and 1959, but, troubled by elbow injuries, he never approached his former brilliance. (He was an All-Star and the American League Rookie of the Year in 1955, led the majors in strikeouts in 1955 and 1956, and was an All-Star and 20-game winner also in 1956.)

But it was the Colavito trade that enraged Indians fans, eventually leading to Terry Pluto's book titled *The Curse of Rocky Colavito: A Loving Look at a Thirty-Year Slump*.[64] After the news broke about their beloved "favorite son" Rocky Colavito being

Chapter 20. "For a Baseball Man, This Is the Ultimate" (1958–1961)

traded, Cleveland fans "hanged Frank Lane in effigy and laid out a likeness of Joe Gordon on slab." Although most of the anger was directed at Lane, manager Gordon, too, it seemed, needed to be castigated for backing up the general manager's decision to trade Colavito.[65]

The Indians opened the 1960 season at home on a cold April 19 day, losing to Detroit, 4–2.[66] Unfortunately, their new outfielder, Harvey Kuenn, pulled a leg muscle during the 15-inning, four-hour and 54-minute game and had to sit out the next five games except for pinch-hitting. The club ended April in a four-way tie for last place with a 4–5 record, 1½ games out of first.

With the arrival of May, they took off like a shot, posting a 17–10 record for the month and launching themselves into second place, just two games behind the Baltimore Orioles. In mid–May, manager Gordon finally obtained the player he'd been hounding Frank Lane for—infielder Ken Aspromonte, from the Washington Senators. Aspromonte had won the 1957 Pacific Coast League batting crown while playing for the San Francisco Seals under manager Gordon. He would record his career-best major league season for the 1960 Indians and later managed the club from 1972 to 1974.

Meanwhile, outfielder Jimmy Piersall's escalating outbursts of temper caused him to be ejected from the first game of a doubleheader at Chicago on Memorial Day. It was reported that he "littered the field with bats, gloves, helmets [from the Indians' dugout] and even a trash can [full of garbage from the White Sox dugout] before making his departure." Ironically, he wasn't even involved in the call that he protested so hotly.[67]

After catching the final out of the nightcap, Jimmy Piersall was hit on the ear by an orange thrown by someone in the grandstands. He retaliated by hurling the ball at White Sox owner Bill Veeck's new "$350,000 exploding scoreboard" and short-circuiting it. The next day, American League president Joe Cronin fined Piersall $250.[68]

Piersall's outbursts at Chicago had followed on the tail of an incident at Detroit, where he was pelted with "nuts and bolts and even firecrackers" from someone in the bleachers. Realizing that some of Piersall's reactions were brought on by the taunting of rival fans, Gordon continued to play his center fielder. Not to mention that Piersall had "hit safely in 15 straight games" until ejected at Chicago. After Cronin fined Piersall, Gordon lamented, "He's been playing so well [batting over .300] we need him in the lineup. We'd have been hurt if we had lost him for a couple of days."[69]

On June 26, the largest American League crowd of the season to date, 57,621 spectators, turned out for a doubleheader at Cleveland's Municipal Stadium against the visiting New York Yankees.[70] Dan Danaceau reported, "He [Piersall] aped [Yankees manager] Casey Stengel after the latter complained about Tito Francona's first game home run. He dropped his bat in disgust after a strike was called on him. Finally he was ejected from the second game after a dispute with an umpire."[71]

The Indians' team physician, Dr. Don Kelly, recommended that Piersall take a rest at his home in Boston for an indefinite period. Frank Lane agreed and communicated with Piersall that he would only return when the doctor agreed to it.[72]

An editorial in *The Sporting News* praised Lane and Gordon: "Attention has been paid here in the recent past to the sympathetic handling of Jim Piersall by the Cleveland Indians and notably by [g]eneral [m]anager Frank Lane and [m]anager Joe Gordon. They were commended for recommending rest for him."[73] However, Yankees manager Casey Stengel later revealed that the Indians had offered Piersall, among other players, to the Yankees before the June 15 trade deadline.[74]

The Indians were slated to play the Chicago Cubs in the 19th Annual National Baseball Hall of Fame (HOF) Game at Cooperstown, New York, on June 27, 1960.[75] Because the HOF Veterans Committee did not vote that year and the Baseball Writers' Association of America did not elect any players for induction into the HOF, the game was scheduled for June instead of July. Cubs pitcher Dick Drott hurled seven innings of no-hit ball until relieved by Moe Drabowsky, who gave up just two hits in the Cubs' 5–0 victory, the first shutout in the history of the Hall of Fame Game.

While Piersall was resting at home, the Indians forged ahead, winning seven of their next eight games. After a week's rest, Piersall rejoined the team to pinch-hit and play left field in the July 4 nightcap. At first, he played well, but the Indians spiraled downward, losing 17 of their next 23 games through the end of July.

For the second year in a row, two Major League Baseball All-Star Games were scheduled, this year only two days apart. The first game was played on July 11 at Municipal Stadium in Kansas City, with the National League winning, 5–3. Two Cleveland pitchers, Gary Bell and rookie southpaw Dick Stigman, were chosen for the American League team (both first-time All-Stars), in addition to first baseman Vic Power and outfielder Harvey Kuenn. The second game was played on July 13 at Yankee Stadium, with the National League shutting out the American League, 6–0.

Following the All-Star Game break, Jimmy Piersall's disruptive behavior began again. After he was ejected in the first inning of the July 16 game, Frank Lane decreed, "[W]hatever the league fines him (Piersall) the club will fine him an equal amount.… No player is any good to us in the clubhouse."[76] At the time, the Indians were in second place, just 1½ games behind the Yankees.

Manager Gordon benched Piersall both games of the next day's doubleheader, except for having him pinch-hit. Between appearances at the plate, Piersall passed the time clowning in the bullpen—pretending to toss basketball shots into a glove and kicking football field goals with the glove. In his two times pinch-hitting, he struck out and flied out, with the Indians losing both games to sixth-place Washington. Gordon fined Piersall a day's pay, saying, "Piersall is no different from anyone else on the club. I expect him to give 100 per cent [sic] when he's playing, and I expect his undivided attention when he's not. We're fighting for a pennant, and … every time he gets tossed out of a game, it hurts our chances."[77]

Frank Lane said that Piersall's clowning "was obviously designed to show up [m]anager Joe Gordon for keeping him [Jimmy] out of the lineup."[78] Lane also spelled out, "If I had been in Gordon's place, I'd have called him [Piersall] in from behind the fence [the bullpen] and … told him that if he opened his trap just once more it would cost him money."[79] The irony of Lane's strategy, however, was that for every fine levied against Piersall, it was reported that his fans were sending him money to reimburse him.[80]

Harold Rosenthal's article in the *New York Herald Tribune* forewarned, "The Jim Piersall situation is bubbling ominously. It could run over during this crucial Yankee-Cleveland series. Cleveland manager Joe Gordon tonight fined Piersall a day's pay—approximately $200—for his lackadaisical performance during the double loss to Washington yesterday [July 17]. Gordon also said Piersall would be fined $500 the next time he is ejected from a game by the umpire. Piersall has been bounced five times this season."[81]

Adding to the club's woes, their home run and RBI leader, shortstop Woodie Held, fractured his finger in two places during the July 18 game against the Yankees and would

Chapter 20. "For a Baseball Man, This Is the Ultimate" (1958–1961)

be out an estimated three to five weeks.[82] Gordon and Lane later lamented about the loss of Held: "[Y]ou don't know how valuable that guy is until you lose him."[83]

With the season more than half over, Lane was baffled by the Indians' disturbing drop in home attendance, saying, "We've got a good team, one that can win the pennant."[84]

By July 20, they had dropped back to third place after losing two of three games at home against the Yankees. Gordon told writer Chuck Heaton, "With the Yankees you can't overpower the hitters. You need some cuteriess [sic]. Our pitchers are young and like to throw that fast ball. The Yankees eat those up."[85]

On July 25 and with the Indians in fourth place after losing three of four games to the seventh-place Red Sox, the *Cleveland Plain Dealer* published an article, headlined "Tribe Players Demand Lane Curb Piersall." The article said, "The Cleveland Indians plan to visit [g]eneral [m]anager Frank Lane when he arrives from Chicago today and demand that he take definite action to curb the antics of teammate Jimmy Piersall.... Seething with animosity toward the eccentric outfielder, Indian players will send their player representative, outfielder Harvey Kuenn, or a committee of players to Lane."[86]

Ejected from a game for the sixth time that season, Piersall again was summoned to the office of American League president Joe Cronin for "some fatherly advice." After paying a $100 fine, Piersall emerged from the meeting, saying, "I am wrong in this situation. From now on I'm just going to play baseball."[87]

Hoping that this time Piersall meant what he said, the players' meeting was called off. Harry Jones wrote, "It would have been the first time in baseball history that players met in protest against a fellow member of the team. The closest thing to it was the [Oscar] Vitt rebellion in 1940."[88]

Frank Lane said, "Gordon is managing the team, and I will endorse any decision he makes in the best interest of the Indians. I'll back him up 100%."[89] Yet neither Lane nor Gordon blamed Piersall for the late July collapse of the Indians as a pennant contender, at least publicly, especially since Piersall was leading the club with 52 RBI. Instead, Lane pinned the cause on disappointing pitching, hitting, and injuries.[90]

But harmony was short-lived. After the club wrapped up a disappointing 4–9 road trip, suddenly Frank Lane announced Joe Gordon's release as manager of the Indians.[91] It also was reported that Gordon would succeed Jimmy Dykes as manager of the Detroit Tigers, and Dykes would manage the Cleveland Indians—described by the media as a manager-manager trade that was a first and only in Major League Baseball history.

At a news conference in Washington, D.C., Frank Lane said that the arrangement to exchange managers had been made "by mutual agreement" with Joe Gordon and was "voluntary on Gordon's part."[92] The Indians had a 49–46 record under Gordon's management and were in fourth place, seven games out of first.

Third base coach Jo-Jo White managed the Indians for one game on August 3. Jimmy Dykes took over for the remainder of the season, posting a 26–32 record and finishing in fourth place, 21 games behind the pennant-winning Yankees. Jim Perry was the only Cleveland pitcher to finish the season with double-digit wins (18–10). But it was the Indians' attendance that took the big hit, with gate numbers down by well over 500,000 from the previous year.

On August 4, the *Cleveland Plain Dealer* published an all-caps, boldface headline on the front page of their sports section, reading, "PIERSALL THE WINNER, INDIANS SAY," followed by a sub-headline, "'Elimination' Battle with Gordon Ends."[93] Sadly, though, it was the Indians players, fans, and organization that ended up as the real losers of the so-called "battle."

The Cleveland Indians unconditionally released Joe Gordon on August 4, and he and Dottie packed their belongings and headed to Detroit for Joe's first game there on August 5. He signed with the Tigers for the balance of the 1960 season, at the same $35,000 salary that the Indians had been paying him. When he took over managing the Tigers, the club had a 45–52 record and were in sixth place, 11½ games behind the Yankees.

In addition to signing for the remainder of 1960, Gordon also was offered a contract for 1961, at the same salary as 1960. Joe was hesitant about signing for a second year, although he reluctantly did so. Not reported at the time of his signing, it was later revealed that he also had a "handshake" agreement with Tigers president William O. DeWitt, Sr., that would let Joe out of his 1961 contract if he [Gordon] was not satisfied with the way things were going at Detroit.[94]

Sportswriters, both then and now, refer to the August 1960 exchange of Cleveland Indians manager Joe Gordon for Detroit Tigers manager Jimmy Dykes as a "trade." In reality, though, the transaction involved the simultaneous release and hiring of two managers by two clubs.[95] Even today, it remains one of the most unusual transactions in baseball history.

Gordon admitted to *Cleveland Plain Dealer* writer Harry Jones that he was departing the Indians "with regret," and added, "But no hard feelings. I've enjoyed managing this ball club and I enjoyed being in Cleveland."[96] After hearing that their manager was leaving, many of Gordon's players contacted him throughout the day to express how sorry they were to see him go. Deeply touched, Joe said, "They're a fine bunch of guys, and I'm going to miss them. If Frank [Lane] and I can sit down and make a few deals[,] I'll get some of them back [at Detroit]."[97]

1960 Detroit Tigers

Ten months before Joe Gordon became manager of the Detroit Tigers in August 1960, longtime baseball executive William O. DeWitt, Sr., had been elected as the club's new president and "top operating officer." It was reported that DeWitt was given "complete autonomy in running the club."[98]

A few days after signing, Joe Gordon requested that his third base coach, Jo-Jo White, be released by the Indians and hired as first base coach at Detroit.[99] Gordon also kept his good friend and longtime Tigers coach Billy Hitchcock on as third base coach.[100] Tigers coach Luke Appling was released by Detroit to join Dykes at Cleveland.

After holding a brief clubhouse meeting with his players, Gordon said, "I told them I didn't contemplate any big changes. I just want them to loosen up and play ball. They should have some fun out there."[101] Following a full day of meetings and photo shoots, the Tigers lost the night game to the Boston Red Sox, 4–2, and Joe acknowledged, "That's about as long a day as I've ever spent in a ball park."[102]

Ominously, just days after Gordon took over managing the Tigers, reports appeared in some Michigan newspapers, saying that Jimmy Dykes was portraying Tigers president Bill DeWitt as a meddler and second-guesser.[103] About that same time, a blatantly false story appeared in a Detroit newspaper, implying that Joe Gordon didn't want

Chapter 20. "For a Baseball Man, This Is the Ultimate" (1958–1961)

president DeWitt in the Tigers' clubhouse. Gordon was reported as "incensed over the story," countering with, "I SAID nothing like that—the writer implied it. And if the writer is trying to create the impression that I'm going to tell Mr. DeWitt what to do, he's wrong. Mr. DeWitt is my boss, and if he wants to come into the clubhouse, he can do it anytime he wants."[104]

Gordon's first road trip managing the Tigers was a four-game series at Cleveland, beginning August 12. The Tigers had just lost six of seven games at home; and, by the same token, the Indians had lost five of their seven games under their new manager, Jimmy Dykes.

During the night game, Gordon was seen standing on the visitors' dugout steps, watching as Jimmy Piersall staged one of his screaming temper tantrums and was ejected for his seventh time, out of a total of eight ejections that season.[105] When asked what he thought of Piersall's antics, Gordon just grinned and said, "I wasn't much impressed.... I'd seen it all before."[106] The Tigers beat the Indians, 6–4, prompting the Flash to acknowledge with a smile, "I must admit it was a very nice one to win." Detroit ended up winning three of their four games at Cleveland.

Things were looking pretty good—at least for a while. The Tigers won eight of their next nine games, including four straight against the visiting Indians. But their hopes were soon dashed during a two-week road trip, followed by more losses at home against the Indians, Red Sox, and Yankees. After that, it was mostly win-a-couple, lose-a-couple, until ending the season still in sixth place with a 71–83 (.461) record, 26 games behind the pennant-winning Yankees.

At 7:00 a.m. on the morning of October 3, just one day after the 1960 season ended, Joe Gordon phoned Detroit Tigers president Bill DeWitt and asked to be released from his 1961 contract.[107]

When the news of his resignation broke, Joe was golfing with friends in Canton, Ohio. He told a newsman, "I have resigned at Detroit and am seeking employment.... If there are reports that I have been hired at Kansas City, I deny them. I'm going to the World Series at Pittsburgh and probably won't give much thought to a job for several days."[108]

Likewise, when questioned about the media reports, Kansas City Athletics general manager Parke Carroll said, "I don't know anything about it. Gordon might have been approached by someone who planned to buy the [Kansas City] ball club. Right now the Athletics wouldn't sign anyone without consulting the group who planned to buy the club."[109] The Athletics' majority owner, 54-year-old Arnold Johnson, had passed away from a cerebral hemorrhage back in March 1960, and the administrators of his estate were trying to sell the club.

Things progressed quickly. Parke Carroll was quoted in an October 4 newspaper article, saying, "Gordon is one of four or five men being considered as acceptable to manage at Kansas City. We are happy that he is available to be hired, and I am going to talk to him about managing our ball club."[110]

1961 Kansas City Athletics

Two days after Joe Gordon asked for his release from the Detroit Tigers, the Kansas City Athletics offered him a two-year contract to manage the A's in 1961 and 1962, at a salary of $30,000 per year. Included in the contract was a clause stating, "Manager to receive bonus of $5,000 each year during term of contract if paid admissions for Athletics home games equal (900,000)." The Tigers unconditionally released Joe Gordon on October 15, and he signed with the Athletics on November 2. Years later, Joe McGuff wrote in *The Sporting News*, "At the time he [Gordon] signed with the A's, the club was in the process of being sold. It appeared a Kansas City group would purchase the club."[111] John E. Peterson, author of *The Kansas City Athletics: A Baseball History, 1954–1967*, wrote that Joe Gordon had "long wanted—to manage a major league club without front office interference."[112]

Since relocating from Philadelphia to Kansas City in 1955, the Athletics had finished in sixth place once, seventh place three times, and last place twice. The team was very much in need of an overhaul, finishing 1960 in the cellar with a record of 58–96 (.377) and trailing the pennant-winning New York Yankees by 39 games. The A's also had seen a disappointing home attendance of 774,944, their lowest total since moving to "The Show Me State."

Joe Gordon said, "I feel we can do a good job in Kansas City. We have a lot of young fellows and that's what I like."[113] However, obtaining ballplayers proved challenging, because the American League was in the process of expanding from eight to 10 teams in 1961. Adding two new teams also necessitated lengthening the season from 154 to 162 games, with each club playing the other nine clubs 18 times apiece instead of 22.

Expansion fever hit Major League Baseball the fall and winter of 1960–1961. The American League saw the creation of two additional clubs, the Los Angeles Angels and new Washington Senators, both of which would begin play in 1961. The previous Washington, D.C., franchise relocated to Minneapolis-St. Paul to become the Minnesota Twins. In mid–December, the two new expansion clubs drafted ballplayers under a complex set of rules, from a pool of players contributed to by the existing eight American League clubs.[114] The National League would follow suit in 1962, adding the Houston Colt .45s (later renamed the Houston Astros) and the New York Mets.

Right before the minor league winter meetings, Joe Gordon announced his three coaches for 1961: Dario Lodigiani, Jo-Jo White, and Ed FitzGerald.[115] Before the 1961 season began, Gordon also brought Ted Wilks onboard to coach the young pitchers.[116]

A's general manager Parke Carroll and manager Joe Gordon attended the minor league winter meetings at Louisville, looking in particular for pitchers and catchers. Sid Bordman wrote, "Because of the major league expansion muddle, most of the teams have put their trading tools back in the cupboard. But Gordon is ready to swap at any time."[117]

The Athletics very much needed a shortstop. Baseball enthusiasts will recognize who they gambled on—rookie Dick Howser, a product of the A's farm system.[118] The gamble paid off. Howser played in 158 games and batted a career-high .280 with 171 hits for the 1961 Athletics, in addition to being named an All-Star for both games (the only player chosen from the A's) and finishing as runner-up American League Rookie of the Year. After a long playing and managing career, Howser also managed the Kansas City Royals to their first world championship in 1985.

On December 20, 1960, it was announced that the flamboyant, self-made multi-millionaire insurance "tycoon" Charles O. "Charlie" Finley purchased 52 percent of the Kansas City Athletics stock from former owner Arnold Johnson's estate.[119] Finley had no prior experience in major league baseball, although, throughout the previous six

Chapter 20. "For a Baseball Man, This Is the Ultimate" (1958–1961)

years he'd been trying to buy a club (the Philadelphia Athletics, Detroit Tigers, Chicago White Sox, and new expansion Los Angeles Angels).[120]

In a surprise move in early January 1961, Finley hired Frank Lane as the A's new general manager, reportedly signing him to a lucrative four-year contract. Lane still had two years remaining on his Indians contract when he departed Cleveland for Kansas City.[121]

Soon after signing with the Athletics, Lane said, "I guess I've been asked a hundred times today: 'How are you and [Joe] Gordon going to get along?' My answer is: We always have, and always will, get along fine.… Actually, I'm tickled to death to have Joe."[122]

Charlie Finley purchased the remaining 48 percent of the Kansas City Athletics stock in mid–February 1961, which gave him sole ownership of the club. Meanwhile, general manager Frank Lane predicted that there was an "outside chance" that the A's would finish the 1961 season in fifth or, "more realistically," sixth place.[123]

The advance squad of veteran and rookie batterymen reported to A's spring training at West Palm Beach, Florida, on February 20, with the balance of the players arriving six days later.[124] Gene Fox wrote in *Sports Guys: Insights, Highlights and Hoo-hahs from Your Favorite Sports Authorities*, that the 1961 Athletics held "one of the franchise's best training camps in it's [sic] history."[125] Gordon enjoyed working with the young players, and, with him as manager, spring training was productive, yet fun—at least for the players.

But things were not as enjoyable for their manager. Fox wrote, "If [Charlie] Finley made life miserable for his broadcasters, it's not too difficult to imagine what life was like for his managers." Fox also related that Kansas City sports reporter and A's broadcaster, Bill Grigsby, had observed, firsthand, an especially contentious, late-night confrontation initiated by Charlie Finley and sprung on Joe Gordon in the George Washington Hotel, the A's headquarters during spring training: "Grigsby said he will never forget the first time he saw Finley belittle a manager [Joe Gordon]."[126] Little known at the time, the ensuing altercation would greatly impact Gordon's future with the Kansas City Athletics.

The A's opened their 1961 season on the road at Boston, winning their first game, then losing two at New York before losing their home opener against the Indians. They ended April with a 5–8 record. Of note, however, was their 20–2 blockbuster victory at home against the Minnesota Twins on April 25.[127]

But as May got underway, Ernest Mehl wrote, "What had been feared has come to pass, and that is weak pitching."[128] Two years earlier, Joe Gordon had talked about managing pitchers: "Take the games to bed with me? Sure I do; everybody does.… Pitchers aren't human beings.… One day they look good, or even one inning. Then, they change for no apparent reason. I don't think anybody knows how to handle pitchers. I just pray."[129]

When the time came in May to pare the club's active roster down to the 25-player limit, owner Charlie Finley overruled Frank Lane's and Joe Gordon's decision to send one of their rookie pitchers to the minors to gain more experience.[130] Instead, Lane and Gordon had to send down their only right-handed pinch-hitter, subject to 24-hour recall. On another occasion, Finley interfered with Gordon and ordered that a pitcher be "given some assignments as a starter." Hints of "feuds" between Finley and Lane appeared in the media.[131] Ernest Mehl wrote, "There have been some predictions that both Lane and Gordon will leave before the year is over, but both deny this stoutly."[132]

By the latter part of May, it was reported in the *Olathe* (KS) *News* that "apparently Finley is taking a very active part in running the team. Wednesday, he stripped [g]eneral [m]anager Frank Lane of much of his trading authority and issued another order to [f]ield [m]anager Joe Gordon about use of his players."[133]

In mid–June, the A's had just returned home from what the media described as a highly successful, three-week, 10-13 road trip, which included 13 games against the top three clubs in the league (Indians, Tigers, and Yankees). The first half of the trip even saw the club topping the .500 mark. It was reported as "the longest road trip in Kansas City [Athletics] history," as well as "generally considered to be the best road trip in the seven years the Athletics have been in Kansas City."[134]

Then, suddenly, with absolutely *no* advanced warning, on June 19, just one day after the A's had lost an 11-inning game to the visiting Los Angeles Angels, 5–3, Charlie Finley fired manager Joe Gordon.[135] Charlie had general manager Frank Lane do almost all the talking during a hastily called press conference, mid-day, before that night's game. The Athletics' 38-year-old outfielder, Hank Bauer, was introduced as the club's player-manager. This was Bauer's first time piloting a club, other than a three-day managing stint in the low minors in 1946.[136]

An "extremely rare" audio recording of the press conference was obtained by nationally syndicated radio host "Dave O," courtesy of Jeff Logan and the Kansas City Baseball Historical Society. The audio gives a fascinating, firsthand, blow-by-blow account of Gordon's firing.[137]

Both Charlie Finley and Hank Bauer were at the press conference, although Frank Lane did most of the talking. Lane indicated that they were making the change to get better results and felt that Bauer would be positively received by the players and fans alike.[138]

Ernest Mehl, sports editor of the *Kansas City Star*, spoke up during the meeting and asked what would be done with Joe Gordon's two-year contract, and whether Gordon had another job lined up. It was then that Frank Lane revealed that Joe Gordon had absolutely *no* knowledge of being fired:

> Gordon's contract will be honored. Ah, we don't know that he has another job, Ernie. In fact of the matter is, we've been trying to reach him all day. I talked to his wife [Dorthy] two or three times. Joe's out fishing [on Lake Lotawana with Harold Ensley of *The Sportsman's Friend* TV show]. And ah, in fact I called Dorthy again just now…. I would say that Joe has no official notice of this. And we haven't been able to…. I talked with Dorthy about two or three times, and I didn't think, ah, I should break it to Dorthy, other than she said she'd definitely have Joe call me by 2:30 because he's out on the lake fishing; and I've been trying to get him for two or three hours. And because of the need to, the need to, of time, the need for time, we were forced to announce this, actually, before Joe has official notification of it…. But he is gunna know within a very few moments, because Dorthy said he would call me.[139]

After announcing Gordon's firing, Lane rambled on for some time about the club's players, future, and new manager, as well as about Joe Gordon. Then Charlie Finley and Hank Bauer each spoke briefly.

Near the end of the press briefing, Gordon had returned home from fishing and received the message to phone Frank Lane. Lane stepped out of the press conference to take Joe's phone call.[140] When Gordon heard that he'd been fired, he asked to talk with

Chapter 20. "For a Baseball Man, This Is the Ultimate" (1958–1961)

Ernest Mehl, wanting to know what was going on. Joe told Mehl, "This is a helluva surprise," in addition to saying that he had no idea why he was let go. He definitely was not expecting to be fired, substantiated by the fact that, just recently, the Gordons were in the process of buying a home at nearby Lake Lotawana.[141]

Charlie Finley's rather vague explanation of why he fired Joe Gordon appeared in a front-page article of the next morning's *Kansas City Times*: "I [Finley] was the man behind that move and I think the heat should be taken off our general manager [Frank Lane].... Not long after I acquired the Athletics one thing became quite obvious to me. Lane had *gordonitis* and Gordon had *laneitis*."[142]

Hearing the news of Gordon's firing, the A's players were "puzzled as well as surprised" and said how much they admired their popular and highly respected manager, and the job he was doing. Infielder Jerry Lumpe said, "Joe was a great guy and he did a great job.... At first I didn't believe it. It just didn't seem possible." First baseman/left fielder Norm Siebern said, "Gordon was a wonderful guy to play for. I thought he was a good manager and he was good to me." Southpaw Bud Daley, who'd been with the A's since 1958 but recently traded to the Yankees, said about Gordon, "He's a great guy and a fine manager. In fact I'd say he's the best manager Kansas City has ever had. I don't think this was Lane's deal. It sounds to me like this was Finley's idea."[143]

Joe, Dottie, and son Joey loved their time in Kansas City. They lived close to a lake, so Joe got to do some fishing. Joey accompanied his dad to A's batting practices to shag balls in the outfield before home games. But just as happened when the Gordons had departed Detroit so suddenly in 1956, Joey just was told to pack his bags, and the family drove home to Sacramento. It wouldn't be until 60 years later, while helping his sister Judy Gordon with this book about their father, that Joey found out why they had to return home so early in 1961.

In a rare instance of reflection about what happened, Joe Gordon was quoted in the *Eugene Register-Guard*: "I suppose there are a lot of things I might say, but what would it accomplish? I don't know whether I'll ever go back into baseball. Things like this make you wonder if you want to stay in this business."[144]

At the time of Gordon's firing, the A's record was 26–33, and they were in eighth place out of 10 teams, yet only 1½ games out of sixth. Moreover, their .441 winning percentage was better than five of their previous six seasons, as well as significantly better than four of those.

Hank Bauer managed the A's for the balance of the 1961 season and all of 1962. Ultimately the club trended downward the remainder of 1961, posting a 35–67 record to end up tied for last place at 61–100 (.379), trailing the pennant-winning New York Yankees by a whopping 47½ games. After a next-to-last-place finish in 1962, Hank Bauer resigned, effective the last day of the season, some say before Finley had a chance to fire him.[145]

The bizarre saga of the 1961 Kansas City Athletics did not end with the firing of Joe Gordon. The proverbial "rest of the story" was revealed on August 22, when Charlie Finley fired general manager Frank Lane during a two-and-a-half-hour press conference held at Finley's insurance office in Chicago. Ironically, like Gordon before him, Lane was fired *in absentia* and first heard the news when he phoned the A's front office to report that he was on his way to the stadium for that night's game.[146]

Reporter Jerry Holtzman said Finley charged that "it was [Frank] Lane who poisoned my mind on Joe Gordon." Finley stated several times during the press conference,

"[T]he biggest mistake I ever made was firing [Joe] Gordon. I fired the wrong man. Lane was the man who should have been fired."[147]

"Dave O" obtained another "extremely rare" audio recording, courtesy of Jeff Logan and the Kansas City Baseball Historical Society, of a phone conversation between "the irate" Charlie Finley and A's broadcaster Monte Moore, recorded on the day Finley fired Frank Lane.[148]

Not surprisingly, Lane's version of what transpired differed markedly from Finley's version. Lane told Ernest Mehl that Finley actually had fired Joe Gordon twice that year, once during spring training, immediately rehiring him; and the last time when the club had a bad day. Lane also said Finley started a rumor that Lane and Gordon were enemies, which both Lane and Gordon said was false.[149]

In 2016, "Dave O" interviewed former Athletics outfielder Jay Hankins who had played under both managers in 1961, Joe Gordon and Hank Bauer. Hankins expressed high regard for Gordon: "They were altogether different managers—Joe Gordon and Hank Bauer. Joe was by far the best manager. I mean, he was a student of the game."[150]

Kansas City has had a long and storied history as a great baseball town—home to the American Association Kansas City Blues, Negro League Kansas City Monarchs, and American League Kansas City Athletics and Kansas City Royals. Charlie Finley continued his hiring and firing of managers and others during his seven years as owner and president of the 1961–1967 Kansas City Athletics, going through seven managers. Although Finley repeatedly professed that he had no intention of moving the A's to another city,[151] he relocated his franchise to Oakland, in time for the 1968 baseball season as the Oakland Athletics. Once there, Finley changed managers multiple times in 13 years (1968–1980), in addition to finally attaining his dream of winning three world championships (1972, 1973, and 1974).

When Joe Gordon passed away in April 1978, writer Red Smith quoted what Dario Lodigiani (Joe's 1936 Oakland Oaks teammate, 1961 Kansas City A's coach, and longtime friend) said: "Funny thing, Joe and [Frank] Lane were real close friends to the end. And Joe got along with Charlie [Finley], too. That's got to tell you something about him [Gordon]."[152] Bill Conlin wrote in the *Sacramento Bee*, "It was a measurement of Gordon that he was never critical of Finley or his methods. The worst critique Joe would make was 'Charlie is Charlie, and you have to understand him.'"[153]

Chapter 21

A Remarkable Career
(1962–1971)

1962–1968 Los Angeles/California Angels

In December 1960, film and TV cowboy star Gene Autry headed a small group of investors approved by Major League Baseball as owners of the new expansion American League Los Angeles Angels.[1] During the club's inaugural year, the 1961 Angels played their home games at old Wrigley Field in Los Angeles. They finished the season in eighth place out of ten teams, nine games ahead of the tied Kansas City Athletics and new expansion Washington Senators, and just a half-game out of seventh place.

On October 6, five days after the 1961 major league season ended, Joe Gordon was offered a contract with the expansion Los Angeles Angels for services as a scout and batting instructor from March through September of 1962. Gordon accepted their offer at a salary of $7,000 for the seven months, as he still was being paid by the Kansas City Athletics for the remainder of his 1961 and 1962 managerial contracts.[2] From 1963 through 1968, the Angels renewed Gordon's contract each year for a salary of $12,000 per year.

Braven Dyer reported in *The Sporting News*, "Always looking ahead, [Angels general manager] Haney hired three of baseball's noted stars to help develop youngsters on Angel farm clubs—Bob Lemon, Joe Gordon, and Johnny Lindell."[3] The coaches and instructors reported early to 1962 Angels spring training at Palm Springs. Whenever the team headed out to play exhibition games on the road, Gordon and Lemon instructed players at the club's farm camps at Fullerton and San Bernardino.[4] Beginning with the 1962 major league season, the Angels played their home games at the newly-built Dodger Stadium (also referred to as "Chavez Ravine") as tenants of the Dodgers.

On August 4, 1962, the San Francisco Giants hosted their first "Old Timers Day" at Candlestick Park, preceding their regularly scheduled game against the Pirates. More than 90 baseball greats were invited to participate, including old timers from the San Francisco Bay area and the former New York Giants. Joe Gordon played second base and co-managed the San Francisco Area Old Timers with Lefty O'Doul. The three DiMaggio brothers (Joe, Dominic, and Vince) played the outfield, thrilling the many local fans. Nearly 50 players were shuffled in and out of the three-inning game, with the former New York Giants shutting out the San Francisco Old Timers, 5–0.[5]

Wrapping up the 1962 baseball season, the Los Angeles Angels' third-place finish and 86–76 (.531) record "stunned the American League," prompting some West Coast sportswriters to nickname the team "Rigney's Remarkables" after their field manager, Bill Rigney.[6] Angels outfielder Albie Pearson, who'd played for the 1957 Pacific Coast

League champion San Francisco Seals under manager Joe Gordon, led the 1962 American League with his career-best 115 runs scored.

During 1963, in addition to instructing at Angels spring training, Gordon was called up periodically during the regular season to "beef up L.A.'s [batting] attack."[7] Catcher Ed Sadowski later talked about that: "Joe Gordon fixed up my hitting some time back when he showed up to give us some batting coaching at Chavez Ravine…. He discovered I was planting too much weight on my rear foot in the box."[8]

During the fall of 1964, the Los Angeles Angels joined up with the San Francisco Giants, Los Angeles Dodgers, and Chicago Cubs in entering a team called the Arizona Instructional League (AIL) Angels in the four-team winter rookie league, which ran through early December. The players ranged from untested rookies to experienced major leaguers. Bob Lemon managed the AIL Angels, with Joe Gordon, Jimmy Reese, and Tom Morgan as coaches.[9] During the remainder of the year, Gordon scouted throughout Northern California and the Northwest.[10] His children still remember that he especially loved "discovering" up-and-coming young "phenoms," as he called them.

During the 1965 season, Angels manager Bill Rigney called up Gordon to help the team with their batting. An article in *The Sporting News* noted, "The arrival of Joe Gordon, the organization's batting instructor, was credited for much of the team's sudden offensive splurge at home. 'Joe and I began three-a-day brand batting practices,' explained Rigney. 'We study and correct the swings of three different players each day.'"[11] The Angels won nine games during their 12-game home stand right before the All-Star Game break.

On September 2, 1965, the Los Angeles Angels officially changed their name to the California Angels in anticipation of moving to the new Anaheim Stadium in Anaheim.[12] Throughout its history, the Angels franchise would go through multiple name changes: Los Angeles Angels (1961–1965), California Angels (1965–1996), Anaheim Angels (1997–2004), Los Angeles Angels of Anaheim (2005–2015), and Los Angeles Angels (2016–present).

One of the California Angels' farm clubs was the Idaho Falls (Idaho) Angels of the Rookie-Advanced Pioneer League in the North-Central Rocky Mountain region of the country. During the 1966 season, the Angels implemented an innovative four-manager rotation schedule for their Idaho Falls club, in order to provide a variety of specialized training for their young ballplayers. The managers included Tom Morgan, Al Monchak, Joe Gordon, and John Fitzpatrick.[13]

About three weeks before his mid–August stint managing the Idaho Falls Angels, Joe Gordon was invited to play in the New York Yankees' Old Timers Game on July 23, 1966.[14] The two-inning game was something special for baseball fans. First, it was the New York Yankees' 20th Annual Old Timers Day.[15] Second, it commemorated the 25th anniversary of Joe DiMaggio's 56-game hitting streak in 1941. Notably, Ken Keltner, the Indians' third baseman who had ended DiMaggio's streak, also was in attendance. Third, Lou Gehrig's widow was there to place a floral wreath on a monument in memory of the 25th anniversary of the passing of "The Iron Horse." For Yankees and Dodgers fans, the game itself was a two-inning rematch, of sorts, of the 1941 World Series between the two ballclubs, with old-timer Yankees picking up right where they'd left off in 1941—winning! In the bottom of the second inning, 51-year-old Joe Gordon singled, and Bill Dickey later hit a sacrifice fly, bringing Gordon home to win the game for the Yankees, 2–1. It also was a sentimental win for former Yankees manager "Marse Joe" McCarthy, who piloted the Yankees' Old Timers squad that day.

In February 1968, it was reported that Bob Lemon, Joe Gordon, and Jimmy Piersall would be tutoring players for the Charros de Jalisco professional baseball team of Guadalajara, Jalisco, Mexico. Piersall had played as a utility outfielder and pinch-hitter for the Angels from midseason 1963 through early 1967. Baseball was said to be booming south of the border, with eight leagues forecast to operate in 1968, five of them affiliated with organized ball in the U.S.[16] Gordon always loved visiting Mexico, and it was said that he spoke Spanish almost like a native.

During Joe Gordon's seven years as a scout and batting instructor for the Angels, he spent most of his time working on the West Coast. Between scouting trips, he even found a little time for hunting, fishing, and golf with his many friends, both in and out of baseball. Joe and Dottie contracted to build a three-bedroom home in the Wilhaggin Estates subdivision of Sacramento, as both of their children were married and living nearby.

1969 Kansas City Royals

The American and National Leagues once again planned on expanding, this time from 10 to 12 teams in each league in time for the 1969 season. The American League added the Kansas City Royals and Seattle Pilots, and the National League the Montreal Expos and San Diego Padres. Each league also was divided into East and West Divisions, with six teams in each division. Ewing Marion Kauffman, a self-made multi-millionaire pharmaceutical entrepreneur and founder of Marion Laboratories, became owner of the expansion Kansas City Royals.[17]

There was considerable speculation about who the Royals would hire as their field manager, with Bill Rigney, Hank Bauer, and Bob Lemon mentioned as the three most likely candidates. Joe Gordon's name also had been brought up, but not as prominently as the others.[18]

At a press conference on September 9, 1968, it was announced that Joe Gordon was being hired as manager of the 1969 Kansas City Royals.[19] The California Angels released Gordon, and a week later he signed a one-year contract with the Royals at a salary of "$40,000 per annum ($30,000 for managing [and] $10,000 for public relations services)." When Gordon was announced as the Royals' field manager, owner Ewing Kauffman said, "I called every general manager in baseball and I talked to Stan Musial. I can assure you that Joe comes highly recommended."[20]

The Royals' executive vice president and general manager Cedric Tallis also talked about Gordon: "Joe is a better man today than when he was managing. When a man goes out [scouting] and tries to find players[,] he realizes they don't grow on trees. Joe has the patience and ability to teach fundamentals that we [the Royals] need. He knows strategy and he has the personality to assist in developing fan interest."[21]

Frank Lane, who'd been general manager of the Cleveland Indians and then the Kansas City Athletics when Gordon had managed those teams, said about the Royals' new pilot, "Gordon is perfect for the Royals. You can't have a better man for a young team. Not only is he patient, but he likes to work with them [the young players] and instruct."[22]

Work began immediately getting ready for the American League expansion draft, held in Boston on October 15. The Royals and Seattle Pilots could draft up to 30 players each, at a cost of $175,000 apiece. Gordon was in a good position to recommend players

Kansas City Royals manager Joe Gordon and his four coaches gather for a photograph at spring training in February 1969. Front row, from left: Owen Friend, Jo-Jo White, Joe Gordon. Back row, from left: Mel Harder and Harry Dunlop (courtesy of Harry Dunlop).

for the Royals, as he'd been scouting the high minor leagues for the California Angels and was familiar with many of the potential draft picks.[23]

Cedric Tallis announced the three coaches selected by Joe Gordon for the upcoming season: Jo-Jo White, third base coach; Mel Harder, pitching; and Harry Dunlop, first base and bullpen. Gordon was quoted saying, "It's the kind of staff I want. All are good baseball men; they work hard and are good with young players. And we're going to be a young club." Rounding out the Royals' coaching staff, Owen Friend was brought onboard as infield coach in early 1969.[24]

In 2021, Judy Gordon was privileged to talk by phone with former Royals coach Harry Dunlop about the 1969 season.[25] Dunlop emailed the following note to Judy in addition to mailing her a photo of the Royals' coaching staff:

> In the expansion draft that winter, the front office of Cedric Tallis, Lou Gorman, and the owner Ewing Kauffman went for mostly young players rather than veterans. It was a good decision, as we ended up with the best record of the four expansion clubs that year. Your dad was the right man to lead these men because of his no-pressure approach. Lou Piniella was the American League Rookie of the Year. Wally Bunker [was] our best starting pitcher with 12 wins, and Ed Kirkpatrick our home run leader [with 14]. We started the season winning four out of our first six games from the Minnesota Twins and Oakland Athletics, the two top-finishing teams of the American League West Division that year. I owe so much to your dad getting me my start as a coach, which lasted 20 years. He will always remain my great friend. Harry Dunlop.[26]

Chapter 21. A Remarkable Career (1962–1971)

The Royals began their spring training at Fort Myers, Florida, on February 21. In mid–March, the *Great Bend* (KS) *Tribune* published an article headlined "Gordon Enthusiastic about Job," quoting Joe: "The owner (Ewing Kauffman) has done a great job promoting the club. They have sold over 7,500 season tickets.... I think this is going to be a pretty good club.... We are young and inexperienced, and we can only improve. There is a lot of talent here. Our philosophy has been to go young at the start. We drafted the best young players we could get."[27]

With just a week of spring training remaining, Gordon was enthusiastic about his young club: "We think we'll be ready to play good baseball. We think we're capable of surprising some people. Of course, a lot of things can happen, but we know we've got some fine young talent."[28]

A week before Opening Day, the Royals traded one of their pitchers and an outfielder to the expansion Seattle Pilots for left fielder Lou Piniella.[29] Years later, Piniella talked about the trade: "Joe Gordon told me that we need some right-handed hitting over here [Kansas City] so we are going to let you play."[30] In his first time at bat, in his first exhibition game for the Royals, Piniella hit a home run.[31] Playing center field on Opening Day, he belted a double and three singles in the Royals' 12-inning win over the visiting Minnesota Twins, 4–3. The following night, he drove in the game-winning run in the 17th inning for another Royals victory.

Joe McGuff reported in *The Sporting News* about the club's first six games of 1969: "The Royals opened their season in the American League West [Division] by playing six games [against] the [Minnesota] Twins and the [Oakland] Athletics, the two top-rated teams in the [D]ivision. Cynics had laughed that the Royals' season would be over almost as soon as it started. Instead of swooning, the Royals surprised everyone by winning four of the six games." Manager Gordon said, "This start means an awful lot to our club. Our players started the season not knowing quite what to expect. Now we're off to a good start and they are beginning to believe in themselves. They think they can win."[32]

The Royals posted a 9–10 April, topping all four of 1969's expansion clubs. However, June's lackluster 10–18 showing occasioned McGuff to write, "During this time of trial, Joe Gordon has blown his top ... and an indeterminate number of Royals have been threatened with demotion to Omaha [the Kansas City Royals' farm club in the Class AAA American Association]. Gordon normally is an easy-going type of manager.... But after the Royals gave a lackadaisical performance in losing three out of four games to Seattle [June 20–22], Gordon was in a kicking mood."[33]

Making it clear that his criticism was *not* directed at all the players, Joe voiced his frustrations: "One thing we can't tolerate is lack of hustle.... We've got some guys down there [Omaha] who would love to play up here [Kansas City]."[34] The Gordons' son, Joey, still remembers two of his dad's pet sayings: "You can tell 'em, but you can't tell 'em much" and "If you could only put a forty-year-old's head on a twenty-year-old's body!"[35]

With about a month of the season remaining, Joe asked Charlie Metro (the Royals' director of scouting and instruction) to join the coaching staff on the field and help with the dozen young players brought up from the Omaha Royals farm club.[36] In mid–September, after having spent a combined 85 years in baseball, two of the Royals' coaches, 60-year-old Jo-Jo White and 59-year-old Mel Harder, announced their retirements, effective the end of the season. Both had been "coaxed" out of retirement in late 1968 by their longtime friend Joe Gordon, for just "one more year."[37]

After posting disappointing records of 11–18 and 10–17 in July and August, things finally turned around. Wrapping up September and October with 15–15 and 2–0 records, they finished the 1969 season in fourth place in the six-team American League West Division with a "surprisingly good" 69–93 (.426) record, only two games behind the third-place California Angels. This was just two games short of Gordon's early-season goal of being the first expansion team to finish its inaugural season in the top half of their Division.[38] The Royals ended their 1969 season as the most successful, *by far*, of the four expansion clubs that year. Their 69 victories were only one short of the record 70 wins for first-year expansion teams, set by the Los Angeles Angels in 1961.[39]

Gordon's confidence in obtaining left fielder Lou Piniella from the Seattle Pilots was well rewarded. Piniella played in 135 games for the 1969 Royals, batting .282 with 11 home runs and 68 RBI. He was voted the 1969 American League Rookie of the Year by the Baseball Writers' Association of America. Later, in an article in *The Sporting News*, Piniella talked with Joe McGuff about manager Gordon: "Looking back on it, it was the way Joe Gordon and Mr. Tallis (Cedric Tallis, Royals' executive vice-president) kept me pumped up that did it. I was a fairly good hitter … but it was Joe who got me thinking, not just swinging. He taught me to be selective up there, to go up there with an idea…. But once I went to Joe's way of thinking—not trying to hit it out [of the park]—things got better for me."[40]

Lou Piniella would go on to distinguished playing and managing careers. In the book, *Pride of October: What It Was to Be Young and a Yankee*, Bill Madden quoted Piniella saying, "I really enjoyed playing for Joe [Gordon]. He gave me my first real chance in the big leagues."[41]

Very unexpectedly, after an impressive season of managing the 1969 Kansas City Royals, 54-year-old Joe Gordon resigned on October 7. The Royals signed him to a two-year contract as a "special assignment scout and instructor" for 1970 and 1971, at a salary of $25,000 per year. In early 1970, he also was named to the Royals' newly created position of coordinator of instruction. Joe enjoyed scouting and instructing, and was called up several times midseason in 1970 and 1971 to work with the Royals' batters.[42]

Royals fans were "stunned" to hear of Gordon's resignation, as they'd been "greatly impressed" with the performance of the youthful team. After Gordon said that he didn't want to manage anymore, Charlie Metro was hired as the Royals' field manager for 1970. Executive vice president and general manager Cedric Tallis told Joe McGuff, "Charlie was Gordon's choice as his successor[,] as well as my choice. I felt Joe's recommendation was important."[43] However, Metro managed only 52 games in 1970, before being replaced by Gordon's former teammate on the Cleveland Indians, Bob Lemon, who would pilot the Royals through 1972.

In his book titled *Safe by a Mile,* published in 2002, Charlie Metro wrote about Joe Gordon and others who were not yet in the National Baseball Hall of Fame: "But there are still some more players, old-timers and those who played more recently, who are undeservedly missing from the Hall. Joe Gordon is one. Joe was a tremendous clutch ballplayer. He always played to beat you. He was a silent leader with his play-making abilities. He made the impossible plays."[44] Happily, on July 26, 2009, 91-year-old Charlie Metro got to know, and hopefully watch on TV, that his good friend Joe "Flash" Gordon was inducted into the National Baseball Hall of Fame. Good things come to those who wait!

Chapter 22

Farewell, "Flash" (1972–1978)

By 1972, 57-year-old Joe Gordon had begun transitioning from baseball to other pursuits, yet he still kept his finger firmly planted on the pulse of the game that he loved. After fulfilling his two-year contract in scouting and instructing for the 1970 and 1971 Kansas City Royals, he obtained his real estate license in April 1972, specializing in selling ranches, recreational, and commercial properties.[1]

The Gordons sold their three-bedroom home in the spring of 1972 and moved to a two-bedroom condominium nearby, where they would live the rest of their lives.[2] It was reported that Joe's baseball retirement income was just $250 per month,[3] so he and Dottie had to depend on their savings and Joe's real estate earnings.

That same year, their daughter, Judy, and her family moved from Sacramento to Idaho Falls, Idaho, where she worked at the National Reactor Testing Station (now known as the Idaho National Laboratory). At the time, the Gordons' son, Joey, was managing a sporting goods store in Sacramento.

Although Joe was retired from baseball, the guest bedroom of the Gordons' condominium was decorated with photographs of the five world championship teams that Joe had played on. His bronzed baseball glove sat atop a dresser, and his desk was positioned near the window, where he would sit and autograph postcards and baseballs for fans who contacted him by mail. In the entryway to their home was a colorful poster of Joe and Dottie in a Granger pipe tobacco advertisement. In the window sill of their kitchen were porcelain figurines of a baseball player arguing with an umpire. Their condo also was decorated with fly fishing rods and a couch upholstered in a fabric featuring pheasants—the home of a sportsman.

Gordon had the same ambitions of being successful in real estate as he did when playing baseball. Dennis Lustig reported for the *Cleveland Plain Dealer* that Joe had sold more than $1 million worth of ranches and land in California, and he was traveling as many as 35,000 miles a year for his job.[4] Joe told Lustig that he "wouldn't be adverse to returning to baseball as a scout but [was] not interested in managing or coaching again." He also said that he'd like to hear from his former teammates and friends, and he gave permission for Lustig to include his home address in the article.

At least once a year, Judy and her family drove from Idaho to visit her parents in Sacramento. Her son, Erik, still recalls the memories of his grandfather taking him fishing for shad on the American River, not far from the Gordons' condo. Many years later, just a day after the announcement of Joe Gordon being voted into the National Baseball Hall of Fame, Erik told writer Nick Draper, "I always thought my grandfather was a fly fisherman, not a baseball player."[5]

Judy's daughter, Sue, spent many summers helping her grandfather as he

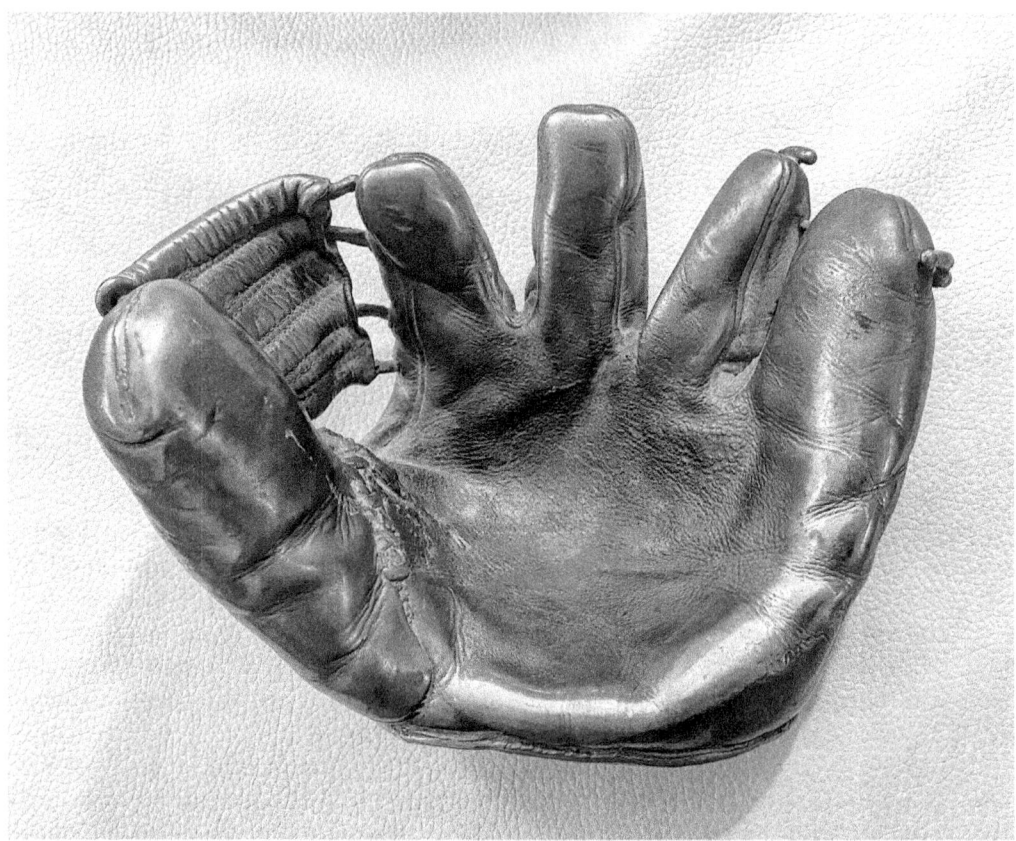

Joe "Flash" Gordon's well-worn, game-used baseball glove had been bronzed and was displayed in the guest bedroom of the Gordons' home in Sacramento, California (Gordon family collections).

autographed cards and baseballs to mail back to fans who had contacted him. She even asked him to autograph a baseball for her, which he did, writing, "To Susy from Grampa Joe."[6]

Judy's oldest son, Mike, sometimes asked his grandfather about the ballplayers pictured in photos at the Gordons' condominium. Mike also remembers the fun they had with their grandfather at the condo swimming pool. Life was never dull in the Gordon household!

The Gordons' son, Joey, still recalls playing golf with his father at Del Paso Country Club in Sacramento. One time when Joe got a hole in one, he said to Joey, "Don't tell anybody. If you get a hole in one here, you have to buy drinks for everyone in the clubhouse." Joey, a near-scratch golfer himself, recently admitted, "I never did beat Dad at golf!" When asked to jot down a few things that he remembered about his father, Joey wrote,

> Let's ignore his obvious talents on the baseball diamond for a minute. I'd rather remember the other things he could do. Just a few come to mind: He could remember people, their names, their children's names, and interesting things about them. Even years later, he was blessed with an amazing memory. He could do fun stuff, such as tap dance, and was a ventriloquist. Remember his ventriloquist sidekick named "Amen" in every elevator? Remember

his crazy faces that made us kids laugh until we almost cried? He was a great pilot. He was an accomplished classical violinist, even played in a symphony orchestra. He also played piano—sort of—and also the harmonica and guitar. He was a champion duck caller and a crack shot. I can remember many mornings with him in the duck blinds at the farm. He was an expert fly fisherman. These, and many more.... I am sure he enjoyed life more than anyone I've ever met. He truly *lived*! He did more in his sixty-three years than most people could do in ten lifetimes![7]

"Grampa Joe" autographed this baseball for his granddaughter, Sue. We believe that this is the last ball Joe Gordon autographed before passing away in 1978 (Gordon family collections).

Despite his keen interest in golf, Joe Gordon remained loyal to baseball and his many friends and fans. On August 9, 1975, along with almost all of his teammates from the 1948 world champion Cleveland Indians, the Flash again put on his uniform to play in a three-inning Old Timers Game against a team of mostly American League All-Stars from 1948. A photo of Joe signing autographs for fans in the grandstands appeared in the *Sunday Plain Dealer*.[8]

Sadly, Joe and Jack Gordon's beloved friend, mentor, and stepfather, 86-year-old Andrew J. "Andy" Lampert, passed away on the last day of December 1975.[9] When notified of Andy's passing, Joe immediately headed to Portland, Oregon, to be with his mother.

In the spring of 1978, Joe golfed several times a week and was proud of having scored a par 72 a week earlier. On Sunday, April 9, he arose for a golf game scheduled with friends at Marysville, California.[10] While eating breakfast, he experienced a sore shoulder, and then chest pains while showering. Dottie phoned their friend, Tom Sertich, who drove them to Sutter Memorial Hospital in Sacramento. Dottie phoned Judy in Idaho and Joey in Texas to tell them that their father had suffered a heart attack. Both children wanted to come home, but certain that Joe was going to recover, Dottie told them not to come.

Interviewed for "Dave O's" website, *Remembering the Royals: Joe Gordon*, former minor league catcher and manager, and multi-year major league coach Harry Dunlop told about phoning Joe the night of April 13 after learning of his heart attack: "I called him at night in the hospital, and he [Joe] says, 'Oh, I'm doing fine.' He says, 'I'm going home tomorrow. Dorthy is coming to pick me up, and I'm doing fine.'"[11]

Dunlop said that he'd heard that Gordon awoke the next morning and got dressed.

While Joe was preparing to go home, Dottie was filling out paperwork to get him discharged from the hospital. He suddenly had another heart attack and died. Sadly, Dunlop recalled, "At least I got to talk to him the night before. That was nice."[12]

According to an article in the *New York Times*, Tom Sertich had visited the hospital on April 14 and said that Joe seemed to be resting comfortably at 11:30 A.M.[13] However, a little more than an hour and a half later, Joe suffered a second heart attack and passed away.[14]

Judy was at work when her mother phoned with the devastating news. Dottie knew that the media would be broadcasting news of Joe's death, and she wanted to let her daughter know about it before hearing it on the radio. Judy did hear it on the news, while she was driving home to get ready to leave for Sacramento.

Grandson Erik still remembers when his mother told him about his grandfather's death. The next day, he read a newspaper story about his grandfather's passing away. It was only then that he realized that his grandfather, Joe "Flash" Gordon, was a *really* famous baseball player. After all, why would a newspaper in Idaho Falls run a story about a baseball player who lived in California?

Per Joe's wishes, there was no funeral held for him, and his ashes were scattered at sea. During the week following his death, Joe's family and a few close neighbors, friends, and former ballplayers visited the Gordons' home to celebrate his life. He would have wanted it that way. Judy still remembers the beautiful bouquet of flowers and kind note sent to Dottie and the Gordon family by New York Yankees owner George Steinbrenner.

In his column, Red Smith wrote, "[T]he obituaries described his [Gordon's] baseball career as best they could[,] but, truly, the way Flash Gordon played ball defied adequate description. He was 175 pounds of rawhide and whalebone, and an acrobat to boot. An all-round athlete with uncommon agility, he had trained as a gymnast and tumbler and he could make plays that were beyond any other second baseman I ever saw."[15]

Tragically, six and a half months after Joe died so unexpectedly, his 65-year-old brother, Jack, passed away at his home, also from a heart attack.[16] During a period of just three years, Louise Gordon Lampert had lost her beloved husband, Andy, and two precious sons. She would remain in her own home in Portland another five years, until passing away on January 7, 1984, just 19 days short of her 91st birthday.[17]

Dorthy Irene "Dottie" Gordon passed away from lung cancer on April 3, 1992, at the age of 78, in Idaho Falls,[18] where her daughter, Judy, and two grandchildren, Erik and Sue, lived. Dottie also had specified that no funeral be held.

Aside from the many memories that Joe and Dottie Gordon left their children and grandchildren, some of their greatest legacies include love of family and the outdoors, and a deeply ingrained sense of loyalty, optimism, humility, and gratitude. We feel eternally blessed to have had such great parents and grandparents.

With Joe "Flash" Gordon's passing in 1978, baseball lost one of the most acrobatic and highly esteemed second basemen in the history of the game. Even today, Joe's legacy lives on, as other up-and-coming second basemen are compared with him and hear their coaches or managers describe how Joe Gordon played the keystone sack. Others, too, tell how he impacted their lives. Interviewed for "Dave O's" website, *Remembering the Royals: Joe Gordon*, former major league player and manager Ken Aspromonte talked about Joe Gordon:

Chapter 22. Farewell, "Flash" (1972–1978)

[Joe was] one of the finest men I've ever come across in the game of baseball, and I was so happy that I ran across him. He helped me in the Pacific Coast League, and he helped me in the major leagues by getting me. And some times [sic] managers do that, and most of the time they don't, and he did. He knew what kind of ballplayer I was, and he went after me and he got me, and I performed well for him at Cleveland, and I was just so sorry that he left, but I'm so happy that he passed through my life, and I'm so sorry that he's gone.[19]

There exist countless accounts similar to Aspromonte's. Players and sportswriters alike shared many stories about Joe Gordon after he passed away. The Gordon family's scrapbooks and "Dave O's" website remain to tell some of these stories about Joe "Flash" Gordon.

Oregon Journal writer Arthur Nelson included a great send-off to Gordon in the final two lines of his newspaper piece: "Joe Gordon—a top baseball player, a man and a legend. Undoubtedly, the legend will live on."[20]

As in life, many people strive to be successful and to make their lives meaningful in their various pursuits. However, it is what they pass on to the next generation that matters the most. Although the assembling of scrapbooks ended upon his death in 1978, Joe "Flash" Gordon's legacy still lives on in baseball and in his family.

Chapter 23

COOPERSTOWN AT LAST (2008–2009)

In 1950, after wrapping up his 11th full season of playing in the American League, 35-year-old Joe "Flash" Gordon retired from playing in the majors. Spanning from 1945, when there were "no rules" regarding retirement or waiting periods for players to be considered for election to the National Baseball Hall of Fame (HOF), through 1970, when "a player may not be on the ballot after 20 years from retirement," the Baseball Writers' Association of America (BBWAA) considered the Flash 12 times. However, he never met the required 75 percent of votes needed for election.[1]

After 1970, Gordon was considered an undisclosed number of times by HOF Veterans Committees (now known as Era Committees). However, until more recently, Veterans Committee ballots and voting results were not disclosed publicly—unless a candidate was elected to the Hall of Fame.[2]

Throughout the years following Joe Gordon's passing in 1978, people would ask, "Why isn't Joe 'Flash' Gordon in the Hall of Fame?" To the authors' knowledge, neither the Gordon family nor anyone else had ever lobbied or campaigned for him to be elected. Yet all along, his family and former teammates and fans *knew* that the Flash well deserved the honor—as they'd seen him play![3]

Meanwhile, Joe Gordon's good friend and fellow Oregonian, second baseman Bobby Doerr, who played for the 1937–1951 Boston Red Sox during the same time period and with a similar record as Gordon's, was voted into the HOF by the Veterans Committee in 1986. Bill James, in *Whatever Happened to the Hall of Fame? Baseball, Cooperstown, and the Politics of Glory*, devoted an entire chapter to comparing the careers of the top two American League second basemen of their era: Joe Gordon and Bobby Doerr. When analyzing their batting statistics, James concluded that Gordon would have had an even more impressive record had he not played his home games at the tough park for right-handed hitters Yankee Stadium and, later, at Cleveland's massive Municipal Stadium.[4]

2008: Cleveland Indians Hall of Fame

Unexpectedly, almost 30 years after Joe Gordon's death, it was announced that the Flash was receiving the recognition that so many players and fans knew he deserved. In February 2008, the Cleveland Indians (now known as the Cleveland Guardians) reported that two of their former players, who had also been their managers, would be inducted into the Cleveland Indians Hall of Fame on August 16, 2008. The two were Joe Gordon (1947–1950 second baseman and 1958–1960 manager) and Mike Hargrove (1979–1985 first

Joe Gordon's Cleveland Indians Hall of Fame bronze plaque is enshrined in Heritage Park at Progressive Field in Cleveland (courtesy Cleveland Guardians).

baseman and 1991–1999 manager, in addition to 1995 and 1997 pennant winners). *Cleveland Plain Dealer* reporter Paul Hoynes quoted honoree Mike Hargrove saying, "I've had a lot of neat things happen to me in my career, but I don't know if I've ever had anything on an individual level that's as special as this. I don't know if there was a better ballplayer to play in Cleveland than Joe Gordon. To go in with him is an honor."[5]

Mike Simpson (Joe Gordon's grandson), Bob Feller (former Indian and Hall of Famer), and Sue (Simpson) Arnold (Gordon's granddaughter) pose for a photograph after the Cleveland Indians Hall of Fame ceremony at Progressive Field on August 16, 2008 (courtesy Cleveland Guardians).

On August 16, Joe Gordon's grandson, Mike Simpson, and granddaughter, Sue (Simpson) Arnold, were privileged to represent the Gordon family at the induction of their grandfather into the Cleveland Indians Hall of Fame. The ceremony was held on the infield of Progressive Field, on a picture-perfect afternoon, right before an Indians game. The Gordon family is especially grateful to the Dolan family for their *outstanding* hospitality shown to Mike and Sue and their families during their visit.

With Sue proudly holding her grandfather's Cleveland Indians Hall of Fame crystal trophy, she and her brother, Mike, had their photos taken with former Indians pitcher and Hall of Famer Bob Feller right after the ceremony. Then Mike, Sue, and their families were taken to Heritage Park to unveil Joe Gordon's beautiful bronze plaque.

2008: Veterans Committee Election to the Hall of Fame Class of 2009

The HOF Veterans Committee was scheduled to meet in early December 2008 to consider players for election to the Hall of Fame Class of 2009. This year there were two ballots: one for ballplayers who had played predominantly before World War II (called the pre–1943 players ballot); and one for those who had played predominantly after World War II (called the post–1942 players ballot).[6]

In the spring of 2008, the BBWAA-appointed, 11-member Historical Overview Committee met at Cooperstown to select 10 candidates for the Veterans Committee's pre–1943 players ballot.⁷ The results were announced on August 25, 2008, composed of the following players: Bill Dahlen, Wes Ferrell, Joe Gordon, Sherry Magee, Carl Mays, Allie Reynolds, Vern Stephens, Mickey Vernon, Bucky Walters, and Deacon White.⁸ Only one of the players was still alive at the time, 90-year-old former first baseman Mickey Vernon. Sadly, he passed away a month after the announcement was made.

In late August 2008, Judy Gordon was surprised to receive a phone call from Hall of Famer Bob Feller. He told Judy that her father was on the pre–1943 players ballot and that the HOF Veterans Committee would be voting in December 2008.⁹ However, recalling that her father had been on HOF ballots in previous years and was not elected, Judy didn't tell anyone in her family and let the upcoming election totally slip from her mind.

The final ballot for the post–1942 players was arrived at separately from that of the pre–1943 players and was announced on September 16, 2008.¹⁰ The HOF Veterans Committee tasked with considering the 10 candidates on the post–1942 players ballot comprised all 64 living Hall of Famers.¹¹

The Veterans Committee considering the candidates on the pre–1943 players ballot comprised 12 members. Seven were Hall of Famers: second baseman Bobby Doerr; left fielder Ralph Kiner; center fielder Duke Snider; pitchers Phil Niekro, Robin Roberts, and Don Sutton; and manager Dick Williams. Four were writers/historians, and one was an executive: Furman Bisher, retired writer/columnist for the *Atlanta Journal-Constitution*; Steve Hirdt of the Elias Sports Bureau; Bill Madden, *New York Daily News* sportswriter and author; Claire Smith, ESPN news editor and sportswriter/columnist; and Roland Hemond of the Arizona Diamondbacks. Each member of the Veterans Committee was allowed to vote for up to four of the 10 candidates on the ballot. A 75-percent threshold was required for election to the Hall of Fame.¹²

On Sunday night, December 7, 2008, unbeknownst to anyone in the Gordon family, National Baseball Hall of Fame and Museum president Jeff Idelson emailed a brief message to Judy Gordon, asking for her phone number in case her father was elected to the HOF. Idelson wrote that he would phone her around 9 A.M. Pacific Time on Monday, December 8—but only if her father was elected.¹³

However, as authors Kevin Warneke and David C. Ogden pointed out in their book, *The Call to the Hall: When Baseball's Highest Honor Came to 31 Legends of the Sport*, "Judy Gordon … hadn't bothered to check her email that night and didn't read Idelson's correspondence until early the morning of the announcement…. [She, however,] understood Idelson's underlying message: 'He'll call only if he (her father) gets in [the HOF]. If not, there's no call.'"¹⁴

Judy briefly discussed Idelson's email with only one of her children, Erik Simpson. Needless to say, she was on "pins and needles," leading up to the appointed time.

In 2016, radio host "Dave O" recorded a phone interview he had with sportswriter and author Bill Madden, who served on the HOF Veterans Committee that considered the 10 candidates on the pre–1943 players ballot in December 2008 at Major League Baseball Winter Meetings in Las Vegas. Madden recalled how the discussions had taken place prior to the vote of the committee members. He told how, at one point, committee member Claire Smith brought up a fact that should be considered about Joe Gordon, which was how helpful he'd been to Larry Doby (the first African American player in the American League) when Doby joined the Cleveland Indians in 1947, and how Gordon had become a friend and mentor to Doby.¹⁵

Madden also told how, as the committee's deliberations continued, Steve Hirdt of the Elias Sports Bureau said that the one Hall of Fame player that Joe Gordon most favorably compared to statistically from that era, was Bobby Doerr. Madden also recalled, "And it just so happened that Bobby Doerr was also on the committee. He was sitting right next to me. So I said to him, 'Well, Bobby, I guess it's up to you now. What have you got to say about Joe Gordon?'" According to Madden, Bobby Doerr replied, "Joe Gordon was a better player than I was."[16]

"That was it," said Madden. "We voted, and Joe got, I think, eleven out of twelve votes [actually, it was ten out of twelve or 83.3 percent]."[17]

"He made it! He's in!"

On the morning of December 8, very close to straight-up 10 A.M. Mountain Time (9 A.M. Pacific Time), Judy Gordon received the most thrilling phone call of her life, when HOF president Jeff Idelson and Jane Forbes Clark, chairman of the HOF Board of Directors, phoned to tell her the news. They offered their congratulations that her father, Joe "Flash" Gordon, had been elected to the National Baseball Hall of Fame! They asked her not to go public with the information until after the announcement was made at a press conference later that morning.[18]

Judy, in tears after hearing the news, phoned her brother, Joey, and her three children, Mike, Erik, and Sue. Joey recalls how he felt when he heard the news:

> I still get tears in my eyes remembering this. Such a great honor for Dad, and so well deserved. What a life he LIVED! When I received the phone call that Dad was elected to the Hall of Fame, I immediately thought, "Such an honor," and I wished he could have been alive to receive it in person. Then I thought about the entirety of his life, and what he'd accomplished in those short 63 years. I compared our rather normal lives, and what most everyone accomplishes over a lifetime. Yes, everyone has a life, but he LIVED! What an amazing journey. We were blessed to be part of it.[19]

Erik also vividly remembers the phone call from his mother that morning: "I was at work, and Mom's number came up on my caller ID. I let the phone ring one time and picked it up."

"Hello," Erik said.

"He made it!" Judy exclaimed, still in tears. "He's in!"

"Oh my God," Erik said. Those were the only three words he could say before tears started streaming down his face. Judy told him that the family shouldn't tell anyone until the Hall of Fame broke the news. As Erik sat in his chair with tears rolling down his face, a colleague came into his office and asked what was wrong. Erik replied, "I can't tell you yet, but it's something good."

Hall of Fame Veterans Committee Announcements

On the morning of Monday, December 8, National Baseball Hall of Fame and Museum president Jeff Idelson opened the press conference with, "Good morning, welcome to the Hall of Fame Veteran's Committee [C]lass of 2009 announcement.... We are going to start with the ballot for those who played after World War II, those players who played in 1943 or later.... The post World War II [V]eterans [C]ommittee is comprised of all 64 living Hall of Famers. They examined the ballot of ten candidates which they themselves screened down to ten from an initial ballot of 21, and all 64 Hall of Famers participated. We had 100% return on ballots. They voted an average of 3.33 votes per ballot. Nobody was elected in the post World War II [V]eteran's [C]ommittee election." Jeff Idelson and Hall of Famer Joe Morgan, vice chairman of the HOF, then took several questions from the press about the voting.[20]

Next, HOF chairman Jane Forbes Clark spoke: "Thank you, Jeff. Good morning. As Jeff mentioned, the second [V]eteran's [C]ommittee election was a review of players who began their careers before 1943.... I have to say, that we could not be more pleased with the discipline and commitment to excellence of all of the voters. We couldn't be more pleased with the process and with the results."[21]

Clark then began reading the names of the players who'd received the fewest number of votes and continued up the list with the names of players with higher vote counts. She read the name of Allie Reynolds, the Indians pitcher who had been traded to the Yankees for Joe Gordon in October 1946. However, Reynolds was one vote shy of being elected.

"And our final candidate is the first member of the [C]lass of 2009 for induction into the Hall of Fame, with ten votes and 83.3% of the ballots cast. I am pleased to announce that the former Yankee and Indians second baseman Joe Gordon has been elected to the National Baseball Hall of Fame."[22]

After briefly describing Gordon's career, Clark continued, "A very deserving candidate, and we are absolutely thrilled that he has been elected to the Hall of Fame and will join any electees which come from the BBWAA election, which we will be announcing on January 12 [2009]."[23]

Soon, the news of Gordon's election was announced by the national news media and MLB.com. In the early part of December 8, the name "Joe Gordon" would be the most-searched name on the Yahoo! search engine. After decades of being off the radar of most baseball followers, Joe Gordon again was being celebrated. Members of the Gordon family received phone calls and notes from players, fans, and others, congratulating them on their father's and grandfather's great honor. Yankees owner George Steinbrenner even invited Judy and her family to Yankee Stadium for a home game. It was a dreamlike time to be contacted by so many people, some of whom Judy and Joey hadn't seen or talked with since their father's days playing and managing.

2009: National Baseball Hall of Fame Induction Weekend

In a follow-up letter to Judy later in December, HOF president Jeff Idelson discussed the upcoming Hall of Fame Induction Weekend scheduled for July 24–27, 2009 at Cooperstown and enclosed a DVD of the 2008 Induction Weekend. Idelson also wrote, "You may deliver a short acceptance speech at the Ceremony—no more than five minutes in length." Idelson said that he would be honored to assist in its preparation.[24]

There was much work to do in getting ready for the 2009 HOF Induction Weekend. Judy and Joey also were invited to loan some of their father's baseball artifacts for the Joe Gordon display at the HOF Museum.

In addition to their daughter Judy, four of Joe and Dottie Gordon's grandchildren (Mike, Erik, Julie, and Seraphina); four great-grandchildren (Andrew, Ananda, Brooke, and Colter); nieces De Ann (Gordon) Morgan and Nancy (Crum) Doyle; and other members of their family and friends gathered at Cooperstown in late July. Due to health issues, Judy's brother, Joey, was unable to attend. In all, 48 family members and special guests made the trip to Cooperstown, which shaped up to be a Gordon family reunion of sorts as well.

Matt Dahlgren and his wife, Jenny, flew to Cooperstown from Southern California to attend the 2009 Hall of Fame Induction Weekend. Matt was the grandson of first baseman Babe Dahlgren, one of Joe Gordon's teammates on the 1937 Newark Bears and 1938–1940 New York Yankees. Matt had always been a Yankees fan and even proposed to Jenny on first base at Yankee Stadium in 2003. He'd learned on MLB.com about Joe Gordon's election to the Hall of Fame and was thrilled. While growing up, Matt had heard a lot about Joe "Flash" Gordon from his grandfather. After he heard Judy Gordon interviewed on MLB.com, he phoned to congratulate her on her father's honor. "I just felt compelled to call her because it was like I knew Joe, as much as I'd heard about him," Dahlgren said. "I've never done anything like that before."[25] After several email conversations, Judy invited Matt and Jenny to be the Gordon family's guests at the 2009 HOF Induction Weekend.

From New Jersey, not far from Yankee Stadium, Dean Hoffman had also listened to the same interview that Matt Dahlgren heard. His reaction was the same. Dean, a New York Mets fan, had heard countless stories from his father and uncle, Ben and Ed Hoffman, about what a great player Joe Gordon was. The Hoffman brothers had learned to play baseball on the streets and sandlots of the Bronx in the shadows of Yankee Stadium in the 1930s. Ben and Ed were loyal Joe Gordon fans, as the brothers had watched the Flash play countless times at Yankee Stadium and felt a strong connection to him. When the Yankees traded Joe Gordon to the Indians in October 1946, Ben was so upset that he ended up becoming an Indians fan.

Dean Hoffman phoned Judy the day after he listened to the interview. He left a message asking that she call his dad and uncle, as it would mean so much to them to speak with their baseball hero's daughter! When Judy called Hoffman several hours later, he told her about his father and uncle, and described them as "Joe Gordon's most loyal fans."[26] Hoffman also arranged a later conference call with his father, uncle, and Judy, and even videotaped the call.

Several months later, an envelope from the Hall of Fame arrived at Dean Hoffman's home, with four tickets to the 2009 HOF Induction Ceremony. He was so moved by the gesture that he phoned the Yogi Berra Museum & Learning Center, located about 30 minutes from his home. He told the curator that he'd been in contact with Judy Gordon, who asked him to speak with Berra about any advice he could give regarding her induction speech. About a week later, Dean Hoffman got a call back from Dave Kaplan, president of the museum, who confirmed that he'd spoken with Yogi Berra, who offered his sage advice to pass on to Judy, which was, "Keep it short."

Several days before the Induction Weekend at Cooperstown, Joe and Dottie Gordon's granddaughter, Seraphina (Joey's daughter)—as well as her husband Rick, daughter Ananda, and some of their friends; several of Judy's friends from Idaho (Jared and Jeremy Underwood, Steve Anderson, Jay Simmons, and Derk Anderson); and Dean and Susan Hoffman—attended a game at Yankee Stadium. The entourage was invited to watch from George Steinbrenner's private suite, while enjoying a beautiful buffet provided by the Yankees. Museum Curator Brian Richards also treated the attendees to a private tour of the New York Yankees Museum.

Chapter 23. Cooperstown at Last (2008–2009)

Just a few days before the 2009 HOF Induction Ceremony, writer Jeff Smith interviewed Joe Gordon's good friend, 91-year-old Hall of Fame second baseman Bobby Doerr, who said, "I'm happy for his family. Joe is just so deserving. He really was an outstanding player. We competed hard on the field, but after the games I'd invite him to dinner at my house in Boston and he'd invite me to his house in New York."[27]

Doerr also had a speaking part in the HOF video titled *Joe Gordon: Hall of Fame Class of 2009*, saying, "When you look at his [Gordon's] record, you know it's a tremendous record, playing in six World Series, and he had to have *something* to do with all of those. I'm just so happy. It's too bad Joe couldn't have been alive to see all this happen."[28]

The Gordon family members and their guests, four dozen in all, arrived in Cooperstown at different times, each stopping to pick up their HOF credentials for the Induction Weekend. Over the course of three days, they would attend multiple events, along with over four dozen Hall of Famers and their families.[29]

On Friday morning, July 24, Judy and her guest from Idaho, Gerry Reilly, were joined by Matt Dahlgren and his wife, Jenny, for a private, behind-the-scenes tour of the National Baseball Hall of Fame and Museum conducted by Senior Curator Tom Shieber, Library Director Jim Gates, and Assistant Curator of New Media Lenny DiFranza. This turned out to be one of their favorite experiences of the entire weekend. Highlights of the tour included getting to see one of Babe Ruth's large scrapbooks and visiting the basement of the museum, where collectibles of players are kept in large file drawers.

On Friday afternoon, Judy, her children and their spouses gathered at the historic 100-year-old Otesaga Hotel. Afterwards, Judy's son, Erik Simpson, walked out onto the balcony of the hotel and noticed a player that he'd seen many times on television—Yankees catcher and Hall of Famer, 84-year-old Yogi Berra. He was sitting at a table talking

The Yankees' longtime catcher and Hall of Famer, 84-year-old Yogi Berra, and Joe "Flash" Gordon's grandson, Erik Simpson, have their photograph taken together on the balcony of the Otesaga Hotel in Cooperstown, on July 24, 2009 (Gordon family collections).

with another gentleman who was getting ready to leave. As Erik approached, the other man got up and left. At this point, Berra was all alone.

Erik introduced himself: "Hi, Mr. Berra. I'm Erik Simpson, Joe Gordon's grandson. You were a teammate of my grandfather's."

"Yes, but only for a short time," Berra replied. "I joined the Yankees near the end of the 1946 season. Your grandfather was traded right after that season to the Cleveland Indians."

"I never heard my grandfather ever talk of his baseball career," said Erik. "To me he was a fly fisherman, golfer, and pilot."

"Oh, yes, I flew with your grandfather once," Berra said.

"Really? You flew in his Beechcraft Bonanza airplane with him?" Erik asked.

"No, on the Yankees plane," Berra replied.

"What do you mean?" Erik asked, puzzled.

"It was my first week with the Yankees, and we were on the Yankees plane going to a game. The plane taxied down the runway and took off. Your grandfather got up out of his seat, walked up to the cockpit, and took over the controls of the plane."

This was a story the Gordon family had never heard before. Erik spoke with Yogi for a few more minutes and had his picture taken with him, before excusing himself and joining his family. The authors are especially grateful to the Yogi Berra Museum & Learning Center, Lindsay Berra, and Edward H. Schauder for helping us obtain permission to include this conversation and photo in our book.[30]

On Friday evening, the Gordon party of eight, which included daughter Judy and four of Joe and Dottie Gordon's grandchildren, attended the Chairman's Event Reception and Dinner held at the home of Jane Forbes Clark, chairman of the HOF Board of Directors. The reception and dinner were held in a huge event tent that, fortunately, had been erected in case of rain, as it poured for most of the evening.

The Gordon family got to meet HOF chairman Jane Forbes Clark, president Jeff Idelson, and the two newest Hall of Fame members elected by the BBWAA, Rickey Henderson and Jim Rice, in addition to many other Hall of Famers. It was one of the most beautiful events the Gordon family members had ever attended. Being in the presence of some of the greatest men ever to play the game of baseball made it an even greater honor.

Early Saturday morning, "Team Gordon" golfers Bill Doyle and Bill Brown played in the Hall of Fame Weekend Golf Tournament at the beautiful Leatherstocking Golf Course. Their foursome also included HOF pitcher Rollie Fingers and former player, broadcaster, restaurateur, and philanthropist Rusty Staub. The 18-hole tournament included breakfast at 6:30 A.M., golf at 8:00 A.M., and an awards ceremony and luncheon afterwards.

The remainder of the Gordon party and their guests gathered for breakfast at the Otesaga Hotel. Joe Humasti, who'd traveled to Cooperstown clear from Nevada, and his baseball-fan cousin, Denny de Freitas from California, shared an album of special photos of Joe Gordon's sandlot days in Portland as a teammate of Humasti's father, Bruno. Included were photos of the boys' 1927 Crosby Juniors sandlot team, their 1931 American Legion Post No. 1 East Side Commercial Club, and their 1932 Jefferson High School varsity baseball team.

After breakfast, the Gordon family and their guests attended a private tour of the HOF Museum and saw the outstanding displays set up to honor the three new Hall of Fame members: Joe Gordon, Rickey Henderson, and Jim Rice. Judy and Joey Gordon,

Judy's son, Erik, and others had loaned artifacts for the beautiful Joe Gordon display, including his World Series championship emblems, 1942 AL Most Valuable Player Award, bronzed baseball glove, items from several of his All-Star Game appearances, an original newspaper drawing, a Joe "Flash" Gordon comic strip, and his *Pilot's Flight Log*.

It was at Joe Gordon's display that Erik got to meet Matt and Jenny Dahlgren for the first time. Matt told Erik that he was the grandson of the Yankees' first baseman, Babe Dahlgren, who on May 2, 1939, had replaced Lou Gehrig at first base when "The Iron Horse" retired from playing. Erik recognized the Dahlgren name from some of the autographed baseballs in the Gordon family's possession. Matt told Erik that his grandfather and Joe Gordon were not just teammates, but good friends. The Yankees had sold Dahlgren to the National League Boston Bees in early 1941, which Matt wrote about in his book, *Rumor in Town: A Grandson's Promise to Right a Wrong*.[31]

Erik remarked how unique it was that he and Matt would meet at Joe Gordon's display at the HOF and talk about their grandfathers' baseball careers. After all, their grandfathers had probably last spoken with each other almost 70 years earlier.

The Gordon family and their guests were invited to the basement of the HOF museum for a private tour of the rarest of baseball artifacts. One item, in particular, got the attention of everyone—a baseball bat once used by Lou Gehrig!

The tour participants also were invited to the museum's Bullpen Theater and shown the video titled *Joe Gordon: Hall of Fame Class of 2009*.[32] The video included historic baseball footage of Joe Gordon, in addition to interviews with some of the HOF Veterans Committee members who had voted Gordon into the Hall of Fame. Claire Smith spoke about how Joe Gordon had reached out to Larry Doby in 1947 and became a mentor and friend to the American League's first African American ballplayer. Former players and historians alike spoke of Gordon's impact as a second baseman with the Yankees and Indians, and his acrobatic play at second base.

Later that afternoon, Judy and Erik were escorted to the Cooperstown High School auditorium to take part in the Inductee Press Conference. They took a seat in front of a dozen or so reporters, who asked several questions about Joe Gordon. Most surprising to everyone was Judy's recollection of growing up in the Gordon household when her dad was playing and then managing in the majors. She told how baseball was not a subject ever discussed in their home. Erik also said that when he spent time with his grandparents, he didn't remember a single instance of baseball ever being discussed. In fact, Erik said that he felt that his grandfather would have been a little taken aback by all the attention he was receiving at the HOF Induction Weekend.

On the evening of July 25, 13 members of the Gordon family attended the Hall of Fame Weekend Cocktail Reception and Dinner at the Otesaga Hotel, along with the attending Hall of Famers. Some of those that the Gordon family members got to meet were Reggie Jackson, Robin Roberts, Harmon Killebrew, Bob Gibson, Bill Mazeroski, and Sparky Anderson. Sports broadcaster Bob Costas also congratulated the Gordon family members. At dinner, Erik sat next to Jim Rice and his wife. Across the table were Rollie Fingers and his wife and in-laws.

After dinner, the Gordon party and the Hall of Famers and their families were taken by trolley car to the Red Carpet Arrivals Public Event. As the trolleys arrived on Main Street in front of the Hall of Fame and Museum, thousands of fans lined the street. A man with a microphone and loudspeaker introduced each Hall of Famer as they exited a trolley car, and the crowd chanted their names over and over. As

Judy exited the trolley, the man asked her to come to the microphone. She spoke a few words, and the crowd immediately broke out into a chant of, "Gordon, Gordon, Gordon!"

The Private Dessert Reception was held that night in the HOF, with 24 members of the Gordon party attending, along with almost all of the Hall of Famers. It was at this event that the family first got to see Joe Gordon's beautiful bronze plaque hanging in the Hall of Fame Plaque Gallery. Beneath his plaque was an emblem recognizing his military service.

As the event began to wind down, the public was invited into the Hall of Fame. Hundreds of people gathered in the Plaque Gallery, where the Gordon, Henderson, and Rice plaques were on display along with all the other Hall of Fame members' plaques. Many people congratulated the family members and asked to have their pictures taken with them.

The 2009 Hall of Fame Induction Ceremony was held on Sunday, July 26, at the Clark Sports Center Outdoor Stage. The Gordon family and their guests arrived about an hour early and spoke with the HOF staff about seating assignments and the agenda. It was a breezy, cloudy day, and rain was forecast to arrive about the time the ceremony was scheduled to begin at 1:30 P.M. Some of the 21,000 baseball fans in the audience already were prepared with umbrellas, parkas, and other rain gear. As the ceremony time approached, the Hall of Famers took their seats at the back of the stage.

It began to sprinkle as the video titled *MLB Hall of Fame Tribute: Joe Gordon* was

Hall of Fame and Museum president Jeff Idelson presents Joseph Lowell Gordon's Hall of Fame plaque to Gordon's daughter, Judy, during the HOF Induction Ceremony in Cooperstown on July 26, 2009. Also pictured are HOF chairman Jane Forbes Clark and Major League Baseball Commissioner Bud Selig (courtesy National Baseball Hall of Fame and Museum).

Chapter 23. Cooperstown at Last (2008–2009)

shown on the big screens near the stage.[33] HOF chairman Jane Forbes Clark delivered a short speech, welcoming Judy's father, Joe Gordon, into the Hall of Fame family. Gordon's HOF plaque was brought out, and Major League Baseball Commissioner Bud Selig read its inscription.

Judy took to the podium with a printed copy of her speech and thanked the HOF executives and staff for treating the Gordon family so kindly leading up to and during the HOF weekend. Soon the rain began to fall, and HOF staff members handed out umbrellas to the families of the new inductees.

Judy continued telling aspects about her father's life that even the most devout baseball historians would not have known. She mentioned Ben and Ed Hoffman being two of Joe Gordon's most loyal fans, to the surprise of Dean Hoffman, who was sitting in the audience behind the Gordon family. She spoke of Joe Gordon and Babe Dahlgren being brought up to the Yankees from the Newark Bears, to the delight of Matt Dahlgren, seated next to Dean.

As she continued her speech, the clouds broke and the sun began to shine. It was a surreal moment that was later mentioned by at least one sportswriter.[34]

Hundreds of miles away, Joe Gordon's granddaughter, Sue Arnold, and her family were driving in Kentucky when they turned on the radio. By chance, they tuned into a station that was broadcasting the Hall of Fame Induction Ceremony. About 10 seconds after tuning in, they heard Judy mention her grandson, Travis Arnold, who was graduating from U.S. Army basic training. They were astonished by the coincidence.

Judy talked about how Joe Gordon was a gymnast, ventriloquist, violin player, and once rode a rodeo bucking horse the full eight seconds when he was in Arizona for Cleveland Indians spring training.

But the most difficult part of her speech was when she talked about her father passing away in 1978: "He insisted against having a funeral. And, as such, we consider Cooperstown and the National Baseball Hall of Fame as his final resting place, to be honored forever." Baseball fans, many with tears in their eyes, rose to their feet and applauded.

HOF inductees Jim Rice and Rickey Henderson then gave their speeches, followed by broadcaster Tony Kubek receiving the 2009 Ford C. Frick Award for "major contributions to baseball" and sportswriter Nick Peters receiving the 2009 J.G. Taylor Spink Award (now known as the BBWAA Career Excellence Award) for "meritorious contributions to baseball writing."

Following the Induction Ceremony, the Hall of Famers were asked to congregate on the lawn of the Otesaga Hotel for a group photo. As the players joined together, they were heard joking about certain crucial plays they'd been a part of, and they teased each other to the laughter of everyone.

Next, the Gordon family was asked to gather on the lawn overlooking beautiful Otsego Lake for a group photo with Joe Gordon's HOF plaque, which would be returned later that day to its place in the Plaque Gallery at the Hall of Fame. With the lake as a backdrop, this was a very poignant moment for the Gordon family.

Before leaving Cooperstown, the family went back to the Hall of Fame to see Joe Gordon's plaque one last time. Erik remembers the sun shining down through the rotunda glass, illuminating the area where the new plaques of Gordon, Henderson, and Rice had been placed. Joe "Flash" Gordon finally had a resting place in Cooperstown and the National Baseball Hall of Fame "to be honored forever." It was a perfect moment, never to be equaled or topped.

2009–2010: New York Yankees Museum

Joe "Flash" Gordon's display during the "Joe Gordon and Rickey Henderson: Cooperstown's Two Newest Yankees" exhibit at the New York Yankees Museum from August 2009 to May 2010 (courtesy Brian Richards).

At the invitation of the New York Yankees and Museum Curator Brian Richards of the New York Yankees Museum, several members of the Gordon family and others loaned items for the museum's display, titled "Joe Gordon and Rickey Henderson: Cooperstown's Two Newest Yankees." The exhibit ran from August 6, 2009, through May 5, 2010.[35]

2010: University of Oregon

Joe Gordon had attended the University of Oregon (UO) from the fall of 1932 through the spring of 1935, helping to bring the Ducks two Pacific Coast Conference Northern Division baseball championships (1934 and 1935). After completing his junior year of college, Joe signed with the Yankees' Newark Bears farm club in June 1935. He continued attending school, just one semester per year, until graduating in 1939. He was inducted into the University of Oregon Athletic Hall of Fame in its inaugural year 1992, and his plaque is displayed at the university's Len Casanova Athletic Center.

Chapter 23. Cooperstown at Last (2008–2009)

On April 2, 2010, the University of Oregon celebrated "Hall of Famer Joe Gordon Day" in honor of their graduate's 2009 Induction into the National Baseball Hall of Fame. Judy Gordon; her cousins De Ann (Gordon) Morgan and Nancy (Crum) Doyle, and Nancy's husband Bill; Hall of Famer Bobby Doerr; Bobby's son Don, a former pitcher for the UO Ducks; outgoing UO Athletic Director Mike Bellotti; and four of Judy's friends from Idaho (Jared and Carter Underwood, and Steve and Zac Anderson) attended UO's baseball game against the league-leading Arizona State University (ASU) Sun Devils.

Bobby Doerr presented the Gordon family with a current University of Oregon baseball jersey with "GORDON" on the back. He also gave Mike Bellotti a gift for the baseball program—a bat that Joe Gordon himself had used in the majors. After some coaching from Bobby Doerr at the pitcher's mound, Judy threw out the ceremonial first pitch of the game, right across home plate. "But on one bounce," Judy says. Jeff Eberhart wrote, "What a way to start a ballgame that would itself become an instant classic!"[36]

Despite being the underdogs, the Ducks broke out into an early lead against the undefeated Sun Devils. ASU started a comeback, scoring two runs, and then lightning and thunder forced the umpires to send the players to their dugouts for a weather delay. But it wasn't rain that followed; it was a winter-like snowstorm driven by high winds.

When the weather broke, the two teams took to the field. After a brief time, the game was again delayed due to weather. When play resumed, ASU took the lead, and it seemed like the Ducks might have to yield to defeat on "Joe Gordon Day." Yet Gordon himself must have been watching from above over his Ducks, as they scored another run to tie the game. In extra innings, neither team was able score until 12:46 A.M., when Oregon scored the game-winning run for the 6–5 triumph in the bottom of the 12th inning. It was reported as the Ducks' first win over a No. 1 ranked team since the 1970s, and the "Sun Devils fell to 24–1."[37] The Ducks had refused to give up; and in "Flash-like" fashion they rose to the occasion when it counted the most. It was a poignant moment. Considering that the game extended well into another day, it turned out being "Joe Gordon Day" for *two* days at the University of Oregon, with what the Flash himself would have expected—a victory!

2010–Present

Members of the Gordon family regularly read articles online about Joe "Flash" Gordon that compare him to other Yankees second basemen or recap past World Series where he was such an instrumental player.

The family was thrilled when Gordon was highlighted in a graphic on TV during the 2020 World Series, for being a reigning Most Valuable Player who hit a home run in the first game of the following year's World Series in 1943. They were proud when he was mentioned during a ceremony honoring Larry Doby at the U.S. Capitol in December 2023. Family members also loaned artifacts and were pleased to see Joe Gordon's prominent role in a new display at the New York Yankees Museum, which opened for two years beginning in August 2024.

When friends visit Yankee Stadium and the New York Yankees Museum, they often send photos of Gordon's autograph or a large photo of him being in an elite class of Yankees who won the Most Valuable Player Award.

At the time of this writing, Joe Gordon has been gone for 47 years. However, his light continues to shine brightly within his family and within a much larger family known as professional baseball. As a son, brother, husband, father, grandfather, and friend, Joe "Flash" Gordon impacted many lives during his short 63 years. As a baseball player, manager, coach, batting instructor, and scout, his impact remains forever woven into the fabric of baseball itself.

Epilogue

After returning home from Cooperstown, the Gordon family members were congratulated by friends and fans who'd read about Joe "Flash" Gordon's 2009 induction into the Hall of Fame or had watched the ceremony. A common phrase that people used when talking to family members was, "That was a once-in-a-lifetime event!" After hearing that a few times, Joe Gordon's grandson Erik Simpson thought to himself, "No; it's rarer than that!"

So, just how rare is it for a baseball player to be inducted into the National Baseball Hall of Fame? Well, it's one of the most exclusive clubs in the world.

According to Wikipedia, the first official baseball game (with a documented score card) on the North American Continent occurred in 1838 in Canada. Since then, tens of millions or perhaps even a hundred million boys and young men have played the sport, with hopes of becoming professional baseball players. Only a tiny fraction of those hopefuls—about 21,000 men—have played baseball professionally since it became a professional sport in the 1870s.

When Joe "Flash" Gordon was inducted into the National Baseball Hall of Fame in 2009, he was the 200th player to receive that honor. As of this writing, in the history of professional baseball, just 278 major league players have received the extremely rare honor of being immortalized as one of the greatest ever to play the game. That means that only one of about every 76 professional baseball players is featured on a plaque at the National Baseball Hall of Fame.

When you factor in every boy who ever swings a bat, the number becomes even more difficult to comprehend. Likely, during the course of baseball history, more than one billion young men or boys have played on an organized baseball team. Of all of those, from the U.S.A. to the Dominican Republic to Japan, just one of several million baseball players will be enshrined in Cooperstown. In fact, more than twice as many people (i.e., over 650) have been in space as have been inducted as players into the National Baseball Hall of Fame (278 at this writing). It is that rare!

Chapter Notes

Due to the large number of sources used in our research and writing, the authors have chosen not to cite those individually where the information is readily available online, such as baseball websites, and so forth.

Many of the newspaper articles and photographs in the scrapbooks compiled by Joe Gordon's mother, Louise, and wife, Dottie, do not identify the writers or photographers, or the names, publication dates, or page numbers of the sources. When citing these, we appended the words "Gordon Family Scrapbooks" to the citations and, if available, included the headline, title, date, or first few words of the article or photo caption. When the actual publication date was not available, we approximated the date from the contents of the article or photograph and prefixed that date with the abbreviation "ab." or "prob." Also, whenever we cited a book but did not include page number(s), it's because page numbers were not available for our eBooks.

Occasionally, when we obtained newspaper articles from online archives, the page numbers listed by the archives did not agree with the page numbers of the actual article or were missing. Wherever possible, the authors have tried to cite the correct page numbers.

The authors are aware that "journalistic embellishment" was somewhat more common in sports articles written during the years when Joe Gordon was active in professional baseball. In order to preserve the authenticity and ambiance of that era, we have quoted from our sources exactly as written, without correcting for spelling, punctuation, or English, except as noted with brackets and ellipses. As for our own writing, we have tried to follow the *SABR Style Guide* of the Society for American Baseball Research.

Introduction

1. Gordon Family Scrapbooks. Considine, Bob. "Pilot Votes Gordon Best All-Around." *Omaha* (NE) *Morning World-Herald*. ab. 7 Oct. 1941.
2. Honig, Donald. *MLB Hall of Fame Tribute: Joe Gordon* [Video]. MLB Advanced Media. 2009.

Chapter 1

1. Joe McCarthy's nickname, "Marse Joe," is thought to have originated from a sportswriter when McCarthy was managing the Chicago Cubs from 1926 to 1930. Back then, the now-obsolete word "Marse" generally was used as a title of respect, short for "Master."
2. Gordon, Joe Lowell. University of Oregon. Grade Report Card. Fall 1936–1937.
3. Gordon Family Scrapbooks. McGee, James K. "Yankees Order Joe Gordon to Report for Trial Next Year." ab. 15 Sep. 1936.
4. Dawson, James P. "McCarthy Looks Ahead with High Hopes as Powerful Yankees Prepare for Race." *New York Times*. 7 March 1937, p. 78.
5. https://moiderersrow.com/new-york-yankees-spring-training-history-since-1903/.
6. "Welcome! Welcome!! 'Yankees' 'Bees.'" Yankees Schedule. St. Petersburg (FL) *Evening Independent*. 13 March 1937, p. 13.
7. Except when cited otherwise, the description of Joe Gordon's arrival at 1937 Yankees spring training is from the following article: Gordon, Joe, as told to Stanley Frank. "A Rookie Wonders." *Street & Smith's Sport Story Magazine*. 1 July 1938, pp. 29–30.
8. Brown, Dr. Bobby. Note to Judy Gordon. 21 Aug. 2019.
9. Gordon, Joe. "Joe Gordon, New Yankee, Tells All About Career." *New York World-Telegram*. 16 Nov. 1937.
10. Smith, Jack. "Front Row for Joe." *Daily News*. 10 June 1942, p. 62.
11. Rennie, Rud. "Ruppert's Roster Flashes Power in All Departments." *New York Herald Tribune*. 11 April 1937, p. 3.
12. Gordon, Joe. "Joe Gordon, New Yankee, Tells All About Career." *New York World-Telegram*. 16 Nov. 1937.
13. Gordon, Joe, as told to Stanley Frank. "A Rookie Wonders." *Street & Smith's Sport Story Magazine*. 1 July 1938, p. 30.
14. Orndorff, Jess W. "The Voice of the Fan: What School Did for Joe Gordon." *The Sporting News*. 23 March 1939, p. 8.
15. Daniel, Daniel M. "Fortune Flashes June Smile on Serious Joe Gordon; Yank Rookie Wins Bride—and Second Base Job Back." *The Sporting News*. 30 June 1938, p. 3.

16. Dawson, James P. "Gomez and Rolfe Outstanding As Yanks Open Practice Games." *New York Times*. 12 March 1937, p. 27.

17. Grapefruit League—a nickname dating back to 1914 for a series of spring training exhibition games played by major league teams each spring in Florida, before the regular season opens; http://springtrainingmagazine.com/history4.html.

18. Reil, Frank. "Yanks Crush Bees, 13-4, in Opening Game." *Brooklyn Daily Eagle*. 14 March 1937, p. 1.

19. Gordon Family Scrapbooks. McDonald, Red. "Yankees Wallop Bees 13 to 4 In Series Opener: Champs Pound 3 Hurlers for Eighteen Hits." ab. 14 March 1937.

20. Gordon Family Scrapbooks. Kase, Max. "View Gordon, Coast Lad, as Lazzeri's Successor." prob. *New York Journal-American*. ab. 16 March 1937.

21. Dawson, James P. "Brilliant Fielding of Dahlgren, Gehrig's Understudy, Wins Ruppert's Praise." *New York Times*. 16 March 1937, p. 27.

22. The Contract Record Card of Joseph L. Gordon indicates that he signed his contract with the Newark Bears on 15 March 1937.

23. Graham, Frank. "Graham's Corner: Speaking of Joe Gordon." *The Sporting News*. 30 Nov. 1955, p. 10.

24. Dawson, James P. "Gomez Hurls Well as Yanks Win, 5-2." *New York Times*. 17 March 1937, p. 32.

25. Rennie, Rud. "Yankee Power Fashions Stars Out of Recruits." *New York Herald Tribune*. 18 March 1937, p. 27.

Chapter 2

1. Gordon Family Scrapbooks. "Mrs. Lowell Gordon, one of the very popular ladies of Oatman, has gone to Los Angeles." *Oatman (AZ) News*. ab. 23 Dec. 1914.

2. Gordon, Joey. Written notes from conversations with Lois Rusche Jenkins, niece of Louise Gordon Lampert. Portland, OR. 1983.

3. United States Census (1900). Deerfield District, Fergus County, MT. 14-16 June 1900.

4. United States Census (1910). Cerbat, Mohave County, AZ. 22-23 April 1910.

5. Marriage Certificate of Lowell Gordon and Lulu Pearl Evans. Globe, AZ. 3 Dec. 1912.

6. Malach, Roman. *Oatman: Gold Mining Center*. Kingman, AZ: Roman Malach, 1975, pp. 19, 21.

7. World War I Draft Registration Card for Lowell Gordon. 12 Sep. 1918.

8. United States Census (1920). Old Trails, Mohave County, AZ. 14 Jan. 1920.

9. Gordon, Joey. Written notes from conversations with Lois Rusche Jenkins, niece of Louise Gordon Lampert. Portland, OR. 1983.

10. Gordon family photo. Jerome Copper. Winter of 1920-1921.

11. Gordon Family Scrapbooks. Obituary of Lulu Gordon's mother, Mrs. James Evans. ab. 23 Jan. 1921.

12. 1st Grade Report Card of Joe Gordon. Holladay School. Portland, OR. 31 Jan. 1921-17 June 1921.

13. Gordon Family Scrapbooks. Cuddy, Jack. "Of All Guys Named Joe, Gordon is the Standout." St. Petersburg, FL. ab. 8 March 1938.

14. De Ferrari, Carlo M., Tuolumne County Historian. Letter to Judy Gordon. 10 Jan. 1999; Vallem, George, and Della. Letter to Judy Gordon. 18 Sep. 1999.

15. De Ferrari, Carlo M., Tuolumne County Historian. Letter to Judy Gordon. 10 Jan. 1999.

16. Death Record of Ben Lowell Gordon. Tuolumne Co. Hospital. Sonora, CA. 12 May 1946; "Ben L. Gordon Dead After Long Illness." *Sonora Union Democrat*. 16 May 1946; Gordon, Judy. Personal visit to Sonora, CA. Feb. 2002.

17. "When gold began to talk, the first word it learned to say was 'Good-bye.'" *Oatman (AZ) News*. 4 Jan. 1919, p. 2.

Chapter 3

1. Zellerbach Paper Co. Gold retirement card awarded to Louise E. Gordon for service from 1921 to 1958.

2. *National Safety News, Vol. 5*. April 1922, p. 24.

3. Report Cards of Joe Gordon. Holladay Grammar School. Portland, OR. 1921-1928; Report Cards of Jack Gordon. Holladay Grammar School. Portland, OR. 1922, 1925, 1926.

4. Daniel, Daniel M. "Fortune Flashes June Smile on Serious Joe Gordon; Yank Rookie Wins Bride—and Second Base Job Back." *The Sporting News*. 30 June 1938, p. 3.

5. Syring, Richard H. "'Flash' Gordon: 'A Good Joe!'" *Oregon Journal—Features*. 2 April 1939, p. 1.

6. Hampson, Fred. "Mother of Joe Gordon Extolls Ballplayers." *Denver Post*. 2 Oct. 1938.

7. Syring, Richard H. "'Flash' Gordon: 'A Good Joe!'" *Oregon Journal—Features*. 2 April 1939, p. 1.

8. Gordon, Joe. "Joe Gordon, New Yankee, Tells All About Career." *New York World-Telegram*. 16 Nov. 1937.

9. Daniel, Dan. "Trigger Gordon of Bombers, Going Back to Second, Put Pennant Click in Infield That Floundered at First." *The Sporting News*. 2 Oct. 1941, p. 3.

10. Gross, Milton. "Money Player." *Collier's*. 18 July 1942, p. 18.

11. Certificate of Marriage of Andrew J. Lampert and Louise E. Gordon. Northminster Presbyterian Church. Seattle, WA. 7 March 1958.

12. Nelson, Stub. "Joe and Johnny: Up from Portland Sandlots to Stardom in the Majors—Gordon and Pesky's Story." *Sunday Oregonian*. 28 June 1942, p. 6.

13. Humasti, Joe. Personal conversations with Judy Gordon. 2013.

14. "Basketball Notes." *Morning Oregonian*. 17 March 1932, p. 23; Syring, Richard H. "'Flash'

Gordon: 'A Good Joe!'" *Oregon Journal–Features*. 2 April 1939, p. 1.

15. Gordon Family Scrapbooks. Gregory, L.H. "I say that from having seen him play soccer...." *Sunday Oregonian*. ab. 10 Oct. 1943, p. 40.

16. Second Annual Portland Area YMCA Track and Field Meet ribbons awarded to Joe Gordon. 25 May 1929.

17. Wright, S.T. "Gordon to Be G.I. Joe." *Morning Oregonian*. 9 Jan. 1944, p. 5.

18. "The Ted Bacon String Orchestra Municipal Concert Program." Ted Bacon Conductor. Portland, OR. 19 Feb. 1928.

19. Harris, Phip. "Joe Gordon Fiddles Way to Tryout with Yankees." *St. Petersburg Times*. 1 April 1938, p. 19.

Chapter 4

1. *The Spectrum: Class of June '32*. Jefferson High School. Portland, OR. p. 64.

2. Goodrich, Hollis. "Jefferson High Proud of Sparkling Graduate." *Portland News-Telegram*. 6 Oct. 1938.

3. Goodrich, Hollis. "Jefferson High Proud of Sparkling Graduate." *Portland News-Telegram*. 6 Oct. 1938.

4. Daniel, Daniel M. "Fortune Flashes June Smile on Serious Joe Gordon; Yank Rookie Wins Bride—and Second Base Job Back." *The Sporting News*. 30 June 1938, p. 3; Report cards of Joe Gordon. Jefferson High School. Portland, OR. 1928–1932.

5. "Jeff Wins Soccer Title." *Morning Oregonian*. 13 Jan. 1932, p. 13; Learned, Frank Marsh. "Prep League Stars Picked by Learned." *Morning Oregonian*. 17 Jan. 1932, p. 23.

6. Oregon State Soccer Football Association membership card certifying Joe Gorden [sic] duly registered as an amateur the season of 1930–1931. 25 Jan. 1931; Photograph of Vikings Soccer Team. Champions of the Portland Soccer Association. 1931–1932.

7. Daniel, Daniel M. "Fortune Flashes June Smile on Serious Joe Gordon; Yank Rookie Wins Bride—and Second Base Job Back." *The Sporting News*. 30 June 1938, p. 3.

8. Daniel, Daniel M. "Fortune Flashes June Smile on Serious Joe Gordon; Yank Rookie Wins Bride—and Second Base Job Back." *The Sporting News*. 30 June 1938, p. 3.

9. Daniel, Daniel M. "Fortune Flashes June Smile on Serious Joe Gordon; Yank Rookie Wins Bride—and Second Base Job Back." *The Sporting News*. 30 June 1938, p. 3.

10. "Year's Review of Sports Brings to Light Many Star Performers in Oregon; Here Are a Few of the Outstanding." *Morning Oregonian*. 1 Jan. 1932, p. 17.

11. Gordon Family Scrapbooks. Grayson, Harry. "Bigger Bat Makes Gordon Bigger Menace." New York. ab. June 1942.

12. "Jeffs Beat Vancouver." *Morning Oregonian*. 3 April 1931, p. 19.

13. Daniel, Daniel M. "Fortune Flashes June Smile on Serious Joe Gordon; Yank Rookie Wins Bride—and Second Base Job Back." *The Sporting News*. 30 June 1938, p. 3.

14. Gordon, Joe. "Joe Gordon, New Yankee, Tells All About Career." *New York World-Telegram*. 16 Nov. 1937.

15. Gordon, Joe, as told to Stanley Frank. "A Rookie Wonders." *Street & Smith's Sport Story Magazine*. 1 July 1938, p. 25.

16. *The Spectrum: Class of June '32*. Jefferson High School. Portland, OR. p. 35.

17. Neuberger, Dick. "32 Preppers Pass .300 Batting Mark." *Morning Oregonian*. 27 May 1931, p. 22.

18. Gordon Family Scrapbooks. Gregory, L.H. "Gregory's Sport Gossip." *The Oregonian*. Summer 1935.

19. Stump, Al. "Mr. Second Sack is Back." *Argosy for Men*. July 1948, p. 19.

20. Gordon, Joe. "Joe Gordon, New Yankee, Tells All About Career." *New York World-Telegram*. 16 Nov. 1937.

21. Syring, Richard H. "'Flash' Gordon: 'A Good Joe!'" *Oregon Journal—Features*. 2 April 1939, p. 1.

22. Gordon, Joe, as told to Stanley Frank. "A Rookie Wonders." *Street & Smith's Sport Story Magazine*. 1 July 1938, pp. 25–26.

23. Neuberger, Dick. "East Side Juniors Win City Pennant." *Morning Oregonian*. 12 July 1931, p. 1.

24. Neuberger, Dick. "East Side Juniors Face Ontario Next." *Morning Oregonian*. 21 July 1931, p. 15.

25. Photo. "Here are twenty young men and their coaches who are going to be very much in the public eye this week." *Sunday Oregonian*. 2 Aug. 1931.

26. "Portland's Junior Ball Team, State Champions, Lose to Seattle at Butte." *The Oregon Legionnaire*. Sep. 1931, pp. 1, 8.

27. Neuberger, Dick. "Portland Juniors Win State Series." *Sunday Oregonian*. 9 Aug. 1931.

28. "Portland Junior Wins." *Sunday Oregonian*. 9 Aug. 1931, p. 2.

29. "Portland Juniors Swamp Idaho Nine." *Morning Oregonian*. 14 Aug. 1931, p. 17.

30. "Seattle Kids Take Portland Down Line." *Morning Oregonian*. 15 Aug. 1931, p. 15.

31. Step, Billy. "The Second Guess." *The Oregonian*. 3 April 1940.

32. Gordon, Joe, as told to Stanley Frank. "A Rookie Wonders." *Street & Smith's Sport Story Magazine*. 1 July 1938, p. 26; Hobson, Howard. "All-Stars Chosen in Prep Ball Loop." *Sunday Oregonian*. 5 June 1932, p. 4.

33. *The Spectrum: Class of June '32*. Jefferson High School. Portland, OR. p. 15.

Chapter 5

1. "State League Formed." *Morning Oregonian*. 22 May 1932, p. 3.

2. Pacific Coast Conference (PCC)—an athletic conference in the western part of the United States from 1915 to 1959, comprising ten participating colleges and universities (including the University of Oregon), with the sport of baseball divided into Northern and Southern Divisions; Schmidt, Ray. "The Joe Lillard Affair." *College Football Historical Society Vol. XXIV, No. III.* May 2011, pp. 1–4.
3. Photo. "State League Shortstop Star." *Morning Oregonian.* 26 June 1932, p. 2.
4. "Girls' Nine to Vie Here. *Morning Oregonian.* 12 June 1932, p. 4; "Girls' Ball Team Here." *Morning Oregonian.* 12 July 1932, p. 15.
5. "Giants Trim Babes." *Morning Oregonian.* 19 July 1932, p. 14; "Giants Booked Again." *Morning Oregonian.* 26 July 1932, p. 12.
6. "Giants Defeat Babes." *Morning Oregonian.* 2 Aug. 1932, p. 18; "Babes Beat Gilkerson's." *Morning Oregonian.* 3 Aug. 1932, p. 14; "West Side Wins Again." *Morning Oregonian.* 4 Aug. 1932, p. 14.
7. "House of David Signed." *Morning Oregonian.* 7 Aug. 1932, p. 4.
8. "Davidites Sweep Series." *Morning Oregonian.* 16 Aug. 1932, p. 12.
9. Daniel, Daniel M. "Fortune Flashes June Smile on Serious Joe Gordon; Yank Rookie Wins Bride—and Second Base Job Back." *The Sporting News.* 30 June 1938, p. 3.
10. Odell, Dick. Zellerbach Paper Co., Eugene Division. Letter to Mrs. Louise Gordon. 19 Jan. 1933.
11. "Babes Win State Title." *Morning Oregonian.* 22 Aug. 1932, p. 14.
12. Gordon, Joe, as told to Stanley Frank. "A Rookie Wonders." *Street & Smith's Sport Story Magazine.* 1 July 1938, p. 26.
13. "56 Freshmen Report." *Sunday Oregonian.* 2 Oct. 1932, p. 2; "Yearling Gridders Awarded Numbers." *Morning Oregonian.* 7 Dec. 1932, p. 16.
14. Gordon Family Scrapbooks. "One of the outstanding players on the frosh nine is Joe Gordon…." Spring 1933.
15. "State League to Open." *Morning Oregonian.* 21 May 1933, p. 3.
16. "Bush League Notes." *Morning Oregonian.* 6 June 1933, p. 14; "Bush League Notes." *Morning Oregonian.* 8 June 1933, p. 14.
17. Daniel, Daniel M. "Fortune Flashes June Smile on Serious Joe Gordon; Yank Rookie Wins Bride—and Second Base Job Back." *The Sporting News.* 30 June 1938, p. 3; "Federals Take Crown." *Morning Oregonian.* 28 Aug. 1933, p. 14.
18. Daniel, Daniel M. "Fortune Flashes June Smile on Serious Joe Gordon; Yank Rookie Wins Bride—and Second Base Job Back." *The Sporting News.* 30 June 1938, p. 3.
19. Gordon Family Scrapbooks. "Joe Gordon's Sigma Chi footballers…." Fall 1933.
20. "GREGORY." *Morning Oregonian.* 19 May 1934, p. 18.
21. Gordon Family Scrapbooks. "Webfoots Batting Average is .312 in Seven Games." ab. 16 May 1934.
22. Gordon Family Scrapbooks. "Baseball Crown Won by Webfoots." Oregon State College. Corvallis. ab. 2 June 1934.
23. Gordon Family Scrapbooks. "Oregon Will Have Veteran Team for '35 P.C.C. Season." University of Oregon. Eugene. ab. 16 June 1934.
24. Gordon Family Scrapbooks. "Ten Varsity Awards Given at Oregon U." University of Oregon. Eugene. ab. 16 June 1934.
25. Pasero, George. "Pasero Says: Flash Gordon." *Oregon Journal.* ab. 24 April 1978.
26. Newspaper photo and article. "Airtight Townie Infield!" Eugene, OR. ab. 24 June 1934.
27. Gordon Family Scrapbooks. "Locals Lose Tilt 13 to 12; Salem at Top of League." prob. 27 Aug. 1934.
28. Gordon Family Scrapbooks. "Colored Stars to Play: House of David's Van Dyke Nine Meets All-Stars." Aug. 1934; "All-Stars Take Game." *Morning Oregonian.* 20 Aug. 1934, p. 11.
29. Cobbledick, Gordon. "Here's the *Flash!*" *Sport.* Oct. 1948, p. 87.
30. "GREGORY." *Morning Oregonian.* 26 Sep. 1934, p. 18.
31. Gordon, Joe, as told to Stanley Frank. "A Rookie Wonders." *Street & Smith's Sport Story Magazine.* 1 July 1938, p. 26.
32. Fisher, Fred. Letter to "Hal." 30 April 1998; Daniel, Dan. "Yankee Star Called Composite of Frisch, Hornsby and Collins." *The Sporting News.* 11 June 1942, p. 1.
33. Gordon Family Scrapbooks. Smith, Jeff. "Gordon to get his due, 59 years after retiring." prob. *The Oregonian.* ab. 25 July 2009, pp. D1, D5; Gordon Family Scrapbooks. "Handballers Forge Ahead in Donut Play." ab. 16 Jan. 1935.
34. Gregory, L.H. "We'll Miss Bill." *The Oregonian.* 24 April 1935.
35. Gregory, L.H. "Gregory's Sport Gossip: Yanks Like Them." *The Oregonian.* 29 April 1935.
36. Gordon Family Scrapbooks. Carmichael, John P. "The Rise of the Golden Boy of Baseball—Joe Gordon." prob. *Chicago Daily News* or *Chicago Herald-Examiner.* prob. early 1940.
37. Parrott, Harold. "Both Sides: Super-Salesman." *Brooklyn Daily Eagle.* 13 Oct. 1941, p. 11.
38. Gordon Family Scrapbooks. "Prize for Bill Essick." ab. 3 April 1935.
39. Gordon Family Scrapbooks. Connelly, Gordon M. "Gala Celebration to Open Oregon Baseball Season." ab. 26 April 1935.
40. Gordon Family Scrapbooks. "Weboots [sic] Skin Beavers, 17 to 0." ab. 27 April 1935, p. 1.
41. Gordon Family Scrapbooks. "Beavers Defeat Duck Nine, 12–7." Oregon State College. Corvallis. ab. 27 April 1935.
42. Gregory, L.H. "Oregon Edges Out Washington 6 to 5." *Morning Oregonian.* 11 May 1935, p. 13.
43. Gordon Family Scrapbooks. Gregory, L.H. "Gregory's Sport Gossip: Scouting for Red Sox." prob. *The Oregonian.* ab. 22 May 1935.
44. Gordon Family Scrapbooks. "Duck Nine to

Meet Orangemen in Last Series of Season." ab. 28 May 1935.

45. Gordon Family Scrapbooks. Gregory, L.H. "Oregon Wallops Orangemen 15–6." *Oregon State College*. Corvallis. ab. 31 May 1935; "Ducks Present Departing Coach with Title; Oregon Wins, 6–3." *Eugene Morning News*. ab. 2 June 1935.

46. Gordon Family Scrapbooks. "Webfooter's Bat Average Tops League." *Oregon State College*. Corvallis. ab. 22 June 1935; "Oregon Gets Five Players on All-Star Nine." *Oregon Daily Journal*. 13 June 1935.

47. Leeding, Harry. "Tower Lights." *Oregon Daily Journal*. 12 June 1935.

48. Gordon Family Scrapbooks. "Oregon Looks Back on 1935 with Pride; Greatest Year in Sports Ever Registered." *University of Oregon*. Eugene. ab. 28 Dec. 1935; Gregory, L.H. "Gregory's Gossip: Joe Gordon Likes It." *Sunday Oregonian*. 5 Jan. 1936, p. 2.

49. Years later, Michael Haupert, Professor of Economics at University of Wisconsin–La Crosse, discovered an entry dated June 3, 1935 in the Yankees' corporate records archived at the National Baseball Hall of Fame and Museum, noting that the Yankees had paid $500 to the Newark Bears to cover Joe Gordon's signing bonus.

50. Parrott, Harold. "Both Sides: Super-Salesman." *Brooklyn Daily Eagle*. 13 Oct. 1941, p. 11.

51. Gordon, Joe, as told to Stanley Frank. "A Rookie Wonders." *Street & Smith's Sport Story*. 1 July 1938, pp. 27–28.

52. "One Club Added by State League." *Morning Oregonian*. 18 Feb. 1935, p. 14; "Koch and Gordon Join Hop Golds." *Sunday Oregonian*. 2 June 1935, p. 2.

53. "Hop Golds Will Be Here Sunday." *Bend (OR) Bulletin*. 11 July 1935.

54. Gregory, L.H. "Gregory's Sport Gossip: Gordon Goes Trojan." *The Oregonian*. 18 Aug. 1935.

55. Gordon, Joe L. Office of the Registrar. The University of Southern California. Report Card for Session ending 6 Feb. 1936.

56. Gregory, L.H. "Gregory's Gossip: Joe Likes It." *Sunday Oregonian*. 5 Jan. 1936, p. 2.

57. Orndorff, Jess W. "The Voice of the Fan: What School Did for Joe Gordon." *The Sporting News*. 23 Mar. 1939, p. 8.

Chapter 6

1. Gordon, Joe L. Office of the Registrar. The University of Southern California. Report Card for Session ending 6 Feb. 1936.

2. McCall, Tom. "Sport Quacks: New York Yankees Farm Out Ex-Oregon Diamond Performers." *Oregon Daily Emerald*. 25 Feb. 1936.

3. Murphy, Eddie. "Yankee Turnovers Await Meyer's O.K." *Oakland Tribune*. 3 Feb. 1937, p. 14.

4. Vermeer, Al. "Vitt Ready to Drag Oaks Out of Woods." *The Sporting News*. 28 Feb. 1935, p. 7.

5. "Meyer Gets Players." *Oakland Tribune*. 13 Feb. 1936, p. 24.

6. Gordon Family Scrapbooks. Murphy, Eddie. "Bell Arrives, Expects Good Season." *Oakland Tribune*. ab. 2 March 1936.

7. McCall, Tom. "Sport Quacks: New York Yankees Farm Out Ex-Oregon Diamond Performers." *Oregon Emerald*. 25 Feb. 1936; Gordon Family Scrapbooks. Murphy, Eddie. "Bell Arrives, Expects Good Season." *Oakland Tribune*. ab. 2 March 1936.

8. Gordon Family Scrapbooks. Murphy, Eddie. "Olds, Oakland Hurler, Hurt by Line Drive." *Oakland Tribune*. ab. 29 Feb. 1936.

9. Gordon Family Scrapbooks. Murphy, Eddie. "Bell Arrives, Expects Good Season." *Oakland Tribune*. ab. 2 March 1936.

10. "Modesto, Cal.: The flashy young keystone combination...." *Sunday Oregonian*. 15 March 1936, p. 3.

11. Gordon Family Scrapbooks. Gregory, L.H. "Beavers Blast Oakland, 8 to 5." *The Oregonian*. ab. 20 March 1936; Gordon Family Scrapbooks. Gregory, L.H. "Gregory's Sport Gossip." *The Oregonian*. ab. 23 March 1936.

12. Gordon, Joe, as told to Stanley Frank. "A Rookie Wonders." *Street & Smith's Sport Story*. 1 July 1938, p. 28.

13. Murphy, Eddie. "Tobin to Stay with Oaks, Signs Contract; Angels Next." *Oakland Tribune*. 29 March 1936; Gordon Family Scrapbooks. Murphy, Eddie. "Tricky Attack to Offset Bat Power of Foes." *Oakland Tribune*. ab. 27 March 1936.

14. Murphy, Eddie. "Tobin to Stay with Oaks, Signs Contract; Angels Next." *Oakland Tribune*. 29 March 1936.

15. Gregory, L.H. "Greg's Gossip: No Bonus to Joe Gordon." *Morning Oregonian*. 31 March 1940, p. 1.

16. National Association Contract Record Cards of Al Raymond Koch. 1935–1941; Koch, Kerry, son of Ray Koch. Phone conversation with Judy Gordon. 2014.

17. Murphy, Eddie. "Kies, Bell and Deviveiros on Bench." *Oakland Tribune*. 8 April 1936, p. 14.

18. Gordon Family Scrapbooks. "Beavers Topple Oakland, 7 to 5." Oakland, CA. ab. 8 April 1936.

19. Frizzell, Pat. "Sport Chat." *Oregon Daily Emerald*. 11 April 1936.

20. Murphy, Eddie. "Oaks Manager Faces Gamble: Ponders Gamble." *Oakland Tribune*. 9 April 1936, p. 28.

21. "Solons Batter Oakland, 14 to 4." *Oakland Tribune*. 7 May 1936, p. 27; Gordon Family Scrapbooks. "Oregon's Joe Gordon has started and finished every ball game...." ab. 15 May 1936.

22. Photo. "Pair of Oaks Face Beavers." *Morning Oregonian*. 2 June 1936.

23. Gregory, L.H. "Oaks Win Opener from Ducks 13–3." *Morning Oregonian*. 5 June 1936, p. 19.

24. Gregory, L.H. "Beavers Topple Oakland, 13 to 4." *Morning Oregonian*. 6 June 1936, pp. 17–18.

25. Murphy, Eddie. "Locals Second After Reds Split Bill." *Oakland Tribune*. 29 June 1936, p. 8.

26. Photo. "Keeping Oaks in Race for 1936 P.C.L. Championship." *Oakland Tribune*. ab. 29 June 1936.
27. Murphy, Eddie. "Coast Race is Hot; Missions Get Setback." *Oakland Tribune*. 17 July 1936, p. 35.
28. "Joe Gordon Shows Real Promise." *Seattle Post-Intelligencer*. ab. 25 July 1936.
29. Byrne, Emmons. "Minors Worth Watching: Joseph (Joe) Gordon of the Oakland Oaks." *The Sporting News*. 30 July 1936, p. 5.
30. Byrne, Emmons. "Sweeney on Gordon: Hustling Joe Best Rookie in the Coast League, Declares Portland Pilot; Better Than DiMaggio." *Oakland Post-Enquirer*. 19 Aug. 1936.
31. Gordon Family Scrapbooks. "Although the Seattle and Portland clubs are doing very well...." Summer 1936.
32. "Coast League (Baseball Standings and Summary)." *Morning Oregonian*. 14 Sep. 1936, p. 14.
33. Gregory, L.H. "Gregory's Sport Gossip: Joe Can't Miss." *Morning Oregonian*. 1 Oct. 1936, p. 17.
34. Wells, Donald R. *The Race for the Governor's Cup: The Pacific Coast League Playoffs, 1936–1954*. Jefferson, NC: McFarland, 2000, pp. 1–3.
35. Wells, Donald R. *The Race for the Governor's Cup: The Pacific Coast League Playoffs, 1936–1954*. Jefferson, NC: McFarland, 2000, p. 13.
36. Wells, Donald R. *The Race for the Governor's Cup: The Pacific Coast League Playoffs, 1936–1954*. Jefferson, NC: McFarland, 2000, pp. 14–16.
37. Wells, Donald R. *The Race for the Governor's Cup: The Pacific Coast League Playoffs, 1936–1954*. Jefferson, NC: McFarland, 2000, pp. 19–20.
38. Wells, Donald R. *The Race for the Governor's Cup: The Pacific Coast League Playoffs, 1936–1954*. Jefferson, NC: McFarland, 2000, pp. 20–27.
39. Wells, Donald R. *The Race for the Governor's Cup: The Pacific Coast League Playoffs, 1936–1954*. Jefferson, NC: McFarland, 2000, pp. 27–28.
40. Gordon, Joe Lowell. University of Oregon. Grade Report Card. Fall 1936–1937.
41. "Joe Gordon, a young infielder...." *The Sporting News*. 28 Jan. 1937, p. 6.
42. Orndorff, Jess W. "The Voice of the Fan: What School Did for Joe Gordon." *The Sporting News*. 23 March 1939, p. 8.
43. Mayer, Ronald A. *The 1937 Newark Bears: A Baseball Legend*. New Brunswick, NJ: Rutgers University Press, 1994, p. ix.
44. Ray, Bob. "Joe Gordon Set for His Big Test with Yanks." *Los Angeles Times*. 6 Feb. 1938.
45. Gordon, Joe. "Joe Gordon, New Yankee, Tells All About Career." *New York World-Telegram*. 16 Nov. 1937.
46. "1937. Spring Training Schedule. 1937." Hotel Sebring. Sebring, FL. 10 March–22 April 1937.
47. Ford, Frank B. "Bears Leaving Florida Confident of Strength." *The Sporting News*. 8 April 1937, p. 9.
48. Effrat, Louis. "Newark Celebrates Inaugural with 8–5 Victory Over Royals." Special to the *New York Times*. 23 April 1937, p. 26; Gordon Family Scrapbooks. "Gordon moved around the short stop sector...." ab. 22 April 1937; Gordon Family Scrapbooks. Moss, Morton. "Oakland Boy Has Eye Set on Lazzeri's Yankee Berth." ab. 23 April 1937.
49. Izenberg, Jerry. Phone conversation with Judy Gordon. 22 Aug. 2015.
50. Izenberg, Jerry. "Gordon, Newark shared bond." *Star-Ledger Archive*. 9 Dec. 2008.
51. https://newarkmemories.com/memories/503.php.
52. Chipman, William J. "Bill Skiff Becomes Favorite for Job as Newark Manager." *The Sporting News*. 28 Oct. 1937, p. 9.
53. "Newark Tossers Having Big Year." *The Oregonian*. 4 July 1937, p. 6.
54. Patterson, Arthur E. "Newark's Sweep Recalls Yankee Surge of 1936." *New York Herald Tribune*. 9 July 1937, p. 23.
55. Gordon Family Scrapbooks. "Second baseman Joe Gordon of the Newark Bears slammed the first pitch...." ab. 8 July 1937.
56. "Youngsters Who Are Helping Bears Make Runaway Race." *New York Herald Tribune*. 9 July 1937, p. 23.
57. Goldberg, Hy. "Sports in The News." *Newark Evening News*. 1937.
58. Fitzgerald, Ed. "Joe Gordon: The Acrobatic Flash." *Sport*. July 1949, p. 19.
59. "Mayer, Ronald A. *The 1937 Newark Bears: A Baseball Legend*. New Brunswick, NJ: Rutgers University Press, 1994, p. 201.
60. "Newark Sweeps Final 2 Games, Finishes 25½ Games in Front." *New York Herald Tribune*. 13 Sep. 1937, p. 20.
61. Werber, Bill, and C. Paul Rogers III. *Memories of a Ballplayer: Bill Werber and Baseball in the 1930s*. Phoenix, AZ: Society for American Baseball Research, 2013.
62. Smith, Jack. "Gordon Signs with Yanks; Brilliant Future Pictured." *The Oregonian*. 12 Feb. 1938, p. 15.
63. Gordon Family Scrapbooks. "Newark Defeats Syracuse, 2–1, on Two Home Runs in Ninth." Newark, NJ. ab. 14 Sep. 1937.
64. Robinson, Murray. "Calling the Turn: Dramatic Classic." *Newark Star Eagle Sports*. 15 Sep. 1937, p. 12.
65. Klein, William. "Bears Sweep Chiefs Series: Gordon's Homer Decides 3–1 Tilt." *Newark Ledger Sports*. 18 Sep. 1937.
66. Mayer, Ronald A. *The 1937 Newark Bears: A Baseball Legend*. New Brunswick, NJ: Rutgers University Press, 1994, pp. 250–251.
67. "Newark Shades Baltimore, 6–5, Amid Fisticuffs." *New York Herald Tribune*. 23 Sep. 1937, p. 30; "Oriole Player and Umpire Fight as Bears Capture 2d Straight, 6–5." *New York Times*. 23 Sep. 1937, p. 34.
68. Mayer, Ronald A. *The 1937 Newark Bears: A Baseball Legend*. New Brunswick, NJ: Rutgers University Press, 1994, p. 253.
69. Mayer, Ronald A. *The 1937 Newark Bears: A*

Baseball Legend. New Brunswick, NJ: Rutgers University Press, 1994, p. 257.
70. Also sometimes written as Governor's Cup.
71. Gordon Family Scrapbooks. "Newark Gains Play-Off Final in Series Sweep." Syracuse, NY. ab. 17 Sep. 1937.
72. "Little World Series Starts Today, with Pitchers Giving Bears Edge." *New York Herald Tribune*. 29 Sep. 1937, p. 26.
73. Mayer, Ronald A. *The 1937 Newark Bears: A Baseball Legend*. New Brunswick, NJ: Rutgers University Press, 1994, p. 266.
74. Laney, Al. "Columbus Downs Newark in Little Series Start, 5–4." *New York Herald Tribune*. 30 Sep. 1937, p. 29.
75. Laney, Al. "Newark Loses to Columbus in 11th, 5–4." *New York Herald Tribune*. 1 Oct. 1937, p. 25.
76. Effrat, Louis. "Columbus Rally Beats Newark, 6–3." *New York Times*. 2 Oct. 1937, p. 15.
77. "10,201 See Newark Stop Columbus, 8–1." *New York Times*. 3 Oct. 1937.
78. "Newark Downs Columbus, 1–0,...." *New York Herald Tribune*. 5 Oct. 1937, p. 28.
79. Spink, J.G. Taylor. "Three and One: Looking Them Over with J.G. Taylor Spink." *The Sporting News*. 13 Oct. 1938, p. 4.
80. "Newark Bears Stage Remarkable Come-Back to Win Junior Series." *The Sporting News*. 14 Oct. 1937, p. 2.
81. Mayer, Ronald A. *The 1937 Newark Bears: A Baseball Legend*. New Brunswick, NJ: Rutgers University Press, 1994, p. 283.
82. Mayer, Ronald A. *The 1937 Newark Bears: A Baseball Legend*. New Brunswick, NJ: Rutgers University Press, 1994, p. 284.
83. Grayson, Harry. "Too Bad Vitt Can't Take Newark Bears." *News-Telegram*. 26 Oct. 1937.
84. Junior Series Receipts." *The Sporting News*. 14 Oct. 1937, p. 2.
85. Gordon Family Scrapbooks. Cuddy, Jack. "Of All Guys Named Joe, Gordon is the Standout." St. Petersburg, FL. ab. 8 March 1938.
86. Gordon, Joe Lowell. University of Oregon. Grade Report Card. Fall 1937–1938.
87. Chipman, William J. "Bill Skiff Becomes Favorite for Job as Newark Manager." *The Sporting News*. 28 Oct. 1937, p. 9; "Newark Bears Stage Remarkable Come-Back to Win Junior Series." *The Sporting News*. 14 Oct. 1937, p. 2.
88. Gordon Family Scrapbooks. "With the same superiority they displayed...." Fall 1937.
89. "Bears Won Lions' Shares of All-League Positions." *The Sporting News*. 1 Dec. 1962, p. 8.
90. McGowan, J.L. "International Gains While 'Shag' Diets." *The Sporting News*. 18 Nov. 1937, p. 9.
91. Photo. "Baseball's No. 1 Men of Year ... In Majors and Minors." *The Sporting News*. 30 Dec. 1937, p. 1.
92. Gordon Family Scrapbooks. "Going down the regular line-up...." Fall 1937.
93. Weiss, Bill, and Marshall Wright. *The 100 Greatest Minor League Baseball Teams of the 20th Century*. Outskirts Press, 2006.
94. Hazen, David W. "Vitt Has Praise for Joe Gordon." *The Oregonian*. 10 Oct. 1937, p. 3.
95. Grayson, Harry. "Too Bad Vitt Can't Take Newark Bears." *News-Telegram*. 26 Oct. 1937.
96. Byrne, Emmons. "'Old Oz,' His Monicker on the Coast, ... Believing His Newark Grads Will Strengthen Yankees." *The Sporting News*. 28 Oct. 1937, p. 9.
97. Ray, Bob. "Joe Gordon Set for His Big Test with Yanks." *Los Angeles Times*. 6 Feb. 1938.

Chapter 7

1. Cartoon. Vermeer, Al. "On Baseball's Hot Spot." *San Francisco News*. 31 Jan. 1938; Smith, Jack. "Gordon Signs with Yanks; Brilliant Future Pictured." *The Oregonian*. 12 Feb. 1938.
2. Gordon Family Scrapbooks. "Joe Gordon, the second-sacker...." early 1938.
3. Orndorff, Jess W. "The Voice of the Fan: What School Did for Joe Gordon." *The Sporting News*. 23 March 1939, p. 8.
4. Ray, Bob. "Joe Gordon Set for His Big Test with Yanks." *Los Angeles Times*. 6 Feb. 1938.
5. "New Second Baseman for New York Yankees." *Los Angeles Times Sports*. 7 Feb. 1938; "Yankee Fans Will See Lots of This." *The Oregonian*. 8 Feb. 1938, p. 15.
6. Smith, Jack. "Gordon Signs with Yanks; Brilliant Future Pictured." *The Oregonian*. 12 Feb. 1938; Haupert, Michael. Haupert Baseball Salary Database, private collection.
7. Gehrig, Eleanor, and Joseph Durso. *My Luke and I*. New York: New American Library, 1976, p. 138.
8. "Freshening Up with Freshmen: Majors in the Making." *The Sporting News*. 17 Feb. 1938, p. 1.
9. Gordon Family Scrapbooks. "Ex-Brownie Figured on for Second Base if Joe Gordon Falls Down or Replaces Frankie Crosetti at Shortstop...." St. Petersburg, FL. prob. late March 1938.
10. Rennie, Rud. "Joe Gordon 'Most-Photographed' as 1,000 Fans See First Practice." *New York Herald Tribune*. 1 March 1938, p. 17.
11. Gordon, Joe, as told to Stanley Frank. "A Rookie Wonders." *Street & Smith's Sport Story*. 1 July 1938, p. 31.
12. Tebbetts, Birdie, with James Morrison. *Birdie: Confessions of a Baseball Nomad*. Chicago: Triumph, 2002.
13. Rennie, Rud. "DiMaggio Ends Holdout, Agreeing to Sign for $25,000, and Will Rejoin Yankees Saturday." *New York Herald Tribune*. 21 April 1938, p. 22.
14. Daniel, Daniel M. "Year 'Round Monthly Salaries, Ruppert Idea to Curb Hold-Outs." *The Sporting News*. 31 March 1938, p. 1.
15. Daniel, Daniel M. "Year 'Round Monthly Salaries, Ruppert Idea to Curb Hold-Outs." *The Sporting News*. 31 March 1938, p. 1.
16. Cawthon, Stanmore. "Yanks Slam Cards, 6–4, Before Record Crowd." *St. Petersburg Times*. 13 March 1938, p. 25.

17. Kieran, John. "Sports of the *Times*: Two-Gun Gehrig, in Person and a Picture." *New York Times*. 23 March 1938, p. 28.
18. Gordon Family Scrapbooks. "The success of the Yankees of 1938...." Sep. 1938.
19. Daniel, Daniel M. "M'Carthy Double-O Okays Joe Gordon." *The Sporting News*. 17 March 1938, p. 3.
20. Gordon Family Scrapbooks. Graham, Dillon. "Rookie of the Year: Joe Gordon." Tallahassee, FL. ab. 1 April 1938.
21. Daniel, Daniel M. "Year 'Round Monthly Salaries, Ruppert Idea to Curb Hold-Outs." *The Sporting News*. 31 March 1938, p. 1.
22. The 1939 World's Fair patches were worn by all three of New York City's major league baseball clubs that year (New York Yankees, Brooklyn Dodgers, and New York Giants).
23. Abramson, Jesse. "Players Gossip, Landis Frets, Fans Boo at Picket Line Delay." *New York Herald Tribune*. 23 April 1938, p. 14; Dawson, James P. "Ruffing Gives Only Four Singles in 7-to-0 Victory over Senators." *New York Times*. 23 April 1938, p. 10.
24. "Yankee Stadium," New World Encyclopedia.com, https://www.newworldencyclopedia.org/entry/Yankee_Stadium.
25. Daniel, Dan. "Yanks Jeer Critics, Cheer Star Rookies." *The Sporting News*. 9 March 1939, p. 3.
26. Levitt, Daniel R. *Ed Barrow: The Bulldog Who Built the Yankees' First Dynasty*. Lincoln: University of Nebraska Press, 2008.
27. Dawson, James P. "Ruffing Gives Only Four Singles in 7-to-0 Victory over Senators." *New York Times*. 23 April 1938, p. 10.
28. "Ball Game Pickets Halt Morris, Lyons." *New York Times*. 23 April 1938, p. 17.
29. Gordon Family Scrapbooks. Patterson, Arthur E. "Crosetti Delivers 3-Run Double and Stars Afield with Gordon." ab. 23 April 1938.
30. Drebinger, John. "Yankees' 5-Run Drive in Third Overcomes Athletics by 5 to 3." *New York Times*. 27 April 1938, p. 26.
31. Dawson, James P. "Yankees Down Red Sox with Aid of Errors;...." *New York Times*. 30 April 1938, p. 11.
32. Dawson, James P. "DiMaggio, Gordon Hurt as Yanks Win;...." *New York Times*. 1 May 1938, p. 1; "DiMaggio Injured in Crash with Gordon." *Los Angeles Examiner Sports*. 1 May 1938, p. 1.
33. Barrow, Edward Grant, with James M. Kahn. *My Fifty Years in Baseball*. New York: Coward-McCann, 1951, p. 163.
34. Newspaper photo. "The Loser in a Tangle with DiMaggio." ab. 2 May 1938.
35. Whittingham, Richard, comp. and ed. *The DiMaggio Albums, Vol. 1: 1932–1941*, 1989.
36. Gordon Family Scrapbooks. "McCarthy Says, 'No Surprise'; Saw Inferiority Complex." prob. late June 1938.
37. Daniel, Dan. "Buzas May Have Shortcomings, But It's Not in Play at Shortstop." *The Sporting News*. 10 May 1945, p. 9.
38. Gordon Family Scrapbooks. "Ex-Brownie Figured on for Second Base if Joe Gordon Falls Down or Replaces Frankie Crosetti at Shortstop;...." St. Petersburg, FL. March 1938.
39. Barrow, Edward Grant, with James M. Kahn. *My Fifty Years in Baseball*. New York: Coward-McCann, 1951, pp. 155–162.
40. Levy, Alan H. *Joe McCarthy: Architect of the Yankee Dynasty*. Jefferson, NC: McFarland, 2005, pp. 5–8; Gordon Family Scrapbooks. "Bears Also Tops in Feats of Magic." Summer 1937; "No Ban on Golf." *The Sporting News*. 7 March 1946, p. 4.
41. Allen, Maury. *Where Have You Gone, Joe DiMaggio?* New York: E.P. Dutton, 1975, p. 91.
42. Cross, Harry. "Gordon, Hit on Head, Pounds 3 Homers for Yanks in Exhibition." *New York Herald Tribune*. 17 May 1938, p. 22; "Yankees' Six Homers Overwhelm Butler." *New York Times*. 17 May 1938, p. 27.
43. Gordon Family Scrapbooks. "Autograph Seekers Break Up Ball Game." Butler, PA. ab. 17 May 1938.
44. "Boys and Girls Break Up Yanks' Game in Seventh." *Chicago Daily Tribune*. 17 May 1938, p. 23.
45. Drebinger, John. "83,533 See Yankees Win Two...." *New York Times*. 31 May 1938, p. 23.
46. Eig, Jonathan. *Luckiest Man: The Life and Death of Lou Gehrig*. New York: Simon & Schuster, 2005, pp. 251–252.
47. Gordon Family Scrapbooks. "Injury May Cost Joe Gordon Post." New York. ab. 3 June 1938.
48. Gordon Family Scrapbooks. Daniel. "Gordon New Hero of Champions." Syracuse, NY. ab. 13 June 1938.
49. Kirksey, George. "Joe Gordon: King of Second Basemen." *Look*. 28 July 1942, p. 48.
50. Marriage License: State of Maryland. Joseph Lowell Gordon and Dorthy Irene Crum. Elkton, MD. 4 June 1938.
51. Ungermann, Kathryn. *The Newton Family History*. Los Altos, CA: Kathryn Ungermann, 1993, p. 160.
52. Gordon Family Scrapbooks. "Yanks Tie Record and Beat Browns." St. Louis, MO. ab. 20 June 1938.
53. Patterson, Arthur E. "Yankees Pelt Tigers, 9 to 3; Gordon Hurt." *New York Herald Tribune Sports*. 26 June 1938, p. 1.
54. Gordon Family Scrapbooks. Smith, Jack. "Gordon Makes Grade at 2d for Yankees." ab. 29 June 1938.
55. Gordon Family Scrapbooks. Mercer, Sid. "Yanks Have .300 Hitter in Gordon." ab. 30 June 1938.
56. Patterson, Arthur E. "Yankees Win, 10–5, Tie 4–4, Sharing Lead with Indians...." *New York Herald Tribune*. 5 July 1938, p. 16.
57. Daniel, Daniel M. "Fortune Flashes June Smile on Serious Joe Gordon; Yank Rookie Wins Bride—and Second Base Job Back." *The Sporting News*. 30 June 1938, p. 3.
58. Gordon Family Scrapbooks. "Name in Book." ab. 26 July 1938.

59. Daniel, Dan. "Close Fight Turns Pressure on Yanks." *The Sporting News*. 28 July 1938, p. 3.
60. "Lou Gehrig Calls Him the Best Ever." *Chicago Daily News*. 30 July 1938.
61. Gordon Family Scrapbooks. "Joe Gordon Gains Boost by Gehrig." *The Oregonian*. ab. 31 July 1938.
62. Gross, Milton. "Money Player." *Collier's*. 18 July 1942, p. 56; Gordon Family Scrapbooks. "Diz Chased and Cubs Lose; Yanks Win, Gordon Battles." Chicago, IL. ab. 30 July 1938.
63. Allen, Maury. *Where Have You Gone, Joe DiMaggio?* New York: E.P. Dutton, 1975, pp. 90–91.
64. Gordon Family Scrapbooks. "Harris Praises Gordon's Ability." *Oregonian-Chicago Tribune Leased Wire*. ab. 15 Aug. 1938.
65. Eig, Jonathan. *Luckiest Man: The Life and Death of Lou Gehrig*. New York: Simon & Schuster, 2005, pp. 255–257.
66. Gordon Family Scrapbooks. Feder, Sid. "Yank Mound Star Blanks Tribe, 13–0." New York. ab. 27 Aug. 1938.
67. Rennie, Rud. "Gordon Hits Pair, Plus 2 Doubles...." *New York Herald Tribune*. 5 Sep. 1938, p. 19.
68. Rennie, Rud. "Gordon Hits Pair, Plus 2 Doubles...." *New York Herald Tribune*. 5 Sep. 1938, p. 19.
69. Eig, Jonathan. *Luckiest Man: The Life and Death of Lou Gehrig*. New York: Simon & Schuster, 2005, p. 257.
70. "Lou Gehrig Heaps Praise on Joe Gordon's Playing." *The Oregonian*. 10 Sep. 1938, p. 17.
71. Gordon Family Scrapbooks. "A Young Man Headed for Greatness." ab. 4 Sep. 1938.
72. Gordon Family Scrapbooks. "Yanks Lose Again to White Sox, 5–2." Chicago. ab. 21 Sep. 1938.
73. Gordon Family Scrapbooks. "New York Takes Third Flag in Row." St. Louis. ab. 18 Sep. 1938.
74. Rennie, Rud. "Browns Sweep Series, Jolting Yankees by 13–1." *New York Herald Tribune*. 20 Sep. 1938, p. 23.
75. Gordon Family Scrapbooks. Mercer, Sid. "Gordon Hit Spree Best of Career." ab. 5 June 1942.
76. Graham, Dillon. "Flash Gordon Well Named." *Lowell* (MA) *Sun*. 28 Sep. 1938.
77. Honig, Donald. *The New York Yankees: An Illustrated History*. New York: Crown, 1981.
78. Gordon Family Scrapbooks. Kahn, James M. "Yanks' Rookie Cast for Hero." Oct. 1938; Souvenir Menu. *New York "Yankees" Special*. Enroute New York to Cincinnati. Oct. 1939.
79. Newspaper photo. "Waiting for Their First Series." *Associated Press*. Sep. 1938; "Facts on Baseball Classic." *New York Times*. 6 Oct. 1937, p. 30.
80. Gordon Family Scrapbooks. "14 Yanks are Vets." Oct. 1938; Patterson, Arthur E. "Yankee Power Promises to Give McCarthy Record Third-Straight World Series Triumph." *New York Herald Tribune*. 2 Oct. 1938, p. B3.
81. Hazen, David W. "Yanks' Joe Gordon Happy Over World Series Chance." *The Oregonian*. 5 Oct. 1938.
82. "Yankees Get Jump on the Cubs by Taking First Game of Series." *The Sporting News*. 13 Oct. 1938, p. 6.
83. Gordon Family Scrapbooks. Dunkley, Charles. "Lee and Ruffing Named Starters." Chicago, IL. ab. 4 Oct. 1938; Gordon Family Scrapbooks. "KEX Will Broadcast World's Series." Chicago. ab. 4 Oct. 1938.
84. Goodrich, Hollis. "Jefferson High Proud of Sparkling Graduate." *Portland News-Telegram*. 6 Oct. 1938.
85. Hazen, David W. "Joe Gordon Stars in Play in First World Series Try." *The Oregonian (Special)*. ab. 5 Oct. 1938.
86. Rennie, Rud. "Yankees Beat Cubs, 3–1, in World Series Opener...." *New York Herald Tribune*. 6 Oct. 1938, p. 28.
87. Gallagher, Jim. "Yankee Brains, not Homers Beat Cubs." *Chicago American*. ab. 6 Oct. 1938.
88. "Gossip of Second Game." *The Sporting News*. 13 Oct. 1938, p. 6.
89. "28,000 Unreserved Seats on Sale Today." *New York Herald Tribune*. 8 Oct. 1938, p. 18.
90. Rennie, Rud. "Pearson to Oppose Bryant as Yankees Seek Third Straight Over Cubs at Stadium Today." *New York Herald Tribune*. 8 Oct. 1938, p. 18.
91. Gordon Family Scrapbooks. "Play-by-Play Traces Win for Yanks Over Cubs, 5–2." New York. ab. 8 Oct. 1938.
92. Photo. "Down, But Not Out." *The Sporting News*. 13 Oct. 1938, p. 6; "Joe Gordon Paces Yankees to 5-to-2 Win Over Cubs." *Sunday Oregonian*. 9 Oct. 1938, p. 1.
93. "Injured Umpire Will Work Today." *New York Times*. 9 Oct. 1938, p. 9.
94. Gordon Family Scrapbooks. Schumacher, Garry. "Infield Ace Crashes a Homer Tying Count and Game Winning Single." ab. 8 or 9 Oct. 1938.
95. Hazen, David W. "Joe Gordon Cubs' Waterloo as Yanks Win Third Game." *The Oregonian*. ab. 8 or 9 Oct. 1938.
96. "Injured Umpire Will Work Today." *New York Times*. 9 Oct. 1938, p. 9.
97. Lieb, Frederick G. "Grand Slam Gives Yankees 24 Wins in 27 Series Games." *The Sporting News*. 13 Oct. 1938, p. 3.
98. Dawson, James P. "McCarthy Calls Yankees Best Ever as Victors Celebrate with Song." *New York Times*. 10 Oct. 1938, p. 23.
99. Gordon Family Scrapbooks. Ferguson, Harry. "Portlander Star of Stars." New York. Oct. 1938.
100. Grayson, Harry. "Joe Gordon Stands Out as Sensational AL Rookie of 1938." *Seattle Star Sports*. 11 Oct. 1938, p. 14.
101. Farrington, Dick. "Seven American and Six National Recruits on All-Freshman Team." *The Sporting News*. 20 Oct. 1938, p. 5.

102. Gordon Family Scrapbooks. Rice, Grantland. "Sportlight by Rice." Los Angeles. ab. 12 Dec. 1938.
103. *Official Baseball Guide.* 1975. p. 270.

Chapter 8

1. Gordon Family Scrapbooks. Ferguson, Harry. "Oregon's 'Flash' Gordon Picked as Bright Young Star of Year." *United Press.* New York. ab. Dec. 1938.
2. "Athletes, Sportsmen, Leaders Saddened by Death of Ruppert." *New York Herald Tribune.* 14 Jan. 1939, p. 19.
3. "Four Trustees to Run N.Y. Club...." *The Sporting News.* 26 Jan. 1939, p. 1.
4. Barrow, Edward Grant, with James M. Kahn. *My Fifty Years in Baseball.* New York: Coward-McCann, 1951, p. 203.
5. Gordon Family Scrapbooks. "Gordon Unsigned but Not Holdout." Feb. 1939.
6. Drebinger, John. "Yankees Forward Contracts to 38." *New York Times.* 22 Jan. 1939, p. 71.
7. Daniel, Dan. "Yanks Jeer Critics, Cheer Star Rookies." *The Sporting News.* 9 March 1939, p. 3; Tofel, Richard J. *A Legend in the Making: The New York Yankees in 1939.* Chicago: Ivan R. Dee, 2002, p. 31.
8. Daniel, Dan. "Yanks Jeer Critics, Cheer Star Rookies." *The Sporting News.* 9 March 1939, p. 3.
9. Gordon Family Scrapbooks. Kirksey, George. "Yank Squad Expected to Repeat This Year." *Oregon Daily Journal.* New York. ab. 6 April 1939.
10. Barrow, Edward Grant, with James M. Kahn. *My Fifty Years in Baseball.* New York: Coward-McCann, 1951, p. 122; Gaven, Michael F. "No Charlie Kellers in Sight, but Over-Supply of Talent is Barrow's Chief 'Worry.'" *The Sporting News.* 19 Oct. 1939, p. 1.
11. Syring, Richard H. "'Flash' Gordon: 'A Good Joe!'" *Oregon Journal—Features.* 2 April 1939, p. 1.
12. "Extensive Plans Made for Baseball's Centennial Celebration." *Pittsburgh Press.* 17 Jan. 1939.
13. Williams, Ted, with John Underwood. *My Turn at Bat: The Story of My Life.* New York: Simon & Schuster, 1969, p. 59.
14. Gordon Family Scrapbooks. Stafford, Dale. "Old Age Winner at Last; 2130-Game-in-Row Player Leaves New York Lineup." Detroit. ab. 2 May 1939.
15. Gordon Family Scrapbooks. Rice, Grantland. "Sportlight by Rice: When Gehrig Cracked." prob. *The Oregonian.* ab. 29 May 1939.
16. https://1939baseball.com/cooperstown_centennial.html.
17. Rennie, Rud. "Gehrig Departs for Mayo Clinic After Playing 3 Innings...." *New York Herald Tribune.* 13 June 1939, p. 25.
18. Gehrig, Eleanor, and Joseph Durso. *My Luke and I.* New York: New American Library, 1976, pp. 10–11.
19. Daley, Arthur J. "Infantile Paralysis Terminates Gehrig's Playing Career." *New York Times.* 22 June 1939, p. 26.
20. "List of Gehrig Records in 15 Years as Yankee." *New York Herald Tribune.* 22 June 1938, p. 25.
21. "Writers Move to Place Gehrig in Hall of Fame." *New York Times.* 8 Dec. 1939, p. 35.
22. Matt Rothenberg, former manager of the Giamatti Research Center at the National Baseball Hall of Fame and Museum, explained in emails to author Judy Gordon: "Lou Gehrig received his formal induction [into the Hall of Fame] in 2013. Since the BBWAA had elected no one [for induction in 2013], and the Pre-Integration Era [C]ommittee elected three deceased individuals [Jacob Ruppert, Hank O'Day, and Deacon White], the decision was made to formally induct [Lou] Gehrig [Class of 1939], Rogers Hornsby [Class of 1942], and the 10 members of the [C]lass of 1945 [Roger Bresnahan, Dan Brouthers, Fred Clarke, Jimmy Collins, Ed Delahanty, Hugh Duffy, Hughie Jennings, Mike "King" Kelly, Jim O'Rourke, and Wilbert Robinson].... [N]o induction ceremonies [had been] held back then, though the elections [had been] held, and all 12 were duly chosen for inclusion in the Baseball Hall of Fame. The actual date [of their formal induction] was July 28, 2013."
23. Rennie, Rud. "American League Adopts Night Games and Unified Baseball with National Loop." *New York Herald Tribune.* 15 Dec. 1938, p. 27.
24. "Yankees and Tigers List Night Baseball on Road." *New York Herald Tribune.* 18 May 1939, p. 27; "White Sox Book 6 Night Games." *New York Times.* 13 Aug. 1939, p. S3.
25. Effrat, Louis. "Yankees Show Little Enthusiasm for Baseball Under Floodlights." *New York Times.* 28 June 1939, p. 25.
26. Gordon Family Scrapbooks. "Gordon Cracks Three Out of Park." Philadelphia. ab. 28 June 1939.
27. Gordon Family Scrapbooks. White, Bill. "New Home Run Record." Philadelphia. ab. 28 June 1939.
28. Henrich, Tommy, with Bill Gilbert. *Five O'Clock Lightning: Ruth, Gehrig, DiMaggio, Mantle and the Glory Years of the NY Yankees.* New York: Carol, 1992, p. 75.
29. Eig, Jonathan. *Luckiest Man: The Life and Death of Lou Gehrig.* New York: Simon & Schuster, 2005, pp. 312–317.
30. Gehrig, Eleanor, and Joseph Durso. *My Luke and I.* New York: New American Library, 1976, p. 172.
31. Tofel, Richard J. *A Legend in the Making: The New York Yankees in 1939.* Chicago: Ivan R. Dee, 2002, p. 138.
32. Harridge, William. American League Professional Base Ball Clubs. Chicago. Letter to Mr. Joseph Gordon. 3 July 1939.
33. "McCarthy Succeeds Ailing Mack as Pilot of A.L. All-Stars...." *New York Herald Tribune.* 2 July 1939, p. 2.
34. Editorial. "An American League Year?" *The Sporting News.* 23 July 1977, p. 18.

35. Gordon Family Scrapbooks. McLemore, Henry. "Sports Parade." New York. ab. 12 July 1939.
36. Gordon Family Scrapbooks. McLemore, Henry. "Sports Parade." New York. ab. 12 July 1939.
37. Patterson, Arthur E. "Classroom Baseball." *Baseball Magazine*. Oct. 1939, pp. 509–510.
38. *Touching All Bases*. The Official American League Motion Picture of 1940. 1 Jan. 1940.
39. Pamphlet. Gordon, Joe. *How to Play Second Base*. Johnstown, NY: John McGlynn, 21 Aug. 1939. AA 309855.
40. "Bears Top Yanks in 11th." *New York Times*. 22 Aug. 1939, p. 23.
41. Patterson, Arthur E. "Yankees Win Two, 7-2, 16-4." *New York Herald Tribune*. 24 Aug. 1939, p. 22.
42. Gordon Family Scrapbooks. "Joe Gordon's improvement in hitting this season...." *The Sporting News*. ab. 24 Aug. 1939.
43. "Germans Bomb Warsaw and Annex Danzig...." *New York Herald Tribune*. 1 Sep. 1939, p. 1B.
44. Photo from Academy of Sport. World's Fair. New York. Christy Walsh, Director of Sports; All America Board of Baseball. Certificate designating Joe Gordon, New York Yankees, as a member of the All America Baseball Team of 1939, approved 16 Sep. 1939. Signed by George H. Babe Ruth, Christy Walsh, and sportswriters from each of the 10 major league American cities.
45. Patterson, Arthur E. "Sundra Captures 10th Straight as Gordon Ties Assist Record." *New York Herald Tribune*. 16 Sep. 1939, p. 18.
46. Gordon Family Scrapbooks. "Yanks Cinch Pennant." New York. ab. 16 Sep. 1939.
47. 1939 MLB Season History—Major League Baseball—ESPN.
48. Daniel, Dan. "Yankees Match Power Against Pitching in Title Clash." *The Sporting News*. 5 Oct. 1939, p. 1.
49. "Derringer and Ruffing Stage Pitching Duel in Curtain-Raiser." *The Sporting News*. 12 Oct. 1939, p. 6.
50. "World Series Contests Seen by Redmond Couple." *Bend* (OR) *Bulletin*. 20 Oct. 1939, p. 3.
51. Gordon Family Scrapbooks. Smith, Jack. "Art Fletcher Hero of 1st—McCarthy." ab. 5 Oct. 1939.
52. Gordon Family Scrapbooks. "Yanks Defeat Reds, 4 to 0." Yankee Stadium, NY. ab. 5 Oct. 1939.
53. Gordon Family Scrapbooks. Dunkley, Charles. "Yank Chief is Happy Man; Crew Noisy in Clubhouse." ab. 9 Oct. 1939.
54. *Official Baseball Guide*. 1975. p. 270.
55. Daniel, Dan. "Over the Fence: This is Best Yankee Club." *The Sporting News*. 19 Oct. 1939, p. 4.
56. Lieb, Frederick G. "Precedent-Smashing Yanks Hailed as Team of Century." *The Sporting News*. 12 Oct. 1939, p. 3.
57. "World Series Contests Seen by Redmond Couple." *Bend* (OR) *Bulletin*. 20 Oct. 1939, p. 3.
58. Event program. "A Dinner by a Few of the Fans for Joe Gordon." Multnomah Athletic Club. Portland, OR. 16 Nov. 1939.
59. Gordon Family Scrapbooks. Leeding, Harry. "Tower Lights." ab. 17 Nov. 1939.

Chapter 9

1. "With all due respect to other stars of the New York Yankees...." *The Sporting News*. 18 Jan. 1940, p. 8.
2. Gordon Family Scrapbooks. "Babe Ruth Credits Joe Gordon for Yankee Dominance." New York. ab. 22 Jan. 1940.
3. Brands, Edgar G. "American Places Nine Men, Led by Yankees with Five...." *The Sporting News*. 11 Jan. 1940, p. 3.
4. Gordon Family Scrapbooks. "Fluttering around Gordon and Priddy at Bovard Field...." Los Angeles. Feb. 1940.
5. Haupert, Michael. Haupert Baseball Salary Database, private collection.
6. Rennie, Rud. "Gordon Thrills Camp Followers in His First Yankee Workout." *New York Herald Tribune*. 2 March 1940, p. 17.
7. Rennie, Rud. "Gordon Accepts Yankee Terms; Salary is Estimated at $12,500." *New York Herald Tribune*. 1 March 1940, p. 23.
8. Drebinger, John. "Yanks Appear Set at Every Position...." *New York Times*. 7 April 1940, p. S5.
9. "Off to the Baseball Wars!" *The Sporting News*. 18 April 1940, p. 8.
10. Strite, Dick. "Highclimber." *Eugene Register-Guard*. 16 Oct. 1940, p. 10.
11. Rennie, Rud. "Yanks Start Against A's Today, Sans DiMaggio, Maybe Ruffing." *New York Herald Tribune*. 16 April 1940, p. 26.
12. Rennie, Rud. "Yanks Start Against A's Today, Sans DiMaggio, Maybe Ruffing." *New York Herald Tribune*. 16 April 1940, p. 26.
13. Gordon Family Scrapbooks. McLemore, Henry. "N.Y. Infield Star Claims Cleveland is 'One to Beat.'" United Press. ab. 18 Feb. 1941.
14. Dawson, James P. "Yanks Lose to Athletics in 10th...." *New York Times*. 17 April 1940, p. 30.
15. Gordon Family Scrapbooks. "The Brilliant fielding of Second Baseman Joe Gordon...." ab. 25 April 1940.
16. Gordon Family Scrapbooks. White, Bill. New York. ab. 19 April 1940.
17. Rennie, Rud. ". . . Yankees Win Stadium Inaugural, 5–3." *New York Herald Tribune*. 20 April 1940, p. 17.
18. Gordon Family Scrapbooks. "Yanks Divide with Boston." New York. ab. 30 May 1940.
19. Drebinger, John. "Six Yankees Picked for Eighth Battle." *New York Times*. 7 July 1940, p. S3.
20. Gordon Family Scrapbooks. Bailey, Judson. "West's Homer Paces Victory for Nationals." Sportsman's Park, St. Louis. ab. 9 July 1940.
21. Daniel, Dan. "11 Yankees Listed as Being on Spot, Fighting for Jobs." *The Sporting News*. 18 July 1940, p. 1.
22. Gordon Family Scrapbooks. Segar, Charles.

"Yanks Get 5 in 3rd on Browns; Ruffing Pitches." St. Louis. ab. 25 July 1940; Patterson, Arthur E. "... Yankees Rout Browns, 13–8, with 16 Hits." *New York Herald Tribune*. 26 July 1940, p. 17.

23. Gordon Family Scrapbooks. McDonough, Pat. "Gordon at Lead-off Puts Pep in Yanks." Aug. 1940.

24. Gordon Family Scrapbooks. "Hitting of Top of Yank Batting Order Credited as Reason for Current Streak." ab. 15 Aug. 1940.

25. Gordon Family Scrapbooks. Mercer, Sid. "Gordon Batting .544 as Leadoff Hitter." ab. 14 Aug. 1940.

26. Drebinger, John. "Yanks Run Streak to 5 in Row...." *New York Times*. 14 Aug. 1940, p. 25.

27. http://www.captainsblog.info/2010/09/09/libeling-lou-iron-horse-sues-to-restore-his-name-80-years-ago-today/2534/.

28. Powers, Jimmy. "Has 'Polio' Hit the Yankees?" *Sunday Daily News*. 18 Aug. 1940, p. C32; Powers, Jimmy. "Slumping Yanks": *Sunday Daily News*. 18 Aug. 1940, p. C32.

29. Powers, Jimmy. "Has 'Polio' Hit the Yankees?" *Sunday Daily News*. 18 Aug. 1940, p. C32.

30. Gehrig, Eleanor, and Joseph Durso. *My Luke and I*. New York: New American Library, 1976, pp. 10–11.

31. Powers, Jimmy. "Our Apologies to Lou Gehrig and the Yankees." *New York Daily News*. 26 Sep. 1940, p. 58.

32. Powers, Jimmy. "Slumping Yanks": *Sunday Daily News*. 18 Aug. 1940, p. C32.

33. Eig, Jonathan. *Luckiest Man: The Life and Death of Lou Gehrig*. New York: Simon & Schuster, 2005, p. 347–348; "Plea for Delay Reveals Gehrig's Suit for $1,000,000 Damages for Libel." *New York Herald Tribune*. 10 Sep. 1940, p. 31.

34. Gordon Family Scrapbooks. "Yank Players Ask Damages in Libel Action." New York. ab. 24 Oct. 1940.

35. Madden, Bill. *Pride of October: What It Was to Be Young and a Yankee*. New York: Warner, 2008.

36. "Yankees Lose 2 Farm Hands in Fall Draw." *New York Herald Tribune*. 4 Oct. 1939, p. 26; "Babich Guns for Champs." *The Sporting News*. 19 Sep. 1940, p. 10.

37. Gordon Family Scrapbooks. "Yanks Win Two." New York. ab. 29 Aug. 1940.

38. Gordon Family Scrapbooks. "Pennant Race at a Glance." *Associated Press*. ab. 5 Sep. 1940.

39. Hurley, Jim. "Joe Gordon's BIGGEST MOMENT." *Sport*. Sep. 1947, p. 70.

40. Gordon Family Scrapbooks. "It looks as if the Giants will have to build the 1941 season around Babe Young...." ab. 9 Sep. 1940.

41. Gordon Family Scrapbooks. Mahon, Jack. "Yanks Rip Nats Twice, 6–5, 9–4." ab. 25 Sep. 1940.

42. Gordon Family Scrapbooks. "A Slogan Starts a Pennant March." Sep. 1940.

43. "'Ifs' of Pennant Race in American League." *New York Herald Tribune*. 26 Sep. 1940, p. 24.

44. Gordon Family Scrapbooks. Rice, Grantland. "The Sportlight: Still Shooting." ab. 25 Sep. 1940.

45. Powers, Jimmy. "Our Apologies to Lou Gehrig and the Yankees." *New York Daily News*. 26 Sep. 1940, p. 58.

46. "Babich Guns for Champs." *The Sporting News*. 19 Sep. 1940, p. 10.

47. Drebinger, John. "Tigers Clinch Pennant by Blanking Indians while Athletics Defeat Yankees." *New York Times*. 28 Sep. 1940, p. 10.

48. Effrat, Louis. "Babich Gives 5 Hits to Down Yanks, 6–2." *New York Times*. 28 Sep. 1940, p. 10.

49. Gordon Family Scrapbooks. Salsinger, H.G. "The Umpire: Disadvantage." 1941.

50. Gordon Family Scrapbooks. McLemore, Henry. "N.Y. Infield Star Claims Cleveland is 'One to Beat.'" *United Press*. Los Angeles. ab. 18 Feb. 1941.

51. Strite, Dick. "Highclimber." *Eugene Register-Guard*. 16 Oct. 1940, p. 10.

52. *Pilot's Flight Log* of Joe L. Gordon. 28 Dec. 1940–14 Sep. 1942.

Chapter 10

1. Gordon Family Scrapbooks. Robinson, Pat. "Yankee Purge to Continue." *International News Service*. New York. ab. 3 Jan. 1941.

2. Kirksey, George. "Yankees Rated as Team to Beat." *Oregon Journal*. 9 Jan. 1941, p. 16.

3. McLemore, Henry. "McLemore Says: "Joe Gordon and Other 'Veterans' of Yankee Squad Must Battle for Posts. *Oregon Journal*. 18 Feb. 1941, p. 13.

4. Brands, Edgar G. "Eight Out of 16 Clubs Place Players on All-Star Team of 1940." *The Sporting News*. 9 Jan. 1941, p. 5.

5. Gordon Family Scrapbooks. "The Joe Gordons packed up their baggage...." Feb. 1941.

6. "Gordon Unsigned." *New York Daily News*. ab. 28 Feb. 1941.

7. Dawson, James P. "Yankees Sell First-Baseman [sic] Dahlgren to Bees in Straight Cash Transaction." *New York Times*. 26 Feb. 1941. p. 25.

8. Many years later, Babe Dahlgren's grandson, Matt Dahlgren, would write a book about what happened to his grandfather during the early spring of 1941; Dahlgren, Matt. *Rumor in Town: A Grandson's Promise to Right a Wrong*. California: Woodlyn Lane, 2007, pp. 121–125.

9. Rennie, Rud. "Yankees Sell Dahlgren to Bees for Estimated $15,000, Sturm Succeeding Him 'for Present.'" *New York Herald Tribune*. 26 Feb. 1941, p. 23.

10. Daniel, Daniel M. "Trigger Gordon of Bombers, Going Back to Second, Put Pennant Click in Infield That Floundered at First." *The Sporting News*. 2 Oct. 1941, p. 3.

11. "Joe Gordon Arrives at Yankee Camp to Talk Contract Matters." *Eugene Register-Guard*. 28 Feb. 1941, p. 10.

12. Daniel, Dan. "Marse Joe Pins Eyes on His

New Kid Infield." *The Sporting News.* 27 Feb. 1941, p. 12.

13. Gordon Family Scrapbooks. "Gordon Question Mark." St. Petersburg. ab. 27 Feb. 1941.

14. Gordon Family Scrapbooks. "Gordon Gets Job at First." St. Petersburg. ab. 3 March 1941; American League of Professional Baseball Clubs: Uniform Player's Contract for Joseph Gordon. 4 March 1941.

15. Daniel, Daniel M. "Trigger Gordon of Bombers, Going Back to Second, Put Pennant Click in Infield That Floundered at First." *The Sporting News.* 2 Oct. 1941, p. 3.

16. Gordon Family Scrapbooks. "Gordon Gets Job at First." St. Petersburg. ab. 3 March 1941.

17. Gordon Family Scrapbooks. Daniel. "Keystone Star Takes Over Job Vacated by Dahlgren." *World-Telegram* Staff Correspondent. St. Petersburg. ab. 4 March 1941.

18. Daniel, Daniel M. "Trigger Gordon of Bombers, Going Back to Second, Put Pennant Click in Infield That Floundered at First." *The Sporting News.* 2 Oct. 1941, p. 3.

19. Gordon Family Scrapbooks. Witwer, Stan. "McCarthy Gives First Base Position to Gordon." *Times.* ab. 5 March 1941.

20. Rennie, Rud. "McCarthy, in Surprise Move, Picks Gordon to Play First Base After Second Sacker Signs." *New York Herald Tribune.* 4 March 1941, p. 26.

21. Gordon Family Scrapbooks. Daniel. "Gordon at 1st, Priddy at 2nd Still Experiments." Washington, D.C. ab. 19 April 1941.

22. Madden, Bill. *Pride of October: What It Was to Be Young and a Yankee.* New York: Warner, 2008; Madden, Bill. Email to Judy Gordon. 30 May 2016.

23. Marazzi, Rich, and Len Fiorito. *Baseball Players of the 1950s: A Biographical Dictionary of All 1,560 Major Leaguers.* Jefferson, NC: McFarland, 2004, p. 313.

24. Gordon Family Scrapbooks. Kirksey, George. "Yankees' Shift of Joe Gordon Interests Rival First-Sackers." San Antonio. Spring 1941.

25. Gordon Family Scrapbooks. Kirksey, George. "Gordon Just Can't Miss: Joe to Handle First for Yankees." San Antonio. ab. 10 March 1941.

26. Kieran, John. "Sports of the *Times*: Looking Around with Lou Gehrig." *New York Times.* 16 March 1941, p. 2S.

27. Gordon Family Scrapbooks. "Play First? Why Not, Says Gordon." *New York World-Telegram.* ab. 4 March 1941.

28. Gordon Family Scrapbooks. McLemore, Henry. "Mrs. Joe Gordon Bit Jittery Over Joe's New First-Base Job." St. Petersburg. ab. 21 March 1941.

29. Gordon Family Scrapbooks. "Yankee Infield is Impressive." 14 March 1941, p. 15.

30. Gordon Family Scrapbooks. "Calling Joe Gordon the greatest all-around player in the major leagues today...." prob. March 1941.

31. *Pilot's Flight Log* of Joe L. Gordon. 28 Dec. 1940–14 Sep. 1942.

32. Gordon Family Scrapbooks. Bailey, Judson. "Yankees Beat Nats, 3 to 0, in Opener." Washington, D.C. ab. 14 April 1941.

33. Gordon Family Scrapbooks. Stan, Francis E. "Win, Lose or Draw." prob. April 1941.

34. Gordon Family Scrapbooks. Daniel. "Gordon at 1st, Priddy at 2nd Still Experiments." Washington, D.C. ab. 19 April 1941.

35. Gordon Family Scrapbooks. Daniel. "Gordon at 1st, Priddy at 2nd Still Experiments." Washington, D.C. ab. 19 April 1941.

36. Rennie, Rud. "Yankees Conquer Indians, 2–0, 5–3." *New York Herald Tribune.* 2 June 1941, p. 17.

37. Newspaper photo. "Yankees Pause in Tribute to Former Teammate—Lou Gehrig." *The Oregonian.* 4 June 1941.

38. Smith, Jack. "Yanks Nip Tribe, 6–4; Trail 1st by Game: Diamond Dust." *New York Daily News.* 17 June 1941, p. 42.

39. Smith, Jack. "Crosetti Spiked; Out Five Days." *New York Daily News.* 17 June 1941, p. 42.

40. Daniel, Daniel M. "Trigger Gordon of Bombers, Going Back to Second, Put Pennant Click in Infield That Floundered at First." *The Sporting News.* 2 Oct. 1941, p. 3.

41. Young, Dick. "Young Ideas." *The Sporting News.* 29 April 1978, p. 15.

42. Broeg, Bob. "DiMag at Best in First of Ten World Series." *The Sporting News.* 4 Sep. 1971, p. 17.

43. Cramer, Richard Ben. *Joe DiMaggio: The Hero's Life.* New York: Simon & Schuster, 2000, p. 170.

44. Kennedy, Kostya. **56**: *Joe DiMaggio and the Last Magic Number in Sports.* New York: Sports Illustrated Books, 2011.

45. Kennedy, Kostya. **56**: *Joe DiMaggio and the Last Magic Number in Sports.* New York: Sports Illustrated Books, 2011; Broeg, Bob. "DiMag at Best in First of Ten World Series." *The Sporting News.* 4 Sep. 1971, p. 17.

46. Broeg, Bob. "DiMag at Best in First of Ten World Series." *The Sporting News.* 4 Sep. 1971, p. 17.

47. McDonough, Pat. "Thomson No. 1 Actor in Two Homer Strings." *The Sporting News.* 22 July 1953, p. 4.

48. Fischer, David. *100 Things Yankees Fans Should Know & Do Before They Die.* Chicago: Triumph, 2012, p. 7.

49. Gordon Family Scrapbooks. Considine, Bob. "DiMaggio Ties Batting Mark Set by Keeler." New York. ab. 1 July 1941; Gordon Family Scrapbooks. Bailey, Judson. "Joe DiMaggio Hits in 45th as Yanks Win." New York. ab. 2 July 1941.

50. Harridge, William. American League Professional Base Ball Clubs. Chicago. Letter to Mr. Joseph Gordon. 30 June 1941.

51. Gordon Family Scrapbooks. Lieb, Frederick G. "Nationals' Big All-Star Error Was in Not Getting Williams Out." ab. 8 July 1941; Boudreau, Lou, with Ed Fitzgerald. *Player-Manager.* Boston: Little, Brown, 1949, p. 51.

52. Gordon Family Scrapbooks. Smith, Jack. "AL Defeats NL, 7–5, in 9th on Williams' Three-Run Homer." Detroit. ab. 8 July 1941.
53. "Yankees Menace Double Play Record." *New York World-Telegram.* 11 July 1941.
54. Gordon Family Scrapbooks. Segar, Charles. "DiMaggio Hits in 50 Straight." St. Louis. ab. 11 July 1941.
55. McAuley, Ed. "Keltner Reaches End of Trail as an Indian." *The Sporting News.* 19 April 1950, p. 13.
56. Gordon Family Scrapbooks. Smith, Jack. "DiMag Streak Halted by Smith and Bagby as Yanks Cop 4–3." Cleveland. ab. 17 July 1941.
57. Gordon Family Scrapbooks. "Yanks Defeat Browns, 1–0." New York. ab. 9 Sep. 1941.
58. Strite, Dick. "Highclimber: By Joe Gordon, Second Baseman, New York Yankees." *Eugene Register-Guard.* 30 July 1941, p. 6.
59. The authors believe this may have been a major league record for the best winning percentage for the month of July, at least up to that time.
60. Gordon Family Scrapbooks. Cobbledick, Gordon. "Plain Dealing: Gordon's Return to Keystone Sack Supplies Spark for Yankees' Sensational Spurt to the Top." *Cleveland Plain Dealer.* ab. 22 July 1941.
61. "Champs of the U.S.A. Set No. 21." Wheaties "Breakfast of Champions." 1941.
62. http://cerealpriceguide.blogspot.com/2013/04/wheaties-cereal-box-price-guide.html.
63. "Tommy Dorsey Entertains Members of 'Yankee' Team." *Bernardsville* (NJ) *News.* 31 July 1941.
64. Gordon Family Scrapbooks. Grayson, Harry. "Bucky Harris Rates Joe Gordon on Best Second Baseman and Gordon-Rizzuto Best All-Time 2nd-Base Combination." ab. 12 Aug. 1941.
65. Gordon Family Scrapbooks. Talbot, Gayle. "Yankee Infield Combination Rated Best in Short Series." New York. ab. 24 Sep. 1941.
66. Daniel, Dan. "Flea and Flash, Skilled Defense." *The Sporting News.* 28 Aug. 1941.
67. McCann, Dick. "Yankees Clinch Flag by Beating Red Sox, 6–3." *Daily News.* 5 Sep. 1941, p. 56.
68. McCarthy, Joe. Handwritten note addressed to Clyde Sayles and Andy Lampert, reading, "Compliments of the New York Yankees from Joe McCarthy." ab. 30 Sep. 1941.
69. Gordon Family Scrapbooks. "Yank Wives Cheer Brooklyn—So Near!" Sep. 1941.
70. Some baseball pundits, however, do not consider either the 1921 or 1922 World Series as "real" Subway Series, because, back then, the Yankees and the New York Giants shared the Polo Grounds as their home stadium; Fischer, David. *100 Things Yankees Fans Should Know & Do Before They Die.* Chicago: Triumph, 2012, pp. 128–129.
71. Newspaper photo. "They're Both a Hit: Two Flashes." ab. 30 Sep. 1941; *International News* photos of Joe Gordon and Alex Raymond at Yankee Stadium. 30 Sep. 1941.
72. http://baseballhall.org/hof/gordon-joe.
73. Gordon Family Scrapbooks. "Yanks Win, 3–2." *New York Daily News.* ab 2 Oct. 1941.
74. Gordon Family Scrapbooks. "Dodgers Beat Yankees 3–2." New York. ab. 2 Oct. 1941.
75. Gordon Family Scrapbooks. Ferguson, Harry. "Joe Gordon Looms as Hero of Series—Unless He Breaks a Leg before Long." New York. ab. 3 Oct. 1941.
76. Gordon Family Scrapbooks. Ferguson, Harry. "Joe Gordon Real Hero of 1941 World Series." New York. ab. 7 Oct. 1941.
77. Newspaper cartoon. Jenkins, Burris, Jr. "The Brooklyn Chain System." prob. 3 Oct. 1941.
78. Gordon Family Scrapbooks. Ferguson, Harry. "Joe Gordon Real Hero of 1941 World Series." New York. ab. 7 Oct. 1941.
79. Powers, Jimmy. "The Power House." *New York Daily News.* 3 Oct. 1941, p. 64.
80. Brooklyn Dodgers Media Guide. 1941.
81. Dunkley, Charles. "Fitz or Higbe Listed Friday." *The Oregonian.* 3 Oct. 1941, p. 3.
82. Gordon Family Scrapbooks. Considine, Bob. "On the Line: Fitzsimmons' Dramatic Exit from Game Should be Remembered for All Time." New York. ab. 4 Oct. 1941.
83. Zeltner, Edward. "Yankees Win 7 to 4 on Owen's Error, Break in 9th Costs B'klyn Game." *New York Daily Mirror.* 6 Oct. 1941.
84. Gordon Family Scrapbooks. "3–1 Win Gives Title to Yankees." Brooklyn. ab. 7 Oct. 1941.
85. Smith, Jack. "Yankees Win Series; Bonham's 4–Hitter Bests Wyatt, 3–1." *New York Daily News.* 7 Oct. 1941, p. 46.
86. Gordon Family Scrapbooks. Corum, Bill. "Sports: Nobody Gave the Yankees This One." *New York Journal American.* prob. Oct. 1941.
87. O'Connor, Leslie M., Secretary-Treasurer. Baseball Office of the Commissioner. Letter to New York American League Club Players. 18 Oct. 1941; Official Baseball Guide. 1975. p. 270.
88. "Joe Gordon's Mother Home." *The Oregonian.* 9 Oct. 1941, p. 3.
89. Gordon Family Scrapbooks. The Old Scout. "MacPhail Picks Best Players." prob. Oct. 1941.
90. Gordon Family Scrapbooks. McLemore, Henry. "From First to Last It Was Joe Gordon." Brooklyn. ab. 7 Oct. 1941.
91. Gordon Family Scrapbooks. McLemore, Henry. "From First to Last It Was Joe Gordon." Brooklyn. ab. 7 Oct. 1941.
92. Henrich, Tommy, with Bill Gilbert. *Five O'Clock Lightning: Ruth, Gehrig, DiMaggio, Mantle and the Glory Years of the NY Yankees.* New York: Carol, 1992, p. 128.
93. Gordon Family Scrapbooks. Williams, Joe. "By Joe Williams: Joe Gordon—The Real Story of World Series." prob. Oct. 1941.
94. Gross, Milton. "Gordon Stands Out as Star of Series." *New York Post.* 7 Oct. 1941.
95. Gordon Family Scrapbooks. Considine,

Bob. "Pilot Votes Gordon Best All-Around." *Omaha Morning World-Herald.* ab. 7 Oct. 1941.
  96. "Joe Gordon's Mother Home." *The Oregonian.* 9 Oct. 1941, p. 3.
  97. Gordon Family Scrapbooks. "Gordon Voted Series 'Finest.'" New York. ab. 7 Oct. 1941; "Joe Gordon Crowned." *The Sporting News.* 16 Oct. 1941, p. 4.
  98. Doerr, Don. Son of Hall of Fame second baseman Bobby Doerr. Email correspondence with Judy Gordon. 22–23 Oct. 2020.

Chapter 11

  1. *Pilot's Flight Log* of Joe L. Gordon. 28 Dec. 1940–14 Sep. 1942.
  2. Private Pilot Airman Certificate No. 133880 issued to Joe Lowell Gordon on 5 Jan. 1942.
  3. Brands, Edgar G. "Yankee Outfielder Heads Squad for Fifth Consecutive Season; Dickey Returns for Sixth Year." *The Sporting News.* 8 Jan. 1942, p. 7.
  4. Berryman, Jim. Cartoon: "First at Second . . . These Keystone Tenders . . . Who Are in Middle in Defense." *The Sporting News.* 15 Jan. 1942, p. 1.
  5. Daniel, Dan. "Joe Gordon Succeeds Gehringer as High Man at Position Whose Guardian Makes or Breaks Team." *The Sporting News.* 15 Jan. 1942, p. 1.
  6. www.archives.gov/publications/prologue/2002/spring/greenlight.html; United States President Franklin D. Roosevelt. "Green Light Letter" to Hon. Kenesaw M. Landis, Commissioner of Major League Baseball. 15 Jan. 1942; http://baseballhall.org/discover/short-stops/keep-baseball-going.
  7. Gordon Family Scrapbooks. "Joe Gordon Off for Florida to Start Training." Eugene. ab. 9 Feb. 1942.
  8. Gordon Family Scrapbooks. Photo of Bill Dickey, Vernon Rickard, Joe Gordon, and Babe Ruth. Wrigley Field. Los Angeles. 18 Feb. 1942.
  9. "Richest Spring Dish for St. Pete Feast." *The Sporting News.* 15 Jan. 1942, p. 6.
  10. "Rolfe, Yankee Third Baseman, May be Forced to Retire Because of Recurring Colitis." *New York Herald Tribune.* 11 March 1942, p. 22.
  11. *Pilot's Flight Log* of Joe L. Gordon. 28 Dec. 1940–14 Sep. 1942.
  12. Private Pilot Airman Certificate No. 133880 Seaplane Rating issued to Joe Lowell Gordon on 10 June 1942.
  13. Wright, S.T. "Gordon—Due to Be G.I. Joe." *Morning Oregonian.* 9 Jan. 1944, p. 5.
  14. Gordon Family Scrapbooks. O'Brien, Pat. "Yanks Bounce Senators, 7–0, in First Tilt." Washington, D.C. ab. 14 April 1942.
  15. Gordon Family Scrapbooks. McShane, Bob. "Speaking of Sports." prob. April 1942.
  16. Leeding, Harry. "Tower Lights: Usually Flashy Joe Gordon Has Awful Time Buying Base Hits Early in Season." *Oregon Journal.* 27 April 1942, p. 12.
  17. Gordon Family Scrapbooks. "Gordon Lost to Yankees 'Indefinitely.'" New York. ab. 30 April 1942.
  18. Gordon Family Scrapbooks. "Gordon Halts Playing Streak." New York. ab. 30 April 1942.
  19. Gordon Family Scrapbooks. "Baseball's Big Six." *Associated Press.* ab. 14 June 1942; https://newyork.sbnation.com/new-york-yankees/2012/7/24/3178445/
  20. Gordon Family Scrapbooks. "Yankees Hit Stride by Chilling Rivals on Big–Inning Bogie." New York. ab. 1 May 1942.
  21. Gordon Family Scrapbooks. "Baseball's Big Six." *Associated Press.* ab. 26 May 1942; Newspaper photo. "Plenty of Basehits in These Four Bats." *The Oregonian.* 27 May 1942.
  22. Considine, Bob. "On the Line: Can Gordon Lead League in Hitting? If the Guy Could Only Field!" *New York Daily Mirror.* 19 May 1942, p. 28.
  23. Gordon Family Scrapbooks. Smith, Jack. "Yanks Win Two, 6–1, 5–4; Gordon Stopped at 29." *Daily News.* ab. 15 June 1942.
  24. https://newyork.sbnation.com/new-york-yankees/2012/7/24/3178445/
  25. Gordon Family Scrapbooks. "Nine Yanks Gain All-Star Squad of A.L." *International News Service.* prob. late June 1942; Gordon Family Scrapbooks. Smith, Jack. "A.L. All-Stars Lead; Boudreau, York Homer." prob. 7 July. 1942.
  26. Gordon Family Scrapbooks. Bailey, Judson. "Lou Boudreau and York Poke Out Four-Baggers." Polo Grounds, New York. ab. 6 July 1942.
  27. Cobbledick, Gordon. "Plain Dealing: Victorious Team is Best Cross Section of A.L.'s Strength Ever to Take Field." *Cleveland Plain Dealer.* 7 July 1942, p. 14.
  28. Patterson, Arthur E. "Military and Baseball Pageant Enthralls Fans at Cleveland." *New York Herald Tribune.* 8 July 1942, p. 21.
  29. Cross, Harry. "American League All-Stars Triumph Over All-Service Nine, 5–0, in Night Game at Cleveland." *New York Herald Tribune.* 8 July 1942, p. 21.
  30. Gordon Family Scrapbooks. "Baseball's Big Six (Three leaders in each league)." *Associated Press.* Chicago, IL. ab. 14 Aug. 1942.
  31. Gordon Family Scrapbooks. "Gordon Atop Hit Parade." *United Press.* New York. ab. 8 Aug. 1942.
  32. Rennie, Rud. "Yankees Set Double-Play Mark with 7 in 11–2 Rout of Athletics." *New York Herald Tribune.* 15 Aug. 1942, p. 14.
  33. Gordon Family Scrapbooks. "Bruce Campbell's 'Eight Magicians.'" ab. 14 Aug. 1942.
  34. Gordon Family Scrapbooks. "Bruce Campbell's 'Eight Magicians.'" ab. 14 Aug. 1942.
  35. Gordon Family Scrapbooks. Daniel, Dan. "Yanks 7 Double Plays in One Game All-Time Mark." Philadelphia. ab. 15 Aug. 1942.
  36. www.espn.com/mlb/story/_/id/24404246/chicago-cubs-turn-mlb-record-tying-7-double-plays-win.
  37. Gordon Family Scrapbooks. Feder, Sid.

"Ruth Swats 2 Homers Off Johnson's Pitches." *Associated Press.* New York. ab. 23 Aug. 1942.

38. Rennie, Rud. "Yankees Split Army–Navy Relief Bill with Senators as 69,136 Pay Homage to Babe Ruth." *New York Herald Tribune.* 24 Aug. 1942, p. 14.

39. Rennie, Rud. "Fans Roar Tribute as Henrich Plays Last Game for Yankees." *New York Herald Tribune.* 31 Aug. 1942, p. 18.

40. Newspaper photo. "Ernie 'Tiny' Bonham not only pitched the Yankees…." *The Oregonian.* 15 Sep. 1942, p. 1.

41. Gordon, Joe. Letter to his mother, Louise Gordon, from Boston. 27 Sep. 1942.

42. Gordon Family Scrapbooks. Considine, Bob. "Ruffing Hurls Masterpiece…." St. Louis. ab. 30 Sep. 1942.

43. Gordon Family Scrapbooks. Considine, Bob. "Cards Whitewash Yanks, 2–0, to Assume World Series Lead." New York. ab. 3 Oct. 1942.

44. Newspaper photo. "Here's the Play That Caused the Big Argument." ab. 3 Oct. 1942.

45. Gordon Family Scrapbooks. Considine, Bob. "Cards Whitewash Yanks, 2–0, to Assume World Series Lead." New York. ab. 3 Oct. 1942; Editorial. "And They Thought the Judge Had Forgotten." *The Sporting News.* 12 Nov. 1942, p. 4.

46. Editorial. "And They Thought the Judge Had Forgotten." *The Sporting News.* 12 Nov. 1942, p. 4; Gordon Family Scrapbooks. "Crosetti Fined $250, Suspended 30 Days." Chicago. ab. 6 Nov. 1942.

47. Gordon Family Scrapbooks. Considine, Bob. "National Champs Near World Series Triumph." New York. ab. 4 Oct. 1942.

48. Gordon Family Scrapbooks. Considine, Bob. "Kurowski Pokes Homer for 4-to-2 Triumph; Long Yank Reign Ended." New York. ab. 5 Oct. 1942.

49. Einstein, Charles, ed. *The Fireside Book of Baseball.* New York: Simon & Schuster, 1956, pp. 233–234.

50. Rice, Grantland. "Veteran Scribe Rates Yankees Far Ahead of Field." *The Oregonian.* 12 March 1946, p. 2.

51. *Official Baseball Guide.* 1975. p. 270.

52. Editorial. "A Four-Way Service in Wartime." *The Sporting News.* 12 Nov. 1942, p. 4.

53. "These World Series Upsets Fooled Fans and Experts." Article from *This Week Magazine* of 29 Sep. 1957 printed in the *New York Herald.* 29 Sep. 1957, p. SM8.

54. Gordon Family Scrapbooks. "Gordon Hunts in Bend Area." Eugene. ab. 15 Oct. 1942.

55. Gordon Family Scrapbooks. Bailey, Judson. "Gordon American League's Most Valuable; Pesky Third." *The Oregonian.* ab. 3 Nov. 1942.

56. "Award 'Floors' Joe at His Eugene Home." *Oregon Journal.* 4 Nov. 1942, p. 19.

57. Brands, Edgar G. "Rickey, Southworth, Williams Receive Top Ranking for Year." *The Sporting News.* 31 Dec. 1942, p. 1.

58. Patterson, Arthur E. "Williams to Receive Baseball Writers' Player-of-Year Trophy at Dinner Feb. 7." *New York Herald Tribune.* 18 Jan. 1943, p. 19; Baseball's Triple Crown is a highly acclaimed achievement by a player who leads or ties the lead for his league in all three batting categories: batting average, home runs, and RBI.

59. Williams, Ted, with John Underwood. *My Turn at Bat: The Story of My Life.* New York: Simon & Schuster, 1969, p. 92.

60. Williams, Ted, with John Underwood. *My Turn at Bat: The Story of My Life.* New York: Simon & Schuster, 1969, p. 263.

61. Tramel, Berry. "Baseball's History Shows OKC Star Will Be MVP." *Oklahoman.* ab. 26 June 2017, p. B3.

62. "Scribbled by Scribes: Williams vs. Gordon Controversy." *The Sporting News.* 12 Nov. 1942, p. 4.

63. Gordon Family Scrapbooks. Turkin, Hy. "Yankees Win Pennant; Chandler Cops in 14th." ab. 26 Sep. 1943.

64. Drebinger, John. "Yankees Homers Help Beat Indians Twice…." *New York Times.* 27 Sep. 1943, p. 25.

65. Levitt, Daniel R. Email to Judy Gordon. ab. 9 May 2016.

66. Brands, Edgar G. "Seven Aces Break into All-Star Line-Up for First Time." *The Sporting News.* 14 Jan. 1943, p. 5.

Chapter 12

1. "Curtailment of Baseball Travel Asked by Transportation Head." *New York Herald Tribune.* 1 Dec. 1942, p. 27.

2. "Majors Postpone Start of Baseball Season to April 21 and Close to Oct. 3." *New York Times.* 6 Jan. 1943, p. 20.

3. Cross, Harry. "Yankees Announce Selection of Asbury Park as Training Site…." *New York Herald Tribune.* 12 Jan. 1943, p. 23.

4. Patterson, Arthur E. "Barrow Predicts Yankees Will Win Pennant Again Despite Loss of Personnel to Services." *New York Herald Tribune.* 26 Jan. 1943, p. 22.

5. Rennie, Rud. "Yankees Acquire Weatherly and Grimes in Trade for Rosar and Cullenbine." *New York Herald Tribune.* 18 Dec. 1942, p. 35.

6. Rennie, Rud. "Yankees Send Priddy and Candini to Senators for Zuber and Cash." *New York Herald Tribune.* 30 Jan. 1943, p. 17.

7. The military draft status III-A (also written as 3-A) included men with dependents, who were not engaged in a national defense occupation. Van Hyning, Thomas. "Atley Donald." SABR Biography Project, https://sabr.org/bioproj/person/atley-donald/.

8. Drebinger, John. "Barrow Forwards Player Contracts." *New York Times.* 30 Jan. 1943, p. 20.

9. "Joe DiMaggio Joins Army Today as Voluntary Inductee;…." *New York Times.* 17 Feb. 1943, p. 27.

10. Strite, Dick. "Highclimber." *Eugene Register-Guard.* 15 Dec. 1943, p. 12.

11. Strite, Dick. "Highclimber." *Eugene Register-Guard.*" 22 Dec. 1942, p. 10; Gordon Family

Scrapbooks. "Joe Gordon in Top Condition." ab. 30 March 1943.
	12. "Plane Crackup, Contract Minor Troubles Faced by Joe Gordon." *Eugene Register-Guard*. 16 March 1943, p. 5; Gordon Family Scrapbooks. "Yankee Infielder Escapes Klamath Plane Accident." Klamath Falls, OR. ab. 16 March 1943.
	13. Gordon Family Scrapbooks. "Luck Deserts Baseball Ace." Eugene. ab. 17 March 1943; "Joe Gordon of the Yankees has quit flying and sold his plane." *The Sporting News*. 8 April 1943, p. 13; The authors have only the first of Joe Gordon's several *Pilot's Flight Log* books, which covers the period from 28 Dec. 1940–14 Sep. 1942.
	14. Rennie, Rud. "Yankee Vanguard Arrives at Asbury Park for Start of Spring Training Today." *New York Herald Tribune*. 15 March 1943, p. 17; Dawson, James P. "Yankees Have Made Final Salary Offers to Gordon and Keller, Says Barrow." *New York Times*. 27 March 1943, p. 18.
	15. Haupert, Michael. Haupert Baseball Salary Database, private collection; Rennie, Rud. "Gordon Accepts Yankees' Terms and Is En Route to Join Squad." *New York Herald Tribune*. 30 March 1943, p. 23.
	16. Dawson, James P. "Gordon Reaches Agreement with Yanks on Salary." *New York Times*. 30 March 1943, p. 24.
	17. Editorial. "And They Thought the Judge Had Forgotten." *The Sporting News*. 12 Nov. 1942, p. 4.
	18. Patterson, Arthur E. "Barrow Predicts Yankees Will Win Pennant Again Despite Loss of Personnel to Services." *New York Herald Tribune*. 26 Jan. 1943, p. 22.
	19. Gordon Family Scrapbooks. McLemore, Henry. "N.Y. Infield Star Claims Cleveland is 'One to Beat.'" *United Press*. ab. 18 Feb. 1941.
	20. "Exhibition Card Set by American League: New York." *New York Times*. 8 March 1943, p. 19; Rennie, Rud. "Spring Bases Call Yankees, 9 Other Clubs." *New York Herald Tribune*. 14 March 1943, p. 1.
	21. Abramson, Jesse. "Flag-Raising Fizzle Fails to Put Jinx on Yankees in Inaugural." *New York Herald Tribune*." 23 April 1943, p. 24.
	22. Rennie, Rud. "Yankees Need Sun and Work, Says McCarthy." *New York Herald Tribune*. 16 April 1943, p. 26.
	23. Morgan, Phyllis. "1943 and 1946 Trips to New York to Live with Dorothy [sic] and Joe Gordon and Their Children…."; Morgan, Phyllis. Letter to Judy Gordon. ab. 2010;. "New York Yankees and the Gordons." Letter to Judy Gordon. 25 Oct. 2004.
	24. Rennie, Rud. "Baseball Inaugurals for Yankees and Dodgers Put Off to Today." *New York Herald Tribune*. 22 April 1943, p. 24.
	25. Abramson, Jesse. "Flag-Raising Fizzle Fails to Put Jinx on Yankees in Inaugural." *New York Herald Tribune*." 23 April 1943, p. 24.
	26. Smith, Jack. "Yanks Nip Nats in 9th, 5–4; 6,225 See Gordon Homer." *New York Daily News*. 23 April 1943, p. 42.
	27. https://www.baseball-reference.com/bullpen/Balata_ball.
	28. Gordon Family Scrapbooks. Cashman, John. "Manager Eyes Gordon Slump." New York. ab. 22 May 1943.
	29. Gordon Family Scrapbooks. "Yankees Trim Athletics, 8–2." Philadelphia. ab. 10 June 1943.
	30. "Big Leagues Ready for All-Star Game." *New York Times*. 11 July 1943, p. S3.
	31. Lieb, Frederick G. "Lieb Dusts Off Old All-Star Sparklers." *The Sporting News*. 13 July 1960, p. 5.
	32. Levy, Alan H. *Joe McCarthy: Architect of the Yankee Dynasty*. Jefferson, NC: McFarland, 2005, p. 292.
	33. Lieb, Frederick G. "Lieb Dusts Off Old All-Star Sparklers." *The Sporting News*. 13 July 1960, p. 5.
	34. Rennie, Rud. "American League All-Stars Defeat Nationals, 5–3, Routing Cooper for Second Year in a Row." *New York Herald Tribune*. 14 July 1943, p. 24.
	35. Patterson, Arthur E. "Yankees Play Spectator Role at Shibe Park." *New York Herald Tribune*. Late City Edition. 14 July 1943, p. 24.
	36. https://thatballsouttahere.com/2015/07/14/phillys-first-all-star-game/; Cross, Harry. "America's Fighters at Fronts Listen in on Majors' Classic." *New York Herald Tribune*. Late City Edition. 14 July 1943, p. 24.
	37. Gordon Family Scrapbooks. Rice, Grantland. "The Sportlight: Yankee Manager Praises Joe Gordon as Ideal Type of Team Player." ab. 7 Aug. 1943.
	38. Gordon Family Scrapbooks. "Browns Win, Gordon Hurt." St. Louis. ab. 10 Aug. 1943.
	39. Gordon Family Scrapbooks. Turkin, Hy. "Stars Top Army, 5–2; Medwick Hits Homer." ab. 27 Aug. 1943.
	40. "Bond Stars Beat Army, 5–2: The Babe and the Big Train…." *New York Daily News*. 27 Aug. 1943, p. 44.
	41. "Star-Laden Army Team Will Play Today Against Yankee-Giant-Dodger Combine." *New York Herald Tribune*. 26 Aug. 1943, p. 19; Drebinger, John. "40,000 War Bond Buyers Thrill to Baseball Spectacle and Variety Program." *New York Times*. 27 Aug. 1943, p. 11.
	42. Daley, Arthur. "Sports of the *Times*: The War Bond Game." *New York Times*. 27 Aug. 1943, p. 11.
	43. Gordon Family Scrapbooks. "Gordon in Old Form at Plate." *New York Journal-American*. ab. 21 Aug. 1943.
	44. Gordon Family Scrapbooks. Turkin, Hy. "Yankees Win Pennant; Chandler Cops in 14th." ab. 26 Sep. 1943.
	45. Gordon Family Scrapbooks. "Yanks Set League Mark; Whip Browns Twice, 5–1, 7–6." ab. 2 Oct. 1943.
	46. Wright, S.T. "Gordon to Be G.I. Joe." *Morning Oregonian*. 9 Jan. 1944, p. 5.
	47. Cross, Harry. "The Setting Was Major league…." *New York Herald Tribune*. 6 Oct. 1943, p. 31.

48. Bailey, Judson. "Yanks Win World Series Opener, 4–2; Gordon Shines Afield, Hits Home Run." *The Oregonian.* 6 Oct. 1943, p. 1.

49. Gordon Family Scrapbooks. Cuddy, Jack. "Gordon, Lanier Hero, Goat of Opening Scrap." New York. ab. 6 Oct. 1943.

50. Effrat, Louis. "Lanier Wild Pitch Topples Redbirds." *New York Times.* 6 Oct. 1943, p. 27.

51. From a graphic displayed on TV sometime after Cody Bellinger hit a home run in Game One of the 2020 World Series. The authors believe this probably appeared on TV during Game Two of the 2020 World Series.

52. Gordon Family Scrapbooks. Bailey, Judson. "Coopers' Father Passes Just Before Game Time; Brothers Refuse to Quit." Yankee Stadium, New York. ab. 6 Oct. 1943.

53. Bailey, Judson. "Yankees Explode in Eighth to Turn Back Cards, 6–2;...." *The Oregonian.* 8 Oct. 1943, p. 25.

54. Gordon Family Scrapbooks. Bailey, Judson. "Yanks Edge Cards, 2–1, Behind Russo to Move within Single Game of Title." Sportsman's Park, St. Louis. ab. 10 Oct. 1943.

55. Gordon Family Scrapbooks. Feder, Sid. "Dickey's Home Run Gives Yankees Series Victory; Final Game Ends 2–0 as Cards Blow Scoring Chances." prob. *The Oregonian.* Sportsman's Park, St. Louis. ab. 11 Oct. 1943, p. 1

56. *Official Baseball Guide.* 1975. p. 270.

57. Drebinger, John. "Yanks' Alertness Vital in Triumph." *New York Times.* 13 Oct. 1943, p. 31.

58. Gordon Family Scrapbooks. "12 New Marks Set in Series." St. Louis. ab. 11 Oct. 1943.

59. Gordon Family Scrapbooks. "'Flash' Gordon Sets Three New World Series Records." St. Louis. ab. 12 Oct. 1943.

60. "Final Composite Score of World Series Contests." *New York Tribune.* 13 Oct. 1916, p. 12.

61. Gordon Family Scrapbooks. "'Flash' Gordon Sets Three New World Series Records." St. Louis. ab. 12 Oct. 1943.

62. Bailey, Judson. "Yanks Win World Series Opener, 4–2; Gordon Shines Afield, Hits Home Run." *The Oregonian.* 6 Oct. 1943, p. 1.

63. Gordon Family Scrapbooks. Fraley, Oscar. "St. Louis Baseball Writers Pan Southworth's Attitude." New York. ab. 12 Oct. 1943.

64. Parker, Dan. "Parker Pens Series 'Standouts.'" *The Sporting News.* 21 Oct. 1943, p. 7.

65. Branagan, Marlowe. "Tower Lights: Cards' Failure to Hit in Pinches Major Reason for Series Failure." *Oregon Journal.* 13 Oct. 1943, p. 14.

66. Gordon Family Scrapbooks. Rice, Grantland. "The Sportlight by Grantland Rice." New York. ab. 13 Oct. 1943.

67. Brands, Edgar G. "No. 1 Men Named in Majors and Minors." *The Sporting News.* 30 Dec. 1943, p. 1.

68. "Joe McCarthy Gets Manager of Year Title." *Chicago Daily Tribune.* 29 Dec. 1943, p. 18.

69. Brands, Edgar G. "No. 1 Men Named in Majors and Minors." *The Sporting News.* 30 Dec. 1943, p. 1.

70. Morgan, Phyllis. "New York Yankees and the Gordons." 25 Oct. 2004.

71. Gordon Family Scrapbooks. "Joe Gordon Collects Deer, Ducks on Trip." Eugene. ab. 28 Oct. 1943.

72. "Gordon Again to 'Quit' Ball." *The Oregonian.* 20 Oct. 1943, p. 1.

73. "Joe Gordon Quits Baseball 'for Good,' And This Time He May Even Mean It." *New York Herald Tribune.* 20 Oct. 1943, p. 25.

74. "Joe Gordon, Tired of Game, Says He Will Quit Baseball for Good." *New York Times.* 20 Oct. 1943, p. 26.

75. Levitt, Daniel R. *Ed Barrow: The Bulldog Who Built the Yankees' First Dynasty.* **Lincoln:** University of Nebraska Press, 2008.

76. "Yanks in Dark on Gordon." *New York Times.* 21 Oct. 1943, p. 33.

77. Carver, Lawton. "Gordon's 'Quit' Decision Still Baseball Puzzle." *The Oregonian.* 22 Oct. 1943, p. 2.

78. Daniel, Dan. "Over the Fence: Yet, There May Be Something to It." *The Sporting News.* 28 Oct. 1943, p. 8.

79. "Gordon Denies Quit Rumor." *The Oregonian.* 3 Nov. 1943, p. 2.

80. "Not Quitting Baseball, Joe Gordon Declares." *New York Times.* 3 Nov. 1943, p. 30.

81. "Major league Clubs Ordered by Landis to Train at Northern Camps Again." *New York Times.* 21 Oct. 1943, p. 33.

82. Drebinger, John. "McCarthy Bars Training at Home While Yanks Are in Atlantic City." *New York Times.* 19 Nov. 1943, p. 26.

83. Patterson, Arthur E. "McCarthy Says Yankees Need Third Catcher, New Outfielder." *New York Herald Tribune.* 19 Nov. 1943, p. 25.

84. Daniel, Dan. "Flash Makes Hash Out of Quitting Yarn. *The Sporting News.* 4 Nov. 1943, p. 6.

85. "Joe Gordon a Walking Ad for 'Ducks Unlimited.'" *New York Herald Tribune.* 19 Nov. 1943, p. 25.

86. Patterson, Arthur E. "Gordon to Enter Armed Service; Yankee Infield Plans Muddled." *New York Herald Tribune.* 17 Dec. 1943, p. 24.

87. "Gordon Scoffs at Quit Talk; Bags 4-Pointer." *The Oregonian.* 29 Oct. 1943, p. 1.

88. Williams, Joe. "Back in Old Stride: Barrow Burrows into Job." *The Sporting News.* 16 Dec. 1943, p. 8.

89. "Gordon Plans to Enter Army This Winter." *The Oregonian.* 17 Dec. 1943, p. 1.

90. Patterson, Arthur E. "Barrow, Back on Job, Declares Yankees Should Repeat in 1944." *New York Herald Tribune.* 18 Dec. 1943, p. 15A.

91. Daniel, Dan. "Gordon's Service Flash Jams Bombers '44 Aims." *The Sporting News.* 23 Dec. 1943, p. 17.

92. Daniel, Dan. "Gordon Plans Physical Test for U.S. Duty." *The Sporting News.* 6 Jan. 1944, p. 14.

93. Polier, Sgt. Dan. "Sports: Joe Gordon is Driving Barrow to a Section 8." *Yank: The Army Weekly.* 23 Jan. 1944, p. 20.

94. "Joe Gordon Quits Baseball 'for Good'; And This time He May Even Mean It." *New York Herald Tribune*. 20 Oct. 1943, p. 25.
95. Gregory, L.H. "Greg's Gossip." *The Oregonian*. 19 Dec. 1943, pp. 1, 3.
96. Strite, Dick. "Highclimber." *Eugene Register-Guard*. 15 Dec. 1943, p. 12.

Chapter 13

1. Woodman, Don. "Baseball Star A-1 in Draft." *The Oregonian*. ab. 17 March 1944; "Gordon Passes Army Pre-Induction Exam." *Oregon Journal*. 17 March 1944, p. 6.
2. "McCarthy Unhappy." *The Oregonian*. 18 March 1944, p. 1.
3. Dawson, James P. "Joe Gordon of Yanks Accepted for Army Service. *New York Times*. 18 March 1944, p. 17.
4. "Gordon Flashes for Oregonians." *Morning Oregonian*. 6 Feb. 1944, p. 2.
5. "Gordon Paces Eugene Stars." *The Oregonian*. 7 April 1944, p. 1.
6. Army of the United States. Enlisted Record and Report of Separation Honorable Discharge for Joseph L. Gordon. 14 Nov. 1945.
7. Gordon Family Scrapbooks. Dooley, Sgt. Ed. "Out of Baseball but Still a Yank." prob. *Sunday Oregonian*. ab. 7 Jan. 1945.
8. Tebbetts, Birdie, with James Morrison. *Birdie: Confessions of a Baseball Nomad*. Chicago: Triumph, 2002; "Tebbetts Brings Waco First Good Baseball Team." *St. Petersburg Times*. 6 April 1944.
9. Spink, J.G. Taylor. "Game Must Find Jobs for 4,000 Vets: Huge Problem Faced Under Preference Act." *The Sporting News*. 26 Oct. 1944, p. 9.
10. Gordon Family Scrapbooks. "Camp Luna Gets Pvt. Joe Gordon." Las Vegas, NM. ab. 17 May 1944.
11. Landis, Kenesaw M. Commissioner of Major League Baseball. Letter to Joseph Gordon. 25 May 1944.
12. Editorial. "Concentration of Players Growing." *The Sporting News*. 11 Nov. 1943, p. 8.
13. Army of the United States. Enlisted Record and Report of Separation Honorable Discharge for Joseph L. Gordon. 14 Nov. 1945.
14. "G-I Joe Shines with Army Nine." *The Oregonian*. 25 May 1944, p. 1.
15. "Gordon's Service Nine Bills Play." *Sunday Oregonian*. 4 June 1944, p. 3.
16. "GI Joe Gordon Shining at Short for Army Team." *The Sporting News*. 15 June 1944, p. 12.
17. "Gordon's Nine Tops." *The Oregonian*. 5 July 1944, p. 2.
18. Gordon, Dottie. Letter to Joe Gordon's mother, Louise Gordon, from Las Vegas, NM. 7 June 1944.
19. "Army Moving Aces from Camp Teams." *New York Times*. 30 May 1944, p. 18; Frye, William. "Army Ends Gold-Brick Teams, Putting Athletes in Combat Units." *New York Herald Tribune*. 30 May 1944, p. 20.
20. Gordon Family Scrapbooks. Dooley, Sgt. Ed. "Out of Baseball but Still a Yank." prob. *Sunday Oregonian*. ab. 7 Jan. 1945.
21. Gregory, L.H. "Greg's Gossip." *The Oregonian*. 2 Aug. 1944, p. 1.
22. Cramer, Richard Ben. *Joe DiMaggio: The Hero's Life*. New York: Simon & Schuster, 2000, p. 211.
23. Army of the United States. Enlisted Record and Report of Separation Honorable Discharge for Joseph L. Gordon. 14 Nov. 1945; "Gordon Aligned with Air Force." *The Oregonian*. 17 July 1944, p. 1.
24. Bedingfield, Gary. *Baseball in Hawaii During World War II*. Baseball in Wartime Publishing, 2021.
25. Karst, Gene. "Big Leaguers' Missionary Work Among GI's to Produce Many Stars for O.B., Says Gordon." *The Sporting News*. 8 March 1945, p. 12.
26. Karst, Gene. "Big Leaguers' Missionary Work Among GI's to Produce Many Stars for O.B., Says Gordon." *The Sporting News*. 8 March 1945, p. 12.
27. Gordon Family Scrapbooks. "Joe Gordon Becomes a Switch Hitter." Summer 1944.
28. Karst, Gene. "Big Leaguers' Missionary Work Among GI's to Produce Many Stars for O.B., Says Gordon." *The Sporting News*. 8 March 1945, p. 12.
29. Gregory, L.H. "Greg's Gossip: Navy Brings in Reinforcements." *The Oregonian*. 18 Sep. 1944, p. 1.
30. Karst, Gene. "Big Leaguers' Missionary Work Among GI's to Produce Many Stars for O.B., Says Gordon." *The Sporting News*. 8 March 1945, p. 12; Magazine photo. McGurn, Sgt. Barrett. "Man at Work." *Yank: The Army Weekly*. prob. Summer 1944.
31. 7th AAF photo (A-2, HQ-7thAAF, APO 953). Joe Gordon and Captain Donal Broesamle. Territory of Hawaii. prob. summer 1944.
32. HQ & HQ Squadron, VII Fighter Command, Office of the Operations Officer, APO 953. Pvt. Joe Gordon, flight logs from 2 Aug. 1944 through 26 Oct. 1944, signed by Captain Donal J. Broesamle.
33. "Nimrod Association of the World." Charter membership certificate. Summer or fall of 1944; Gordon, Joe. Letter to his mother, Louise Gordon, from Territory of Hawaii. 1 Sep. 1944.
34. Gregory, L.H. "Greg's Gossip: Navy Brings in Reinforcements." *The Oregonian*. 18 Sep. 1944, p. 1.
35. Bedingfield, Gary. *Baseball in Hawaii During World War II*. Baseball in Wartime Publishing, 2021, pp. 106, 112; "Service Teams Set for Pacific 'World Series.'" *New York Herald Tribune*. 22 Sep. 1944, p. 25.
36. Gregory, L.H. "Greg's Gossip: Navy Brings in Reinforcements." *The Oregonian*. 18 Sep. 1944, p. 1; Gordon Family Scrapbooks. "DiMaggio, Mize Left Off Central Pacific All-Stars." prob. Sep. 1944.
37. Karst, Gene. "Big Leaguers' Missionary Work Among GI's to Produce Many Stars for O.B.,

Says Gordon." *The Sporting News.* 8 March 1945, p. 12.

38. Photo. "Major Leaguers Manning Mike in Australia." *The Sporting News.* 5 Oct. 1944, p. 19; Gregory, L.H. "Greg's Gossip: Navy Brings in Reinforcements." *The Oregonian.* 18 Sep. 1944, p. 1.

39. Strong, Clarence. *Sports: Service World's Series Special.* Submarine Base, Navy No. 128. 15 Nov. 1944, pp. 1–8.

40. "Service Teams Set for Pacific 'World Series.'" *New York Herald Tribune.* 22 Sep. 1944, p. 25.

41. Bedingfield, Gary. *Baseball in Hawaii During World War II.* Baseball in Wartime Publishing, 2021, pp. 90–100.

42. Except when cited otherwise, information about the first seven games of the 1944 Army–Navy World Series in Hawaii is from: Strong, Clarence. *Sports: Service World's Series Special.* Submarine Base, Navy No. 128. 15 Nov. 1944, pp. 1–8.

43. Drebinger, John. "DiMaggio Headed for Atlantic City." *New York Times.* 22 Nov. 1944, p. 23.

44. Elias, Robert. *The Empire Strikes Out: How Baseball Sold U.S. Foreign Policy and Promoted the American Way Abroad.* New York: New Press, 2010.

45. "Tickets Gone, Seabees Build Stand." *The Sporting News.* 5 Oct. 1944, p. 19.

46. "Navy Sinks Army Twice in Service World Series." *The Sporting News.* 28 Sep. 1944, p. 12.

47. "Joe DiMaggio, Here on Furlough, Says He Knows Nothing About Quitting Army." *New York Herald Tribune.* 22 Nov. 1944, p. 23A.

48. "Navy Guns Blast Army Four Straight to Romp in Pacific World's Series." *The Sporting News.* 5 Oct. 1944, p. 19.

49. Bedingfield, Gary. *Baseball in Hawaii During World War II.* Baseball in Wartime Publishing, 2021, pp. 97–98; "Navy Captures Seven of Nine in Pacific Set." *The Sporting News.* 12 Oct. 1944, p. 16.

50. "GI Joe Gordon Gets Furlough." *Eugene Register-Guard.* 23 Nov. 1944, p. 20.

51. Gordon Family Scrapbooks. Dooley, Sgt. Ed. "Out of Baseball but Still a Yank." prob. *Sunday Oregonian.* ab. 7 Jan. 1945.

52. Gordon, Joe. Letter to his mother, Louise Gordon, from San Rafael, CA. 9 March 1945.

53. Gordon Family Scrapbooks. Dooley, Sgt. Ed. "Out of Baseball but Still a Yank." prob. *Sunday Oregonian.* ab. 7 Jan. 1945.

54. Gordon, Joe. Letter to his mother, Louise Gordon, from San Rafael, CA. 16 Jan. 1945.

55. "Gordon Comes Up with Winner." *The Sporting News.* 5 April 1945, p. 11.

56. Gordon Family Scrapbooks. "Oaks Get Revenge." Boyes Springs, CA. ab. 14 March 1945; Gordon Family Scrapbooks. "Joe Gordon's Hamilton Field Fliers...." San Francisco. ab. 17 March 1945.

57. "Joe Gordon has been placed in charge of the 'March of Dimes' program...." *The Sporting News.* 11 Jan. 1945, p. 14.

58. "Hot Stove League"—A nickname for informal get-togethers of baseball afficionados, taking place after the World Series and before spring training—no games, yet lots of gossip and telling of tall tales, while sitting around a hot stove.

59. Speer, Stan. "Caught on the Fly: Tidbits from the Knife and Fork Circuit—Alameda Party Draws 1,000." *The Sporting News.* 22 Feb. 1945, p. 12.

60. http://vallejomuseum.blogspot.com/2014/06/the-boys-of-summer-visit-mare-island.html; "A group consisting of Ty Cob, Oscar Vitt,...." *The Sporting News.* 22 Feb. 1945, p. 14.

61. Gordon Family Scrapbooks. "Big League Stars to Clash in Benefit Game at Stadium." ab. 7 April 1945; "Stars in Benefit." *San Francisco Examiner.* 8 April 1945, p. 17.

62. AFATC Enlisted Personnel Branch, Washington D.C. War Department Restricted Messageform to Commanding General, Pacific Division, Air Transport Command, Hamilton Field, CA. 25 April 1945.

63. AFATC Enlisted Personnel Branch, Washington D.C. War Department Restricted Messageform to Commanding General, Pacific Division, Air Transport Command, Hamilton Field, CA. 25 April 1945.

64. Army of the United States. Enlisted Record and Report of Separation Honorable Discharge for Joseph L. Gordon. 14 Nov. 1945.

65. Photo of 12 members of the Wheeler Field Wingmen baseball team at their final game in Hawaii. 16 June 1945.

66. Gordon, Joe. Letter to his mother, Louise Gordon, from Oahu, Territory of Hawaii. 16 June 1945.

67. Gordon, Joe. Letter to his mother, Louise Gordon, from Tinian, Northern Mariana Islands. 11 July 1945.

68. Cochran, Jacqueline. "Peace Comes to Tinian." *Liberty.* 27 Oct. 1945, p. 94.

69. Gordon, Joe. Letter to his mother, Louise Gordon, from Tinian, Northern Mariana Islands. 23 July 1945.

70. "In the Service: Star-Studded Army Clubs Stage Series in Marianas." *The Sporting News.* 9 Aug. 1945, p. 13.

71. "Gordon Homers in Army Clash." *The Oregonian.* 30 July 1945, p. 2.

72. "Gordon Used as 'Ringer' in Pacific Softball Game." *The Sporting News.* 9 Aug. 1945, p. 13.

73. Gordon Family Scrapbooks. Newland, Russ. "Fun is Where You Find It: Censors Would Have Had Last Word in Any Event." San Francisco. 13 Aug. 1945.

74. Bedingfield, Gary. *Baseball in Hawaii During World War II.* Baseball in Wartime Publishing, 2021.

75. Gordon, Joe. Letter to his mother, Louise Gordon, from Tinian, Northern Mariana Islands. 11 Aug. 1945.

76. https://blog.newspapers.com/august-15-1945-the-75th-anniversary-of-v-j-day/.

77. Gordon, Joe. Letter to his mother from Tinian, Northern Mariana Islands. 16 Aug. 1945.

78. Silvera, Charlie. Phone conversation with Judy Gordon. 13 July 2015.
79. Flyer. "AAF All Stars POA." Mariana Islands. late Aug. 1945.
80. "N.L. Stars Tie Series in Pacific." *The Sporting News*. 20 Sep. 1945, p. 12.
81. Gordon, Joe. Letter to his mother, Louise Gordon, from Tinian, Northern Mariana Islands. 27 Aug. 1945.
82. "N.L. Stars Tie Series in Pacific." *The Sporting News*. 20 Sep. 1945, p. 12; "Red Schuessler Longs to See Tide Roll." *Birmingham (AL) News*. 8 Oct. 1945.
83. Anton, Todd W. *No Greater Love: Life Stories from the Men Who Saved Baseball*. Burlington, MA: Rounder, 2007, pp. 144–146.
84. Tebbetts, Birdie, with James Morrison. *Birdie: Confessions of a Baseball Nomad*. Chicago: Triumph, 2002.
85. Anton, Todd W. *No Greater Love: Life Stories from the Men Who Saved Baseball*. Burlington, MA: Rounder, 2007, p. 145.
86. Tebbetts, Birdie, with James Morrison. *Birdie: Confessions of a Baseball Nomad*. Chicago: Triumph, 2002.
87. Anton, Todd W. *No Greater Love: Life Stories from the Men Who Saved Baseball*. Burlington, MA: Rounder, 2007, p. 146.
88. Kritzer, Cy. "Rojek, Pacific Vet, Well-Armed for Dodger Infield Fight." *The Sporting News*. 6 Dec. 1945, p. 8.
89. Gordon, Joe. Letter to his mother, Louise Gordon, from Tinian, Northern Mariana Islands. 5 Sep. 1945.
90. Flyer. "USASTAF Special Services Presents Its Major League Baseball Stars." Guam. Sep. 1945; Wood, Hal. "Service Major Leaguers Feel Return Means Hustle." *Oregon Journal*. 18 Oct. 1945, p. 15.
91. Gordon, Joe. Letter to his mother, Louise Gordon, from Guam. 12 Sep. 1945.
92. Gordon, Joe. Letter to his mother, Louise Gordon, from Guam. 20 Sep. 1945.
93. Gordon, Joe. Letter to his mother, Louise Gordon, from Guam. 28 Sep. 1945.
94. "Tebbetts Sent Back to U.S. from Pacific." *Detroit Free Press*. 4 Nov. 1945.
95. Army of the United States. Enlisted Record and Report of Separation Honorable Discharge for Joseph L. Gordon. 14 Nov. 1945.
96. Joseph L. Gordon Corporal of the 58th Bomb Wing Honorable Discharge from the Army of the United States at the Separation Center, Camp Beale, California. 14 Nov. 1945.
97. Gordon Family Scrapbooks. "Gordon Visits Eugene Home." Eugene. ab. 29 Nov. 1945.
98. Gordon Family Scrapbooks. "Gordon Tells Scribe He or Stirnweiss May Be Traded." New York. ab. 8 Feb. 1946.
99. Spink, J.G. Taylor. "Game Must Find Jobs for 4,000 Vets; Huge Problem Faced Under Preference Act." *The Sporting News*. 26 Oct. 1944, p. 9; Obermeyer, Jeff. *Baseball and the Bottom Line in World War II: Gunning for Profits on the Home Front*. Jefferson, NC: McFarland, 2013.

Chapter 14

1. Gordon, Joe. Letter to his mother, Louise Gordon, from New York. 13 Aug. 1946.
2. Levitt, Daniel R. *Ed Barrow: The Bulldog Who Built the Yankees' First Dynasty*. Lincoln: University of Nebraska Press, 2008.
3. www.baseball-almanac.com/teams/yankquot.shtml.
4. Drebinger, John. "M'Phail Will Rule as the Sole Boss in New Yank Set-Up." *New York Times*. 28 Jan. 1945, p. S1.
5. Lauder, Bill, Jr. "Barrow Quits His 26-Year Post with Yankee Empire He Built." *New York Herald Tribune*. 9 Jan. 1947, p. 26A.
6. Barrow, Edward Grant, with James M. Kahn. *My Fifty Years in Baseball*. New York: Coward-McCann, 1951, p. 207.
7. Daniel, Dan. "Weiss Makes His Debut in Role of Yank Trader." *The Sporting News*. 6 Dec. 1945, p. 8.
8. Daley, Arthur. "Sports of the *Times*: A Baseball Empire Changes Hands." *New York Times*. 27 Jan. 1945, p. 16.
9. Daniel, Dan. "Major Leaguers to Play Around World to '46." *The Sporting News*. 27 Sep. 1945, p. 1.
10. Creamer, Robert W. *Baseball in '41: A Celebration of the "Best Baseball Season Ever"—In the Year America Went to War*. New York: Penguin, 1991, p. 109.
11. Daniel, Dan. "More Drastic Overhaul for Yanks Looms." *The Sporting News*. 11 Oct. 1945, p. 10.
12. "Yanks to Maintain Two Spring Camps." *New York Times*. 31 Oct. 1945, p. 27; "Yankee Squad to Train in Two Florida Camps." *New York Herald Tribune*. 31 Oct. 1945, p. 32.
13. Daniel, Dan. "Marse Joe to be Man in a Boat with 70 Yanks and Two Sides of Tampa Bay and Ferry to Ride." *The Sporting News*. 15 Nov. 1945, p. 7.
14. Daniel, Dan. "Yankee Shineup Program Will Include Lights, with Seating Capacity Increased to 80,000." *The Sporting News*. 25 Oct. 1945, p. 8.
15. Gordon Family Scrapbooks. Considine, Bob. "Yankee Team to Break Up; Gordon Plans to Join Navy." *International News Service*. St. Louis, MO. ab. 29 Sep. 1942.
16. Daniel, Dan. "Weiss Makes His Debut in Role of Yank Trader." *The Sporting News*. 6 Dec. 1945, p. 8.
17. Strite, Dick. "Highclimber: January 1 marked the start of a gradual intensified training program...." *Eugene Register-Guard*. 3 Jan. 1946, p. 12.
18. Strite, Dick. "Big Chance Didn't Roll." *The Sporting Goods Dealer*. March 1947, p. 166.
19. "Wives Still Feel War's Impact." *The Sporting News*. 17 Jan. 1946, p. 12; www.tampabay.com/opinion/columns/column-when-d-day-came-to-st-petersburg/2183157/.
20. Daniel, Dan. "Dickey's Role in Yankees'

Setup Hinges on Art Fletcher's Return." *The Sporting News.* 27 Dec. 1945, p. 9.

21. Cooke, Bob. "Yankees Sign Rolfe, Former Third Baseman, as Coach to Fill Post Left Vacant by Fletcher." *New York Herald Tribune.* 8 Jan. 1946, p. 21A.

22. Daniel, Dan. "War Vets in Center Ring of Yanks' Spring Circus." *The Sporting News.* 31 Jan. 1946, p. 6.

23. Smith, Red. "Views of Sport: Join MacPhail and See the World." *New York Herald Tribune.* 26 Jan. 1946, p. 16A.

24. Drebinger, John. "M'Phail Reveals Big Yank Program." *New York Times.* 8 Jan. 1946, p. 19.

25. "15 to Get $20,000 to $60,000." *The Sporting News.* 31 Jan. 1946, p. 1.

26. Rennie, Rud. "Yankees Start Panama Flight this Morning." *New York Herald Tribune.* 9 Feb. 1946, p. 15.

27. Dawson, James P. "Yankees Welcomed in Canal Zone on Arrival for Training Campaign." *New York Times.* 10 Feb. 1946, p. 75.

28. Daniel, Dan. "Latin-American Countries Seek Personal Appearances by Stars." *The Sporting News.* 14 March 1946, p. 2; Photo. "Where Yankees are Putting Up in Panama: Proclaimed by a Huge Sign." *The Sporting News.* 21 Feb. 1946, p. 6; Rennie, Rud. "Yankees Reach Panama; Start Practice Today." *New York Herald Tribune.* 10 Feb. 1946, p. B1; Rennie, Rud. "Little Rizzuto Hands Balboa Biggest Thrill." *New York Herald Tribune.* 14 Feb. 1946, p. 31A.

29. Silvera, Charlie. Phone interview with Judy Gordon. 13 Oct. 2014.

30. Dawson, James P. "Yankees Cut Loose with Long Hitting." *New York Times.* 12 Feb. 1946, p. 30; Rennie, Rud. "Yankees Hot in First Workout (The Canal Zone Heat Was On)." *New York Herald Tribune.* 11 Feb. 1946, p. 23; Dawson, James P. "32 Yankees Start Drills in Panama." *New York Times.* 11 Feb. 1946, p. 35.

31. Dawson, James P. "Yankees Cut Loose with Long Hitting." *New York Times.* 12 Feb. 1946, p. 30.

32. Dawson, James P. "Yankees Cut Loose with Long Hitting." *New York Times.* 12 Feb. 1946, p. 30.

33. Rennie, Rud. "Little Rizzuto Hands Balboa Biggest Thrill." *New York Herald Tribune.* 14 Feb. 1946, p. 31A.

34. "Joe Gordon, second baseman, is not having any trouble...." *The Sporting News.* 21 Feb. 1946, p. 13.

35. Dawson, James P. "Stirnweiss Looms as Third Baseman." *New York Times.* 16 Feb. 1946, p. 8; "Stirnweiss Says He Is Entitled to Pay Increase." *New York Herald Tribune.* 17 Feb. 1946, p. B1.

36. Gross, Milton. "Senor Joe of Los Yanquis Makes Debut as Diplomat." *The Sporting News.* 21 Feb. 1946, p. 6; Dawson, James P. "Rizzuto's Playing Helps His Side Win Yanks' Camp Game." *New York Times.* 17 Feb. 1946, p. 77.

37. Rennie, Rud. "MacPhail Due in Balboa Camp of Yanks Today." *New York Herald Tribune.* 18 Feb. 1946, p. 20; Rennie, Rud. "Yankees Put on Home Run Show for MacPhail." *New York Herald Tribune.* 20 Feb. 1946, p. 27A.

38. Schoor, Gene. *The Scooter: The Phil Rizzuto Story.* New York: Charles Scribner's Sons, 1982, pp. 90–91.

39. Dawson, James P. "Rizzuto Leads Off for Yankees Today." *New York Times.* 21 Feb. 1946, p. 25.

40. Dawson, James P. "Tropical Sun Aid to Breuer's Arm: Yankees Welcomed to Panama by Its President." *New York Times.* 15 Feb. 1946, p. 32.

41. Rennie, Rud. "Yankees Open Panama Tour with All-Stars." *New York Herald Tribune.* 21 Feb. 1946, p. 23.

42. Rennie, Rud. "Yankees Defeat Panama Stars in Their First Exhibition, 5 to 4." *New York Herald Tribune.* 22 Feb. 1946, p. 25.

43. Rennie, Rud. "DiMaggio and Henrich Homers Help Yankees Beat Service All-Stars, 12–4, at Cristobal." *New York Herald Tribune.* 26 Feb. 1946, p. 29.

44. Smith, Red. "Views of Sport: MacPhail Makes His Presence Felt." *New York Herald Tribune.* 27 Feb. 1946, p. 29.

45. "Henrich Fastest Yankee in Going Down to First." *The Sporting News.* 21 March 1946, p. 5.

46. "Star on Way to Florida." *New York Times.* 1 March 1946, p. 24.

47. Dawson, James P. "Yanks Lose, 5–4, in Panama Finale on Bockman's Wild Toss in Ninth." *New York Times.* 4 March 1946, p. 18.

48. Dawson, James P. "Yanks Lose, 5–4, in Panama Finale on Bockman's Wild Toss in Ninth." *New York Times.* 4 March 1946, p. 18; "Yank Outfield Provided Big Punch in Panama Set." *The Sporting News.* 14 March 1946, p. 8.

49. Daniel, Dan. "Yankees from Panama Join Florida Contingent." *The Sporting News.* 7 March 1946, p. 4.

50. Gordon, Joe. Letter to his mother, Louise Gordon, from St. Petersburg. 8 March 1946.

51. Dawson, James P. "Gordon is Spiked as Yanks Lose, 3–2." *New York Times.* 20 March 1946, p. 32; Rennie, Rud. "Cardinals Snap 7–Game Yankee Streak, 3–2, on Homer in 9th...." *New York Herald Tribune.* 20 March 1946, p. 28A.

52. Dawson, James P. "Gordon is Spiked as Yanks Lose, 3–2." *New York Times.* 20 March 1946, p. 32.

53. Gordon Family Scrapbooks. "Gordon Spiked, X-Rays Ordered." St. Petersburg. ab. 19 March 1946.

54. Dawson, James P. "Tigers Vanquish Yankees, 9 to 6, in Contest Holding Seven Homers." *New York Times.* 23 March 1946, p. 21.

55. Cobbledick, Gordon. "Here's the *Flash!*" *Sport.* Oct. 1948, p. 21.

56. "Dave O"—a nationally-syndicated radio host, published writer, and Kansas City Royals historian and enthusiast. Dave generously provided the authors with invaluable historical content and multiple interviews he did with 15 ballplayers and others who had known, or known about,

Joe Gordon. Dave's audio documentary about Joe Gordon's life and career can be found on the website: *Remembering the Royals: Joe Gordon*; https://clubhouseconversation.com/2017/02/remembering-the-royals-joe-gordon/.

57. Gordon Family Scrapbooks. Gibbons, Frank. "Gordon High Flier—Can't Keep Him Down." prob. *Cleveland Press*. June 1958.

58. Gordon Family Scrapbooks. "Joe Gordon Out for Month." St. Petersburg. ab. 20 March 1946.

59. Rennie, Rud. "Yankees Tie Red Sox, 4–4, in Florida Finale." *New York Herald Tribune*. 29 March 1946, p. 25.

60. "M'Carthy Assorts 66 in Two Squads." *New York Times*. 25 March 1946, p. 30.

61. Dawson, James P. "Yankees, Dodgers Kept Idle by Rain." *New York Times*. 9 April 1946, p. 37.

62. Smith, Red. "Views of Sport: Baseball Hungry." *New York Herald Tribune*. 14 April 1946, p. B2.

63. Gordon Family Scrapbooks. Talbot, Gayle. "Major Loops, Talent-Laden, Open Tuesday." New York. ab. 15 April 1946.

64. Daniel, Dan. "Gordon Reveals Row with MacPhail." *The Sporting News*. 28 May 1947, p. 3.

65. Rennie, Rud. "37,472 See Yankees Trounce Athletics, 5 to 0, Behind Chandler in Philadelphia Opener." *New York Herald Tribune*. 17 April 1946, p. 31; Daniel, Dan. "DiMaggio Hailed as No. 1 by Huge Yankee Crowds." *The Sporting News*. 25 April 1946, p. 8.

66. Spink, J.G. Taylor. "Yankee Stadium—Stork Club, Copacabana Wrapped in One." *The Sporting News*. 25 April 1946, p. 2.

67. Rennie, Rud. "55,628 See Yankees Vanquish Senators in Ninth, 7–6, at Streamlined Stadium's Inaugural." *New York Herald Tribune*. 20 April 1946, p. 16.

68. Laney, Al. "Feller Compels Hayes to Share No-Hit Laurels." *New York Herald Tribune*. 1 May 1946, p. 26.

69. Laney, Al. "Yankees Down Tigers, 4–3, on Page's Homer...." *New York Herald Tribune*. 5 May 1946; Gordon, Joe. Letter to his mother, Louise Gordon, from Chicago. 16 May 1946.

70. Rosenthal, Harold. "Yankees Off to St. Louis by Air...." *New York Herald Tribune*. 14 May 1946, p. 30.

71. Dawson, James P. "Three Yanks Connect for Homers as Bevens Checks Browns by 6–2." *New York Times*. 15 May 1946, p. 34.

72. Dawson, James P. "Chandler, Ruffing Win Two for Yanks." *New York Times*. 20 May 1946, p. 16.

73. Cobbledick, Gordon. "Here's the *Flash!*" *Sport*. Oct. 1948, p. 21.

74. https://docs.google.com/spreadsheets/d/1mfjUVrIhBv6HeltZXYZNPFs_VKopDF_unaZ883QPQr0/edit#gid=1613289983.

75. Dawson, James P. "Triple Play Helps Yanks Win, 5–3, Despite Greenberg's 3-Run Homer." *New York Times*. 23 May 1946, p. 24.

76. Dawson, James P. "Yankees Crush Tigers on 17 Hits, Including 3 Homers in a Row, 12–6." *New York Times*. 24 May 1946, p. 22.

77. Levy, Alan H. *Joe McCarthy: Architect of the Yankee Dynasty*. Jefferson, NC: McFarland, 2005, p. 317.

78. Daley, Arthur. "Sports of the *Times*: Exit for Marse Joe." *New York Times*. 26 May 1946, p. S2.

79. "McCarthy, Health Restored, Has Eye on Big League Job." *New York Herald Tribune*. 18 Sep. 1946, p. 13.

80. Henrich, Tommy, with Bill Gilbert. *Five O'Clock Lightning: Ruth, Gehrig, DiMaggio, Mantle and the Glory Years of the NY Yankees*. New York: Carol, 1992, p. 144.

81. Sheehan, Joseph M. "Ruffing of Yanks Trips Senators, 4–0." *New York Times*. 30 May 1946, p. 30; Morris, Everett B. "Year's Smallest Stadium Crowd Sees Ruffing Pitch Three-Hitter." *New York Herald Tribune*. 30 May 1946, p. 23.

82. Gordon Family Scrapbooks. Considine, Bob. "Yankees Bow to Nats, 2–1." New York. ab. 28 May 1946.

83. Drebinger, John. "60,851 See Yanks Score by 6–1, 6–3." *New York Times*. 31 May 1946, p. 15.

84. "Red Sox Average 28 Years Compared to Yanks' 31.5." *The Sporting News*. 24 July 1946, p. 29.

85. Dawson, James P. "Yanks Top Red Sox after 1–0 Setback." *New York Times*. 27 May 1946, p. 28.

86. Drebinger, John. "Hiller is Chased." *New York Times*. 2 June 1946, p. S1.

87. "The Throw to First Did Not Reach There." *New York Times*. 2 June 1946, p. S3.

88. Cobbledick, Gordon. "Here's the *Flash!*" *Sport*. Oct. 1948, p. 20–21; Strite, Dick. "Highclimber: Trigger Joe Gordon wasn't kiddin'...." *Eugene Register-Guard*. 25 May 1947, p. 21.

89. Gordon Family Scrapbooks. McLemore, Henry. "From First to Last It Was Joe Gordon." Brooklyn. ab. 7 Oct. 1941.

90. Fitzgerald, Ed. "Joe Gordon: The Acrobatic Flash." *Sport*. July 1949, p. 88.

91. Drebinger, John. "67,662 See Yankees Split with Indians." *New York Times*. 10 June 1946, p. 33.

92. Gordon, Joe. Letter to his mother, Louise Gordon, from Detroit. 21 June 1946.

93. Woodward, Stanley. "Views of Sport: Happy Stays Late." *New York Herald Tribune*. 10 July 1946, p. 23; Rennie, Rud. "American League All-Stars Crush National, 12–0, Williams Blasting 2 Homers, 2 Singles." *New York Herald Tribune*. 10 July 1946, p. 23; "8 Ball Players Die in Crash of West Coast Bus." *New York Herald Tribune*. 26 June 1946, p. 42.

94. Rosenthal, Harold. "8 Red Sox Players Are Selected for American League All-Stars." *New York Herald Tribune*. 2 July 1946, p. 30A.

95. Rennie, Rud. "DiMaggio Injures Knee and Ankle...." *New York Herald Tribune*. 8 July 1946, p. 23.

96. Rennie, Rud. "American League All-Stars Crush National, 12–0, Williams Blasting 2 Homers, 2 Singles." *New York Herald Tribune*. 10 July 1946, p. 23.

97. "Ted Betters Six All-Star Marks." *The Sporting News*. 17 July 1946, p. 3.

98. Gordon Family Scrapbooks. "Gordon Swap Due Next Year." *New York News.* New York. ab. 13 July 1946.
99. Rennie, Rud. "Indians Down Yankees, 3–2, with 2 in 6th." *New York Herald Tribune.* 14 July 1946, p. B1.
100. Gordon Family Scrapbooks. Walsh, Davis J. "Yank Vets—Headed by Gordon—at Odds with Dickey." *International News Service.* New York. ab. 13 July 1946.
101. Gordon Family Scrapbooks. "Gordon, Etten May be Sold: Rumors Rampant on Yankee Pair." New York. ab. 15 July 1946; Daniel, Dan. "'Rip-Apart' Reports about Yanks Stir Storm." *The Sporting News.* 24 July 1946, p. 1.
102. Gordon Family Scrapbooks. "Gordon Denies Yank Revolt." New York. ab. 17 July 1946.
103. Daniel, Dan. "Gordon Denies Dissension; All of Yanks Back Dickey." *The Sporting News.* 24 July 1946, p. 6.
104. Rennie, Rud. "Yankees Defeat Browns, 3–2, 8–4; Rizzuto Hurt;...." *New York Herald Tribune.* 18 July 1946, p. 23A.
105. Drebinger, John. "Ruffing is Beaten." *New York Times.* 30 June 1946, p. S1; Effrat, Louis. "Yankees Beat Browns, 3–2, 8–4, but Rizzuto is Felled by a Pitch." *New York Times.* 18 July 1946, p. 16.
106. Rennie, Rud. "Tigers Topple New York Club into 3d Place." *New York Herald Tribune.* 1 Aug. 1946, p. 23A.
107. Gordon, Joe. Letter to his mother, Louise Gordon, from New York. 13 Aug. 1946.
108. "Bucky Harris Appointed Assistant to MacPhail." *New York Herald Tribune.* 10 Sep. 1946, p. 8.
109. Kennedy, Doug. "Dickey Says He Won't Stay as Yankee Pilot Next Year." *New York Herald Tribune.* 13 Sep. 1946.
110. Drebinger, John. "Neun to Run Club Until Season Ends." *New York Times.* 14 Sep. 1946, p. 10.
111. Henrich, Tommy, with Bill Gilbert. *Five O'Clock Lightning: Ruth, Gehrig, DiMaggio, Mantle and the Glory Years of the NY Yankees.* New York: Carol, 1992, p. 144.
112. Gregory, L.H. "Greg's Gossip." *The Oregonian.* 10 Feb. 1947, p. 21.
113. Gordon Family Scrapbooks. "Gordon Swap Due Next Year." *New York News.* ab. 13 July 1946; Strite, Dick. "Highclimber: And what do you suppose he was doing?" *Eugene Register-Guard.* 10 Oct. 1946, p. 20.
114. www.baseball-reference.com/bullpen/ Waivers; During Joe Gordon's years in professional baseball, waivers was a complex term, defined as "permission granted by the other teams in Major League Baseball to allow a team to proceed with a player move [or trade] which would not normally be allowed by the rules. In other words, opposing teams waive their objection to the move."
115. "Gordon of Yanks Traded to Indians." *New York Times.* 12 Oct. 1946, p. 24.
116. Gordon Family Scrapbooks. Gregory, L.H. "Greg's Gossip." *The Oregonian.* ab. 11 Oct. 1946.
117. "Deal 'Tickles' Gordon." *The Sporting News.* 23 Oct. 1946, p. 22.
118. Cobbledick, Gordon. "Plain Dealing: Doerr Believes Indians Have Got Themselves a Second Baseman in Joe Gordon and So Does Schulte." *Cleveland Plain Dealer.* 27 Oct. 1946, p. 4C.
119. Gordon Family Scrapbooks. "Doerr Boosts His Rival, Gordon, for Big Season." Sarasota, FL. Spring 1947.
120. Fitzgerald, Ed. "Joe Gordon: The Acrobatic Flash." *Sport.* July 1949, p. 88.
121. Eskenazi, Gerald. *Bill Veeck: A Baseball Legend.* New York: McGraw-Hill, 1988, p. 62.
122. Boudreau, Lou, with Ed Fitzgerald. *Player-Manager.* Boston: Little, Brown, 1949, p. 77.
123. Boudreau, Lou, with Ed Fitzgerald. *Player-Manager.* Boston: Little, Brown, 1949, p. 82.
124. Boudreau, Lou, with Russell Schneider. *Lou Boudreau: Covering All the Bases.* Champaign, IL: Sagamore, 1993, pp. 90–91.
125. Jones, Harry. "Gordon is Man We Need—Veeck." *Cleveland Plain Dealer.* 27 June 1958, p. 29.
126. McAuley, Ed. "Gordon Obtained by Veeck to Jack Tribe Up while Bill Waits for Kids to Fit in Rebuilding." *The Sporting News.* 23 Oct. 1946, p. 17.
127. Allen, Maury. *Where Have You Gone, Joe DiMaggio?* New York: E.P. Dutton, 1975, p. 91.
128. Strite, Dick. "Fish Tales: The sound of a 'quack, quack, quack'...." *Eugene Register-Guard.* 22 Nov. 1946, p. 6.
129. Strite, Dick. "Highclimber: Trigger Joe Gordon...." *Eugene Register-Guard.* 25 May 1947, p. 21.
130. Warfield, Don. *The Roaring Redhead: Larry MacPhail—Baseball's Great Innovator.* South Bend, IN: Diamond Communications, 1987, p. 220.
131. Warfield, Don. *The Roaring Redhead: Larry MacPhail—Baseball's Great Innovator.* South Bend, IN: Diamond Communications, 1987, p. 188.

Chapter 15

1. Gordon Family Scrapbooks. "'Flash' Gordon Signs Contract." Eugene. ab. 14 Jan. 1947; Gregory, L.H. "Greg's Gossip." *The Oregonian.* 10 Feb. 1947, p. 21.
2. Drebinger, John. "Pension Program for Players Voted by Major Leagues." *New York Times.* 2 Feb. 1947, p. S1.
3. Gregory, L.H. "Greg's Gossip." *The Oregonian.* 10 Feb. 1947, p. 21.
4. Spink, J.G. Taylor. "Looping the Loops: Bill Dickey, Professor of Catching." *The Sporting News.* 30 March 1949, p. 8.
5. Daniel, Dan. "Former Yank Great, Dickey, Rates Joe Gordon as Best Defensive Second Baseman." *Indiana* (PA) *Gazette.* 19 March 1949, p. 8.
6. Strite, Dick. "Highclimber: Joe Gordon...." *Eugene Register-Guard.* 12 Jan. 1947, p. 20.
7. http://springtrainingmagazine.com/ history4.html.
8. Strite, Dick. "Fish Tales." *Eugene Register-Guard.* 25 Oct. 1946, p. 8.

9. Veeck, Bill, with Ed Linn. *Veeck—As in Wreck: The Autobiography of Bill Veeck.* Chicago: University of Chicago Press, 2001.

10. Chanin, Abe. "Flash Early Bird at Camp for Bat Tips from Rajah." *The Sporting News.* 26 Feb. 1947, p. 19.

11. Chanin, Abe. "Flash Early Bird at Camp for Bat Tips from Rajah." *The Sporting News.* 26 Feb. 1947, p. 19.

12. McAuley, Ed. "Indian Infield Shaping Up as League's Best." *The Sporting News.* 5 March 1947, p. 16.

13. McAuley, Ed. "Tribe Tunes Up 'Flashiest Foursome' Acrobatic Infield Amazes Camp Observers." *The Sporting News.* 12 March 1947, p. 3.

14. Cobbledick, Gordon. "Here's the *Flash!*" *Sport.* Oct. 1948, p. 18.

15. "Indians Defeat Giants, 3 to 1, in Series Opener." *New York Herald Tribune.* 9 March 1947, pp. 1, 4.

16. Robinson, Eddie. Letter to Judy Gordon. April 2018.

17. Gregory, L.H. "Greg's Gossip: Joe Gordon Happy with Indians." *The Oregonian.* 24 March 1947, p. 21

18. Boudreau, Lou, with Russell Schneider. *Lou Boudreau: Covering All the Bases.* Champaign, IL: Sagamore, 1993, p. 92.

19. "Trout's 5-Hitter Blanks Indians for Tigers, 3–0." *New York Herald Tribune.* 29 April 1947, p. 30.

20. "Trout's 5-Hitter Blanks Indians for Tigers, 3–0." *New York Herald Tribune.* 29 April 1947, p. 30.

21. Boudreau, Lou, with Russell Schneider. *Lou Boudreau: Covering All the Bases.* Champaign, IL: Sagamore, 1993, p. 92.

22. Veeck, Bill, with Ed Linn. *Veeck—As in Wreck: The Autobiography of Bill Veeck.* Chicago: University of Chicago Press, 2001.

23. Zirin, Alex. "Feller Wins 10th One-Hit Game, 2 to 0." *Cleveland Plain Dealer.* 3 May 1947, p. 1.

24. Gordon Family Scrapbooks. "Two Gordon Homers Aid Tribe…." Cleveland. ab. 3 May 1947.

25. Gordon, Joe. Letter to his mother, Louise Gordon, from Cleveland. 6 May 1947.

26. Gordon Family Scrapbooks. "Mullin Boosts Mark to .441." Chicago. ab. 12 May 1947.

27. Gordon Family Scrapbooks. "'Gordon Deal Best Made by Cleveland in Decade.'" Cleveland. ab. 11 May 1947.

28. "Gordon, the Old Flash Again, Causes Flag Talk in Cleveland." *San Francisco Examiner.* 15 May 1947.

29. Stump, Al. "Mr. Second Sack is Back." *Argosy for Men.* July 1948, p. 18.

30. Daniel, Dan. "Gordon Reveals Rows with MacPhail." *The Sporting News.* 28 May 1947, p. 3.

31. Cobbledick, Gordon. "Plain Dealing: Greenberg's Tough Job is Complicated More by Uncertainty of Gordon's Return to Second Base." *Cleveland Plain Dealer.* 20 Dec. 1949, p. 23.

32. Gordon Family Scrapbooks. "Lou and Joe Bobble Only Three Times in 23 Games." ab. 20 May 1947.

33. Photo. "Tribe's Wandering Minstrels." *The Sporting News.* 21 May 1947, p. 11.

34. Boudreau, Lou, with Ed Fitzgerald. *Player-Manager.* Boston: Little, Brown, 1949, p. 80.

35. Moore, Joseph Thomas. *Larry Doby: The Struggle of the American League's First Black Player.* Mineola, NY: Dover, 2011, pp. 41–42; "Cleveland Buys Negro Player, First in the A.L." *New York Herald Tribune.* 3 July 1947, p. 19.

36. Cobbledick, Gordon. "Doby Shows Strong Arm As He Works at 2D Base." *Cleveland Plain Dealer.* 6 July 1947, p. 17A; Moore, Joseph Thomas. *Pride Against Prejudice: The Biography of Larry Doby.* New York: Praeger, 1988; Moore, Joseph Thomas. *Larry Doby: The Struggle of the American League's First Black Player.* Mineola, NY: Dover, 2011, pp. 46–49; Izenberg, Jerry. *Larry Doby in Black and White: The Story of a Baseball Pioneer.* New York: Sports Publishing, 2024.

37. Cobbledick, Gordon. "Doby Shows Strong Arm As He Works at 2D Base." *Cleveland Plain Dealer.* 6 July 1947, p. 17A.

38. "Chicago Crowd Applauds New Infielder's Bid for Hit with 2 on After His Workout with Gordon…." *New York Herald Tribune.* 6 July 1947, p. 2; Schneider, Russell. *The Boys of the Summer of '48.* Champaign, IL: Sports Publishing, 1998, p. 85.

39. Izenberg, Jerry. "Doby's Journey: Momentous Tour for Hall Inductee." *Newark (NJ) Star-Ledger Archive.* 26 July 1998, p. S1.

40. Boudreau, Lou, with Russell Schneider. *Lou Boudreau: Covering All the Bases.* Champaign, IL: Sagamore, 1993, p. 96.

41. Gordon, Judy. Speech for Induction of Joe "Flash" Gordon into the National Baseball Hall of Fame. 26 July 2009.

42. www.espn.com/mlb/columns/story?columnist=morgan_joe&id=1572794.

43. Morgan, Joe. Personal conversation with Judy Gordon. National Baseball Hall of Fame Induction Ceremony. Clark Sports Arena. Cooperstown, NY. 26 July 2009.

44. https://nyyfansforum.sny.tv/forum/general-baseball-forums/around-the-majors/12761-behind-doby-quiet-heroine-stood-guard-by-claire-smith

45. "Doby Makes Debut As Indians Lose, 6–5." *New York Times.* 6 July 1947, p. S3.

46. Moore, Joseph Thomas. *Larry Doby: The Struggle of the American League's First Black Player.* Mineola, NY: Dover, 2011, pp. 50–52.

47. Moore, Joseph Thomas. *Larry Doby: The Struggle of the American League's First Black Player.* Mineola, NY: Dover, 2011, p. 53.

48. Robinson, Eddie, with C. Paul Rogers III. *Lucky Me: My Sixty-Five Years in Baseball.* Lincoln: University of Nebraska Press, 2015; "Doby Bats in Run as Indians Split Twin Bill with White Sox." *New York Herald Tribune.* 7 July 1947, p. 17.

49. Izenberg, Jerry. *Larry Doby in Black and*

White: The Story of a Baseball Pioneer. New York: Sports Publishing, 2024.

50. "Congratulations to Larry Doby on His Introduction [sic] to the Baseball Hall of Fame." *U.S. Congressional Record: Proceedings and Debates of the 105th Congress, Second Session.* Vol 144, No. 28. Washington, D.C. 16 March 1998, pp. S2001-S2002.

51. Schneider, Russell. *The Boys of the Summer of '48.* Champaign, IL: Sports Publishing, 1998, p. 80.

52. Patten, Pat. "All-Star Games Yield Charities $859,000 Total." *The Sporting News.* 9 July 1947, p. 7.

53. "Here's Your Official All-Star Ballot." *Baseball Digest.* Vol. 6 No. 5. July 1947, pp. 60–61.

54. "Line-Ups Selected for All-Star Game." *New York Times.* 29 June 1947, p. S3.

55. Feller, Bob, with Bill Gilbert. *Now Pitching, Bob Feller.* New York: Carol, 1990, p. 152.

56. Gordon Family Scrapbooks. McAuley, Ed. "Hats Off...! Lou Boudreau." ab. 9 July 1947.

57. Heaton, Charles. "Black Credits Baffling Slider; Says Last Bounder Resembled Balloon." *Cleveland Plain Dealer.* 11 July 1947, p. 15.

58. Gordon Family Scrapbooks. "Vic Raschi, Bo Newsom Whip Chisox." Cleveland. ab. 13 July 1947.

59. Gordon Family Scrapbooks. "Attendance Mark Set by Indians." Cleveland. ab. 10 Aug. 1947.

60. McAuley, Ed. "Reynolds Good, Injun Joe Best, Tribe Fans Say." *The Sporting News.* 27 Aug. 1947, p. 10.

61. Jones, Harry. "First Baseman's Ankle is Broken." *Cleveland Plain Dealer.* 24 Aug. 1947, p. 36; Robinson, Eddie, with C. Paul Rogers III. *Lucky Me: My Sixty-Five Years in Baseball.* Lincoln: University of Nebraska Press, 2015.

62. Gordon Family Scrapbooks. "Joe Gordon Shines for Cleveland as Tribe Splits Pair with Bosox." Boston. ab. 11 Sep. 1947.

63. Gordon Family Scrapbooks. McAuley, Ed. "Lou's '48 Status Nears Showdown." Cleveland. ab. 20 Sep. 1947.

64. Jones, Harry. "Gordon's No. 30 is Washed Out." *Cleveland Plain Dealer.* 22 Sep. 1947, p. 18.

65. "Players Pension Plan Goes Into Operation." *The Sporting News.* 16 April 1947, p. 10.

66. The voting for the 1947 American League MVP Award was even closer than it had been for the 1942 award won by Joe Gordon. In 1947, Joe DiMaggio received 202 points vs. Triple Crown winner Ted Williams's 201 points; Drebinger, John. "Yankee Star Leads Williams by Point." *New York Times.* 28 Nov. 1947, p. 36.

67. Gordon Family Scrapbooks. "Indians Best Fielding Club." Chicago. ab. 16 Dec. 1948.

68. Stump, Al. "Mr. Second Sack is Back." *Argosy for Men.* July 1948, p. 95.

69. Goldstein, Doc. "Teeth Chattered in Cleveland Bow, Larry Doby Says." *The Sporting News.* 12 Nov. 1947, p. 10.

70. Hulen, Bill. "Turner, Aiken, Gordon, Beck, Merki Named Tops." *Sunday Oregonian.* 28 Dec. 1947, p. 4; Gordon Family Scrapbooks. Reichler, Joe. "Ted Williams Leads Players on AP Roster." New York. ab. 21 Oct. 1947.

Chapter 16

1. "Boudreau Deal Still Red Hot Says Veeck." *Eugene Register-Guard.* 8 Oct. 1947, p. 12.

2. Brands, Edgar G. "Seventh Year for Jolting Joe." *The Sporting News.* 28 Jan. 1948, p. 13.

3. Haupert, Michael. Haupert Baseball Salary Database, private collection; "Gordon's Contract Received by Veeck." *Eugene Register-Guard.* 5 Feb. 1948, p. 26.

4. Gregory, L.H. "Greg's Gossip: Joe Gordon had a grand year...." *The Oregonian.* 12 Jan. 1948.

5. Cobbledick, Gordon. "Here's the *Flash!*" *Sport.* Oct. 1948, p. 18.

6. Dolgan, Bob. "'Flash' Gordon's on-field acrobatics lifted Tribe." *Cleveland Plain Dealer.* 12 July 1998, p. 4-C.

7. Strite, Dick. "Highclimber." *Eugene Register-Guard.* 18 May 1948, p. 14.

8. Cobbledick, Gordon. "Veeck Applies Psychology in Reshuffling Roommates." *The Sporting News.* 10 March 1948, p. 4.

9. Robinson, Eddie. Phone conversation with Judy Gordon. 7 April 2021.

10. Boudreau, Lou, with Ed Fitzgerald. *Player-Manager.* Boston: Little, Brown, 1949, p. 102.

11. Official Souvenir Program. *Cleveland Indians vs. Boston Braves 1948 World Series.* Cleveland Baseball Corp. Oct. 1948, p. 5.

12. Robinson, Eddie. Letter to Judy Gordon. Dec. 2016.

13. Greenberg, Hank, with Ira Berkow. *Hank Greenberg: The Story of My Life.* Chicago: Ivan R. Dee, 2001.

14. Cobbledick, Gordon. "Here's the *Flash!*" *Sport.* Oct. 1948, p. 18.

15. Schneider, Russell. *The Boys of the Summer of '48.* Champaign, IL: Sports Publishing, 1998, p. 186.

16. Boudreau, Lou, with Ed Fitzgerald. *Player-Manager.* Boston: Little, Brown, 1949, p. 103.

17. Gordon Family Scrapbooks. "Indians Purchase Christopher...." *Cleveland Plain Dealer.* 4 April 1948.

18. Gordon Family Scrapbooks. "Indians Stage Big Rally to Defeat Athletics, 11–5." Cleveland. ab. 6 June 1949.

19. Bromberg, Lester. "Doby Credits Study in Earning Steady Job." *The Sporting News.* 27 Oct. 1948, p. 5.

20. Gregory, L.H. "Greg's Gossip." *The Oregonian.* 21 July 1949, p. 21.

21. Souvenir Program. Cleveland Indians vs. New York Giants. Owls Park, Topeka, KS. 14 April 1948.

22. "Sports Editor Lewis Innocent Culprit in Stanky's 'Murphy Money' Whodunit." *The Sporting News.* 27 March 1957, p. 31.

23. Gordon Family Scrapbooks. "Tribe Blanks Browns." Cleveland. ab. 20 April 1948.
24. Red, Christian. "Eddie Robinson, last living member of 1948 World Series champion Indians...." *New York Daily News*. 20 Oct. 2016; https://www.nydailynews.com/sports/baseball/eddie-robinson-living-member-48-indians-pissed-team-article-1.2838963.
25. Gordon Family Scrapbooks. "DiMag Clouts Three Homers in First Tilt." Cleveland, OH. ab. 23 May 1948.
26. "Gordon Out of Indians Lineup." *Eugene Register-Guard*. 28 May 1948, p. 12.
27. McDonough, Pat. "Indians Boast Top Defensive Mark in Majors." prob. *New York World-Telegram*. ab. 7 June 1948.
28. Gordon Family Scrapbooks. "Gordon Stars for Tribe...." New York. ab. 12 June 1948.
29. Boudreau, Lou, with Ed Fitzgerald. *Player-Manager*. Boston: Little, Brown, 1949, p. 144.
30. "Yanks' New Stadium to be Opened Today." *New York Times*. 18 April 1923, p. 17.
31. "Ruth Will Don Old Uniform Today in Stadium's Silver Anniversary." *New York Times*. 13 June 1948, p. S3; Cooke, Bob. "Ruth's No. 3 Joins His Name in Baseball's Hall of Fame." *New York Herald Tribune*. 14 June 1948, p. 23; "Gordon's Homers Compel Revision in Yank Script." *The Sporting News*. 23 June 1948, p. 4.
32. "Babe Makes Biggest Hit without Bat; Old No. 3 is Finally Retired." *Cleveland Plain Dealer*. 14 June 1948, p. 19.
33. Rennie, Rud. "Yankees Defeat Indians' Feller, 5–3, as Berra and Rizzuto Hammer Out Homers." *New York Herald Tribune*. 14 June 1948, p. 23.
34. Gordon Family Scrapbooks. "Bobby Feller, Lemon Score Mound Wins." Cleveland. ab. 20 June 1948.
35. McAuley, Ed. "Indians Now Shooting at 90,000 Gate." *The Sporting News*. 30 June 1948, p. 7; "$41,533 for Snacks." *The Sporting News*. 30 June 1948, p. 7.
36. Gordon Family Scrapbooks. Cain, Charles C. "Detroit Tigers Blanked, 2–0; Three Walked." Detroit. ab. 30 June 1948.
37. Gordon, Joe. Letter to his mother, Louise Gordon, from Cleveland. 6 July 1948.
38. Paige, LeRoy (Satchel), as told to David Lipman. *Maybe I'll Pitch Forever*. Garden City, NY: Doubleday, 1962, pp. 196, 200.
39. Paige, LeRoy (Satchel), as told to David Lipman. *Maybe I'll Pitch Forever*. Garden City, NY: Doubleday, 1962, p. 200.
40. Gordon Family Scrapbooks. "Rosters of Major League Dream Teams." ab. 13 July 1948.
41. Feller, Bob, with Bill Gilbert. *Now Pitching, Bob Feller*. New York: Carol, 1990, p. 153.
42. Gordon Family Scrapbooks. "Detailed Data on Gleam Game." July 1948.
43. "200 Home Run Club [of] the American and National Leagues of Professional Baseball." Griffith Stadium, Washington, D.C. 19 July 1948.
44. "Majors Seeking Data on Wilson, Klein Kin." *The Sporting News*. 30 June 1962, p. 6.
45. Gordon Family Scrapbooks. "Satchel Paige Beats Nats, 5–3." Cleveland. ab. 3 Aug. 1948.
46. McAuley, Ed. "The Flash." *Sportfolio*. Aug. 1948, p. 55.
47. Gordon Family Scrapbooks. "Gordon Injured in Sunday Tilt." Chicago. ab. 15 Aug. 1948.
48. Strite, Dick. "Highclimber." *Eugene Register-Guard*. 22 Aug. 1948, p. 14.
49. Gordon Family Scrapbooks. "Record Crowd Sees Indians Tie Loop Mark." Cleveland. ab. 20 Aug. 1948.
50. Gordon Family Scrapbooks. "Chisox Score 3–2 Triumph In Late Rally." Cleveland. ab. 21 Aug. 1948.
51. Gordon Family Scrapbooks. "Boston takes Leading Spot in Flag Race." Boston. ab. 24 Aug. 1948.
52. Gordon Family Scrapbooks. "New Yorkers Win in Ninth." New York. ab. 28 Aug. 1948.
53. Gordon Family Scrapbooks. "Tribe Falters." Chicago. ab. 6 Sep. 1948.
54. Cobbledick, Gordon. "Plain Dealing: Gordon Inspired Dejected Indians to Late Pennant Drive in '48." *Cleveland Plain Dealer*. 27 June 1958, p. 29.
55. Gordon Family Scrapbooks. "Tribe 6, Nats 3." Cleveland. ab. 16 Sep 1948.
56. "Pitcher Black in Critical Condition." *Cleveland Plain Dealer*. 14 Sep. 1948, p. 1.
57. "Don Unaware of 'Black Night.'" *Cleveland Plain Dealer*. 21 Sep. 1948, p. 17; Boudreau, Lou, with Ed Fitzgerald. *Player-Manager*. Boston: Little, Brown, 1949, p. 202.
58. Jones, Harry. "Indians Take Series Orders Tuesday." *Cleveland Plain Dealer*. 24 Sep. 1948, p. 1; Official Souvenir Program. *Cleveland Indians vs. Boston Braves 1948 World Series*. Cleveland Baseball Corp. Oct. 1948, p. 29.
59. Gordon Family Scrapbooks. "Chief Wahoo of the Cleveland Indians...." *Eugene Register-Guard*. ab. 25 Aug. 1948, p. 18.
60. Cobbledick, Gordon. "Plain Dealing: Greenberg's Tough Job is Complicated More by Uncertainty of Gordon's Return to Second Base." *Cleveland Plain Dealer*. 20 Dec. 1949, p. 23.
61. "Gordon Home for a Few Days before Going Off to Hunt." *Oregon Journal*. 28 Oct. 1948.
62. "Yankees to Play at Home in Case of Flag Play-Offs." *New York Herald Tribune*. 25 Sep. 1948, p. 15.
63. Gordon Family Scrapbooks. "Joe Gordon, Keltner Star As Tribe Maintains Lead." Cleveland. ab. 29 Sep. 1948.
64. "Almost Every Member of Tribe Named as Key Man, But What About Gordon?" *Oregon Journal*. 30 Sep. 1948, p. 4.
65. Gordon Family Scrapbooks. Reichler, Joe. "Outlaw Plays Villain's Role in 5–3 Upset." Cleveland. ab. 1 Oct. 1948.
66. Gordon Family Scrapbooks. Roden, Ralph. "Sox, Tribe Drive to Pennant Wire." Portland. ab. 3 Oct. 1948.

67. Strite, Dick. "Detroit Hands Indians 7–1 Loss to Force Final Tie with Sox." *Eugene Register-Guard.* 4 Oct. 1948, p. 10.
68. Gordon Family Scrapbooks. Reichler, Joe. "Indians Fall to Prince Hal by 7–1 Margin." Cleveland. ab. 3 Oct. 1948.
69. Boudreau, Lou, with Ed Fitzgerald. *Player-Manager.* Boston: Little, Brown, 1949, p. 208.
70. Lewis, Franklin. *The Cleveland Indians.* New York: G.P. Putnam's Sons, 1949, p. 266.
71. Schneider, Russell. *The Boys of the Summer of '48.* Champaign, IL: Sports Publishing, 1998, p. 130.
72. Boudreau, Lou, with Russell Schneider. *Lou Boudreau: Covering All the Bases.* Champaign, IL: Sagamore, 1993, p. 121.
73. Robinson, Eddie. Note to Judy Gordon. Dec. 2016.
74. Boudreau, Lou, with Russell Schneider. *Lou Boudreau: Covering All the Bases.* Champaign, IL: Sagamore, 1993, p. 121.
75. Boudreau, Lou, with Ed Fitzgerald. *Player-Manager.* Boston: Little, Brown, 1949, p. 211.
76. Schneider, Russell. *The Boys of the Summer of '48.* Champaign, IL: Sports Publishing, 1998, p. 118.
77. Schneider, Russell. *The Boys of the Summer of '48.* Champaign, IL: Sports Publishing, 1998, p. 23.
78. Schneider, Russell. "Schneider Around: Keltner, Gordon, Lemon on hand." *Cleveland Plain Dealer.* 9 Aug. 1975, p. 2-C.
79. Newspaper photo. "1920 Heroes See Triumph." ab. 5 Oct. 1948.
80. Boudreau, Lou, with Russell Schneider. *Lou Boudreau: Covering All the Bases.* Champaign, IL: Sagamore, 1993, p. 125.
81. Borsvold, David. *Cleveland Indians: The Cleveland Press Years, 1920–1982.* Charleston, SC: Arcadia, 2003, p. 53.
82. Dawson, James P. "Wild Celebration by Winning Team." *New York Times.* 5 Oct. 1948, p. 32.
83. McGowen, Roscoe. "M'Carthy Sorry for Players' Sake; DiMaggio Lauds Bearden's Work." *New York Times.* 5 Oct. 1948, p. 32.
84. Boudreau, Lou, with Ed Fitzgerald. *Player-Manager.* Boston: Little, Brown, 1949, pp. 217–219.
85. Boudreau, Lou, with Russell Schneider. *Lou Boudreau: Covering All the Bases.* Champaign, IL: Sagamore, 1993, p. 128.
86. Gordon Family Scrapbooks. "Hard to Top '48." prob. Oct. 1948.
87. "Still the Flash." *Sports Album* magazine. Vol. 1 No. 4. May–July 1949, p. 6.
88. Robinson, Eddie. Letter to Judy Gordon. Dec. 2016.
89. Kaiser, David. *Epic Season: The 1948 American League Pennant Race.* Amherst: University of Massachusetts Press, 1998, p. 62.
90. Daniel, Dan. "DiMaggio in Leadoff Spot in Yank Salary Debates." *The Sporting News.* 12 Jan. 1949, p. 12.
91. Sawyer, Ford. "Williams Runner-Up in Night Averages." *The Sporting News.* 29 Dec. 1948, p. 19.
92. "Indians Nocturnal Scalping Big Factor in Flag Victory." *The Sporting News.* 29 Dec. 1948, p. 19.
93. Strite, Dick. "Highclimber." *Eugene Register-Guard.* 15 Dec. 1948, p. 18.
94. Schneider, Russell. *The Boys of the Summer of '48.* Champaign, IL: Sports Publishing, 1998, p. xii.
95. Schneider, Russell. *The Boys of the Summer of '48.* Champaign, IL: Sports Publishing, 1998, p. 26.
96. Lustig, Dennis. "For 1948 pitching hero Gene Bearden: First win more important than playoff win." *Cleveland Plain Dealer.* 9 Aug. 1975, p. 5-C.
97. Schneider, Russell. *The Boys of the Summer of '48.* Champaign, IL: Sports Publishing, 1998, p. 28.
98. Feller, Bob, with Bill Gilbert. *Now Pitching, Bob Feller.* New York: Carol, 1990, p. 163.
99. Gordon Family Scrapbooks. Newspaper photo sequence. "Was the Umpire Wrong?" prob. 6 Oct. 1948.
100. Schneider, Russell. *The Boys of the Summer of '48.* Champaign, IL: Sports Publishing, 1998, pp. 30, 63–64; McMurray, John. "Phil Masi." SABR Biography Project, https://sabr.org/bioproj/person/phil-masi/.
101. McMurray, John. "Phil Masi," SABR Biography Project, https://sabr.org/bioproj/person/phil-masi/.
102. Gordon Family Scrapbooks. Considine, Bob. "Lemon Cools Braves, 4 to 1, on Eight Hits." Boston. ab. 7 Oct. 1948.
103. Considine, Bob. "Gromek Hurls Indians to Victory, 2 to 1." *Morning Oregonian.* 10 Oct. 1948, p. 2.
104. Boudreau, Lou, with Ed Fitzgerald. *Player-Manager.* Boston: Little, Brown, 1949, p. 235.
105. Photo. "Scalped the Braves." *New York Herald Tribune.* 10 Oct. 1948, p. 1.
106. On December 13, 2023, which would have been Larry Doby's 100th birthday, during a special ceremony at the United States Capitol, The Congress of the United States presented the prestigious *Congressional Gold Medal* to Larry Doby, Jr., and his family, in honor of their father, Larry Doby; "The Congress of the United States Congressional Gold Medal Ceremony in honor of Larry Doby." United States Capitol. Washington, D.C. 13 Dec. 2023; Castrovince, Anthony. "U.S. Mint had never made a Congressional Gold Medal like Larry Doby's". MLB.com. 23 Feb. 2024.
107. "Gordon Brothers, Joe, Jack, Visit in Cleveland Dugout." *Bend (OR) Bulletin.* 13 Oct. 1948, p. 3; Gordon Family Scrapbooks."Greatest Crowd in American Baseball History Sees Boston Defeat Cleveland in Fifth Series Game." ab. 10 Oct. 1948.
108. Paige, LeRoy (Satchel), as told to David

Lipman. *Maybe I'll Pitch Forever*. Garden City, NY: Doubleday, 1962, pp. 222–223.

109. Photo. "Indians' sendoff packed Union Terminal...." *Cleveland Plain Dealer*. 11 Oct. 1948, p. 34; Gordon Family Scrapbooks. "Indian Players Get Sendoff." Cleveland. ab. 10 Oct. 1948.

110. Gordon Family Scrapbooks. Considine, Bob. "Indians Down Braves, 4–3, to End Fracas." Boston. ab. 11 Oct. 1948.

111. Heaton, Charles. "Gene Plays Big Role in 10-Day Drive to Title." *Cleveland Plain Dealer*. 12 Oct. 1948, p. 21.

112. McAuley, Ed. *Bob Lemon: The Work Horse*. New York: A.S. Barnes, 1951, p. 20.

113. Jones, Harry. "Bearden Halts Rally to Save Lemon's 4–3 Victory Over Braves." *Cleveland Plain Dealer*. 12 Oct. 1948, p. 1.

114. Heaton, Charles. "Gene Plays Big Role in 10-Day Drive to Title." *Cleveland Plain Dealer*. 12 Oct. 1948, p. 21.

115. Heaton, Charles. "Gene Plays Big Role in 10-Day Drive to Title." *Cleveland Plain Dealer*. 12 Oct. 1948, p. 21.

116. *Official Baseball Guide*. 1975. p. 270.

117. Boudreau, Lou, with Russell Schneider. *Lou Boudreau: Covering All the Bases*. Champaign, IL: Sagamore, 1993, p. 135.

118. Greenberg, Hank, with Ira Berkow. *Hank Greenberg: The Story of My Life*. Chicago: Ivan R. Dee, 2001.

119. "Cleveland Gives Team Welcome." *Eugene Register-Guard.* 13 Oct. 1948, p. 17; Gordon Family Scrapbooks. Smith, Larry. "Indians Get Big Welcome." Cleveland. ab. 12 Oct. 1948; Photo. "Cleveland Welcomes Its Series Heroes." *Oregon Journal*. 12 Oct. 1948, p. 1.

120. Schneider, Russell. *The Boys of the Summer of '48*. Champaign, IL: Sports Publishing, 1998, p. 36.

121. Robinson, Eddie. Letter to Judy Gordon. Dec. 2016.

122. Brands, Edgar G. "Joe DiMaggio on All-Star Team Eighth Time." *The Sporting News*. 13 Oct. 1948, p. 3.

123. Gillespie, Ray. "Five Newcomers Named on '50 All-Star Team." *The Sporting News*. 3 Jan. 1951, p. 11.

124. Daniel, Dan. "Film Captures Game's Thrills." *The Sporting News*. 8 Dec. 1948, p. 11; Daniel, Dan. "Picture Stresses Skill of Boudreau, Gordon." *The Sporting News*. 8 Dec. 1948, p. 11; Ryan, Jack. "'Pickoff' Controversy Whets Interest in N.Y. Premiere of World Series Film." *The Sporting News*. 1 Dec. 1948, p. 20; "The Double Play Kings of Baseball." *The Sporting News*. 9 Feb. 1949, p. 33.

Chapter 17

1. Chanin, Abe. "Flash Moves Up His 'Good Years'—Two More Now." *The Sporting News*. 9 March 1949, p. 14.

2. Haupert, Michael. Haupert Baseball Salary Database, private collection.

3. Gordon Family Scrapbooks. Gibbons, Frank. "Gordon Hits Homer, Sparkles Afield to Prove He's Ready." prob. *Cleveland Press*. ab. 21 March 1949.

4. Gordon Family Scrapbooks. Gibbons, Frank. "Gordon Develops Sore Arm." Tucson. ab. 31 March 1949; Newspaper photo. "Grounded for several days...." prob. March 1949.

5. Schneider, Russell. *The Boys of the Summer of '48*. Champaign, IL: Sports Publishing, 1998, p. 128.

6. Dickson, Paul. *Bill Veeck: Baseball's Greatest Maverick*. New York: Walker, 2012.

7. Gordon Family Scrapbooks. "Feller Loser as Tribe Bows by 5-to-1 Score." St. Louis. ab. 19 April 1949.

8. Newsspaper article. Yonkers, Bob. "Tribe's 'Old Pros' Have It in Clutch." ab. 23 April 1949.

9. Veeck, Bill, with Ed Linn. *Veeck—As in Wreck: The Autobiography of Bill Veeck*. Chicago: University of Chicago Press, 2001.

10. Gordon Family Scrapbooks. "Henrich Hits Homer, Triple to Spark Win." Cleveland. ab. 2 June 1949; Gordon Family Scrapbooks. Goldstein, Herman. "Gordon's Circus Act is Tops with Wynn." ab. 24 June 1949; Nitz, Jim. "Ken Keltner." SABR Biography Project, https://sabr.org/bioproj/person/Ken-Keltner/.

11. Moore, Joseph Thomas. *Pride Against Prejudice: The Biography of Larry Doby*. New York: Praeger, 1988; Feller, Bob, with Bill Gilbert. *Now Pitching, Bob Feller*. New York: Carol, 1990, p. 172.

12. Boudreau, Lou, with Russell Schneider. *Lou Boudreau: Covering All the Bases*. Champaign, IL: Sagamore, 1993, p. 145.

13. Dudley, Bruce. *Distant Drums: The 1949 Cleveland Indians Revisited*. Bowie, MD: Bruce Dudley, 1989, p. 9.

14. Marsh, W. Ward. "Hollywood Film to Feature City." *Cleveland Plain Dealer*. 8 April 1949; "Chance in Movies Is Yours Today." *Cleveland Plain Dealer*. 7 June 1949, p. 21.

15. Dickson, Paul. *Bill Veeck: Baseball's Greatest Maverick*. New York: Walker, 2012; "Sitter for Indians Freezes, Bakes." *Cleveland Plain Dealer*. 2 June 1949, p. 15; "Fair Sex Hits at Lupica's Perching." *Cleveland Plain Dealer*. 5 Aug. 1949, p. 14; "Indian Sitter Draws Tourists to Perch as Fame Spreads." *Cleveland Plain Dealer*. 3 June 1949, p. 34; "Lupica Hits Dirt; How He Loves It!" *Cleveland Plain Dealer*. 26 Sep. 1949, p. 10; "Fan Atop Flagpole Finds Rain is Wet." *Cleveland Plain Dealer*. 11 July 1949, p. 6; "Indian Pole Sitter Holds New Papoose." *Cleveland Plain Dealer*. 17 Sep. 1949, p. 1.

16. Gordon Family Scrapbooks. "Indians Make Lineup Shift." Cleveland. ab. 6 June 1949; Gordon Family Scrapbooks. "Indians Stage Big Rally to Defeat Athletics, 11–5." Cleveland. ab. 6 June 1949.

17. "Williams, Jackie Robinson Top Record All-Star Game Ballot." *New York Herald Tribune*. 2 July 1949, p. 11.

18. "Red Sox Get Six All-Star Berths, Yankees and Indians Five Apiece." *New York Times*. 5 July 1949, p. 28.

19. Gordon, Joe. "Double Play!" *Boys' Life*. Aug. 1949, p. 13.
20. Gordon Family Scrapbooks. "Tribe 2, A's 1." Cleveland. ab. 1 Sep. 1949; www.cbssports.com/mlb/news/orioles-extra-inning-winning-getting-historic/.
21. Marsh, W. Ward. "Crowds Pack Street and Stillman for Premiere of 'Kid from Cleveland.'" *Cleveland Plain Dealer*. 3 Sep. 1949, p. 8; McAuley, Ed. "Indians' Reel Roles Marked by Realism." *The Sporting News*. 14 Sep. 1949, p. 19.
22. Cobbledick, Gordon. "Plain Dealing: Greenberg's Tough Job is Complicated More by Uncertainty of Gordon's Return to Second Base." *Cleveland Plain Dealer*. 20 Dec. 1949, p. 23.
23. Gordon Family Scrapbooks. "Defeat Erases Last Chance for Cleveland." Boston. ab. 20 Sep. 1949.
24. Gordon Family Scrapbooks. "Veeck Authors Solemn Burial." Cleveland. ab. 23 Sep. 1949; Gordon Family Scrapbooks. "Tigers 5, Indians 0." Cleveland. ab. 23 Sep. 1949.
25. "'Most Loyal' Fan Spends Cold Day." *Cleveland Plain Dealer*. 25 Sep. 1949, p. 32–A; www.espn.com/classic/obit/s/2002/1225/1482290.html.
26. "Lupica Kisses the Dirt; Gifts Erase Futile Vigil." *Cleveland Plain Dealer*. 26 Sep. 1949, p. 1.
27. www.espn.com/classic/obit/s/2002/1225/1482290.html.
28. Gordon Family Scrapbooks. "Tribe 4, Tigers 0." Detroit. ab. 1 Oct. 1949.
29. Gordon Family Scrapbooks. "Tribe 8, Tigers 4." Detroit. ab. 2 Oct. 1949.
30. McAuley, Ed. "Indians a Vanished Tribe, Without '48 Zip." *The Sporting News*. 5 Oct. 1949, pp. 9, 12, 20.
31. Dudley, Bruce. *Distant Drums: The 1949 Cleveland Indians Revisited*. Bowie, MD: Bruce Dudley, 1989.
32. Bang, Ed. "Ryan 7th President of Indians Since '01." *The Sporting News*. 30 Nov. 1949, p. 6; McAuley, Ed. "New Owner Wants to Have Winner 'Right Now.'" *The Sporting News*. 30 Nov. 1949, p. 5; Boudreau, Lou, with Russell Schneider. *Lou Boudreau: Covering All the Bases*. Champaign, IL: Sagamore, 1993, p. 137.
33. Gould, Al. "Gordon Seeks Tribe Release; Wants Pacific Coast Berth." *Oregon Journal*. 28 Nov. 1949, p. 1.
34. Strite, Dick. "Highclimber." *Eugene Register-Guard*. 29 Nov. 1949, p. 16.
35. Gordon Family Scrapbooks. Gibbons, Frank. "Gordon, the Infield Gordon, Saves Another Tribe Victory." Washington, D.C. ab. 24 June 1949.
36. "'Love to Have Joe'—Mulligan." *Oregon Journal*. 28 Nov. 1949, p. 1; Gordon Family Scrapbooks. "Seattle [sic] Interested in Hiring Gordon." Sacramento. ab. 29 Nov. 1949; Gordon Family Scrapbooks. Jarstad, John. "Time Out: Joe Gordon at Boise?" *Idaho Evening Statesman*." ab. Nov. 1949.
37. Newpaper article. "'Out of the Question,' Says Tribe to Gordon." Cleveland. ab. 1 Dec. 1949.
38. Levitt, Daniel R. *Ed Barrow: The Bulldog Who Built the Yankees' First Dynasty*. **Lincoln:** University of Nebraska Press, 2008.
39. Strite, Dick. "Highclimber." *Eugene Register-Guard*. 28 Dec. 1949, p. 8.
40. "Indian Manager 'Hopes Joe Changes His Mind.'" *Eugene Register-Guard*. 29 Nov. 1949, p. 16A.
41. "Gordon 'Winter Fever' Victim. to be Back Says Indian Boss." *Eugene Register-Guard*. 4 Dec. 1949, p. 14.

Chapter 18

1. Gillespie, Ray. "48 Ten-Year Men in Majors, With 31 in American League." *The Sporting News*. 1 Feb. 1950, p. 2.
2. "Major League Rules—Rule 8 Unconditional Release." *Baseball Blue Book 1949*.
3. Bertz, George. "Top New Baseballer: Readers Choose Indians' Gordon." *Oregon Journal*. 14 Feb. 1950.
4. "Joe Gordon Signs Contract." *Eugene Register-Guard*. 15 Feb. 1950, p. 1; Haupert, Michael. Haupert Baseball Salary Database, private collection.
5. "Gordon Accepts Tribe Offer, Will Receive Around $35,000." *Eugene Register-Guard*. 16 Feb. 1950, p. 13.
6. "Gordon Rapping Homers." *Eugene Register-Guard*. 4 April 1950, p. 12.
7. Stone, Jerry. "Rollin' Along." *Salem* (OR) *Statesman*. 12 April 1950.
8. McAuley, Ed. "Keltner Reaches End of Trail as an Indian." *The Sporting News*. 19 April 1950, p. 13.
9. Gordon Family Scrapbooks. "Pirates Dicker for Joe Gordon." Pittsburgh, PA. ab. 12 June 1950; Ruhl, Oscar. "From the Ruhl Book: Gordon as Buc Pilot Prospect?" *The Sporting News*. 21 June 1950, p. 20.
10. Gordon Family Scrapbooks. "Tribe Takes Two." Cleveland. ab. 18 June 1950.
11. Strite, Dick. "Highclimber." *Eugene Register-Guard*. 26 July 1950, p. 12.
12. Jones, Harry. "Gordon's 5 Hits Bag First Game." *Cleveland Plain Dealer*. 18 July 1950, p. 18.
13. "Gordon's Comeback Boosts Pennant Hopes." *Cleveland Plain Dealer*. 18 July 1950, p. 18.
14. Gordon Family Scrapbooks. "Detroit Edge Cut to .002 in Tight Race." New York. ab. 29 Aug. 1950; Gordon Family Scrapbooks. Reichler, Joe. "Mize Shines in Twin Win Over Indians." New York. ab. 30 Aug. 1950.
15. Gordon Family Scrapbooks. "Lou Boudreau Predicts Flag." Boston. ab. 28 Aug. 1950.
16. McAuley, Ed. *Bob Lemon: The Work Horse*. New York: A.S. Barnes, 1951.
17. McAuley, Ed. "'Old Pro' Gordon Calls It Career." *The Sporting News*. 4 Oct. 1950, p. 16.
18. "Portland—Reports from the East Hint that Joe Gordon….." *The Sporting News*. 13 Sep. 1950, p. 28; Gordon Family Scrapbooks. "Suds Boss? Gordon Eyed as Suds Pilot." Seattle. ab. 17 Oct. 1950.
19. Strite, Dick. "Highclimber: Joe Gordon,

who had only one good batting streak...." *Eugene Register-Guard*. 1 Oct. 1950, p. 13.

20. Reserve Clause—the part of a player's contract defining the rights of their club in retaining them upon expiration of their contract. Essentially, Gordon was not free to change clubs unless given his unconditional release.

21. Silvera, Charlie. Phone interview with Judy Gordon. 13 Oct. 2014.

22. "Gordon Doing 'Job Shopping.'" *The Oregonian*. 18 Oct. 1950, p. 2.

23. "'Flash' Okays 2-Year Pact at Big Salary." *The Oregonian*. 19 Oct. 1950, p. 1.

24. "Majors Eyed." *The Oregonian*. 19 Oct. 1950, p. 1.

25. "Major League Rules—Rule 8 Unconditional Release." *The Baseball Blue Book 1949*.

26. "Gordon Free to Join Sacs." *The Oregonian*. 28 Oct. 1950, p. 13.

27. Conlin, Bill. "It Says Here: Flashy Guy." *Sacramento Union*. 7 May 1951, p. 5.

28. As discussed earlier, Joe McCarthy, manager of the 1943 American League All-Star team, did not play *any* of his six Yankees who'd been selected for that year's All-Star Game.

29. "Ted's 14 Picks Best Mark; 12 Stars for Stan." *The Sporting News*. 11 Nov. 1959, p. 4.

30. www.baseball-reference.com/leaders/Gm_2b_top_ten.shtml.

31. www.baseball-reference.com/leaders/DP_2b_career.shtml.

32. http://www.clevelandmemory.org/league/indians100/index.html.

Chapter 19

1. Gordon Family Scrapbooks. Old, John B. "Rookie Pilot Gordon Sets Solons' Pace." Sacramento. ab. 22 May 1951.

2. Branagan, Marlowe. "Tower Lights: Joseph L. Gordon Has Tough Job on Hands in Skipper Debut." *Oregon Journal*. 28 March 1951, p. 2; Spalding, John E. *Sacramento Senators and Solons: Baseball in California's Capital, 1886 to 1976*. Manhattan, KS: Ag Press, 1995, p. 137.

3. Spalding, John E. *Sacramento Senators and Solons: Baseball in California's Capital, 1886 to 1976*. Manhattan, KS: Ag Press, 1995, p. 140.

4. Gregory, L.H. "Greg's Gossip." *The Oregonian*. 25 March 1951.

5. Kane, Tom. "Solons Obtain Boyd, Hairston on Option From Chicago Team." *Sacramento Bee*. 24 March 1951, p. 11.

6. Gordon Family Scrapbooks. Conlin, Bill. "Manager Joe Gordon Seeks Dry Land at Stockton as Cold, Drizzles Hit." prob. *Sacramento Union*. ab. 28 Feb. 1951.

7. Gordon Family Scrapbooks. Kane, Tom. "Gordon Seeks Shelter for Solons as Rain Spoils Opening Drills." *Sacramento Bee*. ab. 2 March 1951.

8. Gordon Family Scrapbooks. "Tough Pilots." Stockton, CA. early March 1951.

9. Gordon Family Scrapbooks. Kane, Tom. "Swift Base Running, Home Run Punch Give Solons 5–4 Victory." *Sacramento Bee*. ab. 27 March 1951.

10. Gordon Family Scrapbooks. Gregory, L.H. "Portland Wins by 10–7, 2–0 in Double Bill." *The Oregonian*. ab. 1 April 1951.

11. Gordon Family Scrapbooks. "Sacs Take 2d Place." San Diego. ab. 21 April 1951.

12. Gordon Family Scrapbooks. Old, John B. "Rookie Pilot Gordon Sets Solons' Pace." Sacramento. ab. 22 May 1951.

13. Gordon Family Scrapbooks. "Solon Manager Joe Gordon visited a movie studio...." Hollywood, CA. ab. 8 May 1951.

14. Gordon Family Scrapbooks. Talbot, Gayle. "Writer Feels Gordon Finest." *Associated Press*. Los Angeles. ab. 27 March 1952.

15. Conlin, Bill. "It Says Here: Flashy Guy." *Sacramento Union*. 7 May 1951, p. 5.

16. Gordon Family Scrapbooks. "Team Spirit: More than Money." ab. 15 May 1951.

17. Gordon Family Scrapbooks. "Judnich is Batting Leader...." San Francisco. ab. 5 June 1951.

18. Gordon Family Scrapbooks. Lipper, Joe. "Gordon is Acclaimed PCL's Hottest Pilot." *Chico (CA) Enterprise-Record*. ab. 14 May 1951.

19. Gordon Family Scrapbooks. "Ears Have It." ab. 6 June 1951.

20. Gordon Family Scrapbooks. Adams, Wilbur. "Between the Sport Lines: 'Joe Boasted.'" prob. *Sacramento Bee*. ab. 15 June 1951.

21. Kane, Tom. "Baseball's Grapevine Says Gordon Will Go to Browns by July 4." *Sacramento Bee*. 23 June 1951; Jones, Harry. "Gordon is Man We Need—Veeck." *Cleveland Plain Dealer*. 27 June 1958, p. 29.

22. Veeck, Bill, with Ed Linn. *Veeck—As in Wreck: The Autobiography of Bill Veeck*. Chicago: University of Chicago Press, 2001.

23. Kane, Tom. "Mulligan Says He Will Not Free Gordon During Season." *Sacramento Bee*. prob. June 1951.

24. Gordon Family Scrapbooks. Landsberg, Morrie. "Bid Rejected by Joe Gordon." Sacramento. ab. 5 July 1951; Gregory, L.H. "Greg's Gossip: No More Big League, Joe Gordon Says." *The Oregonian*. 14 Aug. 1951, p. 19.

25. "Solon outfielder Joe Marty, who suffered a compound dislocation...." *Sacramento Bee*. 22 June 1951, p. 18.

26. Gordon Family Scrapbooks. "Walt Judnich Retains Lead." San Francisco. ab. 25 June 1951.

27. Gordon Family Scrapbooks. "Boyd and Gordon Continue to Pace PCL Batting Race." ab. 15 July 1951.

28. Gordon Family Scrapbooks. "Sacs 7, Oaks 3." Oakland. ab. 19 July 1951.

29. Gordon Family Scrapbooks. Anderson, Lenny. "Joe Gordon's Grand-Slam Homer Defeats Grissom." *Seattle Times*. ab. 28 July 1951; Gordon Family Scrapbooks. "Sacs 4, Oaks 2." Oakland. ab. 21 July 1951.

30. Gordon Family Scrapbooks. "Home Run by Thomas Leads Beaver Attack." Sacramento. ab. 26 July 1951.
31. Gordon Family Scrapbooks. Anderson, Lenny. "Joe Gordon's Grand-Slam Homer Defeats Grissom." *Seattle Times*. ab. 28 July 1951.
32. Gordon Family Scrapbooks. "Suds 5, Sacs 2." Sacramento. ab. 31 July 1951; Gordon Family Scrapbooks. "Sacs 9, Padres 4." Sacramento. ab. 3 Aug. 1951; Gordon Family Scrapbooks. "Sacs Padres Split." Sacramento. ab. 5 Aug. 1951.
33. Gordon Family Scrapbooks. Gregory, L.H. "Beavers Nip Sacs, 6–5; Basinski's Hit Decides." *The Oregonian*. ab. 10 Aug. 1951.
34. Strite, Dick. "Highclimber." *Eugene Register-Guard*. 15 Aug. 1951, p. 15.
35. Conlin, Bill. "It Says Here: Runouts Don't Indicate Dissension on Solons." *Sacramento Union*. 8 Aug. 1951, p. 8.
36. "Sacramento—Manager Joe Gordon missed the select .300 batting circle...." *The Sporting News*. 22 Sep. 1951, p. 19.
37. Gordon Family Scrapbooks. "White Sox Recall Boyd from Sacs." Detroit. ab. 2 Sep. 1951.
38. Gordon Family Scrapbooks. "Rivera Led Coast Loop Batters, Bob Boyd was Second." ab. 10 Sep. 1951.
39. Gordon Family Scrapbooks. "Solons Defeat Seals in Pair." San Francisco. ab. 9 Sep. 1951.
40. Spalding, John E. *Sacramento Senators and Solons: Baseball in California's Capital, 1886 to 1976*. Manhattan, KS: Ag Press, 1995; On a page titled "All-Time Records" in the back of his book, author John E. Spalding wrote that right-hander Bill McNulty hit 55 home runs while playing for the 1974 Sacramento Solons. However, many of McNulty's homers had been hit at Sacramento's Hughes Stadium (the Solons' home stadium that year), with its left-field fence (and 40-foot-high screen) just 232 feet from home plate, considerably less than the league's legal 250-foot minimum. Solons right-hander Gorman Thomas also hit 51 home runs in 1974, many of those at Hughes Stadium.
41. "Joe Gordon Sells Interest in Store." *Sacramento Bee*. 25 Sep. 1951, p. 24.
42. Gordon Family Scrapbooks. L.H. Gregory. "Greg's Gossip: It has leaked out...." *The Oregonian*. ab. 30 Nov. 1951, p. 25.
43. Rennie, Rud. "Minors Create Open Classification as First Step in Setting Up 3d Major League." *New York Herald Tribune*. 7 Dec. 1951, p. 31; "Pacific Coast Loop Wins Open Classification." *New York Herald Tribune*. 1 Jan. 1952, p. 22.
44. Spalding, John E. *Sacramento Senators and Solons: Baseball in California's Capital, 1886 to 1976*. Manhattan, KS: Ag Press, 1995, p. 143.
45. "Gordon Inks New Contract." *Eugene Register-Guard*. 3 Feb. 1952, p. 14.
46. Spalding, John E. *Sacramento Senators and Solons: Baseball in California's Capital, 1886 to 1976*. Manhattan, KS: Ag Press, 1995, p. 143–144.
47. Kane, Tom. "Angels' Ed Chandler Dazzles Solons, 1–0,...." *Sacramento Bee*. 2 April 1952, p. 36.
48. Gordon Family Scrapbooks. "Sacs 4, Angels 2." Sacramento. ab. 4 April 1952.
49. Gordon Family Scrapbooks. "Beavers, Solons Split Long Tilts." Sacramento. ab. 21 July 1952; Gordon Family Scrapbooks. "Bevos, Solons Divide Pair." Sacramento. ab. 22 July 1952; "Injured Solon—Len Attyd, Sacramento Solon...." *Sacramento Bee*. 23 July 1952, p. 27.
50. "Gordon Okay." *Eugene Register-Guard*. 22 July 1952, p. 11; Gordon Family Scrapbooks. "Stars 11, Solons 4." Hollywood, CA. ab. 22 July 1952.
51. "Old-Timers' Game at Stadium Today." *New York Times*. 30 Aug. 1952, p. 7; Koppett, Leonard. "Good Old Days Back in Stadium: RBI-DiMaggio; 2B-Henrich." *New York Herald Tribune*. 31 Aug. 1952, p. 1.
52. Kane, Tom. "Gordon, Solon Pilot for Two Years, Quits." *Sacramento Bee*. 30 Sep. 1952, p. 26.
53. Gregory, L.H. "Greg's Gossip: Joe Gordon 'Standing By' for Detroit?" *The Oregonian*. 23 April 1953.
54. Gregory, L.H. "Greg's Gossip: Red Sox Connection for Joe Gordon?" *The Oregonian*. 24 Sep. 1952.
55. "Gordon to Join Detroit as Boss of Coast Scouts." *The Oregonian*. 9 Oct. 1952:23.
56. Gregory, L.H. "Greg's Gossip: Joe Gordon 'Standing By' for Detroit?" *The Oregonian*. 23 April 1953.
57. "Joe Gordon Opens Tiger Tryout Camp." *Sacramento Bee*. 14 Feb. 1953, p. 14.
58. "Saw Joe Gordon at Glendale...." *Eugene Register-Guard*. 19 March 1953, p. 30.
59. "Three Beavers Sign Pro Pacts." *Eugene Register-Guard*. 9 June 1953, p. 13; Strite, Dick. "Highclimber." *Eugene Register-Guard*. 10 June 1953, p. 25.
60. Strite, Dick. "Highclimber: There is a very strong rumor that Joe Gordon...." *Eugene Register-Guard*. 11 Oct. 1953, p. 30.
61. "The Tigers are setting up a western training camp...." *The Sporting News*. 3 March 1954, p. 13.
62. http://articles.latimes.com/2009/aug/31/local/me-cap31.
63. "Hutchinson Quits Post with Tigers." *New York Herald Tribune*. 1 Oct. 1954, p. 20.
64. Kane, Tom. "Joe Gordon Will Join Detroit's Coaching Staff." *Sacramento Bee*. 8 Nov. 1955, p. 30.
65. Spoelstra, Watson. "Gordon Expected to Help Put New Flash into Bengals." *The Sporting News*. 16 Nov. 1955, p. 4.
66. Spoelstra, Watson. "Decisions on Porter, Bertoia to be Made at Tigers' Early Camp." *The Sporting News*. 18 Jan. 1956, p. 17.
67. Drebinger, John. "Yankees Rally to Rout Tigers...." *New York Times*. 16 March 1956, p. 28; "Joe Gordon May Play 2d for Tigers." *New York Herald Tribune*. 17 March 1956, p. B3.
68. Middlesworth, Hal. "Spike Apologizes for Tiger Blasts, but Gordon Quits." *The Sporting News*. 4 July 1956, p. 10.

69. "Gordon May Quit as Tiger Coach." *New York Herald Tribune*. 28 June 1956, p. B2.
70. "Gordon of Tigers Resigns as Coach." *New York Times*. 29 June 1956, p. 24; Middlesworth, Hal. "Spike Apologizes for Tiger Blasts, but Gordon Quits." *The Sporting News*. 4 July 1956, p. 10.
71. "Tiger Uncertainties Settled." *The Sporting News*. 25 July 1956, p. 12; Devine, Tommy. "Tighe to Put Tougher Twist in Tiger Tale." *The Sporting News*. 24 Oct. 1956, p. 13; "Sport: Scoreboard, [M]ay 6, 1957." *Time*. 6 May 1957; https://time.com/archive/6611763/sport-scoreboard-may-6-1957/.
72. "Seals Drop Joost, Name Gordon Pilot." *New York Times*. 10 July 1956, p. 37.
73. Adams, Wilbur. "Between the Sport Lines." *Sacramento Bee*. 10 July 1956, p. C-1.
74. "Gordon to Boss Seals Next Season." *Eugene Register-Guard*. 11 Sep. 1956, p. 17.
75. "Gordon Gets Big One." *Sacramento Bee*. 4 Jan. 1957, p. 38.
76. "San Francisco Seal Manager Joe Gordon...." *Sacramento Bee*. 27 Feb. 1957, p. 24; "Seals Thump Angels, Bask in Optimism." *Sacramento Bee*. 3 April 1957, p. 22.
77. "Joe Gordon Has Excellent Variety of Youngsters, Oldsters at SF Camp." *Sacramento Bee*. 16 March 1957, p. D-1.
78. Dragseth, P.J. *The 1957 San Francisco Seals: End of an Era in the Pacific Coast League*. Jefferson, NC: McFarland, 2013, Chapter Two: Spring Training.
79. Samuelsen, Rube. "Pacific Coast League: Flag-Hungry Seals Feast on Trailers." *The Sporting News*. 28 Aug. 1957, p. 31.
80. Kane, Tom. "Senators Are Picked for 7th, Seals to Win." *Sacramento Bee*. 11 April 1957, p. D-1.
81. www.history.com/this-day-in-history/baseball-owners-allow-dodgers-and-giants-to-move.
82. Gray, Sid. "Giants Accept San Francisco Offer, Move in 1958 after 74 Years Here." *New York Herald Tribune*. 20 Aug. 1957, p. 1.
83. Holmes, Tommy. "It's Official—Dodgers Go to Los Angeles." *New York Herald Tribune*. 9 Oct. 1957, p. B1.
84. Ward, Alan. "On Second Thought: Gordon Predicts Flag for Seals." *Oakland Tribune*. 5 July 1957, p. 38D.
85. Dragseth, P.J. *The 1957 San Francisco Seals: End of an Era in the Pacific Coast League*. Jefferson, NC: McFarland, 2013, Chapter Six: July.
86. "Hollywood Edges Seals Twice to Take Series 5–2." *Sacramento Bee*. 15 July 1957, p. C-5.
87. "Pacific Coast League." *Sacramento Bee*. 15 July 1957, p. 19.
88. Hannon, Clayton. "Joe Gordon Night: Visiting Seals Top Ems, 5–3 in Exhibition." *Eugene Register-Guard*. 16 July 1957, p. 3B.
89. "Pacific Coast League." *Sacramento Bee*. 22 July 1957, p. 19.
90. Dragseth, P.J. *The 1957 San Francisco Seals: End of an Era in the Pacific Coast League*. Jefferson, NC: McFarland, 2013, Chapter Seven: August.

91. "Job in Majors or Job Hunting: If SF Wins and Giants Move, What Happens to Joe Gordon?" *Eugene Register-Guard*. 11 Aug. 1957, p. 2B.
92. "Lepcio's Wrist Broken." *New York Times*. 31 Aug. 1957, p. 10.
93. "Seals Get Stringer to Fill Second Base." *Sacramento Bee*. 31 Aug. 1957, p. A-10.
94. Dragseth, P.J. *The 1957 San Francisco Seals: End of an Era in the Pacific Coast League*. Jefferson, NC: McFarland, 2013, Chapter Eight: September.
95. "Pacific Coast League: San Francisco." *The Sporting News*. 25 Sep. 1957, p. 40; "Seals Blank Solons 3–0 to Win PCL Flag." *Sacramento Bee*. 14 Sep. 1957, p. D-1.
96. Kane, Tom. "SF Will Bid Farewell to Seals, PCL, at Twin Bill Tomorrow." *Sacramento Bee*. 14 Sep. 1957, p. D-1.
97. Dragseth, P.J. *The 1957 San Francisco Seals: End of an Era in the Pacific Coast League*. Jefferson, NC: McFarland, 2013.
98. "Talk of Giants Was Missing at Seals' Finale." *Sacramento Bee*. 16 Sep. 1957, p. D-1; Dragseth, P.J. *The 1957 San Francisco Seals: End of an Era in the Pacific Coast League*. Jefferson, NC: McFarland, 2013, Chapter Eight: September.
99. Samuelsen, Rube. "Sadness Mixed with Comedy at Seals' Goodbye." *The Sporting News*. 25 Sep. 1957, p. 13.
100. McDonald, Jack. "Flag-Waving Seals Leave 'Em Cheering in Saying Farewell." *The Sporting News*. 25 Sep. 1957, p. 33.
101. "Talk of Giants Was Missing at Seals' Finale." *Sacramento Bee*. 16 Sep. 1957, p. D-1.
102. Kelley, Brent P. *The San Francisco Seals, 1946–1957: Interviews with 25 Former Baseballers*. Jefferson, NC: McFarland, 2002, p. 244; Gordon Family Scrapbooks. "Second Game box score." prob. 16 Sep. 1957.
103. Dragseth, P.J. *The 1957 San Francisco Seals: End of an Era in the Pacific Coast League*. Jefferson, NC: McFarland, 2013, Chapter Eight: September; Samuelsen, Rube. "Sadness Mixed with Comedy at Seals' Goodbye." *The Sporting News*. 25 Sep. 1957, p. 13; Kelley, Brent P. *The San Francisco Seals, 1946–1957: Interviews with 25 Former Baseballers*. Jefferson, NC: McFarland, 2002, p. 245.
104. "Seals Exit Laughing." *New York Times*. 16 Sep. 1957, p. 34.
105. "Seals' Last-Out Ball Put in Shrine." *The Sporting News*. 13 Nov. 1957, p. 7.
106. "Seals Close Out on Comedy Note." *Oakland Tribune*. 16 Sep. 1957, p. 34.
107. "Aspromonte Bat Champ...." *The Sporting News*. 25 Sep. 1957, p. 33.
108. McDonald, Jack. "Flag-Waving Seals Leave 'Em Cheering in Saying Farewell." *The Sporting News*. 25 Sep. 1957, p. 33.
109. Dragseth, P.J. *The 1957 San Francisco Seals: End of an Era in the Pacific Coast League*. Jefferson, NC: McFarland, 2013, Epilogue.
110. Western Union Telefax. Vice President Dick Nixon to the Honorable George Christopher, Mayor of San Francisco. Sep. 1957.

111. Dragseth, P.J. *The 1957 San Francisco Seals: End of an Era in the Pacific Coast League.* Jefferson, NC: McFarland, 2013, Foreword.
112. https://clubhouseconversation.com/2017/02/remembering-the-royals-joe-gordon/.
113. "Giants Trade Minneapolis Franchise to Red Sox for San Francisco Club." *New York Times.* 16 Oct. 1957, p. 43.
114. "Gordon May Pilot AA Club." *Eugene Register-Guard.* 26 Oct. 1957, p. 6.
115. Dragseth, P.J. *The 1957 San Francisco Seals: End of an Era in the Pacific Coast League.* Jefferson, NC: McFarland, 2013.
116. Pearson, Albie. Phone interview with Judy Gordon. 21 March 2014.
117. Gordon Family Scrapbooks. Walter, Bucky. "Gordon Called Smart, Daring Pilot." Cincinnati. 1958.
118. Newspaper advertisement. "Living Insurance by Equitable." *Sacramento Bee.* 16 Sep. 1957, p. D-3.
119. "Gordon Tells of Devil Fish Tow." *Sacramento Bee.* 9 Dec. 1957, p. 24.
120. Kane, Tom. "Joe Gordon is Mentioned for Solon Pilot." *Sacramento Bee.* 9 Dec. 1957, p. C-1.
121. "Gordon Drops Out of Solon Manager Race." *Sacramento Bee.* 21 Dec. 1957, p. D-1.
122. Kane, Tom. "Solon Pilot Choice May be Connected with Player Help." *Sacramento Bee.* 10 Dec. 1957, p. C-1; Gordon Family Scrapbooks. "The Bull Pen: Opportunity Hits Often for Gordon." *Oakland Tribune.* prob. June 1958.

Chapter 20

1. Gordon Family Scrapbooks. "Happy Joe Gordon Takes Over: Lane Greets Manager at Airport." Cleveland. prob. 27 June 1958.
2. Jones, Harry. "Bragan Out, Joe Gordon Hired." *Cleveland Plain Dealer.* 27 June 1958, p. 1.
3. Jones, Harry. "Bragan Out, Joe Gordon Hired." *Cleveland Plain Dealer.* 27 June 1958, p. 1.
4. Editorial. "New Pilots Find Warm Welcome." *The Sporting News.* 9 July 1958, p. 20.
5. Jones, Harry. "Gordon is Man We Need—Veeck." *Cleveland Plain Dealer.* 27 June 1958, p. 29.
6. Heaton, Chuck. "1948 Hero Welcomes Challenge." *Cleveland Plain Dealer,* 27 June 1958, p. 29.
7. Gordon Family Scrapbooks. "McAuley: Tribe's New Boss Big Leaguer in Every Way." prob. July 1958.
8. Gordon Family Scrapbooks. Lebovitz, Hal. "Gordon to Keep Coaches, Won't Platoon Tribesmen." prob. 27 June 1958.
9. Gordon Family Scrapbooks. "Happy Joe Gordon Takes Over." Cleveland. prob. 27 June 1958.
10. Lebovitz, Hal. "Gordon 'Gambled' He'd Get Pilot Offer." *The Sporting News.* 9 July 1958, p. 17.
11. Gordon Family Scrapbooks. Lebovitz, Hal. "Gordon to Keep Coaches, Won't Platoon Tribesmen." prob. 27 June 1958.
12. Editorial. "New Pilots Find Warm Welcome." *The Sporting News.* 9 July 1958, p. 20.

13. Hornick, Charles. R. "Joe Gordon Replaces Bragan as Cleveland Indians Pilot." *Sacramento Bee.* 27 June 1958, prob. p. D1.
14. Kane, Tom. "Believe It or Not!—Gordon, Kress, Jo Jo Join Forces." *Sacramento Bee.* 4 July 1958, p. 18.
15. Schneider, Russell. *The Cleveland Indians Encyclopedia, 2nd Edition.* United States: Sports Publishing, 2001, p. 73.
16. Gordon Family Scrapbooks. Heaton, Chuck. "Gordon Seeks Set Lineup for Tribe." ab. 28 June 1958.
17. Gordon Family Scrapbooks. Gordon Refuses to Concede '58 Flag to Yankees." Cleveland. ab. 7 July 1958.
18. Lebovitz, Hal. "Gordon Relaxed Skipper, But Can Inspire Players." *The Sporting News.* 8 April 1959, p. 15.
19. Kachline, Clifford. "Record 368 Share Series Melon; Each Yank Gets $8,759: Series $ $ $ Breakdown." *The Sporting News.* 22 Oct. 1958, p. 9.
20. Jones, Harry. "Martin Traded to Indians for Narleski and Mossi." *Cleveland Plain Dealer.* 21 Nov. 1958, p. 1.
21. Jones, Harry. "Martin Traded to Indians for Narleski and Mossi." *Cleveland Plain Dealer.* 21 Nov. 1958, p. 1; Jones, Harry. "Lane Eye Turns to Piersall." *Cleveland Plain Dealer.* 22 Nov. 1958, p. 21.
22. Lebovitz, Hal. "'We Can Win'—Tribe Flash from Gordon." *The Sporting News.* 28 Jan. 1959, p. 15.
23. Barmann, George J. "Gordon Labels Team Tribe's Most Colorful." *Cleveland Plain Dealer.* 20 Jan. 1959, p. 23.
24. Lebovitz, Hal. "Flash Wants Tribe to 'Play and Think Way into Shape.'" *The Sporting News.* 25 Feb. 1959, p. 13.
25. Pavlovich, Lou. "'Tribe Greatly Improved by Lane,' Says Medinger." *The Sporting News.* 25 Feb. 1959, p. 13.
26. Lebovitz, Hal. "Gordon Relaxed Skipper, But Can Inspire Players." *The Sporting News.* 8 April 1959, p. 15.
27. Lebovitz, Hal. "Lane's Barbs Seen as Firing Both Teams." *The Sporting News.* 29 April 1959, p. 1.
28. "Wonderful World of Sport: Primer of Cleveland Success." *Sports Illustrated.* 11 May 1959, p. 43.
29. Lebovitz, Hal. "Rocky Joins Lowe and Lou on Four-Homer Honor Roll." *The Sporting News.* 17 June 1959.
30. Cobbledick, Gordon. "Plain Dealing—Game Never Should Have Been Played." *Cleveland Plain Dealer.* 6 Aug. 1959, p. 29.
31. "Cleveland's Joe Gordon Confident—But Cautious." *Crawfordsville* (IN) *Journal and Review.* 16 July 1959, p. 6.
32. Lebovitz, Hal. "Indians Go Over Million at Gate—Goal 1,500,000." *The Sporting News.* 12 Aug. 1959, p. 19.
33. Pennington, Bill. *Billy Martin: Baseball's Flawed Genius.* New York: Mariner Books, 2016.
34. Jones, Harry. "Martin Hit by Pitch, Out 4 Weeks." *Cleveland Plain Dealer.* 6 Aug. 1959, p. 29.

35. Photo. "Keep It Up, Jim." *Cleveland Plain Dealer.* 22 Aug. 1959, p. 19; Jones, Harry. "Batting Around: Martin Gets Off Disabled List." *Cleveland Plain Dealer.* 5 Sep. 1959, p. 21.
36. Cobbledick, Gordon. "Plain Dealing: Lane Gives Gordon Credit for Indians' Success, but Won't Beg Him to Stay." *Cleveland Plain Dealer.* 3 Sep. 1959, p. 29.
37. Lebovitz, Hal "Flash Raises Old Flag Sked on Tepee Top." *The Sporting News.* 16 Sep. 1959, p. 7.
38. Cobbledick, Gordon. "Plain Dealing: Gordon's Chance to Keep Job Gets Slimmer Each Day Lane Remains Silent." *Cleveland Plain Dealer.* 15 Sep. 1959, p. 29.
39. Jones, Harry. "Gordon to Stay if Indians Want Him." *Cleveland Plain Dealer.* 15 Sep. 1959, p. 29.
40. "Gordon Ends Feud with Resignation." *Eugene Register-Guard.* 19 Sep. 1959, p. 6.
41. Editorial: "A Sour Note." *Cleveland Plain Dealer.* 18 Sep. 1959, p. 12.
42. Lebovitz, Hal. "Tepee Tempest Turns to Tea; Flash, Frank Bury Brickbats." *The Sporting News.* 30 Sep. 1959, p. 4.
43. "Gordon Ends Feud with Resignation." *Eugene Register-Guard.* 19 Sep. 1959, p. 6.
44. Wynne, William. Photo. "WE WANT JOE." *Cleveland Plain Dealer.* 21 Sep. 1959, p. 31.
45. Barmann, George J. "54,293 See Sox Win Pennant." *Cleveland Plain Dealer.* 23 Sep. 1959, p. 1; Adams, Wilbur. "Between the Sport Lines." *Sacramento Bee.* 2 Oct. 1959, p. D4; "40,000 to See Tribe, Chisox Clash." *Cleveland Plain Dealer.* 22 Sep. 1959, p. 30.
46. Heaton, Chuck. "Harder replaces Joe as Manager." *Cleveland Plain Dealer.* 23 Sep. 1959, p. 29.
47. Lebovitz, Hal. "Tepee Tempest Turns to Tea; Flash, Frank Bury Brickbats." *The Sporting News.* 30 Sep. 1959, p. 4.
48. "Joe Gordon Rehired by Cleveland; Given New 2-Year Contract." *Eugene Register-Guard.* 23 Sep. 1959, p. 18; Lebovitz, Hal. "Joe, With Two-Year Pact, Can Afford to Wise Crack." *The Sporting News.* 7 Oct. 1959, p. 11.
49. Jones, Harry. "Lane-Gordon 'Talk' Leads to Re-Hiring." *Cleveland Plain Dealer.* 24 Sep. 1959, p. 33.
50. Jones, Harry. "Batting Around." *Cleveland Plain Dealer.* 23 Sep. 1959, p. 31.
51. Kahan, Oscar. "Slicing the Swag: Dodgers and Chisox Split Richest Melon in History of Series." *The Sporting News.* 21 Oct. 1959, p. 16.
52. "A.L. Crowds Up 27%; Slight Drop in N.L." *The Sporting News.* 7 Oct. 1959, p. 9.
53. Kane, Tom. "Jo Jo Calls Future of Tribe Bright." *Sacramento Bee.* 1 Oct. 1959, p. D1.
54. Lustig, Dennis. "From the Summer of '48: Whatever Happened to ... Joe Gordon?" *Cleveland Plain Dealer.* 25 Jan. 1974, p. 1-D.
55. Lebovitz, Hal. "Piersall Standing on TNT, Told Not to Light Matches: Lane Reminds Jim He Was Obtained as Player—Not Clown." *The Sporting News.* 10 Feb. 1960, p. 17.

56. Lebovitz, Hal. "Piersall Standing on TNT, Told Not to Light Matches: Lane Reminds Jim He Was Obtained as Player—Not Clown." *The Sporting News.* 10 Feb. 1960, p. 17.
57. "Tribe Tidbits." *The Sporting News.* 20 Jan. 1960, p. 13; Jones, Harry. "Batting Around." *Cleveland Plain Dealer.* 3 March 1960, p. 30.
58. Lebovitz, Hal. "Tribe Will Strut to Camp with Youngest Club in A.L." *The Sporting News.* 9 March 1960, p. 15.
59. Jones, Harry. "No Snoozing on Firing Line, Tribe Warned." *The Sporting News.* 9 March 1960, p. 15.
60. Jones, Harry. "Piersall Silences Clown Capers, Makes Big Noise with Bludgeon." *The Sporting News.* 23 March 1960, p. 20.
61. Lebovitz, Hal. "Injuns Shape Up as Glove Artists Who Pack Punch." *The Sporting News.* 20 April 1960, p. 27; Jones, Harry. "Weak Pitching Could Drop Tribe to Sixth." *Cleveland Plain Dealer.* 17 April 1960, p. 2-C.
62. Jones, Harry. "Colavito Stunned by Lane Trade." *Cleveland Plain Dealer.* 18 April 1960, p. 33.
63. "Score Dealt to White Sox." *San Diego Union.* 19 April 1960, p. a-17.
64. Pluto, Terry. *The Curse of Rocky Colavito: A Loving Look at a Thirty-Year Slump.* Cleveland: Gray, 2007.
65. Bona, Marc. "Rocky Colavito: 'I am thankful God chose me to play in Cleveland.'" *Cleveland Plain Dealer.* 11 Aug. 2021, p. A1; "Lane Hanged, Joe on Slab; Fans Favor Score Trade." *Eugene Register-Guard.* 19 April 1960, p. 20; Heaton, Chuck. "Okayed 2 Deals, Joe Says." *Cleveland Plain Dealer.* 19 April 1960, p. 29.
66. Cobbledick, Gordon. "Plain Dealing." *Cleveland Plain Dealer.* 20 April 1960, p. 33.
67. Piersall, Jimmy, with Richard Whittingham. *The Truth Hurts.* Chicago: Contemporary, 1984, p. 43; Staff Special. "Piersall Fined $250 for Temper Flareup." *Cleveland Plain Dealer.* 1 June 1960, p. 33.
68. Veeck, Bill, with Ed Linn. *Veeck—As in Wreck: The Autobiography of Bill Veeck.* Chicago: University of Chicago Press, 2001; Piersall, Jimmy, with Richard Whittingham. *The Truth Hurts.* Chicago: Contemporary, 1984, p. 43.
69. Staff Special. "Piersall Fined $250 for Temper Flareup." *Cleveland Plain Dealer.* 1 June 1960, p. 33; Lebovitz, Hal. "Jim Takes Play from Veeck Showpiece by Chicago Shenanigans...." *The Sporting News.* 8 June 1960, p. 15.
70. Danaceau, Paul. "Biggest AL Crowd Sees Indians Split." *Cleveland Plain Dealer.* 27 June 1960, p. 1.
71. Danaceau, Paul. "Tribe Crowd." *Cleveland Plain Dealer.* 27 June 1960, p. 10.
72. "Piersall Disagrees, But He'll Rest." *Eugene Register-Guard.* 28 June 1960, p. 19.
73. Editorial. "Piersall Must Recognize His Problem." *The Sporting News.* 27 July 1960, p. 12.
74. Jones, Harry. "Batting Around." *Cleveland Plain Dealer.* 21 July 1960, p. 29.

75. "Cubs Top Indians with 2-Hitter, 5–0." *New York Times*. 28 June 1960, p. 35.
76. "Lane Says Piersall to Pay Double for Future Fines." *Eugene Register-Guard*. 17 July 1960, p. 13.
77. Lebovitz, Hal. "Gordon Rips Piersall; 'Unfair,' Yelps Jim." *The Sporting News*. 27 July 1960, p. 17.
78. "Piersall Problem, But Can Be 'Handled,' Lane Believes." *The Sporting News*. 27 July 1960, p. 17.
79. Cobbledick, Gordon. "Plain Dealing: Lane Says Piersall 'Can Be Handled.'" *Cleveland Plain Dealer*. 19 July 1960, p. 25.
80. Daniel, Dan. "Players Junk Plans to Hold Squad Confab." *The Sporting News*. 3 Aug. 1960, p. 13.
81. Rosenthal, Harold. "Tense Situation: Gordon, Indians' Pilot, Fines Jim Piersall $200." *New York Herald Tribune*. 19 July 1960, p. 27.
82. Jones, Harry. "Held Injured as Indians Lose, 9–2: Slugger Out for 5 Weeks." *Cleveland Plain Dealer*. 19 July 1960, p. 25.
83. Jones, Harry. "Batting Around." *Cleveland Plain Dealer*. 31 July 1960, p. 2-C.
84. "Tribe's Drop in Attendance Baffles Lane." *The Sporting News*. 27 July 1960, p. 17.
85. Heaton, Chuck. "All Casey Needs is Pitchers." *Cleveland Plain Dealer*. 21 July 1960, p. 30.
86. Jones, Harry. "Tribe Players Demand Lane Curb Piersall." *Cleveland Plain Dealer*. 25 July 1960, pp. 1, 29.
87. "Antics Are Finished, Piersall Promises." *Eugene Register-Guard*. 26 July 1960, p. 3B.
88. Jones, Harry. "Piersall 'Remedy' Meeting Shelved." *Cleveland Plain Dealer*. 26 July 1960, p. 28.
89. Jones, Harry. "Piersall 'Remedy' Meeting Shelved." *Cleveland Plain Dealer*. 26 July 1960, p. 28.
90. Jones, Harry. "Batting Around." *Cleveland Plain Dealer*. 2 Aug. 1960, p. 28.
91. "Gordon, Dykes Swap Managerial Positions." *Eugene Register-Guard*. 3 Aug. 1960, p. 14.
92. "Gordon, Dykes Swap Managerial Positions." *Eugene Register-Guard*. 3 Aug. 1960, p. 14.
93. Jones, Harry. "Piersall the Winner, Indians Say." *Cleveland Plain Dealer*. 4 Aug. 1960, p. 31.
94. Spoelstra, Watson. "Heat on DeWitt After Gordon Quits Bengals." *The Sporting News*. 12 Oct. 1960, p. 7.
95. Cobbledick, Gordon. "Plain Dealing." *Cleveland Plain Dealer*. 4 Aug. 1960, p. 31.
96. Jones, Harry. "Piersall the Winner, Indians Say." *Cleveland Plain Dealer*. 4 Aug. 1960, p. 31.
97. Jones, Harry. "Piersall Winner, Indians Declare." *Cleveland Plain Dealer*. 4 Aug. 1960, p. 34.
98. Middlesworth, Hal. "Hiring of DeWitt 'Bold Move' by Board to Overhaul Tigers." *The Sporting News*. 7 Oct. 1959, p. 7.
99. Schneider, Russell. *The Cleveland Indians Encyclopedia, 2nd Edition*. United States: Sports Publishing, 2001, p. 321.
100. Smith, Ron, "Sports of the Times: Parade Passes Him Up." *Detroit Times*. 5 Aug. 1960, p. 15.
101. Spoelstra, Watson. "Gordon." *The Sporting News*. 17 Aug. 1960, p. 6.
102. Falls, Joe. "Frustration is Same for New Pilot." *Detroit Times*. 6 Aug. 1960, p. 9.
103. Smith, Ron. "Sports of the Times: DeWitt on Spot, Too." *Detroit Times*. 8 Aug. 1960, p. 13; "Dykes Blasts Tigers' Prexy." *Manistee* (MI) *Advocate*. 7 Aug. 1960.
104. Falls, Joe. "In the Clubhouse: DeWitt Welcome? Gordon Yells 'No.'" *Detroit Sunday Times*. 7 Aug. 1960, p. 2-D.
105. Jones, Harry. "Indians Fall in 10th, 6–4." *Cleveland Plain Dealer*. 13 Aug. 1960, p. 17; Falls, Joe. "Sports of the Times: Perfect Day for Gordon Over Tribe." *Detroit Times*. 13 Aug. 1960, p. 9; "Piersall Still at It." *Detroit Times*. 19 Aug. 1960, p. 15.
106. "Piersall's Ejection Antics Just a Re-Run to Gordon." *The Sporting News*. 24 Aug. 1960, p. 10.
107. Spoelstra, Watson. "Heat on DeWitt After Gordon Quits Bengals." *The Sporting News*. 12 Oct. 1960, p. 7.
108. "Gordon to Manage Kansas City Club?" *Eugene Register-Guard*. 3 Oct. 1960.
109. "Gordon to Manage Kansas City Club?" *Eugene Register-Guard*. 3 Oct. 1960.
110. "Athletics Eye Joe Gordon." *Riverside* (CA) *Daily Press*. 4 Oct. 1960, p. B-9.
111. McGuff, Joe. "Old Home Week for Pilot Joe Gordon in Kaycee." *The Sporting News*. 21 Sep. 1968, p. 5.
112. Peterson, John E. *The Kansas City Athletics: A Baseball History, 1954–1967*. Jefferson, NC: McFarland, 2003, Chapter 15.
113. "Kansas City Hires Joe Gordon to Manage Club Next Season." *Eugene Register-Guard*. 5 Oct. 1960, p. 30.
114. Smith, Marshall. "A Mess of Cabbage Degrades Baseball: Greedy Owners Create Two New Teams—And Chaos." *Life*. 19 Dec. 1960, p. 81.
115. McGuff, Joe. "Gordon Names Three Coaches." *Kansas City Times*. 28 Nov. 1960, p. 27.
116. Mehl, Ernest. "Slab Sizzler Herbert Set for Big Year." *The Sporting News*. 12 April 1961, p. 26.
117. Kahan, Oscar. "Minors' Parley Ends Up Behind 8 Ball." *The Sporting News*. 7 Dec. 1960, p. 9; Bordman, Sid. "Boy Battery Pleases Gordon." *The Sporting News*. 14 Dec. 1960, p. 25.
118. Bordman, Sid. "Boy Battery Pleases Gordon." *The Sporting News*. 14 Dec. 1960, p. 25.
119. "Finley Aims for All Kansas City Stock." *Eugene Register-Guard*. 20 Dec. 1960, p. 2B.
120. Michelson, Herb. *Charlie O: Charles Oscar Finley vs. the Baseball Establishment*. Indianapolis/New York: Bobbs-Merrill, 1975, pp. 84–90.
121. Editorial. "Trader Lane Trades Lane." *Cleveland Plain Dealer*. 4 Jan. 1961, p. 12; Photo. "When Lane Got Long-Term Paper." *Cleveland Plain Dealer*. 4 Jan. 1961, p. 23.
122. Jones, Harry. "Lane to Bid for Piersall." *Cleveland Plain Dealer*. 4 Jan. 1961, p. 23; "Lane." *Cleveland Plain Dealer*. 4 Jan. 1961, p. 25.

123. Mehl, Ernest. "A's Will Aim for 5th Place, Frankie Says." *The Sporting News*. 22 Feb. 1961, p. 22.

124. Mehl, Ernest. "Kids Will Get Big Chance for Jobs on A's Slab Staff." *The Sporting News*. 22 Feb. 1961, p. 22.

125. Fox, Gene. *Sports Guys: Insights, Highlights and Hoo-hahs from Your Favorite Sports Authorities*. Lenexa, KS: Addax, 1999, p. 44.

126. Fox, Gene. *Sports Guys: Insights, Highlights and Hoo-hahs from Your Favorite Sports Authorities*. Lenexa, KS: Addax, 1999, p. 42.

127. Nowlin, Bill, Len Levin, Carl Riechers, eds. *Baseball's Biggest BLOWOUT Games*. Phoenix: Society for American Baseball Research, 2020, pp. 244–246.

128. Mehl, Ernest. "Kaycee Clouters Pick Up Steam While Mound Corps Bogs Down." *The Sporting News*. 3 May 1961, p. 27.

129. Young, Dick. "Young Ideas." *The Sporting News*. 20 May 1959, p. 11.

130. "Clubs Trade, Release, Option to Reach Limit." *New York Herald Tribune*. 11 May 1961, p. 28; Editorial. "Finley Shrewd Appraiser of Talent." *The Sporting News*. 14 June 1961, p. 10; "Finley, Lane Feud Grows." *Boston American*. 11 May 1961, p. 21; Cobbledick, Gordon. "Plain Dealing: Lane Sure Bet to Leave A's and Finley for Club Where He Can Call Shots Again." *Cleveland Plain Dealer*. 21 June 1961, p. 29.

131. Nealon, Clark. "Frankie Houston-Bound? Colts Mum." *The Sporting News*. 17 May 1961, p. 28.

132. Mehl, Ernest. "Flash Quickly Spotted Flaws in Hitters from Press Coop." *The Sporting News*. 24 May 1961, p. 4.

133. "A's Reign Tightened by Finley." *Olathe (KS) News*. 25 May 1961, p. 9.

134. McGuff, Joe. "Gordon Is Fired." *Kansas City Times*. 20 June 1961, p. 20.

135. Holmes, Tommy. "Finley Says He Wanted New Pilot." *New York Herald Tribune*. 20 June 1961, p. 24.

136. McGuff, Joe. "Gordon Out as Manager." *Kansas City Times*. 20 June 1961, p. 1.

137. https://clubhouseconversation.com/2017/02/remembering-the-royals-joe-gordon/.

138. https://clubhouseconversation.com/2017/02/remembering-the-royals-joe-gordon/.

139. https://clubhouseconversation.com/2017/02/remembering-the-royals-joe-gordon/.

140. "Lane Acts on Finley's Order." *Cleveland Plain Dealer*. 20 June 1961, p. 31.

141. "Gordon Out, Bauer In as A's Manager." *Eugene Register-Guard*. 20 June 1961, p. 2B.

142. Mehl, Ernest. "Finley Did It." *Kansas City Times*. 20 June 1961, pp. 1, 20.

143. McGuff, Joe. "Dazed Players Tip Hats to Joe, Wish Hank Well." *Kansas City Times*. 20 June 1961, p. 18.

144. "Firing May End Career." *Eugene Register-Guard*. 21 June 1961, p. 4B.

145. "Bauer Resigns, Lopat A's Pilot." *New York Herald Tribune*. 29 Sep. 1962, p. 13; Gordon Family Scrapbooks. "Bauer Takes Bull by Horns." prob. *The Sporting News*. prob. 13 Oct. 1962.

146. Holtzman, Jerry. "Finley Dumps G.M. Lane, Rakes Frankie Over Coals." *The Sporting News*. 30 Aug. 1961, p. 5; "Lane is Tardy in Learning of His Dismissal." *Kansas City Times*. 23 Aug. 1961, p. 1.

147. Holtzman, Jerry. "Finley Dumps G.M. Lane, Rakes Frankie Over Coals." *The Sporting News*. 30 Aug. 1961, p. 5.

148. https://clubhouseconversation.com/2017/02/remembering-the-royals-joe-gordon/.

149. Mehl, Ernest. "Ousted G.M. Blames Boss for Joe Gordon's Dismissal." *The Sporting News*. 30 Aug. 1961, p. 5; Mehl, Ernest. "'A.L. Sent Man to Size Up Cotton Bowl,' Lane Claims." *The Sporting News*. 30 Aug. 1961, p. 6.

150. https://clubhouseconversation.com/2017/02/remembering-the-royals-joe-gordon/.

151. Peterson, John E. *The Kansas City Athletics: A Baseball History, 1954–1967*. Jefferson, NC: McFarland, 2003.

152. Smith, Red. "Joe Gordon—The Yankees' Splendid Flash." *San Francisco Chronicle*. 18 April 1978, p. 44.

153. Conlin, Bill. "Baseball Great Gordon Dead." *Sacramento Bee*. 15 April 1978, pp. E1, E4.

Chapter 21

1. Drebinger, John. "Peace Offer Due in Majors Today." *New York Times*. 7 Dec. 1960, p. 60; Hemond, Roland, with Jean Hastings Ardell. "A Whole New Franchise: Creating the 1961 Los Angeles Angels in 120 Days." *The National Pastime: Endless Seasons—Baseball in Southern California*. Phoenix: Society for American Baseball Research, 2011, pp. 46–48.

2. "What Pilot Could Have Done More Under Circumstances? Friday Asks." *The Sporting News*. 22 Sep. 1962, p. 19.

3. Dyer, Braven. "Vets Rice and Bridges Picked to Help Tutor Angel Kid Talent." *The Sporting News*. 15 Nov. 1961, p. 22; Dyer, Braven. "Haney." *The Sporting News*. 16 June 1962, p. 6.

4. Dyer, Braven. "Seraphs Ship 12 to Farms, 34 Left on Parent Roster." *The Sporting News*. 28 March 1962, p. 22.

5. McDonald, Jack. "Candlestick Party Rekindles Graybeard Feats." *The Sporting News*. 18 Aug. 1962, p. 13; "Souvenir Program: San Francisco Giants Old Timers Day." Candlestick Park, San Francisco. 4 Aug. 1962; Kane, Tom. "ExGiants Whip ExSeals 5–0 in First Annual Candlestick Old Timers Game." *Sacramento Bee*. 5 Aug. 1962, p. D1.

6. Dyer, Braven. "Phenom, 18, Wins Spot on Angel Bench." *The Sporting News*. 13 April 1963, p. 3.

7. Dyer, Braven. "Seraphs' HR Output Sags in L.A. Park." *The Sporting News*. 18 May 1963, p. 18.

8. Dyer, Braven. "Angels Place Emergency Order—New Halo for Sub Sadowski." *The Sporting News*. 25 May 1963, p. 7.

9. Gianelli, Frank. "Big Timers Add Touch of Glamor to Cactus Clubs." *The Sporting News.* 10 Oct. 1964, p. 44.
10. "Tommy Heath Will Scout in Northwest for Angels." *The Sporting News.* 19 Dec. 1964, p. 12.
11. "Angels: Angel Angles." *The Sporting News.* 17 July 1965, p. 42.
12. Newhan, Ross. "From Now On, They'll be Known as California Angels." *The Sporting News.* 18 Sep. 1965, p. 25; "American League: New York at California." *The Sporting News.* 18 Sep. 1965, p. 20.
13. "Monchak Takes Reins as Angels' Field Boss." *Idaho Falls Post-Register.* 12 July 1966, p. 12; "Former Major League Manager Joe Gordon Takes Angel Reins." *Idaho Falls Post-Register.* 12 Aug. 1966, p. 20.
14. "Brooklyn Lives Again: Old-Time Dodgers Beat Themselves." *New York Times.* 24 July 1966, p. 140.
15. Souvenir Program. "Old Timers' Day: Honoring—The 1941 American and National League Champions." 23 July 1966.
16. Hernandez, Roberto. "Baseball Boom in Mexico with 8 Loops Ready." *The Sporting News.* 17 Feb. 1968, p. 38.
17. Fox, Gene. *Sports Guys: Insights, Highlights and Hoo-hahs from Your Favorite Sports Authorities.* Lenexa, KS: Addax, 1999, p. 82.
18. McGuff, Joe. "Old Home Week for Pilot Joe Gordon in Kaycee." *The Sporting News.* 21 Sep. 1968, p. 5.
19. "Name Gordon KC Manager." *Cleveland Plain Dealer.* 10 Sep. 1968, p. 57.
20. "Royals Hire Joe Gordon." *The Oregonian.* 10 Sep. 1968, p. 3.
21. "Royals Hire Joe Gordon." *The Oregonian.* 10 Sep. 1968, p. 3.
22. Wirz, Bob, editor. *Kansas City Royals Inaugural Yearbook.* Kansas City Royals Baseball Club, 1969.
23. Bordman, Sid. "Busy Royals Hire Tutors, Exec Talent." *The Sporting News.* 9 Nov. 1968, p. 44; McGuff, Joe. "Old Home Week for Pilot Joe Gordon in Kaycee." *The Sporting News.* 21 Sep. 1968, p. 5.
24. Bordman, Sid. "Busy Royals Hire Tutors, Exec Talent." *The Sporting News.* 9 Nov. 1968, p. 44; McGuff, Joe. "Royals Tie Up Loose Ends Before Launching." *The Sporting News.* 22 Feb. 1969, p. 40.
25. Dunlop, Harry. Phone interview with Judy Gordon. prob. Feb. 2021.
26. Dunlop, Harry. Email to Judy Gordon. Feb. 2021; Dunlop, Harry. Photo of KC Royals coaches mailed to Judy Gordon. Feb. 2021.
27. "One in a Series: Gordon Enthusiastic About Job." *Great Bend* (KS) *Tribune.* 19 March 1969, p. 8.
28. "Joe Gordon Enthused as Kansas City Royals' Boss." *Salina* (KS) *Journal.* 23 March 1969, p. 18.
29. Piniella, Lou, with Bill Madden. *Lou: 50 Years of Kicking Dirt, Playing Hard, and Winning Big in the Sweet Spot of Baseball.* New York: HarperCollins, 2017.
30. "Dave O." Email to Judy Gordon. May 2018.
31. McGuff, Joe. "Royals See Piniella as Real Rapper." *The Sporting News.* 3 May 1969, p. 18.
32. McGuff, Joe. "Royals Flush with Success Thanks to Rugged Relief." *The Sporting News.* 26 April 1969, p. 18.
33. McGuff, Joe. "Fading Royals Get Singed by Blasting from Irate Gordon." *The Sporting News.* 12 July 1969, p. 20.
34. McGuff, Joe. "Fading Royals Get Singed by Blasting from Irate Gordon." *The Sporting News.* 12 July 1969, p. 20.
35. Gordon, Joey. Phone conversations with Judy Gordon.
36. McGuff, Joe. "Royals Plan Switch for Hernandez' Bat." *The Sporting News.* 13 Sep. 1969, p. 16.
37. McGuff, Joe. "Coaches White, Harder Bid Baseball Good-Bye." *The Sporting News.* 20 Sep. 1969, p. 24.
38. McGuff, Joe. "Royals Plan Switch for Hernandez' Bat." *The Sporting News.* 13 Sep. 1969, p. 16.
39. McGuff, Joe. "'Gordon Taught Me to be a Thinker at Plate,' Says Piniella." *The Sporting News.* 13 Dec. 1969, p. 41.
40. McGuff, Joe. "'Gordon Taught Me to be a Thinker at Plate,' Says Piniella." *The Sporting News.* 13 Dec. 1969, p. 41.
41. Madden, Bill. *Pride of October: What It Was to Be Young and a Yankee.* New York: Warner, 2008.
42. Ferguson, Lew. "Joe Gordon Steps Aside: Charlie Metro Named Manager of Royals." *New London* (CT) *The Day.* 8 Oct. 1969, p. 23; "Baseball Briefs: Kansas City." *The Sporting News.* 10 Jan. 1970, p. 6; McGuff, Joe. "Royals' Roundup." *The Sporting News.* 18 July 1970, p. 34.
43. McGuff, Joe. "Gordon Tells Why He Quit Kaycee Post." *The Sporting News.* 25 Oct. 1969, p. 23.
44. Metro, Charlie, with Tom Altherr. *Safe by a Mile.* Lincoln: University of Nebraska Press, 2002, p. 464.

Chapter 22

1. Certificate of Completion, Real Estate Salesman's License. Lumbleau Real Estate School. April 1972; "Ferrick Realty Proudly Announces Joe Gordon." *Sacramento Bee.* 30 April 1972, p. E2.
2. "Wilhaggin: 4029 Ramel Way." *Sacramento Bee.* 5 March 1972, p. 46.
3. McGuff, Joe. "'Players Must Learn Facts of Life'—Kauffman." *The Sporting News.* 22 April 1972, p. 15.
4. Lustig, Dennis. "From the Summer of '48: Whatever Happened to... Joe Gordon?" *Cleveland Plain Dealer.* 25 Jan. 1974, p. 1-D.
5. Draper, Nick. "Baseball: A long wait: Local family rejoices after relative makes the National Baseball Hall of Fame." *Idaho Falls* (ID) *Post Register.* 9 Dec. 2008, p. D1.

6. Evensen, Kendra. "A humble HERO." *Idaho Falls River City Weekly*. 18 Dec. 2008, p. 11.

7. Gordon, Joey. Email to Judy Gordon. ab. Dec. 2023.

8. Schneider, Russell. "Schneider Around: Keltner, Gordon, Lemon on hand." *Cleveland Plain Dealer*. 9 Aug. 1975, p. 2-C; Schneider, Russell. "'48 Indians have fun and win, too." *Sunday Plain Dealer*. 10 Aug. 1975, p. 2; Photo. "Like old times." *Sunday Plain Dealer*. 10 Aug. 1975, p. 1.

9. Certificate of Death of Andrew J. Lampert. State of Oregon—Health Division. 31 Dec. 1975.

10. Smith, Red. "Joe Only Tried to Beat You." *New York Times*. 17 April 1978.

11. https://clubhouseconversation.com/2017/02/remembering-the-royals-joe-gordon/.

12. https://clubhouseconversation.com/2017/02/remembering-the-royals-joe-gordon/.

13. McGowen, Deane. "Joe Gordon is Dead; Ex-Yankee Star, 63." *New York Times*. 15 April 1978, p. 15.

14. Certificate of Death of Joseph Lowell Gordon. State of California. 14 April 1978.

15. Smith, Red. "Joe Only Tried to Beat You." *New York Times*. 17 April 1978.

16. Certificate of Death of Jack Robley Gordon. County of Humboldt, Eureka, California. 4 Nov. 1978.

17. Certificate of Death of Louise E. Lampert. Oregon Health Division. 7 Jan. 1984.

18. Certificate of Death of Dorthy Irene Gordon. State of Idaho. 3 April 1992.

19. https://clubhouseconversation.com/2017/02/remembering-the-royals-joe-gordon/.

20. Gordon Family Scrapbooks. Nelson, Arthur. "Gordon: One of Oregon's greats." prob. *Oregon Journal*. prob. April 1978.

Chapter 23

1. https://baseballhall.org/hall-of-fame/voting-rules-history.

2. Lang, Jack. "Glove Men Don't Seem to Fit Cooperstown." *The Sporting News*. 24 March 1986, p. 43.

3. Metro, Charlie, with Tom Altherr. *Safe by a Mile*. Lincoln: University of Nebraska Press, 2002, p. 464.

4. James, Bill. *Whatever Happened to the Hall of Fame? Baseball, Cooperstown, and the Politics of Glory*. New York: Simon & Schuster, 1995, Chapter 12.

5. Hoynes, Paul. "Hargrove, Gordon Await Tribe's Hall." *Cleveland Plain Dealer*. 8 Feb. 2008. pp. D1, D3.

6. "Hall of Fame Veteran's Committee Announcement." 2009 HOF Veteran Committee Transcript. ASAP Sports. 8 Dec. 2008; "Joe Gordon Elected to Hall of Fame by Veterans Committee." *National Baseball Hall of Fame NEWS*. 8 Dec. 2008.

7. "Hall of Fame Veteran's Committee Announcement." 2009 HOF Veteran Committee Transcript. ASAP Sports. 8 Dec. 2008.

8. "Ten Finalists Named for Consideration of Pre-1943 Players by 2009 Veterans Committee." *National Baseball Hall of Fame NEWS*. 25 Aug. 2008.

9. Feller, Bob. Phone call to Judy Gordon. late Aug. 2008.

10. "Ten Finalists Named for Hall of Fame Consideration of Players Whose Careers Began in 1943 or Later." *National Baseball Hall of Fame NEWS*. 16 Sep. 2008.

11. "Hall of Fame Veterans Committee Announcement." 2009 HOF Veterans Committee Transcript. ASAP Sports. 8 Dec. 2008; "Gordon elected to Hall by Veterans Committee." *National Baseball Hall of Fame PRESS RELEASE*. 8 Dec. 2008, 1:00 P.M. ET.

12. "Joe Gordon Elected to Hall of Fame by Veterans Committee." *National Baseball Hall of Fame NEWS*. 8 Dec. 2008; "Hall of Fame Veterans Committee Announcement." 2009 HOF Veteran Committee Transcript. ASAP Sports. 8 Dec. 2008.

13. Idelson, Jeff. President, National Baseball Hall of Fame and Museum. Email to Judy Gordon. 7 Dec. 2008, 8:20 P.M.

14. Warneke, Kevin, and David C. Ogden. *The Call to the Hall: When Baseball's Highest Honor Came to 31 Legends of the Sport*. Jefferson, NC: McFarland, 2018, p. 82.

15. https://clubhouseconversation.com/2017/02/remembering-the-royals-joe-gordon/.

16. https://clubhouseconversation.com/2017/02/remembering-the-royals-joe-gordon/.

17. https://clubhouseconversation.com/2017/02/remembering-the-royals-joe-gordon/; "Joe Gordon Elected to Hall of Fame by Veterans Committee." *National Baseball Hall of Fame NEWS*. 8 Dec. 2008.

18. Idelson, Jeff, and Jane Forbes Clark. Phone call to Judy Gordon. 8 Dec. 2008.

19. Gordon, Joey. Email to Judy Gordon. ab. Dec. 2023.

20. "Hall of Fame Veteran's Committee Announcement." 2009 HOF Veteran Committee Transcript. ASAP Sports. 8 Dec. 2008.

21. "Hall of Fame Veteran's Committee Announcement." 2009 HOF Veteran Committee Transcript. ASAP Sports. 8 Dec. 2008.

22. "Hall of Fame Veteran's Committee Announcement." 2009 HOF Veteran Committee Transcript. ASAP Sports. 8 Dec. 2008.

23. "Hall of Fame Veteran's Committee Announcement." 2009 HOF Veteran Committee Transcript. ASAP Sports. 8 Dec. 2008.

24. Idelson, Jeff. President, National Baseball Hall of Fame and Museum. Letter to Judy Gordon. 22 Dec. 2008.

25. Dahlgren, Matt. Phone call with Judy Gordon. Dec. 2008.

26. Hoffman, Dean. Phone call with Judy Gordon. Dec. 2008.

27. Gordon Family Scrapbooks. Smith, Jeff. "Gordon to get his due, 59 years after retiring." prob. *The Oregonian*. ab. 25 July 2009, pp. D1, D5.

28. *Joe Gordon: Hall of Fame Class of 2009* [Video]. National Baseball Hall of Fame and Museum. 2009.
29. https://baseballhall.org/hall-of-famers/past-inductions/2000-2009.
30. Schauder, Edward H. Email to Erik Simpson. 15 Nov. 2024.
31. Dawson, James P. "Yankees Sell First-Baseman [sic] Dahlgren to Bees in Straight Cash Transaction." *New York Times*. 26 Feb. 1941, p. 25; Dahlgren, Matt. *Rumor in Town: A Grandson's Promise to Right a Wrong*. California: Woodlyn Lane, 2007, p. 122.
32. *Joe Gordon: Hall of Fame Class of 2009* [Video]. National Baseball Hall of Fame and Museum. 2009.
33. *MLB Hall of Fame Tribute: Joe Gordon* [Video]. MLB Advanced Media. 2009.
34. McGuire, Mark. "Out of left field, a magic moment." Timesunion.com. 2009.
35. Richards, Brian. Senior Museum Curator. New York Yankees Museum. Email to Judy Gordon. 1 Sep. 2024.
36. Gordon Family Scrapbooks. Eberhart, Jeff. "University of Oregon vs. Arizona State." 2 April 2010.
37. Gordon Family Scrapbooks. Eberhart, Jeff. "University of Oregon vs. Arizona State." 2 April 2010.

Bibliography

Interviews and Other Correspondence

Bedingfield, Gary
Berra, Yogi
Brown, Bobby, Dr.
Dahlgren, Matt
"Dave O"
Doby, Larry, Jr.
Doerr, Bobby
Doerr, Don
Dunlop, Harry
Feller, Bob
Gordon, Joey
Haupert, Michael
Hoffman, Dean
Humasti, Joe
Izenberg, Jerry
Koch, Kerry
Levitt, Daniel R.
Madden, Bill
Morgan, Joe
Pearson, Albie
Richards, Brian
Robinson, Eddie
Silvera, Charlie

Books and Articles

Allen, Maury. *Where Have You Gone, Joe DiMaggio?* New York: E.P. Dutton, 1975.

Anton, Todd W. *No Greater Love: Life Stories from the Men Who Saved Baseball.* Burlington, MA: Rounder, 2007.

Barrow, Edward Grant, with James M. Kahn. *My Fifty Years in Baseball.* New York: Coward-McCann, 1951.

The Baseball Blue Book 1949.

Bedingfield, Gary. *Baseball in Hawaii During World War II.* Baseball in Wartime, 2021.

Borsvold, David. *Cleveland Indians: The Cleveland Press Years, 1920–1982.* Charleston, SC: Arcadia, 2003.

Boudreau, Lou, with Ed Fitzgerald. *Player-Manager.* Boston: Little, Brown, 1949.

Boudreau, Lou, with Russell Schneider. *Lou Boudreau: Covering All the Bases.* Champaign, IL: Sagamore, 1993.

Cramer, Richard Ben. *Joe DiMaggio: The Hero's Life.* New York: Simon & Schuster, 2000.

Creamer, Robert W. *Baseball in '41: A Celebration of the "Best Baseball Season Ever"—In the Year America Went to War.* New York: Penguin, 1991.

Dahlgren, Matt. *Rumor in Town: A Grandson's Promise to Right a Wrong.* California: Woodlyn Lane, 2007.

Dickson, Paul. *Bill Veeck: Baseball's Greatest Maverick.* New York: Walker, 2012.

Dragseth, P.J. *The 1957 San Francisco Seals: End of an Era in the Pacific Coast League.* Jefferson, NC: McFarland, 2013.

Dudley, Bruce. *Distant Drums: The 1949 Cleveland Indians Revisited.* Bowie, MD: Bruce Dudley, 1989.

Eig, Jonathan. *Luckiest Man: The Life and Death of Lou Gehrig.* New York: Simon & Schuster, 2005.

Einstein, Charles, ed. *The Fireside Book of Baseball.* New York: Simon & Schuster, 1956.

Elias, Robert. *The Empire Strikes Out: How Baseball Sold U.S. Foreign Policy and Promoted the American Way Abroad.* New York: New Press, 2010.

Eskenazi, Gerald. *Bill Veeck: A Baseball Legend.* New York: McGraw-Hill, 1988.

Feller, Bob, with Bill Gilbert. *Now Pitching, Bob Feller.* New York: Carol, 1990.

Fischer, David. *100 Things Yankees Fans Should Know & Do Before They Die.* Chicago: Triumph, 2012.

Fox, Gene. *Sports Guys: Insights, Highlights and Hoo-hahs from Your Favorite Sports Authorities.* Lenexa, KS: Addax, 1999.

Gehrig, Eleanor, and Joseph Durso. *My Luke and I.* New York: New American Library, 1976.

Greenberg, Hank, with Ira Berkow. *Hank Greenberg: The Story of My Life.* Chicago: Ivan R. Dee, 2001.

Hemond, Roland, with Jean Hastings Ardell. "A Whole New Franchise: Creating the 1961 Los Angeles Angels in 120 Days." *The National Pastime: Endless Seasons—Baseball in Southern California.* Phoenix: Society for American Baseball Research, 2011.

Henrich, Tommy, with Bill Gilbert. *Five O'Clock Lightning: Ruth, Gehrig, DiMaggio, Mantle and the Glory Years of the NY Yankees.* New York: Carol, 1992.

Honig, Donald. *The New York Yankees: An Illustrated History.* New York: Crown, 1981.
Izenberg, Jerry. *Larry Doby in Black and White: The Story of a Baseball Pioneer.* New York: Sports Publishing, 2024.
James, Bill. *Whatever Happened to the Hall of Fame? Baseball, Cooperstown, and the Politics of Glory.* New York: Simon & Schuster, 1995.
Kaiser, David. *Epic Season: The 1948 American League Pennant Race.* Amherst: University of Massachusetts Press, 1998.
Kelley, Brent P. *The San Francisco Seals, 1946–1957: Interviews with 25 Former Baseballers.* Jefferson, NC: McFarland, 2002.
Kennedy, Kostya. *56: Joe DiMaggio and the Last Magic Number in Sports.* New York: Sports Illustrated Books, 2011.
Levitt, Daniel R. *Ed Barrow: The Bulldog Who Built the Yankees' First Dynasty.* Lincoln: University of Nebraska Press, 2008.
Levy, Alan H. *Joe McCarthy: Architect of the Yankee Dynasty.* Jefferson, NC: McFarland, 2005.
Lewis, Franklin. *The Cleveland Indians.* New York: G.P. Putnam's Sons, 1949.
Madden, Bill. *Pride of October: What It Was to Be Young and a Yankee.* New York: Warner, 2008.
Malach, Roman. *Oatman: Gold Mining Center.* Kingman, AZ: Roman Malach, 1975.
Marazzi, Rich, and Len Fiorito. *Baseball Players of the 1950s: A Biographical Dictionary of All 1,560 Major Leaguers.* Jefferson, NC: McFarland, 2004.
Mayer, Ronald A. *The 1937 Newark Bears: A Baseball Legend.* New Brunswick: Rutgers University Press, 1994.
McAuley, Ed. *Bob Lemon: The Work Horse.* New York: A.S. Barnes, 1951.
Metro, Charlie, with Tom Altherr. *Safe by a Mile.* Lincoln: University of Nebraska Press, 2002.
Michelson, Herb. *Charlie O: Charles Oscar Finley vs. the Baseball Establishment.* Indianapolis: Bobbs-Merrill, 1975.
Moore, Joseph Thomas. *Larry Doby: The Struggle of the American League's First Black Player.* Mineola, NY: Dover, 2011.
_____. *Pride Against Prejudice: The Biography of Larry Doby.* New York: Praeger, 1988.
Nowlin, Bill, Len Levin, Carl Riechers, eds. *Baseball's Biggest BLOWOUT Games.* Phoenix: Society for American Baseball Research, 2020.
Obermeyer, Jeff. *Baseball and the Bottom Line in World War II: Gunning for Profits on the Home Front.* Jefferson, NC: McFarland, 2013.
Official Baseball Guide. 1975.
Paige, LeRoy (Satchel), as told to David Lipman. *Maybe I'll Pitch Forever.* Garden City, NY: Doubleday, 1962.
Pennington, Bill. *Billy Martin: Baseball's Flawed Genius.* New York: Mariner Books, 2016.
Peterson, John E. *The Kansas City Athletics: A Baseball History, 1954–1967.* Jefferson, NC: McFarland, 2003.

Piersall, Jimmy, with Richard Whittingham. *The Truth Hurts.* Chicago: Contemporary, 1984.
Piniella, Lou, with Bill Madden. *Lou: 50 Years of Kicking Dirt, Playing Hard, and Winning Big in the Sweet Spot of Baseball.* New York: HarperCollins, 2017.
Pluto, Terry. *The Curse of Rocky Colavito: A Loving Look at a Thirty-Year Slump.* Cleveland: Gray, 2007.
Robinson, Eddie, with C. Paul Rogers, III. *Lucky Me: My Sixty-Five Years in Baseball.* Lincoln: University of Nebraska Press, 2015.
Schneider, Russell. *The Boys of the Summer of '48.* Champaign, IL: Sports Publishing, 1998.
_____. *The Cleveland Indians Encyclopedia, 2nd Edition.* Champaign, IL: Sports Publishing, 2001.
Schoor, Gene. *The Scooter: The Phil Rizzuto Story.* New York: Charles Scribner's Sons, 1982.
Spalding, John E. *Sacramento Senators and Solons: Baseball in California's Capital, 1886 to 1976.* Manhattan, KS: Ag Press, 1995.
The Spectrum: Class of June '32. Jefferson High School, Portland, OR.
Tebbetts, Birdie, with James Morrison. *Birdie: Confessions of a Baseball Nomad.* Chicago: Triumph, 2002.
Tofel, Richard J. *A Legend in the Making: The New York Yankees in 1939.* Chicago: Ivan R. Dee, 2002.
Ungermann, Kathryn. *The Newton Family History.* Los Altos, CA: Kathryn Ungermann, 1993.
Veeck, Bill, with Ed Linn. *Veeck—As in Wreck: The Autobiography of Bill Veeck.* Chicago: University of Chicago Press, 2001.
Warfield, Don. *The Roaring Redhead: Larry MacPhail—Baseball's Great Innovator.* South Bend, IN: Diamond Communications, 1987.
Warneke, Kevin, and David C. Ogden. *The Call to the Hall: When Baseball's Highest Honor Came to 31 Legends of the Sport.* Jefferson, NC: McFarland, 2018.
Wells, Donald R. *The Race for the Governor's Cup: The Pacific Coast League Playoffs, 1936–1954.* Jefferson, NC: McFarland, 2000.
Werber, Bill, and C. Paul Rogers, III. *Memories of a Ballplayer: Bill Werber and Baseball in the 1930s.* Phoenix: Society for American Baseball Research, 2013.
Whittingham, Richard, comp. and ed. *The DiMaggio Albums, Vol. 1: 1932–1941.* G.P. Putnam's Sons. 1989.
Williams, Ted, with John Underwood. *My Turn at Bat: The Story of My Life.* New York: Simon & Schuster, 1969.
Wirz, Bob, ed. *Kansas City Royals Inaugural Yearbook.* Kansas City Royals Baseball Club, 1969.

Magazines and Periodicals

Argosy for Men. July 1948.
Baseball Digest. Vol. 6, No. 5, July 1947.
Baseball Magazine. Oct. 1939.
Boys' Life. Aug. 1949.

College Football Historical Society Vol. XXIV, No. III. May 2011.
Collier's. 18 July 1942.
Liberty. 27 Oct. 1945.
Life. 19 Dec. 1960.
Look. 28 July 1942.
National Safety News, Vol. 5. April 1922.
Sport. Sep. 1947; Oct. 1948; July 1949.
Sportfolio. Aug. 1948.
The Sporting Goods Dealer. March 1947.
Sports Album. Vol. 1, No. 4, May–July 1949.
Sports Illustrated. 11 May 1959.
Street & Smith's Sport Story Magazine. 1 July 1938.
This Week Magazine. 29 Sep. 1957.
Time. 6 May 1957.
Yank: The Army Weekly. 23 Jan. 1944; ab. summer 1944.

Newspapers and News Services

Associated Press
Bend (OR) *Bulletin*
Bernardsville (NJ) *News*
Birmingham (AL) *News*
Boston American
Brooklyn Daily Eagle
Chicago American
Chicago Daily News
Chicago Daily Tribune
Chicago Herald-Examiner
Chico (CA) *Enterprise-Record*
Cleveland Plain Dealer
Cleveland Press
Crawfordsville (IN) *Journal and Review*
Daily News
Denver Post
Detroit Free Press
Detroit Sunday Times
Detroit Times
Eugene (OR) *Morning News*
Great Bend (KS) *Tribune*
Idaho Evening Statesman
Idaho Falls Post Register
Idaho Falls River City Weekly
Indiana (PA) *Gazette*
International News Service
Kansas City Times
Los Angeles Examiner
Los Angeles Times
Lowell (MA) *Sun*
Manistee (MI) *Advocate*
Morning Oregonian
Morning World-Herald
New London (CT) *The Day*
New York Daily Mirror
New York Daily News
New York Herald
New York Herald Tribune
New York Journal American
New York News
New York Post
New York Times
New York Tribune
New York World-Telegram
Newark (NJ) *Evening News*
Newark Ledger Sports
Newark Star Eagle Sports
Newark Star-Ledger Archive
News-Telegram
Oakland Post-Enquirer
Oakland Tribune
Oatman (AZ) *News*
Oklahoman
Olathe (KS) *News*
Omaha (NE) *Morning World-Herald*
Oregon Daily Emerald
Oregon Daily Journal
Oregon Emerald
Oregon Journal
The Oregon Legionnaire
The Oregonian
Oregonian-Chicago Tribune Leased Wire
The Pittsburgh Press
The Plain Dealer
Portland News-Telegram
Riverside (CA) *Daily Press*
Sacramento Bee
Sacramento Union
St. Petersburg (FL) *Evening Independent*
St. Petersburg (FL) *Times*
Salem (OR) *Statesman*
Salina (KS) *Journal*
San Diego Union
San Francisco Chronicle
San Francisco Examiner
San Francisco News
Seattle Post-Intelligencer
Seattle Star Sports
Seattle Times
Sonora (CA) *Union Democrat*
The Sporting News
Sports: Service World's Series Special
Sunday Daily News
Sunday Oregonian
Sunday Plain Dealer
Timesunion.com
United Press
World-Telegram

Online Sources

http://articles.latimes.com/2009/aug/31/local/me-cap31.
http://baseballhall.org/discover/short-stops/keep-baseball-going.
http://baseballhall.org/hof/gordon-joe.
http://cerealpriceguide.blogspot.com/2013/04/wheaties-cereal-box-price-guide.html.
http://springtrainingmagazine.com/history4.html.
http://vallejomuseum.blogspot.com/2014/06/the-boys-of-summer-visit-mare-island.html.
http://www.captainsblog.info/2010/09/09/libeling-lou-iron-horse-sues-to-restore-his-name-80-years-ago-today/2534/.

http://www.clevelandmemory.org/league/indians100/index.html.
https://baseballhall.org/hall-of-fame/voting-rules-history.
https://baseballhall.org/hall-of-famers/past-inductions/2000-2009.
https://blog.newspapers.com/august-15-1945-the-75th-anniversary-of-v-j-day/.
https://clubhouseconversation.com/2017/02/remembering-the-royals-joe-gordon/.
https://docs.google.com/spreadsheets/d/1mfjUVrIhBv6HeltZXYZNPFs_VKopDF_unaZ883QPQr0/edit#gid=1613289983.
https://moiderersrow.com/new-york-yankees-spring-training-history-since-1903/.
https://newarkmemories.com/memories/503.php.
https://newyork.sbnation.com/new-york-yankees/2012/7/24/3178445/.
https://nyyfansforum.sny.tv/forum/general-baseball-forums/around-the-majors/12761-behind-doby-quiet-heroine-stood-guard-by-claire-smith.
https://1939baseball.com/cooperstown_centennial.html.
https://sabr.org/bioproj/person/phil-masi/.
https://thatballsouttahere.com/2015/07/14/phillys-first-all-star-game/.
https://time.com/archive/6611763/sport-scoreboard-may-6-1957/.
https://www.newworldencyclopedia.org/entry/Yankee_Stadium.
https://www.nydailynews.com/sports/baseball/eddie-robinson-living-member-48-indians-pissed-team-article-1.2838963.

1939 MLB Season History— Major League Baseball—ESPN

www.archives.gov/publications/prologue/2002/spring/greenlight.html.
www.baseball-almanac.com/teams/yankquot.shtml.
www.baseball-reference.com/bullpen/Waivers.
www.baseball-reference.com/leaders/DP_2b_career.shtml.
www.baseball-reference.com/leaders/Gm_2b_top_ten.shtml.
www.cbssports.com/mlb/news/orioles-extra-inning-winning-getting-historic/.
www.espn.com/classic/obit/s/2002/1225/1482290.html.
www.espn.com/mlb/columns/story?columnist=morgan_joe&id=1572794.
www.espn.com/mlb/story/_/id/24404246/chicago-cubs-turn-mlb-record-tying-7-double-plays-win.
www.history.com/this-day-in-history/baseball-owners-allow-dodgers-and-giants-to-move.
www.tampabay.com/opinion/columns/column-when-d-day-came-to-st-petersburg/2183157/.

Films and Videos

Joe Gordon: Hall of Fame Class of 2009 [Video]. National Baseball Hall of Fame and Museum. 2009.
MLB Hall of Fame Tribute: Joe Gordon [Video]. MLB Advanced Media. 2009.
Touching All Bases. The Official American League Motion Picture of 1940. 1 Jan. 1940.

Miscellaneous Sources

AFATC Enlisted Personnel Branch, Washington, D.C. War Department Restricted Message form to Commanding General, Pacific Division, Air Transport Command, Hamilton Field, CA. 25 Apr. 1945.
All America Board of Baseball. Certificate designating Joe Gordon, New York Yankees, as a member of the All America Baseball Team of 1939, approved 16 Sep. 1939.
American League of Professional Baseball Clubs: Uniform Player's Contract for Joseph Gordon. 4 Mar. 1941.
Army of the United States. Enlisted Record and Report of Separation Honorable Discharge for Joseph L. Gordon. 14 Nov. 1945.
Brooklyn Dodgers Media Guide. 1941.
Certificate of Completion, Real Estate Salesman's License. Lumbleau Real Estate School. Apr. 1972.
Certificate of Death of Andrew J. Lampert. State of Oregon—Health Division. 31 Dec. 1975.
Certificate of Death of Dorthy Irene Gordon. State of Idaho. 3 Apr. 1992.
Certificate of Death of Jack Robley Gordon. County of Humboldt, Eureka, California. 4 Nov. 1978.
Certificate of Death of Joseph Lowell Gordon. State of California. 14 Apr. 1978.
Certificate of Death of Louise E. Lampert. Oregon Health Division. 7 Jan. 1984.
Certificate of Marriage of Andrew J. Lampert and Louise E. Gordon. Northminster Presbyterian Church. Seattle, WA. 7 Mar. 1958.
"Champs of the U.S.A. Set No. 21." Wheaties "Breakfast of Champions." 1941.
"Congratulations to Larry Doby on His Introduction [sic] to the Baseball Hall of Fame." *U.S. Congressional Record: Proceedings and Debates of the 105th Congress, Second Session.* Vol 144, No. 28. Washington, D.C. 16 March 1998, pp. S2001–S2002.
Contract Record Cards of Joseph L. Gordon.
Death Record of Ben Lowell Gordon. Tuolumne Co. Hospital. Sonora, CA. 12 May 1946.
Event program. "A Dinner by a Few of the Fans for Joe Gordon." Multnomah Athletic Club. Portland, OR. 16 Nov. 1939.
Fisher, Fred. Letter to "Hal." 30 Apr. 1998.
Flyer. "AAF All Stars POA." Mariana Islands. late Aug. 1945.
Flyer. "USASTAF Special Services Presents Its Major League Baseball Stars." Guam. Sep. 1945.
Gordon, Dottie. Letter to Joe Gordon's mother, Louise Gordon, from Las Vegas, NM. 7 June 1944.

Bibliography

Gordon, Jack. Grade Report Cards. 1922, 1925, 1926.

Gordon, Joe. Letters to his mother, Louise Gordon. 1942–1948.

Gordon, Joe Lowell. Grade Report Cards. 1921–1939.

Gordon, Joey. Written notes from conversations with Lois Rusche Jenkins, niece of Louise Gordon Lampert. Portland, OR. 1983.

Gordon, Judy. Speech for Induction of Joe "Flash" Gordon into the National Baseball Hall of Fame. 26 July 2009.

"Gordon elected to Hall by Veterans Committee." *National Baseball Hall of Fame PRESS RELEASE*. 8 Dec. 2008, 1:00 P.M. ET.

"Hall of Fame Veteran's Committee Announcement." 2009 HOF Veteran Committee Transcript. ASAP Sports. 8 Dec. 2008.

Harridge, William. American League Professional Base Ball Clubs. Chicago. IL. Letter to Mr. Joseph Gordon. 3 July 1939.

Harridge, William. American League Professional Base Ball Clubs. Chicago, IL. Letter to Mr. Joseph Gordon. 30 June 1941.

Haupert, Michael. Haupert Baseball Salary Database, private collection.

HQ & HQ Squadron, VII Fighter Command, Office of the Operations Officer, APO 953. Pvt. Joe Gordon, flight logs from 2 Aug. 1944 through 26 Oct. 1944, signed by Captain Donal J. Broesamle.

Idelson, Jeff. President, National Baseball Hall of Fame and Museum. Email to Judy Gordon. 7 Dec. 2008, 8:20 P.M.

"Joe Gordon Elected to Hall of Fame by Veterans Committee." *National Baseball Hall of Fame NEWS*. 8 Dec. 2008.

Joseph L. Gordon Corporal of the 58th Bomb Wing Honorable Discharge from the Army of the United States at the Separation Center, Camp Beale, California. 14 Nov. 1945.

Landis, Kenesaw M. Commissioner of Major League Baseball. Letter to Joseph Gordon. 25 May 1944.

Marriage Certificate of Lowell Gordon and Lulu Pearl Evans. Globe, AZ. 3 Dec. 1912.

Marriage License: State of Maryland. Joseph Lowell Gordon and Dorthy Irene Crum. Elkton, MD. 4 June 1938.

McCarthy, Joe. Handwritten note addressed to Clyde Sayles and Andy Lampert. ab. 30 Sep. 1941.

Morgan, Phyllis. "New York Yankees and the Gordons." Letter to Judy Gordon. 25 Oct. 2004.

Morgan, Phyllis. "1943 and 1946 Trips to New York to Live with Dorothy [sic] and Joe Gordon and Their Children."

National Association Contract Record Cards of Al Raymond Koch. 1935–1941.

"Nimrod Association of the World." Charter membership certificate. Summer or fall of 1944.

O'Connor, Leslie M., Secretary-Treasurer. Baseball Office of the Commissioner. Letter to New York American League Club Players. 18 Oct. 1941.

Odell, Dick. Zellerbach Paper Co, Eugene Division. Letter to Mrs. Louise Gordon. 19 Jan. 1933.

Official Souvenir Program. *Cleveland Indians vs. Boston Braves 1948 World Series*. Cleveland Baseball Corp. Oct. 1948.

"1937 Spring Training Schedule.1937." Hotel Sebring. Sebring, FL. 10 Mar.–22 Apr. 1937.

Oregon State Soccer Football Association membership card certifying Joe Gorden [sic] duly registered as an amateur the season of 1930–1931.

Pamphlet. Gordon, Joe. *How to Play Second Base*. Johnstown, NY: John McGlynn, 21 Aug. 1939. AA 309855.

Pilot's Flight Log of Joe L. Gordon. 28 Dec. 1940–14 Sep. 1942.

Private Pilot Airman Certificate No. 133880 issued to Joe Lowell Gordon on 5 Jan. 1942.

Private Pilot Airman Certificate No. 133880 Seaplane Rating issued to Joe Lowell Gordon on 10 June 1942.

Second Annual Portland Area YMCA Track and Field Meet ribbons awarded to Joe Gordon. 25 May 1929.

7th AAF photo (A-2, HQ-7thAAF, APO 953). Joe Gordon and Captain Donal Broesamle. Territory of Hawaii. prob. summer 1944.

Souvenir Menu. *New York "Yankees" Special*. Enroute New York to Cincinnati. Oct. 1939.

Souvenir Program. "Old Timers' Day: Honoring—The 1941 American and National League Champions." 23 July 1966.

Souvenir Program. Cleveland Indians vs. New York Giants. Owls Park, Topeka, KS. 14 Apr. 1948.

"Souvenir Program: San Francisco Giants Old Timers Day." Candlestick Park, San Francisco. 4 Aug. 1962.

"The Ted Bacon String Orchestra Municipal Concert Program." Ted Bacon Conductor. Portland, OR. 19 Feb. 1928.

"Ten Finalists Named for Consideration of Pre-1943 Players by 2009 Veterans Committee." *National Baseball Hall of Fame NEWS*. 25 Aug. 2008.

"Ten Finalists Named for Hall of Fame Consideration of Players Whose Careers Began in 1943 or Later." *National Baseball Hall of Fame NEWS*. 16 Sep. 2008.

"200 Home Run Club [of] the American and National Leagues of Professional Baseball." Griffith Stadium, Washington, D.C. 19 July 1948.

United States Census (1900). Deerfield District, Fergus County, MT. 14-16 June 1900.

United States Census (1910). Cerbat, Mohave County, AZ. 22–23 Apr. 1910.

United States Census (1920). Old Trails, Mohave County, AZ. 14 Jan. 1920.

United States President Franklin D. Roosevelt. "Green Light Letter" to Hon. Kenesaw M. Landis, Commissioner of Major League Baseball. 15 Jan. 1942.

Western Union Telefax. Vice President Dick Nixon to the Honorable George Christopher, Mayor of San Francisco. Sep. 1957.

World War I Draft Registration Card for Lowell Gordon. 12 Sep. 1918.

Zellerbach Paper Co. Gold retirement card awarded to Louise E. Gordon for service from 1921–1958.

INDEX

Numbers in ***bold italics*** indicate pages with illustrations

Abbott, Spencer 20
Abernathie, Bill 179
acrobatic 1, 208, 219
African American ballplayers 49, 111, 140, 156, 157, 162, 213, 219
Albrook Army Airfield, Panama 123
All America Baseball Team of 1939 ***60***, 61
All-Service All-Stars 90
Allen, Ethan 58
amateur status 16, 22
American Association 35, 180, 198, 203
American League Pitcher of the Year Award 155
American Legion Junior Baseball 17, 18, ***18***, 19, ***19***, 20, 22, 24, 218
amyotrophic lateral sclerosis (ALS) 46, 56, 68, 76
Anderson, Derk 216
Anderson, Sparky 219
Anderson, Steve 216, 223
Anderson, Walter ***14***
Anderson, Zac 223
Andrews, Ivy ***40***, 49
Appling, Luke 192
Ardizoia, Rugger 109
Arizona State University (ASU) Sun Devils 223
Armed Forces Radio 111
Army-Navy World Series (1944) 110, 111
Arnold, Sue Simpson (granddaughter) 205, 206, ***207***, 208, 212, ***212***, 214, 221
Asbury Park, NJ 97, 98
Aspromonte, Ken 178–180, 189, 208, 209
atomic bomb 115
Attyd, Len 173
autographs 2, ***30***, ***37***, 44, 102, ***102***, ***118***, 205–***207***, 219, 223
Autry, Gene 180, 199
Ávila, Bobby 167, 183

Babich, Johnny 69, 70, 76, 77
Bagby, Jim 78
Baker, Del 170
balata ball 99, 101
Baltimore Orioles (International League) 33–35, 37
barnstorming 22, 24, 33, 40, 41, 65, 87, 122, 128, 147
Barrow, Ed 33, 35, 42–44, 54, 56, 57, 72, 83, 88, 97–99, 105, 106, 121, 130
baseball (college) 22–26
baseball (grammar school) 12, 14
baseball (high school) 16–18, ***20***, 21, 63, 218
baseball glove (bronzed) 205, ***206***, 219
Baseball Writers' Association of America (BBWAA) 56, 64, 72, 86, 94, ***94***–96, 143, 159, 169, 180, 184, 190, 204, 210, 212, 215, 218, 221
batting instructor (Joe Gordon) 1, 180, 199–201, 204, 205
Bauer, Hank 196–198, 201
Bearden, Gene 146, 153–***158***, 160, 161
Beazley, Johnny 93, 101, 109
Bedingfield, Gary 115
Beggs, Joe 25, 34–36
Bell, Gary 190
Bellinger, Cody 103
Bellotti, Mike 223
Bend (OR) Elks 24
Benton, Al 164, 166, 170
Beradino, John 147
Berardino, Johnny 131, 147, 166
Berg, Emil ***14***
Berg, Martin ***14***
Berger, Wally 62
Berra, Lindsay 218
Berra, Yogi 216, 217, ***217***, 218
Berry, Charlie 125
Bevens, Bill 134
Bickel, Fritz 65

Bisher, Furman 213
Black, Don 142, 146, 152
Bockman, Eddie 173
Bonds, Barry 103
Bonham, Tiny 82, 83, 91, 92, 96, 98, 100, 101
bonuses *see* contracts
Boone, Ray 145, 162, 167
Borowy, Hank 92, 98, 101
Bossard, Emil 138
Boston Bees 5, 6, 72, 73, 219
Boston Braves 98, 153, 155–157, 162
Boudreau, Lou 78, 90, 132–146, ***146***, 147, 149, 153–158, ***158***–162, 164–167, 174
boxing (Joe Gordon) 24, 129
Boyd, Bob 170–172
Bragan, Bobby 182
Bresnahan, Roger 101
Breuer, Marv 92
Briggs, Walter O., Jr. 175, 176
Bright, Harry 179
Broesamle, Captain Donal J. 110
Brooklyn Robins 82, 145
Brooks, Ray 22, 23, 27
Brown, Bill 218
Brown, Dr. Bobby 4, 127
Brown, Jimmy 92
Brown, Joe 63
Brown, Mary 63
Bryant, Clay 51
Bullpen Theater 219
Bunker, Wally 202
Butler, Willis 26
Butler Yankees 44

California Angels 199–202, 204
Callison, Prince G. "Prink" 23
Camilli, Dick 174
Camilli, Dolph 112, 174
Camp Luna, NM 107, 108, ***108***, 109
Camp Luna Airtrancos 108, ***108***
Campanella, Roy 162

274 Index

Campbell, Lindsey C. 16, 17, 49
Campbell, William "Bick" 35
Canal Zone 123–125
Canal Zone League All Stars 125
Candini, Milo 97
captain (of a team) 16, 21, 23, 25, 34, 41, 56, 57
Carroll, Parke 193, 194
Casey, Hugh 82
Cavarretta, Phil 50
U.S.S. *Cecil* 119, **119**
"Centennial Year of Baseball" 55, 57
Central Pacific Area Service League 110
Central Pacific Area Service World Series *see* Army-Navy World Series (1944)
Chandler, Albert Benjamin "Happy" 136, 137, 152
Chandler, Spud 36, 45, 49, 51, 61, 78, 90, 92, 93, 98, 100, 101, 103, 105, 107, 125, 128, 132, 134
Chapman, Ben 75
charley horse 65, 66, 71, 98, 128
Charros de Jalisco 201
Cheney, Ben 156, 171
Chicago Cubs 27, 49–52, 91, 104, 133, 137, 142, 190, 200
Chris' Chop House 33
Christopher, George 179
Christopher, Russ 146, 155, 157
Cincinnati Reds 62, 63, 77, 80
Clark, Allie 155
Clark, Jane Forbes 1, 214, 215, 218, **220**, 221
Cleveland Guardians 210
Cleveland Indians Hall of Fame 210, **211**, 212, **212**
Cleveland Indians Man of the Year 155, 184
Cleveland Municipal Stadium 90, 138, 139, 142, 147, 149, 152, 153, 156, 161, 189, 210
Clevenger, Tex 185
coaching (Joe Gordon) 1, 175, 181, 200, 205
Cobb, Ty 93, 112
Cochrane, Mickey 90
Colavito, Rocky 183–185, 188, 189
Coleman, Gordy 188
Collins, Eddie 38, 57, 80, 101, 104
Collins, Ripper 49, 51
Coltrin, Bobby 28
Columbus Red Birds 35, 36
Combs, Earle 90
Concourse Plaza Hotel 45, 99
Congressional Gold Medal 156
contracts 3, 6, 25–28, 30, 35, 39–43, 54, 64, 72, 73, 86, 87, 97, 98, 123, 125, 126, 136, 140, 143, 145, 160, 164–166, 168–171, 173–175, 183, 186–188, 192–196, 199, 201, 204, 205
Cooper, Mort 96, 103
Cooper, Walker 93, 103
Cooperstown, NY 55, 59, 140, 190, 212, 216, 217, 221
Costas, Bob 219
Cramer, Doc 57
Cronin, Joe 48, 57, 61, 67, 142, 180, 189, 191
Crosby Juniors 12, 14, **14**, 17, 218
Crosetti, Frank 4, 25, 42, 43, 48–50, **50**, 51, 56, 58, 59, 73, 76, 88, 92, 93, 98, 103
Crum, Frank Earle (father-in-law) 61, 62
Crum, Irene Arizona (mother-in-law) 62, 68, 80, 90
Crum, Janis (sister-in-law) 26
Crum, Newton (brother-in-law) 24, 26
Cullenbine, Roy 91, 93, 97
Cutshaw, George 104
Cy Young Award 186

Dahlen, Bill 213
Dahlgren, Babe 36, 55–57, 59, 62, 67, 68, 72, 73, 216, 219, 221
Dahlgren, Jenny 216, 217, 219
Dahlgren, Matt 216, 217, 219, 221
Daley, Bud 197
Daniels, Bert 69
Danner, Ford 71
"Dave O" 127, 180, 196, 198, 207, 209, 213
Davis, Curt 81
Dean, Chubby **118**
Dean, Dizzy 49
de Dios Amador, Juan 125
Deedon, Helen 90
de Freitas, Denny 218
de La Guardia, Ernesto 125
Devincenzi, Vic 28
Devine, Joe 28
DeViveiros, Bernie 30, 174
Dewey, Thomas E. 102
DeWitt, William O., Sr. 192, 193
Dickey, Bill 4, **40**, 42, 47, **47**–50, **50**, 51, 56, 57, 59, 61, 62, 64, 65, **65**, 67, 68, 76, 81, 82, 86–**89**, 93, 100, 103, 107, 111, 125, 128–134, 136, 169, 200
Dickey, George 111
Dickey, Violet "Vi" **89**
DiFranza, Lenny 217
Dillinger, Bob 109, 110, 173
DiMaggio, Dominic 110, 111, 130, 199
DiMaggio, Joe 3, 25, 40, 42, 43, 47, **47**–50, **50**, 51, 56, 57, 59, 61, 62, 64–65, 67, 69, 71, 72, 75–78, 80–82, 84, 86, 88–90, 92, 93, 96, 97, 99, 107, 109, 111, 125, 126, 128, 129, 132–135, 143, 147, 155, 162, 199, 200
DiMaggio, Vince 31, 199
Doby, Helyn 141
Doby, Larry 111, 140–144, 146, 147, 149, 151, 155, 156, 158, 159, 162–164, 167, 168, 183, 213, 219, 223
Doby, Larry, Jr. 156
Doerr, Bobby 31, 84, 86, 89–91, 95, 100, 134, 137, 139, 142, 159, 169, 172, 177, 210, 213, 214, 217, 223
Doerr, Don 84, 177, 223
Dolan, Larry & Eva 212
Donald, Atley 34, 36, 61, 65, 68, 92, 97, 98
Donovan, Jerry 176, 179
Doran, Bill 173
Dorman, Harry 17, 20
Dorsey, Tommy 79
Doyle, Bill 218, 223
Doyle, Nancy Crum (niece) 216, 223
Drabowsky, Moe 190
Dragseth, P.J. 177, 179
Drott, Dick 190
Dunlop, Harry 202, **202**, 207, 208
Durocher, Leo 81, 82, 186
Dyer, Eddie 142
Dykes, Jimmy 191–193

East Side Commercial Club 17, 18, **18**, 19, **19**, 20, 24, 218
Easter, Luke 167, 168
Eatch, Jack **14**
Ebbets Field 41, 65, 82, 98, 162
Eberhart, Jeff 223
Edwards, Hank 141
Ellen's Café 14
Embree, Red 135, 138
Ensley, Harold 196
Essick, Bill 3, 5, 24–28, 32, 35, 39, 106
Etten, Nick 98, 129, 134
Eugene Emeralds 177, 178
Eugene Townies 24
Evans, George (uncle) 7, 10
Evans, James (grandfather) 7
Evans, Matilda Grose (grandmother) 7
Evers, Johnny 90, 104
expansion clubs 194, 195, 199, 201–204

Fain, Ferris 109, **118**
Farley, James A. 57, 95, 102
Feller, Bob 57, 64, 70, 77, 90, 128, 134, 138, 142, 143, 145–147, 149–153, 155–157, 159–161, 164, 166, 168, 212, **212**, 213

Index

Ferrell, Rick 42, 89
Ferrell, Wes 213
58th Bombardment Wing Wingmen, West Field, Tinian 113, *114*, *115*
Fingers, Rollie 218, 219
Finley, Charles O. "Charlie" 194–198
firing (of Joe Gordon) 196–198
FitzGerald, Ed 194
Fitzpatrick, John 200
Fitzsimmons, Freddie 82
"Flash" *see* nicknames for Joe Gordon
Flash Gordon (comic strip) 6, 16, 81
Fleming, Les 143
Fletcher, Art 4, 62
Flyers team (on Guam) *118*, 119
flying (Joe Gordon) 71, 75, 86–88, *88*, 94, 98, 106, 110, 127, 180, 207, 218, 219
football (college) 23, 24
football (high school) 17
Ford C. Frick Award of 2009 221
Fox, Nellie 95
Fox, William S. 33
Foxx, Jimmie 52, 59, 61, 65, 68
Francona, Tito 189
Frank Fat's Chinese Restaurant 175
Friend, Owen 202, *202*
Frisch, Frankie 80, 101
Froelich, Ed 123
Furlong Field, Pearl Harbor Naval Base, Oahu, Territory of Hawaii 110, 111

Garbarino, Bill 17, 18, 24
Garcia, Mike 153, 164, 167, 168
Gates, Jim 217
Gehrig, Eleanor 39, 200
Gehrig, Lou 3, 39–42, 44–47, *47*–49, **50**–51, 55, 56, 57, 59, 62, 68–70, 73, 74, 76, 87, 99, 184, 219, 200
Gehringer, Charlie 45–48, 57, 80, 86, 169
Gibson, Bob 219
Gilkerson's Union Colored Giants of Chicago 22
Gill, George *114*, *118*
Gleeson, Jimmy 35, 36
Globe, AZ 7, 8, 10
Gomez, Lefty 25, 48, 49, 56, 58, 59, 61, 68, 102
Goodman, Billy 153
Gordon, Benjamin Lowell Ben (father) 2, 7, 8, **8**, 9, 10, 12
Gordon, Dorthy Irene Dottie Crum (wife) 2, 24, 25, **25**, 26, **33**, 39, 44–47, 49, 52, 53, 62–68, 71, 72, 78, 80, 81, 83,

84, **84**, 86, **87**, **89**, 90, 98, 99, 102, 105, 109, 112, 119, 121, 126, 139, 141, 145, 151, 152, 158, 159, 163, 168, 171, 172, 175, 177, 180, 184, 192, 196, 197, 201, 205, 207, 208, 215, 216, 218, 221
Gordon, Jack (brother) 2, 7, **8**, **9**–11, **11**, 12, **13**, 14, **14**, 15, 17, 21–24, 36, 71, 80, 105, 156, 171, 207, 208
Gordon, Joey (son) 90, 98, 109, 112, **127**, 152, 175, 177, 185, 197, 203, 205–207, 214–216, 218
Gordon, John Riley (grandfather) 7
Gordon, Julie (granddaughter) 215
Gordon, Lulu Pearl Louise Evans (mother) 2, 7–11, **11**, 12, 14–17, 25, 27, 30, 36, 46, 47, 49, 54, 62, 80, 83, 121, 156, 208
Gordon, Martha Ann Darnall (grandmother) 7
Gordon, Seraphina (granddaughter) 215, 216
Gorman, Lou 202
Grayson, Bobby 17
Great Depression 3, 12, 21
"Green Light Letter" 86
Greenberg, Hank 57, 59, 101, 145, 161, 164–166, 169
Griffith, Clark 75
Grigsby, Bill 195
Grimes, Oscar 97, 127, 140, 152
Gromek, Steve 141, 146, 153, 156, 168
Groth, Ernest 153
Grove, Orval 171
Guam 113–115, 117, *118*, 119
Guerriero, Raffaele "Lefty" *108*
Gumpert, Randy 134
gymnastics and tumbling (Joe Gordon) 14, 25, 208, 221

Habein, Dr. Harold 56, 68
Hack, Stan 49, 78, 170
Hadley, Bump 47, 49, 61, 102
Hairston, Harold "Hal" 109, 111
Hairston, Sam 170
Hall of Fame (HOF) *see* National Baseball Hall of Fame (HOF)
Hall of Fame Inductions 2009 1, 2, 141, 169, 215–217, 220, **220**, 221
Hall of Fame plaque 220, **220**, 221
Hamilton Field, CA 10, 109, 112, 113
Hamilton Field Flyers 112
Haney, Fred 170, 199
Hankins, Jay 198
Harder, Mel 145, 183, 187, 202, **202**, 203

Hargrove, Mike 210, 211
Harper, Earl 33
Harridge, William 57, 77, 138, 152
Harris, Bucky 42, 46, 79, 80, 133, 149, 175
Hassett, Buddy 97, 102
Hatton, Grady 179
Haupert, Michael 231n49
Hawaii League 110
Hegan, Jim 141, 142, 146, 157, 162
Held, Woodie 190, 191
Hemond, Roland 213
Henderson, Rickey 218, 220–222
Henrich, Tommy 42, 47, **47**, 49, **50**, 56, 76, 82, 83, 90, 91, 97, 107, 125, 126, 128–130, 134, 155
Heritage Park, Progressive Field, Cleveland, OH **211**, 212
Hershberger, Willard 36
Hickam Field, Oahu, Territory of Hawaii 109, 112
Hildebrand, Oral 61, 68
Hillerich & Bradsby Co. 65
Hirdt, Steve 213
Historical Overview Committee 212
hit for the cycle 69
Hitchcock, Billy 101, **114**, **118**, 175, 192
Hoag, Myril 42, 49
Hobson, Howard 21
Hoffman, Ben 216, 221
Hoffman, Dean 216, 219, 221
Hoffman, Ed 216, 221
Hoffman, Susan 216
holdout 40, 43, 54, 98
Holladay Grammar School 11, 12, 117
Hollywood Stars 170–174, 177, 178
Hop Golds 27
Hornsby, Rogers 56, 80, 93, 137, 145, 170
Hotel Riviera 33
House of Davids of Benton Harbor, Michigan 22
Houston Astros 91, 194
Houston Colt .45s 194
How to Play Second Base (pamphlet) 58–**59**
Howser, Dick 194
Hudson, Sid 101
Hughes, Tommy 101
Humasti, Bruno 14, **14**, **18**, 218
Humasti, Ellen 14
Humasti, Joe 218
Hummel, Walter 122, 172
Hutchinson, Fred 175

Idaho Falls (ID) Angels 200
Idelson, Jeff 213–215, 218, **220**

Index

Inductee Press Conference 2, 219
injuries or other health problems (Joe Gordon or other players) 30, 33, 42–45, 50, 51, 65–67, 75–76, 78, 80, 82, 88, 91, 100, 106, 126–134, 147, 151, 152, 160, 161, 166, 167, 172, 173, 185, 188–191
International League 6, 26, 32–37, 41, 67, 140, 152
International League Governors' Cup 35
Iwo Jima, Volcano Islands 115, *116*, 117
Izenberg, Jerry 33, 140

Jackson, Reggie 103, 219
James, Bill 210
Jefferson High School 14, 16, 17, *20*, 21, 218
Jenkins, Hopkin 16, 49
Jerome Copper *9*, 10
Jewish American ballplayers 157
J.G. Taylor Spink Award 221
Jiménez, Enrique Adolfo 125
Joe Gordon Hardware 122, 135, 172
Joe Gordon: Hall of Fame Class of 2009 (video) 217, 219
Johnson, Arnold 193, 194
Johnson, Billy 98, 103, 104
Johnson, Walter 91, 101
Joost, Eddie 176
Joplin Miners 27, 28, 30
Jorgens, Arndt 55
Judnich, Walt 109, 110, *118*
Junior World Series 35–37
Jurges, Billy 49, 50

Kanelos, Sam 172
Kansas City Athletics 193–199
Kansas City Baseball Historical Society 196, 198
Kansas City Blues 55, 69, 70, 72, 76, 198
Kansas City Monarchs 149, 198, 201
Kansas City Royals 201–202, *202*–205
Kaplan, Dave 216
Kauffman, Ewing 201–203
Keeler, Willie 77
Keen, Colonel Curtis A. 112
Keene, Roy "Spec" *19*
Kell, George 169
Kelleher, Frances *33*
Kelleher, Frank 33
Keller, Charlie 33–37, 61, 62, 67, 81–83, 89, 98, 100, 103, 107, 125, 126, 128, 130, 132
Kellert, Frank 179
Kelly, Dr. Don 189

Keltner, Ken 77, 78, 137, 146, *146*, 149, 151, 152, 154, 155, 158, 161, 166, 170, 172, 200
Kennedy, Bob 155, 166
Keough, Marty 180
Kernoski, John 44
Kerr, Buddy 159
Kiely, Leo 179, 180
Killebrew, Harmon 219
Kiner, Ralph 213
Kirkpatrick, Ed 202
Kirksey, George 72
Klem, Bill 101
Klieman, Ed 143, 146, 153, 157, 170
Knickerbocker, Bill 43, 44
Koch, Ray 23–28, 30
Kress, Red 183
Krichell, Paul 33
Krug, Marty 26
Kubek, Tony 221
Kuenn, Harvey 188–191

LaGuardia, Fiorello 57
Lajoie, Nap 38, 57, 80, 86
Lake Lotawana 196, 197
Lakeman, Al 172
Lampert, Andrew J. "Andy" 12, *13*, 30, 80, 207
Landis, Kenesaw M. 86, 93, 97, 98, 102, 105, 107
Lane, Bill 32
Lane, Frank 182–184, 186–192, 195–198, 201
Lang, Don 109, 110, *114*
Latman, Barry 188
Lazy Vee Ranch 137, 145
Lazzeri, Tony 4, 6, 32, 34, 37, 38, 40, 41, 43, 51, 69, 112, 174
Lemon, Bob 141, 143, 146, 149, 150, 155–*158*, 159, 161–164, 167, 168, 183, 199–201, 204
Leonard, Will 109
Lepcio, Ted 178
letter (in a sport) 16, 17, 21, 24
Letterman's Club (UO) 24
letters (to or from Joe Gordon) 2, 3, 24, 77, 92, 112, 113, 115–117, 119, 121, 126, 132, 133, 138, 149
Levitt, Daniel R. 27, 42, 165
Lewis, Duffy 101
Lien, Al 109
Lilly, Art *114*
Lindell, Johnny 99, 100, 128, 199
Little World Series *see* Junior World Series
Lodigiani, Dario 30, 31, 109, 110, *119*, 194, 198
Logan, Fred "Pop" 4
Logan, Jeff 196, 198
Lombardi, Ernie 57
Londahl, Johnny 23

Lonergan, Dr. Robert C. 126
Los Angeles Angels (American League) 180, 194–196, 199–201
Los Angeles Angels (Pacific Coast League) 37, 87, 170, 173, 178
"Lou Gehrig Appreciation Day" 57
"Lou Gehrig's disease" *see* amyotrophic lateral sclerosis (ALS)
Lowe, Bobby 184
Lumpe, Jerry 197
Lupica, Charles, Jr. 161, 163
Lupica, Charley 161, 163

Mack, Connie 57, 66, 70, 80, 100, 101
Mackey, Biz 146
MacPhail, Larry 81, 83, 102, 121–123, 125, 126, 129–136, 139
Madden, Bill 69, 73, 204, 213, 214
Magee, Sherry 213
Magerkurth, George 92, 93
magicians 43, 68
Majeski, Hank 125
Major League All-Star Team *see The Sporting News'* Major League All-Star Team
Major League Baseball 62, 85, 97, 180, 185, 191, 194, 199, *220*, 221
Major League Baseball All-Star Games 1, 45, 57, 64, 66, 67, 77, 90, 99, 100, 123, 132, 134, 136, 142, 149, 162, 169, 185, 190, 219
Major League Baseball Ball and Bat Fund 100
Major League Baseball Welfare Fund 132
Major League Baseball Winter Meetings 56, 57, 213
Major League Executive of the Year Award 155
Major League Manager of the Year Award 104
Major League Player of the Year Award 95, 105
managing (Joe Gordon) 1, 170, 173, 176, 182–*185*, 186–189, 191–195, 201, 209
Marion, Marty 93, 159
marriage (Joe and Dottie Gordon) 39, 44, 45
"Marse Joe" *see* McCarthy, Joe
Marshall, Cuddles 130
Marshall, Gen. George C. 109
Martin, Billy 184–186, 188
Marty, Joe 112, *114*, 168, 172
Masi, Phil 156
Mavis, Bob 174

Index

Mayo, Eddy 129
Mayo Clinic 55, 68
Mays, Carl 213
Mazeroski, Bill 219
McCarthy, Joe 1, 3–6, 32, 35, 40–44, 48, 54, 55, 57, 64, 67, 72, 73, 75–77, 80, 83, 90, 92, 93, 98–100, 104–107, 109, 120–130, 154, 171, 200
McCormick, Mike 109, 110
McFadden, Don 26
McKechnie, Bill 137, 145, 146
McKeegan, Jim 173
McLish, Cal 185, 188
McQuinn, George 35, 36, 73, 99
Medinger, George 184
Medwick, Joe 61
Mehl, Ernest 196–198
Metheny, Bud 101
Metkovich, George 131
Metro, Charlie 203, 204
Meusel, Bob 69
Meyer, Billy 28, 30
Michaels, Cass 162
Mills, Buster 113, **118**
Milwaukee Braves 47
Minneapolis Millers 180
Minnesota Twins 194, 195, 202, 203
Minor League Baseball 37
Minor League Player of the Year Award 37
Miñoso, Minnie 183, 185
Mission Reds **30**, 31
Mitchell, Dale 155, 162, 164
MLB Hall of Fame Tribute: Joe Gordon (video) 169, 220
Monchak, Al 200
Montebello Merchants 39
Montreal Expos 201
Montreal Royals 33–35
Moore, Dee 35
Moore, Monte 198
Moore, Terry 92
Moran, Billy 180
Moran, Charley 50, 51
Morgan, De Ann Gordon (niece) 216, 223
Morgan, Joe 103, 141, 215
Morgan, Phyllis 98, 99, 105
Morgan, Tom 200
Morris, Newbold 42, 84
Morse, Virgil **14**
Mossi, Don 184
Most Valuable Player (MVP) Award 1, 52, 61, 80, 94, **94**, 95, 101, 103, 105, 123, 134, 143, 155, 169, 174, 219, 223
Most Valuable Player (MVP) voting 1, 52, 61, 80, 94, 120, 143, 155, 169, 183
Mulligan, Eddie 171
Muncrief, Bob 76, 157

Murphy, Johnny 49, 61, 68, 82, 98, 101, 107
Murray, Red 101
Musial, Stan 201
Myers, Billy 62
Myers, George I. 78

Narleski, Ray 184
National Baseball Hall of Fame (HOF) 1, 56, 142, 159, 204, 205, 210, 214, 221, 225
National Baseball Hall of Fame (HOF) Game 190
National Baseball Hall of Fame and Museum 1, 55, 59, 148, 179, 215, 217
National Baseball Hall of Fame Class of 2009 2, 212, 214, 215, 218
National Baseball Hall of Fame Induction Weekend 2, 215–219, 221
National Baseball Hall of Fame Plaque Gallery 2, 220, 221
National Baseball Hall of Fame Veterans Committee 1, 190, 210, 212, 213, 219
National Baseball School 5, 27, 32, 39
National Defense Service List (NDSL) 107, 123
National League All-Stars 142, 162
Negro American League 149, 170
Negro National League 111, 140, 146
Nelson, Frank 173
Neun, Johnny 122, 134
New York Giants 81, 98, 100, 137, 147, 173, 177, 182, 199
New York Highlanders 69
New York Mets 194, 216
New York Yankees Museum 216, 222, **222**, 223
New York Yankees Old-Timers Day *see* Old Timers Games
Newark Bears 6, 26, 27, 32, 33, **33**, 34–37, **37**, 38, 39, 41, 55, 59, 67, 73, 98, 216, 221
Newark Eagles 140, 146
Newcombe, Don 162
Newhouser, Hal 153, 168
nicknames of Joe Gordon 2, 6, 16, 28, 31, 34, 45, 51, 66, 67, 103, 126
Niekro, Phil 213
Niggeling, Johnny 89
night games 56, 59, 78, 99, 122, 130, 155
Nimitz, Admiral Chester W. 110, 111, 114
1939 World's Fair 41, 63
Nixon, Richard 179

no-hitters 47, 128, 142, 149
Northern Mariana Islands 113, **115**, 117, **118**
Northwest League 177

Oakland Athletics 198, 202, 203
Oakland Oaks 3, 27, 28, **29**, **30**, 31, 32, 75, 112, 168, 170, 171, 174, 198
Oatman, AZ 7–9, 52
O'Doul, Lefty 31, 112, 170, 176, 199
Old Timers Games 174, 199, 200, 207
Old Trails, AZ 7, 8, **8**
Omaha Royals 203
Open Classification 173, 180
Oregon State Baseball League 22–24, 27
Oregon State College Beavers 23, 26
Oregon State Soccer Football Association *see* soccer (Joe Gordon)
Orndorff, Jess 5, 27, 32, 39
Ott, Mel 170, 171
Outlaw, Jimmy 129, 152
Owen, Mickey 82

Pacific Coast Conference (PCC) 22, 23, 26, 222
Pacific Coast League (PCL) 27, 28, **30**, 31, 32, 164, 168, 170, 173, 178, 189
Pacific Coast League (PCL) championship 32, 178–180
Page, Joe 139, 143
Page, Phil 36
Paige, Satchel 146, 149–151, 157, 159
Painter, Doc 50
Palm, Mike 172
Panama 123–126, 128
Panama Professional Baseball League All-Stars 125
Patterson, Arthur 123
Pearl Harbor Naval Base, Oahu, Territory of Hawaii 84, 87, 110
Pearson, Albie 178–180, 199
Pearson, Monte **40**, 47, 49, 51, 58, 61, 62, 67, 68
Peckinpaugh, Roger 90
Pelekoudas, Chris 179
pennants 1, 34, 48, 61, 62, 64, 65, 67, 69–71, 76, 78, 80, 91, 95, 97, 98, 100, 101, 105, 129, 130, 134, 135, 137, 143, 145, 147, 151–155, 160, 161, 163, 164, 167–169, 176–178, 180, 182, 185–188, 191
Pennsylvania State Association 44
pensions 39, 136, 142, 143, 150, 166, 180, 185

Perini, Lou 155
Perry, Jim 191
Perry, Ray 174
Pesky, Johnny 94, 130, 131, 153
Peters, Nick 221
Piersall, Jimmy 184, 188–191, 193, 201
Pietsch, Christopher 78
Pilot's Flight Log see flying (Joe Gordon)
Piniella, Lou 202–204
Pioneer League 164, 200
Pitter, Roy **114**
Pittsburgh Pirates 31, 167
player-manager 31, 130, 135, 145, 146, 155, 168–171, 174, 178, 196
playoff game 152–154
Pollet, Howie **114**
Polo Grounds 90, 100
Portland All-Stars 24
Portland Beavers 20, 30–32, 164, 168, 170, 173, 177, 178
Portland Interscholastic Baseball League 17, 21
Portland Interscholastic Soccer League 16
post–1942 players Hall of Fame ballot of 2008 212, 213
Post Office Pharmacy 18
Powell, Jake 49
Power, Vic 185, 190
Powers, Jimmy 68–70
pre–1943 players Hall of Fame ballot of 2008 212, 213, 215
Priddy, Evelyn 73, **74**, 78
Priddy, Jerry 72–**74**, 75, 76, 78, **87**, 88, 93, 97, 109
Private Pilot Airman Certificate see flying (Joe Gordon)
Pujols, Albert 103
Pullman car see railroad travel

R.A. Babb Hardware Co. 23, 122
radio 33, 34, 49, 100, 111, 115, 136, 141, 142, 221
railroad travel 3, 4, 7, 20, 28, 32, 33, 35, 41, 46, 49, 50, 55, 77, 97–99, 101, 103, 128, 147, 153, 155–158
Raymond, Alex 16, 81
records 1, 2, 34, 41, 45–49, 51, 55, 56, 59, 61, 62, 69, 77, 78, 80, 81, 89, 91, 101, 103, 104, 132–134, 143, 149, 151, 155, 156, 158, 163, 167, 169, 172
Reese, Jimmy 200
Reilly, Gerry 217
Reinhart, Bill 22, 23, 25, 27
relief pitching 61, 67, 71, 81, 82, 92, 98, 101, 139, 146, 149, 155, 157, 164, 170, 178, 179, 190
Remembering the Royals: Joe Gordon (website) 207, 208, 209
Renna, Bill 179, 180
Renwick, Helen 180
Renwick, Jack 180
Republic Pictures 161, 163, 171
Reynolds, Allie 129, 134, 135, 139, 143, 147, 213, 215
Rhawn, Bob 126
Ribs and Roasts Dinner, Cleveland Chapter BBWAA 184
Rice, Jim 218–221
Richards, Brian 216, 222
Richards, Vern 20
Richardson, Nolen 34, 36
Rickenbacker, Captain Eddie 102
Riggs, Lew 113, **119**
Rigney, Bill 159, 199–201
Rizzuto, Phil 72, 73, 75, 76, 78, 80, 88, 91–93, 97, 107, 110, 124, 125, 128–133
Roberts, Robin 213, 219
Robinson, Eddie 137, 143, 145, 146, **146**, 147, 154, 155, 157, 158
Robinson, Jackie 49, 111, 140, 142, 162
Rocky River, OH 140, 152, 185
Rogers, Roy 171
Rojek, Stan **114**, 117, **119**
Rolfe, Red 4, 42, 46, 49, **50**, 57–59, 61, 64, 65, 67, 68, 76, 78, 82, 97, 102
Rookie Advanced Pioneer League 200
Rookie of the Year Award 1, 48, 49, 155, 162, 180, 188, 194, 202, 204
Roosevelt, Franklin D. 75, 85, 86
Rosar, Buddy 36, 69, 72, 97
Rose, Pete 77
Rosen, Al 157, 166, 168
Rosenberg, Harry **30**
Rothenberg, Matt 236n22
Rowland, Clarence 173
Ruel, Herold "Muddy" 145, 175
Ruffing, Red 49, **50**, 51, 55, 57, 59, 61, 62, 64, 67, 68, 71, 81, 83, 88, 92, 93, 97, 107, 109, 110, 133
Ruppert, Col. Jacob 6, 33, 35, 36, 39, 40, 42, 49, 51, 54, 121
Ruppert Stadium 32, 33, **33**, 34, 35
Rusche, Bertha Evans (aunt) 7, 10–12
Rusche, Joe (uncle) 7, 10–12
Russo, Marius 69, 71, 75, 82, 83, 98, 103
Ruth, Babe 40, 57, **60**–62, 64, 87, 91, 93, 99, 101, 102, **102**, 103, 148, **148**, 149, 169, 217
Ruth, Claire 102, **102**
Ryan, Ellis W. 164, 165
Ryan Addition, AZ 7, 8, **8**, 9

Sacramento Solons 31, 112, 121, 164, 168–174, 178, 179, 181
Sadowski, Ed 200
Sain, Johnny 156
St. Pete-Bradenton Ferry 127
St. Petersburg, FL 3, 5, **5**, 39–41, 54, 65, **65**, 72, 75, **87**, 122, 126, **127**, 128
Saipan, Northern Mariana Islands 113–115
salaries see contracts
Salem (OR) American Legion Junior Baseball team 19
San Diego Padres (Pacific Coast League) 31, 32, 170, 178
San Francisco Area Old Timers see Old Timers Games
San Francisco Giants 180, 199
San Francisco Seals 31, 112, 170–172, 176, 177, **177**–180, 189, 200
San Rafael, CA 112, 119
sandlots 2, 12, 14, **14**, 17, 43, 63, 216, 218
Schaefer, Germany 104
Schauder, Edward H. 218
Schmidt, Bill 109
Schoendienst, Red 159
Schofield Redlanders 109
Schulte, John 123
Score, Herb 188
scouting (Joe Gordon) 1, 174, 175, 180, 199–202, 204, 205, 224
scrapbooks 2, 14, 121, 209, 121, 209, 217, 227
Seals Stadium 112, 177, **177**
Seaten, John **14**
Seattle Indians 30–32
Seattle Pilots 201, 203
Seattle Rainiers 168, 170, 172, 176
Seeds, Bob 36
Selective Training and Service Act of 1940 120, 123
Selig, Bud **220**, 221
Selkirk, George **40**, 42, 49, **50**, 55–58, 61, **65**, 91, 93, 97
semipro baseball 21–25, 27, 32, 39
Sertich, Tom 176, 207, 208
7th Army Air Force Fighters 110
7th Army Air Force Fliers 109, 110
73rd Bombardment Wing Bombers, Isley Field, Saipan 113, **114**, **115**
Sewell, Luke 76
Shaughnessy, Frank J. 33, 34, 36

Index

Shea, Merv 170
Shaughnessy playoffs 31, 34, 35, 178
Shea, Spec 147
Sheehy, Pete 123
Sheely, Earl 26, 27
Sherry, Magee 213
Shieber, Tom 217
Shisler, Bob 122
Siebern, Norm 197
Siebert, Dick 36
Sigma Chi Fraternity 23–25
Silvera, Charlie 109, *118*, *119*, 123
Silvestri, Ken 125, 126
Simmons, Al 169
Simmons, Jay 216
Simpson, Erik (grandson) 141, 205, 208, 213–215, 217, *217*–219, 221, 225
Simpson, Mike (grandson) 206, 212, *212*, 214, 215
Sisler, George 77, 101
Slaughter, Enos 101, *114*, *118*
Smith, Al 78
Smith, Bob "Riverboat" 178–180
Smith, Claire 141, 213, 219
Smith, Elmer 154
Smith, Vince *118*
Snider, Duke 213
soccer (Joe Gordon) 14, 16
Society for American Baseball Research (SABR) 27, 227
Southworth, Billy 100, 103, 162
Sowers, Dan *19*, 20
Spahn, Warren 157, 162
Speaker, Tris 101, 146, 147
The Spectrum: Class of June '32 (book) 16, 21
Spence, Stan 153
The Sporting News' Major League All-Star Teams 64, 72, 86, 96, 145, 159, 169
Spring, Jack 179
spring training, Cleveland Indians 137, 145, *146*, 160, 165, 166, 184, 188
spring training, Detroit Tigers 174, 175
spring training, Kansas City Athletics 195, 198
spring training, Kansas City Royals *202*, 203
spring training, New York Yankees 3, 5, *5*, 32, 39–41, 54, 55, 64, 65, *65*, 71–73, 75, 86, 87, *87*, *88*, 97, 98, 105, 106, 122, 123, 126, 128, 139, 140
spring training, New York Yankees in Panama 123, 124, *124*, 125, 126
spring training, Newark Bears 6, 32, 33

spring training, Oakland Oaks 28
Stainback, Tuck 103
Stanky, Eddie 183
Staub, Rusty 218
Steinbrenner, George 208, 215, 216
Stengel, Casey 189
Stephens, Bryan 141
Stephens, Vern 94, 159, 213
Stevens, Chuck *114*, *119*
Stewart, Bill 156
Stigman, Dick 190
Stirnweiss, Snuffy 98, 99, 120, 123, 125–129, 132
Stoneham, Horace 180
Stringer, Lou 178
Sturm, Johnny 72, 75, 76, 81, 125
"Subway Series" 80, 81, 84
Sullivan, Haywood 180
Summers, Bill 92, 93, 98
Sundra, Steve 34, 36, *40*, 61, 68
Sutton, Don 213
Suwannee Hotel 3, 40
Sweeney, Bill 31, 170
Syracuse Chiefs 34, 35

Tabor, Jim 68
Tallis, Cedric 201, 202, 204
Tamulis, Vito 34
Taormina, Sal 178
Taylor, Zack 171
Teachers College of Columbia University Summer Baseball School 58, *58*
Tebbetts, Birdie 101, 107, 113, *114*, 117, *118*
Ted Bacon String Orchestra 15, 207
Temple, Johnny 188
Thiel, Bert 178
313th Bombardment Wing Flyers, North Field, Tinian 113, *114*, *115*
tiebreaker game *see* playoff game
Tighe, Jack 175
Tinian, Northern Mariana Islands 113–117
Tinker, Joe 90
Topping, Dan 121, 135
Tornay, Nini 178
Toronto Blue Jays 56
Toronto Maple Leafs 33, 140
track and field (Joe Gordon) 14, 17
trades 97, 131–136, 139, 146, 152, 165–167, 183, 184, 186, 188, 189, 191, 192, 194, 196, 197, 203, 215, 216, 218
train *see* railroad travel
Trautman, George M. 173
Travis, Cecil 77

Tresh, Mike 166
Triple Crown 1, 95, 143
triple play 111, 129, 147, 154, 164, 167
Trosky, Hal 76
Trucks, Virgil 111
Truman, Harry S. 115
Tuttle, William C. 32
20th AAF 113, 115
20th AAF All Stars POA *116*, 117
200 Home Run Club 150, *150*

Uhalt, Frenchy *30*
Underwood, Carter 223
Underwood, Jared 216, 223
Underwood, Jeremy 216
United Service Organizations (USO) 77, 93
U.S. Army Air Corps (USAAC) 107, 108
U.S. Army Air Transport Command 107, 109, 112
U.S. Army All-Stars 125
U.S. Army and Navy Relief Funds 91
U.S. Army basic training 107–109, 221
U.S. Army Camp Cumberland baseball team 101
U.S. military draft 88, 97, 105–107, 173
U.S. Navy 86, 94, 106, 107, 110, 111, 117, 119, 130
U.S. War Department 106, 112
University of Arizona 21
University of Idaho Vandals 23
University of Oregon (UO) Athletic Hall of Fame 222
University of Oregon (UO) Ducks 3, 22–27, 32, 36, 39, 52, 54, 97, 117, 222, 223
University of Oregon (UO) "Hall of Famer Joe Gordon Day" 223
University of Southern California 27, 28
University of Washington Huskies 23, 26
USASTAF Special Services Major League Baseball Stars *118*, 119

Van Dyke Colored House of Davids of Sioux City, Iowa 24
Veeck, Bill 132–135, 137–142, 145–147, 149, 152, 153, 155, 159–161, 163, 171, 182, 189
ventriloquist 68, 206, 221
Vernon, Mickey 183, 213
Veterans Committee *see* National Baseball Hall

of Fame (HOF) Veterans Committee
Vikings team *see* soccer (Joe Gordon)
violin 15, 17, 207, 221
Vitt, Oscar 32, 36, 37, *37*, 38, 112, 191
Voiselle, Bill 157

Wade, Jake 129
Wagner, Honus 101
waivers 134, 165–168
Wakefield, Dick 129
Walker, Gee 46
Walsh, Christy *60*, 61
Walters, Bucky 61, 64, 213
Wambsganss, Bill 154
Washington Nationals 42
Washington Senators (new expansion) 194, 199
Washington State College Cougars 23
Weatherly, Roy 97
Webb, Del 121, 135
Weber, Ben 106
Weinstein, Ed 33
Weisman, Lefty 161
Weiss, Bill 37
Weiss, George 28, 33, 35
Wensloff, Charles "Butch" 101
West, Max *30*, 117
West Side Babes 22, 23
Western Association 27, 28
Westlake Hotel 152, 185
Weyant, Helen 54
Wheaties cereal 78, *79*, 152
Wheeler Field Wingmen 113
White, Deacon 213
White, Ernie 93
White, Jo-Jo 168, 183, 187, 191, 192, 194, 202, *202*, 203
Wicker, Kemp *40*
Wight, Bill 125
Wilburn, Wimpy 35
Wilks, Ted 194
Williams, Dick 213
Williams, Larry 174
Williams, Ted 1, 31, 55, 59, 61, 64, 68, 77, 80, 84, 91, 94–96, 130, 132, 142, 143, 153, 155
Winchell, Walter 44
Wingmen team (on Guam) 119
Winsett, Tom 109, 111
wives 80, *89*, 99, 122, 141, 153
Wolfer's Federals 23
world champions 1, 3, 51, 52, *52*, 55, 58, 62, 70, 82, 93, 104, 105, 129, 134, 147, 148, 157, 158, *158*, 162, 169, 170, 182, 183, 194, 198, 205, 207
World Series emblems 52, *52*, 62, 83, 95, 158, 219
World Series shares 27, 52, 62, 83, 93, 104, 158, 183, 187
World War I 7, 9, 102
World War II 10, 56, 61, 64, 85–87, 90, 97, 99, 101, 102, 107, 109, 113, 115, 143, 168, 212, 214, 215
Wright, Ab 34
Wright, Glenn "Cap" 178
Wright, Marshall 37
Wright, Taft 91
www.baseballinwartime.com 115
Wyatt, Whitlow 77, 81
Wynn, Early 161, 164, 168, 186

Yankee Stadium (significant events) 42, 44, 45, 47, 57, 66, *66*, 75, 81, 91, 92, 102, 121, 128, 130, 139, 147–148, *148*
YMCA Spirit Lake Camp 14, 15
Yogi Berra Museum & Learning Center 216, 218
York, Rudy 45
Young Men's Christian Association (YMCA) 14, 15

Zellerbach Paper Co. 11, 22, 23
Zoldak, Sam 146, 153
Zuber, Bill 97
Zupo, Tony 174

www.ingramcontent.com/pod-product-compliance
Lightning Source LLC
Chambersburg PA
CBHW060337010526
44117CB00017B/2864